ORGANIZATIONAL COMMUNICATION

ORGANIZATIONAL COMMUNICATION
A Critical Approach

Dennis K. Mumby

*The University of North Carolina
at Chapel Hill*

Los Angeles | London | New Delhi
Singapore | Washington DC

Los Angeles | London | New Delhi
Singapore | Washington DC

FOR INFORMATION:

SAGE Publications, Inc.
2455 Teller Road
Thousand Oaks, California 91320
E-mail: order@sagepub.com

SAGE Publications Ltd.
1 Oliver's Yard
55 City Road
London, EC1Y 1SP
United Kingdom

SAGE Publications India Pvt. Ltd.
B 1/I 1 Mohan Cooperative Industrial Area
Mathura Road, New Delhi 110 044
India

SAGE Publications Asia-Pacific Pte. Ltd.
3 Church Street
#10–04 Samsung Hub
Singapore 049483

Acquisitions Editor: Matthew Byrnie
Editorial Assistant: Stephanie Palermini
Production Editor: Eric Garner
Copy Editor: Megan Granger
Typesetter: C&M Digitals (P) Ltd.
Proofreader: Laura Webb
Indexer: Rick Hurd
Cover Designer: Edgar Abarca
Marketing Manager: Liz Thornton
Permissions Editor: Karen Ehrmann

Photos for "Critical Technologies" and "Critical Case
Study" boxes: Courtesy of Dynamic Graphics/liquidlibrary/
Thinkstock.

Printed in the United States of America

Library of Congress Cataloging-in-Publication Data

Mumby, Dennis K.
Organizational communication: a critical approach /
Dennis K. Mumby.

p. cm.

Includes bibliographical references and index.

ISBN 978-1-4129-6315-2 (pbk.)

1. Communication in organizations. I. Title.

HD30.3.M863 2013
306.44—dc23   2012018541

This book is printed on acid-free paper.

13 14 15 16 10 9 8 7 6 5 4 3 2

Brief Contents

Detailed Contents

PART II: THEORIES OF ORGANIZATIONAL COMMUNICATION AND THE MODERN ORGANIZATION

3 Scientific Management, Bureaucracy, and the Emergence of the Modern Organization

6 Communication, Culture, and Organizing   133

PART III: CRITICAL PERSPECTIVES ON ORGANIZATIONAL COMMUNICATION AND THE NEW WORKPLACE   155

7 Power and Resistance at Work   157

8 The Postmodern Workplace: Teams, Emotions, and No-Collar Work   181

9 Communicating Gender at Work   205

10 Communicating Difference at Work 229

11 Leadership Communication in the New Workplace 255

12 Branding and Consumption 281

13 Organizational Communication, Globalization, and Democracy   305

14 Communication, Meaningful Work, and Personal Identity   333

Preface

I have a confession to make (well, two actually). I have never been a huge fan of textbooks. So, you may legitimately ask, what on earth am I doing authoring one? Good question. The simple answer (only partially true) might be that I finally caved to student-consumer pressure to provide something that makes a bit more sense than all those interminable academic articles I assign to students. If I am to be "coerced" into adopting a textbook, I thought, at least I can write one that I actually like!

Okay, so that was just a minor consideration. There are actually several good organizational communication textbooks available, though none of them really fits the way I like to teach this class. In fact, one of my major problems with the typical textbook is that it's written as if from nowhere. It's hard to tell from reading the book if the author even has a particular perspective or set of assumptions that he or she brings to the study of organizational communication. Every textbook reads as though it's an objective, authoritative account of a particular body of knowledge; the author's voice almost never appears. But the truth is that every theory and every program of research you've ever read about in your college career operates according to a set of principles—a perspective, if you like—that shapes the very nature of the knowledge claims made by that research.

Now, this does not mean that all research is biased in the sense of simply being the expression of a researcher's opinions and prejudices; all *good* research is rigorous and systematic in its exploration of the world around us. Rather, I'm saying that all researchers are trained according to the principles and assumptions of a particular academic community (of which there are many), and academic communities differ in their beliefs about what makes good research. That's why there are debates in all fields of research. Sometimes those debates are over facts (this or that is or isn't true), but more often those debates are really about what assumptions and theoretical perspectives provide the most useful and insightful way to study a particular phenomenon.

Certainly, the field of organizational communication is no different. In the 1980s our field went through "paradigm debates" in which a lot of time was spent arguing over the "best" perspective from which to study organizations—a debate in which I participated (Corman & Poole, 2000; Mumby, 1993, 2000). Fortunately, the result of these debates was a richer and more interesting field of study; some disciplines are not so lucky and end up divided into oppositional camps, sometimes for many decades.

Overview of the Book

But what does this have to do with writing a textbook? It's my belief that not only should a textbook adequately reflect the breadth of different perspectives in a field, but it should also adopt its own perspective from which a field is studied. It makes no sense that an author should have to check his or her theoretical perspective at the door when he or she becomes a textbook author—the pretense of neutrality and objectivity is, for me, a non-starter. In fact, I would argue that, from a student perspective, reading a textbook that's explicit about its theoretical orientation makes for a much richer educational experience. It's hard to engage in an argument with someone when that person refuses to state his or her position; when you know where someone is coming from you are better able to engage with his or her reasoning, as well as articulate your own perspective. Dialogue is possible!

So, it's important to me that you know up front who you're dealing with here. For the past 25 years I've been writing about organizations from what can broadly be described as a critical perspective. This means that I am interested in organizations as sites of power and control that shape societal meanings and human identities in significant ways. Thus, I am less interested in things like how "efficient" organizations are (a perspective that some researchers would take) and more interested in how they function as communication phenomena that have a profound—sometimes good, sometimes bad—impact on who we are as people. We spend almost all our time in organizations of one kind or another, and certainly our entire work lives are spent as members of organizations, so it's extremely important to understand the implications of our "organizational society" of various kinds for who we are as people.

Furthermore, the way I have structured this textbook does not mean that it is *only* about the critical perspective. In some ways it is a "traditional" textbook in its coverage of the major research traditions that have developed in the field over the past 100 years. The difference from other textbooks lies in my use of the critical perspective as the lens through which I examine these traditions. Thus, the critical perspective gives us a particular—and, I would argue, powerful—way of understanding both organizational life and the theories and research programs that have been developed to understand it. So as you are reading this book, keep reminding yourself, "Dennis is a critical theorist—how does this shape the way he thinks about organizations and lead him to certain conclusions about the theory and practice of organizational life rather than others?" Also ask yourself, "When do I agree with Dennis, and when do I disagree with him? Why do I agree/disagree, and what does that tell me about my own view of the world?"

In addition to the critical perspective I adopt in this book, I'm also bringing a particular communication approach. Rather than thinking of this book as exploring theories of organizational communication, you can think of it as developing a communication mode of explanation that enables us to understand organizations as communicative phenomena. Organizations can (and have) been studied from psychological, sociological, and business perspectives (among others), but to study them from a communication perspective means something distinctive and, I think, unique. From this perspective, communication is not just something that happens "in" organizations; rather, it is the very lifeblood of organizations. It is what makes organizations meaningful places that connect people together to engage collectively in meaningful activity. The implications of this communication perspective will become clearer as we move through the chapters of the book.

Pedagogical Aids

I've also included some elements that will assist you in getting to grips with the various and sometimes complex issues that we'll be addressing. First, each chapter contains at least one Critical Case Study that enables you to apply the issues discussed in that chapter to a real-world situation. Think of these case studies as an effort to demonstrate the fact that "there's nothing as practical as a good theory." Second, each chapter contains a **Critical Technologies** box that provides some insight into the increasing and now-ubiquitous role of communication technology in everyday organizational life. Because any chapter on technology is quickly outdated these days, the box format seemed the most useful way to go. Third, the book is unique in its inclusion of full chapters on (1) postmodernism and the post-Fordist organization, (2) gender and organizations, (3) difference and organizations, (4) branding and consumption, and (5) the meaning of work. All these chapters in various ways address the changing nature of work and organizations. Finally, each chapter highlights **key terms** in bold throughout the text and lists the key terms at the end of each chapter, along with definitions in the **glossary** at the end of the book.

Ancillaries

In addition to the text, a full array of ancillary website materials for instructors and students is available at **www.sagepub.com/mumbyorg**.

The **password-protected Instructor Teaching Site** at **www.sagepub.com/mumbyorg** contains a test bank, PowerPoint presentations, chapter summaries, and web resources for use in the classroom.

The **open-access Student Study Site** at **www.sagepub.com/mumbyorg** contains web resources, quizzes, and interactive flashcards for key terms to enhance student learning.

The Critical Perspective of the Book

Let me say one last thing about the perspective I adopt in this book. I view this textbook (and, indeed, any textbook) as political in the sense suggested by organizational communication scholars Karen Ashcraft and Brenda Allen (2003):

As they orient students to the field and its defining areas of theory and research, textbooks perform a political function. That is, they advance narratives of collective identity, which invite students to internalize a particular map of central and marginal issues, of legitimate and dubious projects. (p. 28)

As I suggested above, knowledge is far from neutral, shaping our understanding of it in particular ways. The "map" I want to lay out for you will, I hope, enable you to negotiate organizational life as more engaged and thoughtful "organizational citizens." As such, I hope you will be better equipped to recognize the subtle and not-so-subtle ways organizations shape human identities—both collective and individual.

REFERENCES

Ashcraft, K. L., & Allen, B. J. (2003). The racial foundation of organizational communication. *Communication Theory, 13*, 5–38.

Corman, S. R., & Poole, M. S. (Eds.). (2000). *Perspectives on organizational communication: Finding common ground.* New York: Guilford.

Mumby, D. K. (1993). Critical organizational communication studies: The next ten years. *Communication Monographs, 60*, 18–25.

Mumby, D. K. (2000). Common ground from the critical perspective: Overcoming binary oppositions. In S. R. Corman & M. S. Poole (Eds.), *Perspectives on organizational communication: Finding common ground* (pp. 68–88). New York: Guilford.

Acknowledgments

Oh, yes—the second confession. I started writing this book years ago. In fact, I've completed three other book projects since I started this one. There's no single explanation for why it took so long—certainly, changing jobs and becoming a department chair (always a productivity killer) had an impact. To make matters worse, my original publisher was bought out by a much larger company, and my new editor didn't seem invested in the project—a hard lesson in the politics of the corporate world. Bringing ideas to fruition is just as much about the relationships you have with the people around you as it is about your own ability and discipline. And in that regard I finally got lucky—Todd Armstrong at SAGE knew I was working on a textbook and kept pestering me to sign up with him. I'd worked with Todd on several other projects and knew what a smart, energetic, and all-around great person he was. It's due in good measure to Todd that this book has finally seen the light of day. Todd left SAGE before the project was finished, but his successor, Matt Byrnie, and Associate Editor Nathan Davidson kept the project moving along with well-timed feedback and plenty of encouragement. Other SAGE staff, including editorial assistant Stephanie Palermini, Assistant Editor Terri Accomazzo, marketing manager Liz Thornton, and Production Editor Eric Garner proved to be an excellent support team. Last, but not least, Meg Granger was a phenomenal copy editor with a great eye for detail; whatever she gets paid, it's not enough.

Speaking of feedback, this might well be the most reviewed textbook in the history of publishing. Sometimes reviewer feedback can drive you nuts because it's inconsistent and at times even contradictory. But I was lucky enough to get a wealth of constructive and encouraging comments from organizational communication scholars across the field. In alphabetical order, they are, Patrice M. Buzzanell, Theresa Castor, Jennifer R. Considine, Nancy J. Curtin, Maria A. Dixon, Jennie Donohue, Francine Edwards, Kristine Fitch, Marie Garland, Bethany Crandell Goodier, Liane M. Gray-Starner, Di Grimes, Terry L. Hapney Jr., Jessica Katz Jameson, Jeannette Kindred, Erika Kirby, Tim Kuhn, Dan Lair, Kurt Lindemann, Gina Marcello, Caryn Medved, Rebecca Meisenbach, George W. Musambira, Karen K. Myers, Majia Holmer Nadesan, Todd Norton, Andrea M. Pampaloni, Robyn V. Remke, Maria E. Rodriguez, Jennifer Mize Smith, Patty Sotirin, Rob Whitbred, Lynda R. Willer, Mary E. Wilson, Jason S. Wrench, and Heather Zoller, plus a couple of folks who wished to remain anonymous. Reviewing takes a lot of time and energy, and I appreciate everyone's willingness to give detailed comments that, I'm sure, took up time they didn't have.

Thanks also to my excellent colleagues in the Department of Communication Studies at UNC–Chapel Hill—it would be hard to imagine a more stimulating and supportive environment in which to be a scholar and teacher.

The completion of this book was aided greatly by a one-semester Research and Study Assignment from the University of North Carolina at Chapel Hill during fall semester 2011. In addition, the Danish Otto Mønsteds Foundation provided a generous research grant that underwrote a 4-month appointment at Copenhagen Business School (CBS) during spring and summer 2011. My colleagues in the Department of Intercultural Communication and Management at CBS—especially Robyn Remke, Mikkel Flyverbom, Christina Frydensbjerg, Dan Kärreman, Esben Karmark, Eric Guthey, Hans Hansen, Linda Harrison, and Dorte Salskov-Iversen—provided a wonderfully supportive, collegial, and stimulating research environment in which to work. *Tak for alt*! Thanks especially to Mikkel for the loan of the bike! Majbritt Vendelbo was especially helpful with the logistics of moving to and living in a new country.

It will become clear as you read this book that I don't spend a whole lot of time writing while shut up in an office somewhere. I prefer to be out in the world and engaged with people. Most of this book was written "in public," as it were. The bucolic pleasures of Caffé Driade in Chapel Hill provided an ideal writing environment away from the hustle and bustle of campus, in addition to the best espresso drinks anywhere. Thanks to all its baristas and patrons for tolerating my hogging the corner table. In Copenhagen, The Living Room, Log Lady, and Paludan Books were similarly welcoming and accommodating.

Thanks also to Al, Bazza, and Pete (founding members of the Department of Philosophy and Popular Culture at Stoke Rochford University) for organizing annual summer symposia, and for reminding me that it's alright to be out standing in the field, as long as you do some good mantlin' around, god aye.

Finally, thanks to my family for their continued love and support, and for reminding me about life's real priorities.

PART I

Developing a Critical Approach to Organizational Communication

CHAPTER 1

Introducing Organizational Communication

Humans are organizational animals; modern life is defined by organizations and corporations.

Perhaps at no other time in human history have organizations and communication been more central to our lives than they are now. We go to work, attend college and church, do volunteer work, join social groups, shop at numerous stores, internalize thousands of commercials from large corporations, and participate in social media. Human beings are communicating, organizing creatures, and we define ourselves largely through our various organizational memberships and communicative connections.

As simple as this assertion is, it hides a rather complex reality. The organizations that define who we are—and our relationship to them—have become increasingly complicated. Indeed, as systems of communication, we largely take for granted organizations and their role in our lives. We're like the two young fish that one day pass an older fish. The older fish says to them, "Mornin', boys. How's the water?" After he has swum away, one young fish turns to the other and says, "What's water?" Communication and organizations are both a bit like water—we navigate them without really paying much attention to how fundamental they are to our daily lives.

One purpose of this book, then, is to provide you with a map to navigate the water we all swim in and to figure out the complexities of organizational communication processes.

In part, we will be exploring different theories and management perspectives and discussing their strengths and limitations, similarities and differences. But each perspective is more than just an abstract theory that has little to do with the "real world." In many ways, each of them has profoundly shaped the organizational world in which all of us are deeply enmeshed. Indeed, I would suggest that each of these perspectives has, in different ways, shaped who we are as people—a grand claim, I know, but one we will unpack in detail as we move through this book.

In order to lay the groundwork for this claim I want first to identify a common theme that runs throughout these theories—a theme that bears directly on my claim and that will serve as a basic construct in our attempt to understand organizational communication processes. This is the theme of **organizational control**. As a starting point we can define organizational control as "the dynamic communication process through which organizational stakeholders (employees, managers, owners, shareholders, etc.) struggle to maximize their stake in an organization." In this book, then, we will examine organizations as *communicative structures of control*. Let's explore this focus in more detail below.

❖ ORGANIZATIONS AS COMMUNICATIVE STRUCTURES OF CONTROL

In discussing the various theories that have emerged in the fields of management and organizational communication over the past 100 years or so, we will explore how, at its core, each theory is motivated by the problems associated with controlling large numbers of people in specific settings. Beginning in the late 19th century, as capitalism became the dominant economic system, the new corporate organization and its employees became a focal point of study for social scientists in various academic fields. For more than 100 years, researchers have developed various ways of explaining how people can be motivated to come together to perform specific tasks when, more often than not, they would rather be somewhere else doing something different. Such has been the centrality of this problem for social scientists that sociologist Charles Perrow (1986) has claimed, "The problems advanced by social scientists have been primarily the problems of human relations in an authoritarian setting" (p. 53).

This problem of "human relations" in organizations is a complex one, as we will see in the course of this book. One of the defining features of an organization is that it coordinates the behavior of its members so they can work collectively. But while coordination is a nice concept in theory, it is surprisingly difficult to achieve in practice. Particularly in for-profit organizations (where most people work), a number of factors work against the perfect coordination of a large number of people. One of the most important factors is the tensions between the goals, beliefs, and desires of individual organization members and those of the larger organization (see Table 1.1). Because these goals often conflict, they have to be resolved in some way. Telephone company executive Chester Barnard (1938) was among the first to recognize that the way this fundamental tension, or conflict, is usually resolved is by subordinating the goals and beliefs of individual organization members to those of the larger organization.

Table 1.1 Some Tensions Between Individual and Organizational Goals, Values, and Needs

Individual		*Organization*
Maximizing salary	←----------------------→	Minimizing costs
Autonomy	←----------------------→	Commitment and constraint
Job stability	←----------------------→	Organizational flexibility and change
Maximizing leisure time	←----------------------→	Maximizing work time
Behaving spontaneously	←----------------------→	Behaving predictably
Asserting individual values	←----------------------→	Asserting collective values
Developing personal relationships	←--------→	Developing professional relationships
Creativity	←----------------------→	Efficiency
Emotionality	←----------------------→	Rationality
Relaxing the labor process	←-----------------→	Intensifying the labor process
Embodiment	←-----------------→	Disembodiment

In this context, the issue of control becomes central. All organizational and management theories address the individual–organization tension in some way. As such, all organizational theories implicitly pose the question, "How do we get organization members to engage in behavior that they may not spontaneously engage in and that may even be contrary to their best interests?" In other words, "How can we exercise control over employees and get them to function in a coordinated manner?" In many ways, the history of management thought is the history of efforts to develop more and more sophisticated answers to this question. One of the earliest social scientists to focus explicitly on the issue of organizational control was Arthur Tannenbaum (1968), who stated:

> Organization implies control. A social organization is an ordered arrangement of individual human interactions. Control processes help circumscribe idiosyncratic behaviors and keep them conformant to the rational plan of organization. . . . The co-ordination and order created out of the diverse interests and potentially diffuse behaviors of members is largely a function of control. (p. 3)

However, organization members are not simply passive recipients of control mechanisms, blithely accepting each new form of control as it is implemented. On the contrary, the history of management thought is also a history of *struggle*, as employees have individually and collectively resisted management efforts to limit their autonomy in the workplace (Fleming & Spicer, 2007). In this sense, we will examine control as a *dialectical process*. That is, control is never a linear, cause-and-effect phenomenon (like one billiard ball hitting another) but is complex and ambiguous; organizational control mechanisms often produce creative employee responses that produce unintended outcomes for the organization. For example, corporate efforts to engineer organizational culture and instill certain values in employees are sometimes hijacked by employees for their own ends, or else employees create their own countercultures in the organization, rejecting the values communicated by management (e.g., Ezzamel, Willmott, & Worthington, 2001; Smith & Eisenberg, 1987).

Before we can examine these different organization theories through the lens of control, however, we need to do two things. First, we need to develop a coherent and clear notion of what *organizational communication* means. Second, we must develop an overarching framework that allows us to compare the competing perspectives that make up the field of organizational communication. Such perspectives are not conjured out of thin air by scholars and practitioners but emerge out of particular and long-standing research traditions, each with its own agenda. As this book unfolds, we will see that all the research traditions in organizational communication are at least partially explicable in terms of the particular social, political, and economic conditions of the time in which they emerged.

❖ DEFINING "ORGANIZATIONAL COMMUNICATION"

One of the problems in defining the term *organizational communication* is that we are dealing with two phenomena—*organization* and *communication*—that are, individually, extremely complex. Placed in a dynamic relationship with each other, the level of complexity increases greatly. W. Charles Redding (1988)—widely regarded as the founder of the field of organizational communication—provides us with a useful starting point for defining *organization*. While acknowledging the difficulty of providing any universal definition, he argues that all *complex* organizations (i.e., social structures large enough to make face-to-face communication among all members impossible at all times) exhibit the following four essential features: (1) interdependence, (2) differentiation of tasks and functions, (3) goal orientation, and (4) control. Surprisingly, Redding does not include communication as a specific feature, so our fifth defining characteristic of complex organizations is communication processes. We will discuss each of these features in detail.

Interdependence

Organizations exhibit interdependence insofar as no member can function without affecting, and being affected by, other organization members. All complex organizations consist of intricate webs of interconnected communication activities, the integration of which determines the success or failure of the organization. Universities, for example, consist of complex webs of students, faculty, departments, schools, staff, and administrators, each group shaping and being shaped by all the others. While students may seem to be the group with the least agency (i.e., ability to influence others), they nevertheless heavily shape the behavior of the other groups (e.g., by making courses popular or unpopular through enrollment), especially given their role as the primary "customers" of universities.

As organizations have become increasingly complex and global in the past 20 or 30 years, interdependence has become an even more significant and defining feature of organizational life. Many large organizations depend on a complicated array of subsidiaries, outsourcing processes, communication technologies, and leveraged financial structures in order to flourish. Any change in one aspect of this complex system of interdependence can create changes in the entire system. As we saw in 2008, the collapse of several financial institutions had a profound effect not only on the employees of those institutions but on almost everyone in the world, as the global economy went into recession as a result of these failures. The concept of interdependence will be explored in more detail in Chapter 5 on systems theory.

Differentiation of Tasks and Functions

All organizations, however large or small, operate according to the principle of division of labor, in which members specialize in particular tasks and the organization as a whole is divided into various departments. As the 18th century economist Adam Smith illustrated through his description of pin manufacture, many more pins can be produced when the manufacturing process is divided into many specialized tasks than if all the

© iStockphoto.com/gerenme

The control of employees has been a focus of management research for more than 100 years.

tasks are performed by a single individual (Smith, 1776/1937). This feature of organizations truly came into its own in the late 19th and early 20th centuries with the introduction of scientific management principles into most large organizations (Taylor, 1911/1934)—a perspective we will examine in detail in Chapter 3. While the emergence of the "postbureaucratic" organization (see Chapter 8) and job enrichment has somewhat modified this principle, it is still as applicable to today's organizations as it was 200 years ago and remains a basic feature of modern capitalism. Anyone who has worked on a production line or in a fast-food restaurant (e.g., Subway, Taco Bell, McDonald's, etc.) will be well aware of this principle.

Goal Orientation

Organizations, whether nonprofit or for profit, are oriented toward particular goals. Indeed, one could argue that the goals of an organization are what provide it with its particular character, coalescing its members into something more than a random group of individuals. Barnard (1938) makes this goal orientation explicit in his definition of an organization: "An organization comes into being when (1) there are persons able to communicate with each other (2) who are willing to contribute to action (3) to accomplish a common purpose" (p. 82). Universities have education and research as their overarching goals; for-profit companies aim for excellence in their products and, thus, a large market share.

Of course, organizations often have multiple and competing goals, making Barnard's idea of a "common purpose" a complex one. Within a large software company, for example, there may be conflict between the respective goals of the research and development (R&D) and marketing departments. The former might want to spend extra months perfecting a new software program, while the latter might be more interested in getting it to customers quickly and working the bugs out in later versions.

Sometimes company goals can conflict with those of other interest groups, such as community members, employees, or shareholders. In its goal to increase profits, a company might pollute the environment, lay off workers, overlook safety regulations (think BP and deep sea oil drilling) or move its production facilities to countries where labor is cheaper. In recent years shareholder groups have increased their power in publicly traded organizations; in consequence, the "quarterly report" has become a key marker of corporate success, with significant pressure on organizations to produce quick results. In her study of Wall Street investment banking, anthropologist Karen Ho (2009) shows how increased shareholder power has caused many corporations to move away from long-term planning and toward short-term returns on investment—a shift that has had negative consequences for the stability of the economy.

Control Mechanisms

Control is a central, defining feature of complex organizations. As we discussed earlier, the goals and interests of employees and the larger organization frequently conflict, and so various forms of control are necessary to achieve coordinated, goal-oriented behavior. Organizational control is not, by definition, problematic; however, it can often have negative consequences for employees, as we will see below and in later chapters. While Redding presents two forms of control (hierarchy of authority and rules, plans, and roles), I will outline five different control mechanisms that function in the contemporary organization.

Direct Control

The simplest way to control employees is to direct them in explicit ways and then monitor their behavior to make sure they are performing adequately. As such, many organizations function through superior–subordinate relations, where the former has the authority to coerce the latter into working in specific ways. Since the beginning of the industrial revolution, supervisors have been employed to make sure that workers diligently perform their tasks rather than take long breaks or talk to coworkers. As we will see in Chapter 3, in the early stages of industrialization such coercive forms of control were deployed to direct workers who were not used to working in factory settings where "clock time" ruled.

Such close supervision, however, is hardly a relic of 19th and early 20th century factories. Many of you have probably had jobs where your work was closely monitored by a supervisor. In their cleverly titled book, *Void Where Prohibited*, Linder and Nygaard (1998) document restrictions on factory workers' rest and toilet breaks, arguing that such restrictions are more widespread now than they were in the early 20th century. The authors even document cases of workers wearing adult diapers on the production line because of the company's tight restrictions on toilet breaks! In one high-profile case, the Jim Beam company was cited for violating Occupational Safety and Health Administration regulations, when in 2001 the company implemented a policy severely restricting the time and frequency of employee toilet breaks. Direct supervisory control of workers, then, is still very much a feature of the modern organization.

Technological Control

A somewhat less direct form of control is exercised on employees through various kinds of organizational technology (Edwards, 1979). Such technology usually controls both the kinds of work people do and the speed at which they work. Henry Ford's introduction of the moving production line in automobile manufacturing in 1913 is the classic example of such control. From a management perspective, this form of control has the dual benefit of being able to dictate the workers' rate of production and also confining the worker to a particular location (thus limiting the worker's ability to socialize with other workers).

As our economy has shifted from heavy production to a service economy, the forms of technological control have changed. The fast-food industry is a good example of a modern form of technological control, where computer technology carefully regulates (down to the second) every task performed by the employee. At McDonald's, for example, even the dispensing of soda is controlled to make sure exactly the right quantity is released into the cup—the employee has no room at all to exercise discretion (Ritzer, 2000).

In our increasingly service-oriented economy, customers, too, are subject to technological control. In fast-food restaurants, hard seats encourage customers to "eat and run," and menu items are placed in highly visible locations so the customers are ready to deliver their orders as soon as they arrive at the head of the line (Leidner, 1993). In addition, customers are "trained" to line up to place orders and to bus their own trays in order to increase efficiency and productivity. Airport check-in is now mostly self-service, with customers doing the work that used to be done by airline employees—a significant cost savings for the airlines. And many companies (e.g., AT&T and Comcast) are now using online customer discussion forums that enable customers to solve technical problems for each other, thus significantly reducing customer service expenses (Manjoo, 2011).

Thinkstock Images/Comstock/Thinkstock

Technological forms of control often shift work from employees to customers as a way to increase efficiency and profitability.

Finally, technological control in the form of electronic surveillance is widespread in organizations. With such technology, employees can never be certain when they are being monitored and thus are forced to behave at all times *as if* they are under surveillance. The philosopher Michel Foucault (1979) has referred to this form of control as *panopticism*, after the Panopticon—a prison designed by the 19th century utilitarian thinker Jeremy Bentham. Bentham's prison was designed in a circular fashion so a guard in the central watchtower could observe all the prisoners without being visible himself. As such, the prisoners engaged in a form of self-policing. People working in telemarketing, for example, are subject to such surveillance by an invisible supervisor who can eavesdrop on their calls. Similarly, employees doing data-entry jobs often have their keystrokes counted, allowing employers to collect data on their productivity remotely. (See Critical Technologies 1.1 for more on communication technology.)

Critical Technologies 1.1
Defining Communication Technology

In each chapter of this book you will find a text box such as this one that highlights the critical role of communication technologies in organizational life. What is a communication technology (CT)? We will use a broad conception, defining it as anything that mediates and alters the user's relationship to the world. In this sense, CT is not just a tool for the transmission of information but actually shapes our experiences and sense of reality. Put another way, CTs embody a certain kind of human subjectivity and extend our relationship to the world through that subjectivity. In this book, then, we will use a social constructionist, meaning-centered approach to CT, examining the dynamic relationships among CTs, human identities, and organizational communication processes.

While we think of CT as generally being electronic, it is not necessarily so. For example, glasses are a form of CT, altering an individual's relation to the world by enabling him or her to see objects and people not otherwise visible. The invention of the microscope brought a whole new world into view that was not previously known to exist. Thus, both glasses and microscopes are early examples of technologies that change and extend our subjectivities,

altering our relationship to the world and, indeed, the world itself.

One's view of CT depends in part on the perspective one adopts. A functionalist might focus on ways a particular CT can increase organizational efficiency. A critical approach to CT would highlight the ways in which technologies shape organizational power relations. Finally, a feminist perspective might examine how a particular CT has a "gendered" effect on organizational communication processes. For example, critical scholars have studied the use of CT in computerized call centers, examining the dynamic relationship between managerial efforts to control workers through strict routines and employee efforts to resist such control efforts and exercise more workplace freedom (e.g., Taylor & Bain, 2003). A functionalist, or management-oriented approach, on the other hand, would likely focus on how such technology can increase the efficiency of call processing and reduce the "downtime" employees experience.

In future chapters we will use these text boxes to critically examine the various ways in which particular CTs have had a significant impact on organizational life.

Bureaucratic Control

Despite a shift away from bureaucratic organizational forms toward more flexible, less formal structures, bureaucratic control is still common in many organizations (Edwards, 1979). As we will see in Chapter 3, the bureaucratic form is a central—perhaps defining—feature of Western democratic societies, enabling organization members to gain advancement on merit rather than based on one's connections. As a form of control, organizational bureaucracy exists as a system of rules, formal structures, and roles that both enable and constrain the activities of organization members. Concerns about bureaucratic "red tape" aside, bureaucracy can be a highly effective means of coordinating and controlling organizational activity (Du Gay, 2000; Perrow, 1986). For example, the smooth running of your day on campus as you move from class to class would be impossible without an efficient bureaucratic system that carefully coordinates the schedule—timed to the minute—of every single student and faculty member. In this sense, organizational life is unimaginable without at least some level of bureaucracy.

Ideological Control

Ideological control refers to the development of a system of values and beliefs with which employees are expected to identify strongly. From a management perspective, the beauty of ideological control is that it requires little direct supervision of employees. Instead, if employees have been appropriately socialized into the organization's system of beliefs and values, then they should have internalized a taken-for-granted understanding of what it means to work in the best interests of the organization.

In many respects, the "corporate-culture" movement that first emerged in the 1980s (see Chapter 6) represents an attempt by companies to exert ideological control over employees (Peters & Waterman, 1982). Companies often carefully vet potential employees to make sure they "fit" the culture, and then make explicit and carefully calibrated efforts to indoctrinate new employees through training programs such as "culture boot camp." For example, Disney employees are put through an intensive training program where they learn how to maintain the seamless fantasy that is the hallmark of Disney theme parks. Disney keeps a tight rein on its corporate culture; indeed, the Disney employee handbook even dictates the appropriate length and style of sideburns! Similarly, companies such as IBM, Whole Foods, and Southwest Airlines are recognized for their distinctive cultures. The success of Southwest as a low-cost airline has been attributed in no small part to management's cultivation of a culture of fun amongst employees at all levels (Freiberg & Freiberg, 1996).

While this form of control can be an effective means of creating an engaged, energized workforce, it can also be quite oppressive to many organization members, particularly as it often asks the employee to invest his or her very identity, or sense of self, in the company. However, it is a form of oppression that is often disguised as something else—for example, being a "team" or "family" member. Employees who don't fit with the culture may feel alienated from their work. Management scholar John Van Maanen's (1991) account of his experience working at Disneyland is a great example of someone who resists the ideological control to which he is subjected—and loses his job as a result!

Disciplinary Control

Disciplinary control has emerged relatively recently as organizations have shifted from hierarchical, bureaucratic structures to flatter, decentralized systems of decision making. While ideological control is still, in many respects, top-down—with management attempting to impose a particular culture and value system on employees—disciplinary control is distinguished as a "bottom-up" form of control that focuses on employees' own production of a particular sense of self and work identity.

Disciplinary control has emerged as the relationship between organizations and employees has shifted away from the post-World War II social contract of stable, lifetime employment and toward "free agency" and a climate of much greater instability in the job market. This instability is reflected not only in people's high mobility in the job market but also in the fact that "the self" (the identity of each employee) has become a project each individual must constantly work on. Because the project of the self is never finished and must be continuously monitored and improved (in order to meet an ever more competitive work environment), people live in a perpetual state of anxiety about the value of their individual "brand." Thus, individuals constantly engage in forms of self-discipline in which the creation and continual improvement of an "entrepreneurial self" is the goal (Holmer Nadesan & Trethewey, 2000).

Think, for example, about your own day-to-day lives as college students. With adjustment for your own particular college context, I imagine that many of you have schedules similar to the ones reported by journalist David Brooks (2001) in an article called "The Organization Kid," in which he interviewed students at Princeton University: "crew practice at dawn, classes in the morning, resident-adviser duty, lunch, study groups, classes in the afternoon, tutoring disadvantaged kids in Trenton, a cappella practice, dinner, study, science lab, prayer session, hit the StairMaster, study a few hours more." Brooks indicates that some students even make appointments to meet with friends, lest they lose touch. Does this kind of daily schedule sound familiar to you?

Brooks's point is that students willingly (and happily) pursue these punishing schedules because they see it as necessary for the continual process of career advancement; they are basically spending 4 years as professional, goal-oriented students whose goal is continuous self-improvement. I suspect that a high percentage of you are engaged in precisely this kind of self-disciplinary activity in an effort to distinguish yourselves from one another and make yourselves marketable to potential employers.

In disciplinary forms of control, then, the individual is both the subject (autonomously making his or her own decisions and choice of goals) and object (the target of both self-discipline and corporate and other institutional efforts to shape identity) of knowledge. That is, control is exercised through "the constitution of the very person who makes decisions" (Fleming & Spicer, 2007, p. 23). Following the work of French philosopher Michel Foucault (1979, 1980b), control (or power, as he calls it) does not limit people's options or oppress them but, rather, creates the very conditions of possibility in which we act. We see ourselves, for example, as career-oriented, not because humans are "naturally" predisposed to having careers (after all, the idea of a "career" is a pretty recent historical phenomenon) but because there are numerous societal discourses, bodies of knowledge, and experts (who create bodies of knowledge) that construct us as career-oriented (think about the shelves full of books giving "expert" advice on career success at any bookstore, all of which claim to have *the* answer). As such, we become our own entrepreneurial project in which "career" is a defining construct around which life decisions are made.

To understand these five forms of control, it is important to keep three points in mind. First, many organizations use multiple forms of control. For example, an employee might be subject to direct control and bureaucratic control, and be heavily indoctrinated into the company's ideology. Furthermore, while analytically distinct, these forms of control overlap in practice in the workplace—technological control in the form of employee surveillance, for example, may result in employees engaging in forms of self-discipline that render the technology unnecessary.

Second, these forms of control operate with decreasing levels of direct coercion and increasing levels of participation by employees in their own control (control by active consent, if you will). Thus, direct control is the most coercive (telling someone exactly what to do), while disciplinary control is the least coercive (autonomous employee behavior and decision making). However, the development of less explicit and coercive forms of control does not mean that control is no longer an important issue in daily organizational life. Indeed, the development of more sophisticated forms of control suggests a greater need to understand the everyday dynamics of such control and its impact on the lives of organization members (i.e., you and me).

Third, the increasingly sophisticated forms of organizational control require a similarly sophisticated understanding of the role of communication in these control processes. Direct control relies on a simple understanding of how communication works (a message is transmitted from A [supervisor] to B [employee], instructing him or her how to behave), while ideological and disciplinary forms of control depend on a view of communication as complex and central to the construction of employee identities and organizational meaning systems—issues that figure prominently in this book. To get a better sense of this, let's now turn to a brief discussion of communication and its relation to organization.

Communication Processes

Clearly, communication is an important and defining feature of organizations. The fact that this book is called *Organizational Communication* strongly suggests that the terms *organization* and *communication* are closely linked. Indeed, the position we will take in this book is that *communication constitutes organization*—an idea referred to by some organizational communication scholars as the "CCO" approach to organizations (Ashcraft, Kuhn, & Cooren, 2009; Cooren, 2000; Putnam & Nicotera, 2008). Put simply, this means that communication activities are the basic, defining "stuff" of organizational life. Without communication, organizations cease to exist as meaningful human collectives. In this sense, organizations are not simply physical containers within which people communicate; rather, organizations exist because people communicate, creating the complex systems of meaning that we call "organizations."

Similarly, the communication activities of organization members are both made possible and constrained by the institutionalized rules and structures that organizations develop over time (Giddens, 1979). A useful way of thinking about organizations is to view them as complex patterns of communication habits. Just as individuals develop habitual, routine behaviors that enable them to negotiate daily life, so large groups of people develop patterns of communication behavior that enable coordination and collective, goal-oriented activity. A meeting, for example, is a communication phenomenon that is meaningful precisely because it is structured around rules for what counts as a meeting (and which differentiate it from a casual hallway conversation).

Although there are multiple definitions and conceptions of communication, in this book we will adopt a "meaning-centered" perspective, viewing communication as the basic, constitutive process through which people come to experience and make sense of the world in which they live. In other words, communication does not just describe an already existing reality but actually creates people's social reality. For example, organization members who talk about themselves as a "family" create a quite different social reality from that of an organization where a "machine" metaphor is dominant and organization members see themselves simply as cogs in that machine (Smith & Eisenberg, 1987).

From such a perspective, we can define **communication** as follows: *the dynamic, ongoing process of creating and negotiating meanings through interactional symbolic (verbal and nonverbal) practices, including conversation, metaphors, rituals, stories, dress, and space.* As we will see in later chapters, this definition is not accepted by all theories of organizational communication. However, it provides a useful benchmark against which we can examine and critique other perspectives.

Following from the above definition of communication, we can define **organizational communication** in the following way: *the process of creating and negotiating collective, coordinated systems of meaning through symbolic practices oriented toward the achievement of organizational goals.* Again, this definition attempts to capture the dynamic relationship between communication and organization, showing how each produces, and is produced by, the other. While the exact nature of this relationship may be a little fuzzy at the moment, we will continue to return to it throughout the book.

Having identified the main features of the phenomenon that is the subject of this book, we now need to develop a framework from which to examine the various approaches to organizational communication. In the next section of this chapter we will develop this framework in some detail.

❖ FRAMING THEORIES OF ORGANIZATIONAL COMMUNICATION

In order to be able to compare different perspectives on organizational communication, we will develop a **metatheoretical framework**—in other words, a "theory about theories"—that allows us to examine the underlying assumptions on which different theories are based. For example, what assumptions does a particular theory make about how we come to know things (epistemological assumptions)? What assumptions does a theory make about the nature of reality (ontological assumptions)? What assumptions about communication does a particular theory make? Scholars have developed a number of frameworks, each of which has utility in providing a coherent picture of the connections and differences amongst the various research traditions (Burrell & Morgan, 1979; Deetz, 2001; Krone, 2005).

However, the central organizing principle of my framework is the notion that we are living in an age characterized by a "**crisis of representation**" (Jameson, 1984). This phrase can be understood at two levels. First, the idea of "representation" refers to knowledge claims that researchers in various disciplines make about the world. In this context, the term has an *epistemological* dimension (that is, how we come to know things), reflecting some scholars' belief in the possibility of making knowledge claims that accurately reflect, or represent, an objectively existing world. Such a view of knowledge is dominant in the social sciences. The notion of a "crisis" thus reflects the recent emergence of challenges to this dominant model. In the past 30 years or so, multiple and competing ways of knowing have arisen, with each one setting out alternatives to the representational model.

Second, the notion of "representation" can be understood to refer to the issue of "voice." That is, which groups in our society have the opportunity and resources to speak and to represent their own interests and the interests of other groups? This issue has become increasingly complex as society has become more diverse. In the 1950s life was apparently much simpler. Shows such as *Leave It to Beaver* and *Father Knows Best* portrayed a homogeneous national culture with clearly defined values and social roles. In this vision, divorce was almost unheard of, everyone lived in the suburbs, and dad was the all-knowing authority figure who could solve any problem and who had a steady office job that supported the whole family. Mom, of course, was the nurturing housewife who was ready with pipe, slippers, and a home-cooked meal when dad came home from work.

Not only did such a life really exist only in its "ideal" form on TV, but its existence also was rooted in fundamental inequalities. The 1950s was a time of national stability and prosperity for a fairly small segment of the U.S. population—basically, white males. Simply by virtue of their race and/or gender, large segments of the population were denied any voice or even basic human rights such as employment and educational opportunities. The civil rights and feminist movements not only created opportunities for previously disenfranchised groups but also helped shape a worldview in which issues of identity and difference became central. Thus, with the emergence of challenges to a single (white, male) vision of society, various groups began to voice their own visions of the social order that fundamentally rewrote previously accepted premises about what is good, right, and possible. For example, gay rights organizations have challenged dominant definitions of "family," and the feminist movement has helped change long-held beliefs about women's roles in society.

Clearly, the two conceptions of "representation" discussed here are related. As the issue of "voice" has become more complex in the 21st century, so, too, have epistemological issues regarding what counts as acceptable knowledge claims. Where the scientific method once reigned supreme as the tried and tested way to generate universal knowledge, we now have competing perspectives and theories that aim to capture the richness and complexity of human social activity in ways the scientific method cannot.

How does this discussion of the "crisis of representation" relate to my attempt to lay out a useful framework for understanding theories of organizational communication? One way of thinking about the competing worldviews in the social sciences is to see them as presenting increasingly complex challenges to the representational model of knowledge discussed above. Below, I discuss five such worldviews. Each represents a progressive deepening of the "crisis of representation" in the social sciences generally and, more important for us, in the field of organizational communication.

For our purposes I will call these perspectives *discourses*. This term captures the idea that any worldview is made up of a community of scholars who communicate with one another about their research and debate the strengths and weaknesses of the theories they develop. The French philosopher Michel Foucault (1972, 1980b) uses the term *discourse* to describe a system of possibilities for the creation of knowledge. That is, what are the rules of a particular discourse that regulate what counts as a legitimate knowledge claim?

The five discourses I discuss are the following:

1. Functionalism: a discourse of representation

2. Interpretivism: a discourse of understanding

3. Critical theory: a discourse of suspicion

4. Postmodernism: a discourse of vulnerability

5. Feminism: a discourse of empowerment

Each of these discourses takes a particular relationship to what is called the modernist tradition. Broadly speaking, **modernism** refers to both a historical epoch and a way of thinking in which science, rationality, and progress are the dominant themes. Inspired by Enlightenment thought as represented in philosopher Immanuel Kant's Latin injunction,

"Sapere Aude" ("Dare to Know"), modernism is a period in which myth and superstition give way to the idea that each individual, through rational thought, can come to understand the world.

Science represents the pinnacle of modernism in its development of human rational faculties, leading to emancipation from the constraints of the natural world. In the 19th century, the Industrial Revolution and the emergence of the human sciences (sociology, psychology, etc.) are seen as further evidence of the positive effects of modernism on the human condition. Indeed, modernist principles are at the root of Western-style democratic principles. For example, Jean-Jacques Rousseau's "Declaration of the Rights of Man" (which helped inspire the French Revolution in 1792) embodies the notion that each individual has the right to liberty, regardless of his or her station in life. Such a concept was unthinkable in premodern societies, where authority rested with priests and kings by virtue of their God-given right to rule, and everyone was born into a social status that they occupied "naturally" for their entire lives.

Modernism, then, fundamentally altered humans' relationship to the world. Some scholars even argue that modernism is where the very notion of the individual as a rational, thinking being came into existence (e.g., Foucault, 1973). Moreover, the organization as an institutional form is very much a product of modernism; the organization as a bureaucratic structure was the mechanism that helped institutionalize modernist ways of thinking and enabled industrial capitalism to flourish.

Below, I discuss each discourse in greater detail, identifying the model of communication embodied in each.

Functionalism: The Discourse of Representation

This discourse embodies the basic modernist principles in the most straightforward, unproblematic way. The practitioners of this discourse believe that progress and emancipation can best be achieved through a process of discovery, in which the application of scientific principles gradually and progressively illuminates the world for us. This is the dominant discourse in the social sciences today, in which the researcher conducts carefully controlled experiments in order to make causal claims about human behavior. In literature, Sir Arthur Conan Doyle's character Sherlock Holmes is the perfect embodiment of these principles, employing his powers of observation and deduction to solve crimes. The Sherlock Holmes stories were written in the late 19th century, precisely at the time when the idea of Science as the way to Truth and a Better Life was taking a strong hold on society.

In organizational communication, much of the research over the past several decades has been dominated by this discourse. Certainly, early management theories such as scientific management, bureaucracy, and human relations theory were built on the principles of **functionalism**. In addition, much contemporary research into topic areas such as leadership (Barrett, 2011; Eagly & Johannesen-Schmidt, 2001; Yukl, 2006), superior–subordinate communication, organizational socialization (Jablin, 2001), and communication technology draws on this discourse. The goal in such research is to make predictive and generalizable claims about human behavior in organizations. For example, in her research on the relationship between gender and leadership, psychologist Alice Eagly is concerned with trying to measure quantitatively, and make generalizable claims about, the differences and similarities between male and female leaders in organizations.

What assumptions about communication are embedded in this discourse? True to the discourse of representation, communication is conceived as the means by which internal ideas are externalized. In this sense, communication is a vehicle, or conduit, through which thoughts and knowledge about the world can be expressed and shared. Thus, communication about the world and the world itself are two separate entities.

These assumptions are best exemplified by Shannon and Weaver's (1949) widely cited mathematical model of communication. As researchers for Bell Telephone Laboratories, Shannon and Weaver were interested in developing highly efficient systems for transmitting information from senders to receivers. As they state, "The fundamental problem of communication is that of reproducing at one point either exactly or approximately a message selected at another point" (p. 3). But because Shannon and Weaver were engineers, they defined communication largely as an engineering problem, having to do with the relationship amongst such issues as information, noise, channel capacity, and redundancy. Thus, although their model does not do a good job of representing actual face-to-face social interaction, it was for a long time dominant in various areas of communication research. Even today, although frequently criticized by scholars (e.g., Smith, 1970), it still dominates everyday understandings of how communication works.

Management scholar Stephen Axley (1984) has effectively illustrated some of the assumptions of this conduit model, along with its negative consequences for organizational communication processes (see Critical Case Study 1.1). For example, the conduit model ignores significant communication issues such as (1) the potential ambiguity of meaning in all communication acts, (2) the communication by speakers of unintentional meanings, (3) the role of receivers creating the meaning of any communication act, and (4) the need for redundancy in making sure messages are understood by others. In fact, Axley makes a strong case that the conduit metaphor lulls us into the belief that communication is a fairly easy and unproblematic activity that requires little effort. This "success-without-effort" orientation can have severe repercussions in organizations, where the degree of complexity of structures and meaning systems makes good communication a priority. When communication is conceived as relatively effortless and simple, then it is frequently overlooked as the cause of organizational problems. Or, when managers *do* identify "communication problems" in organizations, they frequently apply overly simplistic solutions that overlook the complexity of the communication process.

Interpretivism: The Discourse of Understanding

The interpretive discourse provides an alternative to the representational discourse of functionalism. While **interpretivism** has had an impact on organizational communication research only in the past 30 years, its roots are much older. Sometimes referred to as social constructionism, this perspective sees a direct relationship between communication processes and who we are as human beings. In other words, rather than viewing communication simply as a conduit, or vehicle, for expressing already formed ideas about an objective world, interpretivism sees communication as actually constituting that world. An example of this interpretive perspective is the CCO (communication constitutes organization) theory of communication mentioned earlier in the chapter.

Critical Case Study 1.1
A Conduit Model of Education

In a very real sense, how we *think about* communication has consequences for how we *behave and communicate* with others. Stephen Axley (1984) illustrates this powerfully in an argument regarding the dominance of the "conduit metaphor" in organizations. Following linguist Michael Reddy, Axley suggests that everyday talk about communication is dominated by an information transmission model that operates according to four implicit assumptions: (1) Language transfers thoughts and feelings between people, (2) speakers and writers insert thoughts and feelings into words, (3) words contain those thoughts and feelings, and (4) listeners and readers extract those thoughts and feelings from the words (p. 429). This model is implicit in everyday expressions such as, "He couldn't get his ideas across" and "She tried hard to put her thoughts into words." Let's look at the consequences of this model for the education process.

In U.S. colleges and universities, there is an increasing tendency toward large classes with enrollments of 400 to 500 students. The educational principles embedded in this tendency operate according to a conduit, transmission model of communication. Large class sizes mean that any interaction between professor and students is highly limited, with the dominant discourse being a monologue by the professor. In keeping with this monologue, students view themselves as the passive recipients of information transmitted by the professor. Knowledge consists of information inserted into words and transmitted from the professor's mouth to the students' brains, with lecture notes operating as the repository of such information. Professors try to ensure effective transmission of information by introducing redundancy into the system via the use of PowerPoint, repeating main issues, creating podcasts, putting lectures on iTunes, and so forth.

But the conduit model completely undermines any conception of education as an active and dynamic process in which students and professors engage in dialogues about interpretive possibilities. With pedagogy reduced to the transmission of hard, nonnegotiable facts, we are unable to recognize the extent to which knowledge production is actually a highly contested, contingent, and ever-changing process. The unhappy result is that by the time students do finally get to participate in classes of 20 or 30 (usually in their senior years) they have become little more than efficient note takers. They simply want to know what the Truth (at least in test-taking terms) is so they can write it down. Many students have thus developed a "trained incapacity" in which they apply a monologic model to a dialogic context.

Moreover, one might argue that the dialogic model is inefficient and unproductive in a context where students have become professional self-entrepreneurs who view education as a means to improving their personal "brand equity." The knowledge acquired in courses is useful only if translated into a stellar GPA and well-rounded transcript.

Discussion Questions

1. In groups or individually, develop a definition of communication. In what sense is it similar to or different from the conduit model of communication?

2. To what extent has your experience of college education been similar to the one described here? How has it been different?

3. If you were to create the ideal educational environment, what would it look like? Identify some principles of organizational communication discussed in this chapter that might help you formulate this ideal.

4. Which of the knowledge discourses discussed in this chapter is helpful in informing your understanding of how the educational process operates?

5. Do you agree or disagree with the view of today's students as discussed under "disciplinary control"? Why or why not? How would you describe your own student identity?

As you can perhaps see, this alternative perspective complicates the dominant representational model of human behavior. If communication *constitutes* human identity and reality, then we can no longer easily separate self, other, and world on the one hand and communicating about those things on the other hand. Suddenly, the representational model of knowledge is not quite as unproblematic as it at first appeared to be. No longer is there an objective Truth "out there" waiting to be discovered. Instead, human beings create realities as they interact together. Thus, the belief in predictive, generalizable models of human behavior gives way to a concern with generating deep understandings of the ways in which humans create complex systems of meaning. The philosopher Hans-Georg Gadamer (1989) encapsulates this view of language and communication when he states, "Language is not just one of man's possessions in the world; rather, on it depends the fact that man has a *world* at all" (p. 443).

The interpretive discourse, then, claims a close connection between communication and social reality—a view that has had a profound influence on the field of organizational communication over the past 30 years. Most significantly, there has been a shift from viewing communication as something that occurs *within* organizations to seeing communication as a dynamic process that actually creates organizations (Putnam & Pacanowsky, 1983). This is best illustrated in the emergence of a body of research referred to as "organizational culture" studies. We will be devoting Chapter 6 to this research, but it is worth briefly mentioning here to demonstrate the influence of the interpretive perspective.

The study of organizations as "cultures" has focused heavily on the everyday behavior of organization members, showing how their ordinary communicative practices are the basic "stuff" of what organizations are. In other words, such mundane communication events are seen as *constituting* organizations. Thus, researchers study phenomena such as stories (Boudens, 2005; Humphreys & Brown, 2002; Phillips, 1995; Trujillo & Dionisopoulos, 1987), rituals (Trice & Beyer, 1984), metaphors (Smith & Eisenberg, 1987; Tracy, Lutgen-Sandvik, & Alberts, 2006), and workplace humor (Lynch, 2002; Rhodes & Westwood, 2007). In each case, these communication activities are seen as fundamental to how organization members collectively shape their social reality. Furthermore, researchers in this tradition tend to reject quantitative methods in favor of qualitative forms of research, including oral interviews and participant-observation studies (where the researcher becomes a member of the organization being studied). Here, the goal is to allow organization members' own understanding of organizational life to come to the fore, rather than imposing predetermined categories on members' attitudes and behaviors.

In a study of Disneyland, for example, Ruth Smith and Eric Eisenberg (1987) use oral interviews to show how managers and employees use competing metaphors to characterize their understanding of Disneyland as a place to work. The authors argue that the competing metaphors of Disneyland as a "drama" (held by managers) and as a "family" (held by employees) lie at the root of an industrial dispute that threatens to tear apart the carefully cultivated image of Disneyland as "the happiest place on earth." One of the most interesting features of this study is that it shows how these metaphors are not just ways of talking about life at Disneyland (a representational view) but are fundamental to the shaping of employee identity and experience (an interpretive view). Thus, employees do not just *talk about* Disneyland as a family organization but actually *experience* it through this symbolic structure.

From the interpretive perspective, then, the real world is a symbolic world, and those symbols allow us to live a meaningful, coherent existence. Indeed, many interpretivists would argue that the symbolic world is the only world we can possibly know—we have no direct access to the world around us, which is always mediated by language, symbols, and communicative practices. Similarly, organizations are viewed not as structured containers within which communication (as information transfer) occurs but, rather, as communication phenomena that come into being through the everyday communication practices of their members.

Critical Theory: The Discourse of Suspicion

Like the interpretive approach, the critical perspective views reality as a product of the collective communication practices of social actors. Where it differs, however, is in its focus on the role of power, or control, in the process of reality construction. Critical theorists believe that different social groups have different levels of access to symbolic and communication resources; thus, the way reality gets constructed reflects the ability of powerful groups to shape this process. The notion of **critical theory** as a "discourse of suspicion" therefore focuses on the idea that the exercise of power is often hidden. That is, power is not always exercised coercively by the more powerful on the less powerful but, instead, works in subtle ways to shape the way in which people think about and experience the world.

Critical organizational communication researchers are interested in the ways that communication and power intersect in complex ways (Mumby, 1988). Building on the interpretive view that sees organizations as constituted through communication, critical scholars argue that the process of organizational meaning construction cannot be understood without examining organizations as political structures where power plays a central role. Different interest groups vie to shape the organizational meanings that constitute reality for members; management, for example, might attempt to engineer a certain organizational culture they expect employees to internalize, while employees may actively work to resist that culture (e.g., by making jokes about it or ironically following its principles) because they see it as an effort to manipulate them into working harder (Kunda, 1992). Critical researchers thus ask themselves how certain meaning systems are created through the communication and symbolic practices of organization members and how these meanings, in turn, sustain or resist certain organizational power relations (Deetz & Mumby, 1990).

For example, in my own research on a story told at IBM about a confrontation between a female security guard and Tom Watson, the CEO, I show how this story—while on the surface appearing to celebrate the ability of a low-level employee to "put one over" on the top guy—actually reinforces the strong sense of hierarchy and importance of rule following at IBM (Mumby, 1987). The story creates a social reality for organization members that subtly reinforces what is appropriate and inappropriate behavior. In a similar vein, critical management scholar Michael Rosen (1985, 1988) has studied corporate rituals to show how carefully orchestrated events such as company Christmas parties and corporate breakfasts can function to subtly reassert the worldview of the management élite in the organization.

Placed in the larger context of the modernist project, the critical perspective recognizes that the ideas of progress and emancipation that are so central to the Enlightenment actually represent a double-edged sword. On the one hand, the past 150 years have featured immense progress in science and technology, leading to longer and qualitatively better lives for people. On the other hand, this same progress has resulted in increasingly sophisticated forms of control that subtly exploit people for profit. To use organizational communication scholar Stan Deetz's (1992a) phrase, we live in an age of "corporate colonization" where our identities are heavily shaped by the corporate world. In this sense, the critical perspective aims to critique the voice of "managerialism" that dominates the field of management, and tries to give voice to those in organization who have relatively little power.

Postmodernism: The Discourse of Vulnerability

As an approach to knowledge, **postmodernism** poses the biggest challenge to the representational discourse. Of all the perspectives we have discussed so far, postmodernism is the one that questions most vigorously our common-sense understandings about what we know, and how we know what we know. In this sense, our common-sense view of the world is "vulnerable" to multiple alternative perspectives.

To understand what some scholars have referred to as "the postmodern condition" (Lyotard, 1984), we need to distinguish between two different but related terms. First, *postmodernity* is generally taken to refer to a specific historical period that, as the term suggests, comes after modernity. Precisely when the postmodern era began is open to wide interpretation (some scholars argue that it has yet to begin, that we are still in the modernist era). Some place its roots in the late 19th century with the writings of Nietzsche and his announcement of the "death of God" (i.e., the death of any universal, objective truth and the rise of multiple perspectives on the world). Others regard postmodernity as a much more recent phenomenon.

Architect Charles Jencks, for example, places the postmodern era's symbolic birth at 3:33 p.m. on July 18, 1973—the moment when the Pruitt-Igoe housing project in St. Louis was demolished (Harvey, 1989). Why does this particular moment signal the birth of postmodernity? Jencks argues that the demolition of this housing project symbolically represents the failure of the main hallmark of modernity—the application of rational principles to human, social problems. Certainly, building huge, identical towering structures to provide cheap, low-income housing seemed on the face of it to be a sensible solution to the problem of urban growth. It also satisfied the modernist concern for certainty and control by creating predictable, homogeneous environments. However, the designers of such projects failed to recognize the extent to which such "rational" structures would be deeply alienating to people. With little or no sense of community, these structures functioned more like prisons than homes. There is no better example of the darker side of modernity than this attempt by planners and bureaucrats to develop, in the name of efficiency, an organizational system that almost completely eliminated from people's lives what makes us most human.

The second term associated with the postmodern condition is *postmodernism*. This term refers not to a particular historical period but to a particular way of thinking about the world. Postmodernism is closely associated with an intellectual movement that originated in the 1960s with a group of French scholars—most notably, Michel Foucault and Jacques Derrida. Amongst other things, this movement questions some of the most deeply held principles of modernism. Most significantly, postmodernism challenges and rejects the modernist belief that rationality and science inevitably lead to progress and emancipation. Indeed, many postmodernists argue that it is precisely this unwavering and unquestioning

© iStockphoto.com/Terraxplorer

Modern principles of rationality do not always lead to higher quality of life for people.

belief in the scientific method and rational principles of investigation that has contributed to human suffering. The Pruitt-Igoe housing project discussed previously is such an instance of modernist principles being the problem rather than the solution.

What do postmodern scholars believe in? Part of the problem in answering this question is that laying out a set of foundational postmodern principles actually violates a basic postmodern tenet; that is, there are no foundations! The idea of "no foundations" is an attempt to get at the idea that there are multiple ways of looking at the world and, therefore, multiple potential realities. The influence of this position can be seen in debates over university curricula, where challenges to the so-called "Western canon" argue for the expansion of what counts as knowledge. Instead of requiring students to read only the "Great Books" (written almost exclusively by dead white males), it is argued that students should also be exposed to writers who traditionally have been marginalized by the dominance of Western ideas about Truth. Thus, African American, Asian, Chicana/o, women, gay, and lesbian writers have been integrated into many university curricula.

For postmodernists, then, there is not one, single "grand narrative" that reveals the truth about the world but, rather, many "little stories," each of which constitutes a particular way of seeing. Such multiple stories, postmodernists argue, create alternative realities that challenge the dominant modernist view of Truth as singular and universal.

How do postmodernists view communication? It should be no surprise that they reject the representational view discussed earlier. Indeed, postmodernists do their best to break any connection between communication and the world "out there." In other words, postmodernists reject any "correspondence" view of communication, in which statements somehow reflect an actually existing set of conditions in the world. In fact, some postmodernists reverse the common-sense relationship between communication and reality, arguing that rather than communication being the symbolic representation of a real world, communication is what is real, with the world having a secondary status. In French philosopher Jacques Derrida's (1976) famous words, "there is nothing outside of the text" (p. 157). In other words, all we have access to is discourse—*that* is what is real to us.

An example will help clarify this notion. Paris Hilton is a famous person, known by millions, perhaps billions—but why? She has no apparent talent. She isn't a sports star, a celebrated author, or a singer. The simple, postmodern answer is that she's famous for being famous. She has no substance as such, other than the way she has been carefully "branded," with a particular identity constructed for her (we'll talk in detail about branding in Chapter 12). Now, many stars are "branded," and no one completely escapes the postmodern juggernaut of created meanings, but we could argue that Paris Hilton is the nearest thing there is to pure text, pure discourse! Her fame is totally dependent on her ability to remain in the public eye, on her appearing regularly on my favorite show, *Access Hollywood*; in other words, her fame depends totally on her (in)famy. She is, in this sense, postmodernism personified.

Of course, these days Paris Hilton is passé and other postmodern personalities have usurped her—the entire Kardashian family, The Situation, Snooki, and so on ad nauseam. What all these "celebrities" have in common is that they are all almost purely "text"—they don't really exist outside of the media reality that created them.

How does this translate into the study of organizations? Several postmodern organization scholars have done close analyses of organizational texts, such as stories, to show how they impose a particular meaning on organization members and obscure other possibilities (Boje, 1995; Boje & Rosile, 1994; Calás & Smircich, 1991; Martin, 1990). Sometimes called *deconstruction*—a term coined by Derrida—these interpretive analyses attempt to illustrate how organizations are not the stable structures they appear to be but are actually relatively precarious systems of meaning fixed more by the dominance of a particular worldview.

In addition, many postmodern organization scholars examine the forms of disciplinary control (discussed earlier) that shape the postmodern (sometimes called post-Fordist or postbureaucratic) organizational environment. Scholars examine everything from management theories (how do they construct particular kinds of employee identity?) to the everyday dynamics of workplace control and resistance peculiar to the "culture of enterprise" in the (post)modern organization (Du Gay & Salaman, 1992; Knights & McCabe, 2000b; Townley, 1993b). We will discuss the postmodern, post-Fordist approach to organizational communication in Chapter 8.

Feminism: The Discourse of Empowerment

The feminist approach to organizations is the one that has been around the shortest amount of time, coming to prominence in the 1990s. In terms of the crisis of representation, the most distinctive feature of **feminism** is how it addresses the question of "voice." For the most part, feminist scholars argue, organization researchers have been "blind and deaf" to the question of gender (Wilson, 1996). In other words, for most of its history, the field of management has examined organizational life as if only one gender—men—existed. Moreover, organizations themselves have, until relatively recently, systematically excluded women from anything other than low-paid, entry-level positions.

One of the goals of feminist approaches to organizational communication, then, is to address the exclusion of women's voices from organizational life and to develop research approaches that highlight women's voices (Buzzanell, 1994). However, as we will see in Chapter 9 of this book, there are in reality multiple feminist perspectives, each of which has a different view of the role of women and men in organizations. Liberal feminism, for example, argues for creating a level playing field to provide women voice and opportunity in organizations. Radical feminism argues that creating a level playing field simply leaves patriarchy (male domination) intact, and women need to create alternative organizational forms free from male oppression. Finally, critical feminism takes the position that organizations are "gendered" structures of power; gender is an everyday, constitutive feature of organizational life that implicates both women and men.

From an organizational communication perspective, then, feminist research has focused on exploring the relationships among gender, power, and organization in order to develop more equitable organizational practices and structures. In this sense, feminism is a discourse of empowerment with a specific focus on gender as a construct around which power is exercised. For example, management scholar Rosabeth Moss Kanter's (1977) classic book *Men and Women of the Corporation* was the first to examine closely how the structure of organizations tends to exclude women from managerial positions by hiring them as "tokens" who are set up for failure in a male-dominated environment. Her book documents how men are not necessarily consciously sexist (though in the 1970s many were); rather, the communication environment of corporations—premised on the need to maintain effectiveness and efficiency by hiring and promoting employees who fit in (i.e., white men)—is what puts women at a distinct disadvantage.

As we will see later on, much feminist research has moved away from focusing exclusively on women and is much more interested in how power and organizational communication interact to create different kinds of gendered identities, including both femininity and masculinity. Today, then, and unlike its popular conception, feminism is a long way from its "male-bashing" stereotype and is much more interested in understanding how both women and men are "prisoners of gender" (Flax, 1990). In this sense, many feminist researchers are interested in how both men and women "do gender" (i.e., perform gendered identities) in their everyday organizational lives (Ashcraft, 2005; Collinson, 1988; Mumby, 1998).

In sum, the five perspectives discussed here show an increasing tendency toward questioning our common-sense understanding of the world. Starting from the widely held premise that we communicate in ways that represent or reflect a stable, objective world, we have gradually moved to a position in which the relationship between communication and the world we live in has been rendered complex and problematic. For our purposes, the main consequence of this discussion has been to undermine any simple understanding of the relationship between communication and organization. As I stated early in this chapter, we fail to appreciate fully the difficulties and complexities associated with organizational communication if we view this phenomenon as simply "communication in organizations." By calling into question this widely accepted view, we are better able to "think differently" about organizations and how they function in relation to our everyday lives. Table 1.2 provides a helpful summary of the five perspectives.

Table 1.2 Five Perspectives on Organizational Communication

Perspective	Model of Communication	View of Organization	Conception of Comm-Org Relationship	Conception of Truth/ Knowledge	Representative Metaphors	Research Goals
Functionalist	Communication as information transmission; conduit model	Goal-oriented structures independent from members' actions	Comm takes place *in* organizations; organization as container for communication	External to humans, waiting to be discovered; truth universal and generalizable	Machine Mirror Rational mind Conduit	Prediction and control Generalizable knowledge claims Establish causal relationships
Interpretivist	Communication as dialogic creation of meaning systems	Social/symbolic creations of collective and coordinated actions	Organizations and communication coproduced	Intersubjectively produced by members of a community; emerges through consensus	Culture Community Web Dialogue Narrative	Develop "thick descriptions" of cultures Insight and understanding
Critical	Communication as creation of ideological meaning systems mediated by power relations	Social/symbolic products of different political interests and power struggles	Organizations and communication coproduced; both are medium and product of deep structure power relations	Intersubjectively produced through ideology critique; truth as rational consensus free from ideological distortion	Political system Psychic prison Justice Conflict	Critique of unfair systems of power Emancipation from oppressive organizational structures
Postmodern	Communication as unstable and shifting system of meanings	Organizations consist of multiple, competing, and fragmented realities	Organizations as products of shifting and unstable systems of signification and texts	Multiple truths from different discourses and social groups; truth is local, not universal; "there's nothing outside of the text."	Carnival Hyperreality Rhizome Pastiche	Deconstruction and destabilization of common-sense views of the world Rejection of "grand narratives" and promotion of "little narratives"
Feminist	Communication as creation of gendered meanings and identities; humans "do gender" through communication	Organizations as gendered, coordinated systems of power relations and patriarchal structures	Communication as accomplishment of gendered, collective structures and practices	Privileging of women's experience; "the personal is political"; men and women as "prisoners of gender"	Gender Empowerment Nurturance Connection Difference Patriarchy	Gender equality Revaluing of "women's ways of knowing" Undermining of patriarchal logic Transcending binary thinking

❖ CONCLUSION

This chapter laid out some of the basic assumptions about organizational communication as a field of study. Any time we attempt to understand a particular field, we need to get a picture of the various assumptions on which different perspectives are built. Clearly, organizational communication studies draws on a number of different traditions, reflecting the complexity of the phenomenon we are attempting to understand.

As a way of understanding the field, I presented five different research traditions, or discourses—functionalism, interpretivism, critical theory, postmodernism, and feminism—each of which operates on a different set of assumptions about the nature of communication, organizations, and truth. With these research traditions as a context, we are now in a position to examine more closely the specific research traditions in organizational communication that have emerged in the past several decades.

However, while this chapter has provided us with a sense of the "big picture," we do not yet have a detailed sense of the specific lens or perspective we will use to examine these different theories and bodies of research. As will become clear in the course of this book, it is impossible to examine theory and research without adopting a position oneself (even though many textbooks tend to adopt a "God's-eye view," a view from "nowhere and everywhere"). As I mentioned earlier in this chapter, this book is written explicitly from a critical perspective, and so Chapter 2 will be devoted to a detailed discussion of this perspective. We will discuss the history of the critical perspective and its underlying assumptions, goals, and values. By the end of the chapter, we will have a useful set of principles with which to make sense of the complex terrain that constitutes the field of organizational communication studies.

CRITICAL APPLICATIONS

1. Individually or in groups, identify the different forms of control addressed in this chapter. Think about instances where you have experienced these forms of control. Some will be routine and everywhere; others will be more unusual. How did they make you feel? What were your responses to these experiences? To what degree do you take these control mechanisms for granted? Are there situations where you have tried to resist or circumvent organizational control mechanisms?

2. Discuss the five different perspectives on organizational communication addressed in this chapter. What are their defining features? Using a single organization with which you are familiar, choose three of the perspectives and use the principles of each to analyze the organization. What features of the organization are highlighted and hidden by each perspective? What does this tell you about the nature of research and knowledge generation?

KEY TERMS

communication   14

crisis of
representation   15

critical theory   21

feminism   24

functionalism   17

interpretivism   18

metatheoretical
framework   15

modernism   16

organizational
communication   15

organizational control   4

postmodernism   22

STUDENT STUDY SITE

Visit the student study site at **www.sagepub.com/mumbyorg** for these additional learning tools:

- Web quizzes
- eFlashcards
- SAGE journal articles

- Video resources
- Web resources

CHAPTER 2

The Critical Approach

The critical approach can enable you to navigate the complexities of organizational life.

$\mathbf{I}$n Chapter 1 we framed the field of organizational communication by providing a broad overview of several current research traditions. In this chapter we will take a much more detailed look at the perspective that will be our guide for the rest of this book—the critical approach. By the end of this chapter, you will have the analytic tools that will enable you to understand and critique the various theories, research traditions, and organizational processes we will be examining in the remaining chapters of this book. In developing these analytic tools my goal is to help you become "organizationally literate" such that you can better understand the expanding role of organizations in creating the world in which we live. Being "organizationally literate" enables us to become better organizational citizens, attending more critically to the important organizational processes and practices that shape both our working and leisure activities.

So, we must develop in detail the perspective that provides the guiding assumptions for this book. You may have noticed that the subtitle of this book is "A Critical Approach." In this context, the term *critical* refers not to the everyday, negative sense of that term but, rather, to a perspective on organizations that has emerged in the past 30 years. From this perspective, organizations are viewed as political systems where different interest groups compete for control of organizational resources (Morgan, 2006). The critical approach highlights the goal of making organizations more participatory and democratic structures that are more responsive to the needs of their multiple stakeholders (Deetz, 1995). As we examine different organizational and management theories through the course of this book, we will assess them with this critical approach as our guidepost.

The first goal of this chapter, then, is to provide you with a sense of the various influences and schools of thought that have helped establish a body of critical research in the field of organizational communication. Thus, we will take a historical lens to examine the emergence of the critical approach. A second goal of this chapter is to explain in some detail the principal elements of the critical approach. What are its assumptions? How does it view organizations and organizing practices? How does it conceive of communication? What are its goals and purposes? A third and final goal of this chapter is to show how the critical approach can be used as a way to examine and critique other ways of understanding organizations. As we move forward in the book, each perspective we address will be examined critically.

First, let us turn to an examination of the various historical influences that have led to the emergence of the critical approach.

❖ THE CRITICAL APPROACH: A HISTORY

While there are a number of different historical influences on the critical approach, one common thread tends to run through all these influences—the work of Karl Marx (1967; Marx & Engels, 1947). In the past 100 years or so, Marx's large body of writings has profoundly influenced modern social thought. Indeed, along with sociologists Emile Durkheim and Max Weber, Marx is considered to be a foundational thinker in our understanding of how society functions culturally, politically, and economically. However, the difficulty of Marx's work has led over the decades to a number of different interpretations of his ideas. These different interpretations have, in turn, resulted in the establishment of different research traditions and schools of thought that expand on Marx's original ideas and attempt to make them relevant to contemporary society.

In this section we will first discuss some of the basic elements of Marx's theory of society. Then, we will take a look at two schools of thought that are strongly influenced by Marx but that, at the same time, critique some of the limitations of his work and attempt to provide alternative views of society. These two schools of thought are (1) The Institute for Social Research (commonly known as the Frankfurt School) and (2) cultural studies.

Karl Marx

If we discuss Marx's work in the context of the framework developed in Chapter 1, we can say he was very much a critical modernist (indeed, one could argue that he is the principal founder of the critical modernist perspective). Why is he a critical modernist, and what is the importance of his work for the development of the critical approach?

During his life (1818–1883), Marx was witness to major economic and political upheaval in Europe, as **capitalism** became the dominant economic and political system.

Photos.com/Photos.com/Thinkstock

Karl Marx's writings have significantly influenced how we understand capitalist organizations.

Unlike earlier theorists such as Adam Smith (author of *The Wealth of Nations*, who we will talk about more in Chapter 3), Marx did not celebrate the emergence of capitalism but, rather, criticized the ways in which it exploited working people. As Marx (1967) showed in his most famous work, *Capital*, despite the 19th century's unprecedented growth in production and, hence, in wealth, most of this wealth was concentrated in the hands of a very small minority of people he called capitalists. Even more significantly, Marx showed that this wealth was not directly produced by capitalists but was generated through the exploitation of the laborers who worked for the capitalists in their factories. Marx is a critical modernist, then, in that he both critiques capitalism as an economic and political system of domination and exploitation and outlines an alternative political and economic system (socialism). Thus, he believes in the Enlightenment principle of emancipation and freedom for everyone, regardless of their economic or political status.

How does Marx arrive at this analysis of capitalism as an exploitative system? While his work is immense in volume and extremely complex, we can identify some basic issues.

Marx's Key Issues

First, Marx provides a detailed analysis of the historical development of different economic systems, or forms of ownership. These he describes as tribal, ancient, feudal, and capitalist. Each of these periods represents increasing levels of societal complexity in terms of how goods are produced, the forms of property ownership that exist, and the system of class relations—or social hierarchy—in place. For example, tribal societies featured a hunter–gatherer system of production, little division of labor, and no class system insofar as tribal property was communal. Ancient societies, such as Greece and Rome, were city-states organized around agriculture, with a developed civil and political system. In addition, the class structure consisted of male citizens, women, and slaves, with slaves doing all the direct labor. In the feudal system production was concentrated in agriculture, ownership was in the hands of an aristocratic class that had stewardship over the land, and the class system consisted of serfs who performed labor and the aristocrats who had rights over the serfs.

It was in capitalism, however, that the economic system took on its most complex—and most exploitative—form. Here, production shifted from the countryside to the town and, due to the passing of a series of "Enclosure Laws" that privatized "common land" (which everyone could use) for the exclusive use of the aristocracy, commoners were coercively removed from this land (where they kept livestock and grew produce) and forced to migrate to the developing cities, thus creating a large pool of wage labor for the new factories.

Marx is famous for developing a theory called **historical materialism**—an idea that analyzes history according to different modes of production, each involving shifting forms of property ownership and class relations. Thus, Marx identifies these different modes as common ownership (tribal society), citizen–slave (ancient society), aristocrat–serf (feudal society), and capitalist–wage laborer (capitalist society). In the last three cases, Marx shows that each system consists of an exploiting and an exploited class, with the former living off and dependent on the labor of the latter.

But what does Marx identify as being particularly exploitative about capitalism? Certainly, in the context of early 21st century society, capitalism is usually associated with democracy and freedom, and it has certainly been a driving force behind huge increases in our standard of living over the past 100 years or more. What was it, then, that Marx found so objectionable about this economic and political system?

In his analysis of capitalism, Marx identifies three elements peculiar to this particular economic system.

1. Under capitalism, workers are no longer able to produce for themselves what they need to live. In Marx's terms, they do not possess their own "means of production" (land, tools, animals, machinery, etc.). Because the advent of capitalism in Europe saw the forcible removal of large populations from common land, these dislocated people were forced to sell at the going market rate the only thing that remained to them—their labor power. In this sense, the non-owners of the means of production (workers) are forced to satisfy their own economic needs by selling their labor power to the dominant group (the capitalists). Thus, workers actually perform the economic maintenance of the capitalist class.

2. Marx identifies capitalism as the only system of economic production in which the very foundation of the system is not to make goods in order to produce even more goods but, rather, to turn money into even more money. In this sense, the product a particular company makes becomes largely irrelevant, as long as that company continues to make a strong "return on investment." Thus, the actual "use value" of the product is much less important than its "exchange value."

   This is even truer today than it was in Marx's time. For example, companies such as Procter and Gamble produce everything from bars of soap to potato chips, and media barons such as Rupert Murdoch own companies as diverse as television stations, newspapers, and sports teams. Moreover, financial markets such as Wall

Street do not even make products as such but leverage money itself many times over to make more money. The issue in all these cases is not whether such products are useful but whether, through their exchange value, they can create more wealth for investors. As Marx shows, this means that under capitalism, everything—including workers—becomes a commodity to be bought and sold.

3. The exploitative nature of capitalism is hidden. That is, when workers sell their labor power to capitalists they are not selling a specific amount of labor but, rather, a certain *capacity* to labor for a particular period of time. For example, a worker may be hired to work 10 hours a day at a particular hourly rate (say, $10). The capitalist's goal is to extract as much labor as possible from the worker during that 10-hour period (e.g., by constant supervision, speeding up the work process, etc.). As Marx points out, this means that the labor of the worker produces more value than that at which it is purchased (indeed, the value of the labor is infinitely expandable, limited only by technology, machine efficiency, and the worker's physical capacity). Marx refers to this difference between the value of the labor power, as purchased by the capitalist, and the actual value produced by the laborer as **surplus value**. This is the source of profit for the capitalist. Surplus value is hidden because the worker appears to be paid for a full day's work. However, as Marx shows, the worker is paid for only that portion of the working day that is necessary to maintain the worker, that is, feed and clothe him or her—what Marx calls "necessary labor." The rest of the working day is surplus labor and is actually unpaid.

Summarizing Marx's analysis, sociologist Ken Morrison (1995, p. 81) describes the features of surplus value in the following manner:

1. It is created by the surplus labor of the worker.
2. It is unpaid and hence creates value for the capitalist.
3. It represents deception because it claims to be paid labor.
4. It is at the heart of capitalist exploitation since the worker is not paid for the wealth created.

While Marx was obviously addressing the conditions that existed in 19th century factories, the same principles—and in some cases working conditions—still exist today (indeed, one of the reasons many companies move production overseas is that labor laws regarding minimum wage, length of working day, workplace safety, and so on are less strict or even nonexistent, thus creating more surplus value).

In her participant-observation study of Subaru-Isuzu Automotive, for example, sociologist Laurie Graham (1993) shows how contemporary capitalist organizations attempt to increase the amount of surplus value that workers produce. Graham discusses how workers are grouped into teams and required to perform a long list of tasks on a moving production line. When the plant first opened, the workers struggled to complete the tasks (22 in all) in the designated 5-minute time period. However, through increased efficiency and line speed up, the same tasks were soon performed in 3 minutes and 40 seconds. As Graham indicates,

"Everyone was expected to continually make his or her job more efficient, striving to work to maximum capacity" (p. 160). In Marx's terms, we can say that the workers are producing an increasing amount of surplus value, while the value they accrue to themselves in the form of wages remains the same.

This example is interesting because the workers are apparently happy to work ever harder while receiving no reward for this extra work (except perhaps a pat on the back, although there is a long history of companies firing employees as they become more efficient—hence, paradoxically, it is not always in employees' best interests to work hard!). This apparent willingness to put up with a system of exploitation brings us to the next crucial aspect of Marx's critique of capitalism—his theory of **ideology**. This concept will play an important role in later chapters of this book, so it is important to get a basic understanding of it now.

Marx uses the notion of ideology to show how the economic structure of society directly impacts the system of ideas that prevails at particular points in history. True to his materialist and economic orientation, Marx saw ideas as the outcome of economic activity. Marx argues that not only does our social existence shape how we see the world, but how we see reality depends on the ideas of those who control the means of production. In capitalism, of course, this is the ruling capitalist class. In one of his most famous passages, Marx says the following:

> The ideas of the ruling class are in every epoch the ruling ideas: i.e., the class, which is the ruling material force of society, is at the same time its ruling intellectual force. The class which has the means of material production at its disposal, has control at the same time over the means of mental production, so that thereby generally speaking, the ideas of those who lack the means of mental production are subject to it. (Marx & Engels, 1947, p. 39)

Ideology, then, is the system of attitudes, beliefs, ideas, perceptions, and values that shape the reality of people in society. However, ideology does not simply reflect reality as it exists but also shapes reality to favor the interests of the dominant class and stands in a relationship of opposition, or contradiction, to the working class. What does this mean? In the case of capitalism, it means that, for example, framing the labor process as "a fair day's work for a fair day's pay" ideologically legitimates the accumulation of surplus value by capitalists. As we have seen, however, capitalism obscures the exploitative features of the labor process.

Other examples of ideologies at work include (1) continuous attempts through the 19th and 20th centuries to construct a perception of women as unable to do "men's work" (except during times of war, of course); (2) development of a "myth of individualism," in which success is seen as purely the product of hard work and intelligence (the "Horatio Alger" myth) and failure becomes the responsibility of the individual; and (3) the historical creation of white racial superiority over non-white races (in a later chapter we'll look at how the issue of what groups get to count themselves as white has been fiercely contested during the history of the United States). There are many more such examples, but all function to structure reality in a way that serves the interests of the dominant class. Thus, while Marx shows that economic interests structure ideologies, he also shows that such ideologies take on a life of their own, inverting reality in a way that marginalizes some groups and privileges other, dominant groups.

In sum, Marx's writings have had a profound impact on our understanding of the relationships among economics, social reality, and the class structure of society. Taken together, his ideas of historical materialism, worker exploitation, and ideology demonstrated the importance of looking beneath "mere appearances" to examine the underlying social relations in capitalist society. In this sense, he provided an incisive critique of how capitalism turned everything into commodities (including workers themselves) and alienated people from natural productive activity.

Finally, we must remember that Marx was not only an economist and philosopher but also a revolutionary. Indeed, he saw one of the principal goals of philosophy as social change. In one of his most frequently quoted passages, he states, "The philosophers have only interpreted the world differently, the point is to change it" (Marx & Engels, 1947, p. 199). With Frederick Engels, he wrote *The Communist Manifesto*, an explicit call to workers around the world to engage in revolutionary struggle, containing the memorable line, "Working men of all countries unite! You have nothing to lose but your chains!" (Marx & Engels, 2008).

Critiquing Marx

While Marx's work is central to an understanding of the critical approach, his work also has significant limitations that have led scholars to revise his ideas over the past 100 years.

The first, and perhaps most obvious, criticism is his belief in the evolutionary nature of the economic model of history that he developed. Marx believed that he had developed a set of universal principles that, much like Darwin's theory of the evolution of species, explained the inevitable development of political and economic systems around the world. Thus, for Marx and his followers, just as feudalism had naturally evolved into capitalism, so capitalism would evolve into socialism.

The belief in the inevitability of this process was rooted partly in Marx's contention that capitalism was so exploitative and so beset with problems and paradoxes that it was bound to fail. Like slavery and feudalism before it, an economic system that kept the vast majority of people in poverty for the benefit of a few surely could not continue to survive. Marx argued that the basic contradictions of capitalism (e.g., that while the working class *produced* wealth directly through their labor, the capitalist class *accumulated* that wealth exclusively for itself) would eventually become so apparent that people would revolt. Indeed, in the middle of the 19th century, conditions in English factories had become so appallingly oppressive and poverty was so widespread that strong revolutionary movements gained considerable support amongst the general population. Similarly, in the United States, the late 19th and early 20th centuries saw massive wealth, poverty, and social unrest existing side by side. Trade unionism had strongly increased its membership, and the women's movement was actively demanding social and political reform.

However, as we all know, capitalism did not collapse (at least not in Western Europe and the United States). In fact, the one major revolution of the early 20th century took place in a country—Russia—that was relatively underdeveloped industrially (thus violating Marx's principle that revolution would occur only in advanced capitalist countries). Despite a number of crises, including the Depression of the 1930s, capitalism continued to be the dominant economic system. So, from a historical point of view, Marx's "evolutionary" position has proven problematic.

A second—and related—criticism of Marx is his almost exclusive focus on the economic features of capitalism. While his development of an economic, materialist view of society is important, he tends to overemphasize the extent to which the economic structure of a society determines its cultural, political, and ideological features. As later scholars showed, there is no easy one-to-one correspondence between economics and social reality. One cannot say, for example, that all members of the working class will develop a similar ideological point of view. As we know, there are many working-class people who share a conservative ideology and many upper-class people who have radical ideologies (the billionaire businessman George Soros would be a good current example). In this sense, while Marx's model suggests that economics determines class, which in turn determines ideology, later scholars have shown this position to be extremely suspect.

Finally, because he was writing in the middle of the 19th century, Marx was unable to foresee the significant changes that capitalism would go through in the next 100 years or so. As we have said, capitalism did not collapse as Marx predicted, and later scholars would have to account for the ways in which capitalism was able to adapt to changing economic and political circumstances. While subsequent generations of Marxist scholars would not abandon principles of social change, they nevertheless needed to develop theories that would explain why capitalism continued to reign supreme despite the continued existence of poverty and exploitation.

In the next two sections we will discuss two "neo-Marxist" schools of thought that have strongly influenced both social theory generally and critical organizational communication studies more specifically. Both schools have critiqued Marx's original writings and attempted to adapt his work to the analysis of modern capitalism.

The Institute for Social Research (the Frankfurt School)

The Institute for Social Research, founded in Frankfurt, Germany, in 1923, has had a major impact on European and U.S. theory and research over the past several decades. In the past 30 years it has grown in importance for scholars in the field of communication, particularly those studying mass media, rhetoric, and organizational communication. Established by a group of radical German Jewish intellectuals, most of whom came from well-to-do backgrounds, the work of this school was an attempt to reinterpret Marxist thought in the light of 20th century changes in capitalism. In particular, Frankfurt School members were interested in understanding capitalism not only as an economic system (which, as we have seen, was Marx's main focus) but also as a cultural and ideological system that had a significant impact on the way people thought about and experienced the world. Important Frankfurt School members included Max Horkheimer (who was the school's most influential director), Theodor Adorno, Herbert Marcuse (who became a significant figure in the 1960s student movement), and Walter Benjamin.

These researchers were concerned that, in the 40 years since Marx's death, Marxist theory had become overly dogmatic. Indeed, the basic tenets of Marxist thought had become akin to a system of religious principles seen as universally and indisputably true. For Frankfurt School members, "the true object of Marxism . . . was not the uncovering of immutable truths, but the fostering of social change" (Jay, 1973, p. 46). In broad terms, then, the work of the Frankfurt School was an attempt to make Marxist theory relevant to the changing nature of capitalism in the 20th century (Kellner, 1989).

In responding to Marxism's apparent failure to predict the demise of capitalism, the scholars of the Frankfurt School embarked on a research agenda that attempted both to retain the spirit of Marxism and to move beyond its rather simplistic model of inevitable economic evolution. In short, the Frankfurt School wanted to continue the examination and critique of capitalism that Marx had begun, but they decided to take this project in a different direction than that pursued by Marx and his followers.

What was this new direction? While the scholars of the Frankfurt School pursued many diverse research agendas, there are two themes around which much of their work tended to coalesce. First, the Frankfurt School researchers believed that orthodox Marxism was in error in focusing principally on the economic aspects of capitalism. While the economic foundations of a society strongly influence the structure and processes of that society, Frankfurt Schoolers believed it was just one element in a more complex model of society. As such, they rejected the model of **economic determinism** (which argued that the nature of society was causally determined by its economic foundation) of orthodox Marxism. In its place, Frankfurt Schoolers developed a **dialectical theory** through which they viewed society as the product of the interrelationships among its cultural, ideological, and economic aspects. This theory became known as *critical theory*—a term still used today to describe a great deal of neo-Marxist theory and research.

Second, Frankfurt School members were interested more broadly in the nature of knowledge itself and in examining the course that modernist, Enlightenment thought was taking in the 20th century. While they believed in the Enlightenment-inspired ideals of human emancipation and happiness, many were concerned that the 20th century had witnessed the perversion of these ideals. As we will see below, many Frankfurt School researchers developed a profound skepticism about the possibilities for fulfilling the goals of the Enlightenment project. Both of these themes are discussed next.

Critical Theory and the Critique of Capitalism

Given the failure of classical Marxism to predict the demise of capitalism, the Frankfurt School turned its attention to studying the processes by which capitalism was able to legitimate and sustain itself despite the existence of paradoxes and contradictions that Marx argued would lead to its overthrow. This shift in focus involved turning away from the traditional Marxist "base-superstructure" model of society (in which the economic base is seen as determining the ideological and political superstructure). In its place, the Frankfurt School developed a "dialectical" model, arguing for an interdependent relationship between the cultural and ideological elements of society on the one hand and the economic foundations of society on the other.

In their examination of the cultural and ideological aspects of society, Frankfurt School researchers were particularly interested in the then-recent emergence of various forms of mass media such as radio, television, film, and popular music. Frankfurt School scholars made the claim that these media functioned as control mechanisms through which general consent to capitalism was maintained. Horkheimer and Adorno (1988) coined the term **culture industry** to describe the coming together of popular forms of mass culture, the media, and advertising to create a "totally administered society" that left individuals little room for critical thought. For example, in describing the role of advertising in consumerism, Horkheimer and Adorno state:

> What is decisive today is . . . the necessity inherent in the system not to leave the customer alone, not for a moment to allow him any suspicion that resistance is possible. The principle states that he should be shown all his needs as capable of fulfillment, but that those needs should be so predetermined that he feels himself to be the eternal consumer, the object of the culture industry. . . . The paradise offered by the culture industry is the same old drudgery. (pp. 141–142)

According to Horkheimer and Adorno (1988), the development of the culture industry was one of the principal means by which capitalism could simultaneously perpetuate itself through the continuous creation of new needs and produce a mass consciousness that "buys into" the ideological beliefs of capitalist consumer society. As Jacques (1996, p. 153) states, "The same industrial processes which have resulted in the mass production of goods and services have been applied to the mass production of needs themselves."

Thus, the term *culture industry* suggests three ideas: (a) popular culture is mass-produced just like cars, laundry detergent, and candy; (b) it is administered from above and imposed on people rather than being generated by them spontaneously; and (c) it creates needs in people that would not otherwise exist but are nevertheless essential for the continued survival and expansion of capitalism and maintenance of the status quo. (See Critical Case Study 2.1 for an example of how this process works.) These ideas will be taken up in much more detail in Chapter 12 when we discuss branding and consumption.

Critical Theory and the Critique of Enlightenment Thought

In addition to developing a critical theory of society and capitalism, Frankfurt School members sought to analyze the relationship between Enlightenment thought and 20th century forms of science and rationality. Although they saw themselves very much working in the tradition of Enlightenment rationality, they considered that the confluence of capitalist modernity, science, and instrumental forms of thinking had led to the perversion of the Enlightenment project. In one of their most famous statements on the 20th century's "fall from grace," Horkheimer and Adorno (1988) comment, "In the most general sense of progressive thought, the Enlightenment has always aimed at liberating men from fear and establishing their sovereignty. Yet the fully enlightened earth radiates disaster triumphant" (p. 3).

Critical theory thus involves an examination of why—particularly in the 20th century—humankind, "instead of entering into a truly human condition, is sinking into a new kind of barbarism" (Horkheimer & Adorno, 1988, p. xi). For Frankfurt School researchers, the main answer to this question lies with the emergence of science and technology and the dominance of instrumental reasoning. While Adorno and Horkheimer do not argue that science and technology are bad *per se*, they suggest that society's focus on objectification and quantification has led to an extremely narrow conception of knowledge that is unreflective. In this sense, Horkheimer and Adorno claim that Enlightenment thought has become totalitarian, serving the interests of domination and supplanting more radical forms of thought (Kellner, 1989, p. 89). Indeed, where the Enlightenment supposedly

Critical Case Study 2.1
McDonaldizing "Fridays"

You are probably familiar with the Rebecca Black song "Friday." It's the one that went viral on YouTube in early 2011 with more than 160 million hits and was dubbed by some the worst pop song of all time (I won't post a link here, as I don't want to further rot anyone's brain, but you shouldn't have any trouble finding it online). My interest here is not in the song itself but in the organization that released it. Ark Music Factory (AMF) is a company that specializes in producing and marketing music sung by teens to a teen audience. On its website (arkmusicfactory.com) it actively recruits teens (mainly teenage girls, as far as I can tell) who want to become pop stars. For a fee, AMF will provide "a song made specifically" for the wannabe pop star and will also create a music video. When I went to the company's website, AMF was marketing a 14-year-old girl called Lexi St. George, who was getting the full "will she be the next big pop star?" treatment. By the time you read this, she will probably have disappeared into obscurity.

In many respects, AMF is a perfect example of how the "culture industry" operates. Music is reduced from a creative act to a rationalized, McDonaldized formula in which a product is carefully tailored to appeal to a particular set of audience demographics. In some ways, the actual song is unimportant—what matters is its manufacture as a commodity that will be widely consumed. Moreover, the singer is rationalized, too—she is provided with a carefully prepackaged image that will be eagerly consumed by the target audience. Indeed, I was struck by the similarity

between Rebecca Black's and Lexi St. George's videos, right down to the synthesized, electronic quality of their voices.

At their best, art and music provide insight into the human condition; rationalized, mass-produced pop culture is intended to narcotize us and encourage us to part with our hard-earned money—critical thinking is the *last* thing it needs.

Discussion Questions

1. What's your opinion of the kind of pop culture artifacts that companies such as AMF produce? Are they harmless fluff, or do they have a wider social impact?

2. Identify other examples of mass-produced, rationalized activities or items; what impact do they have on your daily life?

3. Take an "inventory" of your day from getting up to going to bed. How many times a day do you engage in activities that involve rationalization processes? What, if anything, does this tell you about your life?

4. Can you identify any activities you engage in that *do not* involve rationalization processes?

5. In groups, discuss the possibilities for "enchanting a disenchanted world" (Ritzer, 2005)—that is, for having experiences not rationalized through mass production and calculation. How easy is it to have these experiences?

---

stands for progress and greater freedom, Horkheimer and Adorno see a logical progression from factories to prisons to the concentration camps of Nazi Germany (keep in mind that they are writing as Jewish intellectuals in the immediate aftermath of World War II).

In summary, we can say that the critical theory of the Frankfurt School was *both* a critique of the existing conditions of capitalist society *and* an instrument of social transformation aimed at increasing human freedom, happiness, and well-being (Kellner, 1989, p. 32). However, like the classical Marxism it critiques, the Frankfurt School version of critical theory also possesses some limitations. We will briefly address these limitations next.

Critiquing the Frankfurt School

The most problematic element in Frankfurt School research is its narrow conception of the role of mass culture in society. It is probably fair to say that Adorno and many of his colleagues had a rather elitist notion of what counted as "culture," developing a rather rigid distinction between "high" and "mass" culture. For Adorno, only "high" culture was authentic, being able to produce the kind of insight and critical reflection that would result in social transformation. On the other hand, he saw the mass-produced culture of the "culture industry" as completely without redeeming value and as simply reproducing the status quo in capitalist society.

But this rigid separation of high and mass culture ironically ran counter to Adorno's (1973) espousal of a dialectical approach to the study of society. Through this polar opposition, Adorno and his colleagues overlooked the possibility that mass, popular culture could function as other than instruments of social control. Missing from the Frankfurt School's approach to popular culture was the idea that perhaps the consumers of the culture industry were more than simply unwitting dupes who accepted at face value everything the mass media produced. As later scholars show, there is no single "culture industry," nor is there one way in which people interpret the products of that industry. Indeed, one could argue that popular culture is a "contested terrain" in which conservative and radical meanings and interpretations compete together for dominance.

For example, hip-hop music is arguably both a multimillion dollar production of the culture industry and a means by which marginalized members of society—particularly young, African American men—express their frustration at social and political injustice. But this music does not have a singular meaning. To the politically conservative it represents a threat to traditional family values. To many women—both black and white—it is seen as an example of the violence and misogyny often aimed at women.

Thus, Frankfurt School researchers both overestimated the power of the culture industry to create a "totally administered society" in support of capitalism and underestimated the ability of the average person to develop interpretations that contest "administered" meanings. However, there is little doubt that the culture industry represents an extremely powerful and dominant force in modern society, and its effects are widespread. How else can one explain the fact that more people vote in *American Idol* than during a presidential election? Or how many people follow Ashton Kutcher's tweets? In this sense, while the Frankfurt School certainly overestimated the power of the culture industry, we should not underestimate its ability to influence social reality and shape meaning in society.

In sum, the Frankfurt School represents an important contribution to our understanding of the relationships among capitalism, culture, and power. It is central to our attempts to understand how people's experiences of the world are shaped at an everyday level. As we will see in later chapters, modern organizations have become extremely adept at shaping our perceptions, feelings, and identities, both as organization members and as consumers of corporate products. The reality is that we live and work in a corporate world, and very little of who we are is *not* affected in some fashion by corporate structures, processes, and systems of communication.

Cultural Studies

The research tradition known as **cultural studies** has had a major impact on scholars in a wide variety of fields, including English, media studies, sociology, and communication. In this section we will examine some of the principal elements of this work and discuss its implications for a critical approach to organizational communication.

As we saw earlier, Frankfurt School scholars used the term *culture industry* to describe the emergence and negative effects of popular culture in society, but scholars associated with cultural studies use the term *culture* in a different way. They critique the distinction between "high" and "low" culture, arguing that such an opposition was not only elitist but also limited the ways in which popular ("mass") culture could be conceptualized. Thus, over the past four decades, researchers in the cultural studies tradition have taken popular culture as a serious object of study, examining the complex ways in which it structures social reality. Researchers have studied cultural phenomena such as soap operas (Gledhill, 1997), teenage girls' magazines (McRobbie, 2000), and shopping malls (Fiske, 1989; Morris, 1998).

How, then, do researchers in the cultural studies tradition define the notion of "culture"? In its most basic sense, "culture" refers to the system of shared meanings that unites members of a particular group or community. Such shared meanings are developed through "systems of representation" (Hall, 1997a, 1997b) that enable us to make sense of the world in particular ways. The language we speak is the most obvious example of a representational system, but others include the clothing we wear, music, films, photography, and so forth. Indeed, everything has the potential to become part of a system of representation and thus come to "mean" something to a particular community.

Drawing on the work of Swiss linguist Ferdinand de Saussure (Culler, 1976) and French philosopher Roland Barthes (1972), cultural studies researchers show that the elements or signs that make up these systems of representation are both arbitrary and conventional. In other words, there is no natural or intrinsic meaning associated with a particular sign, and its meaning rests on an agreed-on set of rules, or conventions, that govern how the signs are coded. De Saussure further showed that the meaning of a sign does not depend on what that sign refers to (e.g., "tree" and the object that grows in your garden) but on its relationship to other signs in the same system of representation. In this sense, meaning arises out of *difference*. De Saussure referred to this scientific study of systems of representation as **semiology** (today, the term **semiotics** is most used to describe this area of study).

Let's take a simple, everyday example to illustrate this principle. As drivers, we are all dependent on traffic lights to regulate our driving behavior, and our understanding of traffic lights depends on our ability to learn the coding system that translates the lights into meaningful signs. Thus, red means "stop," yellow means "get ready to stop" (or, to some people, "drive faster"!), and green means "go." However, there is nothing natural about these meanings or about the relationship between the colors and what they refer to. Such meanings are arbitrary and conventional and only work because everyone agrees on their meanings. If everyone agreed to use a blue light to mean "stop," then this system of representation would work just as well. But there's another important principle at work here. Not only is the connection between the lights and what they refer to arbitrary, but their meaning is determined by the lights' relationship to, and difference from, each other. Thus, red means, or signifies, "stop" only because it can be differentiated from yellow and green. In this sense, meaning arises within a system of differences. This principle is borne out by the fact that in Britain the "representational system" of traffic lights is slightly more complex. Even though the same colors are used, an extra element of difference is added through the lighting of red and yellow together after the red—this combination of colors means "get ready to go" and prepares drivers for the appearance of the green light. Again, however, this combination is meaningful only in its difference from red, yellow, and green as they appear separately.

One of de Saussure's great achievements was to show that language—or any system of representation—is not something that arises from within us but, instead, is fundamentally social, requiring that we participate in the system of rules and conventions in order to be understood and share meaning. In this sense, systems of representation are what create the very possibility for culture and society and what—in a very real and concrete sense—create who we are as people (i.e., they create our identities).

Cultural studies researchers have taken up and explored these basic principles in studying the various systems of representation that constitute culture and society. However, as their work illustrates, most systems are much more complex than the traffic light example above. One of their findings has been that the meaning of particular signs or the combination of signs is not fixed but can change over time, or can function simultaneously with multiple meanings, depending on the ways in which signs are combined. Thus, we are not passive receivers of representational processes; instead, we have to interpret and make sense of them actively. Indeed, signs are not meaningful until they have been interpreted in some fashion. Again, an example will help explain this point.

© iStockphoto.com/raisbeckfoto

Capitalism needs to expand continually into new markets to survive.

The McDonald's "Golden Arches" is one of the most instantly recognizable signs in the United States, perhaps in the world. But what does this sign mean? At its most simple level, the sign is associated with a particular product—hamburgers and fries. But that is probably the most insignificant part of its meaning. As a corporation, McDonald's spends millions of dollars in advertising, attempting to "fix" the meaning of the golden arches in particular ways. Thus, they produce image advertising to create associations of efficiency, cleanliness, affordability, and quality of product. Through advertising, the arches also have become synonymous with family and solid American values. The golden arches have also come to represent the connection between capitalism and democracy. In the 1990s the opening of McDonald's stores in former Soviet Bloc countries was portrayed in the media as the triumph of free-market capitalism and democracy over planned economies and totalitarian governments. There's even a political theory that claims that no two countries where McDonald's stores have opened have ever gone to war (this theory held true until Israel invaded Lebanon in 2006)!

However, as cultural studies researchers have shown, the meaning of a sign is never fixed or final, being subject to constant slippage and contestation between different interest groups. While the McDonald's corporation would love to be able to control and fix the meaning of the arches fully and absolutely, the arbitrariness of signs and the active interpretive processes of different people make this impossible. Thus, interpretations have arisen that *resist* and challenge the process of meaning production in which McDonald's engages. For example, environmental groups have targeted McDonald's for its unsound ecological practices, such as clearing large areas of forest to raise cattle for hamburger meat. Similarly, health groups have criticized the high fat content of McDonald's food, despite the latter's efforts to present itself as catering to health-conscious customers.

Critics of the impact of McDonald's on society have even coined a new term—*McDonaldization* (Ritzer, 2000)—to describe the proliferation of prepackaged, instant, easily consumable products and lifestyles. In this context, McDonald's is seen as an icon for the ways in which capitalism has contributed to a fragmented, soulless way of life. In fact, the term *culture industry* would apply quite well to this process of McDonaldization.

Researchers in the cultural studies tradition, then, analyze the systems of representation that make up the cultures in which we live. In this sense, they are interested in the process of "meaning construction"—that is, in the various ways people collectively use different signifying practices or discourses to produce the social reality in which they live. However, as cultural studies scholars have shown, these processes do not occur randomly, spontaneously, or even consensually. The reality is that some people or groups of people have greater influence over the "meaning construction" process and are better able to get others to share in their view of the world. To use a cultural studies term, such groups have greater "cultural capital" (Bourdieu, 1977) in the sense that they have extensive economic, political, and symbolic resources at their disposal through which to influence the structure of social reality.

In the next section, then, we will examine how these principles can be used to examine organizations as communication phenomena. In other words, what insights can we gain into organizations by thinking of them as sites for complex and collective acts of meaning construction? From a critical perspective, what does it mean to view organizations as sites of everyday culture? Table 2.1 which follows compares the three critical perspectives we have discussed in this chapter.

Table 2.1   Comparing Marx, the Frankfurt School, and Cultural Studies

Issue	Marx	Frankfurt School	Cultural Studies
View of capitalism	• System of exploitation through wage labor • Mode of production that will fail, to be replaced by socialism • Exchange value over use value	• Economic, political, and cultural system of exploitation • Highly adaptable to change • Creates narrow, instrumental view of knowledge that serves status quo	• Close relation between economics and systems of representation • Capitalism neither inevitable nor bound to fail; contested through alternative meanings and subcultures
Conception of culture	• Determined by economic system • Ideology works to create dominant meanings/ideas that serve ruling class (capitalists)	• Popular culture administered from above through culture industry • Only high culture has meaning	• High/low culture distinction rejected • Culture produced through everyday life and creative activity of knowing actors
Role of ideology	• Maintains status quo: "Ideas of ruling class are ruling ideas"	• Works through culture industry to maintain status quo	• Place where meanings are contested; change can occur
Possibilities for resistance and/or social change	• Inevitable because of contradictions in capitalism • Workers will unite and overthrow capitalism, creating socialist system	• Unlikely because of dominance of culture industry	• Resistance occurs at everyday level in subcultures • Capitalism not overthrown but reformed through incremental change

❖ UNDERSTANDING ORGANIZATIONAL COMMUNICATION FROM A CRITICAL PERSPECTIVE

The critical approach adopts a number of assumptions about organizations as communicative phenomena. In this section we will examine those assumptions in detail.

Organizations Are Socially Constructed Through Communication Processes

In the past 30 years or so there has been wide acceptance of the idea that organizations are not "objective" structures but, rather, exist as a result of the collective and coordinated

Critical Technologies 2.1
Mediating Everyday Life

From a critical perspective, researchers are interested in how technologies mediate between people and the world, constructing social realities that have political consequences. Gary Shteyngart's funny and disturbing novel *Super Sad True Love Story* is set in the near future and depicts the United States as a declining former superpower where no one reads, everyone is obsessed with their credit and "F*#kability" ratings, and media and retail are the jobs everyone aspires to. In the novel, everyone wears an "Apparat" (a sophisticated web browsing device) that provides a constant stream of information not only about current media events but about everyone in the immediate environment, including their "C" and "F" scores, which determine power and social status.

Is this novel purely fictional, or an all-too-possible portrait of what geographer Simon Thrift (2005) calls the "increasing mediatization of everyday life" (p. 7)? Certainly the rise of social media has fundamentally changed our relationship to the world. Students seem increasingly unable to get through a class period without checking their smartphones, and it's not unusual to see many students walking across campus, heads down, as they check their latest texts/tweets/Facebook messages. Indeed, as social media become more pervasive, we seem to be increasingly isolated from the people in our immediate environment. It's not unusual to see families out to dinner "together," each absorbed with their mobile devices with no interaction among family members. People even feel compelled to text while driving—an activity that's as dangerous as drunk driving. Moreover, Twitter's reduction of ideas to 140 characters does little to foster dialogue or

encourage careful reflection about complex topics. Indeed, one might argue that the tendency to communicate ideas in ever-smaller units produces a trained incapacity to engage with longer, more complex arguments. In my experience, it's increasingly difficult to get students to read longer essays (how many of you have thought, "This chapter is too long!"? How many of you have used social media while reading it?).

Social media have also had an effect on organizing processes. During the popular uprisings in Egypt and Tunisia in early 2011 people used social media to organize government protests quickly. In the United Kingdom, the pressure group UK Uncut used social media to organize creative demonstrations against government cuts to public services. Such use of social media overcomes the need for hierarchical, centralized organizations and enables the quick development of loosely networked coalitions of like-minded people. UK Uncut is a great example of this, as an initial conversation about government cuts among 14 people in a pub quickly developed into a network of thousands of activists. An example of a UK Uncut event can be found here: http://www.youtube.com/watch?v=YbDVE-OHqic

From a critical perspective, scholars have argued that power is connected to mobility; exploitation and marginalization are increasingly the condition of those who are immobile or unconnected (Boltanski & Chiapello, 2005). Global capitalism moves at increasingly fast speeds and is the province of the powerful and the highly networked. In this sense, perhaps social media provide a means for the disenfranchised to connect with one another and resist authoritarianism.

---

communication processes of its members. Communication is not something that happens "in" organizations; rather, organizations come into being through communication processes (Pacanowsky & O'Donnell-Trujillo, 1982; Putnam, 1983; Putnam & Pacanowsky, 1983). Such a position is often referred to as a "social constructionist" approach because of its belief that language and communication do not simply reflect reality but actually create the realities in which we live. Consistent with the interpretive perspective discussed in Chapter 1, this position views "organizational reality" as a linguistic and communicative construction.

From this perspective, scholars study various forms of symbolic practice such as storytelling, metaphors, and humor in an attempt to understand the role they play in creating the reality that organization members experience (e.g., Browning, 1992; Lynch, 2002; Smith & Eisenberg, 1987; Trujillo & Dionisopoulos, 1987). Like the cultural studies tradition, this work is concerned with the ways in which people collectively create systems of meaning. Thus, an underlying premise of this research is that *social actors are active participants in the communicative construction of reality*. As I mentioned in Chapter 1, in recent years a group of organizational communication scholars have developed what is called the CCO approach—the communicative construction of organization—that looks at how routine organizational conversations and texts (reports, mission statement, etc.) shape organizational reality (Ashcraft, Kuhn, & Cooren, 2009; Cooren, 2000). From this perspective, documents are viewed not as simple providers of information but as themselves having agency that shapes people's behaviors in significant ways (Brummans, 2007).

Organizations Are Political Sites of Power and Control

Not only are organizations communicatively constructed, such construction processes are influenced by processes of power and control. In other words, organizational meanings do not simply arise spontaneously but are shaped by the various actors and stakeholder interests. In this context, the critical approach to organizations explores the relationship between the social construction process discussed above and the exercise of power.

There are many ways to conceive of organizational power (e.g., Bachrach & Baratz, 1962; Clegg, Courpasson, & Phillips, 2006; Dahl, 1957; Lukes, 1974; Pfeffer, 1981b), and we will examine some of these in more detail in Chapter 7. However, the critical approach views power as the process by which organization members' identities are shaped to accept and actively support certain issues, values, and interests. Thus, the critical approach's view of power is consistent with Italian philosopher Antonio Gramsci's (1971) concept of **hegemony**. For Gramsci, the notion of hegemony referred to the struggle over the establishment of certain meanings and ideas in society. He suggested that the process by which reality was shaped was always a contested process and that the hegemony of a particular group depended on its ability to articulate ideas that are actively taken up and pursued by members of other groups. In his own words, Gramsci defines hegemony as

> the "spontaneous" consent given by the great masses of the population to the general direction imposed on social life by the dominant fundamental group; this consent is "historically" caused by the prestige (and consequent confidence) which the dominant group enjoys because of its position and function in the world of production. (p. 12)

As we saw in discussing control in Chapter 1, organizations for the most part do not exercise power coercively but rather through developing consensus about various work issues. According to organizational communication scholars Phil Tompkins and George Cheney, organizations engage in "unobtrusive control" in which members come to accept the value premises on which their organization operates and actively adopt those premises in their organizational behavior (Cheney, 1991; Cheney & Tompkins, 1987; Tompkins & Cheney, 1985). Another way to think of this process is that organizational power is exercised when members experience strong identification with that organization (Barker, 1993, 1999).

However, the critical approach does not argue that processes such as concertive control and identification are by definition problematic. Clearly, collective action and members' identification with an organization are necessary for that organization to thrive. Rather, the concern is with the extent to which the assumptions identification and control are based on are open to examination and freely arrived at. Whose interests do these assumptions serve? Are organization members identifying with and taking on value systems that, when closely examined, work against their own best interests?

As Stan Deetz has shown, organizations consist of multiple stakeholders (managers, workers, shareholders, community members, customers, etc.), but rarely are these multiple and competing interests represented in organizational decision making (Deetz, 1995; Deetz & Brown, 2004). For example, while a corporation may reap huge profits from moving its operations to a country where labor is cheap, such a move can be devastating (economically, culturally, and psychologically) for the community left behind. Who gets to define the premises on which such a decision is made? What right do host communities have to expect responsible behavior from resident corporations? Who gets to define "responsible behavior"?

Thus, the conception of power with which the critical approach operates is one that emphasizes the "deep structure" of organizational life (Giddens, 1979). That is, what are the underlying interests, values, and assumptions that make some forms of organizational reality and member choices possible and foreclose the possibility of other choices and realities? Furthermore, how are these underlying interests shaped through the communication practices of the organization?

Therefore, when we say organizations are *political* sites, we mean that they consist of different underlying vested interests, each of which has different consequences for organizational stakeholders. The dominant interests are those that are best able to utilize political, cultural, and communicative resources to shape organizational reality in a way that supports those interests. These dominant interests often engage in forms of "discursive closure" (Deetz, 1992a) that limit the ways in which people can think, feel, experience, speak, and act in their organizations. This leads us to the third critical assumption about organizations.

Organizations Are Key Sites of Human Identity Formation in Modern Society

Following a number of scholars in management and organization studies, we can argue that organizations are not just places where people work but, more fundamentally, function as important sites for the creation of human identity (Deetz, 1992a; Knights & Willmott, 1999; Kuhn, 2006; Kuhn et al., 2008). Deetz, for example, argues that the modern corporation has become *the* primary institution for the development of our identities, surpassing the family, church, government, and education system in this role. In this sense, we are all subject to processes of **corporate colonization**—a concept that reflects the extent to which corporate ideologies and discourses pervade our lives (we'll discuss corporate colonization in more detail in Chapter 7).

Several researchers have examined how the boundaries between work and other aspects of our lives are becoming increasingly blurry and, thus, harder to manage. The emergence of "no-collar" work (usually creative "knowledge work" that occurs in decentralized organizations with flexible but highly demanding work schedules) in the past 15 to 20 years has put even more pressure on a coherent, stable sense of identity because it breaks down the boundaries between work and other spheres of life almost completely (Ross, 2003). As Andrew Ross has shown, while such no-collar work often occurs in humane, participative organizational environments, the hidden costs to our sense of self (in terms of losing any sense of identity independent from work) can be high. We will look more closely at this issue in Chapters 8 and 14.

Organizations Are Important Sites of Collective Decision Making and Democracy

The above three defining features of the modern organization situate it as a central institution of contemporary society. As such, we can argue that the workplace not only is an important context in which people's identities are constructed but also represents one of the principal—if not *the* principal—social and political realms within which decisions that affect our daily lives get made. There are two ways in which the critical approach examines issues of decision making and organizational democracy.

First, several researchers in organizational communication and related fields have begun to question traditional, hierarchical organizational structures, arguing that the quality of organizational life is enhanced with the development of more participatory structures (Cheney, 1995; Harrison, 1994; Rothschild-Whitt, 1979; Stohl & Cheney, 2001). Rothschild-Whitt (1979), for example, compares the traditional, bureaucratic organization with what she calls the "collectivist" organization—a structure that emphasizes shared power and widely dispersed decision-making responsibilities. And George Cheney (1995) has conducted field research on the Mondragón system of worker-owned cooperatives in the Basque region of Spain, examining the democratic decision processes by which they operate. Most of this research emphasizes both the need to develop more humane and democratic workplace practices and also argues that greater democracy can be more effective for the organization in its utilization of human resources.

Second, the critical approach moves beyond the immediate workplace and examines how organizations shape the meaning systems with which we make sense of the world. In this sense, the critical study of organizations is not only about the *cultures of organizations* but also about the *organization of culture* (Carlone & Taylor, 1998). Similar to Deetz's notion of "corporate colonization," this work examines how the modern corporation has shaped people's values, interests, and beliefs; that is, how do organizations structure our experience of the world? What are the consequences of these structuring processes for our identities as human beings? We will examine this issue in later chapters on identity and the meaning of work, and branding and consumption.

Organizations Are Sites of Ethical Issues and Dilemmas

Finally, because the critical approach argues for a close relationship between organizations and democracy, it is, by definition, concerned with organizational ethics (Lyon & Mirivel, 2010; May, Cooren, & Munshi, 2009). In this sense, "ethics" is not an issue that can be addressed or not but is rather a fundamental feature of organizational life. A critical approach to **organizational ethics** argues that, by virtue of their structure as systems of competing interests and power relations, organizations are continuously in the process of making decisions that affect people's lives in often fundamental ways.

Of course, we are all familiar with situations, often reported in the media, where organizations behave in unethical ways, usually by placing profits before the welfare of their employees or members of the public. The tobacco industry's failure to make public the harmful effects of smoking is perhaps the most extreme example of this kind of unethical behavior. More recently, pharmaceutical companies such as Merck have aggressively marketed antidepression drugs with the full knowledge that clinical trials had shown them to put many patients at risk of heart attack (Lyon, 2011). However, many ethical questions are much more complex and difficult to figure out. For example, is it ethical for organizations to introduce a policy of random drug testing for employees? In this instance, how does one balance the right to privacy against a company's right to curtail behaviors that may negatively affect employee performance? What are the ethical dilemmas involved in acts of whistle-blowing (Jensen, 1996)? How does a whistle-blower manage the tensions between loyalty to his or her company and responsibility to the larger community or society?

From the perspective adopted in this book, ethics are part of the fabric of everyday organizational life. In this sense, ethics are closely tied to communication issues and systems of power (Kersten, 1991; Mumby, 2011a). Thus, ethics are political in that while there are certainly different and conflicting ethical positions in organizations, some ethical systems come to dominate over others. In such circumstances, the choice of one set of ethics over another often has less to do with its ethical superiority than with the political power of those who espouse the dominant ethical position. As Kersten (1991) states, "The critical questions here are not only 'Whose ethics are dominant?,' but also 'What are the consequences of this dominance?'"

What, then, constitutes ethical communication? We can say that communication is ethical when it (a) promotes genuine dialogue and understanding amongst different organizational stakeholders, (b) contributes to individual and relational growth amongst organization members, (c) recognizes the possibility of different organizational realities operating simultaneously, (d) acknowledges the multiple and often conflicting interests of different organizational stakeholders, and (e) facilitates democratic and participatory decision-making processes across all levels of the organization.

Of course, such criteria for ethical communication are relatively easy to state but much more difficult to achieve in practice. And, certainly, by such standards much of the communication of everyday organizational life would be considered unethical. However, simply because these goals are difficult to achieve does not mean they are not worth striving for. Indeed, such criteria are quite consistent with models of organizational practice being developed by a number of researchers in U.S. business schools (e.g., Fletcher, 1998).

❖ CONCLUSION

The purpose of this chapter has been to provide you with an overview of the major characteristics of the critical approach to organizational communication—an approach that is the foundation for the rest of the book. As such, we discussed some of the major theorists and traditions associated with the critical approach. First, we examined the writings of the most famous exponent of the critical approach, Karl Marx, focusing mainly on his critique of 19th century capitalism. Second, we explored the limitations of Marx's ideas and suggested the need to "modernize" his perspective to account for 20th century changes in the capitalist system. Third, we saw how such changes are reflected in the writings of two later critical traditions—the Institute for Social Research (better known as the Frankfurt School) and the cultural studies tradition.

Both these schools of thought shift their attention to the cultural and ideological features of capitalism, examining the relationships between capitalism and popular culture. While the Frankfurt School adopted a rather elitist perspective, clearly distinguishing between "high" and "mass" culture (the "culture industry"), the cultural studies school focused more on the radical potential of popular culture and its possibilities for resisting the dominant values of commodity capitalism. We also brought our discussion back to focus more directly on organizational issues, examining the features of organizational communication as viewed from a critical perspective.

We are now in a position to examine the various theories and bodies of research that make up the field of organizational communication. Armed with the analytic tools we have discussed in these first two chapters, we can begin to get to grips with the long history of organizational communication as a field of study and to understand the historical, cultural, and political forces that have shaped the role of organizations in our society.

CRITICAL APPLICATIONS

1. Reflect on your relationship to popular culture. What are some of the ways you participate in and/or consume it? How invested are you in various aspects of popular culture (music, fashion, etc.)? Would you describe your relationship to popular culture as better described by the Frankfurt School perspective or the cultural studies perspective? Why?

2. Develop as complete a list as possible of the various organizations to which you belong. How would you describe your membership and participation in each? To what extent do they shape your identity as a person?

3. Examine the series of dots below. Try to connect them all with no more than four straight lines and without taking your pencil off the paper. How difficult was this to accomplish? How does this exercise reflect the way in which ideology works?

· · ·

· · ·

· · ·

KEY TERMS

capitalism   30

corporate colonization   47

cultural studies   40

culture industry   37

dialectical theory   37

economic determinism   37

hegemony   46

historical materialism   32

ideology   34

organizational ethics   49

semiology/semiotics   41

surplus value   33

STUDENT STUDY SITE

Visit the student study site at **www.sagepub.com/mumbyorg** for these additional learning tools:

- Web quizzes
- eFlashcards
- SAGE journal articles

- Video resources
- Web resources

PART II

Theories of Organizational Communication and the Modern Organization

CHAPTER 3

Scientific Management, Bureaucracy, and the Emergence of the Modern Organization

© iStockphoto.com/samxmeg

Many political, cultural, and economic factors have led to
the emergence of the modern organization.

In this chapter we will take a historical perspective to make sense of our status as "organizational beings." In particular, we will explore the "prehistory" of organizational life and examine some of the economic, political, and cultural conditions that led to the emergence of the modern corporation. This is not intended to be a comprehensive history; instead, it will serve to highlight some of the most important societal transformations that, in the past 200 years or so, have profoundly altered our sense of what it means to be human.

In addition to this historical perspective, we will examine some of the early theories of management and organizational communication that—in conjunction with huge shifts in the way we live—emerged early in the 20th century to explain and regulate the newly emergent organizational life. It is important to recognize that these theories did not emerge in a vacuum but are closely connected to the kinds of social and political tensions society was experiencing at the time. The two most influential theories of this time were scientific management, developed by Frederick Winslow Taylor, and bureaucratic theory, developed by one of the founding figures of sociology, Max Weber. In addition to these two theories, we will also be examining related theorizing and research that emerged around the same time. Finally, we will use the critical perspective to assess the strengths and weaknesses of these early theories.

55

❖ THE EMERGENCE OF THE MODERN ORGANIZATION

While many economic, political, and cultural factors led to the emergence of what we would recognize today as the modern, corporate organizational form, two factors are particularly worthy of mention—the emergence of industrial conceptions of time and space. Put simply, the modern organization depends for its existence on the willingness of its employees to appear together at a specific place and time. Of course, the recent emergence of the virtual organization complicates this claim, but most of us still have to "go" to work in a real, rather than a virtual, sense.

This statement is so obvious that it seems barely worthy of mention. In order to survive, organizations depend on people to come to work and stay for a set period of time. However, this has not always been the case. Indeed, the very idea that people should work for someone else and thus earn a wage is an idea of fairly recent invention. As late as the middle of the 19th century, working for an employer (as opposed to working for oneself) was called "wage slavery." For the average U.S. citizen, such a notion directly contradicted the principles of freedom and independence on which the United States was established. In fact, in the early 19th century around 80% of U.S. citizens were self-employed; by 1970 this number had decreased to a mere 10% (Braverman, 1974). To be described as an "employee"—a term that came into widespread use only in the late 19th century and was originally used exclusively to describe railroad workers—was definitely not a compliment. As management scholar Roy Jacques (1996) argues, "Before the late nineteenth century in the U.S., there were workers, but the employee did not exist" (p. 68).

This shift from a society consisting of "workers" to one consisting of "managers" and "employees" is key to understanding the historical transformations that led to the emergence of an "organizational society." This shift involves both a change in the kinds of jobs people held and a more fundamental transformation of collective beliefs, values, and cultural practices. Moreover, a change occurred in the forms of discipline and control to which people were willing to consent. In Foucault's (1979, 1980b) terms, the employee as a particular "subject" (i.e., an object of scrutiny about whom knowledge is produced) was created as a definable and measurable entity. Similarly, managers as an identifiable social group were also created to administer and control the newly emergent employee. To understand our origins as corporate or organizational beings, we will explore the elements of this creation process.

Time, Space, and the Mechanization of Travel

Most of us are familiar with the fact that the Industrial Revolution produced a major transformation in the structure of Western society. In Europe and the United States, the invention of steam power and the emergence of mechanical, high-volume production profoundly altered people's relationship to work. Broadly speaking, a major shift occurred in which society was transformed relatively rapidly from an agricultural, mercantile system to an industrial, capitalist system. In Britain—the first nation to experience an industrial revolution—this process began around 1780. In the United States, industrialization did not get fully under way until almost 100 years later. In both cases, however, the changes in how most people lived were profound. The process of mechanization not only enabled the production of vast quantities of goods but also fundamentally altered the economic, political, and cultural landscape.

Of course, this process did not happen by accident. Indeed, a whole set of societal changes occurred that made industrialization possible. One of those changes involved the creation of a mass population of workers who could be employed in the new factories. As I indicated earlier, self-employment was the norm; so what occurred to begin this shift to wage employment? In Britain and other parts of Europe this shift occurred with the passing of a series of "enclosure" laws. For hundreds of years, many people in Britain (mostly the poor) had access to "common lands" on which they could raise livestock and grow food (even today we use the term *commons* to describe a gathering place open to all, regardless of social status). The enclosure laws took away such commons rights, awarding these areas to landowners who made vast fortunes through rents and sheep farming. Those who were dispossessed could no longer provide for themselves and thus were forced to sell their labor to others.

In the United States, of course, there was no enclosure system; indeed, the government provided ordinary people with incentives to colonize the apparently limitless supply of land. The U.S. Industrial Revolution relied for its labor on the large numbers of immigrants that arrived in the late 19th and early 20th centuries. In fact, many of those immigrants left their home countries as a result of the enclosure system in Britain and much of Europe.

In addition to these important political developments, the shift to industrial capitalism was rooted in technological change. The creation and emergence of steam power functioned literally as the engine of the Industrial Revolution. It made possible the efficient, cheap, mass production of goods and allowed the development of a national transportation system that could rapidly move people and goods. However, there were other—equally significant—consequences of the emergence of mechanical power. In many respects these consequences were just as important in the emergence of the organizational society in which we all live. Here, I am referring to a profound shift in human consciousness and perception of reality that accompanied the emergence of railway transportation.

Historian Wolfgang Schivelbusch (1986) argues that the invention of the railway was a major factor in the transformation of humans' experience of time and space. Specifically, he suggests that the mechanical motion of the steam engine was rooted in regularity, conformity, and potentially unlimited duration and speed. For the first time in human history, transportation was freed from its natural, organic limitations, and its relation to the space it covered was changed drastically. With steam power, "motion was no longer dependent on the conditions of natural space, but on mechanical power that created its own new spatiality" (p. 10). Schivelbusch points out that a frequently used metaphor in the early 19th century to describe locomotive power was that it "shoots through like a bullet." Railroad tracks crossed rivers, carved through towns, and bored directly through mountains. In the face of such mechanical power, nature lost its awesome majesty, and the arrival of "the infernal machine" heralded a new, "rational" way of looking at the world.

From a 19th century perspective, the invention of mechanical forms of transportation was a double-edged sword. From the point of view of industry, steam-powered transportation represented the breaking of nature's fetters on economic development. No longer subject to the unpredictability of horses and wind power, transportation became much more efficient and predictable for business purposes. Against this modernist perspective was regret at the loss of a close relationship between humans and nature. The new travel technology alienated people from the natural relationships among the traveler, his or her vehicle, and the landscape through which the journey unfolded. Riding a horse or traveling in a stagecoach had a natural rhythm and sense of exertion, movement, and distance traveled that was lost in train travel. While such a perspective seems quaint from a 21st century point of view, it nevertheless indicates the fundamental change that mechanical travel introduced in people's experience of the world.

As we shall see, the railway traveler who felt alienated from his or her natural surroundings had much in common with the worker who experienced alienation from his or her work in the newly industrialized organization (of course, these were frequently the same people!). In order to better understand this process, however, we must look more closely at how this new industrial consciousness emerged in the workplace. That is, we need to examine how the craftsperson of the 18th century became the industrial employee of the 19th, 20th, and 21st centuries—the employee about whom so many management and organization theories have been developed.

Time, Space, and the Industrial Worker

The transformation of society from a primarily agrarian to an industrial system witnessed changes not only in the way goods were manufactured but also in people's relationship to and experience of work. The mass production of goods by mechanical means required a completely different kind of worker from the craftsperson of preindustrial times. We have already seen how political developments such as the enclosure system created workers as "raw material" for the new factories. However, the new worker had to embody a different set of work habits that were necessary for the new form of industrial work discipline. The development of these new work habits can be traced to the emergence of a new understanding and measurement of time.

Historian E. P. Thompson (1967) identifies the shift from task time to clock time as being a defining feature in the emergence of industrial capitalism. **Task time** refers to an organic sense of time in which work is shaped by the demands of the tasks to be performed. For example, the lives of the people living and working in a seaport are shaped by the ebb and flow of the tides, regardless of the "objective" clock time. Life in a farming community is shaped by the seasons; working long hours in the harvest season contrasts with the more limited amount of labor in the winter months. Similarly, the lives of independent craftspeople and artisans are oriented around the tasks they perform and are not dictated by the hands of the clock.

Thompson (1967) shows how, in preindustrial Britain, little of life was subject to routine, with work involving "alternate bouts of intense labour and of idleness" (p. 73). For the most part, people worked when they needed to and thought nothing of mixing leisure with labor. Thompson argues that this task orientation toward time is more humanly comprehensible than labor dictated by the clock and represents a lack of demarcation between work and life in general. From the perspective of clock time, however, such an orientation toward work appears wasteful.

In the struggle between employers and employees in early industrial capitalism, time proved to be *the* significant point of contention. As more and more people shifted from self-employment to working for others, employers attempted to impose a sense of time— clock time—that was alien to most workers but essential to the development of systematic and synchronized forms of mass production. As such, under the employer–employee industrial relationship, time was transformed from something that was passed to something that was spent—time became a form of currency. In this new relationship, it is not the task that is dominant but the value of the time for which the employer is paying the worker. (See Critical Technologies 3.1 below.)

However, the introduction of clock time into the workplace marked a period of considerable struggle between employers and employees, in which the former attempted to erode the old customs and habits of preindustrial life rooted in task time. For example, in the late 1700s Josiah Wedgwood was the first employer to introduce a system of "clocking in" for workers (Thompson, 1967, p. 83), dictating the *precise* time that employees started and finished work. In addition, early industrialists recognized that schooling could socialize

Critical Technologies 3.1
Timepieces and Punch Clocks

The shift from task time to clock time was a key development in industrial capitalism, and political struggles regarding time were (and still are) a widespread feature of capitalist–labor relations (Stevens & Lavin, 2007). E. P. Thompson (1967) documents the words of one early 19th century worker who reports the level of exploitation to which he and his fellow workers were subjected:

The clocks at the factories were often put forward in the morning and back at night, and instead of being instruments for the measurement of time, they were used as cloak for cheatery and oppression. Though this was known amongst the hands, all were afraid to speak, and a workman then was afraid to carry a watch, as it was no uncommon event to dismiss any one who presumed to know too much about the science of horology [timekeeping]. (p. 86)

Interestingly, it is precisely at the moment when industrialization required a much greater synchronization of labor that an explosion of watches and clocks occurred amongst the general population. This played an important role in socializing the average person into the new industrial "time consciousness." By the early 1800s watches and clocks were possessed widely and were considered not only convenient but a mark of prestige. Even today watches are given as gifts to mark long service with a company.

Along with the introduction of personal timepieces came factory owners' widespread use of punch clocks. These devices recorded the precise time that workers "clocked in" and "clocked out" of work. Again, a great deal of worker–management conflict developed (and still exists) around this technology. As a college student, I spent my summers working for a company that required hourly workers to clock in every morning. The punch clock required that we clock in by 7:30 a.m.—if we clocked in at, say, 7:32 a.m., we would not be officially "on the clock" until 7:45 a.m. On the other hand, if we were stupid enough to clock out at 4:59 p.m., we would get paid only until 4:45 p.m. Theoretically, then, the company could get 28 minutes of free labor from a worker. Employees would try to "game" the system by, for example, clocking in for someone else if it looked as though that person might be a couple of minutes late; or they might drive slowly back to the depot after making a delivery to make sure they didn't have to clock out too early.

In Charlie Chaplin's film *Modern Times*, there's a scene in which Chaplin runs out of the factory where he works after "losing it." On the street outside, Chaplin accosts a woman, who calls for help from a passing police officer. As Chaplin runs back into the factory to escape the pursuing officer, he takes time to stop and punch his time card. It's a great example of how the technology of the punch clock helped instill in workers a sense of industrial time and functioned as an important technology of control in shaping people's work lives.

future workers into the discipline of industrial time. Thus, a number of late-18th century social commentators viewed education as "training in the habit of industry," referring not to specific skills but to the discipline required for industrial work (Thompson, 1967, p. 84).

The introduction of clock time, then, was not only crucial for the development of mass-production techniques but also as a means of controlling a workforce for whom independent work was the norm. As Thompson (1967, p. 80) points out, the shift to clock time was not simply a technological advancement but, more significantly, made possible the systematic exploitation of labor. Once time became a form of currency—something that was paid for—then employers used all possible means to extract as much labor as possible from their workers. In fact, much of the workplace conflict in the 19th and early 20th centuries

Ryan McVay/Photodisc/Thinkstock

The creation of "clock time" was closely linked with industrialization and efforts to control factory workers.

revolved around the length of the working day, with workers' unions playing a significant role in reducing the amount of hours employees were required to work. Nevertheless, the basic principle that workers could be required by employers to work a certain number of hours was accepted relatively early in the Industrial Revolution.

In case this discussion appears rather detached from our early 21st century work experience, let me illustrate the extent to which time is still intimately connected to issues of power and control in the workplace. Management scholar Joanne Ciulla (2000) points out that the level of power and prestige a person holds in his or her job is connected quite closely to the amount of discretionary work time they possess. Generally speaking, the more one is considered a professional, the less one is tied to clock time and the more one is invested in the nature of the tasks one performs.

For example, as a university professor, I have a considerable amount of discretion over how I organize my time. As long as I fulfill my professional obligations (teaching, advising, committee work, research, etc.), how and where I spend that time is entirely up to me (in fact, as I write this, I'm sitting in a coffee shop!). I don't have to clock in when I come to work or clock out when I leave. So, even though I may work 60 hours in a given week, the clock dictates relatively little of that time. On the other hand, for an assembly-line worker, the clock and speed of the assembly line dictate the entire working day. Such a worker has little or no control over how his or her time is spent and, as in the case of the Jim Beam company (see Chapter 1), he or she may not even have discretion over when bathroom breaks are taken (Linder & Nygaard, 1998).

Each of these examples demonstrates the close connection between organizational power and one's control over clock time. As we will see later in this chapter, the 20th century witnessed a more and more discriminating measurement of clock time in the workplace. While 19th century owners and managers considered it a major accomplishment to gather workers together in the same place at the same time, 20th century managers developed much more precise forms of control.

In the first part of this chapter, we have been examining the historical, political, and communication contexts for the emergence of the modern organizational form. As we can see, the issue of control figures prominently. In order for organizations to function as collective, coordinated, goal-oriented social structures, fundamental shifts had to occur in the experience and meaning of work. While it took a number of decades, the average worker had to be trained to internalize, accept, and maybe even celebrate the idea of working for someone else in a synchronized, coordinated manner for a specified time period.

As the 20th century progressed, however, the simple coordination of employee activity was no longer the ultimate goal of organizations. As numerous management researchers were soon to show, there were many sources of untapped potential for increasing the productivity of organizational employees. In the rest of this chapter, we will explore in detail two of the earliest theories that attempted to further systematize life in the modern organization. First, we turn to scientific management.

❖ SCIENTIFIC MANAGEMENT: "TAYLORING" THE WORKER TO THE JOB

Frederick Winslow Taylor's (1911/1934) theory of **scientific management** was the first systematic attempt to develop a set of principles regarding the management of workers.

While the organization and control of workers had been a major preoccupation of employers since the beginning of the Industrial Revolution, Taylor's ideas transformed how control was exerted. However, to appreciate fully the impact of scientific management on control in the workplace, we need to understand the nature of work as it had developed under industrial capitalism. With this context, we will be able to see more clearly the ways in which Taylor's theory revolutionized management–worker relations.

Sociologist Harry Braverman (1974, p. 52) argues that work within industrial capitalism has three general features:

1. As we saw in our discussion of Marx in Chapter 2, workers are separated from the means by which to engage in the production of goods. As such, they can produce goods only by selling their labor power to others. Marx calls this process **expropriation**.

2. Workers are freed from any legal constraints (such as slavery or serfdom) that prevent them from freely selling their labor power to capitalists (although the development of company towns in the late 19th and early 20th centuries tended to put severe limits on a worker's freedom to sell his or her labor power).

3. From the capitalist's point of view, the purpose of employing workers is the expansion of a unit of capital that belongs to that capitalist. This is how the capitalist is able to make a profit.

An important principle in operation here is that the worker does not sell an agreed-on amount of labor but, rather, the *power* to labor for an agreed-on amount of time. In theory, human labor is infinitely expandable, and, thus, the capitalist seeks various ways to increase the productivity of the worker during a given time period (e.g., speeding up the production line).

It has long been established that one of the best ways to increase productivity is through the division of labor. Adam Smith (1723–1790) provides the most famous analysis of how the division of labor operates to increase productivity in his famous economic treatise, *An Inquiry Into the Nature and Causes of the Wealth of Nations* (Smith, 1776/1937). Using the example of the production of pins, Smith shows that, by dividing pin manufacture into 18 different operations, productivity is increased immensely.

The division of labor, first presented by Adam Smith well over 200 years ago, is an essential feature of all societies. As Braverman points out, however, the division of labor takes two different forms. First, the *social* division of labor divides society into different occupations and has been a feature of all societies for thousands of years. Second, the *manufacturing* division of labor is a specific feature of capitalist society and divides humans. That is, not only are the operations in making a particular product (e.g., pins) separated from one another; they are also assigned to different workers. Thus, the skill needed to make pins is not embodied in a single worker but, rather, is fragmented among many. While the social division of labor maintains the organic connection between the worker and his or her craft, the manufacturing division of labor ruptures that connection and turns the craftsperson into an unskilled detail worker.

In examining scientific management, we will be particularly interested in the manufacturing division of labor because Taylor concentrates his efforts here in his attempt to transform the nature of work. Let us now examine his theory more closely.

Taylor's Principles: The "One Best Way"

As an engineer at the Midvale Steel Company in Pennsylvania, Taylor spent his entire professional career attempting to develop more efficient ways to work. From shoveling piles of pig iron to the science of cutting metals in machine shops, Taylor was single-minded in his efforts to develop the "one best way" to perform various tasks. Starting in 1880, and continuing for 26 years, Taylor performed between 30,000 and 50,000 experiments on steel cutting alone (Taylor, 1911/1934, p. 106).

The development and implementation of the principles of scientific management, however, were by no means simply a technological issue. More than anything else, Taylor's system addressed the relations between employers and employees. In the late 19th and early 20th centuries, Taylor was confronted with a work environment characterized by high levels of antagonism between workers and managers. Much of this conflict revolved around efforts by employers to intensify the work process (i.e., get workers to work harder) and corresponding attempts by workers to restrict their output. Taylor referred to this deliberate restriction of output by workers as **systematic soldiering**—a problem he saw as *the* central problem in the workplace. While what he referred to as "natural soldiering" involved "the natural instinct and inherent tendency of men to take it easy" (Taylor, 1911/1934, p. 19), systematic soldiering resulted "from a careful study on the part of the workmen of what will promote their best interests . . . with the deliberate object of keeping the employers ignorant of how fast work can be done" (p. 21).

At first glance, systematic soldiering appears to defy logic. Why would workers wish to restrict their output and at the same time hide from their employers how fast a particular job could actually be done? This seems especially odd given that most workers in Taylor's time were paid according to a piece rate (i.e., a given amount for each "piece" produced) and thus, theoretically, would receive higher wages the more they produced. As Taylor shows, however, systematic soldiering is a rational response by workers to the logic of the workplace. For the most part, systematic soldiering occurred because employers tended to reduce the piece rate as the workers' output increased. As such, workers had to work harder to earn the same amount of money. Thus, they would attempt to find the minimally acceptable output level that would both maintain wages and insulate themselves from employer attempts to reduce labor costs.

The process of systematic soldiering was not an act by individual workers but, rather, was based on collective decision making by groups of workers. Workers policed one another to make sure no one was engaging in "rate busting"—a practice that could jeopardize the piece rate (and, potentially, coworkers' jobs). Indeed, such collective decision making was possible in part because many workers in the late 19th century were still organized into work groups within factories that reflected the old guild system.

For example, Ciulla (2000) documents the case of "iron rollers" in the Columbus Iron Works who worked in 12-man teams, with each team negotiating with the employer how much iron they would roll and their fee. They then made a collective decision regarding what portion of the fee each member would receive. These groups worked according to a strong moral code, the most important element of which was an agreement to produce only as much as their union had agreed on. A constant struggle was waged between these workers and the owners, who wanted increased output. According to Ciulla, "worker restriction of output symbolized unselfish brotherhood, personal dignity, and cultivation of the mind" (p. 92).

In developing his principles of scientific management, Taylor's objective was to replace this old system of **ordinary management**—a system he perceived as arbitrary and based on "rules of thumb"—with a rational system rooted in sound scientific principles. Such a system, he argued, demonstrated conclusively that the workplace did not have to be rooted in conflict and antagonism between mutually exclusive interests but, instead, could be based on cooperation and mutual benefit. From his perspective, scientific management turned a zero-sum game into a win-win situation.

Taylor outlines four basic principles of scientific management:

1. *Scientific job design.* Each element of the work task is designed according to scientific principles, thus replacing the old "rule-of-thumb" method of "ordinary management."

2. *Scientific selection and training of individual workers.* Each worker is matched to the job for which he or she is best suited and then trained in the necessary skills. This differs from the system of ordinary management, where workers chose their own work and trained themselves.

3. *Cooperation between management and workers.* In order to ensure that all the work being done corresponds to scientific management principles, managers supply a supportive supervisory environment that provides workers with a sense of achievement.

4. *Equal division of work between management and workers.* Under this principle, management assumes the responsibility for scientifically designing tasks and planning ahead. Under the old system, workers were responsible for both the planning and labor of work. Under the new system, managers develop the laws and formulas necessary to design and plan tasks scientifically.

Taylor argues that the only way in which these principles can be enacted is through what he calls a "complete mental revolution" in society in which both workers and managers fully recognize the benefits of working under the new system. In an argument consistent with Adam Smith's idea of "enlightened self-interest," Taylor claims that scientific management simultaneously increases productivity, cheapens the cost of consumer goods, and raises the income of workers. As a result, the population's real income is greatly increased and the entire country's general standard of living improves.

In *The Principles of Scientific Management* Taylor provides the reader with a series of vivid illustrations to make his case for "the one best way" to perform work tasks. The most famous example is his discussion of the "science of shoveling." In his research at the Bethlehem Steel Company, he shows how a worker named "Schmidt" increased his daily productivity from 12 ½ tons of pig iron shoveled to 47 tons. Taylor achieved this large increase in productivity by carefully observing the work process for several days, redesigning the task (e.g., by experimenting with the size of the shovel and varying rest periods), and choosing an appropriate worker who was physically capable of working at this higher rate. In this example, Taylor promised to pay Schmidt $1.85 per day instead of his usual $1.15. Thus, under Taylor's system, a 60% increase in wages is more than offset by an almost 300% increase in productivity.

From its inception, scientific management was an extremely controversial system. Indeed, in January 1912 Taylor was called to appear before a congressional committee set up to investigate the effects of his system on workers. While much of the opposition to scientific management came, not surprisingly, from labor unions, the system also encountered opposition from factory owners and captains of industry. From the latter's point of view, the idea that management skills were rooted in scientific principles rather than being inherent in a superior class of men ("captains of industry") was difficult to accept.

However, for Taylor, scientific management was more than just an efficiency system designed to improve productivity—it was something akin to a moral crusade. Historian Martha Banta (1993) has pointed out that *The Principles of Scientific Management* is written not so much like a typical scientific treatise but rather in a strong moral tone. As such, the principles of scientific management reflected Taylor's need "to eliminate immoral waste motion in the workplace and to replace dissonance with harmony in society at large" (p. 113). Indeed, Taylor's system was consistent with the progressive ideology of the time, in which science and efficiency were connected to social harmony (Fry, 1976, p. 125).

This connection between efficiency and societal harmony is a good indication of the extent to which many of the leading thinkers of the day saw "the question of organization" as *the* central issue facing society as a whole. At the turn of the century, mass immigration, African Americans moving north into industrial areas, women entering the workforce, and labor unrest were all seen as disrupting the smooth functioning of society. As such, the emergence of the scientific, machine model of organization appeared to provide a way to assimilate the new worker into the fabric of society. A formula to describe this historical period might be written as follows:

$$science \rightarrow rationality \rightarrow efficiency \rightarrow moral\ virtue \rightarrow social\ harmony$$

From a communication perspective, Taylor's principles encapsulate the idea that a progressive society rests on the clear and convincing communication of ideas. As becomes clear from reading Taylor's work, he is fully convinced that the only thing preventing full adoption of his principles is a lack of clear understanding of how his system operates. Thus, the provision of information in a clear manner and the use of vivid practical examples will ensure the wide acceptance of his system. Moreover, the way his system is practically implemented requires a model of communication consistent with the discourse of representation discussed in Chapter 1. That is, success of the system depends on the clear transmission of information about how a specific task should be performed. Taylor even recommended that managers prepare job cards that gave workers precise instructions for their tasks; in this way, there could be no misunderstandings or ambiguities about the nature of the work.

Next, we turn to a discussion of two of Taylor's contemporaries and collaborators—Frank and Lillian Gilbreth.

The Contributions of Frank and Lillian Gilbreth

While Taylor was the principal exponent of scientific management, he was certainly not alone in that endeavor. Almost as famous in their application of scientific principles to

Smithsonian Institute Archives

Along with her husband, Frank, Lillian Gilbreth refined scientific management and helped introduce its principles into the home.

work were the husband and wife team of Frank Bunker Gilbreth (1868–1924) and Lillian Moller Gilbreth (1878–1972). Immortalized in the book *Cheaper by the Dozen* (Gilbreth & Carey, 1948)—so called because Frank and Lillian had 12 children—the Gilbreths became famous for their development of time and motion studies. Although they were initially advocates of Taylor's system, they became rather disillusioned with Taylor's focus on time as an indicator of how efficiently a job was being performed (Graham, 1997, p. 547). Instead, they argued that managers should focus on motion rather than time (Graham, 1999, p. 639).

Using the new technology of motion pictures, the Gilbreths studied workers' movements by analyzing tasks according to **Therbligs**—the basic units of motion that make up all work tasks (can you spot where the word *Therbligs* comes from?). Using this unit of analysis, the goal was to redesign work tasks, making them more efficient by eliminating any unnecessary movements. The objective was not only to increase the efficiency of work (the Gilbreths promised a 33% reduction in unnecessary movements in any task) but to reduce the amount of fatigue experienced by workers. Given that one of the complaints about Taylor's system was that it pushed workers beyond limits of physical endurance, this goal caught the attention of managers, and the Gilbreths were widely sought after as organizational consultants.

A second important difference between the Gilbreths' system and Taylor's is that the former paid close attention to the psychological dimensions of work. While Taylor based his system on the belief that workers were motivated primarily by economic incentives, the Gilbreths believed that worker satisfaction in performing tasks was key to achieving optimum performance (Graham, 1997, 1999). Indeed, the Gilbreths developed the term *happiness minutes*, referring "both to the reduced fatigue that efficient workers would experience . . . and to the greater enthusiasm workers displayed once they began thinking about their own efficiency challenges" (Graham, 1999, p. 641).

Thus, the Gilbreths argued for the need to increase workers' job satisfaction by correctly matching individuals to jobs, minimizing the fatigue experienced in the work process, and giving workers personal reasons to work efficiently. In addition, they advocated tapping into employee expertise and involving them in decision making by, among other things, placing suggestion boxes in the workplace. As sociologist Laurel Graham (1999) points out, "Roughly a decade before Elton Mayo's famous 'Hawthorne Experiments' at Western Electric [see Chapter 4], Lillian Gilbreth made both the psychological attributes of the worker and the social characteristics of the work situation central to modern management" (p. 640).

While it would be easy to dismiss the Gilbreths' system as manipulative and aimed at further exploiting workers, evidence suggests they had a genuine concern for workers. Their break with Taylor's system was due in part to their perception that it treated workers simply as bodies, neglecting the psychological dimension of work that is necessary for job satisfaction. Indeed, in his consulting work, Frank Gilbreth had a policy of signing contracts with both managers and unions before taking on a particular job, suggesting a genuine concern for labor issues (Graham, 1999, p. 640).

However, the story of Frank and Lillian Gilbreth has an interesting twist. In 1924, Frank Gilbreth died unexpectedly of a heart attack, leaving Lillian as the sole breadwinner for her surviving 11 children. Despite the fact that they had been equal partners in their consulting business, Lillian found herself suddenly unable to earn a living this way. Given the climate of the times and the prejudice against educated women, she had to find alternative ways of supporting her family. Thus, in the years between 1924 and 1930 she remade herself as a nationally renowned expert in the application of scientific management principles to the home. As she herself explained in a 1925 magazine interview, "The search for the One Best Way of every activity, which is the keynote today in industrial engineering, applies equally well to home-keeping and raising a family" (quoted in Graham, 1999, p. 633).

For example, in discussing ways for women to increase their efficiency in the kitchen, Gilbreth recommended that they plot their movements by carrying a ball of string and pinning the string every time they changed direction. In this way, a woman's movements around the kitchen could be "graphed out" (Gilbreth, 1927). Such information could be used to rearrange the kitchen appliances in order to minimize unnecessary motion and hence reduce fatigue.

From the perspective of the scientific and progressive philosophy of the time, Lillian Gilbreth was fighting against a traditional, romantic view of the home that saw it as a haven from the harsh realities of modern, industrial life. Any changes in traditional household methods were viewed by many as undermining the sanctity and morality of the family unit. Thus, Gilbreth's task was not only to introduce science and efficiency into the home but also to connect this efficiency with morality. She had to disassociate morality from household drudgery and show that modernization "would increase job satisfaction without threatening the ideal of a nuclear family in a private home with a full-time homemaker" (Graham, 1999, p. 657). Thus, Gilbreth was able to show that a healthy—and, therefore, moral—home life was made possible only through the scientific achievement of an efficient home. Thus, once again, we see the connections among efficiency, morality, and social (in this case, family) harmony that were so prevalent in this era.

How, then, can we assess scientific management? In the next section we examine, from a critical perspective, some of its problems and limitations.

A Critical Assessment of Scientific Management

Sociologist Harry Braverman provides perhaps the most systematic critique of Taylor's system. Writing from a critical perspective, Braverman (1974) argues that scientific management is an "attempt to apply the methods of science to the increasingly complex problems of the control of labor in a rapidly growing capitalist enterprise" (p. 86). According to Braverman, Taylor assumes a capitalist perspective, recognizing the antagonistic relations between capital (represented by the employers) and alienated labor. His basic goal is to adapt the workers to the needs of capital. However, workers are not adequately controlled, because they maintain their hold over the labor process, generally knowing more about how the work is done than do managers. For Taylor, then, control over the labor process must be placed in the hands of management in order to realize the full potential of labor power.

Braverman claims that Taylor succeeds in his task by making a fundamental division between the conception of work and its execution. While in the old craft system, conception and execution were united in a single worker (for example, a shoemaker both designs a shoe and makes it), under Taylor's system, the unity of labor is broken in order to control it. By placing all knowledge about work in the hands of managers, workers lose control over how work gets done. This division between mental labor and physical labor serves to alienate workers from their jobs, insofar as they become mere appendages to the work process. Their autonomy and decision-making ability are minimized. Furthermore, as managers gain a monopoly over work knowledge and work is further divided into different tasks, workers become increasingly deskilled.

Braverman (1974) summarizes the effects of scientific management in the following, rather poignant, manner: "In the setting of antagonistic social relations, of alienated labor, hand and brain become not just separated, but divided and hostile, and the human unity of hand and brain turns into its opposite, something less than human" (p. 125).

We can argue, then, that for Taylor *the focal point of organizational control was the human body*. In his effort to take control of the labor process from workers and place it in the hands of management, he advocated the development of a vast body of knowledge about work processes, the object of which was to discipline the worker's body so it performed work in precise and calculated ways (Foucault, 1979). This legacy is still with us, as we will see in the next section.

A second, related, criticism of Taylor is that he viewed the individual worker as his basic unit of analysis and neglected the social dimension of work (a management focus that would emerge in the wake of the Hawthorne Studies, which produced the human relations movement—see Chapter 4). Indeed, Taylor saw any kind of communication and cooperation amongst workers as problematic precisely because it led to such problems as systematic soldiering. For Taylor, then, group communication in the workplace was dysfunctional because it interfered with the "one best way" of performing tasks. In this sense, Taylor's conception of communication is rooted in one-on-one information transmission between manager and worker.

Third, Taylor had a rather limited view of workers, seeing them as motivated exclusively by economic incentives. Any notion that workers might fulfill higher-order, psychological needs through satisfying work was completely absent from Taylor's model. Furthermore, his descriptions of the workers he studied suggested a rather paternalistic view of their abilities. He describes "Schmidt," for example, as being "so stupid and so phlegmatic that he more clearly resembles in his mental make-up the ox than any other type" (Taylor, 1911/1934), even though, by Taylor's own account, Schmidt was building his own house. Certainly, in comparison with Frank and Lillian Gilbreth's psychological model of the worker, his perspective captures little of the complexity of the worker's relation to his or her work and the larger organization.

Fourth, Taylor can be criticized for elevating scientific management to a moral system that had the ability to cure society's ills. Certainly, such conceit is consistent with the larger social movement of his time that equated rationality and efficiency with moral good. However, the idea that society as a whole should function according to his machine-like "one best way" is somewhat problematic. However, much of the enthusiasm for scientific management can be explained by the sense that society was disordered and full of social and political unrest. If everyone followed Taylor's principles (including in their daily lives), then order would be restored.

Finally, as I have already suggested, Taylor operated with a very limited conception of communication, though it was consistent with prevailing views of his time. For him, communication was a largely mechanical process compatible with the conduit model (Axley, 1984) discussed in Chapter 1. While Taylor talks about cooperation between management and workers, his conception of organizational communication seems limited to managers accurately transmitting information about work tasks to employees.

The Legacy of Scientific Management

The conventional wisdom of management thought suggests that scientific management quickly fell into disfavor and, with the emergence of human relations theory, largely disappeared as a viable way to manage employees. The reality, however, is very different. As Braverman (1974) points out, scientific management disappeared from general visibility not because it was rejected but because it became a widely accepted, taken-for-granted way of organizing work. Once Taylor's principles became a defining feature of the workplace, it was necessary to create various theories and models (such as human relations theory) to adjust the worker to the alienating nature of the work experience. Indeed, one need not look far to see the effects of Taylorism in today's workplace.

The fast-food industry is probably the most visible and successful practitioner of scientific management principles. There is no better example of this success than McDonald's, which has elevated the principle of the "one best way" to new heights (Leidner, 1993; Ritzer, 2000, 2004). Each McDonald's is run by closely following a 700-page operations manual, and no aspect of the business of selling hamburgers escapes careful control and routinization. It would certainly make no sense to walk into a McDonald's and ask, "What's good today?" Neither employees nor customers have much autonomy in the decisions they make ("value meal" items, for example, cut down on the amount of time it takes for people to place orders). Ritzer (2000) has argued that the basic features of "McDonaldization" are efficiency, calculability, predictability, and control—four elements that are highly consistent with Taylor's vision of scientific management.

The customer-service industry in general applies scientific management principles in a systematic way. For example, sales representatives in department stores often receive electronic messages on their cash registers instructing them to "call the customer by his or her first name." Many retail stores enforce strict guidelines about how quickly a customer should be greeted upon entering the store. A student once told me that the store she worked for required its sales representatives to greet customers within 19 seconds of their entering the store! And we have all experienced annoying telephone sales techniques in which the caller follows a script carefully designed to limit the kinds of responses the unlucky recipient of the call can make.

In recent years the power of computer software has taken scientific management of work to new heights. The grocery chain Meijer, for example, uses a computer system to measure the efficiency and speed of checkout clerks, with timing beginning automatically when each customer's first item is scanned. Each clerk is given a weekly efficiency score, and too many weeks below a baseline 95% score can result in termination. One of the effects of this efficiency effort (in addition to reducing labor costs) is that daily pleasantries between customers and checkout clerks have been significantly reduced (O'Connell, 2008).

Ryan McVay/Digital Vision/Thinkstock

Grocery stores use computer technology to monitor checkout employees' efficiency in bagging purchases.

What all these examples share is the effort to create an efficient, routinized system that maximizes control over both employee and customer. Each is consistent with Taylor's basic goal of separating the conception of work from its execution and disciplining the worker's body to perform tasks in a way that will secure profitability for the company. This is particularly true in the service industry, where the point of contact between customer and company employee is the primary source of revenue generation.

Finally, perhaps the most troubling legacy of scientific management is the degree to which Taylor's principles have entered our personal lives. Society is practically besieged by experts telling us how to lead "efficient" everyday lives. Every bookstore displays several rows of books written by "experts" who have a plan for making us more fulfilled people. These "self-help" books are based on the idea that there is "one best way" for us to conduct our lives. No one seems to notice the paradox of there being literally dozens of "one best ways." Books such as Steven Covey's (1989) *Seven Habits of Highly Effective People* preach a gospel that roots happiness in our ability to routinize our lives and locates personal empowerment in predictability. Ironically, many companies now use the principles of self-help gurus to train their workers as they search for new ways to incorporate private aspects of the self into work (Carlone, 2006; Carlone & Larson, 2006).

❖ BUREAUCRATIC THEORY: MAX WEBER AND ORGANIZATIONAL COMMUNICATION

Max Weber (1864–1920)—pronounced "Vayber"—is an important figure in the social sciences whose work is wide-ranging, complex, and difficult to classify (Clegg, 1994). Strangely, though, if you examine the way his writings have been presented in the fields of organizational communication and management, the diversity and complexity of Weber's works disappear. For the most part, he is presented almost exclusively as the theorist responsible for developing the bureaucratic model of organizational behavior. Most textbooks give Weber a page or two, restricting themselves to describing the features of bureaucracy as outlined by Weber (1978).

We will take a somewhat different approach to Weber and paint a broader picture of his work. Indeed, the first thing you should know about Weber is that he was not really an organizational theorist or researcher at all but, rather, a sociologist and philosopher. Weber was interested in studying organizations but only to the extent that they were examples of the broader social, political, and economic processes he was interested in explaining.

What, then, was Weber's main focus? In brief, most of his work sought to explain the historical development of various civilizations through the examination of political, legal, religious, and economic systems (Morrison, 1995). He asked questions such as, "What is the connection between religious systems and the development of particular economic structures and organizational forms?" For example, his famous study titled *The Protestant Ethic and the Spirit of Capitalism* (Weber, 1958) analyzes the influence of protestant religious doctrine on the development of capitalism in the United States and Europe. In this study, he shows how work and the "gain spirit" were elevated in the 19th century to a moral duty in everyday life—accumulating wealth was seen as a means to acquire grace and salvation.

Weber's writings can be compared to those of his countryman Karl Marx, in that both were interested in tracking the historical development of different societal forms. However, Weber differs from Marx in important ways. First, Weber disagreed with Marx that the job of philosophers was to change the world by linking theory to political action. Rather, Weber saw the primary goal of scholarship as developing a descriptive body of historically valid truths (although we will see later that Weber was not averse to engaging in social critique). Second, Weber rejected Marx's theory of historical materialism that sought to explain society through a primarily economic model. Weber argued instead that no single causal model could explain societal development and change. He saw economics as only one element in a broader model that included examination of political, legal, and religious elements (Kalberg, 1980; Morrison, 1995). As such, his writings attempt to show the interconnections amongst these various features of society.

One of the issues that most interested Weber was the forms of power he identified as having emerged historically in various societies. Specifically, he was interested in how a particular form of authority emerged with the modern, capitalist state, replacing earlier forms of authority associated with monarchies and feudal systems. Below, we will discuss Weber's forms of authority and address their importance for understanding contemporary organizations.

Weber's Types of Authority

In discussing the development of social order in different societies, Weber makes a distinction between power and authority. *Power* is a general term used to describe the ability of those in power to exercise their will, despite resistance by others (Weber, 1978, p. 53). In this sense, it describes the most crude, overt forms of domination. For example, a professor has the power to give a student a failing grade, regardless of that student's protests. This is the form of power in which Weber is least interested. On the other hand, *authority* refers to a society's development of a system of rules, norms, and administrative apparatus to which people adhere. In such a system, leaders are legitimately able to exercise authority over others, who are expected to obey. Weber identified three forms of legitimate authority, which he identified as characteristic of three different forms of social order.

Charismatic Authority

Literally speaking, *charisma* means "gift of grace," and Weber argued that one important source of authority derived from the identification of a particular individual as having exceptional—perhaps even supernatural—abilities and qualities. Certainly, religious figures such as the Pope and Billy Graham partly derive their authority from their charismatic abilities. People follow them precisely because they are seen as having the gift of grace and as transcending the routines of everyday life through their possession of special powers. Such figures do not have to engage in brute force or coercion; rather, their authority is rooted in their followers' belief in the validity and truth of their powers (Morrison, 1995, p. 285).

However, **charismatic authority** is not limited to religious leaders. History is full of charismatic figures—both good and evil—such as Hitler, Martin Luther King Jr., John F. Kennedy, and Nelson Mandela. Each of these figures had a charismatic presence that secured the allegiance of millions of people. Charismatic authority is also a significant feature of organizational life. In the late 19th and early 20th century "captains of industry" such as John D. Rockefeller and J. P. Morgan were heroic figures of their day. In the 21st century, industry leaders such as the late Steve Jobs and Donald Trump are identified as charismatic figures with magical abilities when it comes to making money.

© iStockphoto.com/EdStock

Steve Jobs met Weber's conception of a charismatic leader.

Weber argues that one of the features of charismatic authority is that it tends to emerge in times of crisis and social unrest. For example, Hitler came to power as a result of the economic and political instability experienced in Germany in the 20 years after World War I. Martin Luther King Jr.—by virtue of his rhetorical powers—was able to unite diverse groups to pursue the goal of civil rights for all. Nelson Mandela (1995) was a charismatic figure even while in jail under the apartheid system, and in post-apartheid South Africa he has been a unifying force, appealing to both white and black South Africans.

Another feature of charismatic authority is its tendency toward instability and social chaos. Because such authority is rooted in a single individual, its potential for disruption is quite high. Perhaps the most extreme example of this is in the case of religious cults, where the actions of mentally unstable charismatic leaders have led to the deaths of many followers. Jim Jones and David Koresh in the United States are two examples of such leaders. Similarly, the assassination of Martin Luther King Jr. in 1968 contributed to a period of great civil unrest and political instability in the United States. Many organizations also experience instability or failure when a charismatic leader is no longer in charge. For example, many people are wondering how Steve Jobs' death will affect Apple and its ability to create iconic, must-have electronic products.

Traditional Authority

In Weber's second form of authority, legitimacy is derived from tradition and custom. **Traditional authority** is rooted largely in the inherited right of an individual to expect obedience and loyalty from others. The legitimate exercise of authority, then, comes not from any kind of special powers of the person but from adherence to a tradition that may go back hundreds of years.

Probably the best example of traditional authority is a monarchy. Kings and queens derive their authority not from any specific skills or individual characteristics but by an accident of birth. While Weber associates traditional authority with a bygone age (mainly feudal systems), such authority still exists even in corporate life. For example, in family-owned businesses, sons and daughters frequently inherit the reins of power from parents. Such appointments may have little to do with expertise; indeed, even when children are groomed for many years to inherit businesses, developing considerable skill, the organization is still operating within a traditional system of authority. For example, Australian media mogul Rupert Murdoch employs two of his children in prominent positions in his company.

Another good example of traditional authority is the operation of an "old-boy" or "old-school-tie" network in an organization. Employees gain power based not on their abilities but because they have gender and racial characteristics that fit the prevailing value system of the organization. Employees not exhibiting such characteristics tend to be marginalized. For years, women managers have fought against informal organizational structures where important decisions are made on the golf course or at private clubs—places from which women have traditionally been excluded. College fraternities and sororities might also be seen as structured along traditional systems of authority. Organizational structures and belief systems are rooted in age-old customs and values handed down from generation to generation, and potential members are closely vetted to make sure they fit the typical member profile (Bird, 1996; DeSantis, 2007).

Rational–Legal Authority

Weber's final system of authority is the most important and the one he argues is at the foundation of the modern form of Western democracy. **Rational–legal authority** is the form underlying the bureaucratic model. The term *bureaucracy* means "rule of the bureau," or office, and refers to a system based on a set of rational and impersonal rules that guide people's behavior and decision making. People owe allegiance not to a particular individual or set of customs and beliefs but to a set of legally sanctioned rules and regulations. Amongst the features of bureaucracy identified by Weber (1978, pp. 956–958), the following are the most important for our purposes:

1. A hierarchically organized chain of command with appropriately assigned responsibilities.
2. A clearly defined system of impersonal rules that govern the rights and responsibilities of office holders.
3. The development of written regulations that describe the rights and duties of organization members.
4. A clearly defined division of labor with specialization of tasks.

5. Norms of impersonality that govern relations between people in the bureaucracy. Employees behave and make decisions according to the rules of their positions rather than personal ties to others.

6. Written documentation and use of a file system that stores information on which decision making is based.

Weber argued that the bureaucratic system, with its foundation in rational–legal authority, was technically superior to the other forms of authority in a couple of ways. First, bureaucracy was democratic insofar as it treated everybody equally and impersonally. While at first glance an "impersonal" organizational decision-making system might seem lacking in human qualities, it remains an important feature of most organizations in the Western world and ensures that people are treated according to their merits and abilities.

Second, Weber argued that the rational–legal authority system and its bureaucratic structure promoted the development of capitalism (Morrison, 1995). This is because bureaucracy enhances the speed of business operations by maximizing efficiency and functioning according to a set of calculable rules. In addition, because of its impersonal structure, business people are increasingly encouraged to make decisions for economic rather than emotional reasons. As Morrison states, "When fully developed, bureaucracy adheres to the principle of *sine ira et studio*—without hatred or passion" (p. 299).

Weber's three authority systems do not represent three mutually exclusive forms of organization. Indeed, it is not unusual for all three kinds of authority to be found in a single organization. There are certainly plenty of examples of organizations that are highly bureaucratic but also employ charismatic figures and have strong traditions to which members adhere. My own university, the University of North Carolina at Chapel Hill, is recognized as both a top-notch research university and a powerhouse in the world of men's college basketball. As such, it simultaneously embodies rational–legal, traditional, and charismatic forms of authority. For students, the process of "getting an education" partly involves figuring out a highly complex system of bureaucratic rules that regulates everything involved in obtaining a degree. At the same time, the university's prestige is derived not only from its educational excellence but also from its history and tradition, not a small part of which is the success of the university's men's basketball team. As such, the team's former and much-revered coach, Dean Smith, holds significant charismatic authority, despite having retired many years ago. The current coach, Roy Williams, is similarly revered (and, not accidentally, a former assistant of Dean Smith), having won two national championships at UNC—it's not unusual to see bumper stickers around Chapel Hill that state, "In Roy We Trust!"

Of course, all organizations—even large bureaucracies—have elements of all three forms of authority. Indeed, an organization based on exclusively rational–legal principles would be an extremely sterile and soulless place to work.

Weber's Critique of Bureaucracy and the Process of "Rationalization"

Weber was not simply an uncritical advocate of bureaucracy. As such, it is important to address the extent to which he was skeptical about the direction in which a bureaucratized, rational society was heading (Clegg, 1994; Kalberg, 1980). Although he was not a critical theorist in the sense that Marx and the Frankfurt School researchers were, his model of society nevertheless had a strong critical element.

Much of this critical element centered on Weber's analysis of what he called the **rationalization** process in modern society. For Weber, rationalization referred to the process by which all aspects of the natural and social world become increasingly subject to planning, calculation, and efficiency. Such rationalization was an important hallmark of modernity, he argued. But while rationalization was an efficient process that helped fuel the massive growth of capitalism, it also led to a narrowing of human vision and limited appreciation of alternative modes of existence. While a rationalized world is a predictable, efficient, and calculable world, it is not necessarily a fulfilling world in which to live. In recognizing these negative consequences, Weber referred to the "iron cage of bureaucracy" in which everyone had become imprisoned.

Innumerable examples of this rationalization process are all around us. The shift from shopping at the local "mom and pop" store to shopping at department stores and malls is one example of everyday life being rationalized and stripped of enchantment. While department stores may be cheaper, more efficient, and offer a wider selection of goods, they undermine our sense of community and destroy our connections to one another. As we saw earlier in our discussion of the legacy of scientific management, department stores try to compensate for this process of rationalization by employing greeters and instructing employees on how to be "friendly" to customers. Of course, the irony is that this kind of "emotional labor" (Hochschild, 1983) is itself a form of rationalization. Many businesses engage in the commercialization of human feeling and emotion in order to improve their efficiency and profitability.

The rationalization process is not confined to the corporate world, however. Any social context that can be subject to rational calculation exhibits such qualities. For example, universities are increasingly subject to rationalization as administrators look for ways to increase organizational efficiency and accountability. So, for instance, professors are under increasing pressure to provide quantitative assessments of their classroom performance. Whether such assessments provide actual evidence of classroom performance seems less important than the fact that these measures exist as "data" administrators can use when lobbying the state legislature for funding. In the same vein, many students adopt a "means–end" approach to education, in which the actual process of learning is viewed as less important than the grades (and, ultimately, the job) received. In this instance, the educational process is rationalized to fit within an instrumental worldview.

The Legacy of Bureaucracy

Weber was a theorist who tried to make sense out of the process of modernization as it occurred in the 19th and early 20th centuries. His aim was not to provide a model of organizational life but, rather, to show how various systems of rationality and authority emerged in different historical and cultural contexts. Moreover, he was concerned with how these systems of rationality enabled people to make sense of the world and order it into meaningful regularities (Kalberg, 1980, p. 1174).

Weber, then, was a modernist theorist but not an uncritical advocate of the modernization process. While he recognized the superiority of bureaucracy and its underlying democratic impulses, he also expressed great concern about the ways modernity limits the richness and possibilities of human existence. Indeed, despite Weber's writing in the early part of the 20th century, the process of rationalization is arguably even more applicable to current organizational life than in Weber's own time. In this sense, Weber's writings are quite prophetic.

Sociologist George Ritzer's (2000) work, mentioned earlier in the chapter, takes up Weber's notion of "rationalization," showing how this process has come to pervade every aspect of our lives, organizational and otherwise. Like Weber, Ritzer is concerned that rationalization has led to the "disenchantment" of everyday life, with everyone subject to a daily diet of calculated, mass-produced, carefully controlled, predictable experiences.

Critical Case Study 3.1
Rationalizing Emotions

My oldest brother hates the service in U.S. restaurants. Sure, he thinks the service is fast and efficient, but he can't stand the way servers try to create a synthetic connection with the customer ("Hi, my name is Julie, and I'll be your server—how are you guys this evening?!"). He feels manipulated, arguing that it's simply an effort to sell more food and increase the size of the tip. He much prefers the service in Spain, where being a server can be a career, the pay is good, and service is discreet, knowledgeable, and professional.

But one of the legacies of both scientific management and bureaucracy is efforts to micromanage and rationalize social interaction, and emotional labor in the service industry is part of that legacy. In recent years, scholars have documented how for-profit organizations increasingly co-opt employees' emotional expressions as a way to increase profitability (Raz, 2002; Tracy, 2000, 2005). Sociologist Arlie Hochschild (1983) coined the term *emotional labor* to describe this process of putting emotion to work for profit. In describing Hochschild's study of flight attendants' use of emotional labor, Kathy Ferguson (1984) states:

> The flight attendant's smile is like her makeup; it is on her, not of her. The rules about how to feel and how to express feelings are set by management, with the goal of producing passenger contentment. Company manuals give detailed instructions on how to provide a "sincere" and "unaffected" facial expression, how to seem "vivacious but not effervescent." Emotional laborers are required to take the arts of emotional management and control that characterize the intimate relations of family and friends . . . and package them according to the "feeling rules" laid down by the organization. (p. 53)

In her ethnographic, participant-observation study aboard a cruise ship, organizational communication scholar Sarah Tracy (2000) describes similar control efforts, discussing in detail how she became a "character for commerce," largely forfeiting any rights to personal emotions not expressed in the service of the cruise line.

The reality is that in a 21st century service economy we all expect efficient, friendly, and helpful service from employees. We generally give little thought to the stresses and strains the employee might be experiencing as we revel in the knowledge that the customer is "king." On the other hand, many of you have worked or currently work in such positions and so have intimate knowledge of the kinds of emotional labor employers expect of you to ensure that customers have a positive experience. You know what it's like to work a long shift, all the time having to maintain a sunny and positive disposition as you interact with customers who are often demanding and surly.

In class or group discussion, address the following questions related to emotional labor:

1. Discuss your own experiences both giving and receiving emotional labor in service contexts. What limitations, if any, should be placed on employers' ability to use employees' emotions as a way to sell their products and services? What are the limits of customer rights to demand friendly and attentive service from employees?

2. Discuss the following comment by Herb Kelleher, former CEO of Southwest Airlines, responding to the question, Aren't customers always right?: "No, they are not. And I think that's one of the biggest betrayals of employees a boss can possibly commit. The customer is sometimes wrong. We don't carry those sorts of customers. We write to them and say, 'Fly somebody else. Don't abuse our people.'" (Freiberg & Freiberg, 1996, p. 268).

There are numerous examples of rationalization, but let me just briefly provide two:

- "Theme" restaurants such as Applebee's, Chili's, TGI Friday's, etc., all of which have rationalized the process of creating a "unique" dining experience for customers. Think about how Jennifer Aniston's manager criticizes her for not exhibiting enough "flair" in the movie *Office Space* and you'll get the picture of how creativity gets rationalized and bureaucratized.
- The conduit model of education discussed in Chapter 1 certainly fits the process of rationalization. Education focuses less on the engaged learning process and more on the efficient and calculated production of graduates with marketable skill sets.

Lest I leave you with the wrong impression, the legacy of bureaucracy is by no means all bad. Although Weber worried about rationalization and the iron cage of bureaucracy, he still saw the bureaucratic institution as the bedrock of Western democracies. And, to a large degree, this is still the case. While we will see in later chapters that many commentators have criticized the bureaucratic organization for being too cumbersome and inflexible in times of rapid change and fast, global capitalism, some theorists have argued that it remains an essential feature of our organizational society (Du Gay, 2000; Perrow, 1986). In fact, one might argue that the emergence in the past 20 years of "postbureaucratic" organizations with flexible structures, decentralized decision making, rapid adaptability to changing environments, and so forth (see Chapter 8) has created greater opportunities for corporate malfeasance (e.g., think about the various corporate and financial institution scandals in the past few years) as well as a more unstable work environment for employees. The idea of "*sine ira et studio*—without hatred or passion" is still an essential characteristic of organizational life that helps create greater opportunities for everyone's advancement.

❖ CONCLUSION: A CRITICAL ASSESSMENT OF "CLASSIC" THEORIES OF ORGANIZATION

The classic theories of scientific management and bureaucracy have both made significant contributions to the nature of organizational life as we know it today. Although both theories are widely regarded as limited in their conception of organizational behavior, the effects of each are still felt in the modern organization, with both scientific management principles and rationalization processes widely applied. The machine metaphor of order, efficiency, and predictability underlying both perspectives has by no means been abandoned, although it is practiced in a more sophisticated manner than in the days of Taylor and Weber. Table 3.1 provides a summary comparison of these two important theories.

From a critical perspective, how might we characterize the relationship between Taylor's and Weber's views of organizations and society? First, Taylor's writings can be described as prescriptive, while Weber's are largely descriptive. In other words, Taylor is arguing vigorously for the adoption of his principles as a way to improve work performance. Weber, on the other hand, is providing a comparative analysis of the systems of authority and rationality that emerged in various societies. In some ways, Taylor's model is less about social science than it is about promoting a set of work principles. In contrast, Weber is a trained social scientist interested in the systematic exploration and analysis of human social behavior.

Table 3.1   Comparing Scientific Management and Bureaucratic Theory

Issue	*Taylor's Scientific Management*	*Weber's Bureaucratic Theory*
Conception of communication	Transmission of information from supervisor to worker	Transmission of information along formal bureaucratic channels
Metaphor of organizing	Organization as machine	Organization as machine
Level of analysis	Microlevel focus on time and motion of work tasks	Macrolevel focus on organization's role in society
Main focus of critique	"Ordinary management" and "rule-of-thumb" decision making	Rationalization of life; "iron cage of bureaucracy"
Focal point of control	Worker's body	System of impersonal rules and regulations; "rule of the bureau"
View of authority	Located with managers who have monopoly over knowledge of work	Located with officeholder who represents legal–rational system of impersonal rules
View of the employee	Executor of work tasks; motivated by extrinsic rewards	Occupier of bureaucratically defined role; motivated by opportunities for promotion
View of organization–society relationship	"Complete mental revolution"; through scientific management, organizations will create wealth and maintain social harmony	Bureaucratic organization as main embodiment of democracy in Western industrial societies
Current legacy	Defining element of many work processes and ways of thinking	Still defines many organizations, though challenged by the postbureaucratic organizational form

Second, Taylor and Weber differ greatly in terms of the levels of analysis at which they are working. We might describe Taylor's work as operating at the "micro level," focusing on the individual worker (or, more specifically, the individual worker's *body*). Weber, in contrast, has a "macro-level" focus; his interest lies in explaining the conditions underlying the development of whole societies.

Third, both Taylor and Weber are modernist theorists insofar as they believe in the role of science and rationality in human progress and liberation from oppression. However, Taylor's belief in the "one best way" suggests his uncritical equation of science and truth. For him, science and rationality are the only roads to truth and social harmony. For Weber, science and rationality are viewed with much greater skepticism. While the rationality of modern human society reflected liberation from myth and superstition, it also signaled entrapment in the iron cage of bureaucracy and rationalization. The accompanying "disenchantment" of the world led to an impoverished sense of community and human identity. Thus, Weber is much more critical of the path that modernization and capitalism have taken than is Taylor.

Finally, we can compare their conceptions of communication. In comparison with some of the theories we will discuss in later chapters, both Taylor and Weber have relatively crude models of communication. For Taylor, communication involves merely the correct transmission of information to employees about how a particular task should be performed. In this sense, he adopts a simplistic transmission model of communication. Weber's model of bureaucracy contains a similar conception, in that communication is conceived as the task of transmitting information amongst employees through a formal organizational structure. However, Weber's perspective is a little more complex if we view his larger theory of society as an examination of how people develop a system of values with which to make sense of our world. In studying the relationship between Protestantism and capitalism, for example, Weber is examining how a particular value system was used to order the world in a particular way.

Having examined closely two of the earliest theories of management and organization, in the next chapter we turn our attention to the human relations school of organization. As we will see, this next perspective introduced an important shift in how organizing processes were understood.

CRITICAL APPLICATIONS

1. Reflect on your own relationship to time. As you think about your daily routine, how much of your time is dictated to you by external factors (work, school, etc.), and how much is under your control? What does this tell you about the nature of your daily life?

2. Make a "field trip" to a chain restaurant and take a notepad along with you. Observe how the restaurant operates and make a note of all the instances where you can detect scientific management and rationalization processes at work. Also make a note of your own feelings as you go through this dining experience. What are your expectations, and how do you feel at the end of the experience?

KEY TERMS

charismatic authority   72

clock time   58

expropriation   62

ordinary management   64

rationalization   76

rational–legal authority   74

scientific management   61

systematic soldiering   63

task time   58

Therbligs   66

traditional authority   74

STUDENT STUDY SITE

Visit the student study site at **www.sagepub.com/mumbyorg** for these additional learning tools:

- Web quizzes
- eFlashcards
- SAGE journal articles

- Video resources
- Web resources

CHAPTER 4

The Human Relations School

The human relations school focuses on the social aspects of work.

The problems advanced by social scientists have been primarily the problems of human relations in an authoritarian setting.

—Perrow (1986, p. 53)

In this chapter we take a close look at a perspective that has been instrumental in redefining how we view human behavior in the workplace. The research associated with this perspective is widely referred to as the **human relations school**. In many ways, the work initially performed by the founding researchers of this school still provides the touchstone for many of the central questions that present-day organizational communication and management scholars are asking themselves—questions having to do with the *social* dimensions of organizational life.

If we frame our discussion of this perspective in terms of the central issue of control, we can see a profound shift in where the focus of organizational control lies. While scientific management located control in the very body of the worker, shaping precisely how tasks were to be performed, and bureaucracy controlled employees through a complex system of impersonal rules and regulations, the human relations model shifted focus to the psychological and social aspects of work. In other words, the human relations school—as its name suggests—addressed workplace control by paying attention to the attitudes, feelings, and relational concerns workers brought to their work. For the first time, managers were actually interested in what workers were thinking and feeling. The early pioneers of this perspective were researchers such as Elton Mayo (widely regarded as the founder of the human relations movement) and Mary Parker Follett.

Moreover, this shift in focus had important implications for communication processes. While scientific management and bureaucratic theory both focused on the creation of formal communication channels along which important organizational information was transmitted, human relations theory recognized for the first time the importance of informal communication processes for organizational effectiveness.

To understand the implications of this important development, however, our discussion must first be placed in a larger historical and political context. As I have suggested before, new theories and bodies of research do not just spontaneously emerge but frequently are responses to, or reflections of, developments and events in the wider society. In this sense, the human relations school is very much a product of the political and economic turmoil of the early decades of the 20th century. Let's turn to an examination of its historical emergence.

❖ PLACING THE HUMAN RELATIONS MOVEMENT IN ITS HISTORICAL AND POLITICAL CONTEXT

In both the United States and Europe, the decades of the late 19th and early 20th centuries were a time of great social and political turmoil. Highly authoritarian and coercive working conditions had led to increasing unrest amongst workers and a considerable rise in organized action against factory owners. In the United States between 1881 and 1905, there were 37,000 strikes involving 7 million workers in a total workforce of 29 million (Bederman, 1995, pp. 13–14). Unions thus became a major political force, with membership rising from 487,000 to 2,072,700 between 1897 and 1904 (Perrow, 1986, p. 57). Tragedies such as the Ludlow massacre in 1915 (where a 7-month strike at a coal mine, owned by John D. Rockefeller Jr., ended with 10 men, 2 women, and 12 children being shot dead by government soldiers) and the 1911 Triangle Shirtwaist Factory fire in New York City (where 141 women and men working in sweat-shop conditions burned to death) raised public consciousness about labor conditions. In 2011, on the 100th anniversary of the Triangle fire, *The New York Times* published an excellent set of articles documenting the incident (http://topics.nytimes.com/top/reference/timestopics/subjects/t/triangle_shirtwaist_factory_fire/index.html).

Such incidents led to several reform initiatives that attempted to improve conditions not only in the workplace but in local communities as well. In addition, and in light of the deprivations created by industrial capitalism, there was widespread interest in alternative political systems such as socialism and communism (O'Connor, 1999b). Furthermore, the need for increased production during World War I (1914–1918) led factory owners (pressured by the government) to provide workers with increased rights, including the creation

Library of Congress

The Ludlow massacre was a pivotal event in U.S. labor relations. The congressional investigation into its events led to improved labor laws, including the 8-hour workday.

of workers' councils, the passing of the Adamson Act (guaranteeing an 8-hour workday), and a nondiscrimination policy against unionized workers (O'Connor, 1999b, p. 119).

In the aftermath of the "Great War" there was a widespread sense that social, political, and economic reform was necessary in order to address the many inequities that had emerged in the previous 50 years or so. In the 1920s wealth disparities between rich and poor reached unprecedented levels (not unlike today!), and the Great Depression further intensified social conflict, providing momentum for change in work practices. Thus, the question of "democracy" was on the lips of many of the great thinkers of the day, although there was considerable debate about the form that democracy should take. Management scholar Ellen O'Connor has offered some interesting observations on this debate (O'Connor, 1999a, 1999b). She has suggested that there are important connections amongst the ways this debate developed in the wider society, the role of organizations in this debate, and the eventual emergence of the human relations movement.

O'Connor argues that two distinct camps developed out of the debates about democracy and its application to industrial contexts. On one side were those political scientists and social theorists (represented, for example, by John Dewey and Mary Parker Follett) who advocated the application of principles of civic democracy to the workplace. These **industrial democrats** called for increased levels of participation by workers of all levels in industrial decision-making processes. John Dewey pointed out the irony of fighting a war to save democracy, only to return to a highly authoritarian system in the workplace (O'Connor, 1999b, p. 119).

On the other side of the debate, and heavily opposed to increased industrial democracy, were the **realist democrats**, who included the likes of Harold Lasswell, Elton Mayo, and

Wallace Donham (dean of the Harvard Business School, and Mayo's primary supporter). Arguing that the industrial democrats held an idealist and misplaced faith in "the masses," this group argued for a more "realist" conception of industrial democracy, in which administrative élites took a leading role in the development of industrial policy. Much of the realists' argument drew on recent developments in psychology and studies of crowd behavior and mass propaganda to support their claim that only experts could make objective decisions about such policy. As Harold Lasswell stated,

> The findings of personality research show that the individual is a poor judge of his own interest. . . . The time has come to abandon the assumption that the problem of politics is the problem of promoting discussion among all the interests concerned in a given problem. (Quoted in O'Connor, 1999b, p. 120)

Only the administrative élite, it was argued, were qualified to engage in such discussion through the generation of objective facts.

Ellen O'Connor (1999b) summarizes the significance of the debate between the industrial democrats and the realist democrats in the following way: "What appeared to be a theoretical debate about the future of democracy was actually a highly politicized discussion about manager–employee relations, industry–government relations, and particularly the balance of power between management and workers" (p. 120).

It is probably no surprise to anyone that the realist democrats' position prevailed. Industrial leaders turned to people such as Elton Mayo and Wallace Donham to help resolve the problems of industrial conflict in a way that would enable the former to retain their considerable power. The human relations movement was to help provide the solution, and Elton Mayo was its principal architect. Let us turn to a more detailed discussion of this pioneer in the field of management.

❖ ELTON MAYO AND THE HAWTHORNE STUDIES

In his early work on industrial relations, Elton Mayo (1880–1949) argued that the experience of the average worker in industry ran parallel to the experience of posttraumatic stress victims during wartime. In other words, the workplace produced an extreme sense of alienation in the worker, leading to a form of "negative reverie" and detachment from the work environment (O'Connor, 1999a, p. 226). Mayo's answer to this problem was to propose that, through counseling, the workers could be psychologically adjusted to their work and thus experience it as meaningful and worthwhile.

Following sociologist Emile Durkheim, Mayo saw the workplace—specifically one's occupational group—as the primary medium for the creation of human identity. However, Mayo argued that the industrialization process had destroyed the tight social bonds between workers, thus alienating individuals from the social world. According to Mayo, "the central problem of a changing society was how to develop and maintain cooperative systems; preindustrial societies depended on the spontaneous cooperation of skilled groups and modern society must re-create these conditions" (Smith, 1998, p. 231). For Mayo, workers did not have the time or ability to re-create these conditions themselves.

Instead, "social collaboration can only be restored through the creation of administrative élites trained in techniques of social organization and control coupled with a readiness to move away from a belief in simplistic political solutions" (p. 237). For Mayo, Western-style democracy was one such simplistic political solution.

Thus, just as Taylor saw his system of scientific management as having ramifications well beyond the workplace, we see the same with Mayo. For him, the development of a cooperative system in the industrial workplace had implications for the social system as a whole. He saw the widespread industrial and social conflict of his day as the product of political agitators and politicians who exploited class antagonisms. Mayo argued that the development of an administrative élite who could instill cooperative principles in the minds of agitation-prone workers would be superior to the existing system of democracy.

Wallace Donham (the aforementioned dean of the Harvard Business School) certainly saw Mayo as a kindred spirit and expressed similar views to those of Mayo:

> Capitalism is on trial, and on the issue of this trial may depend the whole future of western civilization. . . . Our present situation both here and in all the great industrial nations of the world is a major breakdown of capitalism. Can this be overcome? I believe so, but not without leadership both in business and in government, a leadership which thinks in terms of broad social problems instead of in terms of particular companies. (Quoted in O'Connor, 1999b, p. 125)

Mayo had a well-developed political philosophy that placed the solution to industrial and societal ills not in a broad agenda of social and economic reform but in the application of psychological principles to the transformation of individual (worker, not management) attitudes and dispositions toward the labor process. It is important to keep these points in mind as we examine arguably the most famous set of experiments conducted in the history of the social sciences—the Hawthorne studies (Roethlisberger & Dickson, 1939).

The Hawthorne Studies

The **Hawthorne studies** were conducted from 1924 to 1933 at the Western Electric (a subsidiary of AT&T) Hawthorne plant in Cicero, Illinois. In a progressive series of experiments—some lasting many years—the researchers attempted to investigate the importance of a variety of physical, economic, and social variables in terms of their effects on employee behavior and attitudes. Given the importance of this body of research for our understanding of subsequent approaches to organizational issues, let's spend some time laying out the various experiments.

The Illumination Studies (1924–1927)

The initial set of Hawthorne experiments was conducted closely along classic scientific management lines. Carried out by Hawthorne engineers, these experiments were intended to discover the effects of variations in lighting on employee productivity. Using two groups of workers, the researchers gradually increased the level of illumination in one group (the experimental group) while keeping illumination constant in the other (the control group). In all other ways, the two groups were identical. In keeping with their initial hypothesis, the researchers found that the productivity of the experimental group increased along with the level of illumination. Strangely, however, the productivity of the control group increased as well. Furthermore, even when the researchers began to decrease the level of lighting in the experimental group back to its original level, worker productivity continued to go up. It even continued to increase as the lighting fell below normal levels. Only at the point when lighting levels were extremely low did worker productivity drop (Perrow, 1986, p. 80).

The researchers were baffled by these results—clearly, some variable other than the level of illumination had caused the increased production levels. Some of the researchers speculated that participation in the experiment might be having some kind of psychological effect on the workers, thus encouraging increased output. To investigate this alternative hypothesis, a second set of studies was set up.

The Relay Assembly Test Room (RATR) Studies (April 1927–February 1933)

In this new experiment, five women were separated from the rest of the workforce and set to work in a special test room. The women were subject to a number of experimental changes in the conditions of their work, including a much less variable work task, shorter working hours, more rest pauses, freer and friendlier supervision, and a new wage incentive system. The women's output increased by 30% over the first 2 years of the study, and the researchers came to the conclusion that, although the physical changes and new incentive system had some effect on productivity, much of the increase in productivity could be explained by the new system of friendly, "laissez-faire" supervision (Roethlisberger & Dickson, 1939).

Two more experiments—the second RATR study (August 1928–March 1929) and the Mica Splitting Test Room study (October 1928–March 1930)—were conducted to further investigate the findings of the initial RATR study. Again, the researchers concluded that increased productivity levels could be attributed mainly to the new supervisory system. In later years, this phenomenon, in which workers respond to the personal attention paid to them by supervisors, became known as the **Hawthorne effect**. For the first time, social scientists seemed to have established the significance of the "human" element in the work process. In other words, and contrary to Frederick Taylor's views, workers appeared to be motivated not merely by economic incentives (extrinsic motivation) but also by their experience of, and attitudes toward, the work process itself (intrinsic motivation). What workers were thinking and feeling while working became subject to intense scrutiny.

In addition to the set of experimental studies described above, the Hawthorne studies had two other components.

The Interview Program (September 1928–January 1931)

Armed with the knowledge that workers actually possessed a whole set of opinions, thoughts, and feelings about their work, investigators launched a massive interviewing campaign aimed at providing employees with the opportunity to express those thoughts and feelings (Bramel & Friend, 1981; Perrow, 1986; Roethlisberger & Dickson, 1939). This element of the Hawthorne studies was very much influenced by Mayo's philosophy and reflected his belief that such "nondirective counseling" (as he envisioned these interviews) provided a way for workers to become mentally well-adjusted to the workplace.

It should be stressed that the purpose of these interviews was not to collect information from workers in order for management to address their concerns but, rather, to allow workers to "let off steam" (they were called "ventilation" interviews) and thus experience psychological and emotional improvement in their attitudes toward work. Roethlisberger and Dickson (1939, p. 227) pointed out that the workers seemed to appreciate being recognized as individuals by the company.

The Bank Wiring Observation Room Study (November 1931–May 1932)

The last study at Hawthorne was one of the earliest examples of qualitative, naturalistic (as opposed to experimental) research in the workplace. Based on the observation of a group of male workers, the goal of the study was to examine the natural development of informal group relations without interference from researchers. The most important finding of this study was that the workers engaged in a classic case of "systematic soldiering," developing a strong set of group norms aimed at restricting output.

At first glance, this discovery seems to contradict findings of the earlier studies regarding the importance of "human relations" for the development of productive workers. For Mayo and his colleagues, however, the significance of this study lay in its identification of workers as forming social groups and developing elaborate norms and sentiments to shape their relationship to the work process.

Implications of the Hawthorne Studies

The significance of the Hawthorne studies and their findings cannot be overestimated. Although there is plenty to critique (and we will get to that next), the research of Mayo and his colleagues had a profound influence on the course of research in organizations for the next several decades. The findings produced many important implications for the further study of organizational life. These are summarized below.

1. *Discovery of the informal work group*. Unlike Frederick Taylor, who associated the work group with systematic soldiering, Mayo argued that group cohesiveness could, in the right context, lead to a more cooperative and productive workforce, especially with appropriate "attitude adjustment" through counseling. This "discovery" of the informal workgroup was a catalyst for several decades of research on small-group relations (Perrow, 1986; Roy, 1959).

2. *Importance of informal communication*. While classical theories argued that informal communication was largely detrimental to the functioning of organizations, the human relations movement emphasized its positive, social aspects and its contribution to worker satisfaction (Roy, 1959).

3. *The Hawthorne effect*. As a result of the Hawthorne studies, worker attitudes to work and feelings of satisfaction became a focus of organizational research. The Hawthorne effect seemed to suggest a great deal of untapped potential in terms of managers' abilities to motivate workers. "A happy worker is a productive worker" became a mantra for the human relations movement. (See Critical Case Study 4.1 for a modern-day version of this mantra.)

4. *Impetus for leadership research.* With Mayo's emphasis on the importance of "administrative élites" appropriately trained in techniques of social control, later researchers attempted to establish the criteria for "good leadership," spawning numerous leadership models (Bass, 1990; Yukl, 2006).

5. *Early systems focus.* Although Mayo's interest lay primarily in the psychology of individual workers, the Hawthorne studies showed the importance of taking a more systemic approach to attitudes and norms in the workplace. In this sense, the Hawthorne researchers can be seen as early contributors to a systems perspective on organizational communication (see Chapter 5).

6. *Use of qualitative methods.* The Hawthorne researchers were amongst the first to utilize naturalistic, qualitative methods in the workplace (Smith, 1998, p. 237). In this sense, they were considerably ahead of their time if we consider that, in management and organizational communication studies, qualitative research has only in the past 25 years been accepted into the mainstream of these fields.

7. *Solution to industrial conflict?* The Hawthorne studies, coupled with Mayo's political philosophy, seemed to provide a solution to the intense industrial conflict that was a pervasive feature of the workplace in the 1920s and 1930s. If Mayo's emphasis on the psychological adjustment of the workers to industrial life could be implemented, then industrial peace and cooperation between workers and managers would be the result. The preindustrial "organic community" could be reestablished in the workplace.

In some ways, the findings of the Hawthorne studies seemed too good (and too simple) to be true, and in the decades after the publication of their findings, they were subject to severe critique from a variety of quarters.

Critical Case Study 4.1
Reframing Happiness at Zappos

The idea that "a happy worker is a productive worker" has not gone completely out of fashion, despite the lack of evidence connecting the two things. Indeed, with the corporate culture movement in the 1980s (which we'll examine in Chapter 6) and the recent emergence of "funsultants" (which we'll discuss in Chapter 8) the idea of creating a happy, committed workforce returned to the top of the agenda of companies everywhere. These days, however, the emergence of the service economy has made "happiness" a key construct for companies as they compete to retain and grow their customer bases. Some companies understand that keeping customers happy means keeping employees happy, too. An example of an organization that tries to integrate employee happiness, customer happiness,

and e-commerce is Zappos—a company from which many of you have probably ordered items.

In a 2009 interview with *Inc.* online magazine, Zappos CEO Tony Hsieh (pronounced "Shay") states that his entire business philosophy is built on the principle of happiness for both customers and employees (Chafkin, 2009). Indeed, Zappos is widely regarded as one of the most innovative companies around when it comes to keeping customers happy. In addition, it regularly appears on *Fortune* magazine's list of the 100 best companies to work for. What's interesting is that Zappos doesn't do this by paying employees well or giving them lots of benefits; the annual salary for an hourly worker is about $23,000, and although they get full health care benefits, Zappos doesn't offer lots of other perks such as onsite child care and matching pension contributions.

The uniqueness of Zappos lies in how it constructs its culture around happiness and weirdness. Potential employees must pass a "culture" interview during which they're asked questions such as, "On a scale of 1 to 10, how weird are you?" (a higher score is better than a lower score). Alcohol also figures into interviews, many of which Hsieh conducts himself. His goal is to put job applicants into social situations to see if they can connect emotionally with other people. Hsieh explains that Zappos is all about PEC—personal emotional connection with the customer.

Once hired, all employees go through 2 weeks of classroom training that teach them how to answer customer calls. At the end of the training period, employees are offered $2,000 to quit the company. "Our training team had gotten good at figuring out who wasn't going to make it, and we were thinking, how do you get rid of those people?" says Hsieh. Zappos saves money by paying these employees to quit, weeding out people who would probably quit anyway and enabling loyal employees to make a public commitment to the company by not accepting the offer. When Chafkin comments to Hsieh that Zappos seems not unlike a religious cult in how it instills core values in employees, Hsieh doesn't disagree: "I think there's a lot you can learn from religion. This is not just a company. It's like a way of life."

On the company website, an employee defines Zappos culture as

> the overall environment; space, attitude, freedom, management style, and actual physical surroundings which all work together to create a total milieu which attempts to make each individual better and happier on a whole, so that each one of us will then spread this to each other, our customers, and everyone we encounter. (http://www.zapposinsights. com/culture-book)

The "Zappos Family Core Values" on which this culture is built are as follows:

1. Deliver WOW through service
2. Embrace and drive change
3. Create fun and a little weirdness
4. Be adventurous, creative, and open-minded
5. Pursue growth and learning
6. Build open and honest relationships with communication
7. Build a positive team and family spirit
8. Do more with less
9. Be passionate and determined
10. Be humble (http://www.zapposinsights.com/ culture-book)

Chafkin's article provides an example of these core values at work in Hsieh's telling of a story about an employee dealing with a female customer who wanted to return a pair of boots she had ordered for her husband, who died in a car crash the day after she ordered them. Without checking with his supervisor, the employee sent flowers to the woman's home:

> "At the funeral, the widow told her friends and family about the experience," Hsieh said, his voice cracking and his eyes tearing up ever so slightly. "Not only was she a customer for life, but so were those 30 or 40 people at the funeral." Hsieh paused to compose himself. "Stories like these are being created every single day, thousands and thousands of times," he said. "It's just an example that if you get the culture right, then most of the other stuff follows." (Chafkin, 2009)

Questions for Discussion

1. Using both McGregor's Theory X/Theory Y and Likert's four-system model, discuss Zappos' approach to human resources. How would you classify Zappos according to these two models?

2. Examine the core values of the "Zappos Family." What insights do they give you into the organization?

3. We will be examining emotions in more detail in Chapter 8, but discuss Zappos' focus on encouraging employees to connect with customers emotionally. What do you think of this strategy, and what's your opinion of the story about the woman whose husband was killed?

4. Do you have any experience working for a company like Zappos? What was it like from an employee perspective? Check out the Zappos Insights website (http://www.zapposinsights.com/) and discuss what you find there.

❖ A CRITIQUE OF THE HAWTHORNE STUDIES

We can divide the criticisms of the Hawthorne studies into two categories. First, the studies were critiqued on *empirical* grounds. A number of commentators argued that when the Hawthorne data were subject to close scrutiny, the researchers' claim of a connection between worker satisfaction and productivity did not hold water (Argyle, 1953; Carey, 1967; Francke & Kaul, 1978). Second, several critics challenged the Hawthorne findings on *ideological* grounds, questioning the study's (or, more accurately, Mayo's) highly conservative vision of worker–management relations. Let's examine the empirical criticism first.

Reexamining the Empirical Data

As we have seen, the fame of the Hawthorne studies was derived largely from the researchers' claim that a new, more relaxed form of supervision was responsible for an increase in worker satisfaction, which in turn led to an increase in productivity. Although there were competing explanations (including the impact of a new pay incentive system), Mayo and his colleagues ruled these out in favor of "social factors."

Sociologist Alex Carey (1967) provides an interesting and detailed statistical reexamination of the Hawthorne data. While his analysis is quite complex and cannot be reproduced in its entirety here, a couple of his claims are worth mentioning. First, he examines the results from the first RATR study, focusing particularly on the variable of friendly supervision. He points out that the researchers initially experienced problems with two of the five women in the study who took literally the supervisors' directive to do as they wished—in other words, they spent too much time talking and "goofing off" and not enough time working. Thus, the level of discipline was increased to reduce this behavior. When the two women did not respond to the tightening of supervision, they were dismissed and replaced by two women who were seen as more cooperative. These two new group members were highly motivated and were instrumental in raising the output of the group; so, once again, the system of friendly supervision was implemented.

One does not have to be a highly trained social scientist to see why this calls into question the results of the study. First, the replacement of the two women clearly compromised the controlled experimental conditions of the study. Second, and following from this first point, Carey suggests that the causal relationship between friendly supervision and productivity is actually the reverse of that suggested by the researchers. In other words, rather than friendly supervision resulting in increased productivity, there is evidence that the increased productivity caused by the introduction of the two new women led to friendlier supervision.

Carey also points out that data from both the second RATR study and the Mica Splitting Test Room study provide plenty of evidence that the use of preferred incentive systems had much more to do with increased productivity than did the system of supervision. For example, in the second RATR study, the implementation of a new group incentive system (in which earnings were based on the average output of the whole group) produced an immediate 12% increase in productivity. However, when this incentive system was discontinued after 9 months (apparently because of discontent amongst other workers not involved in the study), output dropped immediately by 16%.

There is, therefore, a significant discrepancy between the available evidence and the conclusions the Hawthorne researchers drew from that evidence. Why has this discrepancy been largely neglected by social scientists? Charles Perrow suggests that the reason is largely political. In the wake of the Hawthorne studies, huge amounts of money were invested by businesses, government agencies, foundations, and universities in efforts to provide further empirical evidence of the connection between worker productivity and various social factors, including leadership styles and group norms (Perrow, 1986, p. 84). The various interests involved in such efforts had little incentive to explore the possibility that the original study that made such research possible was seriously flawed. Indeed, to this day—and despite several decades of research—there is little evidence to suggest any strong causal connections among social factors, worker satisfaction/morale, and productivity.

Critiquing the Ideology of the Hawthorne Researchers

A number of different criticisms have been aimed at the perceived conservative ideology that underlies Mayo's philosophy of organizational life and its role in the larger society. The interpretations of the Hawthorne data, it has often been argued, reflect this conservative ideology. We will discuss these criticisms below.

The Wholly Negative Role of Conflict

Under Mayo's philosophy, there is no legitimate role for conflict in the workplace. With cooperation and social collaboration being the watchwords for the rehabilitation of both industry and society, conflict is viewed as an unacceptable workplace phenomenon.

Bramel and Friend (1981) argue that Mayo explained any workplace conflict and resistance as due to worker psychology (i.e., workers were behaving irrationally and emotionally). They suggest that Mayo never considered the possibility that worker resistance might be due to the competing and antagonistic interests of capitalism on the one hand and workers on the other. For example, the evidence of output restriction in the Bank Wiring Room experiment can be interpreted as legitimate worker resistance to the possibility of layoffs (if workers produce more, then management can lay off workers without decreasing production levels). Such an interpretation clearly falls outside the scope of Mayo's philosophy of cooperation.

Rational Manager Versus "Sentimental" Worker

Mayo maintained a clear ideological split between the rationality of the managerial élite and the nonrationality of the workers. On many occasions in the account of the Hawthorne studies (Roethlisberger & Dickson, 1939), workers are described as being ruled by the "logic of sentiment." Mayo and his colleagues seemed convinced that, unlike managers, the average worker was unable to understand the nature of working conditions objectively. By definition, then, any resistance on the part of the worker was irrational and had nothing to do with the material conditions of organizational life.

Thus, the early human relations movement was heavily paternalistic in its view of the average worker, with little interest in making real changes in the quality of workers' lives. Rather, the goal was to adjust workers' attitudes to accept existing organizational conditions more readily. As such, human relations theory did nothing to change the strongly hierarchical structure of existing organizations.

Gender Bias in the Hawthorne Studies

Gender plays a hidden, but crucial, role in the Hawthorne studies. Some commentators have pointed out that the subjects in the first RATR study were all women, while those in the Bank Wiring Room study were all men (Acker & Van Houten, 1974; Marks, 1999). While at first this may seem to have little bearing on the studies, this gender dichotomy might explain how the researchers arrived at some of their conclusions.

In their analysis of the first RATR study, Acker and Van Houten (1974) attempt to place the issue of gender in a larger social context. They provide a demographic analysis of the five women chosen for the study. Of the five women, four were single, aged 19 to 20, and lived at home in first-generation, European immigrant households with a strong, patriarchal system of authority. In addition, each woman was required to give her wages to her parents, receiving a small allowance in return (Acker & Van Houten, 1974, p. 154).

Acker and Van Houten (1974) argue that if one takes into account their socialization into a male-oriented home environment, economic dependence, and the existence of a similar patriarchal authority system in their workplace, these women would be particularly responsive to the authority of the all-male research team studying them. That is, they would be eager to please the researchers in order to stay in the test room. Acker and Van Houten describe the women as being subject to a "power multiplier effect." In other words, "the sex power hierarchy in the home and in the factory were congruent; and when there is such congruence, sex power differentials outside the organization act as a multiplier, enhancing the authority of male superiors in the workplace" (p. 154). Thus, it is quite possible that much of the Hawthorne effect is attributable to gender dynamics and not to a general feature of the work environment set up by the researchers.

Summary

In summary, human relations theory is traditionally presented as a paradigm shift in management approaches to work and employees. At one level this is true, given the wealth of research the Hawthorne studies spawned. On the other hand, one can argue that human relations theory is simply the flip side of the scientific management coin. That is, while scientific management took the worker's body as the focal point of control efforts, human relations theory focused on the psychology of the worker—his or her attitudes and feelings about work. Thus, control practices shifted from body to mind, but with little or no change in the nature of work itself. Indeed, it might be said that human relations theory did not *replace* scientific management but, rather, complemented it with efforts to mentally adjust workers to the industrial labor process. As such, this theory was arguably a significant force in the affirmation of the status quo at a time of considerable industrial and political unrest.

In the next section, we look at the work of a theorist and practitioner whose ideas were considerably more radical—Mary Parker Follett.

❖ MARY PARKER FOLLETT: BRIDGING THEORY AND PRACTICE

When one reads the work of Mary Parker Follett (1868–1933), it is very clear that she was decades ahead of her time in the way she addressed organizational issues such as leadership, control, communication, power, democracy, and authority (Follett, 1918/1998, 1924, 1995b, 1995c). Indeed, a number of commentators have suggested that present-day theory and research are only just catching up with the sophistication of Follett's ideas (Bennis, 1995; Dixon, 1996; Graham, 1995; Kolb, Jensen, & Shannon, 1996; Parker, 1984).

Yet, despite her celebration by many as a "prophet of management" (Graham, 1995), Follett remains a shadowy figure whose work today is rarely cited and infrequently read. In fact, I would speculate that most organizational communication students (and even some instructors) have never heard of her. How might we explain this apparent anomaly? What circumstances led to her being almost completely erased from the history of management and organizational communication research? In answering these questions, we will address two issues. First, we will lay out the elements of Follett's perspective on organizations, thus developing some insight into why she is considered such a prophet. Second, we will examine some potential explanations for why her work basically disappeared from the management and organizational communication fields after her death.

Follett's Theory of Organization

To grasp Follett's perspective on organizations adequately, we need to be able to think unconventionally about organizational communication theory and research. Follett was an unconventional thinker in a number of ways. First, she was not a professional academic or organizational consultant and thus developed her ideas outside of mainstream academic theory and research. Second, her education at the Harvard Annex for Women (later Radcliffe College), Cambridge University in England, and postgraduate study in Paris exposed her to a wide range of thinkers in philosophy, politics, sociology, and psychology. As such, her education had a distinctly European flavor that was reflected in her philosophy of organization. Finally, her ideas about "organization" transcended the corporate model, developed as they were in the first two decades of the 20th century in her work with community groups in the Boston area. Thus, when Follett spoke about the principles of "organization," she was referring not only to business organizations but also to "organizing" as a basic feature of community and social life.

What, then, was Follett's basic philosophy of organization? Follett was strongly influenced by the philosophy of pragmatism—a distinctly American philosophy developed by thinkers such as William James and John Dewey. In contrast with the dominant view of science in the early 20th century as producing absolute truth, pragmatists believed that humankind could survive only by adopting an attitude of constant experimentation and doubt toward the world. For pragmatists, truth was always uncertain and shifting and dependent on the creative processes of reasoning and testing of ideas. In this sense, truth was not static and independent of human thought but dependent on dialogue and reflection.

For Follett, pragmatism was a way of thinking that could be realized through its application in everyday life. As such, she was both a thinker and an activist who saw pragmatism as a potential change agent that could shift society toward greater democracy (Carter, 1992). The vehicle for such change, according to Follett, was the groups and organizations people belonged to as members of their communities.

When she spoke of "organizations," however, Follett did not have in mind the bureaucratic, hierarchical structures that dominated the landscape of her time (and, in many respects, our own). Instead, she envisioned flat, nonhierarchical collectives that could empower people to improve their everyday lives. In this sense, Follett's primary concern was not really with organizational life as such but, rather, with "reinventing the citizen" (Drucker, 1995, p. 7). That is, she wanted to generate a conception of society that would better enable ordinary people to realize their potential more fully and hence improve their quality of life. Given this general conception of Follett's orientation, let's now examine some of the specific concepts she developed as a way to realize her view of organizations in society.

The notion most central to Follett's conception of organization is the idea of the **circular response**. The intent of this concept is to capture the ongoing, dynamic, and ever-changing character of the interactions amongst people. Although she does not use the term *communication* explicitly, the idea of "circular response" is clearly a rather sophisticated conception of the communication process. In developing this notion, Follett is interested not in the senders or the receivers of communication but, rather, in the process of *relating*. As she states, "reality is in the relating, in the activity-between" (Follett, 1995c, p. 36). In this sense, circular response is an attempt to get at the dynamic, process-oriented, constantly shifting conditions under which people relate to one another. Follett captures the idea that when two or more people communicate, the very act of communicating changes everyone involved, as well as the environment in which the process of communication is occurring: "I never react to you but to you-plus-me; or to be more accurate, it is I-plus-you reacting to you-plus-me. . . . By the very process of meeting, we both become something different" (pp. 58–59).

Follett's dynamic view of communication was quite different from the model embedded in the dominant, scientific management view of the workplace, in which communication was simply conceived as a way to transmit orders to workers about job tasks. Indeed, as we saw in the first chapter with the critique of the conduit model, Follett's insights into the communication process were still not fully grasped and implemented some 60 years later.

A number of other important concepts emerge out of Follett's notion of the circular response. Her ideas about conflict, the giving of orders, and power are all related to her dynamic conception of communication. Let's deal with each in turn.

Follett distinguishes three different ways of dealing with conflict in organizational life. The first is through *domination*, where the interests and goals of one person are simply asserted over those of another. For example, management's firing workers for going on strike would be an example of resolving conflict through domination.

The second way of dealing with conflict is through *compromise*. Here, both parties give up something in order to resolve the situation. For example, in contract negotiations, a union might choose to give up its demand for higher wages in order to secure a "no-layoffs" agreement from management. In agreeing to this, management gives up its ability to reduce the labor force during economic downturns.

Follett's third—and favored—form of conflict resolution she calls **integration.** Integration involves finding a solution to a conflict in which neither side has to make a sacrifice. By way of illustration, Follett (1995a) provides the following example:

> In the Harvard library one day, in one of the smaller rooms, someone wanted the window open, I wanted it shut. We opened the window in the next room, where

no one was sitting. This was not a compromise because there was no curtailing of desire; we both got what we really wanted. For I did not want a closed room, I simply did not want the north wind to blow directly on me; likewise the other occupant did not want that particular window open, he merely wanted more air in the room. (p. 69)

In resolving conflict through integration, the goal is to find a resolution in which each party's desires are satisfied and no one has to sacrifice anything. Follett admits that not all conflicts can be resolved in this way, but she suggests that through creative engagement (via the circular response) where each party involved makes all differences explicit, development of such integrative resolutions is frequently possible.

Follett's efforts to address conflict as a significant workplace issue distinguish her from Mayo, who saw conflict in wholly dysfunctional terms. While Mayo viewed conflict as a symptom of industrial sickness and worker maladjustment promoted by workplace agitators, Follett saw it as "friction," a part of the natural dynamics of social life that could help promote creativity and original solutions to problems. Her approach to conflict emphasized commonality of purpose amongst the participants, thus promoting a spirit of workplace cooperation (Selber & Austin, 1997). In this sense, her ideas are consistent with modern-day approaches to workplace conflict.

Follett's belief in workplace cooperation is reflected in her conception of issues of *power*, *authority*, and the *giving of orders*. Again, her ideas about these concepts sharply contrast with the dominant management thinking of her day, where authoritarian rule and strict hierarchy were standard practice. For Follett, there are two forms of power: "power-over" and "power-with." Power-over reflects the normal exercise of power in which managers simply assert their authority over workers. On the other hand, power-with is "a jointly developed power, a co-active, not a coercive power" (Follett, 1995b, p. 103). In this conception, Follett integrates into her view of organizations a notion of empowerment consistent with the participative management approach that emerged in the 1960s with the work of theorists such as Douglas McGregor and Rensis Likert (see pages 98 and 100). In such a view, the ability to exercise power arises not out of one's position in the organizational hierarchy but, rather, out of the expertise and ability one can bring to a particular situation. Indeed, one of Follett's best-known concepts is what she refers to as the **law of the situation**, which refers to the idea that in exercising power or giving orders, one's authority arises out of the needs of the situation. In this way, authority and the giving of orders are "depersonalized"—orders are followed not because of the power of a certain individual but because of the recognition by everyone involved that the situation demands a particular course of action.

A contemporary example of the law of the situation is the way in which organizational decision making occurs amongst team members. Ideally, team members make decisions about productivity, time off, changes in the manufacturing process, and so on, not because someone in authority imposes such decisions on them. Instead, team decisions involve a dynamic process of circular responses that leads to recognition of what the situation demands. For example, if a customer needs an emergency shipment of the company's product, then team members might collectively decide to stay after regular work hours to make sure the order is filled. This decision arises out of the "law of the situation," invoked through a jointly developed sense of power.

In sum, Mary Parker Follett's theory of organization was decades ahead of its time. For her, organizations existed not to control people's behavior but, ideally, to enable people to reach their potential as citizens and community members. As both a thinker and activist, she was strongly committed to the realization of democracy through the development of a participatory community life (Carter, 1992). For Follett, the "new state" (the title of one of her books) consists of a "union of individuals who have worked in groups, who have become more empathic, more systemic, more aware because of their experience" (Carter, 1992, p. 74).

As I indicated earlier, however, Follett virtually disappeared from the history of management thought after her death in 1933. Why were such provocative and insightful ideas neglected for so long? We discuss this question below.

The Strange Case of the Disappearing Theorist

The simplest answer to Follett's "disappearance" might have to do with her gender. As a woman in a male-dominated world, perhaps her ideas were just not taken seriously. Rosabeth Moss Kanter (1995) suggests that Follett's writings spoke in a "female voice" that did not fit well with the hard-edged management ideas of the time (e.g., scientific management). Harvard Business School Dean Wallace Donham unwittingly provides some rather disturbing insight into the open prejudice women experienced at this time. When asked if he would admit women to his school, he replied, "Well, to be candid, we are not interested in training women, for if they are attractive they get married, and we don't wish to take on unattractive ones" (quoted in Stivers, 1996, p. 162). However, the question of gender is not the only possible explanation for the field's neglect of Follett.

A second potential explanation has to do with the nature of Follett's work. At a time when the fledgling field of management wasn't exactly overflowing with sophisticated theorizing about organizational life, Follett's writings exhibited a rich and complex understanding of organizations and their importance in 20th century industrial society. Management scholar Rosemary Stewart (1996) even suggests that Follett's writings have attracted little attention since her death because they are "too rich"! Indeed, her work is an elegant mixture of systems theory (before it was labeled as such), psychology, and pragmatist philosophy. It is for this reason that Follett is sometimes classified as a "bridge" or "eclectic" theorist, in that her work "bridges" or draws together insights from a number of different perspectives.

Thus, while most well-known management thinkers are associated with a single idea (Taylor and Mayo come immediately to mind), her writings are not easily classifiable into any single perspective with a clearly identifiable "trademark" notion. Other theories can be encapsulated in phrases such as "the one best way" (scientific management) and "a happy worker is a productive worker" (human relations theory), but Follett's writings do not lend themselves to such slogans. The fact that much popular management literature today still relies on such memorable—though often empty—phrases ("who moved my cheese?," "thriving on chaos," etc.) suggests that we have made little progress in our understanding of organizational life since Follett's time.

A third possible reason for the neglect of Follett's writings concerns their political implications (Stivers, 2006). As I indicated earlier in this chapter, Follett's work was associated with the industrial democrats—a group that believed (in opposition to the realist democrats) in a stronger system of democracy that went beyond the representative democracy prevalent in the United States. Follett was a strong believer in greater levels of grassroots participation in social groups, which she saw as the defining feature of a strong, participative democracy (Dixon, 1996). Indeed, she rejected the very idea of society as consisting of separate individuals, arguing that "there is no such thing as the 'individual,' there is no such thing as 'society'; there is only the group and the group-unit—the social individual" (Follett, 1918/1998, p. 21). Such a position is politically radical and certainly did not fit with traditionally conservative management thinking. Management scholar Rosabeth Moss Kanter (1995) suggests that Follett's philosophy has a utopian and romantic character: "Her ideas are rooted in American optimism and egalitarianism, yet they also run counter to American individualism and belief in social engineering" (p. xvii).

In sum, Elton Mayo wanted to maintain the status quo, while Mary Parker Follett wanted to transform it. We are all perhaps a little bit poorer for the fact that Mayo is remembered while Follett is largely forgotten.

❖ HUMAN RESOURCE MANAGEMENT

The years following World War II (1939–1945) were boom years for the U.S. economy and, in many ways, marked the institutionalization of the modern corporate organization. As markets expanded and a stable, growing economy and full employment became the norm, so the large-scale corporate bureaucracy came into its own. This was the age of the "organization man" (Mills, 1951; Whyte, 1956). Sociologists Luc Boltanski and Eve Chiapello (2005) argue that this period, with the dominance of the large corporation, can be described as the second "spirit" of capitalism. While in the first spirit the dominant, heroic figures were the capitalist entrepreneurs and the captains of industry, in this second spirit the corporate manager is the dominant figure. The manager possesses the skills necessary (rationalizing work, long-term planning, marketing, product standardization, leading employees, etc.) to enable the corporation to maximize profits and grow. In this second spirit, capitalism gains its legitimacy from wealth creation that spreads throughout society, creating a large and stable middle class whose members have lifetime employment.

However, this period of a stable, growing economy and full employment also created a problem from a managerial perspective. While in the early days of capitalism coercion and threats were enough to motivate employees, this was no longer the case. The 1920s and 1930s had witnessed labor struggles, a Great Depression, and the creation of New Deal legislation that limited conflict between workers and management. The result of all this was that workers were in a more powerful position after World War II than before it. Stable, well-paid employment and strong unionization meant that management could no longer simply use coercion or the threat of firing to motivate workers.

This is the political context for the arrival of human resource management (HRM) on the organizational scene. HRM is usually framed as a genuine effort to motivate workers by recognizing their value to the organization—their human resources. And this is certainly true in part. But what is often overlooked is that HRM is also a response to a legitimacy crisis in management; that is, managers appeared to have little influence over the motivation and productivity of their workers. Employees saw work as the place where they took care of their lower-level needs (physiological and safety) but not as the place where their higher-order needs (love/belonging, esteem, self-actualization) were satisfied; these were reserved for life with friends and loved ones (Maslow, 1987). HRM, then, represents an attempt to tap into these higher-order needs and make work relevant to the achievement of human potential. As Douglas McGregor (1960), one of the theorists we will discuss below, states:

> Few managers are satisfied with their ability to predict and control the behavior of the members of their organization. . . . Many managers would agree that the effectiveness of their organization would be at least doubled if they could discover how to tap the unrealized resources in their human potential. (p. 4)

In the rest of this section, then, we will discuss the work of two of the most important HRM theorists, whose work is still impacting management theory and practice today: Douglas McGregor and Rensis Likert.

Douglas McGregor's Theory X and Theory Y

In developing a model of work motivation, McGregor (1960) explicitly frames his theory in terms of influence and control. McGregor argues that managerial authority is still largely based on an old, outdated model of authority founded primarily on coercion of employees. This model is problematic because it ignores the fact that the means of enforcing authority is no longer available in the same way; workers do not have the same kind of dependence on managers that they once had.

McGregor (1960) terms this traditional philosophy of management control **Theory X** and describes its view of workplace control in the following way:

1. The average human being has an inherent dislike of work and will avoid it if he can.
2. Because of this . . . most people must be coerced, controlled, directed, threatened with punishment to get them to put forth adequate effort toward the achievement of organizational objectives.
3. The average human being prefers to be directed, wishes to avoid responsibility, has relatively little ambition, and wants security above all. (pp. 33–34)

McGregor claims that as long as Theory X continues to be the guiding philosophy behind management strategy, then organizations will fail to realize the full potential of workers as human beings. As such, he argues that management philosophy must shift from coercion to what he calls "selective adaptation," in which the power to influence workers is not a function of coercive authority but rather the selection of the means of influence that circumstances require (notice the similarity to Mary Parker Follett's "law of the situation" here). This alternative perspective recognizes the high degree of interdependence among managers and workers in achieving organizational objectives. If managers recognize this, then the philosophy of management they will adopt will reflect an effort to achieve the human potential of their employees.

McGregor (1960) calls this philosophy **Theory Y** and describes its assumptions in the following manner:

1. The expenditure of physical and mental effort in work is as natural as play or rest.
2. External control and the threat of punishment are not the only means for bringing about effort toward organizational objectives. Man will exercise self-direction and self-control in the service of objectives to which he is committed.
3. Commitment to objectives is a function of the rewards associated with their achievement.
4. The average human being learns under proper conditions not only to accept but to seek responsibility.
5. The capacity to exercise a relatively high degree of imagination, ingenuity and creativity in the solution of organizational problems is widely, not narrowly, distributed in the population.
6. Under the conditions of modern industrial life, the intellectual potentialities of the average human being are only partially utilized. (pp. 47–48)

As you can see, the management philosophy of Theory Y reflects a very different view of human nature than does that of Theory X. Theory Y situates work as providing the possibility for human growth and the realization of higher needs of esteem and self-actualization, as described by Maslow (since Maslow is covered in every Psych 101 class, I'm not going to waste your time discussing him here). Work becomes motivating, and not drudgery, precisely because workers recognize that their higher needs can be realized through the degree of autonomy and responsibility they are given.

Thus, while the central principle of Theory X is direction and control, the goal of Theory Y is integration (again, note the connection to Follett). McGregor (1960) defines integration as the "creation of conditions such that the members of the organization can achieve their own goals *best* by directing their efforts towards the success of the enterprise" (p. 49). In other words, Theory Y requires that both the organization's and the individual's needs be recognized if employees are to achieve their potential and organizations are to reach their objectives. Indeed, McGregor describes Theory Y as "an invitation to innovation" (p. 57).

Interestingly, McGregor explicitly states that Theory Y is not a permissive, anything-goes management style that is a response to the authoritarian styles of earlier decades. Instead, he views it as an effort to cultivate a sense of responsibility and autonomy in employees, using techniques such as employee performance appraisals. Ultimately, the goal is a higher degree of participation in decision making by lower-level employees. Importantly, McGregor argues that, unlike Theory X, Theory Y places ineffective organizational performance squarely in the laps of managers who are unable to get the best out of the human resources who work for them. Workers don't refuse responsibility or avoid work because they are lazy but because managers fail to provide an organizational climate that taps into their human potential.

Let's now look at an exact contemporary of McGregor's who develops a more complex approach to the problem of HRM.

Critical Technologies 4.1
"Wilfing" Your Life Away

Wilfing is a term used to denote the experience of being online. Derived from the acronym WWILF ("What was I looking for?"), it describes the manner in which we interact with the virtual world. We do a little work, check our e-mail, check out a YouTube link someone has sent us, respond to a text message, play Angry Birds for 10 minutes (is it possible to play for *only* 10 minutes?), respond to another text message, and so on, ad infinitum. We go online to check a specific thing, and then, like Alice disappearing down a virtual rabbit hole, we don't emerge until half the morning has evaporated before our very eyes. Science fiction author Carey Doctorow has captured this experience with his description of the Internet as "an ecosystem of interruption technologies" (quoted in Leith, 2011, p. 18), and certainly that's an evocative and fairly accurate way of describing the wilfing experience.

The larger question, however, is how this virtual ecosystem is shaping our lives and identities. Some commentators claim that this ecosystem requires a novel form of intelligence that enables people to think in less linear ways. Others have suggested that it has led to a decreasing ability to think critically and in a sustained manner about issues. Either way, wilfing is probably here to stay.

From an employer perspective, wilfing raises issues of time theft (Stevens & Lavin, 2007). If employees are wilfing on company time rather than working, then it could be considered a form of stealing. From an employee perspective, wilfing can be a fun distraction but also a source of frustration; the realization that hours of one's life have disappeared with little to show for them can be thoroughly depressing.

Of course, neither McGregor nor Likert could have anticipated this workplace development, but it would have been interesting to see how they explained it via their respective models. They might argue that wilfing would be more pervasive in Theory X and exploitative–authoritative forms of organizing, as it's a way for people to avoid work; in Theory Y and participative organizations, employees would be too busy unleashing their creative potential to engage in such wasteful activities.

What's your own experience of wilfing, and how does it tie in to the psychology of work discussed in this chapter? Is the amount you wilf tied to how you're feeling about work, school, or life in general? How do you feel after an extended wilfing session?

Rensis Likert's Four Systems Approach

Published a year after McGregor's book, Likert's (1961) *New Patterns of Management* picks up many of the same themes. Indeed, the book starts out with an explicit recognition that workers will not accept coercive forms of management as they had in the past. Likert puts his framework in a broader political context when he states, "The trend in America, generally, in our schools, in our homes, and in our communities, is toward giving the individual greater freedom and initiative" (p. 1). This may seem a quaint remark today, but it gives some sense of the historical context in which Likert was conducting his research.

Based on research conducted at the Institute for Social Research at the University of Michigan beginning in 1947, Likert (1961) argues for what he calls "a generalized theory of organization" (p. 1) that reflects the management practices of the highest-producing companies. Conducting a comparative analysis, he makes the case that all organizations can be classified into one of four systems, or leadership styles, that reflect the degree of employee participation in organizational decision making. The leadership styles in this **four systems approach** are as follows:

1. *Exploitive–authoritative*: An autocratic organization, similar to McGregor's Theory X form; motivation occurs through fear and threats; information flows

down the hierarchy; management communication is viewed with great suspicion by subordinates; decisions concentrated with top management; orders issued and expected to be followed without question; high employee turnover; mediocre productivity.

2. *Benevolent–authoritative*: Motivation occurs through both rewards and threats; communication is mostly downward, with limited upward communication; orders are issued, with possible opportunity for comment at lower levels; moderately high employee turnover; fair to good productivity.

3. *Consultative*: Motivation occurs through rewards, with some low-level participation in decisions; goals are set or orders issued after consultation with subordinates; moderate employee turnover; good productivity.

4. *Participative*: Motivation occurs through rewards; there is group participation in setting organization goals; lots of communication occurs downward, upward, and with peers; decision making is distributed throughout the organization; employee turnover is low; excellent productivity.

The features of these four organizational systems are abstracted from a table that Likert presents at the end of his book, comparing the four forms across seven different dimensions that encompass 42 different characteristics. The seven dimensions are (1) type of employee motivation, (2) character of communication processes, (3) character of interaction–influence processes, (4) character of decision-making processes, (5) form of goal setting, (6) character of control processes, and (7) performance characteristics. Likert argues that each organizational form has, among its features, its own internally consistent set of relationships and that it's not possible, for example, to graft the communication processes of a benevolent–authoritative organization onto a participative organization. Because of this, Likert argues that each type of organization constitutes a "system" (a perspective we will discuss in the next chapter).

Likert, of course, advocates adoption of the participative form, arguing that—like McGregor's Theory Y—it most effectively taps into human resources and, for good measure, is also the most productive organizational system. From a communication perspective, Likert provides a fairly in-depth discussion of the relationship between formal and informal communication. He argues that in the exploitive–authoritative system, formal and informal communication are at odds; the level of suspicion between workers and organizational leadership creates an informal communication system that opposes the formal system. On the other hand, in the participative organization, informal and formal communication systems are one and the same, with a unified approach to organization goals. Likert's position thus supports early Hawthorne research that suggested the potentially productive nature of informal communication. Likert is also an early advocate of participative *group* decision-making processes, which, as we will see in Chapter 8, have become a routine feature of 21st century organizations.

Critiquing Human Resource Management

HRM represents a significant move beyond human relations theory, largely because it appears to be a genuine effort to address questions of human motivation, arguing for the creation of work contexts where employees can better realize higher-order needs. Where human relations theory largely paid lip service to addressing employee concerns (recall the "ventilation" interviews in the Hawthorne studies), HRM addresses directly the question of employee involvement in organizational decision making and goal setting (see Table 4.1 for a comparison of human relations, Follett's theory, and human resource management). McGregor describes two—admittedly rather stereotypical—models of organizational leadership. Theory X represents the archetypal soul-destroying bureaucracy, while Theory Y reflects the ideally supportive and innovative organizational climate where employees are as happy to be at work as at play. Likert presents four organizational systems that reflect progressively participative models of organizing, culminating in the ideal of the participative system. What, then, are the limitations of this work?

First, as Charles Perrow (1986) indicates, HRM is notorious for treating all organizations the same, regardless of the kinds of work in which they engage. The reality is that different

Table 4.1   Comparing Human Relations Theory, Mary Parker Follett's Bridge Theory, and Human Resource Management

Issue	*Human Relations Theory*	*Follett's Bridge Theory*	*Human Resource Management*
View of perspective control	Mental adjustment of worker to work	Law of the situation	Create knowledge about employees in order to tap into need for self-actualization
View of communication	Informal communication creates social group	Dialectical, process-oriented; circular response	Both formal and informal communication are important; psychologically focused on shaping attitudes
View of organization	Organic community of social relations	Context for creative thought and community problem solving	Context for bringing together individual and managerial objectives
View of organization–society relationship	Organizations can cure societal conflict through training of administrative élite; maintain status quo	Organizations are structures through which a more democratic society can evolve; change status quo	Organizations provide context for realizing individual freedoms and potential and producing innovations
Underlying philosophy of organizing	Create cooperative, conflict-free worker–manager relations	Create community and empower average citizens	Create supportive environment that enables employees to realize their potential

forms of work lend themselves more or less easily to the kinds of participative models McGregor and Likert endorse. For example, working on a production line, where the speed of the line dictates how one works, does not lend itself well to high levels of motivation and self-actualization. On the other hand, a software company where employees work in small creative teams is a work context that is, by definition, more participative (and probably more self-actualizing). However, HRM rarely takes such different organizational contexts into account; differences in size, technology, goals, environment, and so forth are ignored.

Second, from a critical perspective, we might argue that HRM is like human relations theory on steroids in its efforts to produce knowledge about employees. I suspect that McGregor and Likert would be amazed by the various evaluation instruments that organizations use to collect information about employees—personnel evaluations, 360-degree feedback, various personality tests, executive coaching, and so forth. As management scholar Barbara Townley indicates, over the past few decades HRM has accelerated the view of the employee as an object of knowledge that can be more and more precisely controlled (Townley, 1993a, 1994). As such, the rationale of HRM is to create the individual employee as "something both useful and docile" (Burrell, 1988, p. 227). While early factory work and even the bureaucratic form were not very interested in the individual worker, other than to train him or her appropriately, HRM takes to new heights the idea of the employee as knowable, both from a managerial perspective and from the perspective of the individual employee. For example, Majia Holmer Nadesan's (1997) analysis of companies' use of personality testing shows not only how such tests construct employees as knowable objects but also how employees themselves question their abilities because of such tests, thus creating anxieties and insecurities (an issue we will take up in later chapters).

❖ CONCLUSION

The human relations/human resource management (HRM) school of thought represents an important shift in management philosophy, particularly in regard to the question of organizational control. While scientific management focused on the worker's body and bureaucratic theory placed control in rational systems of rules, human relations/HRM shifted the locus of control to worker psychology, exploring various ways to change the attitudes and motivations of workers. This does not mean that scientific management and bureaucracy disappeared as forms of control (indeed, they are both very much alive and well today) but, rather, that an additional layer of sophistication was added to management control methods.

As McGregor (1960) makes very clear, the shift to psychological forms of control was necessary because coercive methods were no longer effective motivators for workers; the shift to worker psychology was thus, in part, a response to the legitimacy crisis that management faced. Human relations/HRM is the first attempt to consider the possibility that work can be meaningful, and not just a "*form of punishment* which is the price to be paid for various kinds of satisfaction away from the job" (p. 40; italics in original).

From a communication perspective, human relations/HRM research is not very sophisticated. Because of the psychological focus, communication is generally conceived as the manifestation of individual attitudes and as information flows up, down, and across the organization. However, the shift to a focus on the importance of informal communication as a potential source of satisfaction and workplace participation represents an advance beyond scientific management and bureaucratic theory. The irony is that the theorist who had the most sophisticated and radical view of the communication–organization relationship, Mary Parker Follett, has been largely forgotten by management researchers and practitioners alike.

In Chapter 5 we will address a perspective that represents a significant shift from the individual, psychological focus of human relations/HRM and instead examines organizations as holistic systems of communication.

CRITICAL APPLICATIONS

1. Assess your experience in any work situations in which you have been involved. To what extent did you feel motivated to work hard? Why or why not? What were the factors that determined your level of productivity?

2. Using McGregor's Theory X and Theory Y, engage in a group discussion in which you compare and contrast experiences with X and Y organizations. What is your experience with communication processes in each organizational type? How do they differ?

KEY TERMS

circular response   94

four systems approach   100

Hawthorne effect   86

Hawthorne studies   85

human relations school   81

industrial democrats   83

integration   94

law of the situation   95

realist democrats   83

Theory X   98

Theory Y   99

STUDENT STUDY SITE

Visit the student study site at **www.sagepub.com/mumbyorg** for these additional learning tools:

- Web quizzes
- eFlashcards
- SAGE journal articles

- Video resources
- Web resources

CHAPTER 5

Organizations as Communication Systems

A systems perspective focuses on the interdependence
and connectedness of organizational life.

How do we know an organization when we meet one? On its surface, this seems like a simple question to answer. Organizations have names, physical structures, leaders, mission statements, and so forth. We walk through the front door of a building, crossing a boundary and "entering" the organization. We could go to an organization's website and find its mission statement, organizational chart, and employee directory. We could also make an appointment to meet an organization representative who might explain to us the goals of the organization and its commitment to serving the community. Each of these examples represents an attempt to encounter the organization and get to know what kind of organization it is and what it does. But all these efforts are doomed to failure because they are necessarily partial and limited in their approach. One might say they are "reductionist" in the sense that they attempt to understand the organization by reducing it to one of its features.

In this chapter, we will explore a perspective on organizational communication that rejects this reductionist approach and instead examines organizations from a systems perspective. In many respects the systems approach represents a revolutionary change, not only in the study of organizations but also in the natural and human sciences. The paradigm shift the systems perspective brought to the study of the world around us significantly changed how we look at that world and, indeed, what the world looks like.

In the section below we will put the systems perspective in its historical context and discuss its basic tenets. In the following section we will address the systems perspective as a way to understand organization life. Finally, we will look at various "riffs" on systems theory, including the work of Karl Weick and of Niklas Luhmann.

❖ SITUATING THE SYSTEMS PERSPECTIVE

The emergence of the systems perspective represents a fundamental shift in the dominant metaphor for talking about both the natural and the social world (Skyttner, 2005). For more than two centuries prior to systems theory, the dominant explanatory metaphor had been the machine—the idea that everything in the universe can be understood in a mechanistic fashion. Starting in the early 18th century the ambition of the newly emerging sciences was to control, predict, and conquer nature. Everything in the universe—both natural and human—could be explained in terms of causal, linear relationships. In this model, humans and animals were seen as nothing more than elaborate mechanical beings that could be understood through dissection and examination of their individual parts. The human heart, for example, could be explained as a hydraulic pump that obeyed mechanical laws. Newtonian physics, with its unchangeable laws, best embodied this determinist, cause-and-effect model of the world (drop an apple and gravity will cause it to fall to the ground).

Thus, determinism and reductionism together defined the pursuit of knowledge about both the human and natural world. Through the scientific method, reality could be reduced to basic, indivisible elements that provide the building blocks for higher-order explanations of phenomena: In physics, analysis revolves around the atom; in biology, the cell; in linguistics, the phoneme (the basic, indivisible unit of sound). This approach examines phenomena in isolation, controlling for or ignoring the effects of the surrounding environment. The laboratory experiment, with its careful control of experimental conditions, exemplifies this perspective on knowledge.

In an organizational context, Frederick Taylor's principles of scientific management are the best realization of this mechanistic, reductionist model. Taylor analyzed work by breaking it down into its basic, irreducible elements and then redesigning these elements into the "one best way." In this sense, his methods were both deterministic and reductionist.

The emergence of the systems perspective challenges all these assumptions about the way the world works. Early examples of this approach include Albert Einstein's theory of relativity, Werner Heisenberg's uncertainty principle, and Max Planck's quantum theory. Einstein, for example, showed how space and time are inseparable; a star millions of light years away is not only distant in space but in time as well. Moreover, he showed how two events separated in space that are judged to occur simultaneously by one observer can be seen as happening at different times by another observer. Without going into further detail (and thus moving beyond my own limited comprehension!), these theorists shifted science away from studying objects per se and toward thinking of reality in terms of processes and transformations. As a result, the determinism and reductionism of the mechanical age became the indeterminacy and perspectivism of the systems age. Such scientists work with probabilities, not certainties.

Ludwig von Bertalanffy (1968), considered one of the founders of what he called **general system theory**, describes this shift in the following manner:

> We come, then, to a conception which in contrast to reductionism, we may call perspectivism. We cannot reduce the biological, behavioral, and social levels to the lowest level, that of the constructs and laws of physics. . . . The mechanistic world view, taking the play of physical particles as ultimate reality, found its expression in a civilization which glorifies physical technology that has led eventually to the catastrophes of our time. Possibly the model of the world as a great organization can help to reinforce the sense of reverence for the living which we have almost lost in the last sanguinary decades of human history. (p. 49)

In speaking of the world as a "great organization," von Bertalanffy references the inter-relatedness and interdependence of all things, human and natural—the central principle of systems theory. You might note that his statement also holds a strong moralistic tone: The mechanistic worldview has brought us great technological progress but has also been catastrophic for the human race, encompassing two world wars and a nuclear arms race. Writing in the 1950s and 1960s, at the height of the Cold War, von Bertalanffy (1968) argues for both the scientific and moral superiority of systems theory, claiming that it represents "a way out of the chaos and impending destruction of our present world" (p. 52). The mechanistic worldview has undermined our sense of humanity and connection to one another; the systems approach restores and explores that connection, demonstrating that the individual is not "a cog in the social machine" (p. 53) but an important element of a wider, interconnected community. In some ways this position is quite similar to the philosophy expressed by the Frankfurt School theorists we discussed in Chapter 2.

❖ THE PRINCIPLES OF THE SYSTEMS PERSPECTIVE

What, then, does it mean to adopt a systems approach to the study of the human and natural world? Von Bertalanffy (1968) defined general system theory (GST) as "the general science of wholeness" (p. 37). With this definition, von Bertalanffy argued that as a world-view, GST sees all systems as having characteristics in common, regardless of their internal structures. Thus, everything from the structure of biological cells to the social and economic structure of societies shares common features that explain its functioning. In this sense, von Bertalanffy viewed GST as a universal perspective that brings together all fields of study by providing them with a common language and shared set of principles. We can say, then, that with GST von Bertalanffy attempted to provide a holistic framework that brings together research from various fields to produce a comprehensive view of human beings, nature, and society. Put simply, the systems approach represents a shift from the dominance of the "machine" metaphor in understanding human behavior (including organizations) to the dominance of the "organism" metaphor.

Given this framing, let's lay out the basic principles of GST. As we discuss them, however, keep in mind that, like a system itself, all the principles we will discuss should be seen as interconnected and interdependent, rather than as separate, mutually exclusive elements. In other words, the definitions are only meaningful in relationship to one another.

Interrelationship and Interdependence of Parts

A system—biological or social—is made up of elements that function, well, systemically. That is, a change in one part or element of the system can have an effect on the entire system. From a systems perspective, change is not linear and causal but, rather, affects the entire system. Similarly, one element of a system depends on many other elements of the system to function effectively.

The phenomenon of climate change is an example of this process at work on a global scale. As humanly created emissions increase and the "greenhouse effect" raises temperatures around the globe, there is no single, causal effect of this but, rather, multiple effects across the ecological system: rapid melting of arctic ice; melting of glaciers and mountain snow; destruction of coral reefs around the world (which are highly sensitive to temperature change); more extreme weather conditions, including wildfires, heat waves, and strong hurricanes. As an example of the lack of linearity and predictability in system relationships, a potential effect of climate change on my home country of the United Kingdom is *falling* temperatures due to the possibility that melting polar ice will push the Gulf Stream (a source of the United Kingdom's temperate climate) farther south, perhaps even producing another ice age.

Organizationally speaking, collective activity is difficult to imagine without interdependence of activities, people, and units. In a university setting, for example, students, faculty, administration, staff, and alumni function in an interdependent manner. Students rely on faculty for classes, on staff for various services (registration, counseling, food, degree processing, etc.), on alumni to fund fellowships and help maintain the university's reputation, and on administration to give the university direction, shape its mission, and provide a safe and dynamic learning environment. Faculty need students to teach and to provide their raison d'être, staff to take care of organizational bureaucracy, and administration to uphold the system of tenure and promotion. Such interdependence produces "butterfly effects." For example, a lengthy economic recession can create indirect effects such as larger class sizes: A recession means higher unemployment, which reduces a state's tax base, leading to reduced budget allocations to colleges; thus, fewer instructors and professors are hired, and class sizes must increase in order for students to graduate on time.

Holism

When von Bertalanffy defines GST as "the general science of wholeness," he is referring to the quality of **holism**. Holism involves the principle that when elements in a system function interdependently, the result is different from the sum of the parts; in other words, a system is *nonsummative*. This quality distinguishes a system from a mere aggregate or collection of elements. For example, a collection of automobile parts will not function as a car unless it is assembled in the correct, interdependent manner; an assembled car plus oil and gasoline functions as a holistic system in a way that the aggregated parts do not.

In human organizational processes, collective interdependent activity functions holistically to enable decision making and creativity that would not be possible with aggregated individuals working independently. For example, in the TV industry, shows such as *The Daily Show*, *The Colbert Report*, and *30 Rock* employ teams of writers to create scripts; such teams function holistically in the sense that their creativity emerges from the energy of their dynamic interactions—a creativity that would not result from each writer working independently.

However, holism can also have a negative effect (note that, previously, I indicated that the whole is different from, not greater than, the sum of the parts). Psychologist Irving Janis (1983) has demonstrated this with the phenomenon of "groupthink," where the holistic quality of groups leads to poor decision making. Such groups develop highly interdependent members, but in the decision-making process they eliminate dissenting opinions and consider only information that supports and confirms the group's worldview (Janis uses the term *mindguard*—a kind of information bodyguard—to describe a group member whose role is to protect the group from information that might challenge this worldview). Thus, groups with this dynamic function as relatively closed systems, limiting information input from their surrounding environment. Janis analyzes policy decisions such as President John F. Kennedy's decision in 1961 to send a group of CIA-trained Cuban exiles to invade Cuba in an effort to overthrow the government of Fidel Castro. The decision was

Jupiterimages/Comstock/Thinkstock

Employees working interdependently in teams can be more creative and better problems solvers than employees working individually.

ill-advised, and the invading force was defeated in 3 days. A more contemporary example would be President George W. Bush's decision in 2003 to invade Iraq on the basis of flimsy evidence about the existence of "weapons of mass destruction." President Bush's decision-making team chose to ignore evidence to the contrary and relied on information that supported their case for invasion.

Input, Transformation (Throughput), and Output of Energy

All **open systems**, both biological and social, exchange information and energy with their environments. This information and energy is taken into the system, transformed through various system processes, and put out as something different. For example, the human body takes in food, liquid, and oxygen, and through various biological processes transforms these into heat, action, and waste products. An organization takes in money, people, information, and raw materials, and through various organizational processes transforms these into products for consumption or services to a community.

For example, a university system has numerous inputs, including state and private funds (including research grants), materials for building infrastructure, employees (faculty, part-time instructors, staff—clerical, custodial, food service, and administrators), and students (graduate and undergraduate). These various inputs interact in multiple ways and, in the process, are transformed into outputs that are quite different from the initial inputs. Raw materials are transformed into classroom and lab spaces where professors and students interact, ultimately (we hope!) creating more knowledgeable and experienced citizens and skilled employees; faculty interact with one another and use university resources (libraries, databases, grants, etc.) to produce original knowledge that in turn becomes a new system input, perhaps being taught in college classrooms worldwide or even winning a Nobel prize (an event that transforms a university's reputation); graduate students interact with faculty and utilize university resources, ultimately earning the title "Dr." and becoming inputs into other university systems.

Negative Entropy

One of the founders of systems theory, Kenneth Boulding (1985), states that "a system is anything that is not chaos." In this sense, an open system exhibits **negative entropy**. What does this mean? According to Isaac Newton's second law of thermodynamics, entropy is a universal condition by which all forms of organization naturally move toward disintegration and randomness. **Entropy**, then, is a measure of the relative degree of disorder that exists within a system at a given moment in time; the more disorder, the more entropy exists. Open systems have the ability to counter entropy, or disorder, and are thus "negentropic." However, over time all systems, regardless of their degree of openness, move toward entropy and die; systems can arrest entropy, but they cannot eliminate it. Thus, biological systems grow and develop over time and then degrade, sometimes over decades or centuries. Organizations and societies thrive and grow but eventually deteriorate and succumb to entropy.

By virtue of their lack of interaction and information exchange with their environments, **closed systems** are, by definition, entropic and cannot resist disorganization and disintegration (McMillan & Northorn, 1995). Examples of such closed social systems are cults, which close themselves off from the rest of society in order to prevent contamination from unbelievers; societies ruled by autocratic governments (North Korea, the former Soviet Union); and secret societies, such as the Freemasons.

It's important to point out, however, that *open* and *closed* are relative terms; no system is ever completely open or closed. A completely open system would have no structure or boundaries and would lack distinctiveness from its environment; as such, it would cease to exist as a distinct system. In this sense, openness is always selective on the part of organizations—a process we will examine more closely below. Similarly, a completely closed system is unthinkable; even a cult needs to communicate with its environment to recruit new members.

Equilibrium, Homeostasis, and Feedback

Systems that are open and negentropic maintain equilibrium through a process of **homeostasis**. All systems maintain a degree of permeability with their environments, thus allowing information and energy to flow back and forth across the system's boundaries. Because of this permeability, organizations are able to receive information that provides intelligence about their own functioning in relation to their environments (which include other organizations). Such feedback enables system performance to be monitored and corrected if necessary. In this sense, open systems are able to adapt effectively to changes in environmental conditions, thus combating entropy.

The simplest (and most oft-cited) example of a system that maintains homeostasis (or "steady state") through feedback is a thermostat. A thermostat operates according to what is called "negative feedback"—that is, feedback that corrects a deviation from the norm and is therefore error activated. Thus, a thermostat detects variations in room temperature and sends signals to the heating and cooling system to adjust its performance; if the heating unit heats a room beyond the preset temperature (e.g., 70 degrees), an error signal will be sent to the heating system to turn it off. Anyone who has had class in a room where the thermostat is broken and the heating unit continuously blows hot air (thus creating a system lacking in equilibrium) will appreciate the thermostat's importance!

The system of feedback and regulation is obviously much more complex for social systems such as organizations, which receive information from multiple environmental sources and must make constant adjustments to maintain homeostasis. Indeed, a complex organizational system operates according to two kinds of feedback: negative (or deviation-counteracting) feedback and positive (or deviation-amplifying) feedback. For example, an automobile company must assess feedback from a variety of environmental sources, including parts suppliers, the economy (what is the price of raw materials, including oil?), customer tastes, and so forth. Currently, for example, U.S. automobile companies are shifting some of their production away from large, gas-guzzling vehicles and toward smaller, "green" (electric and hybrid) vehicles. However, such vehicles are still a very small part of the automobile market, and so car manufacturers will have to monitor their environments (including customer tastes, government mandates for more fuel-efficient vehicles, creation of more efficient technologies, etc.) and adapt to changes in order to maintain their competitiveness.

Systems can also combat entropy through deviation-amplifying feedback, in which systems engage in growth and expansion. Deviation-amplifying feedback is positive feedback in which deviation away from a norm occurs. In this process, more energy is taken into a system than is put out, and, thus, the system grows. However, systems cannot grow continuously and must return to a homeostatic, steady state if they are to survive. An organizational system in deviation-amplifying mode will often expand to take over parts of its environment, including other competing organizations. For example, in recent years the airline industry has experienced several mergers, with American Airlines taking over TWA, US Airways buying America West, and United merging with Continental. The logic of such mergers is that market share increases and the larger system is less vulnerable to environmental changes.

However, deviation-amplifying feedback will destroy a system if that system does not return to a homeostatic, steady-state condition at some point. For example, the "dotcom" boom and bust of the late 1990s/early 2000s is a perfect example of how a deviation-amplifying feedback loop creates a doomed system. The founding of the Internet and World Wide Web in the early 1990s stimulated the massive growth of Internet startup companies ("dotcoms"). Everyone wanted to get in on the act, and investment capital was available to anyone who had an idea for an online company. Basically, all a new company had to do was put "e-" before its name or ".com" after it to see investment capital pour in and its stock price shoot up. The problem was that most of these companies operated at a loss, expecting that market share (and, hence, profits) would come later; thus, money was invested on the possibility of future earnings that, for the vast majority of these new companies, never materialized. Eventually, many companies used up all their cash and could not attract more investors. In March 2000 the stock market crashed, with the NASDAQ (the tech stock index) losing 10% of its value in one day. Fifty percent of startups failed, with thousands of people losing their jobs. Companies and investors banked on the deviation-amplifying cycle continuing indefinitely—something that violates a basic system principle.

© iStockphoto.com/BackyardProduction

The recent housing bubble is a classic example of a deviation-amplifying system that got out of control.

Similarly, the financial meltdown of 2008 was the result of a deviation-amplifying loop in which banks kept selling millions of "subprime" mortgages (because they were hugely profitable), creating a "housing bubble" that burst when interest rates rose and millions of homeowners discovered they could not meet their mortgage payments. Banks got into severe financial trouble, and several closed. The resulting effort to regain equilibrium involved negative (deviation-counteracting) feedback in which getting bank loans went from being very easy to being extremely difficult. Businesses discovered they could not borrow the money they needed to stay afloat, and many went bankrupt. Such an example illustrates how highly interdependent elements of a system are and how deviations from a state of equilibrium can quickly result in the destruction of a system.

Hierarchy

One of the most important features of a system is its ordering into a **hierarchy**. Systems are not structured on a single level but, rather, process information and function dynamically across multiple levels. As such, any system is made up of interrelated and interdependent subsystems and is itself a subsystem within a larger suprasystem. All these hierarchically ordered levels are interrelated, and any change in one level will produce changes throughout the system.

For example, at the University of North Carolina, my department can be viewed as an open system with a distinct identity and permeable boundaries, allowing it to take in resources such as a budget, students, faculty, and alumni contributions. But it's also a subsystem within the College of Arts and Sciences, which houses about 70 departments and

© iStockphoto.com/leluconcepts

Systems are hierarchical, consisting of subsystems and suprasystems.

programs and against which our department competes for budget allocations and student majors. Thus, an increase in budget allocation or undergraduate majors for other departments might negatively affect our own system. The College of Arts and Sciences is also only one college among several on the UNC–Chapel Hill campus and must compete for resources with other colleges, such as the business school, the medical school, the schools of social work and public health, and so forth. But it doesn't stop there. The UNC–Chapel Hill campus is 1 of 17 in the North Carolina university system, so the chancellors from each campus must compete for resources at the state level, lobbying the state legislature in Raleigh. One could go even further, arguing that the state of North Carolina competes with other states for businesses to relocate there (North Carolina is a center for high-tech, medical, and pharmaceutical companies); competing successfully means higher tax revenues for the state, which can lead to an increase in state allocations for higher education, leading ultimately to a bigger budget for my department.

It's important, then, always to think of systems hierarchically and to view them as both made up of subsystems and embedded within suprasystems.

Goal Orientation

All systems are goal oriented, and through the process of feedback (both positive and negative) they are able to adjust their activities in order to maintain progression toward their goal. A simple example is the cruise control "servo-mechanism" on an automobile, which will constantly compare the set speed to the actual road speed, increasing road speed when it falls below the set speed and decreasing it when it goes above. This simple cybernetic feedback loop uses information to compare the actual performance of a mechanism with a preset goal, making appropriate adjustments to the mechanism's performance (Wiener, 1948).

Of course, in social systems such as organizations, **goal orientations** are far more complex; indeed, it is quite possible for organizations to have multiple and possibly competing goals. The research and development unit of a company, for example, might have a goal of creating the highest-quality products, while the marketing division of the organization might want to get the product to market as quickly as possible to meet consumer demand. Similarly, a university might have the goal of being known as a top research institution, but this goal often competes with that of providing the best-possible education for undergraduates (because research faculty don't teach as frequently as at teaching-oriented colleges and class sizes are often bigger and taught by inexperienced graduate students).

Equifinality and Multifinality

The principles of equifinality and multifinality are the final properties of an open system that we will discuss, and they reflect the dynamic, process-oriented, and interdependent character of a system. **Equifinality** refers to the fact that "a system can reach the same final state from differing initial conditions and by a variety of paths" (Katz & Kahn, 1966, p. 30). On the other hand, **multifinality** refers to the ability of a system to reach multiple goals and states from the same initial conditions and inputs. With a closed system, knowledge of the initial condition means that one can predict the final state; for example, the result of a chemical reaction in a test tube is known if one knows the composition of the initial substances. With an open system, however, the degree of complexity and interdependence means that no such prediction is possible. Indeed, the principles of equifinality and multifinality capture the creativity and dynamism of an open system.

For example, organizational communication scholar Mike Pacanowsky (1988) has shown how Gore Company (the maker of Gore-Tex) uses a nonhierarchical "lattice" structure of organizing, in which employees are given autonomy to make connections with others in ways that will facilitate creativity in product creation and manufacturing. In such a system equifinality rules, as there are literally thousands of permutations in terms of how employees interact and create functioning workgroups.

Similarly, a supermarket might exhibit the principle of multifinality, realizing multiple goals from the same initial conditions. While for managers and owners the primary goal of inputs is profit making, other stakeholders might pursue different goals. For example, customers see the goal as feeding their family in a healthy way (and might encourage the supermarket to stock organic products); *single* customers might view the supermarket as a dating system, with the goal of meeting potential mates; and employees might see the supermarket as part of a larger employment system, with the goal of moving up the hierarchy or on to a more prestigious organization.

In sum, when the systems perspective emerged in the 1960s it represented a radical new approach to the study of both the biological and human social world. Organizationally speaking, the systems perspective is a response to the failure of the psychological approach (as reflected in human relations and human resource management) to address the role of organizational structure and collective behavior in the organizing process. In this sense, the systems perspective rejects the individualistic approach of human relations and human resource management and instead looks at organizational behavior as occurring within interdependent systems. Let's now turn to a closer look at how the systems perspective has influenced the study of organizational communication.

❖ ORGANIZATIONS AS SYSTEMS OF COMMUNICATION

In their classic systems study *The Social Psychology of Organizations*, social psychologists Daniel Katz and Robert Kahn (1966) state that "social organizations are flagrantly open systems" (p. 20). However, as they themselves indicate, this "flagrant" openness does have its limitations; as we have already discussed above, a system that is completely open ceases to be a system. In fact, one of the most important tasks that a system performs is in selectively receiving information and resources through a process of coding and interpretation. For example, the human body selectively processes inputs; if we eat something that cannot be digested or is poisonous, the body will not process it and will evacuate it.

Human organizations such as corporations, nonprofits, volunteer groups, street gangs, fraternities and sororities, and so on can all be viewed as open systems with relatively permeable boundaries that must selectively code and interpret potential inputs. What all these groups have in common is their status as *communication* systems. In other words, while organizational systems consist of various kinds of inputs, throughputs, and outputs, their

Critical Technologies 5.1
Organizing Food

If Ludwig von Bertalanffy were alive today, I suspect he would be appalled by the stuff we put in our bodies, or at least by the technology that gets it there. As a systems theorist, he would view the modern food industry as a perfect (and terrifying) example of how the mechanical, reductionist view of the world has "found its expression in a civilization which glorifies physical technology." Factory farming has effectively utilized technology to create a massive fast-food industry, and, as Eric Schlosser (2002) describes in his book *Fast Food Nation*, the industry represents a systemic threat to our health and well-being.

From a systems perspective, it's fascinating and disturbing to examine the ways that the technology for producing vast quantities of cheap, unhealthy, and hugely profitable food has changed society. Food conglomerates such as ConAgra, IBP, Cargill, and Archer-Daniels-Midland exercise massive control over what we eat. ConAgra, for example—which owns more than 60 food brands, including Chef Boyardee, Jiffy Pop, and Peter Pan peanut butter—controls about 25% of the U.S. beef industry. Unlike the pretty pictures you see in TV commercials, cattle are raised in huge factory farms that not only produce prodigious amounts of waste (about 50 pounds per cow per day) but create significant environmental problems. A factory outside Greeley, Colorado, produces more waste than the cities of Boston, Denver, Atlanta, and St. Louis combined, and, unlike human waste, it's dumped untreated into pits called "lagoons."

The big slaughterhouses owned by ConAgra can process up to 5,000 cattle a day. Work in the slaughter and meatpacking industry is among the most dangerous in the nation and is performed mainly by low-wage, migrant workers. Injuries and maiming are routine. The speed of the production line (key to profits) means that in the dismembering of animals, it's not unusual for excrement to contaminate the meat. Indeed, E. coli from a single animal can contaminate 32,000 pounds of ground beef. According to the Centers for Disease Control, each year about one quarter of the U.S. population experiences food poisoning, most cases of which are never reported (Schlosser, 2002, p. 195). Many of these incidences of food poisoning are a product of the industrialized nature of food processing.

Moreover, one of the modern technologies that profoundly affect our lives without us knowing it is the production of chemicals to enhance the flavor of food. According to Schlosser (2002), about 90% of what Americans spend on food is for processed food. Processed food has no real taste (and not much nutritional value), and so the multibillion-dollar "flavor industry" has to add the missing—and crucial—element.

Take McDonald's fries. Until 1990 their "unique" flavor was derived from being fried in a mixture of 7% cottonseed oil and 93% beef tallow—a deadly combination that contained more saturated fat per ounce than McDonald's hamburgers (Schlosser, 2002, p. 120). So, under pressure from consumer groups, McDonald's switched to pure vegetable oil. However, this changed the well-recognized flavor of the fries. So McDonald's turned to "food technology" (i.e., chemistry) to solve the problem. As a result, the taste of your favorite fries is chemically produced.

It's the same story with hamburgers. As a result of the way cattle are slaughtered and the manner in which meat is treated, the patty that arrives on your hamburger bun is processed to the point where it's unrecognizable as meat from a cow; indeed, a single patty can contain meat from hundreds of different cows. Again, chemistry comes to the rescue. Schlosser (2002) reports his experience at a New Jersey research facility devoted to developing flavors for food:

> After closing my eyes, I suddenly smelled a grilled hamburger. The aroma was uncanny, almost miraculous. It smelled like someone in the room was flipping burgers on a hot grill. But when I opened my eyes, there was just a narrow strip of white paper and a smiling flavorist. (p. 129)

So the taste of your Big Mac and accompanying large order of fries is produced in a laboratory somewhere in New Jersey. Still want to have that hamburger and fries for lunch? To get a better sense of how the food industry system works, check out the documentary *Food, Inc.* and the related website (http://www.foodincmovie.com), or watch the short parody of *The Matrix* that addresses factory farming (http://www.themeatrix.com).

status as complex "collections of people trying to make sense of what is happening around them" (Weick, 2001, p. 5) is what differentiates them from other kinds of systems.

While earlier theories of organizational communication are dominated by information transfer conceptions of the communication process—much like Axley's (1984) conduit model, discussed in Chapter 1—the systems perspective provides us with a more complex communication model that, for the first time in the study of organizations, focuses on social actors' meaning and sense-making processes, examining communication as something that is meaningful only within—and, indeed, creates—a larger social context.

While they are not organizational researchers, psychologists Paul Watzlawick, Janet Beavin, and Don Jackson (1967) developed a systems view of communication in their classic book *Pragmatics of Human Communication*. This book is famous in part for the development of a communication axiom that you have probably come across in other communication courses: "One cannot not communicate" (pp. 48–51). While this has become a rather trite and overused phrase among students of communication, it points to at least four important features of a systems approach to communication:

1. All behavior is communicative. A person sitting alone at a crowded bar and staring straight ahead might be communicating that he or she doesn't want to communicate with anyone; a professor who closes his or her door might be communicating that he or she doesn't want to be disturbed (hint, hint!).

2. Intent is not necessary for communication to occur. Someone can intend not to communicate but, in the process, communicate anyway. Communication is thus an interpretive process. For example, the person at the bar might be trying to be enigmatic and mysterious, in the hope that someone will approach him or her. The professor may have closed his or her door to keep out noise from the hallway but is quite open to visitors. However, from the standpoint of understanding communication processes, intent is much less important than the interpretive frame people use in making sense of behaviors.

3. Communication is relational and contextual. Meaning and sense making are shaped by the social context and the participants involved—that is, by the system in which it occurs. For example, I've noticed that students often find it weird to run into professors off campus, as if we don't live normal lives in other social contexts. (I once had a student come up to me in a bar and ask incredulously, "What are *you* doing here?")

4. From a systems perspective, a key feature of sense making is the process of punctuation. In other words, everyday life consists of ongoing streams of behavior, which punctuation (like periods and commas in written texts) organizes into meaningful units. For example, the stream of everyday organizational behavior is punctuated into meaningful units by identifiable events, such as meetings, casual conversations, breaks, rituals (formal and informal), and so forth. Different people can punctuate the same stream of behavior differently, thus making sense of it in competing ways. Watzlawick et al.'s (1967) classic (and rather dated) example is the husband who claims he withdraws from his wife because she nags at him, while his wife claims she nags at him because he withdraws from her. These competing punctuations make sense of the couple's relational dynamic in

diametrically opposite ways. Watzlawick et al. argue that individual behavior and sense making can be understood only by examining it from the perspective of the communication system within which it occurs (in this case, the couple's interaction) and that their conflict can be solved only through communicating about their communication process (i.e., "metacommunication"), thus breaking this cycle of blame. This is a great example of how looking at individual behavior in isolation completely misses how sense making works; only a systems analysis is able to address interdependencies and how meaning gets constructed in a collective way.

How, then, can we examine organizational communication processes from a systems perspective? In the remainder of this chapter, we will examine a couple of contemporary examples of systems approaches to organizational communication.

Karl Weick and Organizational Sense Making

Karl Weick is a bit of a maverick. He teaches in a business school, but his writings constantly undermine the idea that organizations are places where people make rational decisions based on analysis of carefully gathered information. Management researcher John Van Maanen (1995) argues that Weick doesn't develop theories about organizations but, rather, engages in "allegorical breaching"; that is, he tells stories to represent abstract ideas in ways that undermine our common-sense views of how organizations work.

To give you a sense of how Weick (1979) thinks, let me quote from the opening of his book *The Social Psychology of Organizing*:

> This book is about organizational appreciation. To understand organizing is to appreciate events such as these:
>
> A professor, named Alex Bavelas, often plays golf with other professors. Once, he took the foursome down to the golf course, and they were going to draw straws for partners. He said, "Let's do this after the game."
>
> The story goes that three umpires disagreed about the task of calling balls and strikes. The first one said, "I calls them as they is." The second one said, "I calls them as I sees them." The third and cleverest umpire said, "They ain't nothin' till I calls them." (p. 1)

In some ways, this quote captures all the elements of Weick's view of organizations. First, it's important to draw attention to the title of his book: *The Social Psychology of Organizing*. This title is nearly identical to that of Katz and Kahn's book, mentioned earlier, but Weick's shift from noun to verb form is significant, reflecting his view of collective activity as ongoing, process oriented, and dynamic. People don't work in organizations; they engage in organizing processes and continually try to make sense of the processes in which they are participating. As Weick (2001) states, "In the last analysis, organizing is about fallible people who keep going" (p. xi). Think about how different this is from most theories about organizations. It captures an essential element of most people's organizational experience: Quite often, we don't know what the heck is going on, and so we spend a lot of our time figuring it out. Thus, "organizations are collections of people trying to make sense of what is happening around them" (p. 5).

This idea is well captured by the first story above about the golf outing. Think about the level of confusion that would be created if Bavelas's suggestion were taken up. First, as a member of the foursome, you wouldn't know who to root for. If one of the other players sinks a long putt on the fifth green, does that hurt you or help you? Is he your partner or your opponent? Every shot played has a level of ambiguity that's almost too much to bear. Second, the game can be made sense of only in retrospect; that is, it's not until after the game when partners are revealed that the foursome can look back and reconstruct what happened over the previous few hours. Interestingly, Weick notes that none of the players were willing to take up Bavelas's suggestion—it created too much ambiguity for them.

Weick argues that the "crazy foursome" in this story actually epitomizes a lot of what happens in organizational life (no, not that a lot of golf gets played). That is, as they organize, people engage in lots of "**retrospective sense making**," where they "reconstruct plausible histories" (Weick, 1979, p. 5) after the fact to provide rational accounts of their organizational behavior and decision making. But such retrospective sense making papers over the reality that, in the ongoing process of organizing, people rarely behave in such a rational manner. Let me give an example to illustrate Weick's perspective.

Every semester, instructors have to make decisions about which textbook to adopt for a particular course. Frequently, this is a routine decision, especially if the instructor has taught the course before—in which case, he or she adopts a previously used textbook. However, maybe the instructor is teaching the course for the first time or is fed up with the text currently being used. In an ideal world, and consistent with rational models of organizational decision making, the instructor would engage in a careful information search, reviewing all the available textbooks, and then decide which one best meets his or her instructional goals for the course. The reality is probably quite different. With the deadline for textbook orders looming (and increasingly demanding e-mails from the department chair), the instructor realizes it's impossible to review all the possible adoptions, especially with a large pile of papers that need grading. So he or she pulls a couple of texts from the bookshelf (complimentary copies from publishers), looks through the table of contents in each, and decides that one of them covers more topics with which he or she is familiar. An e-mail is sent to the campus bookstore, and life becomes a little less ambiguous. Indeed, it's possible that you're reading this textbook precisely because of this mode of decision making and not because of your instructor's recognition of its inherent genius!

Now, if you were to ask your instructor why he or she adopted this particular text, your instructor would probably tell you that it's the best one on the market and that it fits best with his or her own teaching philosophy for this course. Your instructor would probably not admit to ordering it at the last minute, and might even describe the extensive information search conducted before choosing this text. Weick would say that this instructor is a perfect example of a "fallible person who keeps going"—someone who lives in an organizational world that is inherently ambiguous but that demands rational behavior from everyone. Hence, the role of retrospective sense making—constructing rational accounts after an organizing process that is actually messy and ambiguous. People do this not because they are incompetent or liars but because it's impossible either to make sense of all the available information or to meet the expectations of the rational model of behavior by which organizations pretend they operate. Sometimes people can't make sense of what they do until after they have done it. Or, as Weick (1979) states, "How can I know what I think until I see what I say?" (p. 5).

In the second story, we have three philosopher umpires. The first believes that there's an objective world out there in which balls and strikes exist as facts, and it's just a question of describing that objective reality; a pitch *is* a ball or a strike. That's how most people view organizational life. The second umpire believes in a subjective, rather than objective, reality. Reality is determined by individual perceptions, and, thus, there are as many realities as there are people to perceive them. However, if this were the case, how would people ever talk to each other and how would organizing as collective action ever take place, given that collective action requires at least some level of shared reality? In saying, "They ain't nothin' till I calls them," the third umpire is the cleverest, because he identifies an important element of organizational life; that is, people play a key role in creating the environments to which they then respond. By calling "ball" or "strike," the third umpire enacts an organizational environment that everyone—players, managers, spectators—must make sense of. But, until he makes the call, there's nothing to interpret. Moreover, with this story, Weick illustrates the central role of language and communication in organizing systems; communication does not function simply as a vehicle for information transmission but, rather, creates organizational possibilities. If a pitch is nothing until it's called, then naming brings a particular reality into being.

Here, we can identify an important sense in which Weick's perspective moves beyond the systems approach we discussed in the first part of the chapter. While traditional systems research looks at how organizations as open systems adapt to changing environments, Weick argues that organizations actually create, or enact, their own environments, which they must then make sense of. His theory of organizing is therefore aimed at providing insights into the ways people organize—not to achieve predefined goals and make rational decisions but, rather, to cope collectively with the uncertain and equivocal information environments in which they find themselves. For Weick, then, organizing is about seeing everyday life as an ongoing sense-making accomplishment, in which people engage in the continuous process of making their situations rationally accountable to both themselves and others (like the instructor giving a rational account of his or her textbook choice) and, in the process, reduce equivocality or uncertainty.

This perspective is reflected in Weick's model of enactment, selection, and retention, which we will discuss below.

Weick's Model of Organizing: Enactment, Selection, and Retention

Weick (1979) defines organizing as "a consensually validated grammar for reducing equivocality by means of sensible interlocked behaviors" (p. 3). He presents this **equivocality (uncertainty) reduction** process as a three-stage model of **enactment, selection, and retention** (see Figure 5.1). For Weick, equivocality reduction is *the* key function of organizing. As you try to make sense of this model, you should think about it not as a static thing but as an effort to depict an ongoing, dynamic, and never-ending process that people collectively engage in as they go about their daily organizational lives. In this sense, it represents collective sense-making activity in which people who function interdependently (i.e., systemically) constantly engage.

Figure 5.1   Karl Weick's Model of Organizing

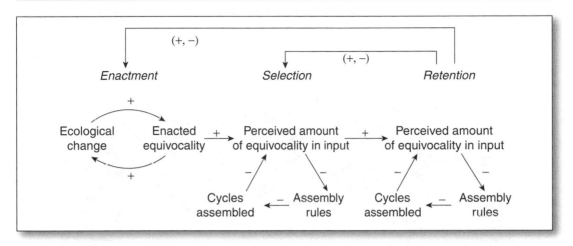

SOURCE: Weick (1979).

Again, Weick's model is unique in his attention to what he calls an "enacted" environment. That is, organizations as systems not only respond and adapt to environmental (ecological) changes but also create their own environments by virtue of what they choose to pay attention to. As Weick (1988) states, enactment refers to the fact that "when people act, they bring events and structures into existence and set them in motion" (p. 306). Organizations inhabit communication environments that they selectively perceive, and this selective perception and creation of environments is subject to sense making.

Once an equivocal organizational environment is enacted, organization members must decide how to make sense of it and select sense-making processes. Weick argues that rules and cycles are the two principal mechanisms that organization members employ. Cycles are series of interactions made up of **double-interacts**, which Weick sees as the basic unit of organizing. A double-interact is actually three interrelated acts of communication: A-B-A. For example, a supervisor (A) may say to a subordinate (B), "Can you get that report to me by 9 a.m. tomorrow?" This instruction may not be clear to the subordinate, thus increasing the amount of equivocality in her communication (i.e., sense-making) environment. Because of this equivocality, she responds, "Do you mean the final version of the report, or just a first draft?" The supervisor (A) responds, "Just the first draft." Thus, through this double-interact (A-B-A), equivocality is reduced. Of course, this is an extremely simple example, and Weick argues that daily processes of organizing actually consist of thousands of such interactions.

On the other hand, rules are established organizational practices for making sense of equivocality. Rules are employed in contexts that are less equivocal (often because there is a precedent for them and, hence, the existence of rules), while cycles tend to be adopted more when equivocality is high. Selection processes that are successful in reducing equivocality are retained (retention stage) as organizational memory to be used should similar equivocal situations arise in the future; however, this doesn't guarantee that such rules will work at a later time, given the changing and dynamic nature of systems. Indeed, Weick argues that memory should be treated as a pest; too much retention of tried-and-tested rules often limits an organization's flexibility in responding to equivocal situations. Weick uses the term *requisite variety* to refer to the idea that complex enacted environments require similarly complex responses from the organization; in other words, complex situations do not lend themselves well to simple solutions (application of organizational rules) and vice versa.

Pixland/Pixland/Thinkstock

Group assignments can suck, but they can also provide important insights into how teams make decisions and cope with equivocality.

Let's briefly explore an organizing context to which this model can be applied. Imagine that your professor sets a written assignment that requires you to team up with three other class members and write a 25-page research paper that analyzes an organization using two different theoretical perspectives. Your professor's only instructions are that the paper must be written like a scholarly article and must include a minimum of 15 different citations of scholarly research in addition to those assigned in class; also, it must conform to APA standards for style and format. Using Weick's model, we can say that your professor has enacted an organizational environment that greatly increases the level of equivocality you experience. In other words, your world (at least in terms of this class) has gone from relatively predictable (your level of coping is fairly high) to highly uncertain. The professor's enactment thus invokes a sense-making effort on the part of you and your classmates.

In terms of selection (i.e., sense-making) processes, you quickly realize that your existing recipes and rules (i.e., what's retained in your organizational memory from previous organizing experiences) for written assignments don't work. You've never written such a lengthy research paper before, never mind one that's written like a "scholarly article," and you're not even sure what counts as "scholarly research" (do magazine or online articles count?). You kind of know what a "citation" is, but what the heck is APA? What's more, your friendly local fraternity/sorority doesn't have a copy of a similar assignment in its collection of papers and exams from other classes. None of the online paper-writing services is any help either (I'm not condoning these, just acknowledging their existence).

So, what do you do? Weick (1989) argues that "to understand organizing is to understand jazz" (p. 242). Jazz is an improvisational musical form in which "a little structure goes a long way" (p. 243); all the musicians in a jazz group work from a loose theme, or structure, and then improvise with one another in creating something original. Your group paper assignment can be addressed in the same way. Using the principle of "requisite variety," any simple formula (organizational memory for paper writing) must be viewed with suspicion given the complexity of the assignment, and we can think of the professor's instructions as the loose structure around which the group can engage in improvisational double-interacts and cycles of communication to engage in sense making and equivocality reduction.

For example, your group might begin with a brainstorming session, throwing out ideas for the paper. A plan of action might be created as a result of this session, not necessarily as a solution to the identified problems but, instead, as a way to motivate action. Weick (1995) indicates that plans are often useful less as rational, goal-oriented solutions to problems and more as a "binding mechanism" (p. 127) that brings people together and encourages collective activity. What action might the plan motivate? One (or all) of the group might go meet with the professor (a radical and scary notion, I realize) and ask her for more explicit instructions: What counts as a scholarly article (in my experience, students sometimes have difficulty distinguishing scholarly and more popular publications)? What is APA, and why does it have to be used? Where can the 15 scholarly research publications be located?

Your professor might refer you and your group to some online scholarly databases and tell you to go to the library. Your visit to the library might involve some wandering around in the stacks (some of my best research discoveries have occurred through "wandering" and not because of any carefully planned search). Based on what your meanderings lead you to, you may have an actual conversation with a real, flesh-and-blood librarian who points you to some more resources and might even send you to another librarian who has specialized knowledge about the topic you're researching. Meanwhile, another member of your group has a conversation with a friend, who tells him about this great company he's just started working for and how they have this really interesting corporate culture that would be fascinating to study. Just like that, you have your study site.

And so it goes. This is just one small illustration of how a relatively complex and equivocal communication environment can evoke an equally complex sense-making effort on the part of the organization members involved. As Weick (2001) points out, there is no single solution to this situation. Engaging in sense making and equivocality reduction is rather like being a mapmaker; an infinite number of plausible maps can be created of the same territory. However, the organizational sense-making problem is compounded because the terrain keeps changing; thus, the members' task is to carve out temporary stability in a continuous flow of behavior.

Similarly, there's no single answer to the paper-writing problem. Weick argues that part of the answer to effective organizing is to recognize that plausibility—not accuracy—is the goal.

Plans are not really solutions, there are no simple cause–effect answers to problems, and Point B can be reached from Point A in an infinite number of ways (and, anyway, the location of Point B will change over time). Creating a group paper that is plausible rather than accurate is the goal; that is, it provides an interesting narrative account (among the many possible) of the organization studied, drawing on a small part of a vast scholarly literature.

From Weick's perspective, students (or any organization members) make the mistake of thinking that the vision of the organization's order that exists in their heads is actually how organizations operate. In fact, organizations act and then think, make sense of actions after the fact, create plans in order to have something for people to follow, and generally behave in a less-than-rational way. In other words, organizing is never tidy, despite the best efforts of management researchers to make it so. As Weick (2001) states,

> To appreciate organizations and their environments as flows interrupted by constraints of one's own making is to take oneself a little less seriously, to find a little more leverage in human affairs on a slightly smaller scale, and to have a little less hubris and a little more fun. (p. xi)

A Critical Perspective on Weick

Weick is generally classified as a systems theorist (hence, his appearance in this chapter), but he would fit just as well in Chapter 6 on the cultural perspective given his focus on the ways people organize through processes of sense making—a central issue in the next chapter, as you will see. Moreover, although Weick doesn't talk about power and control in a direct way, as would a critical theorist, he is critical of traditional models of organization that depict human beings as strategic, goal oriented, and rational in their decision making. As he states, "Efforts to maintain the illusion that organizations are rational and orderly in the interest of legitimacy are costly and futile" (Weick, 2001, p. xi). Indeed, Weick argues that, put into practice, such traditional models are actually detrimental to effective decision making, and even to personal health; his analyses of both the Mann Gulch firefighter tragedy (Weick, 1993) and the Tenerife air disaster (Weick, 1990) show how narrow definitions of organizational effectiveness based on hierarchy and formal organizational structure can cost people their lives (see Critical Case Study 5.1).

Critical Case Study 5.1
Airlines and Equivocality

On March 27, 1977, two Boeing 747 "jumbo jets" collided on the runway at Tenerife airport, killing 583 passengers and crew. The planes, originating from New York and Amsterdam, respectively, had been diverted to Tenerife on their way to the Canary Islands because of bad weather. The crash occurred when KLM Flight 4805 commenced its takeoff run while Pan Am Flight 1736 was still taxiing on the takeoff runway and slammed into the side of the other aircraft; low clouds at Tenerife airport obscured the Pan Am plane from the KLM flight crew's view. Weick's (1990) analysis of the factors that led to the crash addresses a number of issues, including the small size of the Tenerife airport, the limited experience of the control tower crew in dealing with large aircraft, pressure on the aircraft to take off, and unpredictable weather conditions. However, much of his study focuses on the KLM cockpit crew's interaction immediately prior to takeoff:

> The communication from the tower to the [Pan Am plane] requested the latter to report when it left the runway clear. In the cockpit of the KLM, nobody at first confirmed receiving these communications until the Pan Am responded to the tower's request that it should report leaving the runway with an "OK, we'll report when we're clear." On hearing this, the KLM flight engineer asked, "Is he not clear then?" The captain did not understand him and he repeated, "Is he not clear that Pan American?" The Captain replied with an emphatic "Yes." Perhaps influenced by his great prestige, making it difficult to imagine an error of this magnitude on the part of such an expert pilot, both the copilot and flight engineer made no further objections. The impact took place about 13 seconds later. (p. 574)

Such was the system of hierarchy on the flight deck that neither the copilot nor the flight engineer felt free to challenge the pilot's decision to take off, despite not having received clearance from the control tower.

More than 30 years after this event, in late May 2011, I was on an American Airlines flight from Boston to London. About a minute into the flight, as we were making our initial ascent, I noticed two flight attendants—sitting directly in front of and facing me—talking to each other in a rather animated way. Both had concerned looks on their faces, and one of them kept looking out the window at the right engine. Then she picked up a phone and made a call. The next thing I knew, another flight attendant came rushing forward from business class and consulted with the two flight attendants. Then she rushed back to the front of the plane. As casually as I could, I leaned forward and asked the flight attendants what was going on. "The noise of the right engine is much louder than it should be; we're recommending to the captain that he turn back to Boston." Sure enough, a couple of minutes later the captain's voice came over the PA, announcing that he was going to jettison fuel and return to the airport.

The next few minutes were a bit nerve-racking, to say the least, but we landed safely back at Logan airport. After we taxied back to the gate, I sat and watched as a meeting took place right on the gangway (my seat was next to the exit door), involving the captain, first officer, flight engineer, two mechanics, and two flight attendants. They all stood in a circle talking. I couldn't hear what was being said, but one of the

flight attendants was pretty animated and clearly getting her point across. Eventually, the two mechanics came onboard and ran some tests on the engine. A few minutes later the captain announced that they couldn't find anything wrong but that they were going to change to another aircraft anyway. We took off again from Boston about 3 hours after the original departure time.

What's extraordinary about this incident is that it could not have happened 30 years ago. Why? Because in the wake of accidents such as the one in Tenerife, airlines have widely instituted a more team-based authority structure amongst flight crews. Now, common sense tells us that the last place you need democracy and shared power in decision making is on the flight deck of a jumbo jet, where in critical situations you want to feel as though someone is in charge. And we're all used to the iconic father-figure captain who is completely professional, highly competent, and fully in charge of the crew and passengers. But as Weick's analysis shows, it's precisely this kind of strict hierarchy that creates a decision-making context in which challenging questionable decisions is almost impossible. On the Boston-to-London flight the decision to turn back was ultimately the captain's, but he made that decision based on a flight attendant's perception that an engine sounded different from normal. If that same system had been in place 35 years ago, there's a good chance that 583 people would not have perished.

Developing a more flexible structure in which sense making and reducing equivocality is not just one person's responsibility but everyone's leads to a safer and more adaptive system. Who would have thought it? Think about that next time you fly somewhere.

Questions for Discussion

1. How might Weick's model of enactment, selection, and retention be used to compare and contrast the two scenarios discussed above, in terms of both effective and ineffective organizing?

2. As you look at the interaction among the flight crew described by Weick, what strikes you most? How would you describe the language used by the crew, and why might it be problematic?

3. Using Weick's model, analyze an organization with which you are familiar. In what ways do the organization and its members enact environments? How is equivocality engaged with? How are rules and cycles invoked? To what degree is organizational memory (retention) relied on or treated with healthy skepticism?

Weick's critics would argue that his perspective overemphasizes the nonrational features of organizational life and downplays the degree to which organizations can successfully implement plans that have been carefully and thoughtfully developed through rational decision making. But Weick might point out that, in some ways, his vision of organizational life has become more fully realized in recent years as organizations have shifted away from rational bureaucracies toward more fluid, decentralized structures that give employees more flexibility in decision making. Either way, Weick provides us with an incredibly creative, insightful, and, moreover, practical view of organizational life. His aim is not just to contribute to abstract theorizing but also to get managers to think differently and creatively by thinking in circles, not straight lines, and by "mutating metaphors"—shifting from "machine" metaphors and cause–effect thinking to alternatives, like organizing as improvisational jazz. What do you think? Do you want to belong to organizations that deploy machine metaphors or that think like Weick?

Niklas Luhmann and the Autopoietic Organization

The work of German sociologist Niklas Luhmann (1927–1998) is probably the most innovative attempt to develop a systems perspective, particularly in its application to the realm of social systems theory. Indeed, he can even be interpreted as extending Weick's work in an interesting and radical manner. It is impossible to encapsulate Luhmann's work fully here, especially if I tell you that he published around 70 books and nearly 400 articles in his academic career. However, I will try to explain some of the basic elements of his systems perspective and suggest how they might provide us with a novel way to understand organizational communication processes.

As with Weick and other systems researchers, Luhmann's work does not fit into the category of testable theory; instead, Luhmann is trying to develop a grand, universal theory that helps us understand all of social life. In this sense, it is a systems theory of society (Seidl, 2005). Moreover, it's probably fair to say that some of Luhmann's ideas are novel to the point of strangeness, particularly when first encountered, because they overturn many of our intuitive understandings of the social world and how it works.

The central concept in Luhmann's systems theory of the social world is the notion of **autopoiesis**. Although this word sounds as though it refers to an automatic poetry-writing machine, it actually comes from the Greek *auto* (self) and *poiesis* (creation, or production) and means "self-production." The term was originally coined by Chilean biologists Humberto Maturana and Francisco Varela as a way to answer the question, "What is life?" How are living and nonliving systems different? Living, biological systems, they argued, are autopoietic, or self-producing. For example, living cells are autopoietic because they reproduce their own molecules; they are not imported from their environment. All autopoietic operations are produced internally—that is, by the system itself. Similarly, all operations of autopoietic systems engage in self-reproduction. Thus, only a cell can reproduce its molecules, and only these molecules can produce a cell. In this sense, an autopoietic system is operatively closed.

However, unlike our earlier discussion of general system theory, this does not mean that an autopoietic system is closed off from its environment (confused yet? Me, too). Rather, **operative closure** refers to the fact that no operations can enter or leave the system. On the other hand, autopoietic systems exchange energy and information with their environments. However, such exchange is regulated by the autopoietic system itself; a cell's operations determine when and how nutrients from its environment are turned into cell molecules.

In developing his systems theory of society, Luhmann (1995) argues that the principle of autopoiesis can be applied to understanding how social systems—including organizations—work. He argues that while biological systems reproduce themselves on the basis of life, social systems reproduce themselves on the basis of communication. Communication, then, is the centerpiece of Luhmann's theory; indeed, communication is the operational process that makes social systems possible. All social systems are *nothing but* communication, each with their own autopoietic system of production and reproduction. Moreover, every social system will create its own specific communication operations. As Alex Viskovatoff (1999) states in discussing Luhmann's perspective:

> Since social systems are autopoietic systems, they must by definition keep on
> producing their elements, which are communications. If a social system, whether
> it be an organization or a whole society, were to stop producing communications,
> it would simply cease to exist. (p. 487)

However, for Luhmann, the fundamental purpose of a social system is not the preservation of its *existence* (as we saw in traditional systems theory, through processes of adaptation) but rather the production and preservation of *difference*. That is, a system exists as such because it can, through its communication processes, differentiate itself from its environment. This difference is what gives a system its unity and meaning. A system is therefore nothing except its difference from its environment (think about how similar this is to the idea we discussed in Chapter 2, regarding communication as a system of differences, using stop lights as an example).

Luhmann argues further that a system's environment is specific to that system, because each system communicatively constructs its own environment by making particular attributions to it (this idea is not unlike Weick's notion of enactment, discussed earlier). Indeed, a system's operative closure through specific communication processes is what makes it open to its environment, because these processes are what allow a system to perceive its environment.

Management scholar Christian Borch (2011) suggests that Luhmann's systems approach is a theory about the reduction of complexity in different social realms. Since the complexity of the world is so overwhelming, we can lead meaningful lives only if we are able to reduce the level of complexity we experience. Viewing organizations as self-reproducing, autopoietic systems that construct the world communicatively is a way to explain the mechanisms of complexity reduction. As Luhmann (2005) himself states, "The autopoiesis of organizations is kept going precisely by the fact that uncertainty is not only reduced but also renewed" (p. 62). In other words, an autopoietic system reduces uncertainty by selectively constructing its environment, but then this very act of selection produces new "irritations" (as Luhmann calls them) in the system's environment that require processing, and so on.

Moreover, Luhmann does not view autopoietic systems as having any real permanence; rather, they exist only in the moment they communicate, and their continued existence thus depends on their ability to produce new communication. In this sense, autopoietic social systems are in a constant process of renewal. Thus, social systems have structure only to the extent that the ongoing processes of communication produce norms and expectations in the system. These expectations limit and direct what an autopoietic system pays attention to in constructing its environment, thus reducing complexity and uncertainty in the system.

Let's look at a brief example to illustrate our discussion. Keep in mind that, for Luhmann, *all* social systems are by definition autopoietic, so we could pick literally any organization to examine. Just to be different, let's look at the subculture of "Goths" as an autopoietic social system. Goths fulfill the main condition of an autopoietic system in that they construct themselves as independent and different from their environment through their nonconformist lifestyle. Their taste in clothing, makeup (for men and women), music, art, and literature defines them as separate from the environment they inhabit. These elements must be continuously produced and reproduced through communication processes in order for the group to maintain itself as a system of difference and as a relatively stable structure (i.e., a set of expectations for behavior and communication). Thus, certain styles of clothing must be worn (e.g., Victorian, neo-punk, black/dark, etc.), certain forms of music must be listened to and discussed (e.g., Siouxsie and the Banshees, The Damned, The Cure, etc.), and certain literature must be read (e.g., Anne Rice's vampire novels). If the group stops these various activities, it ceases to be a system.

Goths thus meet the conditions of both operative closure and openness to their environment. First, conditions of operative closure are met in that no operations from other systems can be incorporated into the Goth system; moreover, this system of operative closure shapes group member expectations and serves to reduce complexity, limiting what can be selected by the Goth system. For example, Goths would not adopt expectations regarding dress that operate within preppy or jock culture; those are separate and independent autopoietic systems that have their own self-reproducing mechanisms. Anyone who showed up at a lunchtime gathering of Goths in the school cafeteria wearing chinos and flip-flops and talking about their shopping trip to Banana Republic would probably be ridiculed (with heavy irony, of course). Second, the Goth system is open in two ways: (1) It can attract new followers, and (2) it pays selective attention (because of its operative closure) to its environment—for example, Goths might pay attention to the media demonization of Goth culture and thus see themselves as an embattled subculture, strengthening their sense of identity and difference.

Of course, if it is not possible for them to maintain their difference as a system, then they will, by definition, fall apart. For example, one might argue that the recent mainstreaming of elements of Goth culture in popular culture—with the *Twilight* book and movie series, for instance—has diminished its status as nonconformist, thus potentially threatening its position as an independent system; members might actually leave the culture because they no longer construct it as different and nonconformist.

In sum, the Goth culture maintains its sense of unity and meaning as a system insofar as it is able to establish its difference from its environment through operatively closed communication processes. Goth culture exists in the moment-to-moment as members communicatively reproduce a structure of expectations about the culture. Again, the same kind of analysis can be conducted on any system, according to Luhmann, given the autopoietic status of all systems.

A Critical Perspective on the Autopoietic Organization

Luhmann's work has not been widely explored by organizational communication researchers in the United States, but he has a much stronger following in Europe (e.g., Martens, 2006; Seidl, 2005; Seidl & Becker, 2006, 2005). The difficulty and complexity of his work are rather daunting, but his reworking of systems theory provides some important insights into organizing processes. One might even argue that he transforms systems theory from a rather staid, functionalist perspective on organizations (organizations as adaptive mechanisms) to one that is radically constructionist in nature, treating organizations as nothing but communication. For Luhmann, organizations are not "things" that have a stable existence; they exist only to the degree that they are able to construct difference communicatively from their (communicatively constructed) environment.

Although Luhmann is not viewed as a critical theorist (nor did he describe himself as one; he saw himself as a descriptive theorist with a goal of explanation, not critique), his research is quite amenable to being read from a critical orientation. For instance, his concept of autopoiesis can be viewed from a critical perspective to explain how structures of power are produced and reproduced. Organizational communication scholar Stan Deetz (1992), for example, uses the concept of autopoiesis to explain how the "discourse of managerialism" is a self-reproducing system that communicatively constructs organizational life as exclusively about efficiency, profit, rationality, power, and so forth. This discourse functions as an operatively closed system that does not permit incorporation of other conceptions of organizing that might include, for example, discussions of work–life quality, democratic decision making, personal well-being, and so forth. In this sense, from a critical perspective the concept of autopoiesis can be used to examine how the powerful can reproduce the conditions that maintain their power.

Finally, Luhmann's presentation of counterintuitive ideas and his upsetting of conventional thinking enables us to think in radically different ways about organizing and everyday experience. For example, Luhmann argues: "Humans cannot communicate; not even their brains can communicate; not even their conscious minds can communicate. Only communication can communicate" (quoted in Seidl & Becker, 2006, p. 20). Such a notion is hard to get one's head around, especially in light of our earlier discussion of the famous communication axiom, "One cannot not communicate." However, the idea that "only communication can communicate" has much in common with some of the postmodern principles we will discuss in Chapter 8. That is, Luhmann "decenters" the idea of a coherent human individual and argues instead that humans are a conglomeration of various autopoietic systems (though they are not systems themselves). So, from Luhmann's systems perspective, a "person" is the name employed to describe how humans are addressed by various systems through communication. In doing this, Luhmann extends systems theory's efforts to reject psychological explanations of the human–society relationship.

❖ CONCLUSION

The systems approach to organizational communication is a powerful and insightful perspective that represents a significant advance beyond earlier perspectives on organizational communication. Most important, it represents a shift from psychological, individual-focused explanations of organizational behavior (how can individuals be motivated more effectively?) to a perspective that attempts to explain organizational communication systemically and dynamically; in other words, individual behavior becomes meaningful only when examined as part of a set of wider, interdependent processes. Thus, organizational communication behavior has to be understood contextually and holistically, not by dividing it up and looking at individual parts.

However, traditional systems theory has been subject to a number of criticisms, two of which we will briefly mention here. First, we can identify what has been called the "correspondence" problem (Monge, 1982). Simply put, too often something of a disconnect has occurred between the principles of the systems perspective and empirical studies conducted under this framework. As organizational communication scholar Peter Monge has argued, researchers have often employed methods of data collection and analysis that are unable to capture the dynamic and interdependent properties of a system. In other words, it's hard to capture the holistic qualities of a system using reductionist methods that divide up the parts of that system.

Second, it can be argued that overall systems theory is a relatively conservative perspective that focuses on the ways organizations as systems engage in processes of regulation and adaptation. Indeed, the extensive use of the biological metaphor in systems theory that equates human, organizational systems with organic processes leads almost inevitably to viewing organizations from a "survival-of-the-fittest," Darwinian orientation; the "fittest" organizations are those best able to adapt to environmental variations and thus survive. One might question whether this perspective is the best way to think about human systems.

However, the work of both Karl Weick and Niklas Luhmann suggests that systems theory does not have to be read in such a conservative way. Both scholars develop perspectives that challenge us to rethink our conventional understandings of organizational life. They suggest that organizations are not the stable structures they appear to be but, rather, are nonrational, precarious, and, most important, made up of complex communication processes that are the very "stuff" of organizing. Both scholars place meaning and sense making at the center of their respective orientations—issues we will take up in more detail in Chapter 6.

CRITICAL APPLICATIONS

1. Using this class as your object of study, conduct a systems analysis of its organizing processes. What are its various inputs, transformations, and outputs? How does it function holistically? Is it made up of subsystems? What processes of feedback and adaptation can you identify?

2. Watch the short animated film *The Meatrix* (available at www.themeatrix.com), and discuss how it provides a critically oriented systems analysis of the food industry.

KEY TERMS

autopoiesis   126

closed systems   110

double-interacts   121

enactment, selection, and
retention   120

entropy   110

equifinality   114

equivocality (uncertainty)
reduction   120

general system theory   107

goal orientations   114

hierarchy   113

holism   108

homeostasis   111

multifinality   114

negative entropy   110

open systems   110

operative closure   126

retrospective sense
making   119

STUDENT STUDY SITE

Visit the student study site at **www.sagepub.com/mumbyorg** for these additional learning tools:

- Web quizzes
- eFlashcards
- SAGE journal articles

- Video resources
- Web resources

CHAPTER 6

Communication, Culture, and Organizing

The corporate culture approach seeks to create a shared reality for organization members.

The emergence of the "cultural" approach in the late 1970s and early 1980s represents what might be termed a "paradigm shift" in the field of organizational communication (Kuhn, 1970). This new perspective offered a radically different set of conceptual tools with which to examine organizations, creating a body of knowledge that stood in stark contrast to the dominant functionalist perspective. Moreover, it provided tools for management practitioners that offered a different philosophy of work and organizational life.

Why was the emergence of this new perspective so important? In brief, the cultural approach offered a radically different way to think about the relationship between communication and organization. For the first time, scholars began to take seriously the notion that organizations are communication phenomena that only exist because their members engage in complex patterns of communication behavior. Put another way, scholars viewed organizations as structures of meaning created through the everyday symbolic acts of their members (Keyton, 2011; Martin, 1992; Putnam & Pacanowsky, 1983). By studying communication phenomena such as stories (Boje, 1991; Browning, 1992; Martin, Feldman, Hatch, & Sitkin, 1983), metaphors (Koch & Deetz, 1981; Smith & Eisenberg, 1987), and rituals (Trice & Beyer, 1984), researchers developed rich understandings of the ways members both constructed and made sense of their organizational realities.

In this chapter, we are going to examine that paradigm revolution and explore the 30 years or so of research that has significantly altered our understanding of organizations as humanly created phenomena. First, we will discuss a few of the reasons for the emergence of the cultural approach.

❖ THE EMERGENCE OF THE CULTURAL APPROACH

By the 1970s, the large, bureaucratic, and homogeneous organizational form that had dominated the post-World War II era of unprecedented growth and stability had started to show its age. As such, a number of economic, political, and social factors came together that provided the impetus to look for new ways of approaching organizational life. First, the 1970s witnessed much greater economic instability, with high inflation and low economic growth. This was fueled in part by two energy crises (in 1973 and 1979), both of which were linked to political upheaval in the Middle East, with oil-producing countries limiting oil supplies to the United States. Related, management–labor relations were also in crisis, with frequent and widespread strikes in both the United States and Europe as unions fought to retain job benefits established in the 1950s. Moreover, U.S. corporations were facing increasingly strong global competition for markets, especially from Japan. For example, in the wake of the oil crises, Japanese automobile companies were quick to exploit U.S. companies' failure to produce fuel-efficient cars.

Furthermore, and as I mentioned in Chapter 4, from a social perspective the large bureaucratic organization was seen as dehumanizing. While theorists such as Taylor and Mayo focused mainly on blue-collar workers and efforts to improve the experience of industrial labor, it became increasingly clear in the second half of the 20th century that white-collar, managerial work could be just as alienating. Classic texts such as C. Wright Mills's (1951) *White Collar*, William H. Whyte's (1956) *The Organization Man*, and Arthur Miller's (1949) *Death of a Salesman* document struggles to maintain dignity in the face of a machine-like, impersonal organizational environment.

The employees who came of age in the 1970s, however, rejected the conformity of the megabureaucracy their parents accepted, and adopted a more individualistic approach to work that sought something beyond a 9-to-5 job and a paycheck at the end of the week. In this sense, intrinsic rewards and meaningful work that produced "personal growth" (a phrase that would have been alien to the 1950s white-collar worker) became just as important as extrinsic rewards. The so-called "me" decade (Wolfe, 1976) that was part of the 1960s and 1970s cultural revolution (hippies, flower power, and all that) thus had a profound influence on organizational life.

In many respects, then, the rational manager who was the guardian of bureaucracy in the second spirit of capitalism (Boltanski & Chiapello, 2005) was losing his luster (in 1960s terms, he was pretty "square"), and a movement was building for something new—an alternate way of organizing that was better able to tap into the greater complexities and aspirations of people's lives. While human resource management had begun this transformation, it really didn't take full hold until the cultural approach arrived on the scene.

This economic, political, and social transformation provides the frame for a number of research-related reasons why the cultural approach emerged as a new way of studying organizational life. Perhaps foremost amongst these is the very concept of "culture" itself, which provided a vivid and transformative way of examining organizations as communication phenomena. Put another way, researchers acquired a new metaphor with which to make sense of organizational life. Beginning in the late 1970s and early 1980s, there was a strong sense that the traditional forms of organizational research (most of which fit into the "discourse of representation" that we talked about in Chapter 1) had become stagnant and were offering little in the way of new insights into organizational communication.

In particular, some researchers were becoming critical of the dominant paradigm and its attempts to show causal relationships between various communication variables and organizational outcomes such as effectiveness and productivity (Mumby, 2007). Such an approach, it was argued, reflected a managerial conception of what was important to study in organizations. In other words, because managers were primarily interested in knowing how changes in organizational communication could lead to greater efficiency and productivity, that's what researchers studied.

The cultural approach, however, began from a different premise. As organizational communication researchers Mike Pacanowsky and Nick O'Donnell-Trujillo (1982) state,

> The jumping off point for this approach is the mundane observation that more things are going on in organizations than getting the job done. . . . People in organizations also gossip, joke, knife one another, initiate romantic involvements, cue new employees to ways of doing the least amount of work that still avoids hassles from a supervisor, talk sports, arrange picnics. (p. 116)

As such, the cultural approach started from the notion that one should not study organizations just to improve their efficiency and make people better employees, but also because they are interesting and complex communication phenomena in their own right. Understanding how they operate thus provides greater insight into an important element of the human condition.

Of course, the idea of "culture" as a metaphor for the study of organizations did not originate in the field of organizational communication. Since the 19th century, anthropologists had been studying "exotic" cultures, partly as a way to understand those societies that were being colonized by Western nations. In the 20th century, anthropology turned its gaze closer to home and began to study the changing structure of U.S. society, particularly in the urban environment. Foremost in this movement was the University of Chicago School of Sociology, led by Robert Park. Much of this work was directed toward studying emergent social problems and social groups, and giving voice to ordinary people as they dealt with these problems in their everyday lives (e.g., Liebow, 1967; Whyte, 1981).

Another source for the emergence of the cultural approach was the "interpretive" tradition that had been part of the human sciences since the early 19th century. As we discussed in Chapter 1, this tradition (which we labeled the "discourse of understanding") focuses on language and communication as the principal medium through which human beings create social reality for themselves. In such a view, language and communication do not simply represent social reality but, rather, constitute it. In the field of communication, this interpretive focus started to have an impact in the mid-1970s as scholars began to draw on this tradition to provide alternative conceptions of communication processes (Deetz, 1973a, 1973b; Hawes, 1977).

However, the anthropological and interpretive traditions come together in the writings of Clifford Geertz, whose development of an interpretive approach to anthropology has significantly influenced organizational communication studies. Indeed, Geertz's (1973) definition of culture is probably the most widely cited conception in organization studies:

> The concept of culture I espouse . . . is essentially a semiotic one. Believing, with Max Weber, that man is an animal suspended in webs of significance he himself has spun, I take culture to be those webs, and the analysis of it to be therefore not an experimental science in search of law, but an interpretive one in search of meaning. (p. 5)

There are a number of important elements to this definition of culture. First, Geertz argues for a *semiotic* conception of culture. As we saw in Chapter 2, semiotics is the study of the ways in which sign systems, or systems of representation, come to create social reality for people. In this sense, Geertz adopts a meaning-centered conception of culture—culture doesn't exist in people's heads but in the shared (i.e., public) rites, rituals, artifacts, conversations, and so forth in which people engage.

Second, Geertz suggests that the "webs of significance" that make up culture have a dual life. On the one hand, they are formed by people, who actively participate in the creation of their culture. At the same time, culture acts back on its members, shaping and constraining their conception of the world. Just as a spider both creates and is limited by its web, so people create and simultaneously are limited by their culture.

Third, and related, the "web" metaphor emphasizes the notion that culture is not a "thing"; rather, it exists in the moment-to-moment—people "spin" their cultures in an ongoing and dynamic fashion as they go about their daily lives (Frost, Moore, Louis, Lundberg, & Martin, 1985).

Finally, Geertz describes the analysis of culture as an interpretive rather than experimental science. This is significant because it highlights another important element in the emergence of the culture paradigm in organizational communication studies: a shift away from the quantitative study of communication variables (and the search for laws of human behavior) toward the qualitative study of collective sense making in real-life settings. Geertz (1973) argues that the interpretive study of culture involves "**thick description**"—that is, the development of narrative accounts that provide rich insight into the complex meaning patterns that underlie people's collective behavior. We will examine several examples of such thick description later in the chapter.

For several reasons, then, both corporate leaders and organization researchers were primed to rejuvenate their respective domains. The notion of "culture" appeared to provide just such a catalyst for rejuvenation. Books such as Peters and Waterman's (1982) *In Search of Excellence* and Deal and Kennedy's (1982) *Corporate Cultures* tapped into a desire by managers to rethink how organizations operated and, in many ways, to revive the flagging image of the manager as a dull bureaucrat. Thus, examining organizations from a cultural perspective seemed to provide managers with a new way to motivate employees, reinvigorate corporate productivity, and meet the challenges of a changing global economy. For organization researchers, the cultural approach provided a new frame that had the potential to revitalize their area of inquiry, making it more relevant to organization members.

In the next section, we will examine more closely the assumptions that underlie the different conceptions of the cultural approach to organizational communication.

❖ TWO PERSPECTIVES ON ORGANIZATIONAL CULTURE

To understand the cultural approach, it is important to keep in mind that the notion of "culture" is a metaphor that provides us with certain insights into organizational communication processes (Morgan, 2006). Just as the machine metaphor of organizations highlighted issues of efficiency, predictability, and effectiveness, and the organism metaphor highlighted growth, adaptation, and complexity, so the culture metaphor highlights a particular way of examining organizations.

From the cultural perspective, organizations are systems of beliefs, values, and taken-for-granted norms that guide everyday behavior. The lens of "culture" enables us to focus on the ways in which people communicatively construct systems of meaning that shape and embody these beliefs and values. Adopting a cultural perspective, Charles Bantz (1993) defines organizational communication in the following manner:

> The collective creation, maintenance, and transformation of organizational meanings and organizational expectations. . . . Communication is the medium through which organizations, as symbolic realities, are constructed by humans. (p. 1)

From a cultural perspective, then, organizations do not exist independently from their members; rather, organizations are only real to the extent that their members engage in various communication activities.

Within the organizational culture literature, however, this basic principle is explored and conceptualized in a number of different ways. For our purposes, we will discuss in detail two prominent approaches: the pragmatist approach and the purist approach.

The Pragmatist Approach: Organizational Culture as a Variable

The conception of organizational culture as a variable has a distinctly managerial orientation to it. From a management point of view, interest lies in attempting to assess the impact of an organization's culture on its performance. Thus, in identifying culture as a variable, managers are interested in measuring how one feature of the organization (the culture) affects the larger organization. From this perspective, "organization" and "culture" are distinct entities. This is important because one can show the effect of one variable on another only if they can first be shown as separate. Another way to think of this variable approach is that from this perspective, culture is seen as something that an organization has—it is one feature amongst others such as technology, structure, and environment.

Management scholar Joanne Martin (1985) refers to this variable perspective as the **cultural pragmatist** approach to organizations. From this pragmatist orientation, culture is a key element in efforts to increase employee commitment and performance and, thus, in improving company productivity and profitability. Because the pragmatist sees culture as a variable, it can—by definition—be manipulated and changed. Thus, from this perspective, one of the principal roles of managers is to intervene in, diagnose, and, if necessary, change an organization's culture—in other words, to "engineer" the culture to meet corporate goals (Kunda, 1992; Sathe, 1983, 1985). The good manager is attuned to the cultural aspects of his or her organization and is able to manipulate that culture in the best interests of the organization. From a pragmatist perspective, then, there is a very strong means–end orientation at work; culture is a means by which particular ends (commitment, profit, etc.) are reached. As such, the pragmatist, variable approach assumes a causal relationship between culture and organizational performance—a strong, functional culture strengthens employee identification with their organization, while a weak, dysfunctional culture weakens that sense of identification.

The pragmatist approach also assumes that successful organizations possess a single, unitary culture that all employees buy into. Martin refers to this as an "integration" approach to culture; that is, ideally, all organization members are integrated into a single worldview and set of values that guide their behavior and decision making (Martin, 1992). Such "strong" organizational cultures exercise the kind of ideological control we discussed in Chapter 1; when all members internalize a set of values, they can be counted on to act in the best interests of the organization without any direct control by supervisors.

Finally, we can say that the pragmatist approach adopts a strongly prescriptive orientation. By this, I mean that cultural pragmatists provide guidance for the shaping of strong, functional cultures. Peters and Waterman's (1982) book *In Search of Excellence*, mentioned earlier, is a classic and widely read example of such a prescriptive approach. The basic premise of this book is that those companies identified as "excellent" (the authors discuss companies such as IBM, 3M, Disney, and McDonald's) have certain features in common and that companies wishing to emulate these exemplars of excellence need to adopt these features, too.

The pragmatist, variable approach also adopts a distinctly functionalist orientation to organizational culture. That is, culture is seen as having specific functions within the organization. These functions include the following:

1. *Creating a shared identity amongst organization members.* By developing a strong culture, members are more likely to share a single vision of the organization and its overall beliefs and values. Such a shared vision enhances the potential for members to make decisions that are consistent with organizational goals. For example, Disney, which has a very strong corporate culture, carefully schools its employees ("cast members") in the company vision, thus ensuring that each person identifies with the role they must play (Van Maanen, 1991). Subaru-Isuzu Automotive spends more time training new employees in the features of its culture than in teaching them the mechanics of their jobs (Graham, 1993).

2. *Generating employee commitment to the organization.* A strong, shared identity amongst employees also increases the possibility that those employees will be

highly committed to the organization. Pragmatist research is full of stories about "organizational heroes" who exemplify the kind of commitment a strong culture can produce. For example, on my campus we have a global studies center named after FedEx, which gave a large sum of money to the university for the right to have its name on the building. The director of the center told me that one time a UPS delivery person expressed reservations about delivering packages to a building that bore a competitor's name. I suspect this employee was highly committed to his employer.

3. *Enhancing organizational stability*. The creation of a strong culture, a shared identity, and high employee commitment minimizes organizational turnover, reduces the chances of distrust and worker–management conflict, and enhances the stability of the organization. Conversely, employees who do *not* buy into the corporate culture are likely to create conflict and organizational instability. Companies will frequently tolerate creative "mavericks" who behave in unconventional ways but nevertheless identify with the company's values; on the other hand, employees who deviate too far from corporate values are likely to be removed (Sathe, 1983). Similarly, in maintaining organizational stability, companies will look to hire employees who "fit in" with the corporate culture.

4. *Serving as a sense-making device*. Socializing employees into a strong organizational culture results in a highly internalized sense of the realities of organizational life. Employees develop a shared set of taken-for-granted norms and principles that help them negotiate the complexities of day-to-day organizing processes. Indeed, an important part of being socialized into any organization involves learning the culture of that organization. And the consequences for *not* quickly learning a culture can be severe. In his study of an Internet startup company, sociologist David Stark (2009) reports speaking to a new employee, recently recruited from IBM, who talked excitedly about working for a company that had an informal, laid-back culture (no more IBM suits!). However, he said, nobody had yet told him what his job was. This new employee was fired by the end of the week; he hadn't figured out that he was supposed to take the initiative and create a role for himself in the company—a very different culture from the one he was used to at IBM.

The pragmatist approach to organizational culture thus represents an important body of research oriented to organizational intervention. Culture is defined as a tool that provides managers with a way to shape the organizational reality that employees experience. The primary motivation for the pragmatist approach is to explore the link between culture and organizational performance. If managers can successfully intervene in and shape organizational culture, then organizations can improve their effectiveness and competitiveness. In the next section, however, we will discuss a very different approach to culture—one that rejects many of the primary assumptions of the pragmatist perspective.

Critical Technologies 6.1
Communication Technology and Organizational Culture

When Peters and Waterman (1982) wrote their classic book *In Search of Excellence*, stressing the need for strong corporate cultures in excellent companies, they could hardly have anticipated the revolutionary technological changes that have forever altered people's relationship to work. While this chapter focuses on organizational culture and the way organization members collectively engage in sense-making activities, communication technology has complicated people's relationship to their organizations and the possibilities for constructing meanings. Communication technologies are a double-edged sword in that they both provide faster, more efficient ways for people to connect with one another and make organizations more porous, less stable communication structures. Communication technologies "decenter" organizations in that they reduce the need for employees to come together in the same location every day. As such, the "distributed organization" (where many employees spend some or much of their time working off-site and "telecommuting") is becoming a standard phenomenon of organizational life, with telework growing by about 20% a year in the United States and around the world (Golden & Fromen, 2011, p. 1452). From a cultural perspective, what implications does this have for an organization's ability to develop and maintain a strong organizational culture? What is its impact on employees' ability to develop a strong sense of identification with their company?

If some of the research on telework and distributed organizing is anything to go by, then there is some evidence that employees are negatively impacted by a lack of regular, face-to-face interaction with coworkers and peers. Management researchers Kevin Rockmann and Michael Pratt (2011), for example, suggest that when a significant number of employees are regularly engaged in telework away from the organization site, both teleworkers *and*

employees working on-site can experience isolation and lack of organizational identification—the latter because there are not enough coworkers around to talk to.

Similarly, in a survey of more than 11,000 workers, Timothy Golden and Allan Fromen (2011) report that non-teleworking employees who have a manager who teleworks are likely to experience degraded job feedback, less clarity regarding tasks, a reduced sense of empowerment, fewer opportunities for professional development, and difficulty in gauging appropriate workloads. In terms of work outcomes, such workers may experience reduced job satisfaction, a less positive organizational climate, and a greater need to seek other employment.

Finally, Melissa Gregg's (2011) study of part-time and "free-agent" employees who frequently work online from home shows that these workers often rely on social media and online communities to establish a sense of work culture. Given their lack of a shared physical workplace culture, many of these workers rely on social media such as Facebook and LinkedIn to provide a virtual work culture. Moreover, such online communities are often the *only* stable element in free agents' work lives, given their high mobility between jobs and companies.

One other factor to consider is that Peters and Waterman's (1982) original idea of a single, unified organizational culture with which employees identify was always problematic given that most large organizations consist of multiple subcultures. Moreover, such "strong cultures" are often aimed only at a core group of employees, with many other employee groups (e.g., custodial workers, temp/agency workers) deliberately marginalized in the organization as a way to limit identification in contexts where organizations are frequently "reengineered" and the tenure of many employees is brief (Gossett, 2003).

The Purist Approach: Organizational Culture as a Root Metaphor

The assumptions underlying the **cultural purist** perspective stand in sharp contrast to those of the pragmatist approach. First, rather than viewing culture as one organizational variable amongst many, purists see culture as a basic, root metaphor for understanding organizations (Morgan, 2006; Smith & Eisenberg, 1987). In other words, culture is not something an organization *has*, or possesses; rather, from this perspective, an organization *is* a culture. In this sense, the notion of culture works as a basic framing device to shape our fundamental sense of organizational reality. Second, because an organization *is* a culture, it follows that organizations exist only insofar as members engage in the various communicative practices that make up the culture of the organization. Thus, where the pragmatist sees culture as one aspect of an organization amongst many, the purist argues that the organization can be understood as a meaning-based social collective only by viewing it through the lens of culture.

Third, cultural purists question the idea that organizational cultures can be manipulated to meet the needs and goals of the organization. They argue against the culture management approach for a number of reasons:

1. Organizational culture is emergent and not something shaped by managers. In this sense, culture evolves spontaneously, reflecting people's needs and experiences.

2. Due to the complexity of organizational culture, it is impossible to establish any causal connections between culture and organizational outcomes, such as employee performance; culture is just too messy to quantify, measure, and make predictions about. As management scholar Mats Alvesson (1993) argues, "The general conclusion which can be drawn from . . . investigations of the link between organizational culture and performance is that the idea of culture very often promises more than it delivers" (p. 42).

3. Organizations do not have a single, unitary culture that all members share. Many organizations—especially large ones—are made up of a complex array of often competing subcultures that make it difficult to argue that employees share a single corporate vision (Martin, 1992). Management scholar Ed Young (1989) has shown that even in organizational cultures where members share the same objects, sayings, rituals, etc., interpretations of these cultural artifacts can vary across the various groups that make up the organization. In his study of a British clothing manufacturer, he shows how the meanings of important cultural manifestations, such as the "Royalty Board" (where workers posted anything related to the Royal Family), company outings, and the wearing of poppies on St. George's day, were interpreted very differently by two distinct groups of workers—one group consisting of older, married women and the other group consisting of younger, single women. However, managers in this organization perceived these "shared" cultural artifacts as evidence of a single culture and were largely unaware of the rather intense conflict on the shop floor that centered on the significance of these cultural expressions.

4. Attempts to manage organizational culture often manipulate employee feelings and emotions and are therefore unethical. Mats Alvesson (1993) argues that an instrumental, functionalist perspective that largely serves the interests of managers underlies the pragmatist approach. As such, the interests of other organizational groups are largely ignored in favor of a bottom-line approach. For example, an organization that emphasizes a "team" culture often places heavy

pressure on individuals to "come through" for the team. Such pressure makes it difficult for workers to express anything but performance-related concerns. For example, a single working mother who misses a day to look after a sick child has to justify to all the other team members why she did something that demonstrated a lack of loyalty to the team (Mumby & Stohl, 1992).

For a number of reasons, then, cultural purists view the pragmatist approach as problematic. What, then, are the elements of the purist approach? We have already drawn attention to its conception of culture as a root metaphor for framing the study of organizations. Let's explore its features in greater detail.

A Broader Conception of "Organization"

At the beginning of this chapter, we discussed how the cultural approach had broadened traditional understandings of what counts as an appropriate type of organization to study. While the pragmatist approach largely focuses on corporate organizations (which would make sense, given its managerial orientation), the purist perspective has included a large array of organizations in the scope of its studies. For example, Nick Trujillo and Bob Krizek have studied baseball parks (Krizek, 1992; Trujillo, 1992); Dean Scheibel (1992, 1996) has studied the socialization of medical students and communicative performances in bars; Sarah Tracy (2000, 2005) has researched two closely related organizations—prisons and cruise ships; Alexandra Murphy (2003) has studied strip clubs; and Alan DeSantis (2003, 2007) has studied smokers at a cigar store and campus Greek organizations.

Because of this broad-based approach, cultural purists are generally uninterested in examining the relationship between culture and organizational competitiveness. Rather, their interest lies in understanding organizational life as complex, dynamic, and constituted in an ongoing fashion through communicative processes. Moreover, they are interested in understanding organizations "from the native's point of view" (Geertz, 1983)—in other words, from the perspective of the members of the culture being studied, allowing members' own sense making to emerge in the course of research. This is very different from the pragmatist approach, where managerial definitions of organizational culture prevail.

The Use of Interpretive, Ethnographic Methods

Earlier in the chapter we discussed the influence of anthropologist Clifford Geertz in the emergence of organizational culture research. Much of this influence is centered around his development of an interpretive approach to the study of culture. From the purist perspective, this has translated into an explosion of research that employs qualitative, field-based methods to develop "thick" descriptions of organizational cultures. When researchers employ the methods of **ethnography**, it means they are immersing themselves (often for a period of months, sometimes years) in a culture so they can become intimately familiar with the sense-making efforts of its members. Ethnographic research, then, does not set up experimental conditions but, instead, studies naturally occurring, everyday behavior and communication processes (Taylor & Trujillo, 2001). A number of implications are associated with this development, but perhaps the best way to explain it is by example.

Organizational communication researcher Bob Krizek (1992) gives an excellent example of thick description in an essay called "Goodbye Old Friend: A Son's Farewell to Comiskey Park." Krizek's goal in this essay is to provide the reader with a vivid account of the last baseball game in the Chicago White Sox's old Comiskey Park before it was closed and torn down. To accomplish this, Krizek draws on interviews with fans, detailed accounts of his own experiences and perceptions at the final game, and recollections of attending White Sox games as a child with his father (the "friend" in the title of the essay is a double reference to both the park and his father). The result is a powerful account that brings to life the sights, sounds, and emotions of that final game. Here's a brief extract from the essay to provide you with a sense of how an ethnographic "thick description" creates a vivid picture of a particular cultural context:

> Research was secondary on my mind that Thursday evening as I instinctively negotiated the ramps and stairways to those . . . upper deck seats. With all the Park renovations in the late seventies and the eighties (the years when ballparks were invaded by corporate skyboxes), the finding was based more on intuition than geographic certainty. Prompted by the climb to the upper deck, my twenty-pound equipment bag, and the anticipation generated by the moment, I arrived winded. I paused, filled my lungs with a few deep breaths, and then held one especially large mouthful of Comiskey Park air as I sank into the chair closest to the aisle. For one brief moment, the confidence of adulthood drifted away, replaced by the feelings of a lost six-year-old boy. I began to cry. This may have been the first time I truly missed my dad or genuinely mourned his passing. (pp. 88–89)

More than anything else, the account provides the reader with compelling insight into what the closing of the park *means* to the people in attendance. Krizek shows that the park is not just a place where baseball games happen but that, more important, it is a site of collective memory and a place where a strong sense of community and belonging has developed. For the fans in attendance, the tearing down of the park involves the destruction of that site of memory and community; indeed, as Krizek vividly demonstrates, it involves the destruction of part of their own identities.

Krizek's study is, thus, not "objective" in the sense of presenting a "fair and balanced" perspective. For example, he does not interview the owners or managers of Comiskey Park. Rather, he is emotionally invested in the fans' perspective and describes the closing through their eyes and sense-making efforts. Indeed, it is precisely because of his emotional involvement with the subject matter that he is able to provide such a rich and compelling account of the closing of Comiskey Park. As such, it provides powerful insight into the human condition—the ultimate goal of all research.

Of course, not every thick description requires Krizek's level of emotional involvement. Indeed, field research varies from a complete "observer" role, in which the researcher has no direct contact with organization members, through a "participant-as-observer" role, where the researcher participates in organizational life but members are aware of his or her status as a researcher, and to a "complete participant" role, where members are unaware of his or her status as a researcher (Bantz, 1993).

A classic example of this last type of study is Donald Roy's (1959) famous ethnography of a manufacturing company. Although Roy's study was written with a strong "human relations" orientation, it is actually one of the earliest examples of a full participant study of a specific organizational subculture. Roy took a job at a "clicking" machine in a room with three other workers and immersed himself in the workplace culture. Roy's status as a researcher was completely unknown to his workmates, and, thus, he was able to participate fully in the daily rituals the workers developed to help offset the extreme tedium of the tasks they were performing. Roy shows how the daily rituals of "banana time," "coke time," "peach time," "fish time," and so forth gave meaning to the workday and helped time pass far more quickly in an extremely monotonous work environment. His findings showed that the social interaction among the workers increased their level of job satisfaction.

A more contemporary example is communication scholar Alan DeSantis's (2003) ethnographic, **participant-observation** study of a cigar shop. What I love about this study is that, as its title suggests, it is literally about "a couple of white guys sitting around talking." DeSantis takes the most mundane and ordinary of circumstances (a group of men hanging out in a cigar shop, enjoying a cigar, and discussing issues of the day) and effectively illustrates how, through their everyday talk, they collectively construct a distinct social reality.

DeSantis focuses on one particular aspect of this communicative construction of reality—the men's collective rationalization regarding the health hazards associated with smoking. He shows how in the course of their interactions the men engage in "symbolic convergence" (Bormann, 1983); that is, their individual realities start to converge as they collectively create a social reality about smoking. DeSantis illustrates in great detail how the men construct a reality that both denies and rationalizes away the health hazards of smoking. This rationalization contains five themes that arise routinely in the course of conversations among the men: (1) all things in moderation; (2) cigar smoking has health benefits; (3) medical research that shows smoking is hazardous to health is flawed; (4) cigars are not like cigarettes and don't have the same health risks; and (5) life is dangerous, and smoking is a minor risk in the grand scheme of things.

DeSantis's study is particularly insightful in illustrating how, when confronted with a mountain of scientific evidence, the men have an amazing ability to construct communicatively a reality that essentially functions as an alternate universe. Even when one of the men dies from a heart attack at a relatively young age, they are able collectively to rationalize this event and construct the man's death as stress-related, not smoking-related. In sum, DeSantis's study is a perfect example of how "man is an animal suspended in webs of significance that he himself has spun."

The Study of Organizational Symbols, Talk, and Artifacts

The purist approach to organizational culture places a heavy focus on the study of cultural expressions—that is, the various symbols, conversations, artifacts, and practices that are the visible manifestation of a given culture. The main difference between the pragmatist and purist approach to the study of these manifestations is that the former treats them as the outward expression of an underlying "objective" culture that can be measured and quantified. The purist approach, however, argues that it is through these various communicative practices and processes that organizational culture actually comes into being. In this sense, the various symbolic forms do not represent something else but are the culture themselves. This is important, because it points to the public character of both culture and the sense-making processes in which organization members collectively engage to create their social reality (Geertz, 1973, 1983).

Pacanowsky and O'Donnell-Trujillo (1982) argue that in order to understand the way in which organization members engage in the communicative accomplishment of sense making, culture researchers must try to answer the following two basic questions: (1) What are the key communication activities through which organizational sense making occurs? and (2) In any particular organization, what are the features of this sense-making process? (p. 124). The first question requires researchers to identify the public, communicative features of organizational culture; the second question asks researchers to interpret these communication processes to understand how people make sense of the culture they inhabit.

What, then, are the various symbolic forms that culture researchers have tended to focus on in making sense of organizational culture? Pacanowsky and O'Donnell-Trujillo (1982) identify the following expressions of culture and sense making: (1) relevant constructs, (2) facts, (3) practices, (4) vocabulary, (5) metaphors, (6) rites and rituals, and (7) stories. Let's examine each of these "cultural indicators" separately, with a special emphasis on storytelling (which we'll give a whole section of its own).

Relevant Constructs. All organizations and social collectives identify objects, individuals, events, and processes that punctuate the daily life of the organization and allow members to structure their experiences. For example, the construct of "meeting" makes sense to most organization members as a relatively structured event that can be differentiated from more loosely scripted behaviors such as informal chats by the coffee machine. For students, **relevant constructs** are things such as grades, class meetings, assignments, "partying," and so forth. All these labels help students organize their experiences as members of a particular culture.

Similarly, subcultures within larger cultures have an additional set of constructs that differentiate their members' experience from the experiences of members of the larger culture. For example, members of Greek organizations identify with constructs such as "brotherhood" and "sisterhood" in a way that members of the larger student body likely do not. If you speak to your professors, many of them will tell you that the construct of "tenure" organizes much of their professional lives at the beginning of their careers; in almost everything they do, they have to ask themselves the question, "Will this help me get tenure?"

Facts. Every organizational culture has a body of "social knowledge," shared by members, that enables those members to navigate the culture. This social knowledge does not consist of **facts** in the sense of "objective truths" but, rather, consists of a shared understanding about what is significant and meaningful to the organization and its members. For example, the "fact," often propagated by college students, that "if your roommate dies you automatically get a 4.0 GPA for the semester" tells us something about the ways in which students collectively construct a shared social reality (Scheibel, 1999). Although objectively untrue, such a "fact" provides insight into several features of student sense-making activities, including (a) the intense pressure school frequently places on students, (b) the heavy focus on grades as an indicator of success, and (c) the ongoing search for ways to "beat the system." DeSantis's (2003) study of cigar smokers, discussed earlier, is also an excellent example of a body of "facts" (e.g., smoking is not harmful) that are central to the creation of a particular organizational reality.

Practices. Organizational life is made up of a set of ongoing **practices** that members must engage in to accomplish the process of organizing. From a cultural perspective, a focus on such practices provides insight into the routine features of everyday organizational life. In addition, this focus draws attention to the way the sense-making process is an ongoing, moment-to-moment, practical accomplishment for social actors. For example, a "meeting" is not only a significant organizational construct but also a set of practices in which members must engage in order to accomplish organizational business. Not only must members know their roles, rules for addressing agenda items, and so forth, but they also must be aware of the extent to which such meetings may embody cultural understandings of what can be said, what can't be said, what hidden agenda items are present, and so on.

In his study of a high-tech engineering firm, management scholar Gideon Kunda (1992) shows how company meetings are places where people engage in a variety of behaviors, including "grandstanding," attempting to belittle rival project groups, subtly criticizing the dominant culture of the organization, and making power plays and alliances. None of the issues are official agenda items, but they illustrate how being a member of a culture involves understanding and participating in the ongoing and practical accomplishment of everyday organizational life.

Vocabulary. Often one of the most distinctive features of a culture is members' use of a specific **vocabulary**, or jargon, that describes important aspects of the culture. Such jargon frequently serves as a kind of "badge" signifying membership of the culture, and anyone who doesn't know the jargon can be immediately identified as an "outsider." For example, in his ethnographic study of mostly homeless men who sell used books and goods on the sidewalk in Greenwich Village in New York City, sociologist Mitch Duneier (1999) reveals a distinctive vocabulary that the men use to describe what they do. Phrases like "table watcher," "laying shit out," "place holder," and "mover" signify a complex pattern of social roles and collective meanings that serve to impose order on the chaotic environment of the street.

Sometimes organization members' vocabularies are used as a way to denigrate nonmembers. In their study of a police department, Nick Trujillo and George Dionisopoulos (1987) show how police officers routinely use terms such as *scrote*, *dirtbag*, and *maggot* to describe members of the public. Such terms framed the way the officers approached interactions with people they encountered on their patrols. Similarly, Tracy and Scott (2006) describe firefighters' routine use of the term *shitbum* to describe indigents who make 911 calls and *shitbox* to describe the ambulances that take "shitbums" to the emergency room. Again, such terms do not simply describe a person or object but, instead, communicatively organize the collective experience and professional identities of firefighters as they engage in routine interactions with members of the public. In other words, vocabularies don't just describe organization realities—they shape them.

Metaphors. The study of organizational **metaphors** has become an important way for culture researchers to interpret the sense-making processes of organization members (Grant & Oswick, 1996; Kirby & Harter, 2002; Koch & Deetz, 1981; Smith & Eisenberg, 1987; Smith & Keyton, 2001). Researchers argue that metaphors are used not simply to describe the world but, rather, as a fundamental part of our perceptions and experience of the world. Philosophers George Lakoff and Mark Johnson (1980) claim that "our basic conceptual system, in terms of which we think and act, is fundamentally metaphorical" (p. 1). By studying organizational metaphors, then, culture researchers can develop some important insights into how organization members experience and make sense of their organization (see Critical Case Study 6.1).

A good example of how metaphor analysis can provide such insight is Tracy, Lutgen-Sandvik, and Alberts's (2006) study of workplace bullying. Through interviews and focus-group meetings with targets of workplace bullying, the study analyzes victims' efforts to make sense of the painful experience of being bullied. Starting with the basic question, "What does it feel like to be bullied?" Tracy et al. identify a series of metaphors that interviewees articulate. In speaking about the experience of bullying, respondents described it variously as a game or battle, a waking nightmare, water torture, and a noxious substance.

© iStockphoto.com/photomorphic

Rites and rituals symbolically mark significant moments in organizations and the lives of their members.

In metaphorically describing the bullies, interviewees used the metaphors of dictator, two-faced actor, and evil demon. Finally, in describing themselves as targets of bullying, respondents spoke of slaves or property, prisoners, children, and heartbroken lovers. Thus, for example, in describing bullies as "two-faced actors," respondents made sense of how, while bullies made their lives miserable in one-on-one situations, around other employees or supervisors they played the role of the perfect organization member, making it difficult for targets of bullying to be taken seriously. Similarly, in using the metaphor of "heartbroken lover" respondents were attempting to address their experience of feeling betrayed in a job they loved.

Studies such as this illustrate the importance of the culture-as-root-metaphor approach in two ways. First, they allow researchers to enable

Critical Case Study 6.1
Organizational Culture and Metaphors

With the rise of the cultural approach to organizations and the more intense focus on communication, researchers started to pay much more attention to the kind of talk people used to make sense of their organizations. Because of this, metaphors became a particular focus for researchers. Metaphors can be defined as understanding and experiencing one kind of thing in terms of another. For example, when someone says, "I won the argument," they are understanding one thing (having an argument) in terms of another (war or sport). As we have seen in this chapter, metaphors don't simply describe an already existing organizational reality but, rather, function as fundamental ways for people to organize their experiences.

Organizational communication scholars Ruth Smith and Eric Eisenberg (1987) provide a fascinating example of the importance of metaphors in structuring organizational reality in their study of a management–employee conflict that resulted in a worker strike at Disneyland. In their study, Smith and Eisenberg argue that Disneyland was experienced through two competing "root metaphors"—Disney as drama and Disney as family. The drama root metaphor constructed organizational experience as providing entertainment, putting on a show, wearing costumes (not uniforms), having onstage and backstage areas, and so forth. The drama metaphor also emphasized "the business of show business," in which Disneyland was seen as a profit-making enterprise. While the management of Disneyland emphasized the drama metaphor, many of the employees experienced Disneyland as a family, in which employees were brothers and sisters, everyone looked out for one another, and Walt Disney (long since dead) was seen as the spiritual "head" of the family. As one employee stated, "The people who work here treat each other as a family, there seems to be a common cause. . . . We're family presenting family entertainment; it's like we're inviting someone to our home to entertain them" (p. 374).

However, as Smith and Eisenberg (1987) show, these two root metaphors represent competing worldviews—one representing Disney as a for-profit business, the other constructing Disney as a benevolent family where everyone pulls together and takes care of one another. Thus, when Disney management began to implement pay freezes, benefit cuts, and layoffs, employees regarded this as a fundamental violation of the principles on which Disney had been founded. As one employee stated,

> Walt Disney's philosophy was to bring families together so that they could have fun. . . . The philosophy is now let's make as much money as [we] can. . . . We're numbers now, we're not people to them anymore. (p. 374)

Such was the perceived conflict between the two competing metaphors that employees went on a 22-day strike in response to what they perceived as the poor treatment of family members. Interestingly, management responded by trying to reinterpret the family metaphor, arguing that during difficult times families had to make sacrifices and tighten their belts if they expected to survive. However, this reinterpretation failed to catch on among employees.

Smith and Eisenberg (1987) argue that while the overt (first-order) conflict may have been focused on economic issues (pay freezes, etc.), a deeper, more far-reaching (second-order) conflict focused on the basic philosophy regarding how Disneyland should be run. The two competing metaphors of "drama" and "family" represented two largely irreconcilable perspectives on this philosophy. In this sense, then, we can see that the two metaphors are not just ways to describe an already existing organizational reality but, rather, fundamentally shape reality for organization members.

Questions for Discussion

1. Think of organizations to which you belong. Can you identify metaphors that members use to describe the organization? How does this shape the experience of organization members?

2. In groups, brainstorm possible metaphors that might be used to describe organizations. Some common metaphors are organizations as family, team, machine, political system, tribe, etc. For example, an "organization as machine" metaphor would emphasize efficiency, well-oiled parts, precision, impersonality, and so forth. Be as creative as possible in your brainstorming. What features are associated with each metaphor, and how would they shape organizational life?

organization members to make sense of their own reality, rather than their reality as shaped by managerial efforts to "engineer" culture. In this particular study, for example, the organization members' own metaphors provide a "linguistic shorthand to describe long, difficult-to-articulate, and devastatingly painful feelings associated with workplace bullying" (Tracy et al., 2006, p. 171). Second, these studies show how such research can be used to address real-world organizational issues. Workplace bullying is a widespread organizational problem that affects many employees (Lutgen-Sandvik, 2003), and Tracy et al. (2006) illustrate how this issue can be better understood by speaking directly to the people who experience it.

Rites and Rituals. The fact that all organizations practice various kinds of **rites and rituals** suggests that, over time, organizational reality sediments into stable and patterned forms. Rites and rituals emerge partly from a need for organization members to experience order and predictability in their lives. Such rituals can be as informal as a daily greeting between two colleagues or as formal as the pomp and circumstance of a graduation ceremony. All such rituals contribute to the social order of an organization and aid members in the creation of a shared social reality in which they can invest their professional identities (Trice & Beyer, 1984). They can mark the passage into a new phase of one's life (such as a graduation ceremony or getting married), or they can serve to further integrate members into a culture. An office holiday party, for example, can serve as a "rite of integration" that increases common bonds and further commits members to their organization (Rosen, 1988).

Rites of "enhancement" (Trice & Beyer, 1984) can increase the status and power of organization members through public recognition of their accomplishments while at the same time placing the organization in a positive light. For example, at high-profile, high-energy ceremonies, the Mary Kay company gives awards to successful representatives, with the top sellers receiving pink Cadillacs (Waggoner, 1997).

Finally, rites of "degradation" (Trice & Beyer, 1984) occur when organizations experience problems and top organization members must perform a ritual acknowledgment of such problems in an effort to address them (or create the perception that they are being addressed). For example, in 2011 when News Corporation CEO Rupert Murdoch appeared before a British parliamentary committee in the wake of the *News of the World* phone-hacking scandal, he was engaging in a "rite of degradation" in an effort to limit damage to his global enterprise. The fact that he stated to the committee, "This is the most humble day of my life," served to mark the event explicitly as a ceremonial rite of degradation.

Organizational Stories

Organizational storytelling has become one of the most extensively researched features of work and organizational culture (Boje, 1991; Brown, 1990; Brown, 2006; Browning, 1992; Langellier & Peterson, 2006; Martin et al., 1983; Mumby, 1993). Part of the reason for this is that people like both to tell and hear stories, and so this form of cultural expression is a pervasive feature of everyday organizational life. Organizational culture researchers thus view storytelling as one of the most important ways in which humans produce and reproduce social reality. Rhetoric scholar Walter Fisher (1985) has gone so far as to argue that human beings are "homo narrans"—that is, storytelling beings. In other words, our identities as humans are largely dependent on our ability to construct coherent narratives about ourselves. Such stories can range from personal narratives that individuals tell about themselves to "grand narratives" that embody the identity of an entire nation. Thus, one might argue that the grand narrative of the United States is the American Dream—a story of individual freedom, opportunity, and an entrepreneurial spirit. Each new group of immigrants has attempted to find a place within this grand narrative.

Organizational communication scholar Kristen Lucas (2011) provides an insightful analysis of tensions between the American Dream and what she describes as the "Working Class Promise." In her study of working class families' narratives about their work lives, she identifies the Working Class Promise as "a commitment to uphold the core set of shared values revered by working class communities . . . and, by extension, to maintain one's working class membership and identity" (p. 358). The four core values she identifies are (1) a strong work ethic, (2) a commitment to providing for one's family, (3) a belief in the dignity of all work and workers, and (4) a sense of humility, without arrogance or pretentiousness.

Lucas (2011) suggests that the Working Class Promise is a narrative that operates as a moral imperative, much like the American Dream narrative. However, she argues that the two narratives operate in tension with each other, presenting paradoxical views of social mobility. On the one hand, the American Dream narrative argues that being working class "is a starting point, a social position one should strive to rise above"; on the other hand, the Working Class Promise positions being working class as "an esteemed endpoint, a social position one should strive to maintain" (p. 365). Thus, Lucas identifies a contradiction between the American Dream as a social structure that one can climb and the Working Class Promise as a value system that one feels connected to, perhaps for life. These two narratives, existing in tension, are hard to reconcile if one has, at least socioeconomically, moved beyond one's working-class origins. I'm sure that many of you (like me) are members of the first generation in your family to go to college, and so I suspect you may experience the same kind of tension between loyalty to the Working Class Promise and the promise of the American Dream. In other words, is it possible both to live the American Dream and to stay true to the values of the Working Class Promise?

Management scholar Joanne Martin and her colleagues (1983) provide a particularly interesting early example of research looking at organizational storytelling. In analyzing stories from a range of organizations, they discover that many of the stories exhibit common scripts. For example, stories might be told around such scripts as, Can the little person rise to the top? How will the boss react to mistakes? Is the big boss human? Will I get fired? Martin et al. illustrate how stories with these same scripts occur across a range of organizations, often in both positive and negative versions. They dub this phenomenon the "uniqueness paradox" to get at the idea that stories intended to express an organization's uniqueness actually occur across a range of organizations.

For example, in a frequently recurring script about the importance of following organizational rules, Martin et al. (1983) recount one version of the story in which a female security guard tells Tom Watson, CEO of IBM, that he can't enter a secure area because he isn't wearing the right ID badge; Watson reacts positively and sends one of his staff to get the ID. In a parallel story, a secretary at Revlon challenges CEO Charles Revson when he violates a rule about not removing the employee sign-in sheet from its location. In this instance, the secretary is fired for daring to challenge the big boss. Thus, the moral of the IBM version of the story is, "Even the big boss follows the rules, so you should, too." On the other hand, the moral of the Revlon version is that rules apply arbitrarily and capriciously; the more power you have in the company, the less the rules apply to you. Thus, two similarly structured stories provide diametrically opposite morals about organizational rule following.

I actually have my own independent confirmation that Martin et al.'s (1983) idea of the "uniqueness paradox" is a widespread organizational phenomenon. At three different universities at which I have taught (Rutgers, Purdue, and University of North Carolina), I have heard a story that is always connected to a famous statue on campus. The story relates to the presence (or absence) of virgins at the university (the story is typically about female students). At Rutgers, a story circulated about "Willie the silent" (a statue of William of Orange), who, it was said, would whistle when a virgin walked by (of course, he never whistled). At Purdue the same story was told about the stone lions outside the administration building (who would roar in the presence of a virgin). At UNC, it is said that Silent Sam (a statue of a confederate soldier) will fire his gun when a virgin walks by. Each story, then, is intended to convey a unique feature of the university's culture while simultaneously being common to many campuses—hence, the uniqueness paradox.

From the perspective of a researcher wishing to understand the culture of an organization, the question is, what does such an organizational story mean? What does it tell us about the ways members of these organizations make sense of their social reality? A simple surface reading might be, "All the female students on campus are sexually active." But, of course, we know this isn't true; students and young people generally adopt a variety of orientations regarding their sexual activity, or lack thereof.

Instead, I interpret the story as saying something about anxieties and tensions around sex on college campuses. Given the status of college life as a transition period to full adulthood and independence, there is a great deal of pressure on students to figure out how sexually active, or inactive, they should be: Who's a friend? Who's a "friend with benefits"? What counts as a date, rather than just hanging out with someone? And, of course, no one wants to appear sexually naïve or inexperienced, even if they are. In her study of student sexuality, Kathleen Bogle (2008) argues that on today's college campuses the idea of the traditional date has largely disappeared, replaced by the "hook-up." Student stories about their sex lives suggest that freshman women are more likely to "hook up" than are their upper-classmen sisters. Again, this perhaps tells us something about the anxiety college students feel about their sexual identities—something they are maybe closer to figuring out by their senior year.

What concepts like the "uniqueness paradox" tell us about organizational stories is that they have a distinct moral imperative (Bruner, 1991); that is, through the story structure, they move us toward a particular moral conclusion about some aspect of organizational reality. Stories are not just random descriptions of events but, rather, perform a sensemaking function in teaching us what is important to pay attention to. In other words, stories are told only about things that are worth having stories told about them! Such worthy events can range from "a funny thing happened at the office today" to stories about the fulfillment of the American Dream of wealth and prosperity. As a moral imperative, the

American Dream narrative instructs us to value the individual over the collective, work hard, earn lots of money, and believe in a meritocratic system in which everyone, regardless of origin, can succeed.

In sum, narratives are important communication processes that can significantly shape organization members' sense-making efforts. We all love to hear a good story; indeed, we're happy to hear a story multiple times if it's good! This suggests how much the narrative form resonates with us and how effective stories are in shaping realities. Stories are symbolically powerful not so much because of their relationship to reality (often they are fictional) but because of the way they provide us with a coherent and compelling reality. At an everyday level they provide us with organizing scripts that tell us what to pay attention to; at a macrosocietal level (the American Dream, the Working Class Promise) they shape and express value systems and overarching ideologies. Indeed, as management scholar Barbara Czarniawska (1997) compellingly states, "Organizational stories capture organizational life in a way that no compilation of facts ever can; this is because they are carriers of life itself, not just 'reports' on it" (p. 20).

Summarizing the Two Perspectives

The pragmatist and purist approaches represent two distinct ways of conceptualizing and studying organizational culture. The pragmatist approach is more managerially oriented, emphasizing the ways managers can intervene in and shape culture to fit the needs and goals of the organization; culture is viewed as an independent variable that can be manipulated to achieve particular organizational consequences. The purist perspective, on the other hand, rejects the idea that organizational culture can be manipulated, and argues instead that one should adopt culture as a "root metaphor," thus providing a powerful frame for understanding the complexities of organizational life. In this latter perspective, the notion of culture is used to get at the complex, precarious, and emergent features of daily organizational life. Heavy emphasis is placed on organizational actors as active and knowledgeable participants in the social construction of organizational reality.

Which of these approaches is better? The answer is that it depends on your particular interest in organizational culture. As a manager, you might well be interested in the link between culture and organizational performance (although, as we discussed earlier, this link is notoriously difficult to demonstrate and measure). On the other hand, as a culture researcher, you may have no interest in performance issues whatsoever, confining yourself to gaining insight into the endless complexities and nuances of human meaning-making processes. Thus, as with most theories, there is no absolute truth involved—just ways of seeing and not seeing. The two perspectives are compared and contrasted in Table 6.1.

❖ CONCLUSION

In this chapter we closely examined the cultural approach to the study of organizations. We laid out the origins of this body of research, showing how it emerged in response to particular economic, political, and social issues. In addition, we examined two of the main research traditions of the cultural approach: the pragmatist and purist perspectives on

Table 6.1 Comparing Pragmatist and Purist Approaches to Organizational Culture

Issue	Pragmatist Approach	Purist Approach
Conception of culture–organization relationship	Culture as a variable; an organization *has* a culture	Culture as a root metaphor; organization *is* a culture
Role of communication	Means by which organization members are socialized into culture	Process through which members constitute organizations as cultures
View of culture	Unitary view: Ideally, organizations have a single culture with which everyone identifies	Pluralist view: Organizations consist of multiple, often competing subcultures
Orientation to knowledge	Functionalist: Allows intervention in organizational culture; promotes culture engineering	Interpretivist: Deepens understanding of human collective behavior and meaning construction
Research orientation	Managerial view: Engineers culture from top down; creates culture with which employee will identify	"Native's point of view": Studies culture from bottom up, allowing members' meanings to shape findings
Research goals	Tie strong cultures to increased organizational effectiveness and competitiveness	Provide "thick description" of culture; increase understanding of complexity of organizational life

organizational culture. As we have shown, these two approaches adopt quite different assumptions about both the relationship between organizations and culture and the reasons for studying organizational culture.

As a preview to Chapter 7, Mats Alvesson (1993) has suggested the need for an "emancipatory" approach to organizational culture. By this he means that organizational communication researchers must counteract "parochialism" (narrow-mindedness or short-sightedness) and instead develop perspectives that capture the full complexity of organizational life—what Alvesson calls "eye-opening" studies. In this chapter we examined some of those studies—research that gets us to think about organizations differently, moving beyond a purely managerial point of view (where efficiency and profit are the defining criteria).

In Chapter 7 we will expand this emancipatory, "eye-opening" perspective by examining more closely a key issue in the critical approach to organizations—power and control.

CRITICAL APPLICATIONS

1. Conduct an oral interview with someone who works full-time. Ask this person about what his or her work means. How is work tied to this person's sense of identity as a

human being? How is work related to other aspects of his or her life? Make extensive notes during the interview and/or ask your interviewee for permission to record the interview. What themes can you identify in the interview that provide insight into how your interviewee makes sense of his or her work life?

2. Conduct a participant-observation study of an organization to which you belong. This can be a place of work, a club, or any other social group. Provide an analysis of the organization's culture using Pacanowsky and O'Donnell-Trujillo's (1982) question as a starting point: What are the key communication activities through which organizational sense making occurs? Focus on members' use of stories, constructs, rituals, metaphors, and so forth. In other words, provide an analysis of the organization's culture—how do the members collectively produce meaning through communication processes?

KEY TERMS

cultural pragmatist   138

cultural purist   140

ethnography   142

facts   145

metaphors   147

organizational storytelling   149

participant-observation   144

practices   146

relevant constructs   145

rites and rituals   149

thick description   136

vocabulary   146

STUDENT STUDY SITE

Visit the student study site at **www.sagepub.com/mumbyorg** for these additional learning tools:

- Web quizzes
- eFlashcards
- SAGE journal articles

- Video resources
- Web resources

PART III

Critical Perspectives on Organizational Communication and the New Workplace

Power is often associated with corporate symbols, such as a corner office.

CHAPTER 7

Power and Resistance at Work

Power is to organizations as oxygen is to breathing.

—Clegg, Courpasson, and Phillips (2006, p. 3)

In the previous chapter we talked about how organizations are sites of culture and meaning, where members engage in the collective construction of reality through various communication processes. In this chapter we will look closely at the processes of power and resistance that undergird the practices of meaning creation. **Power** is a pervasive feature of organizational life, of even the most routine organizational events. By examining how organizational power operates, we gain a stronger understanding of organizations as political sites—that is, as places where various actors bring different and competing interests and resources (economic, political, and symbolic) to the table.

We will also examine organizational power primarily from a communication perspective, looking at how the exercise of power is closely tied to the ability of organizational actors to marshal symbolic resources and shape organizational meanings. And we will look at how the exercise of power is always a contested process; that is, people routinely resist efforts to shape meanings and often construct alternate meanings of their own. Examined through this lens, we can better understand organizations as dynamic phenomena that are key sites of human identity formation and decision making in society (Deetz, 1992a).

First, let's look more closely at the various approaches to power that have been developed over the past several decades.

❖ PERSPECTIVES ON POWER AND ORGANIZATIONS

> *Power corrupts. Absolute power corrupts absolutely. But it rocks absolutely, too.*
>
> —"Demotivational" poster from Despair, Inc.
> (www.despair.com/power.html)

The concept of "power" is a complex and slippery notion that many social scientists in a number of different fields have attempted to explore. It is a very important concept because it is a defining feature of all social relations. The problem is that in some social contexts power is a clear and defining feature of those contexts, while in others it is less visible. For example, superior–subordinate and professor–student relations are characterized by relatively overt differences in the power associated with each position. A professor has power "over" a student in the sense that he or she dictates course content, decides what will be talked about in class, and, most important from a student perspective, assigns grades. Indeed, in such a context there is an expectation that power will be exercised in certain ways. I suspect that students wouldn't think very highly of a professor who came into class every day and said, "So what do you want to talk about today?" Of course, this oversimplified example overlooks the fact that there are many different teaching models, some of which empower students more, but it's hard to ignore that, ultimately, students adopt a relationship of dependence with their professors. This places the latter in a position of power.

On the other hand, how would we characterize the power issues in a work team where everyone participates equally in decision-making processes? Certainly, the team system has been touted as an important innovation that moves organizations toward decentralized, flatter structures, thus empowering workers. Hence, the team system cannot be examined quite so easily based on a simple conception of power that focuses on the direct influence of superiors over subordinates in the organization. As organizations become more complex, so do the ways in which organizational power operates. Clearly, then, we need to develop more complex notions of power in order to explain how it works at an everyday level.

Below, we will examine several different theories of power, exploring their strengths and weaknesses and discussing the various insights they provide for understanding organizational life.

Power as Social Influence

Social psychologists John French and Bertram Raven (1959) examined supervisor–subordinate relations in developing a model of power as a process of social influence. They argued that power-as-influence occurs when a psychological change takes place in the person or persons being influenced. As a result of their research, they developed five bases for social influence:

1. *Positional power.* Sometimes called legitimate power, this occurs by virtue of a person's position in an organizational hierarchy. I exercise power by virtue of my role as a department chair; as the occupant of that office, I am able to exercise social influence over others in a way that I couldn't as a regular faculty member. For example, I can mediate and rule in a dispute between two faculty members or set policy regarding use of the department copier (I know, my life is incredibly exciting!).

2. *Referent power.* This form of power is rooted in the charisma of the person exercising influence. Charismatic people possess traits that attract followers who wish to identify with that person. For example, I suspect you have found yourself wanting to do well in a class where you find the instructor charismatic.

3. *Expert power.* This power resides in a person's ability to provide to an organization knowledge and expertise that other members do not possess. For example, in a study of a French tobacco factory, Michel Crozier (1964) discovered that a group of lowly maintenance workers had a great deal of power because they were the only employees who knew how to repair the factory's aging machines.

4. *Reward Power.* This involves the ability to provide subordinates with resources that result in positive feelings about themselves and the organization. Giving employees promotions, pay raises, or a better parking space are all examples of reward power.

5. *Coercive power.* This is the most explicit form of power and is the mirror image of reward power. It is generally used in getting a subordinate to do something he or she wouldn't typically do, and is most often punitive. Subordinates are subject to coercive power when they are influenced by their perception that a negative outcome will occur if they don't carry out a superior's request. For example, if your instructor tells you that you will receive a failing grade if you turn in an assignment late, he or she is attempting to use coercive power.

Two points about French and Raven's model are important to note. First, these bases for power overlap. For example, someone who possesses positional power is also likely to yield coercive and reward power because of his or her organizational authority. Second, all these forms of power are relational; that is, they function only by virtue of a relationship of interdependence between the power holder and the subordinate. For example, a superior holds coercive power only if able to produce a psychological change in the person he or she is trying to influence. If you don't care about getting a failing grade for a late assignment, then the instructor has no power over you. Similarly, the ability to exercise reward power may wane over time; rewards such as pay raises may lose their effectiveness if the nature of the work is soul destroying.

Power, then, is not a *thing* that someone in authority can possess. Rather, **power is** *exercised through a dynamic process in which relations of interdependence exist between* *actors in organizational settings*. Some actors have more resources than others, but such resources are useful only if others prize them. Similarly, no one is without power; regardless of how limited or constraining a situation is, it is possible to act in the face of power. For example, even a prisoner can go on hunger strike. The sociologist Anthony Giddens (1979) refers to agency as the ability to "act otherwise." In other words, we are never simply billiard balls on a table reacting in a mechanical fashion to the pool cue of power.

So, as we develop the idea of power in this chapter, we will examine increasingly complex understandings of power as a relational, dynamic process. Moreover, unlike French and Raven's focus on interpersonal power in the superior–subordinate relationship, we will look at power as a broader social process that operates both at the level of everyday life and in societal-level discourses.

Debates about the nature of power became particularly focused in the 1950s, 1960s, and 1970s in the field of political science. During this time, scholars attempted to examine systematically the issue of who holds and exercises power in society. Attempts to answer this question developed roughly into two camps: the **pluralists** (Dahl, 1957, 1958, 1961; Wolfinger, 1971) and the **elitists** (Bachrach & Baratz, 1962, 1963; Hunter, 1953; Mills, 1956). The debate between these two camps became known as the **community power debate.** The pluralists argued that power was equitably distributed throughout society and that no particular group had undue influence over decision-making processes. The elitists, on the other hand, claimed that power was concentrated in the hands of a privileged few who controlled political agendas. The pluralists adopted what can be called a **one-dimensional view of power**, while the elitists developed a **two-dimensional view of power**. Let's examine the two perspectives more closely.

The One-Dimensional Model of Power

As a member of the pluralist camp, Robert Dahl argued for a behavioral model of power. He defined power in the following way: "A has power over B to the extent that he [or she] can get B to do something that B would not otherwise do" (Dahl, 1957, pp. 202–203). Dahl thus defined power in terms of direct influence—for him, power is exercised when one person or group is able to influence directly (and measurably) the behavior of another person or group. For example, a boss exercises "power over" an employee when that employee chooses to forgo an evening out when instructed by the boss to deliver a report by 9 a.m. the following morning. The employee's behavior is directly influenced by her boss, which causes her to do something she would not normally do (stay at work to finish a report rather than going out with friends).

Dahl saw the presence of conflict as being a condition for the exercise of power. In other words, two people or groups bring two different perspectives or agendas to an issue, with each party having a preferred decision or course of action. The individual or group with the most power is the one that has issues resolved in its favor. Dahl used this model of power in his study of conflict and political decision making in New Haven, Connecticut, showing that no particular group exercised a disproportionate amount of power over decision outcomes (Dahl, 1961). In other words, a plurality of interests was represented (hence, the name of the perspective).

The Two-Dimensional Model of Power

The political elitists challenged Dahl's model of power, arguing that it was too simplistic and unable to capture the full complexity of how power actually worked in society. Thus, in response to Dahl, Peter Bachrach and Morton Baratz (1962, 1963) developed a model that captured what they called "the two faces of power." In this model, they argued that not only is power exercised when someone persuades another person to engage in behavior he or she otherwise *would not* have, but it is also exercised when someone *prevents* someone else from doing something he or she otherwise *would* have. This model of power captures the exercise of power as involving both decisions and nondecisions. This view can be captured in the following statement: "A has power over B when A prevents B from doing something that B would otherwise do."

For example, imagine that you are the owner of a small retail store and you attend a public meeting of your city planning committee to complain about a plan to approve the building of a new Wal-Mart on the outskirts of town. You feel that such a plan would hurt many small business owners in the downtown area. However, the meeting is dominated by Wal-Mart representatives who present a barrage of facts and figures about why this new store would help revitalize the town's economy and provide 500 new jobs in the area. Under such circumstances you feel intimidated and unable to state your own position and thus remain silent.

Bachrach and Baratz would argue that in this instance Wal-Mart's representatives exercise power because they are able to shape the discussion to serve their own needs and limit dissenting opinions. Borrowing a term from Schattschneider, Bachrach and Baratz (1962) refer to this process as "the mobilization of bias." This means that

> power is . . . exercised when A devotes his energies to creating or reinforcing social and political values and institutional practices that limit the scope of the political process to public consideration of only those issues which are comparatively innocuous to A. To the extent that A succeeds in doing this, B is prevented . . . from bringing to the fore any issues that might in their resolution be seriously detrimental to A's set of preferences. (p. 948)

To explain this concept, let's extend the Wal-Mart example a bit further. Such "mobilization of bias" would exist if Wal-Mart representatives were able to shape the discussion at the public meeting so that it addressed only issues that were relatively unthreatening to Wal-Mart. For example, it would be in their best interest to minimize discussions about damage to local businesses, negative environmental impact, and increased traffic congestion. If such debate were minimized and Wal-Mart representatives were able to restrict discussion to issues such as how big the store was going to be, how much the city's tax revenues would increase, or how many local people would be employed by the store, then one could argue that power was being exercised. Again, notice that no open conflict is occurring. Rather, the key issue is that "mobilization of bias" takes place, such that some (potentially conflictual) issues are organized out of public discussion, while others are strategically organized into the discussion.

Bachrach and Baratz's model of the two faces of power thus recognizes that overt conflict or difference between parties does not have to be present for the exercise of power to occur. Indeed, their model suggests that a more subtle exercise of power involves the ability to prevent potential conflict from being expressed in an overt fashion. Thus, they argue that power is not distributed evenly across different stakeholders, as the pluralists suggest, but is instead heavily skewed toward "political élites"; these élites are able to use their resources to "mobilize bias" and shape debates in ways that serve their own interests.

The Three-Dimensional Model of Power

Political scientist Steven Lukes (1974) has added an important third perspective to the debate over the nature of power. Lukes argues that while both Dahl and Bachrach and Baratz provide useful conceptions of how power works in society, both are limited because they see power as a purely behavioral phenomenon. That is, power is exercised when people's behaviors are affected in some way (i.e., people are persuaded to do something or persuaded *not* to do something). Lukes suggests that both these views of power presume some kind of conflict: in Dahl's case overt conflict, in Bachrach and Baratz's case covert conflict. This is a problem, Lukes argues, because power can also be exercised in situations where no form of conflict—either overt or covert—exists.

Lukes thus developed a three-dimensional model that extends the conception of power. His position is summarized in the following quote:

> A may exercise power over B by getting him to do what he does not want to do, but he also exercises power over him by influencing, shaping, or determining his very wants. Indeed, is it not the supreme exercise of power to get another or others to have the desires you want them to have—that is, to secure their compliance by controlling their thoughts and desires? (Lukes, 1974, p. 23)

Lukes is not pointing here to some kind of mind-control program. Rather, he is highlighting a form of power that is widespread in society and that, in fact, functions as the very basis of modern capitalism. Capitalism is successful precisely because businesses spend large sums of money to convince us that we absolutely must have a particular product they just happen to manufacture. That is, they shape our very wants and needs (an issue we'll look at in detail in Chapter 12, on branding and consumption).

Examples of this phenomenon abound. For instance, think about how almost every year at Christmastime a form of mass hysteria grips parents as they attempt to buy for their children the "must-have" toy of the season. Without fail, the media report tales of people fighting each other in department stores or paying many times the retail price to secure the precious item. Whether it's Beanie Babies, Tickle Me Elmos, or the latest Xbox, the scenario is the same year after year. Clearly, parents are not coerced into buying these toys, and they exercise free will in making such purchases. However, Lukes would argue that this example illustrates the exercise of power insofar as companies are able to create and shape people's very needs. People don't need such products until they are persuaded by slick advertising campaigns that they are indispensable to a happy and fulfilling existence. Such a process isn't limited to coveted Christmas gifts; it occurs with virtually every product on the market, right down to mundane items such as toilet paper and cleaning products, where commercials attempt to persuade homemakers that a particular brand will increase the quality of family life.

This form of power is also a part of daily organizational life. Organizations spend a great deal of time and money getting employees to identify with organizational beliefs, values, and goals. Indeed, the pragmatist approach to organizational culture that we discussed in the previous chapter is an excellent example of Lukes's third dimension of power in operation. Rather than simply telling employees to do something (one-dimensional view) or limiting opportunities for expressing alternative views (two-dimensional view), it is much better from a managerial perspective to cultivate in employees a way of thinking and acting that is consistent with the overall value system of the organization. One of the reasons why companies are increasingly adopting personality tests as part of the interview process is that they provide them with more data about how potential employees may "fit in" with the culture of the organization (Holmer Nadesan, 1997).

In this sense, it is perhaps the ultimate exercise of power for organizations to cultivate in employees a sense of identification that leads them to behave spontaneously in ways that serve the best interests of the organization (Barker, 1993, 1999; Tompkins & Cheney, 1985). For example, companies such as Disney and McDonald's have their own "universities" that not only provide employees with particular job skills but also socialize them into the Disney or McDonald's system of values. Once employees have internalized these values, their decision making and behavior are much more likely to be consistent with the larger organizational philosophy. McDonald's, for example, refers to such strongly identified employees as "having ketchup in their veins." In Chapter 8 we will see how the emergence of a team-based organizational structure (sometimes referred to as a postbureaucratic organization) is heavily grounded in the principle that team members can both function autonomously and make decisions consistent with organizational philosophy.

This **three-dimensional view of power** therefore argues that conflict (either overt or covert) is not a necessary condition for the exercise of power. The existence of a consensus amongst different groups does not mean that power is not being exercised. Instead, this view sees power operating at a "deep-structure" level, shaping people's very interests, beliefs, and values. But how does this happen? What is the mechanism by which large groups of people come to share a similar worldview? In order to understand this process more clearly, we turn to a discussion of the concept of ideology.

❖ ORGANIZATIONAL COMMUNICATION AND IDEOLOGY

Ideology and power are closely connected. When Marx (1947) states that "the ideas of the ruling class are in every epoch the ruling ideas" (p. 39), he is recognizing that those in power do not simply rule by coercion but, equally important, shape the ways in which people think about and experience the world. In this sense, ideology (as the term suggests) operates in the realm of ideas and meanings.

In this sense, a simple way to understand the concept of ideology is to see it as providing the link between meaning and power. That is, ideology functions as an interpretive lens through which people come to understand what exists, what is good, and what is possible (Therborn, 1980). In other words, ideology shapes people's sense of reality, provides them with a taken-for-granted frame for judging what is good and bad or right and wrong in that reality, and both enables and constrains their thinking about what realities are possible. Let's develop these ideas through an example.

One of the most central features of U.S. society is the ideology of individualism. The notion of "the individual" is meaningful for all Americans, and it comes with a whole set of associations. For example, it refers to a particular set of freedoms enshrined in the Constitution (freedom of expression, freedom of religion, freedom of assembly, the right to bear arms, etc.). In this sense, the idea of "the individual" embodies a set of principles that have to do with the freedom of each person in society to live life as he or she sees fit, unencumbered by government intervention (within the law of the land, of course). The principle of individualism also has strong connections with the economic system that prevails in U.S. society. The notion of the free market embodies the idea that anyone who has the ability, work ethic, and desire for success will be successful and that every corporation (enshrined in law as an "individual") is free to pursue profit, unencumbered by heavy-handed government regulations. Thus, the "Horatio Alger" myth is very strong in U.S. society, celebrating as heroic those people whose lives consist of some kind of "rags-to-riches" story. Certainly, many immigrants came to the United States precisely because they believed that, through hard work and diligence, they could make their fortunes.

In the work context, the ideology of individualism is, if anything, becoming increasingly significant. Indeed, as we will see in later chapters, the idea of the "social contract" between companies and workers (which provided job security) has largely disappeared. In its place, employees are expected to "brand" themselves as unique individuals who provide employers with a competitive advantage over other companies.

The American notion of individualism, however, is an ideological construct. In other words, it is not a naturally occurring, objective feature of U.S. society but, rather, is a socially constructed phenomenon that gives shape and meaning to people's lives. This can easily be demonstrated by comparing the United States with other societies. For example, in many European countries the ideology of individualism is not nearly as strong; indeed, the ideology of collectivism is much stronger. This does not mean that "the individual" is unimportant but, rather, that the rights of the individual are situated in the context of the larger society. For example, higher income-tax rates (viewed by many in the United States as an infringement on individual rights) are seen as a contribution to the greater good (guaranteeing, for example, health care for every citizen).

We can also think of ideology as a communication phenomenon. That is, ideology operates principally through the formal and informal communicative practices of daily life (Critical Case Study 7.1 illustrates how organizational stories function ideologically). In this sense, communication processes are ideological in that they shape our relationship to the world and to other people, highlighting some ways of viewing the world and hiding others. Cultural studies researcher Stuart Hall (1985) provides an excellent example of the communicative, discursive character of ideology. Focusing on his own experience as a Jamaican who has lived in two different societies (Jamaica and Britain), Hall clearly demonstrates how the phenomenon of "race" is ideological in that it is closely tied to the ways it is constructed through communication. For example, Hall explains how, as a young man growing up in Jamaica, his racial identity grew out of a complex system of finely graded discursive categories that reflected the colonial history of the country. Thus, he was frequently described as *colored*—a term used to mean both "not white" *and* "not black." In this context, *colored* was a term that designated him as a member of "the 'mixed' ranks of the brown middle class, a cut above the rest—in aspiration if not in reality" (p. 108). As such, great stress was placed on a system of hierarchically arranged distinctions that signified one's place in society in terms of class, status, and race.

However, when Hall emigrated from Jamaica to England as a young adult in the 1950s, he discovered a much simpler classification system at work. There, as a racial signifier, the term *colored* was largely synonymous with the term *black*. Given that Britain in the 1950s was an extremely homogenous society with a minimal nonwhite population, the terms available to signify race operated according to a simple, binary system—white/not white. Terms such as *black* and *colored*, then, had the same meaning, that is, "not white." Thus,

Critical Case Study 7.1
Ideology and Storytelling

A lot of research has looked at organizational stories not only as sense-making devices that contribute to organizational culture (see previous chapter) but also as communicative forms that function ideologically to maintain and resist structures of organizational power (Brown, 1998; Clair, 1993b; Humphreys & Brown, 2002; Mumby, 1987; Witten, 1993). A few years back, I published an article that conducted an ideological analysis of a famous story that circulated at IBM and told of an encounter between a female security guard and Thomas Watson Jr., then IBM's CEO. The story focused on

> a twenty-year-old bride weighing ninety pounds whose husband had been sent overseas and who, in consequence, had been given a job until his return.... The young woman, Lucille Burger, was obliged to make certain that people entering security areas wore the correct clear identification.
>
> Surrounded by his usual entourage of white-shirted men, Watson approached the doorway to an area where she was on guard, wearing an orange badge acceptable elsewhere in the plant, but not a green badge, which alone permitted entrance at her door. "I was trembling in my uniform, which was far too big," she recalled. "It hid my shakes, but not my voice. 'I'm sorry,' I said to him. I knew who he was alright. 'You cannot enter. Your admittance is not recognized.' That's what we were supposed to say."

> The men accompanying Watson were stricken; the moment held unpredictable possibilities. "Don't you know who he is?" someone hissed. Watson raised his hand for silence, while one of the party strode off and returned with the appropriate badge. (Mumby, 1987, p. 121)

Using the discussion of ideology in this chapter, conduct an ideological analysis of this story. Put yourself in the place of an IBM employee being told this story, and think about how it might influence your sense-making efforts regarding the company. Use the three functions of ideology discussed in the chapter to focus your analysis. Pay attention to how the story is constructed. For example, what's the significance of the description of Burger as "a twenty-year-old bride weighing ninety pounds"? How does this particular choice shape the power of the story and give it impact? What do you think the moral of the story is intended to be? How might it be interpreted differently from a managerial perspective and from an employee perspective?

In class, provide examples of other organizational stories you have heard or been told as a member of an organization. What has been the impact of these stories? Why are they so significant in the organization? Can you identify how they might work ideologically to shape the reality of the organization?

If you want a "crib sheet," you can read my article (Mumby, 1987), listed in the references at the end of this book.

the status associated with being "colored" (as opposed to "black") in Jamaican society was completely absent in British society, as all "nonwhites" were viewed as a single, undifferentiated mass.

We can take several important issues from this example. First, Hall shows how terms do not have a single, fixed meaning but, rather, take on significance according to their position within the larger system of discourse and meaning that makes up a particular culture or society. Indeed, this example is similar (although with much more profound implications) to our discussion in Chapter 2 about how traffic lights signify meaning. Second, Hall illustrates how communication does not simply represent an objectively given world but actively functions to shape that world. In this instance, the discourse available to construct "race" as a category shapes how people view one another. Finally, Hall (1985) shows how "meaning is relational within an ideological system of presences and absences" (p. 109). Not only is meaning rooted in difference; it is also ideological in that it both shapes and reflects the systems of power relations in society. In this example, "whiteness" is always marked as the positive, taken-for-granted term—the one to which everyone aspires and the one in relation to which "blackness" is constructed. Thus, in Jamaica, "colored" has a higher status than "black" precisely because it is closer to "white"; in Britain, "colored" and "black" lose their distinctiveness because they are both "nonwhite" and, thus, equally inferior. We will address race and organizations in much more detail in Chapter 10.

However, there is another feature of ideology that we must address. As the mediating element between meaning and power, ideology does not simply reflect the dominant system of meanings and ideas (and hence reflect the ideas of the dominant group). Rather, ideology both represents a particular reality and obscures the underlying power relations of that reality. In this sense, ideology complicates our relationship to other people and the world. Sociologist Anthony Giddens (1979) suggests three ways in which ideology obscures the relationship between societal meanings and the power relations that underlie those meanings: Ideology (1) represents particular group interests as universal, (2) obscures or denies contradictions in society, and (3) naturalizes social relations through the process of reification. Let's briefly discuss each of these functions in turn.

Ideology Represents Particular Group Interests as Universal

The first function of ideology addresses the way the power differences between different social and economic groups are hidden. In this function, ideology manages the relationship between power and meaning by presenting the interests of a particular group in society as being representative of, and inclusive of, all groups. In most Western countries, for example, capitalism is universally accepted as the economic system that is in everyone's best interest. However, only a tiny percentage of the population are actually capitalists. Most of us don't own capital and have to work for someone else in order to make a living. Despite this, the interests of a small number of people are represented, through ideology, as being universally shared by everyone. While we see capitalism as a positive and democratic system that we take for granted, rarely do we reflect on whose interests are served by this system and whose are marginalized. Indeed, the Occupy Wall Street movement, with its slogan of "We are the 99%," can be seen as an effort to draw attention to the way capitalism largely serves the interests of the 1%.

Ideology Obscures or Denies Contradictions in Society

Ideology also obscures basic contradictions that operate in everyday organizational life. A contradiction is a basic or logical incompatibility between two coexisting statements or states of affairs in the world. For example, the "Horatio Alger" myth, discussed earlier, operates ideologically in its obscuring of basic contradictions in society. That is, the myth constructs a social reality that emphasizes equal opportunity and a "pull yourself up by your own bootstraps" value system while obscuring the deep economic and political inequalities that exist among various groups in society.

For example, Figure 7.1 presents the results of a study that surveyed a random sample of more than 5,000 people regarding their perceptions of how wealth is distributed in U.S. society (Norton & Ariely, 2011). The study reveals a huge disparity between people's perceptions of wealth distribution and the actual distribution of wealth in society. What's even more fascinating is that people's view of the ideal distribution is way more equitable than

Figure 7.1   Actual, Estimated, and Perceived Ideal Wealth Distribution in the United States

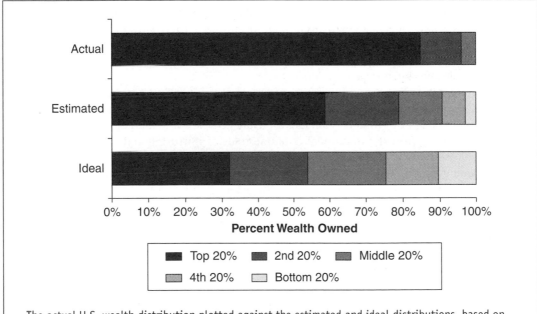

The actual U.S. wealth distribution plotted against the estimated and ideal distributions, based on more than 5,000 randomly surveyed respondents. "Estimated" indicates how Americans *think* wealth is distributed, and "Ideal" indicates how they would *like* it to be distributed. Because of their small percentage share of total wealth, both the "4th 20%" value (0.2%) and the "Bottom 20%" value (0.1%) are not visible in the "Actual" distribution (Norton & Ariely, 2011).

their perceptions: Asked to choose their ideal distribution of wealth, 92% picked one that was even more equitable.

Critical scholars would argue that ideology functions to obscure the contradictions between the narratives of equality and justice that inform the perceptions of most U.S. citizens and the actual inequality that the figure above makes apparent.

Ideology Functions to Reify Social Relations

As we have discussed, social actors construct the social reality they inhabit. Viewed from this perspective, organizations exist only through the communication activities of their members (Ashcraft, Kuhn, & Cooren, 2009). One of the functions of ideology, however, is that this communicative construction process is frequently hidden, and organizations are seen as objective structures existing independent of communication behavior. We can use the term *reification* to describe this ideological process (Lukács, 1971); that is, ideology makes social relations and institutions appear natural and objective. When humanly created phenomena are reified in this fashion, they appear to lie outside the influence of human behavior.

There are lots of examples of the process of ideological reification in society. For instance, gender roles were for a long time seen as natural, biological characteristics of men and women. The idea that men went out to work and women stayed home to cook, clean, and raise children was seen as predetermined by our biology. In recent decades, however, these roles have been shown to be cultural, socially constructed products that kept in place unequal power relations between men and women. While such power differences still exist in many ways, the assumption that men and women are biologically suited to particular social roles has been largely undermined.

In organizational contexts, certain positions are still reified within traditional gender roles. For example, a large "pink-collar" sector in organizations persists, involving jobs occupied mostly by women. Such jobs typically involve some kind of support role and, in many cases, reflect the traditional feminine roles of nurturing and caretaking. Positions such as secretary and nurse are representative of these pink-collar occupations.

Ideology, then, works to manage the relationship between communication and power by shaping the ways social reality is constructed. Returning to the above discussion of Lukes's work, we can say that ideology constructs a social reality in which potential conflicts between different groups are never allowed to rise to the level of full consciousness. In other words, people don't challenge or resist their social reality because they lack awareness of the contradictions on which it is based. For example, a woman who claims that "a woman's place is in the home" is, one could argue, under the sway of an ideology of patriarchy, in which men define the role of women as involving economic, political, and cultural servitude to men. Ideology, then, is accepted and actively upheld by *both* the dominant and subordinate groups, but only the former benefits from that ideology. Thus, it is in the best interests of the dominant group to maintain and reproduce that ideology.

However, ideology does not work that simply. Indeed, because it is largely about meaning and systems of signification, dominant ideologies are frequently challenged and vulnerable to change. Struggle always exists around ideologies, as different social groups compete to shape the meanings that make up social reality. As Stuart Hall (1985) states, "Ideology also sets limits to the degree to which a society-in-dominance can easily, smoothly, and functionally reproduce itself" (p. 113). While ideology functions to maintain the status quo, change is never far away. At various points in the past hundred years, for example, change has occurred through social movements challenging the dominant ideology: The women's suffrage movement in the 19th and early 20th centuries challenged the prevailing political status quo and won the vote for women; in the 1960s, the civil rights movement challenged racial discrimination and gained equal rights for nonwhites; and in the 1960s and 1970s, the feminist movement challenged patriarchy and changed perceptions of what women can do. Perhaps the Occupy Wall Street movement will, in hindsight, be seen as the catalyst for a shift toward greater economic justice in society.

In the next section, then, we will examine this process of struggle, looking at the ways organizations attempt to exercise control over organization members through ideological processes and how employees frequently resist such attempts to shape organizational reality (Fleming & Spicer, 2007).

❖ EXAMINING ORGANIZATIONAL COMMUNICATION THROUGH THE LENS OF POWER AND IDEOLOGY

Scholars in the critical organizational communication tradition are interested in studying organizations as sites of power and resistance. That is, they examine the ways organizations seek to control and shape the behavior of their employees, as well as the various means by which employees attempt to resist and escape these methods of control (Fleming & Spicer, 2007; Mumby, 1988). Researchers in the critical tradition explore organizational life through the concepts we discussed in the first part of this chapter—communication, ideology, and power. From a critical perspective, organizations are viewed as sites of collective communication behavior where power is distributed unequally amongst organization members. Critical researchers are interested in the various ways "struggles over meaning" occur. In other words, how does organizational reality get defined, and who are the various groups and social actors that engage in this struggle? Because the resources for this struggle are not shared equally, some groups and individuals have more influence in this struggle over meaning.

As organizational communication scholars, critical researchers are particularly interested in how different kinds of communication practices play central roles in this struggle over organizational reality and meaning. Researchers have studied communication phenomena such as stories (Brown, 2006; Helmer, 1993; Mumby, 1987; Witten, 1993), rituals (Rosen, 1985, 1988), metaphors (Deetz & Mumby, 1985; Kirby & Harter, 2002; Smith & Keyton, 2001), and everyday conversation (Boden, 1994; Holmes, 2006), among other phenomena, to try to understand how power and resistance work at an everyday level.

Critical researchers also employ an additional concept in studying the relationships among communication, power, and resistance—the concept of **hegemony** (Gramsci, 1971). As we saw in Chapter 2, hegemony refers to the ways a dominant group is able to get other groups to consent actively to the former's conception of reality. Hegemony operates when the taken-for-granted system of meanings that everyone shares functions in the best interests of the dominant group.

Critical sociologist Michael Burawoy (1979) provides an interesting example of hegemony "at work" (bad pun intended) in his ethnographic study of a machine tool factory. Burawoy begins his study by asking a question that upsets the taken-for-granted (i.e., dominant managerial) way of thinking about employees in the workplace. While a managerial orientation would start with the basic question, "Why don't workers work harder?" Burawoy begins with the question, "Why do workers work as hard as they do?" This simple shift in focus reorients our usual way of thinking about work. The hegemony of the managerial approach (i.e., a focus on efficiency, productivity, and profit) is so ingrained in all of us that it is hard for us to think any other way. Burawoy's question challenges our taken-for-granted sense of how the world works (i.e., that employees don't work as hard as they could and managers have the right to get them to work harder). His question makes the alternative assumption that employees already work harder than anyone has the right to expect them to; the real question is why is this the case?

> It wasn't long before I too was breaking my back to make out, to make the quota, to discover a new angle, and to run two jobs at once—risking life and limb for that extra piece. What was driving me to increase Allied's profits? Why was I actively participating in the intensification of my own exploitation and even losing my temper when I couldn't? (p. xi)

Burawoy's answer to this alternative question is an interesting one that draws heavily on issues of power, ideology, and hegemony. He argues that the workers create for themselves a game called "making out" in which their workplace identities become strongly invested in their ability to maximize their output and, hence, their pay (which is based on a piece-rate system). Different jobs in the plant have varying degrees of difficulty and thus vary in terms of workers' ability to "make out" (i.e., maximize pay) on a particular job. The workers thus engage in a process of negotiation for particular jobs, rates (how much they must produce to get a pay bonus), and information about how to maximize output on certain jobs. Thus, without management asserting any direct control at all, workers produce a culture in which all must adhere to the rules of the game of "making out" in order to be considered full-fledged members of that culture. In this sense, the game functions ideologically to produce a system of hegemony, creating a taken-for-granted organizational reality that serves the interests of the management (i.e., maximizing efficiency and profitability).

One of the ways ideology and hegemony work, then, is in creating a process of identification between employees and their organization (Cheney, 1991; Cheney & Tompkins, 1987). Organizational control is at its most effective when a sense of "we-ness" exists between employees and their company. When employees fail to differentiate between their own identities and that presented by their company, a strong sense of organizational identification exists and employees will actively pursue the interests of the organization.

From a critical perspective, the process of identification is not by definition problematic but becomes so only when a company uses it merely to promote efficiency and productivity over and above the well-being of its employees. For example, is a particular company actively promoting a sense of identification while at the same time ultimately treating employees as disposable commodities? In recent years, we have seen lots of examples of companies that exhort workers to make strong commitments to their organization, only to "downsize" them when profits fall. Sometimes companies lay off employees not because they are losing money but because they need to keep shareholders happy and improve quarterly earnings reports.

The critical perspective views this kind of organizational behavior as problematic for several reasons. First, it is exploitative in that it views workers as mere resources to be used and then discarded when they are no longer needed. Second, it is unethical because it misrepresents the relationship between employees and the organization. That is, the organization uses various identification techniques to create a sense of community amongst organization members, but in the final analysis, this sense of community is a fragile one that is frequently sacrificed to protect the company's bottom line. Finally, such behavior is problematic because it frequently distorts the role of work in employees' lives. In today's unstable corporate environment, employees are increasingly required to identify with their organizations in ways that eclipse other spheres of their lives, such as family and recreation. Critical researchers are thus concerned with how corporations work to create an organizational reality that swallows up employees' identities. Critical organizational communication scholar Stan Deetz (1992a) has referred to this phenomenon as the process of **corporate colonization**. Let's develop this idea in more detail.

Organizational Communication and Corporate Colonization

Deetz's (1992a) notion of corporate colonization is a useful way of coming to understand the role of the modern corporation in contemporary life. Deetz claims that the corporation has become *the* dominant institution in society, largely eclipsing religious, family, and community institutions in producing meaning, identity, and values. He argues that corporations not only attempt to shape our work lives but all other spheres of our lives, too. Thus, just as a powerful country might colonize less powerful countries as a way of extending its sphere of influence (e.g., the British Empire in the 19th century), so the modern corporation works to colonize all aspects of modern life.

Following philosopher Jürgen Habermas, Deetz (1992a) describes this process as the "colonization of the lifeworld," where *lifeworld* refers to the structures of beliefs, values, and meanings that make up our sense of community. The "corporate colonization of the lifeworld" thus highlights the modern corporation's efforts to shape fundamentally our beliefs, values, and meaning systems—that is, our very sense of identity as human beings in a social world.

One example of this process that occurs outside the immediate work setting involves the role of the corporation in our education system. Deetz (1992a) argues that the educational process has been subject to corporate colonization in a number of ways. First, the classical education aimed at developing a critically aware citizenry has been eroded by a view of education as involving skills training in preparation for the corporate world. In this sense, the development of a well-rounded individual takes a back seat to corporate needs for "well-trained" workers.

Second, students are increasingly being asked to take on the role of consumer, adopting a passive consumption orientation in their relationship to education (McMillan & Cheney, 1996). As we saw in Chapter 1, this consumer model tends to go hand in hand with a conduit model of communication that emphasizes information gathering over genuine engagement and struggle with difficult ideas. In this sense, education is viewed as a product to be consumed rather than an ongoing process to be engaged in. As a result, many students see cheating and plagiarism as acceptable means to reach a particular end (good grades and a marketable degree).

Third, knowledge itself tends to be presented in a prepackaged and easily consumed form, usually in the shape of textbooks—the medium "par excellence" for the dissemination of knowledge-as-information-transmission. Textbooks are rarely controversial, being strongly market driven and appealing to the lowest common denominator amongst students (Agger, 1991). In this sense, textbooks are defined more as commodities than as learning tools. Indeed, the fact that students routinely sell their textbooks at the end of the semester rather than keeping them as a learning resource further confirms the commodified, disposable nature of knowledge in the university that has been colonized by corporate ideology. As Deetz (1992a) suggests, textbooks teach the lesson that "learning should be quick and easy. Careful learning is costly and to be avoided" (p. 30). As a critical researcher who is writing a textbook (definitely a contradiction in need of examination!), my job is to help undermine dominant notions of what a textbook should be like and promote a sense of learning as engaging and dynamic. Only you can be the judge of whether I've succeeded or not.

The education system thus serves as an excellent example of how the "corporate colonization" process impacts our sense of identity and community. Our high schools and universities are increasingly subject to a corporate ideology that says learning should be an instrumental process that efficiently prepares students for entrance into the work world. In this sense, school molds us into good corporate "subjects."

Deetz (1992a) suggests further that the workplace itself is a critical site of decision making and identity formation in contemporary society. Who we are as people is strongly connected with our identities as workers (Kuhn, 2006). Corporations are well aware of this and thus spend a great deal of time, energy, and money indoctrinating people with their corporate philosophy. As a way of illustrating how this process of corporate colonization and identity formation occurs in the workplace, let's take a more detailed look at a specific example of critical research.

Engineering Culture

In a study of a high-tech engineering firm, Gideon Kunda (1992) provides a rich and detailed analysis of efforts to instill the dominant corporate culture in every employee. Using the term **normative control** (similar to the concept of "ideological control" discussed in Chapter 1) to describe this process, Kunda shows how the strategic practices of the corporate culture are aimed at the employee's very sense of self. Kunda describes the process of normative control in the following manner:

> The attempt to elicit and direct the required efforts of members by controlling the underlying experiences, thoughts, and feelings that guide their actions. Under

normative control, members act in the best interest of the company not because they are physically coerced, nor purely from an instrumental concern with economic rewards and sanctions. . . . Rather, they are driven by internal commitment, strong identification with company goals, intrinsic satisfaction from work. . . . In short, under normative control it is the employee's *self*—that ineffable source of subjective experience—that is claimed in the name of the corporate interest. (p. 11)

In his ethnographic study Kunda (1992) illustrates how those aspects of the self that have traditionally been considered private are increasingly "coming under corporate scrutiny and domination" (p. 13). Kunda shows how the company co-opts personal emotions, values, and beliefs in order to get employees to identify strongly with corporate goals.

For example, the company runs a "culture boot camp"—a 2-day workshop that indoctrinates new employees into the culture of the organization. The goal is not to teach employees about the formal structure of the company but how to "make sense" of the everyday organizational reality. Thus, new employees learn about the company's slogan, "Do what's right"—a phrase frequently uttered but never clearly defined. Indeed, it is the "strategic ambiguity" (Eisenberg, 1984) of this phrase and its multiple possible interpretations that aid in the process of normative control; the lack of a clear meaning leads employees to spend much time trying to figure out the corporation's expectations. As a result, employees invest a great deal of themselves in their work—working long hours, figuring out organizational politics, and taking work home—in the effort to be successful.

One of the consequences of this level of investment in the company is the phenomenon of "burnout"—a state in which employees experience a physical or even mental breakdown due to their high level of commitment to their work. The burnout phenomenon is a good example of the ambiguity that pervades the corporate culture. While members treat burnout as a serious and problematic condition that signals a loss of the ability to self-manage (coworkers with burnout are often treated as though they have a communicable disease), there is also a certain amount of pride and prestige within the culture attached to this condition; in other words, it is a visible demonstration of one's commitment to the company.

Kunda's study, then, draws attention to how even white-collar workers are subject to ever-increasing levels of control by their organizations. Indeed, we might argue that white-collar workers are subject to even greater levels of control than are blue-collar workers, precisely because the former often have a much closer identification between their sense of self and their jobs. Interestingly, in Kunda's study, only the professional employees are subject to normative control, while secretarial staff, temporary workers, and security guards are not integrated into the corporate culture, have few demands placed on them in terms of investment of self-identity, and thus occupy rather marginal organizational roles.

Resisting Corporate Colonization

As we discussed earlier, employees often resist organizational control efforts, and critical scholars have increasingly focused on the various ways organization members engage in individual and collective acts of resistance to corporate colonization efforts (Ball, 2005; Carlone & Larson, 2006; Ezzamel, Willmott, & Worthington, 2001; Fleming, 2007;

Humphreys & Brown, 2002; Mumby, 2005; Prasad & Prasad, 2000; Trethewey, 1997). This research recognizes that employees have a great deal of insight into the daily routines and practices of organizational life. Organization members frequently make sense of their organizational lives in subversive ways that run counter to the dominant corporate ideology. Thus, organization members can often carve out alternative ways of being an organization member. Many of these activities cannot be classified as outright resistance to organizational power but frequently involve either "undercover" forms of resistance (Scott, 1990) or else subtle efforts to co-opt dominant meanings to serve alternative purposes (e.g., Knights & McCabe, 2000a).

From a critical perspective, the efforts of organization members to engage in various forms of resistance point to significant ways in which the process of corporate colonization can be undermined. Such resistance is important because it not only represents a different way of looking at organizational life but also suggests the ways organizations exist as sites of contested meanings where alternative sense-making processes can develop. Let's examine more closely an example of research that focuses on employee resistance to corporate hegemony.

Digital Vision./Digital Vision/Thinkstock

Flight attendants are particularly subject to emotional labor.

The Hidden Resistance of Flight Attendants

A good example of an organizational environment that reflects the trend toward increasing levels of control over employees is the airline industry. With higher fuel prices and falling (or nonexistent) profit margins, the airlines have become increasingly concerned with staying competitive in a turbulent market. As a service industry, airlines focus heavily on interactions between employees and customers because they know the profitability of their company depends on the success and pleasantness (for the customer) of such interactions.

In a study we first encountered in Chapter 3, sociologist Arlie Hochschild (1983) examined the lengths to which airlines go to control the ways employees—particularly flight attendants—conduct themselves in interactions with customers. She showed that the demands of their job require flight attendants to engage in **emotional labor**—that is, "the management of feeling to create a publicly observable facial and bodily display" (p. 7). Flight attendants are required to employ their emotional expressions in the service of the company's need to please customers and make a profit. Thus, emotional labor "requires one to induce or suppress feeling in order to sustain the outward countenance that produces the proper state of mind in [passengers]" (p. 7).

Flight attendants are therefore trained to engage in a careful management of their public presentation of self, always exhibiting warmth and friendliness, even at times when their natural tendency might be to express very different emotions (e.g., when they are tired, frustrated, or dealing with the demanding jerk in Seat 23C). This corporate management of emotions is a form of control that can have serious consequences for the psychic well-being of employees who regularly experience large differences between felt emotions and publicly expressed emotions.

Corporations' ability to manage and control employee emotions and behavior, however, is not complete. In fact, employees can be amazingly inventive in their efforts to resist organizational control. For example, Hochschild (1983) illustrates how flight attendants respond to company efforts to get them to smile more often and "more sincerely" at more passengers. She states:

> The workers respond to the speed-up with a slowdown: they smile less broadly, with a quick release and no sparkle in the eyes, thus dimming the company's message to the people. It is a war of smiles. . . .
>
> The smile war has its veterans and its lore. I was told repeatedly, and with great relish, the story of one smile-fighter's victory, which goes like this. A young businessman said to a flight attendant, "Why aren't you smiling?" She put her tray back on the food cart, looked him in the eye, and said, "I'll tell you what. You smile first, then I'll smile." The businessman smiled at her. "Good," she replied. "Now freeze, and hold that for fifteen hours." Then she walked away. In one stroke, the heroine not only asserted a personal right to her facial expressions but also reversed the roles in the company script by placing the mask on a member of the audience. She challenged the company's right to imply, in its advertising, that passengers have a right to her smile. (pp. 127–128)

This example brings into sharp focus one of the key ways employee resistance occurs. That is, rather than engage in direct confrontation with the corporation (through strikes, for example), employees organize their resistance around the inherent ambiguity of corporate meanings. In this case, flight attendants engage in resistance by playing with the definition of what it means to smile. While they follow the company's requirement to engage in frequent smiling, they invest their smiles with their own meaning rather than the company's intended meaning. Their smiles say, "We resent company efforts to control our smiles!" rather than "I love my job, and I'll do everything I can to make your flight pleasant!" The flight attendant who confronted the businessman challenged the company more directly by questioning its right to control every aspect of her life. Nevertheless, her act of resistance is still rooted in the meaning implied in a smile or in its absence, and in her rejection of the dominant meaning of a smile. You might say that the flight attendants are engaged in a kind of "emotional systematic soldiering" (see Chapter 3).

Organizational communication scholar Alexandra Murphy (1998) has extended Hochschild's study by focusing more directly on flight attendant resistance to corporate control over their expressed emotions. In her study, she is interested in the **hidden transcripts** (Scott, 1990) of flight attendant resistance—that is, discourse and behavior that occur "offstage," outside the immediate view of those in power in an organization. Murphy identifies three distinct forms of resistance in her analysis: (1) resistance to gender hierarchy and status, (2) resistance to the regulation of movement and space, and (3) resistance to the regulation of appearance.

1. *Resistance to gender hierarchy and status.* While part of the public role of flight attendants is to function in a feminized, nurturing role, Murphy shows how flight attendants frequently violate this role behind the scenes. For example, employing humor and irony, flight attendants often undermine the authority of the (usually male) pilot by making fun of company guidelines that require them to keep pilots fully hydrated during flights by bringing them drinks. As one flight attendant stated:

> When I ask the pilots if I can get them a drink, I always ask them, "So, do you need to be hydrated? I don't want you all to die of dehydration in the next hour and a half." And then I throw in that my father is a urologist, and perhaps they might want me to remind them to go to the bathroom so that they don't get a kidney infection, too! Usually I only have to go in there once. They get their own drinks after that. (Murphy, 1998, p. 513)

2. *Resistance to the regulation of movement and space.* Murphy shows that one of the ways in which the airline attempts to control flight attendant behavior is by carefully restricting their movements during initial training. Female flight attendants are required to live on-site in a special training center where visitors (especially male ones) are not allowed and movements are carefully monitored with curfews and sign-in/sign-out procedures. There is also a resident "housemother," called "Momma Dot." The trainees describe this facility variously as the "convent" and "Barbie Bootcamp" (Murphy, 1983, p. 517).

Murphy (1983) shows how this attempt to restrict trainee movement is by no means complete, however, as the women engaged in various strategies to maneuver around the efforts to control them. For example, they manipulated the sign-in/out system in order to subvert the curfew and set up a communication system that informed them when "Momma Dot" was in her room and the coast was clear for them to leave the premises. Similarly, when, as qualified flight attendants, rumors of "ghost riders" (i.e., company supervisors who go undercover as passengers to check the quality of service) would circulate, the flight attendants shared information about ways to spot these "passengers." Thus, despite company efforts to regulate movement and space carefully, flight attendants became experts at circumventing these efforts.

3. *Resistance to regulation of appearance.* In recent years, flight attendants have been less subject to the careful control of appearance-related factors such as age and weight.

Female flight attendants no longer fall exclusively into the 120-pound, 20-something category. However, airlines still have tight regulations about such appearance factors as makeup, hairstyle, nail length and color, height of shoe heel, and so forth. Such regulations are an area of struggle for female flight attendants, who frequently rebel against the feminine image they are expected to project and opt for comfort and practicality instead. For example, some flight attendants wear shoes with heels only when a supervisor might see them. Others apply their makeup in a company-prescribed manner only for their yearly appearance checks. Thus, like the meaning of the smile, flight attendants resist company definitions of what it means to have a "professional" appearance. Again, because the meaning of the term *professional* is open to interpretation, flight attendants can strategically manipulate it for their own purposes.

It is certainly true that none of these examples of employee resistance is particularly profound or radical. Individually, they do little to challenge the existing power structure of the airline industry. However, it is worth noting that as a direct result of charges filed with the Equal Employment Opportunity Commission by a group of flight attendants against one airline, the practice of using standard weight tables to evaluate flight attendants was discontinued. (In her study, Murphy states that many trainee flight attendants referred to Sunday evening as "Ex-Lax night" as they attempted to conform to the weight standards of

Critical Technologies 7.1
Social Media as Resistance

The emergence over the past two decades of the Internet and social media has changed possibilities for organizational resistance and dissent. At a societal level, Twitter has proven to be more than just a way to keep up with Ashton Kutcher's every move, emerging as a critical organizational tool for protesters during the uprisings in Egypt and Tunisia in early 2011. It assisted antigovernment protesters' coordination efforts by allowing the fast dissemination of crucial information about protest gatherings. At the organizational level, disgruntled employees can use the anonymity of the web to criticize their place of work. Organizational communication scholars Loril Gossett and Julian Kilker (2006) report that thousands of websites are dedicated to such criticism, with names that often end in "sucks." Gossett and Kilker focus on one such website, RadioShackSucks.com, and show how it provides a forum for employees, ex-employees, and consumers to voice their feelings and opinions about the well-known electronics retailer. The advantage of such sites is that they provide a vehicle for resistance and dissent that lies outside the formal purview of the company. As such, employees who may feel vulnerable expressing dissent through formal

organizational channels are provided with an alternative forum. In addition, while dissenters and whistle-blowers often feel isolated from other organization members, such forums provide a sense of community and an experience of shared views with like-minded contributors to the site, thus providing opportunities for collective organizing.

Companies take such websites very seriously and, indeed, Gossett and Kilker (2006) report that in 2004 Radio Shack took out a court injunction against RadioShackSucks.com to prevent it from operating. In 2005 the company and the website reached a legal settlement that permitted the site to continue operating but restricted its ability to identify Radio Shack employees and managers by name.

Such use of social media also has a dark side. In the summer of 2011 rioters in various areas of London and other U.K. cities used Twitter and Facebook to stay one step ahead of the police and coordinate looting and burning in various communities. In one hotly debated case, two young men were given 4-year prison sentences for attempting to organize looting through social media, even though both efforts failed in their intended outcomes.

the Monday weigh-in sessions.) This is one example of the ways collective—rather than individual—forms of resistance to organizational power can lead to changes in working conditions for employees.

❖ CONCLUSION

This chapter has examined the dynamics of communication, power, and resistance as played out in organizational life. Starting from the premise that it is impossible to understand organizational communication processes without focusing on issues of power, critical scholars attempt to explore how organization members negotiate the complexities of organizational meaning systems. From a critical perspective, understanding organizational power involves gaining insight into how the struggle over organizational meaning occurs. Who has the resources to shape the meaning of the dominant organizational culture? In what ways are organization members subject to the hegemony of this dominant meaning system? How do organization members with fewer resources create alternative, resistant meanings for themselves? What communicative resources (stories, rituals, metaphors, etc.) do organization members utilize in this struggle over meaning? All these questions are central to critical organizational communication researchers in their efforts to explore the complexities of everyday organizational life.

I hope the above discussion has illustrated to you the complexities of control processes in everyday organizational life. Organizations do not simply exert control over passive employees. Rather, organization members actively contribute to organizational sense-making processes and frequently resist corporate efforts to impose a particular reality on them. However, in addressing power and resistance processes in organizations, it is important to keep in mind that we are not examining two distinct and separate processes. We oversimplify organizational life if we view some activities as reproducing the dominant organizational ideology and see others as resisting it. A more appropriate way of thinking about control and resistance is to see these activities in an interdependent relationship with one another. Just as the meaning of communication can be ambiguous, so the ways in which communication behavior fits into the overall control processes of an organization can be, too.

In this chapter we have focused on these issues through an in-depth exploration of the concepts of power, ideology, hegemony, corporate colonization, and resistance. We examined various conceptions of power, showing how Lukes's three-dimensional conception of power most adequately captures the intricacies of the influence process in organizations. Our exploration of the concept of ideology provided further insight into this process by showing how socially constructed ideas and meanings become reified, and their origins and interests hidden. Finally, we discussed how these concepts can be used to examine organizational life by looking at the phenomenon of corporate colonization. Here, we explored the ways corporate colonization is both widespread in our daily lives and subject to various forms of resistance by social actors.

CRITICAL APPLICATIONS

1. Conduct a "power analysis" of your day. How many different situations can you identify in which power is a contributing factor to your communication behavior? How many different perspectives on power can you identify in your analysis?

2. Can you think of work situations in which you have actively (or passively) resisted organizational control efforts? What was your motivation in these situations? What do you think should be the limits of the degree to which organizations can dictate or shape employee behavior?

KEY TERMS

community power debate   160

corporate colonization   171

elitists   160

emotional labor   175

hegemony   169

hidden transcripts   176

ideology   163

normative control   172

one-dimensional view of power   160

pluralists   160

power   157

three-dimensional view of power   163

two-dimensional view of power   160

STUDENT STUDY SITE

Visit the student study site at **www.sagepub.com/mumbyorg** for these additional learning tools:

- Web quizzes
- eFlashcards
- SAGE journal articles

- Video resources
- Web resources

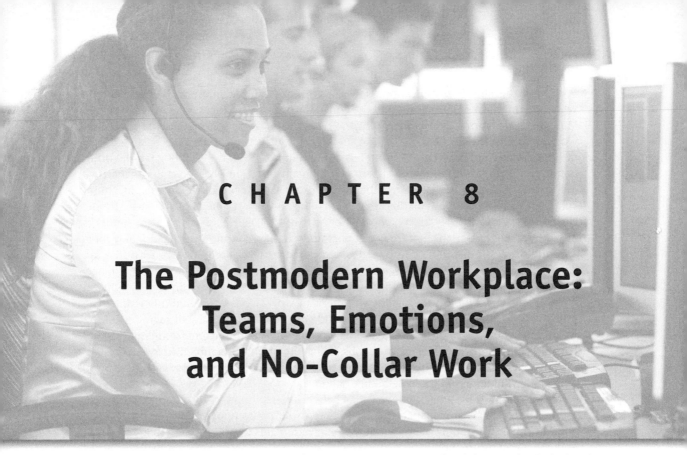

© iStockphoto.com/monkeybusinessimages

The postmodern workplace is built on new technologies and knowledge work.

CHAPTER 8

The Postmodern Workplace: Teams, Emotions, and No-Collar Work

The idea of the "postmodern organization" suggests the rejection of the principles of the modernist, bureaucratic organization that has been the benchmark for corporate and government structures for the past 100 years (Bergquist, 1992; Clegg, 1990). Where the modern organization embodied principles of stability, predictability, hierarchy, rules, and clear structure and function, the postmodern organization is organized around such issues as constant change, instability, flexibility, and empowerment. Business gurus speak of "thriving on chaos" (Peters, 1988) and "managing the art of irreversible change" (Bergquist, 1992). Furthermore, the postmodern organization is less about producing things and more about providing services, harnessing information technology, and developing brand identities (Klein, 2001). According to most business commentators, over the past 30 years we have shifted from a production-based to a service- and information-based economy. And because of the association of the old modernist, production-based organization with Henry Ford and his use of the moving production line, the new organizational form is often called "post-Fordist" (Harvey, 1989).

181

Clearly, this shift in organizational form has profound implications for both the people who work in those organizations and the consumers who buy their products and services. Many commentators have argued that the new organizational form has led to greater worker empowerment and participation, greater job satisfaction, and a more balanced view of the relationship between work and leisure (Bergquist, 1992; Roth, 2000). On the other hand, some scholars argue that the postmodern organization simply represents an increase in the level of organizational control that can be exercised over employees, albeit in a more subtle and unobtrusive fashion (Barker, 1999; Collinson, 2003; Deetz, 1992b, 1994b, 1994c; Knights, 1990; Kunda, 1992). Whichever view is true (and, as we'll see, there are elements of truth to both sides), the picture of the postmodern, 21st century organizational form is a complex one. Indeed, the complexities and paradoxes of contemporary work life are summed up by an issue of the *New York Times Magazine* devoted to the new workplace, titled "The liberated, exploited, pampered, frazzled, uneasy new American worker" (2000).

In recent years, however, this "new" American worker has earned another title—the **precariat** (Kalleberg, 2009; Ross, 2008). The title applies to workers in all segments of the workforce who find themselves in extremely precarious economic environments and are constantly under threat of losing their jobs, which are often "outsourced" to other companies in other countries. This phenomenon is heavily tied to the process of globalization, which we will address in some detail in Chapter 13.

It seems important, then, that we gain a better understanding of the changes in organizational life that have reshaped the landscape of the contemporary workplace. Indeed, whatever the truth about the postmodern organization, it is important to keep in mind that as current and future members of the workforce, you will be faced with many of the issues that will be discussed in this chapter.

First, in the next section, we will discuss the perspective on power that is typically associated with researchers who adopt a postmodern perspective on organizational life—disciplinary power. In particular, we will examine the work of French philosopher Michel Foucault, whose view of power has strongly influenced how scholars think about contemporary organizational life. Then, after comparing the Fordist and post-Fordist organizational forms, we will look at three specific features of the post-Fordist organization and how it shapes our everyday work lives.

❖ DISCIPLINARY POWER AND THE POSTMODERN ORGANIZATION

The postmodern perspective we discussed in Chapter 1 provides a new way of thinking about power and control, particularly as conceived in the work of French philosopher Michel Foucault. Stuart Hall (1997b) argues that Foucault's writings enable researchers to develop more sophisticated conceptions of how power operates in society. Rather than viewing power as something that is imposed on people from above (a modernist view of power) or that emanates from a single source (e.g., a dictator or the capitalist class), Foucault views power as widely dispersed in society, functioning like a network (or, as he puts it, in a capillary fashion). Furthermore, Foucault argues that power should not be viewed negatively (i.e., as oppressing people) but, rather, as *productive*. As he states, power "doesn't only weigh on us as a force that says no, but . . . it traverses and produces things, it induces pleasures, forms of knowledge, produces discourse" (Foucault, 1980b, p. 119).

By calling power "productive," Foucault is not arguing that it is good, or positive. Instead, he is trying to move us away from the traditional conception of power as prohibiting, coercing, or preventing (a form of power he calls "sovereign power") and toward a view in which power is studied as a basic, constitutive feature of everyday life (which he calls **disciplinary power**, as discussed in Chapter 1). Indeed, part of his strategy is to shift our perspective away from looking at power on a grand scale and, instead, toward examining the way power works at a "micro" level, permeating everything we do. Foucault shows that power works in this fashion through the emergence of various discourses that both create and provide possibilities for thinking about and acting toward particular phenomena.

For example, in his various historical (what he calls "genealogical") studies, Foucault has examined phenomena as diverse as sexuality, madness, and forms of punishment (Foucault, 1979, 1980a, 1988). In each case he shows that such phenomena "only exist meaningfully *within* the discourses about them" (Hall, 1997b, p. 45). Thus, modern conceptions of sexuality began to emerge only with the proliferation in the 19th century of various discourses that attempted to define and control sexuality (Foucault, 1980a). Foucault makes the interesting point that if we use a negative, coercive model of power, then we see the Victorian era only as repressing sexuality and "sweeping it under the carpet." However, his discursive, productive model of power illustrates how it is only through a general "incitement to discourse" about sexuality during this period that it becomes definable and controllable in certain ways.

For example, it is in the Victorian era that homosexuality is first officially separated from "normal" sexuality and criminalized. Hence, homosexuals for the first time are created as an identifiable and separate group that can be constructed as "deviant" and hence controlled. Thus, power, through discourse, produces a particular "regime of knowledge" that makes possible a certain identifiable form of subjectivity, or identity (homosexuality) in order that it can be "disciplined" (to use Foucault's term).

Thus, Foucault's most important contribution to the postmodern study of organizations (even though he wasn't an organization researcher) is that he provides an insightful conception of the relationships among discourse, power, identity, and institutions. Indeed, in recent years Foucault's writings have been widely used by management and organizational communication researchers alike as a way of generating insight into the post-Fordist organization, particularly given the ways that it uses new forms of disciplinary power to shape employee identities (Burrell, 1988; Clegg, 1989, 1994; Deetz, 1994a; Jermier, Knights, & Nord, 1994; Kondo, 1990; Tracy, 2000). We will examine some of this research below.

❖ THE POSTMODERN ORGANIZATION: FROM FORDISM TO POST-FORDISM

The shift to the postmodern organization implies the emergence of particular kinds of organizational structures, processes, and sensibilities that distinguish it from the modern organization. In other words, when we talk about the postmodern organization, we are referring to an organizational form that has a particular, identifiable set of features, as well as a particular way of thinking about work. As is the case with other changes in organizational forms we have discussed in earlier chapters, the postmodern organization did not appear out of nowhere. Rather, it is a response to transformations in the economic and political climate of industrial nations. In brief, we can argue that the emergence of this new organizational form occurred as a result of a more volatile and competitive economic environment, in which the relatively slow-to-change bureaucratic form was no longer viewed as functional. As such, many organizations developed leaner, meaner, and more flexible structures that could quickly respond to perceived changes in the increasingly globalized economic environment.

However, this shift is also political in that, beginning in the 1980s, shareholders became a much more powerful force than ever before in organizations, and companies became increasingly beholden to their quarterly reports (Ho, 2009). Decisions to "right-size," reorganize, reengineer (or whatever term was current) thus became more about short-term returns to shareholders than about the long-term health of the organization. As we talk about this transformation, then, it's important to keep in mind that changes in the workplace and the nature of work and organizing are as much about power and politics as they are about creating more efficient, more effective organizations.

First, let's compare and contrast the features of the modern, Fordist organization and the postmodern, post-Fordist organization.

The Fordist Organization

Fordism can be characterized by the following features:

1. *A highly bureaucratic organizational structure.* This involves a clear chain of command, rigidly defined roles, and an extremely centralized decision-making system. The military is the archetypal example of such a bureaucratic form, where strict adherence to chain of command is imperative for the execution of military strategy. In civilian life, government agencies tend to be highly bureaucratic in structure.

2. *A highly differentiated labor process.* In the Fordist organization, most production jobs are generally unskilled or semiskilled, with the labor process itself broken down into its basic components. Workers may have little or no knowledge of how the entire production process operates. For example, McDonald's produces a 700-page operations manual that dictates in minute detail every employee task and organizational function. Charlie Chaplin's film *Modern Times* is a classic parody of work on the Fordist assembly line.

3. *Large economies of scale.* Many Fordist organizations are designed along mass-production principles, with huge levels of investment in plants, machinery, and a large workforce. Profitability is based on the ability to produce goods in large quantities, cheaply and efficiently. For example, the Foxconn company in China—a major outsourcing firm that makes iPads, Kindles, and Xboxes, among other products—employs more than 800,000 workers. Despite small profit margins on its products, its net income in 2010 was $2.2 billion, due mainly to its sheer size and large economies of scale.

4. *Standardization of products.* The more standardized a product is, the more cheaply and efficiently it can be produced (because the work process does not have to be changed constantly to adjust to product variation). Henry Ford once famously said that the consumer could have any color car he wanted, as long as it was black!

5. *Stable, lifetime employment.* While this characteristic varied from industry to industry, the employment norm in the 1950s and 1960s (the height of the Fordist organization) was for employees to spend their entire working lives with the same organization. A social contract between workers and employers ensured job security and benefits in exchange for company loyalty.

6. *The transfer of these Fordist principles to society as a whole.* In this sense—and particularly after World War II—Fordism became not just a system of production but also a lifestyle for people. This meant mass consumption of standardized products, homes in the suburbs that all looked alike, and the creation of a mass popular culture. One of the reasons why Henry Ford introduced the $5, 8-hour workday in 1914 was to help stimulate the economy by providing workers with sufficient disposable income and leisure time. Ford also tried to make sure that his employees were responsible workers and consumers; employing an army of social workers, he monitored their home lives for signs of "deviant" behavior outside the workplace (drunkenness, immoral sexual behavior, etc.).

Of course, the Fordist organization is not obsolete. Many corporations still produce large quantities of standardized goods, and some industries are relatively immune to changes in the economy. However, there has been a significant shift in the past 30 years to a post-Fordist, postmodern organizational structure.

The Post-Fordist Organization

The basic characteristics of **post-Fordism** are as follows:

1. *The development of a more flexible organizational structure.* Geographer David Harvey (1991) has outlined three dimensions of flexibility that characterize the post-Fordist organization. These include (a) flexibility in relation to the work process itself (e.g., job enrichment, work teams, decentralized decision making, etc.); (b) flexibility in labor markets (the extensive use of subcontracting and part-time and temporary employees); and (c) greater geographic mobility, including the development of telecommuting and the shifting of manufacturing to wherever labor is cheapest (i.e., outsourcing).

2. *The development of a "dedifferentiated" labor process* (Clegg, 1990). Post-Fordist organizations have increasingly recognized the importance of their "human capital" (i.e., employees) and tap into the large stock of knowledge workers possess about the work they do. The "knowledge worker" thus takes center stage; work is not divided among many deskilled workers but comes together in the knowledge worker. Hence, employees are not provided with a narrowly defined job description and set of rules and guidelines; rather, they are encouraged to use their initiative to carve out their own sphere of responsibility and competence (Stark,

2009). For example, in his study of Gore Company (makers of Gore-Tex), Mike Pacanowsky (1988) describes how new employees are not given a job description but, rather, are encouraged to develop their own networks and define their own roles in the company.

3. *Limited production runs and the development of "niche" markets.* While the post-Fordist organization has shifted toward dedifferentiation of the work process, it has moved in the opposite direction in the area of consumption, targeting specific groups of customers. Such an orientation to the market can succeed only if companies develop flexible and adaptable systems of production. This involves the use of "just-in-time" (JIT) production methods (i.e., the maintenance of minimal inventories that speed up production and allow fast retooling for new products) and the employment of information technologies to allow companies to adapt quickly to changing consumer patterns. Thus, it is fairly routine these days to be able to order items ranging from sneakers to automobiles that are tailored to the specific desires of the consumer. For example, I suspect a number of you have ordered sneakers online for which you designed your own color scheme and perhaps added a stitched, personalized message.

4. *The increased commodification of everyday life and the creation of products as lifestyles* (Hall, 1991). While Fordism is a production-based economy, post-Fordism is a consumption-based economy with a massive shift toward the creation of services and lifestyles for people. As such, the brand takes center stage in post-Fordism. While we will devote Chapter 12 to branding and consumption, it's important to note here that while branding of products has been around for 150 years, it has taken a particular turn in the past 20 years, as companies increasingly shape people's everyday lives and identities through branding (Klein, 2001). In this sense, people are increasingly defined (and define themselves) as consumers rather than as citizens. Moreover, in a consumption-based economy, everything is potentially brandable, from individual people to water. This shift from a production-based to a consumption-based economy is perhaps best encapsulated by Nike Chairman Phil Knight's invocation of the mantra, "Brands, not products." In other words, post-Fordist companies do not sell products but, rather, lifestyles and systems of meaning.

5. *Increasingly unstable, insecure employment.* Workers in the post-Fordist organization face an increasingly precarious work environment, as companies constantly adapt to changing economic conditions and the need to stay competitive in a turbulent marketplace. Few industries provide the stable, lifetime employment of the Fordist era, with workers changing jobs an average of 11 times during their working lives. Part-time and temporary work is increasingly the norm, and companies frequently outsource work to countries with lower labor costs and less-restrictive labor laws. Moreover, the shift to a consumption-based economy has led to a decline in blue-collar manufacturing work and an increase in low-wage pink-collar (female) and white-collar work in the service sector (Kalleberg, 2009).

6. *A blurring of the modernist distinction between work and home.* Along with the increasingly precarious employment picture are greater demands on employees' sense of self. Although companies no longer provide stable employment, they frequently demand a level of commitment from employees that goes well beyond 9 to 5. Post-Fordist organizations often not only expect employees to take work home but also try to create the home at work. For example, corporate campuses are self-contained worksites that often provide all the amenities (child care, Bible study, medical facilities, gyms, etc.) for a "well-rounded" life (Mansnerus, 1999; Useem, 2000). Richard Florida (2003) has stated that, in many respects, the implicit statement to employees behind such work culture engineering is, "No need to go wandering off; stay right here at work" (p. 123). In other words, many of the distinctions between work and other aspects of our lives (including family and social life) have been subtly and not-so-subtly eroded by the post-Fordist work environment. Although many of these perks have disappeared with the long-term economic recession, companies still try to create employees whose sense of self is intimately tied to their professional selves. If we add to this picture the communication technologies that enable work to be performed almost anywhere, then it is clear that a corporate logic and value system pervades all spheres of life in the post-Fordist organization. As we discussed in Chapter 7, the idea of "corporate colonization" (Deetz, 1992a) effectively characterizes this increasing blurring of the corporate world and the social world of self, family, and community. What happens, then, when the company we work for is the primary provider of the sense of community that makes us human? What are the consequences of privatizing community? If corporations are creating branded lifestyles for us as consumers, and creating communities in the places where we work, what's left of our lives that is not a postmodern corporate construction?

Now that we have compared the Fordist and post-Fordist organization (see Table 8.1 for a summary of their differences), let's examine in a little more detail three of the central features of the latter. First, we will look at a feature of the shift to a more decentralized organizational form and examine work teams. Second, we will address the fact that post-Fordist organizations are more consumption based and service oriented by looking at the phenomenon of emotional labor. And third, we will examine the emergence of "no-collar" and precarious work in the current economic and organizational environment.

❖ THE POST-FORDIST ORGANIZATION: TEAMS, EMOTIONS, AND NO-COLLAR WORK

Teams at Work

In many respects, the emergence of **work teams** and the "team-based organization" (Mohrman, Cohen, & Mohrman, 1995) is a throwback to an earlier period in the history of work when workers functioned together in skilled, self-organizing groups, largely

Table 8.1   Comparing Fordist and Post-Fordist Organizations

Fordist Organization	Post-Fordist Organization
Inflexible bureaucratic hierarchy	Flexible, decentralized structure
Lifetime work, social contract	"Free agency," temporary workers, the "precariat"
Differentiated, deskilled labor process	Dedifferentiated, enriched labor process
Manual work	Knowledge work
Production oriented: • Large economies of scale • Mass production • Fixed production • Standardization of products	Consumption oriented: • Small economies of scale • Limited production and niche markets • Flexible production (e.g., JIT) • Branding—products as expressions of individual "lifestyles"
Separation of work and home	Blurring of work and home
"Old technologies" (machines, moving production lines)	"New technologies" (communication systems, virtual workplaces)
Bureaucratic control	Disciplinary control

determining how (and how quickly) work was performed. Indeed, if you recall our discussion of scientific management in Chapter 3, one of Taylor's principal goals in developing a new system of work was to break up the informal group that—through systematic soldiering—dictated the pace of work. Such work groups did not exist only in factory settings but also in industries such as coal mining, where miners worked in teams not as a way to limit output but as the most effective way to perform a difficult, dirty, and dangerous job.

Interestingly, some of the earliest research on organizational teams was conducted on coal miners by industrial psychologist Eric Trist and his colleagues (Trist & Bamforth, 1951; Trist, Higgin, Murray, & Pollock, 1963). In this research the focus was on the relationship between different forms of work organization and the introduction of new technologies into the British coal-mining industry after World War II. Trist and Bamforth (1951) describe the organization of work in the traditional "hand-got" (nonmechanized) form of mining in the following manner:

A primary work-organization of this type has the advantage of placing responsibility for the complete coal-getting task squarely on the shoulders of a single, small, face-to-face group which experiences the entire cycle of operations within the compass of its membership. For each participant the task has total significance and dynamic closure. . . . Leadership and "supervision" were internal to the group, which had a quality of *responsible autonomy*. (p. 6)

Trist and Bamforth (1951) indicate that in these groups (usually 2–4 workers) each member possessed a full range of work skills, such that each could substitute for any of the others. Moreover, each worker "had craft pride and artisan independence" (p. 6). Workers chose their own workmates, resulting in stable relationships that sometimes lasted for many years. If a worker was injured or killed, it was not uncommon for his workmates to care for his family. Trist and his colleagues examined how the introduction of technology and the shift to "longwall" mining (involving groups of 40–50 men) changed the nature of work and largely destroyed the system of "responsible autonomy."

This early research set the stage for several decades of study regarding the effectiveness of workplace teams. Although there are numerous definitions and types of teams, a useful starting point is the following definition by management scholars Susan Cohen and Diane Bailey (1997):

A team is a collection of individuals who are interdependent in their tasks, who share responsibility for outcomes, who see themselves and who are seen by others as an intact social entity embedded in one or more large social systems. (p. 241)

This definition stresses the interdependence of team members, not only in terms of the work tasks they must perform but also regarding their mutual perceptions as constituting a distinct social collective. In this sense, work teams are inherently communicative.

Research on work teams has investigated numerous factors relating to their performance in organizations (see Cohen & Bailey, 1997, for a review of this research). These include the following:

- *Task design*. How does the composition and complexity of tasks affect team performance?
- *Group composition*. How do factors such as team size, diversity, and experience of members impact work teams?
- *Organizational context* includes factors such as the reward system and the form of supervision work teams experience.
- *Internal processes* relate to the degree of collaboration and/or conflict in which team members engage.
- *Group psychological traits* involve the ways in which the degree of cohesiveness and group norm development affect team performance. What is the affective tone of the group? Is it positive or negative?
- *Effectiveness*. Team effectiveness has been examined not only in terms of productivity but also through other factors such as job satisfaction, commitment, amount of absenteeism, and turnover.

The management fascination with work teams has become even more intense given the shift to post-Fordist organizational forms. As organizations have become more decentralized and less hierarchical, work teams are seen as the ideal decision-making structure in an economic environment that requires flexibility, adaptability, and innovation. From a management perspective, then, the advantages of work teams include the following:

- Empowerment of workers by enabling them to play a more direct role in organizational decision making
- Development of a workforce that is multiskilled rather than deskilled
- Development of holistic team synergies (think systems theory) that often result in more innovative decision making
- Subordination of individual employees' agendas to the collective task of the team
- Higher-quality decisions as a result of the pooling of team member talents
- Functional autonomy, with little need for direct supervision
- Greater commitment of employees to organizational goals
- Increased organizational productivity

However, while management researchers and practitioners alike have extolled the virtues of work teams as a way to both improve the organization's bottom line and empower workers, a number of critical scholars have placed these claims under considerable scrutiny. Let's look at some of these criticisms.

Critiquing Work Teams

While there is a large body of research that attempts to establish the effectiveness of work teams, a significant number of researchers have questioned their role in organizational life (Barker, 1993, 1999; Doorewaard & Brouns, 2003; Ezzamel & Willmott, 1998; Knights & McCabe, 2000b; Sewell, 1998; Sinclair, 1992).

Management scholar Amanda Sinclair (1992) is pretty unambiguous in her critique of the existing research on work teams, describing it as "the tyranny of a team ideology" (p. 611). Sinclair argues that management research on teams seems less interested in empirical investigation of their merits and limitations and more interested in creating an ideology that uncritically celebrates their virtues. She argues that, "the hegemony of the [team] ideology has created a tyranny of oppressive stereotypes fed by a team-building industry" (p. 621), where teams are presented as the models of consensus building and where critical issues such as power, leadership, and conflict are underplayed. Sinclair indicates that research often ignores the fact that team membership can be stressful and dissatisfying, and that power seeking by group members is a routine feature of team life. Sinclair does not argue that teams are inherently bad; rather, she expresses concern that a narrow ideology is driving research.

The idea of teams as "management by stress" (Parker & Slaughter, 1988) is taken up by a number of critical researchers. In her ethnographic study of a Subaru-Isuzu automobile plant, sociologist Laurie Graham (1993) examines how the apparent increase in worker control and participation enabled by the Japanese system of **kaizen** (a process-oriented continuous improvement method of work; literally, "change for the better") actually resulted in tighter control and more stress on employees. Workers were assigned to teams of 12 that performed a specific set of tasks in the vehicle assembly process. Graham refers to "tact time" as the time required for each worker to complete all the tasks assigned to him or her on each vehicle as it moved through the work station. At her station, Graham performed 22 tasks in the 5 minutes allotted (as the plant got more efficient, this time was cut to 3 minutes and 40 seconds). Stress arose from a number of sources, including workers who worked too slowly and then experienced peer pressure from teammates to speed up; team leaders putting pressure on members to work faster; management speeding up the work process; and arbitrary, last-minute requests from management to work overtime.

Although the philosophy of kaizen is intended as a participatory model of work where employees are directly involved in the improvement process, Graham (1993) documents the amount of stress workers experience, indicating that the goal of kaizen "was for workers to be working every second of every minute" (p. 160). Interestingly, in a study in the same plant some years later, organizational communication researcher Heather Zoller (2003) reported that tact time had shrunk to 1 minute and 54 seconds and that a number of workers were experiencing repetitive stress injuries as a result of their work.

But perhaps the most intriguing examination of autonomous work teams is organizational communication scholar Jim Barker's case study of a high-tech company's shift from a traditional bureaucratic organizational structure to a flatter, decentralized form of decision making (Barker, 1993, 1999). He shows how the shift simultaneously gave employees a much greater level of participation in the organization's daily functioning and introduced a system of power and control far more pervasive and insidious than the previous bureaucratic system. Indeed, it is a great example of Foucault's disciplinary power in operation.

Barker shows how the company literally switched overnight from its traditional, bureaucratic decision-making system to a decentralized system in which employees were organized into autonomous work teams with complete control over decisions about the work process. Faced with this new structure, employees were at first unsure how to behave. What if they did something wrong? The company president assured them that there were no "wrong" decisions and that, while he was available for advice, he would not intervene in their discussions about how to organize their work. Barker illustrates how, over time, this apparent freedom in decision making evolved into a system of self-generated **concertive control** that informed everything the team members did.

Following Tompkins and Cheney (1985), Barker (1993) argues that under concertive control the locus of authority shifts from the impersonal bureaucratic system of rules to the "value consensus of its members and its socially created generative rules system" (p. 412). In other words, while in a bureaucratic structure employees might come to work on time because the rules say they must and they'll get in trouble if they don't; under a system of concertive control an employee will arrive on time because the team members have collectively generated a "value premise" within which timeliness is seen as integral to both the successful performance of work and the team's own definition of excellence. In this sense, employees are unable to argue that the system of rules was simply imposed on them. Furthermore, employees operate according to a self-generated set of values rather than a set of bureaucratic rules, the reasons for which may not even be apparent.

In Barker's (1993) study, then, he describes how this system of concertive control emerges from the employee teams, creating a level of oversight and surveillance that is far more extensive than anything that occurred under the old bureaucratic model. In other words, the form of control exercised is from the bottom up rather than the top down. As one team member states, "I don't have to sit there and look for the boss to be around; and if the boss is not around, I can sit there and talk to my neighbor or do what I want. Now the whole team is around me and the whole team is observing what I'm doing" (p. 408).

Barker's study makes clear that in the post-Fordist workplace one of the principal struggles for power and control occurs around the construction of workplace identities. Again building on the work of Foucault, scholars have explored how employees have become particular "objects of knowledge" who are "disciplined" to behave as a "good employee" (lest they be revealed as a bad employee!). This move also includes employees' view of *themselves* as objects of self-knowledge; that is, by virtue of the panoptical effect of disciplinary discourses, employees routinely scrutinize their own behaviors and attitudes to see if they match up to espoused organizational standards.

Interestingly, Melissa Gregg's (2011) study of the impact of communication technology on work–home relationships seems to support the findings of researchers such as Barker and Sinclair. Gregg shows that even virtual work teams can have a coercive, disciplinary effect on employees. Indeed, consistent with critical research on teams, she finds that members of online teams feel greater pressure to be in regular communication with other team members than they would with their managers in a conventional organizational hierarchy. Not surprisingly, appropriate e-mail etiquette proved to be the hardest issue to negotiate in virtual teams, with team members feeling the need to be responsive to maintain team solidarity and yet often frustrated by the sheer volume of e-mails sent by some team members. In fact, online communication often seemed to function as a substitute for face-to-face interaction, or else was used to avoid dealing with an issue more directly with a phone call. Ultimately, Gregg argues that the work team "is one of several coercive dimensions of office culture exacerbated by new media technologies" (p. 74). Critical Technologies 8.1 addresses the issue of communication among virtual team members.

Before we end our discussion of work teams, let's briefly look at one high-profile case of the failure of a team system. In 1992 Levi Strauss, makers of the iconic Levi's jeans, converted its U.S. plants from a piecework system, in which each individual worker was paid according to his or her productivity at a single, specialized task (sowing zippers, attaching belt loops, etc.), to a team-based system, in which teams of 10 to 35 workers were paid according to the total output of the group (King, 1998). While the shift was heralded as an important effort to empower workers, reduce stress, and improve productivity, the opposite actually happened. As *Wall Street Journal* reporter Ralph King (1998) states:

> [The team system] led to a quagmire in which skilled workers . . . found themselves pitted against slower colleagues, damaging morale and triggering corrosive infighting. . . . Threats and insults became more common. Longtime friendships dissolved as faster workers tried to banish slower ones. (p. 1)

Moreover, in the first year of the team system, productivity fell by almost 25% while labor costs rose by the same amount. At the same time, the wages of the top performers under the old piece-rate system fell, while the slower workers saw their wages increase under the new system (because of the group payment system). As a result, faster, more-skilled workers cut back on their productivity. As one worker stated, "You felt cheated because you are making less, so why give them 120%?"

Critical Technologies 8.1
Virtual Teams

While most organizational teams work in face-to-face contexts, the increasingly global nature of work and organizing means that work teams are often virtual. That is, team members are often separated by thousands of miles and several time zones, perhaps "meeting" together on an irregular basis. Such virtual teams find it harder to develop a strong team dynamic and connections among members. The development of trust among members can be a particular problem. One of the ways virtual team researchers have attempted to address this problem is by developing communication rules that apply specifically to the virtual team context. Communication researchers Joseph Walther and Ulla Bunz (2005) lay out these communication rules for virtual teams:

Get started with tasks right away. Teams tend to procrastinate anyway over tasks, but the problem is worse in a virtual situation where members may have more difficulty coordinating.

Communicate frequently. Communicating a lot tends to increase trust among members and limits misunderstandings. It also prevents tasks piling up toward the end of the team members' time together.

Multitask getting organized and doing substantive work simultaneously. Face-to-face teams usually get organized and define and allocate tasks before executing them. But this linear approach can be counterproductive in virtual teams. Often it is more effective and a better use of precious time to start some substantive tasks before settling on group processes.

Explicitly acknowledge that you have read one another's messages. Often members of virtual teams assume a common stock of knowledge when it does not actually exist, so it's important that messages are explicitly acknowledged so everyone stays on the same page.

Be explicit about what you are thinking and doing. While the use of Skype and other forms of video conferencing have increased the role of nonverbal communication in virtual teams, much communication still takes place through text-only media. Explicitly communicating ideas and actions with other team members helps improve trust and increase the stock of common knowledge.

Set deadlines and stick to them. Because there is less perceived accountability in virtual groups, it's important that team members can be counted on and that tasks are accomplished in a timely manner. Timely completion also increases trust among team members.

Some of these rules may seem obvious, but sometimes it's taking care of the little, apparently obvious things that can be the difference between success and a failed team process. There's a strong likelihood that you will participate on virtual teams during your professional life, and these are not bad rules to live by. However, given Melissa Gregg's (2011) research on virtual work teams, discussed above, it's also important to "metacommunicate" about the communication process. For example, discussions about what "communicate frequently" means for team members might help avoid problems in team processes; frequent communication may build trust, but it can also produce frustration when overdone.

Ironically, Levi Strauss had long been seen as an industry leader, frequently being ranked as one of the best companies to work for, and had made the decision to switch to a team-based system as a way of protecting its U.S. plants from the competition of cheap jeans made overseas. But in the wake of the shift, workers experienced much greater levels of stress and morale plummeted. Many workers experienced peer pressure and even coworker threats if they failed to maintain productivity. "You can't pit one person against the other and expect it to work," said a worker who quit due to the stress created by the team environment. In 1997, Levi-Strauss closed 11 of its U.S. factories and laid off 6,000 employees—one third of its U.S. workforce.

So how should we assess work teams? They are certainly not a panacea for organizational problems, nor are they inherently evil. Under the right circumstances they can empower workers, increase the quality of the work experience, and improve decision making. But team systems have to be implemented carefully and with input from all the interested stakeholders, including the employees themselves. In addition, team members must be given adequate training in team processes, including task, decision-making, and leadership skills. Too often team systems fail because they are imposed on workers from above—ironic, if you think about, because they are meant to empower employees and make work more participatory.

Let's now turn to a discussion of the relationship between emotions and work in the post-Fordist workplace.

Emotions at Work

With the emergence of a service-based, post-Fordist economy in the past 30 years researchers in the fields of organizational communication, management, and sociology have examined many of the consequences of bringing emotion into the work environment (e.g., Bolton, 2005; Fineman, 2000; Martin, Knopoff, & Beckman, 1998; Pierce, 1995; Raz, 2002; Tracy, 2000, 2005). Here, we are not concerned with the spontaneous expression of emotion (joy, sadness, empathy, guilt, and so forth) that people routinely experience in their everyday organizational lives. Rather, this research looks at organizational situations in which management deliberately and systematically harnesses employee emotions as a way to improve the bottom line. Any service industry involving direct interaction between employees and customers—from airlines to hotels to restaurants to telephone call centers, and so forth—utilizes emotion in this manner, and it is a relatively new means by which organizations exercise control over employees.

In Chapters 3 and 7 we briefly discussed the phenomenon of **emotional labor**, first developed by sociologist Arlie Hochschild (1983) as a way to explain how organizations increasingly draw on employees' emotions in addition to their physical and intellectual labor. Emotional labor involves situations in which employees are required to express emotions according to the emotional display rules developed by companies in order to maximize customer satisfaction. According to Hochschild, these are situations in which emotions are "processed, standardized and subject to hierarchical control" (p. 153). In this context, emotions are used as a way to increase, as Karl Marx might say (and as discussed in Chapter 2), the "surplus value" of work. As organizational communication scholar Sarah Tracy (2005) indicates, "For service professionals . . . a pleasant emotional façade is part of the commodity being bought and sold" (p. 263). And, of course, this is something we have all come to expect as consumers in a service economy; we are easily irritated when we do not receive prompt and courteous "service with a smile" in response to all our requests, however demanding they might be.

However, such service positions can be highly stressful. One of Hochschild's (1983) main findings was that service industry employees often experience "emotional dissonance"; that is, a conflict between the emotional displays in which they are required to engage and the inner feelings they are actually experiencing. Such emotional dissonance can lead to a variety of problems, including stress, job burnout, emotional numbness, alienation from self, and a general cynicism toward work.

Sarah Tracy (2000) provides a vivid and insightful analysis of her own experience as a member of the staff aboard a cruise ship and details the ways her emotions were used instrumentally by the cruise company to entertain the guests aboard the ship. In her role as a member of the entertainment staff, she was informed by a colleague that "I should turn on my smile in the morning and not turn it back off again until I went to sleep" (p. 108). Her dominant experience was one of being a member of a "total institution" (an organization, like a prison or mental institution, that dictates every aspect of a person's life) that regulates how she should feel, act, and dress. In other words, she was required to draw continually on her personal feelings and emotions in order to provide the best possible service to the cruise line's customers. Tracy experienced extreme emotional dissonance when, after receiving news that her grandmother had passed away, she had to work a regular shift on the cruise ship, including performing in a stage show and "dancing around in costume with a bunch of drunk passengers" (p. 116).

This is certainly a vivid example of how, in the post-Fordist organization, employees are increasingly being asked to utilize what are considered key dimensions of our sense of self. This focus on emotional labor is a key feature of what many commentators have noted is an increasingly fuzzy boundary between work and home. Companies are increasingly utilizing aspects of our personal lives traditionally considered separate from work. Emotions used to be a fairly personal thing, but they are now fair game for corporate control. In other words, the issues that the (post)modern worker faces involve not only work entering the nonwork realm but also personal life entering work (Fleming, 2009).

And, increasingly, it is not only the point of interaction between employees and customers that is the focus of managerial attention. Journalist Dominic Rushe (2007) reports that many companies—from Google to Southwest Airlines to Anheuser-Busch—explicitly cultivate "cultures of fun" at work, leading to the emergence of "fun-sultants" who charge big bucks to show executives how to make their work environments more fun and exciting for employees. As the saying goes, fun is now serious business. The rationale for this is, in part, that workers from the post–baby-boom generations (X, Y) are not prepared to adopt the same workaholic attitude as their baby-boomer parents did, and, hence, they demand not only a greater work–life balance but also work that is not just daily drudgery.

Critical management scholar Peter Fleming (2009) has explored in detail this emergence of a "culture of fun" and a "just be yourself" ethos in the contemporary organization, arguing that such a development involves the manufacture of "individualized conformism" (p. 8). Fleming suggests that corporate efforts to get employees to bring their "authentic" selves to the workplace are the next step in the evolution of control processes. Here, the blurring of work and personal lives enables corporations to utilize previously protected aspects of the self for economic gain.

Fleming illustrates how workers are encouraged to be themselves but only to a point; self-expression is carefully circumscribed to include only those behaviors and identity-management activities that serve the company. Thus, Sarah Tracy was not able to "be herself" and express sadness at her grandma's passing, except out of sight of passengers. And Southwest Airlines' culture of fun encourages self-expression, but it's amazing how many of the same jokes one will hear over the PA on different Southwest flights! Similarly, the "spontaneous" songs of employees at Cold Stone Creamery are carefully prescribed by the corporation, with its website addressing potential employees in the following manner:

Wanted: People Who Know How to Have Fun!

Cold Stone Creamery is the hottest retail food concept in the nation, and you just may have what it takes to join the team. Because we're such a fun place to work (it's ice cream, after all), we attract a large number of applicants, allowing us to hire some of the best people around. If you've got the right stuff, we'd love to hear from you! (http://www.coldstonecreamery.com/jobs/best_jobs.html)

Interestingly, Cold Stone Creamery holds auditions, not interviews, and describes employees as "creating an experience for every person who walks in the door." And you thought you were just buying ice cream. Personally, I can't bear to go into Cold Stone Creamery, because all that carefully engineered fun drives me nuts; I object to the fact that someone thinks I need to be entertained while standing in line for ice cream! Call me a curmudgeon. I do find it fascinating, however, that in a world where everything is branded, it's no longer possible for us just to buy something—we are required to have an *experience*. But the experience is carefully prescribed for us; in this sense, the customer's participation in the culture of fun is no more spontaneous than that of the employee.

Fleming's insight is important because it illustrates how the blurring of work and personal life is not just a problem because we might end up always working (is that guy in the coffee shop with the laptop working or hanging out?) but because we are being required to give up more and more of ourselves—including our emotional expressions—in the service of profitability. We become accountable not just for the satisfactory, perhaps even exceptional, performance of a task but also for the kind of psychological identity (manifested in a particular kind of communicative performance) that we bring to the workplace. Moreover, the "just be yourself" corporatization of fun obscures the fact that workers are still subject to many forms of control, from various forms of technological control to ideological and disciplinary control mechanisms. In this sense, the culture of "just be yourself" does not amount to freedom from control but, rather, freedom *around* existing controls (Fleming, 2009, p. 33).

Critical management scholar Catherine Casey (1995) nicely summarizes the current state of many workplaces when she states:

The new colluded self is no longer permitted to be quietly compliant and dedicated. Rather, the new employees must be, as the popular management writers Peters and Waterman urged that they become, "charged up people" who "feel great" and who are "unleashed" to become "winners" for the corporation and for themselves. (p. 191)

I must say it makes me tired just reading that quotation (and it suggests that all employees must be Charlie Sheen types with tiger blood!). But the reality is that many workplaces increasingly demand intimacy and emotional expression from us in a context where we might feel uncomfortable sharing those personal aspects of our identities. "Fun-sultants" may be everywhere, but many workers resent the efforts of companies to co-opt their identities in this manner.

Critical Case Study 8.1
What Does Drinking Coffee Have to Do With Organizational Communication?

When I was in graduate school in the 1980s, I used to hang out in coffee shops, doing homework or chatting with friends. Back then, the only kind of coffee you could get was the generic stuff that came from a bottomless glass carafe and was generally served by a waitress in a pink polyester uniform. I still like to hang out in coffee shops, but the coffee-drinking experience has changed drastically in the past 20 years. As I write these very words, I'm sitting in a Starbucks—a coffee company that has grown exponentially in the past 15 years, going from 165 stores in 1992 to 13,501 worldwide in 2000 to 16,858 at the end of fiscal year 2010 (http://www.starbucks.com/about-us/company-information).

Starbucks is a postmodern company that understands better than most the power of branding its products. Indeed, it is not so much in the business of selling coffee as of "taking a generic product and branding it so completely that it becomes a spiritual/designer object" (Klein, 2001, p. 138). In other words, Starbucks is in the "meaning creation" business. How does it achieve this? Starbucks describes itself in its annual reports as providing a "comforting third place" for its customers. Starbucks locations evoke a New Age, spiritual feel, with their earthy décor, comfortable chairs, and employees in denim and khakis (incidentally, employees are not allowed to wear perfume or cologne, as that would pollute the coffee smell!). As their mission statement says: "When our customers feel this sense of belonging, our stores become a haven, a break from the worries outside, a place where you can meet with friends. It's about enjoyment at the speed of life—sometimes slow and savored, sometimes faster. Always full of humanity" (http://www.starbucks.com/about-us/company-information/mission-statement).

But this effort to provide coffee/chicken soup for the soul hides a business strategy and ethic that is anything but New Age in orientation. In fact, Starbucks has more in common with businesses such as Wal-Mart and McDonald's than one might at first suspect. Starbucks' business strategy is built on the principle of "clustering" (Klein, 2001, p. 136). Rather than spreading its stores out evenly across the country, Starbucks saturates a particular area with stores until the competition in that area becomes so intense that sales figures drop even in individual Starbucks stores (Starbucks calls this "cannibalizing" its stores, i.e., new stores take customers from old stores). However, total sales continue to increase. This clustering generally has the effect of driving the competition (usually independently run stores) out of business. Indeed, Starbucks "clusters" in a particular area only when it is fairly certain it can quickly become the dominant retailer in that area.

Although Starbucks' clustering strategy is a little different from Wal-Mart's "big box" technique (i.e., building huge stores—averaging 92,000 square feet—on the edge of towns where taxes are low and selling items at lower prices than any competitors), the effect is pretty much the same. Because of its massive resources, Starbucks can afford to engage in an aggressive market strategy that, while potentially causing problems for individual stores, leads to greater overall profit and the elimination of competition.

If we bring a critical lens to bear on Starbucks, then, we can see that there is a contradiction between the company's earthy, community-oriented, New Age image and its business strategy. While its branding efforts aim at creating a spiritual experience out of the act of drinking coffee, the reality is that Starbucks' intent is to dominate the coffee retail market and homogenize (standardize) the café culture. As Naomi Klein (2001) points out, this is one of the ways in which the concept of "public space" is being redefined. Traditionally, public space has—as its name suggests—belonged to the public and has provided the venue where ordinary citizens can gather, debate the political issues of the day, and give voice to their beliefs. Increasingly, however, postmodern values and business practices are privatizing such space and limiting public debate and dissent.

For example, shopping malls—owned by private companies—have replaced the marketplace and town square and will have protesters arrested for trespassing. Similarly, coffee houses have been a staple of democracy both in the United States and in Europe for more than 200 years, providing a venue for citizens to come together to discuss ideas great and small, profound and trivial. It would be a great pity if the coffee house as public space became an

(Continued)

(Continued)

experience completely defined by a corporate ethic of standardization. I'd hate to see the disappearance of counterculture cafés with mismatched furniture, servers with attitude, and a generally bohemian feel.

Discussion Questions

1. Have you ever been to a Starbucks? What was your experience like?

2. How would you describe the "culture" of Starbucks? How is it different from having coffee at your local diner or independent coffee shop?

3. In what ways is Starbucks a postmodern organization? In what ways is it modernist?

4. To what extent do you think Starbucks has been successful in its branding efforts?

Doing "No-Collar" Work

Under the old Fordist regime, when organizations were fairly stable structures and workers could generally expect long-term employment at a single organization, the kinds of work people engaged in were classified into blue-collar, white-collar, and pink-collar occupations. Blue-collar workers generally worked with their hands and were paid a wage based on the number of hours worked, white-collar workers were a professional class paid a salary not tied to hours worked, and pink-collar workers were usually female support staff who did mainly clerical work. Each of these terms represents a different relationship to the labor process, but a relationship that is relatively clearly defined: white-collar workers work with ideas and generate organizational knowledge; blue-collar workers do the work of actually making things; pink-collar workers provide the auxiliary support that greases the wheels of the corporate enterprise.

In contrast to this classification, there is now much talk about the **no-collar worker** (e.g., Ross, 2003), who, in many respects, is the product of the post-Fordist, knowledge-based economy in which we now find ourselves. To understand the significance of this shift to no-collar work, or what sociologist Richard Florida (2003) has called the "rise of the creative class," we can briefly compare the new no-collar worker to a classic account of the nature of white-collar work. Writing more than 60 years ago, sociologist C. Wright Mills (1951) depicted the shift in the United States from an economy consisting mainly of farmers, entrepreneurs, and small-business owners in the 19th century to one characterized by the "white-collar man . . . the small creature who is acted upon but who does not act, who works along unnoticed in somebody's office or store, never talking loud, never talking back, never taking a stand" (p. xii).

Mills (1951) compares the psychological hardship of such work with the physical hardship of 19th century factory workers, arguing that the white-collar worker is just as alienated from his work as the industrial worker was:

The salaried employee does not make anything, although he may handle much that he greatly desires but cannot have. No product of craftsmanship can be his to contemplate with pleasure as it is being created and after it is made. Being alienated from any product of his labor, and going year after year through the same paper routine, he turns his leisure all the more frenziedly to *ersatz* diversion that is sold him, and partakes of the synthetic excitement that neither eases nor releases. He is bored at work and restless at play, and this terrible alternation wears him out. (pp. xvi–xvii)

Here we see the classic description of the white-collar worker subject to the indignities of the bureaucratic form of organization, who, in the process, loses any sense of freedom and autonomy. He is alienated from both his own labor and his sense of self. For Mills, white-collar workers sell not only their time and energy but their personalities as well (a critique of "emotional labor" that predates Hochschild's famous study by more than 30 years). Mills's critique provides us with insight into how the modernist institutional form could be alienating not only to blue-collar workers and the working class generally but also to the middle-level white-collar bureaucrats whose job it was to keep the wheels of the bureaucratic machinery well oiled.

Of course, white-collar work is still alive and well in the 21st century—middle managers, bureaucrats, and office employees doing mundane clerical work have hardly disappeared from organizational life. What is different from the era Mills wrote about, however, is the level of job insecurity experienced. While the white-collar workers of the 1950s and 1960s might experience work as alienating and unrewarding, at least they could typically expect to have such jobs for life. Today, white-collar work can be dull, alienating, *and* unpredictable and lacking in job security.

© iStockphoto.com/sandoclr

The alienating nature of white-collar work that Mills wrote about in the 1950s is still a part of the corporate landscape today.

How, then, is the no-collar worker different from Mills's classic white-collar worker? First, no-collar workers have a much more nonconformist relationship to work that reflects the changes that have occurred in work and the workplace over the past 30 years or so. The very name "no-collar" signifies this changed relationship: "white-collar" invokes the business suit and tie and a "buttoned-down" approach to work; "blue-collar" represents the work shirt, oil, and dirt; and "pink-collar" suggests a feminine, auxiliary role. "No-collar," on the other hand, invokes images of graphic T-shirts and jeans in the workplace—an extension of "casual Fridays" to the entire work week!

Second, no-collar workers bring a very different sensibility to work, treating it not as a traditional career or a route to mega-salaries but, rather, as a vehicle for creativity that puts to good use their skills as "knowledge workers." In this sense, no-collar workers do not exhibit the same kind of loyalty to companies typically associated with employee identification and commitment; they frequently see themselves as "free agents" who take their highly market-able skills to the highest bidder. This approach to work is consistent with sociologist Richard Sennett's (1998) view that the current conditions of the new economy make flexibility and mobility a "moral virtue" for workers in unstable employment conditions. For example, in his study of a high-tech organization experiencing a highly unstable economic environment, Andrew Ross (2003) reported that employees would frequently consult a website called Fuckedcompany.com (a site that itself was f#@*ked in 2007!). This website was useful to employees because it reported rumors about layoffs and downsizing at various organizations, frequently providing information before employees at the affected companies heard about it! In this way, employees could be constantly on the lookout for new jobs.

Third, "no-collar" suggests something not only about the employees themselves but also about the structure of the organizational environment in which they work. Thus, creativity is not cultivated through the establishment of formal hierarchical organizations but by providing a flat, decentralized decision-making structure that enables knowledge workers to maximize their creative talents. Furthermore, no-collar work is typically characterized by a significant breakdown in the traditional boundaries between work and other aspects of one's life. After all, creative thinking cannot be confined to a 9-to-5 workday! As one of Andrew Ross's (2003) respondents said, "I simply did not know where the work stopped and I began" (p. 76).

Finally, perhaps the most important feature of no-collar work (particularly in its con-nection to professional identity) is that the work performed is only peripherally connected to making things. As we saw above in Mills's analysis, white-collar workers experienced a sense of alienation because the product of their work was not something tangible. However, as we will discuss in the chapter on branding, the value of a product as a "thing" is only a small part of its actual value; the value added through the brand and the meaning, ideas, and emotion built into the product is much more important. In this sense, no-collar work-ers are quite different from white-collar workers in the way their work is tied to the produc-tion and manipulation of ideas, symbols, and meanings, rather than to things. As Andrew Ross (2003) states:

> By the time the no-collar people appeared on the center stage of American history . . . making things was increasingly something that happened overseas, in developing countries. At home, adding value was the name of the profit game, and

Thinkstock/Comstock/Thinkstock

No-collar workers pursue a nontraditional career path in creative work. However, they often experience job insecurity and are unable to separate work from their private lives.

> it was all-important in any description of jobs and services. Standard commodities had a basic market worth, but their value could be boosted by intangible qualities like ideas, brands, stories, or designs. (pp. 52–53)

In this sense, no-collar workers can be described as what economist Robert Reich (1991) has called **symbol manipulators**—those workers who create ideas and knowledge and find ways to transform them into branded, marketable products. Such symbol manipulators, Reich argues, are at the top of a hierarchy of work categories, given the nature of their work and the ways in which they add value to the economy. As we will see in the chapter on branding, the worth of a company lies in the branded, "symbolic" value of its products and image, and workers employed as "symbol manipulators" are precisely the employees who play a key role in creating this value.

In the context of post-Fordism, then, no-collar work presents both possibilities and constraints. On the one hand, no-collar work provides a potentially enriching knowledge environment where employees are given the opportunity to realize their creative potential in an exciting and rewarding workplace (I realize this last sentence reads like a job ad!). No-collar work is typically knowledge work that is not "deskilled" by scientific management and bureaucracy in many of the ways we discussed in Chapter 3. Moreover, no-collar work thrives in work environments that are nonhierarchical and that enable employees to provide significant input into organizational decision making. Finally, no-collar work involves not only a flexible work environment that gives employees the freedom to work on their own schedules but also provides many work amenities we would typically associate with life away from work.

On the other hand, it might be argued that no-collar work makes a virtue out of the precariousness and instability of the post-Fordist economic environment, in which layoffs have become a basic element of employer strategies to restructure organizations not considered profitable enough, at least by the standards of the all-important quarterly earnings report. Thus, while the idea of the "free agent," no-collar worker can be appealingly romantic, it also reflects some serious, long-term changes and consequences for the relationships among people, work, and society (Gill & Pratt, 2008; Kalleberg, 2009; Ross, 2008).

First, it reflects a decline in the mutual attachment between employers and employees, whereby employers were interested in maintaining a high-quality workforce and workers were interested in long-term employment. Second, the idea of precarious work has spread to all professions and sectors of the economy, not just low-wage work; even in the colleges and universities where you are students, since 1975 the percentage of part-time and non–tenure-track instructors has increased from 43% to about 70% (Kalleberg, 2009, p. 9). Third, the emergence of the "precariat" reflects a growth in the perception of job insecurity and, hence, stands as a threat to many workers' sense of identity. Fourth, the growth of precarious work reflects a shift of risk from employers to employees; with much work being contingent and temporary, employers are able to reduce investments such as health care and pension schemes for workers. Fifth, the shift to precarious work has contributed to a massive increase in income inequality, to the point where the middle class in the United States is under threat.

Finally, the growth in the class of workers called "the precariat" negatively affects communities. When employment is precarious, people often have to move to find work, and newcomers are sometimes afraid to put down roots in a community. As such, there may be a lack of social engagement, indicated by declining membership in voluntary and community organizations. Moreover, increase in precarious work can coincide with an upsurge in immigrants to a community (due to globalization processes we'll address in Chapter 13); immigrants are often willing to work for lower wages and in poorer working conditions than will native-born workers.

❖ CONCLUSION

It is clear that the postmodern, post-Fordist organizational structure has profoundly affected the way organizations—as communication systems—function. In some respects, the postmodern organization appears to provide increased possibilities for employee participation in organizational life—the development of decentralized forms of decision making, such as work teams, gives employees a level of autonomy that was unthinkable in the modernist, bureaucratic, and Taylorized organization. In addition, organizations are increasingly seeing employees as important human resources that function optimally when provided with an environment that is comfortable, humane, and responsive to the complexities of 21st century lifestyles and demands. Given that we spend a large chunk of our adult lives working in organizations, it is important for our sense of well-being that we experience this time as fulfilling.

On the other hand, a number of issues should give us pause as we think about work life in the 21st century. As Deetz (1992a) has pointed out, there is a danger that the process of "corporate colonization" will continue to swallow up dimensions of our lives that, in an ideal world, would remain independent from work. In the mid-1990s a *Business Week* article pointed out that with the erosion of the work–home distinction, "work anywhere, anytime is the new paradigm" (Hamilton, Baker, & Vlasic, 1996, p. 109). As such, "privacy is being replaced with productivity, hierarchy with teamwork, and status with mobility" (p. 108). Where should we draw the line between our "private" selves and our "corporate" selves? How much of a role should we give to corporations in raising children? In shaping our social lives? In telling us how we should feel? As the boundaries of the workplace become increasingly ill defined (through technology, virtual work environments, corporate restructuring, etc.), how do we prevent our conception of self from becoming synonymous with the organization's conception of a productive individual?

The great irony of the postmodern organization is that as employees are given greater autonomy at work, new ways must be found to exercise control over those same employees. The velvet glove of the 21st century has replaced the iron fist of the 19th and 20th centuries. Decentralized forms of control may be more subtle than direct control, but this very subtlety makes them all the more effective—and harder to identify and resist. The real issue, however, is what we give up when we rely more and more on the corporation to fulfill the needs in our lives. As the distinction between private and public spheres increasingly breaks down in the postmodern organization and as the corporation comes to hold increasing sway over our noncorporate lives, we need to be aware of the potential loss of freedom this entails. And perhaps the most significant freedom is the ability to build a sense of self and community that is free of corporate influence.

CRITICAL APPLICATIONS

1. In groups, identify and discuss the features of the postmodern, post-Fordist organization. Using these features, how would you redesign your college or university? In other words, what would a postmodern college or university look like? In what ways would its communication and decision-making systems be different? Explore some concrete examples of how things would operate differently. How might your lives as students be different?

KEY TERMS

concertive control   191

disciplinary power   183

emotional labor   194

Fordism   184

kaizen   190

no-collar worker   198

post-Fordism   185

precariat   182

symbol manipulators   201

work teams   187

STUDENT STUDY SITE

Visit the student study site at **www.sagepub.com/mumbyorg** for these additional learning tools:

- Web quizzes
- eFlashcards
- SAGE journal articles
- Video resources
- Web resources

Gender is not just a women's issue, but much of the early research equated women and gender.

CHAPTER 9

Communicating Gender at Work

Women have won the right to do as much as men do. They just haven't won the right to do as little as men do.

—Quindlen (2003, p. 74)

In recent chapters we have examined new developments in the study of organizational communication—developments that take seriously the idea that organizations are sites where issues of communication, power, and identity come together in complex ways. In this chapter, we will take that focus a step further by examining research that explores the relationships among gender, communication, and organization. While a great deal of research has been conducted on gender issues in the past 30 years or so, it is only relatively recently that scholars in the field of organizational communication have begun to examine systematically how gender is a defining feature of the organizing process. Much of this research has arisen out of a strong interest in feminist approaches to the study of organizations, so in this chapter we will address both gender and feminism.

I'm sure all of you have opinions about feminism. Some of you might describe yourselves as feminist; some might claim a distinct antagonism toward feminism; and some of you may consider yourselves feminist but wouldn't share this position publicly. Many of you might participate in a discussion of feminism by starting with the disclaimer, "I wouldn't say I'm a feminist, but . . ." (Ashcraft, 1998), and then go on to talk about forms of sex discrimination you have experienced or witnessed. Your standpoint on feminism is probably shaped by a lot of things, including your upbringing, your religious beliefs, and your gender (see Critical Case Study 9.1 at the end of this chapter for my mom's opinion of feminism!). For example, it's relatively rare for men explicitly to describe themselves as feminist, given the traditional association of feminism with women's rights.

In this chapter, I'm not interested in persuading you that you should be a feminist. However, I *am* interested in painting a picture that might get you to think about gender and feminism in a way that's more sophisticated than the rather simplistic portrayal that generally appears in the media, where feminist issues appear in fairly black-and-white terms. As journalist Susan Faludi (1991) showed in her book *Backlash*, since the early 1980s the mass media have consistently portrayed feminism as extremist and representative of only a small minority of women—Rush Limbaugh's "feminazi" epithet being one example among many.

The reality is that any attempt to portray feminism as a single, unified, collective movement is doomed to failure. There are many feminist perspectives, some of which you might agree with and others you might reject (Tong, 1989). In this sense, as an approach to the study of human behavior, feminism is much like any other area of study in its multiple and sometimes divergent efforts to understand how society works.

So what is **feminism**? Do the various feminist perspectives share any features and issues? Clearly, all forms of feminism are, by definition, committed to the improvement of women's situations, given that women have historically been systematically excluded from full participation in the various realms of society. In this context, the feminist scholar bell hooks (2000) defines feminism as "a movement to end sexism, sexist exploitation, and oppression" (p. 1). While this is a pretty broad and generic definition, it does point to a key question common to all feminist approaches; *that is, how do we understand, explain, and critique the relationship between gender and power?* In other words, to what extent can the distribution of power in society be understood through the analysis of gender? While studying gender cannot account for all the ways power and oppression work in society, it provides a number of different insights into how social structures rest on gendered assumptions. Thus, we can think of the long history of feminism as involving increasingly sophisticated efforts to explore the relationship between gender and power.

For example, the original first wave of feminism from the mid-19th through the early 20th centuries defined oppression principally in terms of women's disenfranchisement from the right to vote. The second wave of feminism that began in the early 1960s was a much broader movement, concerned with such issues as reproductive freedom, domestic violence, rape, and the participation of women in domains—such as upper management and the political arena—that were previously reserved for men. Thus, the second wave viewed oppression in much more sophisticated terms, identifying forms of exploitation (e.g., sexual harassment and domestic violence) that had not previously been brought into public consciousness (MacKinnon, 1979).

Finally, the past 25 years or so have witnessed a growing recognition that women are far from a homogeneous group and that oppression and exploitation are experienced in myriad ways. In fact, the second wave of feminism has rightly been criticized for privileging the voices of white, middle-class women and excluding working-class women and women of color from its agenda. In the early 1980s, for example, bell hooks (1981)—an African American feminist—wrote a book titled *Ain't I a Woman* that drew attention to the white middle-class worldview that dominated the second wave of feminism. Today, the project of feminism includes not only women of color but also men.

How do these issues relate to the study of organizational communication? In the next section we will briefly consider three different feminist perspectives and their impact on the study of organizations. There are many more than three perspectives that we could discuss, but these three provide some useful insights into the ways feminism has significantly affected how we think about our everyday organizational lives.

❖ FEMINIST PERSPECTIVES ON ORGANIZATIONAL COMMUNICATION

Although feminism as a movement has been around in various forms for 200 years, it was only in the 1970s that it began to have a significant impact in academia and only in the early 1990s that organizational communication scholars began to examine organizations from a feminist perspective. In this section we will examine three different feminist perspectives, each of which provides us with a different lens for examining organizations. These perspectives are (1) liberal feminism, (2) radical feminism, and (3) critical feminism. While these perspectives overlap in some fashion, each presents us with different ways of examining issues such as patriarchy, domination, gender, equality, emancipation, and so forth. In addition, each perspective provides different ways of understanding and examining organizational life; indeed, the nature of societal institutions and organizations is very much a focal point of feminist analysis and critique. A summary of the three perspectives can be found in Table 9.1 later in this chapter (page 220).

Liberal Feminism: Creating a Level Playing Field

Liberal feminism is a product of late 18th and 19th century liberal political theory and is perhaps most associated in its early days with the writings of Mary Wollstonecraft (1792/1975) and John Stuart Mill (1869/1970). Liberal feminism is both a critique and an extension of the Enlightenment tradition we discussed in Chapter 1. While this perspective firmly believes in Rousseau's "declaration of the rights of man," it critiques the fact that women were excluded from that declaration. Thus, while (male-oriented) Enlightenment liberal political theory developed the principles of liberty, fraternity, and equality, liberal feminism critiqued its failure to include women in this new conception of individual rights. Thus, the 19th century women's movement had as its goal the expansion of individual rights to include the other half of the population. In the 19th and early 20th centuries, much of this effort toward expanding women's rights was directed toward gaining women the right to vote. This is generally referred to as the "women's suffrage" movement. Once the right to vote was secured in 1920, this first wave of the women's movement dissipated somewhat.

However, the 1960s saw the emergence of a second wave of feminism that emerged partly out of disenchantment with the emerging civil rights and student movements (which tended to marginalize the role of women activists) and partly in response to Betty Friedan's (1963) landmark book *The Feminine Mystique*. In identifying what she called "the problem with no name," Friedan gave voice to many middle-class, educated women who experienced a deep sense of malaise as a result of their limited opportunity for fulfillment through anything other than their roles as wives and mothers. The AMC show *Mad Men*, which is set in an advertising firm in the 1960s, provides fascinating insight into the gendered nature of society and professional life only 50 years ago. What's particularly interesting about the show is not only its depiction of the restrictive roles available to women (mainly those of wife and secretary) but also its portrayal of corporate masculinity—sexually aggressive, hard drinking (with the ever-present liquor tray in the office), and homogeneous. Although a fictitious show, *Mad Men* provides us with some interesting cultural insights into why a book such as *The Feminine Mystique* struck a chord with so many women and provided an impetus for the second wave of feminism.

Thus, whereas the first wave of the women's movement saw women's oppression located primarily in denial of the right to vote, the second wave expanded its conception of oppression to include such issues as equal employment opportunity, sexual harassment, domestic violence, and reproductive rights. The rallying cry, "The personal is political," stressed the idea that what patriarchal society had traditionally defined as individual, personal issues (domestic violence, child care, relational abuse, etc.) actually had much more profound and far-reaching implications for the ways in which society defined women and their roles. In this sense, the second wave of feminism was a time of consciousness raising, in which feminists attempted to draw attention to the various institutional mechanisms that limited women's full participation in society.

In what ways can these concerns be related to organizational communication issues? From a liberal feminist perspective, the principal concern has been with expanding access to work and career opportunities for women. The past several decades have seen efforts on a number of different fronts to "level the playing field" in order for women to compete for jobs on an equal basis with men. For example, in 1964 Title VII of the Civil Rights Act was passed, prohibiting employment discrimination on the basis of sex, race, or religion. In addition, affirmative action programs and Equal Employment Opportunity laws have mandated equal access to job opportunities for women.

Despite these legislative efforts, women still lag behind men on a number of different organizational fronts. For example, many women continue to experience the **glass ceiling** phenomenon, where they reach a certain level of the organizational hierarchy and then have great difficulty progressing any further. Indeed, in 2010 women still constituted only 14.4% of executive office positions in Fortune 500 corporations (Soares, Regis, & Shur, 2010), up from 12% in 2000 (Walsh, 2000). Furthermore, because many organizations are still male dominated, women are not as able to develop the kinds of social networks and support systems that facilitate movement up the corporate ladder.

Comstock Images/Comstock/Thinkstock

The glass ceiling limits women's ability to reach the highest levels of corporate life.

Where women *are* able to move into particular occupations, they frequently tend to fill "occupational ghettoes"—professions that are "pink collar" or "pink velvet collar" and are thus defined as "women's occupations." These include secretarial work, nursing, pediatrics, elementary school teaching, temporary employment, and so forth. When women are able to move into a profession that has previously been dominated by men, the salaries in such professions tend to fall. Recently, researchers have identified a phenomenon that complements women's "glass ceiling" experience—the **glass escalator** (Williams, 1992). This phenomenon suggests that while women in male-dominated organizations frequently have difficulty advancing, men in female-dominated professions (e.g., nursing, grade school teaching) experience a pressure toward upward mobility that sees them promoted more quickly than women. Thus, even in professions where women have a distinct numerical superiority, they still experience difficulty in their efforts to progress professionally.

One of the earliest and most important liberal feminist efforts to address the role of gender in organizational life was Rosabeth Moss Kanter's (1977) book *Men and Women of the Corporation*. In her 5-year-long investigation of a large corporation, Kanter identified a number of different factors that prevented women from advancing in this organization. Two phenomena in particular are significant for us in understanding how gender and organizational communication are closely linked: (1) tokenism and (2) homosocial reproduction.

Tokenism refers to a condition whereby a person finds him or herself identified as a minority in a dominant culture. In Kanter's (1977) study, women were the tokens because of their minority status in the corporation, but anyone who is a member of a minority group can be given "token" status" (e.g., African Americans, Latinos/as, individuals with disabilities, etc.). The important thing about tokens is that they are visible (because they *look* or behave differently from other organization members), and they come to be viewed as representatives of their minority group rather than as individuals with particular traits and skills. This visibility means that any mistake they make tends to be amplified while, ironically, competent performance is overlooked. In other words, ability is often eclipsed by physical appearance, according to Kanter. As such, token organization members frequently have to work much harder than do dominant group members in order to get recognition and rewards. Thus, tokens are under tremendous pressure and are, in effect, set up for failure. Furthermore, any failure is taken as indicative of the performance of members of the token group, rather than as a failure of the individual person.

From a communication perspective, tokenism is a perceptual phenomenon created by the members of the dominant culture; people are not tokens unless others communicatively construct them as such. Kanter indicates that tokenism is a "perceptual tendency" characterized by high visibility, contrast, and assimilation. That is, a token (a) has a high organizational profile; (b) is perceived as contrasting significantly with the dominant culture, such that members of the dominant culture exaggerate both their differences from the token and commonalities amongst themselves; and (c) is assimilated into the stereotype of his or her token group and not allowed by members of the dominant group to function as an individual. In this sense, tokenism is a creation of the perceptual and communication practices of those who shape the dominant culture of the organization.

In such contexts, people who experience tokenism feel that all their actions and decisions are scrutinized in a manner that members of the dominant culture do not experience. As such, they can never afford to function merely adequately and often end up working much harder than the average organization member in order to be perceived as competent. As Anna Quindlen's (2003) quote at the beginning of this chapter indicates, women (and all minorities) have yet to earn the right to work as little as men do!

Homosocial reproduction is a condition that functions in tandem with tokenism and describes an organizational context in which, to put it simply, "the men who manage reproduce themselves in kind" (Kanter, 1977, p. 48). In her interviews with male managers, Kanter discovered that they preferred to work with people who were like themselves, mainly because it facilitated a relatively predictable environment in which communication with colleagues was easy and comfortable. In this sense, women employees inserted a level of unpredictability that upset the smooth flow of communication and decision making. Put in the terms discussed in Chapter 6, we might say that male managers were comfortable being part of a single, coherent organizational culture that reflected their view of the corporate world. Women undermined that coherence.

Thus, phenomena such as "the old boys' network" and the "old school tie" are part of the process of homosocial reproduction, whereby men hire other men who look a lot like them and come from similar backgrounds—white, middle class, educated at particular schools, and so forth. In such a context, it becomes extremely difficult for women to assimilate into a culture where they do not immediately understand the taken-for-granted meanings at work, and where the "in-group" perceives them as "alien" before they have even had a chance to prove themselves.

Of course, much has changed in the 35 years since Kanter's study. But while it is no longer unusual for women to be in management positions, they still frequently experience barriers to advancement that limit their success when compared with similarly qualified men. For example, just a few years ago Wal-Mart faced charges that it systematically discriminated against its female employees. In a class-action lawsuit, a federal judge ruled that the lawyers for the plaintiffs

present largely uncontested, descriptive statistics which show that women working in Wal-Mart stores are paid less than men in every region, that pay disparities exist in most job categories, that the salary gap widens over time even for men and women hired into the same jobs at the same time, that women take longer to enter into management positions, and that the higher one looks in the organization, the lower the percentage of women. (Ackman, 2004)

Jupiterimages/Pixland/Thinkstock

Sexual harassment is still a relatively widespread feature of organizational life.

Such evidence indicates that women still experience more obstacles in progressing up the corporate hierarchy than do men. Furthermore, instances of sexual harassment and intimidating work environments for women and minorities are still relatively common. I imagine that many women (and some men) reading this will be able to recall professional contexts in which they have felt uncomfortable because of unwanted attention from a colleague or superior. Incidents such as these frequently leave the recipient feeling inadequate, powerless, and unable to perform work tasks adequately.

In general, then, a liberal feminist perspective takes what might be described as an "entryist" approach to organizational communication, in which efforts are aimed at providing ways for women to receive the same professional opportunities and support as men do. For example, at General Electric the corporation's "Women's Network"—established to improve women's access to high-ranked GE positions—coaches women managers in public-speaking skills, in making effective presentations, and in "exuding leadership qualities" (Walsh, 2000, p. 13).

Furthermore, many companies now have parental leave programs in place that permit women (and often men) to take paid leave around the birth of a child without compromising their professional status and career chances in the firm. However, the United States is years behind many other (particularly European) industrialized nations in providing adequate parental-leave programs for women. For example, in a study examining the parental leave laws in 21 countries, the United States ranked 20th in the amount of "protected job leave" available to parents (Ray, Gornick, & Schmitt, 2008). Switzerland ranked last with 14 weeks of protected leave, while Spain and France ranked first with more than 300 weeks. The United States offers a combined 24 weeks of protected leave for a two-parent family. Moreover, while almost all countries provide direct financial (government-paid) support for parents (varying between 3 months and 1 year of "full-time equivalent" paid leave), the United States is one of only two countries that offers no paid parental leave. Finally, "only about one-fourth of U.S. employers offer fully paid 'maternity-related leave' of any duration, and one-fifth of U.S. employers offer no maternity-related leave of any kind, paid or unpaid" (p. 1). Figure 9.1 (Ray et al., 2008, p. 6) provides information on all 21 countries in the study and certainly displays some interesting comparative data on the efforts of most of the top industrialized nations to provide parental leave for their citizens. The United States does not fare well in this comparison.

Often, when women do take advantage of such programs, they find themselves less competitive in terms of raises, promotions, job opportunities, and so on. As such, women (and men) are often loathe to participate in company parental-leave programs even when they are available, for fear it will indicate they are not serious about their careers. For example, in their study of one workplace with a parental-leave policy, organizational communication scholars Erika Kirby and Kathy Krone (2002) discovered that employees often adopted an attitude of "the policy exists but you can't really use it," indicating a considerable gap between the official company leave policy and the ways employees made sense of it within the culture of the organization. In academia, female professors have often been hesitant to take maternity leave (during which their tenure clock stops) for fear their colleagues will not see them as serious academics.

In general, then, the liberal feminist perspective has done much to draw attention to the difficulties professional women often face in organizational settings, including pay inequities, lack of advancement opportunities, tokenism, and so forth. However, this approach also has certain limitations. First, in leaving unquestioned the basic structure and assumptions of contemporary organizational life, this perspective places the onus on women adapting to a male-dominated organizational environment. For example, "exuding leadership qualities" usually means adopting masculine standards of leadership premised on control, taking charge, and being directive; women who make such adaptations are frequently accused of being "unfeminine" or "bitchy." Hence, adapting to the status quo often leads women into a "catch-22" situation where both "masculine" and "feminine" forms of behavior are problematic.

Figure 9.1 Total and Full-Time Equivalent (FTE) Paid Parental Leave for Two-Parent Families

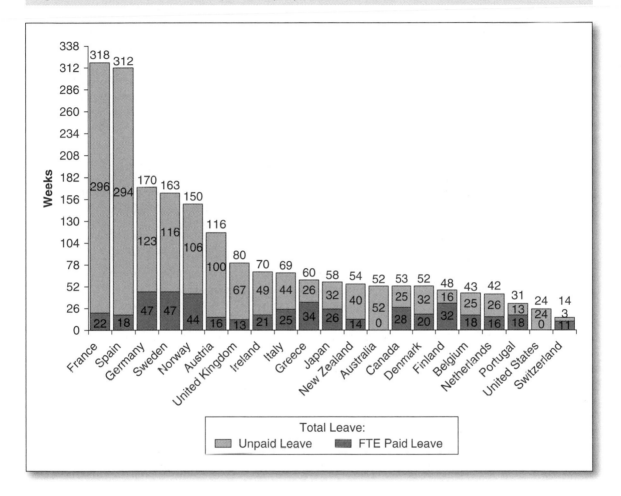

Second, the liberal feminist perspective can be described largely as a "women in management" approach to organizational issues (Calás & Smircich, 1996). As such, its focus has been on white, middle-class women, to the neglect of minority and working-class women. For example, while liberal feminism has drawn attention to the difficulties "career women" face in juggling work and home life, struggling against the glass ceiling, and developing support networks, it has often ignored the fact that many women (a) have little choice about whether to work or stay home, (b) are often in low-wage jobs with little or no hope of advancement, and (c) are more subject to sexual harassment than are women in higher-level positions. Thus, the research on so-called "supermoms," who make the choice both to have a career and fulfill domestic life with children, often overlooks the fact that many poor and working-class mothers have no option but to work, given the decline in real income over the past 30 years. Many of the blue-collar occupations that could support a family on a single income have largely disappeared from the American economic landscape, forcing many women into low-income jobs that are the only means of family survival.

Third, the liberal feminist perspective has tended to treat gender as a variable, regarding masculinity and femininity as unproblematic categories. As we will see in our later discussion of the critical feminist perspective, gender is more usefully understood not as an organizational variable but, rather, as a constitutive feature of organizational life that shapes everyday meaning and sense-making practices. From this perspective, gender is viewed not as a role one takes on or casts off depending on the social setting but, instead, as intimately tied up with the ways we construct our identities.

Radical Feminism: Constructing Alternative Organizational Forms

Like the second wave of liberal feminism, **radical feminism** has its roots in the political movements of the 1960s and arose out of disenchantment with the sexism of those movements. However, it developed in a very different direction and is rooted in a different set of premises than liberal feminism.

Radical feminism is "radical" in the sense that it is "woman centered" (Calás & Smircich, 1996). That is, while liberal feminism seeks women's access to male-dominated institutions, radical feminism proposes alternative institutional forms rooted in women's values. In this sense, radical feminism takes feminine qualities that have traditionally been devalued in a patriarchal society and revalues them, placing them at the center of an alternative vision of society. Thus, traditional "feminine" qualities such as emotion, nurturance, sensitivity, and connectedness—qualities that have occupied a secondary status to rationality, competitiveness, and independence in patriarchal society—are reframed as the basis on which an alternative vision of the world can be built. Radical feminism therefore emphasizes "women's ways of knowing" as an alternative to the perceived failure of men's stewardship of the world (which, radical feminists would argue, has led to wars, poverty, persecution, famine, etc.).

Radical feminists are thus interested in the transformation of various features of society through the development of alternative ways of thinking, feeling, and acting. As radical feminist Audre Lorde (1984) stated in her critique of patriarchy:

> [Feminism] involves learning how to take our differences and make them strengths. *For the master's tools will never dismantle the master's house.* They may allow us temporarily to beat him at his own game, but they will never enable us to bring about genuine change. And this fact is only threatening to those women who still define the master's house as their only source of support. (p. 112; emphasis in original)

Thus, while liberal feminism generally tends to downplay the differences between men and women, arguing that women are just as competent as men and able to perform traditionally male-dominated roles, radical feminism—following Lorde—argues that the very assumptions on which patriarchal society is built are problematic and inherently oppressive to women. Thus, society needs to be built on a set of principles that reject patriarchy and embrace matriarchy.

Radical feminists argued that this could be done through the establishment of women-based groups and organizations structured according to a different set of values and operating principles. Beginning in the 1960s and 1970s, these organizations were aimed at providing contexts that were free from the oppressive conditions that frequently characterized male-dominated bureaucracies and thus provided women with a forum for "consciousness raising"—that is, a context in which women could come to a better understanding of themselves and others that was untainted by dominant patriarchal ideologies.

In many ways, this was very much a utopian project; it was a collective effort to develop alternative organizations and groups that provided women with spaces in which to create an alternative vision of what the world might be like based on a very different set of principles. For example, many of these women's organizations had no hierarchy, preferring to engage in decision making through developing consensus, and leadership roles tended to rotate regularly amongst members of the organization. Furthermore, many of these organizations described themselves as "collectives," to distinguish themselves from the traditional bureaucratic forms of patriarchy.

Sociologist Joyce Rothschild-Whitt (1979) characterizes such collectivist organizations as having the following features:

- Authority resides in the collective as whole, not individuals who occupy an office.
- There is minimal stipulation of rules rather than the universal, formal rules of a bureaucracy.
- Social control is based on mutually shared values rather than supervision or use of impersonal rules and sanctions.
- Social relations are personal and of value in themselves, as opposed to the role- and rule-based relations of bureaucracies.
- Recruitment and advancement are based on friends and shared values rather than specialized training and formal certification.
- Individual incentives focus on furthering the organization's values and political goals, rather than securing economic rewards.
- Power is distributed in an egalitarian manner, rather than being determined by the office one holds. Any individual's power is strictly limited by the collective as a whole.
- Division of labor is minimized, with members sharing many jobs and functions; the separation of mental and manual work is minimized. In the bureaucratic organization job specialization and division of labor are maximized.

As we can see, then, such collective organizations attempted to reject completely the bureaucratic model and the hierarchy and impersonal organizational environment it implied. Instead, radical feminist organizations valued an organizational structure and form that emphasized the opportunity for individual women to contribute to a larger vision of what life could be like in a non-oppressive, more egalitarian society where women could more fully realize their identities. While such an approach to organizing certainly has its merits, the utopian project of radical feminism remains unrealized for a number of reasons.

First, it adopts what might be described as an "essentialist" approach to gender issues. That is, women are valued because of what are seen as their natural characteristics—nurturance, emotionality, caring, connection, and so on—which are viewed as superior to masculine tendencies of rationality, independence, hierarchy, and individualism. Such an approach succeeds not only in suggesting that women have "natural" characteristics but that men do also. This leads to a very bifurcated, bipolar view of the world, in which women and men live in different universes. In addition, the characterization of women and men as having natural characteristics suggests little possibility for change.

Second, radical feminism adopts a "separatist" philosophy, in which women can fully realize their possibilities only through the creation of social structures and institutions free from patriarchal values and ideologies. In other words, such feminist organizations often have a "women-only" rule. Under some circumstances, such a separatist philosophy makes good sense (e.g., women's support groups for victims of rape, domestic abuse crisis centers, etc.); in such contexts, the presence of men can provoke extreme anxiety in the women seeking support and counseling. On the other hand, we could argue that in many circumstances such a separatist philosophy simply represents a reversal of the kind of sexism male-dominated organizations have long practiced.

Third, the very separatist philosophy of some feminist organizations frequently led to their demise, largely because, in reality, there is no such thing as an organization not interconnected with many different organizations and its environment. As we saw in the chapter on systems theory, organizations that cannot adapt to environmental changes tend toward entropy and disorder, and certainly this was the case with many of the feminist organizations of the 1970s; their separatist philosophy proved to be their downfall, and many went out of existence. Those that did survive and thrive learned the importance of adaptation and interdependence with other organizations. Maguire and Mohtar (1994), for example, show how a feminist women's crisis center was able to remain true to its feminist values of advocacy for women while at the same time developing close ties with state funding agencies and the local police department. Furthermore, Karen Ashcraft (2000, 2001) focuses on a contemporary feminist organization's efforts to adopt a "hybrid" structure that combines feminist values with the bureaucratic formalization of organizational goals and principles—a form of control Ashcraft describes as "feminist-bureaucratic." Finally, management scholars Joanne Martin, Kathleen Knopoff, and Christine Beckman's (1998) study of The Body Shop international corporation demonstrates how even a large, multinational, for-profit organization can combine bureaucratic, postbureaucratic, and feminist principles to create a progressive corporate structure that allows organization members to be expressive and emotional in their work.

In general, then, radical feminist principles in their pure form were typically unable to survive the realities of their social, political, and economic environments. Instead, radical feminist goals tended to adapt to the practicalities of everyday organizational life. While on the one hand this may seem like a compromise of basic principles, on the other hand it recognizes the need for organizations and their members to address the changing character of the real world.

Critical Feminism: Viewing Organizations as Gendered

The last perspective we will consider is what I call **critical feminism**. For me, this is the perspective that is the most interesting and useful for understanding the relationship between gender and organizational communication. The critical feminist approach has a number of advantages.

First, it views gender neither as an individual variable (liberal feminism) nor as a natural, stable feature of women and men (radical feminism) but, rather, as a socially constructed phenomenon that is subject to change. For example, in the past 100 years what counts as "feminine" and "masculine" has altered considerably as the norms for gender-appropriate behavior have shifted over time. For instance, the phrase "woman leader" is not the oxymoron it was 50 years ago (though it's interesting that we'd never think of saying "man leader"—an indication that the term *leader* is still heavily gendered). In the early 1980s I remember having a discussion about gender issues with students in a class I was teaching; two male students in the class indicated that they would never be able to work for a woman boss because it would be demeaning for them and would run contrary to the "natural" differences between men and women. I can't imagine any but the most conservative of men taking such a position today.

Second, the critical feminist perspective views gender not as an organizational variable that can be isolated and studied separately from other organizational phenomena; rather, gender is seen as an integral and constitutive feature of daily organizational life. In this sense, we can think of organizations as "gendered." Sociologist Joan Acker (1990) defines this term in the following manner:

> To say that an organization . . . is gendered means that advantage and disadvantage, exploitation and coercion, action and emotion, meaning and identity, are patterned through and in terms of a distinction between male and female, masculine and feminine. Gender is not an addition to ongoing processes, conceived as gender neutral. Rather, it is an integral part of those processes, which cannot be properly understood without an analysis of gender. (p. 146)

This definition gets at the idea that gender is not only a routine feature of daily organizational life but also impossible to escape because it lies at the very foundation of how we define ourselves, the world, and others. All our identities, sense-making efforts, and organizational meanings are therefore gendered. Thus, many jobs are gendered and hence coded as either masculine or feminine. Secretarial work, nursing, and grade school teaching are gendered as feminine, while airline pilot, bank manager, and surgeon are coded as masculine. This does not mean, of course, that men can't be nurses or that women can't be surgeons—many are. The point is that the organizational roles themselves are gendered such that the people occupying them have particular expectations placed on them by the organization and those around them. In other words, gender is a structural feature of organizations rather than simply a characteristic of individuals.

For example, a female airline pilot might have to work very hard in her organizational performance to be seen as equally competent as her male colleagues (aren't we all still at least a little surprised to hear a female voice coming from the cockpit over the PA system?). As Karen Ashcraft (2005) has shown, the airline industry historically has deliberately constructed an image of the airline pilot as coolly rational, professional, in control, and paternalistic—a gendered professional identity intended to make us feel safe while we are flying in a metal tube at 30,000 feet. Similarly, the role of flight attendant has been deliberately constructed in a gendered manner to convey warmth, nurturance, and attentiveness; this feminized role perfectly complements the masculine role of the pilot. Thus, the creation of an organizational reality that allows us to fly with at least some level of comfort and calm is heavily dependent on gendered organizational identities and scripts in which the man takes care of the rational, technical, mechanical aspects of flying and the woman tends to the emotional, bodily dimensions of the experience. To take the analysis one step further, we can say that the experience of flying as a safe activity depends on a mind–body split, in which the masculine is associated with the mind and rationality and the feminine is associated with the body and emotions.

Third, and following from the idea of organizations as gendered, the critical feminist perspective focuses on the ways organization members "do gender" (West & Zimmerman, 1987). This notion enables us to understand how, as social actors, we are constantly engaged in performances of gendered identity that are highly context driven and for which we are held accountable by others on a moment-to-moment basis. This doing of gender encompasses everything from the way we dress to how we talk to the kinds of activities we engage in, as well as the meanings we construct. In other words, our very identities are involved in the process of doing gender.

The notion of **gender accountability** is extremely important in this process. As sociologists Candace West and Don Zimmerman (1987) argue, each of us is constantly being held accountable for our adequate performance of masculinities and femininities, with each performance judged in terms of the social context in which it occurs. For example, David Collinson's (1992) study of male blue-collar workers in a truck factory illustrates how workplace humor is central to the adequate performance of working-class masculinity. Through practical jokes, the workers communicate to one another on a daily basis what it means to be a "real man"; that is, someone who does hard, physical, dirty work can engage in the banter and horseplay of the workplace, can brag about his sexual prowess, and so forth. Anyone who is unable to pass this test of masculinity (e.g., the white-collar workers in the main office who do only clerical work) is not considered to be appropriately masculine. In Collinson's study, then, masculinity is an ongoing performance and accomplishment that has to be reasserted by the shop-floor workers on a daily basis.

One of the best examples I have come across of how gender is both an ongoing accomplishment and contextual came from a student in one of my classes recently. I was asking for examples of gendered behavior for which one is held accountable, and a male student (who was also a football player) said that his family made fun of him for flossing his teeth! They said it was not very manly for a big guy! For me, this is a great example of how everything we do is potentially open to gendered interpretations and, hence, to evaluation and accountability. Who would have thought that such a routine, mundane piece of behavior as flossing could take on gendered meanings? Furthermore, the example shows how highly contextual gendered performances are; what is appropriately gendered behavior in one context may well be highly inappropriate in another.

Fourth, the critical feminist perspective conceives of gender as an ongoing accomplishment of both women and men. Certainly this is quite different from liberal feminism, which mostly views gender as a "woman question," and radical feminism, which largely views men as part of the problem. Critical feminism, on the other hand, explores the ways women and men are implicated together in gendered organizing processes. Feminist scholar Jane Flax (1990), for example, argues that both men *and* women are "prisoners of gender" and that we need to examine how both masculine and feminine identities are constructed in modern society. The usefulness of this approach is that it does not simply isolate women and femininity as problems to be addressed. Instead, masculinity is examined as something that is every bit as socially constructed as femininity is. It also recognizes that, as Flax suggests, men are in many ways just as constrained by societal gender scripts as women are. For example, men are often held to standards of "hypermasculinity" and required to behave in macho and aggressive ways; such standards frequently limit how men are legitimately able to express emotion and tenderness.

In recent years, organizational communication scholars have started to examine workplace masculinity in order to better understand how gender and organizing work together. We have already mentioned David Collinson's (1992) work on working-class masculinity and the ways it requires a particular kind of gender performance in order for workers to be seen as real men. In contrast, Karen Ashcraft's (2005) work on commercial airline pilots illustrates how a quite different performance of masculinity is required to maintain a legitimate professional identity. Pilots are held accountable for performances that exhibit rational decision making, coolness under pressure, paternalism ("This is your captain [father] speaking"), and technical proficiency.

For example, when US Airways Flight 1549 crash-landed in the Hudson river a few years ago after striking a flock of birds, the pilot, Chesley "Sully" Sullenberger, was universally praised for his cool and calm behavior under pressure and was rightly called a hero. What's interesting about this story, though, is that his copilot, Jeffrey Skiles, received little mention in the news stories even though he played a critical role in the successful landing. One explanation for this is that we rarely think of a commercial pilot as part of a team whose members work together but, rather, as an individual who is solely responsible for the decisions made in the cockpit. I suspect that the strongly masculine identity of the airline pilot has much to do with this image.

Thus, the critical feminist perspective allows us to explore the ways gender becomes encoded and communicated in multiple and complex ways in daily organizational life. Indeed, I would imagine that all of you can think of ways you perform different gendered identities in different social contexts, with an awareness of the attendant sanctions for not performing appropriately. For example, it's no accident that the derogatory statement, "That's so gay" (typically used by teenagers to describe any behavior seen as stupid, negative, or effeminate), is premised on a belief that a particular performance of gender and sexuality is problematic and outside what counts as "normal." It's also interesting that it's a phrase used mainly by teenagers—precisely the group that most struggles with emerging identities and for whom ridicule by others for inadequate gender performance is a daily possibility.

This brings us to the final way in which critical feminism provides insight into the relationship between gender and organizing. *Namely, it enables us to look closely at the relationships among gender, organizational communication, and power*. While gender is socially constructed and changing, such constructions do not occur in a haphazard manner. Rather, they are the result of relations of power in organizations and society. Generally speaking, those groups who have the most power and resources have the most influence on the ways gender identities are constructed. Moreover, those groups in power construct these gendered identities in ways that benefit them the most.

The simplest example of this process at work is the way that, historically, men have largely shaped the gendered identities available to both women and men, with feminine identities being constructed as inferior to masculine identities. Such constructions (e.g., women as emotional/irrational, subject to hysteria, maternal, etc.) were traditionally used as a means to justify women's exclusion from many spheres of society (government, industry—except in limited roles—law, etc.). In the airline industry, for example, the argument for excluding women from the cockpit included the claim that a woman who was menstruating might act irrationally and place passengers in danger! And of course, legally speaking, women historically were considered to have no rights and were viewed literally as the property of their husbands. Such a view of women in society is hard to sustain without discourses and sense-making practices that construct women as weak, irrational, needing paternalistic care, and so forth. In addition, the perspective of history allows us to see just how socially constructed these views of women were (although, of course, these social constructions had very real political and economic consequences).

In contemporary organizational life, the relationship between gender and power shapes everyday work and professional contexts. Angela Trethewey (2001), for example, shows how middle-aged professional women are subject to a societal "master narrative of decline" in which they are positioned as less attractive and less powerful by virtue of their aging bodies; professional women often experience aging as a time of loss and isolation. Such a narrative typically does not apply to male professionals, who are generally viewed as more experienced, distinguished, and powerful as they age. Trethewey's point is that women

Table 9.1   Comparing Liberal, Radical, and Critical Feminist Perspectives

	Perspective		
Issue	*Liberal Feminism*	*Radical Feminism*	*Critical Feminism*
View of organizations	Create barriers to women's advancement (e.g., glass ceiling)	Inherently patriarchal; need alternative orgs. rooted in women's ways of knowing	Gendered forms that construct systems of power and meaning
Conception of gender	Social roles played by men and women; gender as variable	Gender as essential features of women and men	We are always accountable for our gendered performances
View of communication	Communication as expression of gender roles; communication styles reflect gender	Built on patriarchal meanings; need to create alternative, woman-centered forms of communication	Communication and power inextricably linked; communication creates gendered identities
Goal of emancipation	Create equal opportunities for women and men	Create a world based on feminist principles, free from patriarchy	Free both women and men from systems of power that make both "prisoners of gender"

professionals inevitably have to confront and make sense of the narrative of decline, choosing either to reproduce it by buying in to the idea that they need to work out more, get plastic surgery, and so on, or to resist it and reject the idea of youth and beauty as superior to the aging process.

Critical Technologies 9.1
Gender, Technology, and Power

Feminist perspectives on technology are as varied as its approaches to organizational communication. Indeed, it's possible to map out liberal, radical, and critical feminist approaches to technology, all of which take differing perspectives on the relationships among gender, technology, and power. All three approaches ask the basic question, what role does technology play in creating and embedding gendered power relations in society (Wajcman, 2010)? Moreover, all three perspectives agree that, historically, technology has been a male domain that has excluded women and that femininity has been constructed as incompatible with technology and technical professions. However, each approach differs in how to conceive the gender–technology–power relationship.

Liberal feminism typically views technology as a politically neutral form that has traditionally been male dominated. In other words, technology is not seen as gendered per se but as historically controlled by men. The solution to this problem is to create a level playing field that enables women to participate in technology-related fields at the same level as men. For example, women make up less than 25% of workers in STEM (science, technology, engineering, and math) fields, and so various programs encourage high school and college women to join STEM fields in order to close the "gender innovation gap" (Beede et al., 2011). One stated reason for this gap is lack of female role models. Saabira Chaudhuri's (2008a) article in *Fast Company* features the 10 "most influential women in web 2.0." However, Chaudhuri was forced to write a follow-up to this article in response to the "overwhelming majority" of sexist comments, including responses such as, "I'd hit each one of them"; "There are no women on the internet"; and "Do her, do her, Oh who hasn't done her, do her, lose the pigtails and we'll talk" (Chaudhuri, 2008b). Chaudhuri's follow-up essay dealt with how hard it is for women to get into the web 2.0 world, and maybe looking at these comments there's little wonder why.

While liberal feminists picture male control of neutral technologies, radical feminists view technology itself as deeply imbued with gendered power relations and as inherently patriarchal. Men not only control technology but also define it in male terms; men construct technology for men. Thus, Cynthia Cockburn's (1984) study of a print workers' union shows how, even as the technology shifted from heavy machinery to computers and more deskilled work, male workers were able to redefine their jobs and preserve their status as skilled craftsmen, thus continuing to marginalize women workers. Similarly, Karen Ashcraft's (2005) study of airline pilots (discussed in this chapter) illustrates how the profession is constructed in a strongly masculine way, with the mastery of airplane technology as a key aspect of this construction process; women are barred from the cockpit and marginalized in the "soft," feminine skills of passenger comfort.

Finally, critical feminists view technology neither as politically neutral nor as inherently patriarchal but, rather, as both limiting and liberating, both material and socially constructed. Some critical feminists with a postmodern emphasis have argued that the new virtual reality blurs the distinction between human and machine, masculine and feminine, allowing users to assume alternative identities and make gender differences much more fluid. In this sense, the virtual world is liberating; networks rather than hierarchy, brains rather than brawn rule the day. However, Judy Wajcman (2010) argues that "the possibility and the fluidity of gender discourse in the virtual world is constrained by the visceral, lived gender relations of the material world" (p. 148). A popular virtual world such as Second Life, for example, offers both antiestablishment values and the ability to take on alternate identities, as well as a site for virtual pornography and sadomasochistic sex acts—environments that are not typically women friendly.

From a feminist perspective, then, technology is neither completely oppressive nor completely liberating, but it *always* has implications for gender and power relations.

❖ MASCULINITY AND ORGANIZATIONAL COMMUNICATION

As I indicated earlier, when people think about gender and feminism they typically think about women's issues. This is partly because, for much of its history, feminism has been concerned with women's rights and advancement, but it's also because, from a "common-sense" perspective, women have gender and men do not. However, as we have already learned, masculinity is just as much a product of social constructions and power relations as femininity is. The case is simply that those groups possessing the most power tend to position themselves as the norm and therefore are relatively invisible. Hence, masculinity typically has not been held up to the same kind of scrutiny as femininity has. So, in this section, we will take a closer look at the relationship between masculinity and organizing.

Historian Gail Bederman (1995) shows that the term *masculinity* came into common usage only in the early 20th century and replaced the term *manliness* in describing appropriate male behavior and identity. From the early to mid-19th century the term *manliness* was used to describe "honor, high-mindedness, and strength stemming from . . . self-mastery" (p. 12). *Manliness* had strong moral connotations, describing a virtuous form of life characterized by gentility and respectability; in complementary fashion, true womanhood involved the pious, maternal guardianship of virtue and the domestic sphere. This conception of manliness was seen as the foundation on which virtuous men could build their fortunes in an entrepreneurial society. Thus, "middle-class men were awarded (or denied) credit based on others' assessment of the manliness of their characters, and credit raters like Dun and Bradstreet reported on businessmen's honesty, probity, and family life" (p. 14).

In the late 19th century, however, this conception of "manliness" changed as the economic landscape shifted from small-scale businesses to the large-scale corporations of industrial capitalism; between 1870 and 1910 the percentage of middle-class men who were self-employed dropped from 67% to 37%. Moreover, middle-class male identity and authority were being challenged on two fronts: by women demanding universal suffrage and by working-class men and immigrants who were increasingly gaining political power through unions (there were 37,000 strikes between 1881 and 1905 in a workforce of only 29 million) and through election to city governments (Bederman, 1995, p. 14). If we add to this scenario a newly diagnosed medical condition called "neurasthenia" (a nervous disorder caused by excessive brain work in an increasingly competitive economy) from which doctors claimed middle-class businessmen were increasingly suffering, then "manliness" as a form of identity was under significant threat.

Bederman (1995) claims that in the face of this threat, middle-class men attempted to remake and revitalize their sense of manhood. For example, social contexts traditionally associated with working-class men, such as saloons and music halls, were increasingly adopted by middle-class men, and values such as physical prowess, aggressiveness, and strong sexuality were seen as desirable traits. Moreover, middle-class men began to take up activities such as sparring and adopted boxing as a spectator sport.

Interestingly, Bederman (1995) indicates that in the late 19th century, as men worked to reshape manhood, they adopted new terms used to denigrate behaviors seen as unmanly. *Sissy*, *pussyfoot*, and *stuffed shirt* were all coined "to denote behavior which had once appeared self-possessed and manly but now seemed overcivilized and effeminate" (p. 17).

In contrast, a new term increasingly emerged to refer to all behaviors that embodied the new, virile sense of manhood—*masculinity*.

In many ways this "new" form of masculinity (which Bederman says was firmly established by 1930) is still hegemonic, or dominant, today. *Aggressiveness, strong heterosexuality, assertiveness, independence, individuality*, and so forth are probably terms that most men (and women) would use to describe what it currently means to be "masculine." The important thing to keep in mind is that this form of **hegemonic masculinity** is not a natural feature of men but is the product of specific historical, economic, political, and social conditions and is open to change and transformation.

In studying workplace masculinity, the focus of many organizational researchers has involved, as management scholar Jeff Hearn (1996) puts it, "deconstructing the dominant—making the one(s) the other(s)" (p. 611). In other words, shining a light on masculinity means exploring how it is constructed as a dominant gender and also enables us to think about other ways in which masculinity might be performed (Connell, 1993, 1995). As Mills and Chiaramonte (1991) put it, organizations provide a gendered "metacommunicative" frame; that is, they communicate about the appropriate gendered communicative practices in which we should engage.

Of course, such frames do not *dictate* how we must enact our gendered identities—masculine or feminine—but, as I indicated above, we are always held accountable for our gendered performances, hence rendering us open to sanctions if we do not perform adequately. Women are often sanctioned if they fail to act in an appropriately "feminine" manner (whatever that might mean), while men are often sanctioned for exhibiting behavior that is not appropriately masculine (again, the meaning of this varies from context to context).

It is important to note, though, that when we talk about masculinity we are not referring to individual men or women and the ways they act. Instead, masculinity refers to a set of routines, scripts, and discourses that shape behavior. In this sense, masculinity is less a personality trait and more a set of meanings and institutional frames through which we are held accountable for our gendered performances. In addition, masculinity as a gendered practice makes sense only in relation to femininity; neither stands alone as a meaningful identity.

Let me give you an example from my own life. During my summer breaks when I was in college I worked for an agricultural contractor called Farmwork Services that provided crop-spraying services to local farmers (not many young adults have such romantic and rewarding summer employment!). Many of the men I worked with (and they were all men, apart from one female clerical worker in the office) were relatively uneducated (some never finished high school), and all were poorly paid, earning wages barely above the poverty line. It would be fair to say that all of them were very much working class. All, however, had strong mechanical and technical skills; one had trained as a JCB driver (a JCB is a large, earth-moving machine), another could fix any engine around, and another had extensive body-shop experience. In one way or another, all had practical skills that I most certainly did not have.

When I think back to that time, it's clear to me that much of the interaction among us was rooted in, and expressive of, a particular kind of working-class masculinity, not dissimilar from that of the workers in David Collinson's study discussed earlier. Of course, there was the usual banter and joking about sexual performance (questions like, "Did you get any [sex] last night?" abounded), as well as the ritual daily passing around of the "Page Three girl" in *The Sun*—a daily tabloid that always featured a topless model.

But beyond these more obvious expressions of masculine heterosexuality, working-class masculinity was also performed in more subtle ways. For example, there were informal, though strictly enforced, rules about who sat in which chair in the crew room. As a new employee I made the mistake of sitting in a senior employee's seat and was told in no uncertain terms to move, finally being allocated the least-desirable seat by the drafty crew room door. Also, early in my employment I made the mistake of picking up and reading a newspaper sitting on the seat next to me. The owner of the newspaper berated me for this faux pas; what I quickly discovered was that a newspaper became common property in the crew room only when its owner had read it to his satisfaction; opening a crisp, clean newspaper for the first time was the owner's prerogative and no one else's.

Finally, one of the most distinctive ways in which masculinity was performed was through employees' careful separation of book knowledge and white-collar work on the one hand, and practical knowledge and blue-collar work on the other hand. Much of the employees' identities as men was tied up in the practical skills they possessed, whether that involved working complex equipment, repainting company vehicles, or spraying crops with chemicals. Moreover, despite the fact that they were more poorly paid than the white-collar office workers and managers, they frequently compared themselves favorably with them, arguing that the managers knew little about the "real work" they did. In fact, one of the employees who had expertise in spray painting vehicles turned a 2-day job into 3 days of work because he knew his supervisor had no idea how such a job was done. Such resistance to managerial control is not unusual as workers attempt to maintain some degree of autonomy in work environments where they have little power.

Work at Farmwork Services, then, was defined in part by the working-class masculine identities employees enacted in the workplace. These identities were constructed partly through identification with a particular kind of work—hard, physical labor that required engagement with and mastery of something tangible—and partly through opposition to other forms of identity that did not pass muster on the masculinity front. The latter included white-collar masculinity that involved "paper pushing" or "book knowledge" and any form of femininity (most of the men I worked with placed women in two categories— sex objects and faithful or nagging wives—but either way they were placed in a subordinate position).

While this kind of masculinity is quite common, the reality is that there are multiple forms of workplace and professional masculinity. For example, the airline pilot identity we discussed earlier would clearly not pass the masculinity test at Farmwork Services, but it nevertheless involves a very strong sense of masculine identity that is intricately connected to the kind of work pilots engage in. Indeed, as Karen Ashcraft (2007) suggests, there is even a gender hierarchy among airline crew members, with captains at the top and first officers and flight attendants arranged below them. As one airline captain states:

Being a Captain is a different world. . . . You're the helper as the copilot, and if something comes along, it's just like being with your dad in a way. . . . But as Captain, I feel like those [the crew] are all under my protection, or they're my responsibility, but it's a happy responsibility. . . . And your other fellow crew members have a lot more confidence in you. . . . [Q: So is it kind of like being a dad?] It is. It is! You're the dad of the crew. These are your kids, you know, kind of. (p. 22)

Again, as was the case with Farmwork Services' workers, we can see how a gendered identity is always constructed in relationship to other identities that are perceived as different or lacking. In this instance, airline pilots gain their authority in the cockpit not merely because of their technical expertise (although, obviously, that is an important part of it) but because those around them continually—and communicatively—reinforce and hence legitimate that identity. For example, Ashcraft (2007) reports an incident where a flight attendant scolded a newly promoted captain who was folding a blanket in the passenger cab, saying, "You're a Captain. Captains don't fold blankets." Thus, "she instructs the Captain that her work is beneath him" (p. 25).

As we discussed above, gender roles are not simply acted out in individualistic ways but, rather, are produced through interactions with others who hold us accountable for playing out those roles. Such accountability leaves us open to sanction when we fail to meet the standards of the organization or those around us—even if those other people occupy subordinate positions in the organizational hierarchy.

For example, author Joseph Finder (1987) provides an interesting account of his experience working as a secretary in a large corporation (the title of the article, "A Male Secretary," gives some insight into how gendered the traditional secretarial role is). He describes how everyone who visited the office where he worked would try to make sense of his role there by asking questions such as, "Are you filling in for the regular secretary?" or "Are you working here temporarily?" Even his boss would try to avoid giving him certain tasks, such as photocopying, and would frequently stop by his desk to talk sports ("How about those Red Sox?") in an effort to reassert a "normal" masculine relationship. Interestingly, even his female secretarial coworkers refused to accept his presence there or his claims that this was his "real" job, choosing instead to encourage him to move on to "better things" (which of course he eventually did, becoming a successful writer).

To me, this is a great example of how gendered organizational structures and ideologies constantly reassert themselves and reify established power relations, with those in subordinate positions often working to reproduce such power relations, even when they are not in their own best interests. Thus, rather than see the presence of a male secretary as a possibility for challenging traditional gender roles and creating the potential for change, the women secretaries instead choose to hold Finder accountable for his gender violation, hence reproducing their own subordination to gender ideologies that limit their own professional mobility.

Masculinity, then, is worthy of our consideration because it is usually taken for granted in the wider culture and has profound implications for how we view men, women, and their relationships with each other. As we have seen, masculinity is every bit as socially constructed as femininity, and what counts as masculine behavior is dependent on a number of contextual factors, including historical precedent, economic conditions, class, race, organizational culture, and so forth. I am personally interested in masculinity in part because I think it shapes contemporary organizational life in numerous ways. As I indicated earlier in the chapter, quoting Jane Flax, both men and women are "prisoners of gender," and, as such, we need to understand how contemporary conceptions of masculinity (and the kinds of femininity that complement them) both enable and limit possibilities for personal growth and development in organizational life.

The idea that masculinity, like femininity, is socially constructed means it is potentially open to change and transformation. Thus, although one might argue that the kind of hegemonic masculinity Bederman (1995) describes is still dominant in organizations and society more broadly, it is certainly the case that competing, or alternative, masculinities exist. Eric Anderson's (2009) notion of "inclusive masculinity," for example, challenges the idea that masculinity is always rooted in homophobia and antifemininity. His ethnographic study of members of fraternities and university sports teams such as soccer and rugby reveals a greater openness to alternative masculinities, such as gay and more feminine men, than has usually been seen as typical for such social contexts, where domination, aggression, competition, sexism, and homophobia are thought to prevail. "Inclusive masculinity" doesn't necessarily challenge or overthrow hegemonic or orthodox masculinity but, instead, broadens the range of possibilities for legitimate expressions of masculinity. If we think back to our earlier discussion of gender and accountability, we might say that Anderson's study suggests that young men in the contexts he studied (university sports teams and fraternities) are less likely to hold one another to a narrow definition of what "counts" as appropriately masculine behavior. In your experience, do you agree with this assessment?

Critical Case Study 9.1
Why My Mom Isn't a Feminist

Everyone has an opinion about feminism, including my mom. At 87, she's experienced a lot in her life. She left school at 14 to care for her new baby sister because her mother was too sick to do it herself. She worked in a munitions factory during World War II and then got married in 1945, when she was 20. She had four children (all boys) and has run a household her entire life. When my brothers and I were old enough, my mom wanted to go out to work, but my dad wouldn't let her. He said it was his job to be the breadwinner and her job to look after the children (and him, of course) and keep house. It was years before my mom was "allowed" to take a number of different part-time jobs. Now that my dad has passed away she freely admits that, even though she's a good cook, she hated having to cook meals every day and get them on the table at a certain time for my dad and us kids to eat. In many respects, being a widow has given her a degree of freedom to decide her own schedule that she never had as a married woman.

Politically, I would describe my mom as left of middle. She's in favor of gay rights and believes in equal opportunities for everyone, regardless of race, gender, or sexuality. But she wouldn't describe herself as a feminist. In fact, I've often heard her refer to "those feminists" in a derogatory manner. As far as she's concerned, "those feminists" have gone too far and are responsible for the more extreme effects of "political correctness." She often cites as an example "the fact" that it was feminists who were responsible for "Benny Hill" being taken off TV because it was considered derogatory toward women! And my mom really liked Benny Hill!

Why would my mom be antifeminist? In many ways, she's precisely the kind of woman the 1960s and 1970s second wave of feminism was interested in reaching. In lots of ways she has been denied opportunities in her life because she grew up in a male-dominated society. She was denied an adequate education because of her sex (her *brother* wasn't expected to leave school and take care of the new baby). She wasn't allowed to have a career because of a husband who insisted on traditional sex roles. And all her energies and sense of fulfillment had to be channeled into raising children and making a home—a role that was basically complete by the time she reached her early 50s. In many ways, she perfectly fits the profile of the frustrated homemaker Betty Friedan (1963) depicts in *The Feminine Mystique*—the book that helped launch the second wave of feminism. If anyone was a candidate for consciousness raising, it was my mom!

Discussion Questions

1. Would you describe yourself as feminist? Why or why not?

2. Where have your ideas about feminism come from?

3. How have your ideas about feminism changed, if at all, after reading this chapter?

4. How relevant to your everyday life are the gender issues addressed in this chapter?

5. Can you think of any situations in which you were held accountable for your performance of gender and found lacking? How did this make you feel? In what ways, if any, did you change your behavior?

6. To what extent are you conscious of gendered aspects of your sense of identity? How does this affect your behavior? Give some examples.

❖ CONCLUSION

In this chapter we have examined the relationship between gender and organizing. To begin with we discussed three different feminist perspectives that provided us with three very different lenses for viewing the gender-organization perspective. While all three perspectives are useful in their own right, the critical feminist approach best captures the ways in which gender is a socially constructed, communicative phenomenon. Moreover, the critical feminist approach enables us to think of gender as an ongoing accomplishment of everyday organizational life that always occurs in the context of power relations; everyone is held accountable for the performance of gender, but some people are held more accountable than others. Finally, the critical feminist perspective enables us to see gender not as simply a characteristic of individuals but, rather, as an endemic, defining feature of organizational life. In claiming that organizations are gendered, we are saying that the very meanings, structures, routines, and norms of organizing are rooted in particular understanding of male and female, masculine and feminine. By examining the relationship between gender and power in this way, we can develop a better understanding of how gender issues thread themselves in complex ways through everyday organizational life.

In the last part of the chapter we looked at masculinity and organizational communication. This is important in part because, as a rule, men and masculinity are the neutral norm against which gender performances are measured. By unpacking masculinity and its meanings we can better understand how what is "normal" and "natural" comes into being and, thus, how what complements the normal (femininity, alternative masculinities, etc.) is positioned in society and in organizational life. This opens up the possibilities for thinking about what alternatives to "hegemonic masculinity" might look like.

Overall, we have tried in this chapter to think about gender and organizational communication in more complex ways than it is typically discussed. Through this process we can better reflect on the role gender plays in everyday organizational life.

CRITICAL APPLICATIONS

1. Conduct a "gender analysis" of yourself. How would you describe your own gendered identity? Keep in mind that this is different from your sexuality; it refers to the ways you engage in a gendered performance as you engage with others in social situations. Do you see yourself as highly masculine/feminine? Metrosexual? Why? What is it about your gender identity that enables you to classify yourself in this way?

2. Think about some examples from your everyday organizational life that illustrate how gender is socially constructed. What consequences does this social construction process have for the way organizations operate and make decisions?

KEY TERMS

critical feminism 216	glass escalator 209	liberal feminism 207
feminism 206	hegemonic masculinity 223	radical feminism 214
gender accountability 218	homosocial reproduction 210	tokenism 209
glass ceiling 208		

STUDENT STUDY SITE

Visit the student study site at **www.sagepub.com/mumbyorg** for these additional learning tools:

- Web quizzes
- eFlashcards
- SAGE journal articles

- Video resources
- Web resources

CHAPTER 10

Communicating Difference at Work

Increased difference and diversity characterize the 21st century organization.

> *Fear of difference is dread of life itself.*
>
> —Mary Parker Follett (1924, p. 301)

Why is studying difference important? A simple answer to this question is that the advent of the "new workplace" and the shift away from the bureaucratic form has been accompanied by the development of a more inclusive workplace. There is, in other words, a lot more difference around. As such, it is important to get an understanding of the complex dynamics of difference in current organizational life. More profoundly, however, as questions of identity become increasingly central to work life, we need to understand how difference plays a central role in human identity construction. While we will address identity and the meaning of work in Chapter 14, in this chapter we will focus on difference as a central organizing principle of the workplace.

Although it has traditionally been a neglected area of study, a number of organizational communication scholars have begun to examine the question of difference and to think about how it can be addressed from a communication perspective (Allen, 1996, 2003, 2007; Ashcraft, 2011; Mumby, 2011b). From this viewpoint, differences such as race, class, gender, sexuality, and so forth, are not natural but are historical, political, and economic constructs that require a lot of communicative labor to maintain them (Dempsey, 2009). However, arguing that forms of difference are socially constructed does not negate their real-world consequences. Indeed, we will discuss the ways the communicative construction of difference shapes the material and economic realities of difference in its various forms. The organization of difference in the workplace, then, is very much a consequence of the communicative labor that has occurred across several generations.

Following the suggestion of organizational communication scholar Karen Ashcraft (2011) we will address difference by asking the question, "How does communication organize work through difference?" In other words, rather than think of difference as a set of individual characteristics ("natural" or otherwise) or as something that exists "in" organizational settings (e.g., "We have a diverse workforce"), we will think of difference as an organizing principle that—through communication processes—shapes the meaning, structure, and very practice of work.

❖ DEFINING DIFFERENCE

How might we define **difference**? Borrowing a conception from communication scholars Mark Orbe and Tina Harris (2001) that they developed to define race as a category of difference, we can say that *difference is a social construction "that has been used to classify human beings into separate value-based categories"* (p. 6). A number of interconnected issues are associated with this definition:

1. Difference is connected to power; that is, those in power construct differences that create systems of enfranchisement and disenfranchisement. In this sense, differences are not benign or neutral in their effects.

2. All differences are not created equal. Each pair in a binary system of difference is characterized by a dominant, more highly valued pole and a subordinate, less-valued pole. In the following pairs, for example, the first item in the binary pair is historically dominant and valued, while the second is subordinate and less valued: man/woman, white/black, heterosexual/homosexual, able-bodied/disabled, white collar/blue collar. All binary differences contain a positive and a negative element.

3. Related, difference contrasts with and complements what is defined as normal. That is, the dominant term in each of the pairs above is normalized and becomes the largely invisible (because it is the taken-for-granted norm) lens through which the lesser term is measured. A "deviation" from the norm is that which is different and hence targeted for classification and investigation. For example, as we will see below, "whiteness" is the invisible, normalized racial category against which other racial categories are constructed, classified, and assigned value.

4. Difference is communicatively constructed. That is, differences are produced and maintained through various forms of talk, texts, and interactions. Racial

differences, for example, are maintained and reproduced through something as mundane as a job application form or as significant as anti-miscegenation laws in the United States, which operated from the late 17th century until (in some states) the 1960s.

Differences are therefore not naturally occurring; they are social constructions that get normalized and institutionalized in organizations. Such institutionalization serves the interests of the dominant group, who will often go to great lengths to preserve that dominance if it appears under threat by anyone regarded as different. Historically, dominant groups have organized in both formal and informal ways to marginalize difference, including, for example, opposition to women's suffrage, Jim Crow legislation in the U.S. South, and criminalization and demonization of homosexuality (including its classification as a mental disorder until the early 1970s).

But wait a second, I hear you say. How can you argue that differences are not naturally occurring when they clearly exist in the world? We have men and women, white people and people of color, heterosexuals and homosexuals, and so on. This is, of course, true. However, it's also false. Race, for example, is a humanly constructed category. Society (well, the people in power in society) has taken an arbitrary difference between groups of people (one that makes up an infinitesimal part of our DNA) and has constructed a massive cultural, political, and economic edifice around it. In this sense, "race" as a category is a powerful ideological construct rooted in an arbitrary, insignificant biological variation among humans. Just because it is a "mere" construct, however, does not mean that race does not organize the world in ways that have genuine material and economic consequences for people, as the examples above suggest.

Thus, we can argue that what is most interesting and central to our understanding of difference is the process by which particular differences are structured into society and identified as important, while others are not. In other words, following the anthropologist Gregory Bateson (1972), we can ask the question, what are "the differences that make a difference?" Which differences are coded in ways that make them central to how we make sense of the world and construct systems of meaning around them?

Let's now look more closely at two important forms of difference and examine their relationship to organizational communication: (1) race and (2) sexuality.

❖ RACE AND ORGANIZATIONAL COMMUNICATION

Putting Race and Organization in Historical Context

It's very evident in reading books such as William H. Whyte's (1956) *The Organization Man* or Rosabeth Moss Kanter's (1977) *Men and Women of the Corporation* that for most of the 20th century, organizations were dominated by white males (again, think *Mad Men*). As we saw in the previous chapter, this was functional if you were a white male, but it pretty much sucked if you were not.

In fact, the idea that difference and diversity among employees was a good thing did not even register as an issue with mid-20th century managers. In the 1950s and 1960s (and even into the 1970s) managers did not walk around thinking, "We really need to make our organization more diverse—if only I could attract lots of female and minority employees." The white maleness of most organizations was just a fact—the way things were and always had been, with no need for justification. In this sense, whiteness was the invisible, taken-for-granted norm against which everything was measured. Indeed, the presence of the occasional token woman or person of color in managerial positions often reaffirmed the white male norm, especially as these token employees often failed, hence providing justification for the "natural order" of the work world.

For example, Helen Richey was hired in 1934 as the first female pilot for a major airline. Such was the outcry from male pilots (with the main argument being that her menstrual cycle would affect her judgment!) that the airline severely restricted her duties, and she resigned in less than a year. The next female airline pilot was not hired until the 1970s (Ashcraft & Mumby, 2004).

Furthermore, this white male norm obscured the fact that while women and minorities were largely absent from managerial and professional positions, they have always been a significant presence at lower levels of organizations, occupying unskilled and semi-skilled positions in factories and on production lines throughout the history of industrial capitalism.

Management scholars Stewart Clegg, David Courpasson, and Nelson Phillips (2006) even argue that there was a strong racial element to the surveillance Henry Ford's Sociological Department imposed on Ford's employees. The department consisted of teams of investigators whose job was to make sure that workers at Ford were living a clean, sober, industrious, and thrifty private life worthy of their $5-a-day wage. Many Ford workers in the early 20th century were African Americans who had migrated from the South in search of work. Clegg et al. argue that much of the motivation for the surveillance program was a larger society-level "moral panic" that focused on the apparent connections among African American migration, alcohol, and jazz music. Such moral panics, they argue, were "barely coded concerns for the contagion of white society by black bodies and black culture" (p. 59). As a 1921 edition of *Ladies Home Journal* stated:

> The effect of jazz on the normal brain produces an atrophied condition of the brain cells of conception, until very frequently those under the demoralizing influence of the persistent use of syncopation, combined with the inharmonic partial tones, are actually incapable of distinguishing between good and evil, right and wrong. (Quoted in Clegg et al., 2006, p. 59)

It is easy to see here how a form of culture originating with African Americans is constructed in the popular imagination as a threat to (white) social order. This is just one small example of how difference is simultaneously constructed and marginalized in an effort to maintain the status quo.

The relationships among race, ethnicity and work are particularly fascinating when we examine U.S. history in the late 19th and early 20th centuries. While the United States is generally described as a "nation of immigrants" and a "great melting pot," this period of massive immigration from Europe (and the intense competition for jobs) is also a period during which many debates took place about national identity and, more specifically, which immigrant groups counted as "white." Such debates were hardly academic and had a profound effect on the ability of particular immigrant groups to find work.

For example, as labor historian David Roediger (2005) shows, Italian immigrants were discriminated against by being constructed as nonwhite, and frequently as black. Roediger reports that the Italian diaspora in the United States was racialized both as "the Chinese of Europe" (a group historically barred by law from working in the United States after their work on the railroad system was completed) and linked closely to Africans. Indeed, in a fascinating insight into how Italian immigrants were "othered" (i.e., marginalized) through racial classification, Roediger states: "The one black family on the *Titanic* was until recently lost to history in part because 'Italian' was used as a generic term for all the darker skinned passengers on board" (p. 47). Roediger also indicates that in the Jim Crow South, Italians were sometimes assigned to black schools. When in 1911 a white Louisiana lynch mob killed 11 Italians, their perceived identity as "nonwhite" was a significant factor in the actions of the mob.

In a similar manner, Hungarians and Eastern Europeans more broadly were identified in the early 20th century as nonwhite. Known by the racial slur "Hunky" (a corruption of Hungarian) or "Bohunk" (Bohemian-Hungarian), the term shifted from a specific reference to Hungarian immigrants and became applied more widely to unskilled immigrant workers from central and Eastern Europe. One early 20th century Texas planter worried that "Bohunks wanted to intermarry with whites," adding that, "yes, they're white but they're not our kind of white" (Roediger, 2005, p. 43).

From a 21st century perspective such a system of classification seems to defy logic. However, it provides important insight into the degree to which "race" as a "difference that makes a difference" has little to do with biology and "natural" divisions among racial groups and everything to do with the broader political, economic, and historical context that shapes human behavior and decision making. The "strangeness" of the classification system in operation here suggests how truly contextual efforts to construct difference can be; they are rooted less in "natural" or essential criteria and much more in efforts to construct systems of inclusion and exclusion that protect the interests of particular groups at particular points in history (in these instances, white males).

These examples also suggest to us how fluid and changeable identities can be, and how such changes happen through political and economic factors. Thus, the fact that Italians, Hungarians, Irish, Greeks, Austrians, and so forth are no longer "othered" (at least for the most part) has less to do with people simply becoming more enlightened and more to do with changing political and economic circumstances in which an expanding economy needed more workers to work in various industries as well as to contribute to economic well-being by purchasing consumer goods. Constructions of forms of difference such as race, gender, and sexuality, amongst others, then, have much to do with context—historical, cultural, economic, and political.

Race and the Contemporary Workplace

It is perhaps not surprising to learn that race is both widely examined and partly ignored in the study of work and organizations. For the most part, when race and ethnicity are taken seriously by theorists and practitioners it is usually in the context of **managing diversity** and cultivating a workplace that reflects the demography of the wider population in terms of race, gender, and ethnicity. Such claims are typically made in terms of a "business case" for diversity; that is, organizations that do not develop a diverse workforce are deemed to be hurting their bottom line because they are not drawing on the full range of skill sets offered by the entire working population (e.g., Martino, 1999; Moss, 2010; Ross, 1992).

On the other hand, the heavy focus on "managing diversity" means that race is rarely treated as a central theme in research on organizations. In other words, race is a focus of study only under certain circumstances, typically involving a deviation from the white norm (as in the perceived need, for example, to diversify the workforce, or in investigating minority leadership styles). However, just as we saw in the previous chapter how a focus on gender issues is not synonymous with studying women employees (men "do gender," too), so a focus on race and ethnicity need not be exclusively about people of color; white people also "do race," but mostly in an invisible manner by virtue of their taken-for-granted "neutral" status.

Thus, rather than think of race as relevant only in the context of "minority" issues, we would need to think about it as an everyday feature of organizational life. Moreover, a view of organizations as "raced" (similar to how we can think of organizations as "gendered") means that we need to explore the relationships among race, organizing, and power. It's less useful to think of race as being about individuals who possess a certain racial or ethnic identity, and more useful to view race as a structural aspect of organizations and society that shapes meanings, values, and identities. As we have seen, differences are produced by power (who controls what differences make a difference?), and so race is more fruitfully understood as a sedimented system of meanings and practices that have differential effects on organization members, depending on their social location.

Such a position enables us to go beyond seeing the race–organization relationship as simply about managing cultural differences between individual people in order to improve organizational effectiveness. Instead, we can think about how, from a critical perspective, power relations are created and sustained by the communicative production of difference. Let's briefly examine one area of research in organizational communication to provide a sense of how thinking about race as an everyday feature of organizational life might change our perceptions of work and organizing.

Organizational communication scholar Brenda Allen's (1996, 1998, 2000) analysis of organizational socialization shows how thematizing race can alter our understanding of how these processes work. For the most part, research on this topic has taken the white professional worker as the universal norm for explaining how new employees move through stages of organizational socialization. In perhaps the most famous and widely adopted model, Jablin (2001) lays out different stages of socialization: anticipatory socialization, assimilation, and exit. In the first stage, people gather information about work from friends, family, school, the popular media, and so forth, all of which creates certain expectations about the nature of work. In the second stage, a worker enters an organization and goes through an assimilation process characterized by organizational efforts to integrate the worker into its formal and informal norms and values, and efforts on the part of the worker to tailor a position to his or her own goals, interests, and expectations. Jablin argues that at some point a "metamorphosis" occurs in which the worker adjusts his or her expectations, resolves organizational conflicts, and develops her or his own individualized job role. Finally, exit occurs when the worker leaves the organization for a different position.

Adopting feminist standpoint theory and writing from her perspective as an African American scholar, Allen provides a critique of Jablin's model, arguing that its supposedly "universal" principles do not very accurately capture the experience of many women and workers of color. Feminist standpoint theory argues that knowledge must be grounded in people's lived experiences (standpoints) and that differences between the lived experiences of men and women, white people and people of color, provide the opportunity for knowledge claims that reflect the situated experiences of women and minorities. Thus, Allen's life experience as an African American woman enables her to bring a different lens to the process of organizational socialization—a lens that does not unreflectively mirror the "universal" model of socialization.

Drawing on her experience of being socialized as a faculty member into a U.S. university setting, Allen (1996, 1998) describes how her socialization experience cannot be fully accounted for by Jablin's model. For example, Allen notes that a woman of color is likely to encounter negative experiences on a much more regular basis than the socialization literature suggests. As the only black woman faculty member in her department, and one of very few on campus, she was regularly confronted by everyday acts of stereotyping that required a great deal of energy for her to process and make sense of. A few of these "socialization" experiences included the following:

- During a conversation at a faculty reception, a white female faculty member asked her to sing a "negro spiritual."
- After the first day of class a white male student informed her that he was dropping her class because he had already fulfilled his ethnic studies requirement (even though the class was not about race or ethnicity).
- A colleague told her that another colleague was overheard telling a group of students she was not qualified for her job and was hired only because she is a black woman.
- She was called on to do a variety of tasks her white colleagues were not asked to do, such as serving on task forces on minority issues, having dinner with visiting minority job candidates, giving advice to minority students who were not in her classes, and so forth.

Note that these behaviors do not involve outright racism (though bullet points one and three do flirt with it) but, rather, point more to the ways in which the broader organizational culture in which Allen works institutionalizes and normalizes a white worldview. Allen's blackness is not only constructed as different and exotic but as over-determining who she is as an individual. Her socialization experience suggests that her white colleagues largely reduce her to her blackness. In this sense, everyday organizational communication processes construct Allen as an **outsider within** the professional culture into which she is being socialized (Hill Collins, 1991).

Thus, Allen's research on organizational socialization effectively illustrates the limits of research that generalizes the white experience in organizations to all people—the everyday experience of an increasingly significant portion of the workforce is largely overlooked.

It is important to stress one other point about Allen's research. Earlier we indicated that to examine organizations as "raced" is to move away from a perspective that sees race as largely about individual and cultural differences. For example, it is quite possible to frame the examples of Allen's experience listed above as simply interpersonal differences and cultural insensitivities on the part of the people involved (one could argue, for example, that the female faculty member who asked to hear a "negro spiritual" was simply trying to be welcoming and acknowledge Allen's cultural heritage). However, such a position ignores the degree to which Allen's experiences occur within a set of power relations rooted in white patriarchy. As such, the "default" way of thinking, talking, and sense making reflects white, patriarchal norms that regularly position Allen as an "outsider within."

It's fairly easy to demonstrate that this is the case. As a thought experiment, imagine that, at the faculty reception, out of the blue Allen asked the white female faculty member to sing a song from a Broadway musical. We can immediately see how such a request is pretty absurd, if not demeaning, particularly in a professional context. Such a frame of reference seems especially absurd because it assumes that, as a white woman, the faculty member would know any Broadway tunes or identify with that genre. As such, this counter-example reveals how a particular interpersonal encounter is not just about personal bias or misunderstanding (it can be that, too) but is situated within larger relations of power.

In sum, the process of organizational socialization looks very different from the perspective of an "outsider within" such as Allen. Because of the historically sedimented assumptions about organizational life and the predominantly white viewpoint they reflect, there is little that Allen can take for granted as she "learns the ropes" of the organization—stuff that many of you reading this book (and me, too!) can take for granted: assumption of your competence until evidence proves otherwise (rather than the reverse); formal and informal ready-made networks that provide an instant support system (rather than having to seek out actively or perhaps create a network from scratch); relative anonymity that lets you get on with your job (rather than high visibility in which every mistake is noted); and mentors who share your experience (rather than no mentors, or mentors who have little in common with your life experience).

Another way race tends to get marginalized in organizational communication is through a heavy focus on the corporate context. As Ashcraft and Allen (2003, p. 14) argue, white-collar workplaces and workers have largely been treated as the universal setting for the study of organizations. In some respects this is understandable, given that the corporate firm has been the main object of analysis for management research for the past 100 years or more. And, of course, white males have dominated this organizational context for the vast majority of that period. However, this perspective overlooks the fact that a significant percentage of people do not work in such contexts, occupying either low-income, "dirty-work" positions (Ashforth & Kreiner, 1999; Ashforth, Kreiner, Clark, & Fugate, 2007), working minimum-wage jobs in the service sector, or even working outside the formal economy altogether.

Studying these other organizing practices and forms can help us get a better handle not only on the complexity of various organizational forms but also on the struggles of women and men of color in negotiating life at the margins of the economy. Let me talk about a study that illustrates this alternative perspective on organizations.

In *Sidewalk,* sociologist Mitch Duneier (1999) provides a rich and interesting example of organizing processes in the face of extreme social, political, and economic conditions. In a long-term ethnographic study, he documents life on the streets of lower Manhattan for a predominantly African American group of book vendors who sell their wares from stalls set up on the sidewalk (hence, the title of the book). Most of these men are homeless, many have criminal records, and a number are former or current drug addicts or alcoholics. What's particularly interesting about this study is Duneier's focus on how the men collectively create a fragile but functional community that helps them redevelop a sense of self after "hitting bottom." For example, in the face of efforts by the city to restrict their space to sell books, they develop an informal code of conduct that allows everyone access to space.

Furthermore, Duneier's (1999) study functions as an explicit critique of accepted policy on the homeless. In contrast to conventional wisdom that says the homeless should be treated like "broken windows" and removed from the street (public policy analysts have determined that broken windows and other signs of decay in a neighborhood lead to more crime and must be cleaned up if an area is not to deteriorate), Duneier argues that these men actually serve a positive function in the neighborhood in which they work. He argues that, in fact, the booksellers serve as "eyes on the street," contributing to a sense of social order in the neighborhood in which they work.

Duneier's (1999) study thus extends our understanding of organizations in at least two ways: (1) He provides a rich analysis of an organizational form usually excluded from management and organization research, and (2) he studies this community not from a managerial perspective but from the point of view of the members of that community (for example, his chapter on "going to the bathroom" seriously challenges white, middle-class assumptions about that most delicate and private of behaviors).

Other researchers have conducted studies that similarly focus on racial groups typically marginalized in the study of organizations. For example, Patricia Zavella (1985) looks at the Mexican cannery workers and their use of family networks in the workplace, and Louis Lamphere (1985) examines the ways white ethnic garment workers create a culture of workplace resistance by "bringing the family to work" through celebration of birthdays, marriages, births, and so forth.

In sum, moving away from an almost exclusive focus on the corporate worksite and white(-collar) workers will enable us to gain a greater appreciation of the broad scope of work experiences.

Interrogating Whiteness and Organizational Communication

As I indicated earlier, if we are to take race seriously in studying and understanding organizations, then we need to treat it in a thematic way and not just as a problem that crops up under particular circumstances. Race should not only be an issue when, for example, instances of racial bias come to the fore or when organizations recognize the need for great workforce diversity.

One of the ways to address race as an everyday, routine feature of organizational life is to explore **whiteness** as a socially constructed racial category (Frankenberg, 1993; Grimes, 2001, 2002; Martin & Nakayama, 1999). In this context, whiteness is not the same as being a white person. Rather, we can think of whiteness as "a set of institutionalized practices and ideas that people participate in consciously and unconsciously" (Parker & Mease, 2009,

p. 317). Thus, we can distinguish between the institutionalized practices and ideas that make up whiteness as a societal discourse or narrative, and the behavior, talk, and ideas of specific white people. From this perspective, we can explore the ways white people—either consciously or unconsciously—protect their own "normal status" by reproducing whiteness, or else challenge and interrogate the discourse of whiteness.

As a socially constructed racial category, whiteness is simultaneously taken for granted, largely invisible, and the yardstick for judgment. An example will perhaps help illustrate this point. Rhetoric scholar Carrie Crenshaw (1997) reports the following meeting with a white student from her communication and diversity course:

> [She] came to me in tears struggling with her beliefs about race. She volunteered her reluctance to return home because her family members were racist. We talked at length, and at the end of our conversation she thanked me with a smile and said, "I'm glad you're white. You're so much more objective than other professors." (p. 253)

Crenshaw finds this incident interesting (and disturbing to her own sense of identity) because it illustrates a pretty rare occurrence in everyday talk—white people talking about and naming whiteness. For the most part, whiteness goes unnamed while remaining the "hidden-in-plain-sight" norm against which deviations from that norm are judged. In explicitly naming Crenshaw as white, the student did a couple of things: (1) She equated whiteness with objectivity, thus suggesting that nonwhite people are unable to be objective about issues of race (because they "have" race, whereas white people do not), and (2) she placed Crenshaw herself in a position of privilege, better able to rule on matters of race precisely because she is perceived as having no race. In this sense, one might argue, the student's naming of Crenshaw as white is less about placing her in a specific racial category and more about imbuing her with the supposed objectivity that comes with her "nonracial" whiteness.

This example also nicely illustrates an earlier point I made about race—it is relevant not only when identifiable racial incidents occur but also when performed at the level of everyday life, in the moment-to-moment of routine organizing (such as a student meeting with a professor). In this sense, race is structured into everyday life through ideological struggles over meaning. Whiteness, then, "functions ideologically when people employ it, consciously or unconsciously, as a framework to categorize people and understand their social location" (Crenshaw, 1997, p. 253). Thus, the student (probably unconsciously) uses whiteness ideologically to position her professor in a specific social location—a neutral arbiter on racial issues. By implication, of course, such a position also does the ideological work of positioning professors of color as lacking objectivity because they are "raced" in a visible manner (at least as framed from the position of the invisible white norm).

One of the benefits of "interrogating whiteness," then, is that it makes visible the ways that race and power come together in routine ways to reproduce the organizational status quo. Interrogating whiteness is about "making the center visible" (Nakayama & Krizek, 1995); that is, it highlights the processes through which whiteness itself is both obscured as a category and the norm against which organizational life is defined. A brief example will illustrate this point.

The term *affirmative action* refers to efforts to recruit underrepresented groups into colleges, government organizations, and corporations. It is based on recognition that minority groups have historically been denied professional and educational opportunities because of their minority status; in other words, for many generations, most organizations were bastions of white male privilege, and affirmative action is an attempt to correct that. In recent years, affirmation action has come under fire (including legal challenges) for giving undue preference to underqualified minorities and denying opportunities to qualified white applicants.

Interestingly, *Wall Street Journal* reporter Daniel Golden (2006) reports that—at least in the case of college admissions—this is a misleading view of affirmative action. His study shows that a form of affirmative action is practiced at élite institutions (Harvard, Princeton, Yale, etc.), where the children of rich white alums are admitted even though they may fail to meet the minimum admission standards. In fact, Golden suggests that such students are admitted at a higher rate than are racial minorities—the students who are supposed to benefit from affirmative action policies. This issue is broader than college admission policies, because élite institutions (government, the law, the media, Wall Street, etc.) still recruit heavily from the Ivy League. For example, former President George W. Bush was admitted to Yale because of family connections, not because of his academic qualifications.

In this example we see a very different conception of affirmative action—one that is about white privilege and white preferential treatment. It undermines our conventional understanding of affirmative action and shows how easily we can slip into thinking of it as simply about favoring members of minority groups. It demonstrates how the "conventional wisdom" about affirmative action operates from a perspective of whiteness, where white privilege generally becomes invisible and is therefore not subject to scrutiny. When affirmative action is focused on racial minorities, it is *always* under scrutiny and subject to questioning and challenge.

In fact, we could argue that, at the level of everyday organizational life, a subtle, informal form of affirmative action operates for whites—particularly middle-class professional white men, such as me. Indeed, I might argue that I walk around with what Peggy McIntosh (1990) has described as the **invisible knapsack**—a set of privileges and practices that white people carry around with them that largely protect them from everyday injustices. For example, I don't have to worry about students doubting my competence when I walk into the classroom on the first day (worrying about it halfway through the semester when students have had the chance to watch me in action is a different matter, but I'm given the benefit of the doubt until I prove otherwise!). I go to meetings and see lots of people around the room who look just like me. I don't have to worry too much about the way I dress and if I look appropriately professional. When I express opinions in meetings or at public gatherings, the viewpoints I express are generally viewed as reasonable and rational, and people will not question whether my motives are race based. In other words, it's simply easier for me to negotiate daily organizational life with a white face, because the organizations I inhabit are socially constructed in my image.

Finally, let me state that in talking about "whiteness" and white privilege my intention is to move us away from the idea that racism is mainly about uneducated individuals who hold and express racist beliefs. Few people do that explicitly these days (although, ironically, it seemed to become okay again when the United States elected a black president). Rather, as I said above, the idea is to focus on a *system* of power and domination that we all, to a greater or lesser degree, participate in. This does not make all white people racist; instead, it suggests that we need to develop greater awareness and self-reflexivity about the ways that we—often unconsciously—participate in systems of inclusion and exclusion.

Critical Case Study 10.1
Interrogating Mumby Family Whiteness

I grew up in a rural, sparsely populated region of Britain called Lincolnshire. It was, and is, racially and ethnically homogeneous, although there has been some immigration over the past few years, mainly from Eastern and Southern Europe. When I was growing up there, it was rare to see a nonwhite face, and during my high school years in the 1970s I don't recall any minority students in a school of 350. However, that doesn't mean that issues of race didn't figure in the Mumby family narrative. A couple of stories from my childhood will help illustrate how, even in white families, race can subtly and not-so-subtly construct its sense of identity.

Story 1: When I was very young, my dad (who was a police officer) went on a weeklong detective training course. When he came back he told the story of the one African (Kenyan) officer on the course who took a bath every night. My dad interpreted this as an (over-the-top) effort on this officer's part to prove that he had good personal hygiene, thus dispelling the common stereotype of Africans. It probably never occurred to my dad that this guy was simply engaging in his usual bathing routine and that the British working-class habit of bathing once a week (when I was a kid Sunday night was bath night) was probably pretty gross to him. I remember looking at the black-and-white photograph of the (all-male) students from this course and seeing the one black face smiling from the back row among a sea of white faces. I wondered what that experience was like for him. What kinds of daily jokes, insults, and stereotyping did he have to endure?

Story 2: When I was 16, my older brother Alan decided to emigrate to Jamaica to teach in a high school. The night before he left, the family was sitting together in the kitchen and Alan turned to my dad and said, in his usual provocative way, "You never know, Dad, I might meet and marry a nice Jamaican woman." Right away my dad responded, "I bloody well hope not!" When my brother inquired (again, mischievously) why that would be a problem, my dad paused and then said, "It's not fair on the kids—they're neither one thing nor the other."

Now, the irony of this story is that my brother did, in fact, meet and marry a Jamaican woman (the vice principal at the high school where he taught), and they had a son, Andrew. Sadly, a year after Andrew was born, my

sister-in-law died from a brain aneurism and my brother subsequently moved back to the United Kingdom so my mom could help him raise his son. What's fascinating is that Andrew became the apple of my dad's eye. This "neither one thing nor the other" kid created a bond with his white, conservative granddad that lasted until the day my dad died. In fact, Andrew became a Church of England vicar and prayed with my dad as he lay on his deathbed, dying of cancer.

From my perspective, both of these stories challenge the ways whiteness gets constructed, even in the apparently whitest of families. In the first story, the blackness of the Kenyan officer is the foil against which the "superiority" of white culture is demonstrated; he can wash all he likes, but it won't wash away his blackness. But, of course, my dad's ideological construction of blackness actually reveals more about British working-class whiteness than African blackness. In the second story, the abstract idea that someone of mixed race is "neither one thing nor the other" creates a binary racial system in which anyone "in between" is a nonperson who is not classifiable. You're either white or not white—you can't be both. This abstract notion collapses when confronted by a real, flesh-and-blood person who defies any racial stereotypes one might have. While my dad didn't exactly lose all his prejudices (who does?), his relationship with his Jamaican–British grandson significantly reshaped his (racial) view of the world.

Discussion Questions

1. In what ways is race narrated and encoded in your own family? Whether you're white or a student of color, how is race both silent and voiced in your family?

2. To what degree is your racial or ethnic background important to you? How, if at all, does this manifest itself in your life?

3. What's your experience with race in work or other organizational contexts? Can you identify instances where race was an explicit element of an organizational decision or behavior?

4. Can you identity examples of race as socially constructed, either from your own life or from popular representations of race?

❖ THE BODY, SEXUALITY, AND ORGANIZATIONAL COMMUNICATION

Why discuss the body and sexuality as a form of difference? From a critical perspective, it makes sense for a couple of reasons. First, employees' bodies and sexuality have for a long time been a focal point of control for organizations. For example, management scholar Gibson Burrell (1984) argues that with the growth of industrial capitalism organizations sought actively to control employee sexuality because it was perceived to interfere with their productivity. As we discussed earlier, Henry Ford's Sociological Department attempted to monitor his employees' behavior outside of work, including their sexual behavior and personal hygiene (Jeffrey Eugenides's 2002 novel, *Middlesex*, has a wonderful description of a Ford researcher visiting the home of a Greek immigrant Ford employee to check on his home life). More broadly speaking, the bureaucratic form generally functions to eliminate or suppress the idea of employees as sexual beings with bodies and desires.

Second, and related, everyday organizational life teems with sexuality. After all, people are sexual beings, and despite bureaucracies' best efforts to monitor and restrict its expression we do not check our sexuality at the door when we go to work. Organization members flirt, have romantic relationships, sometimes dress provocatively, and experience work at least in part through their bodies. Work, in this sense, has a very sensuous dimension. Because of this increasing recognition of organizations as sites of sexuality, a number of researchers have begun to take seriously the idea that organizations, sexuality, and the body come together in important ways (Brewis & Linstead, 2000; Fleming, 2007, 2009; Hearn, Sheppard, Tancred-Sheriff, & Burrell, 1989; Pringle, 1989; Spradlin, 1998).

Third, and finally, sexuality is worth our consideration as a form of difference because, increasingly, organizations are not so much attempting to eliminate employee sexuality from the workplace as exploit it as a potential way to increase productivity. By incorporating what traditionally has existed in the private sphere of home and relationships, companies are increasingly encouraging employees to "just be yourself" at work (Fleming, 2009), including expressions of sexuality. The idea here is to bring the energy and vitality of the private sphere to the workplace.

In this section, then, we will examine three different ways to frame organizational sexuality: (1) instrumental uses of the body and sexuality, (2) sexual harassment in the workplace, and (3) resistant/emancipatory functions of sexuality.

Instrumental Uses of the Body and Sexuality

In the first frame, the body and sexuality are seen as organizational resources that can be exploited for the gain of the organization (Burrell, 1992). Organizations carefully monitor and control expressions of sexuality, as well as harnessing it as a commodity that has value to the organization. In some organizations, such harnessing of sexuality for profit is explicit and obvious. For example, advertisers have recognized for decades that "sex sells," and today many commercials have overtly sexual messages that attempt to connect the purchase of products with enhanced sexual prowess. But perhaps more significantly, organizations are increasingly encouraging and harnessing employee sexuality as a way to enhance customer "brand experience" and corporate profitability (Fleming, 2009).

Meika Loe (1996) provides an example of this kind of management of sexuality and the body in her ethnographic study of "Bazooms" restaurant (an entertaining pseudonym for Hooters). Loe shows how the female body is gendered (and sexualized) in a specific way to create an organizational environment that maximizes the sale of burgers and chicken wings. Loe took a job as a "Bazooms girl" to study the ways the women are sexualized through dress, mandatory choreographed performances, and deliberate corporate efforts to present them as dumb (e.g., a Bazooms calendar features the months out of order because "the Bazooms girls put it together"). The effect is to create an image of the Bazooms girl as an "all-American" girl-next-door type who is always smiling, always ready to have fun, and always attentive and approachable to the (mostly male) customers. Loe notes in her study how male customers felt free to make lewd, suggestive comments to the women and how the women employees had to develop strategies to fend them off. Of course, the idea is to sell menu items by suggesting to customers that the "girls" are sexually available; such a notion is ridiculous at one level, but the reality is that few customers actually go to Hoo–, er, I mean Bazooms, for the food!

While this might be seen as an extreme example from the food-service industry, as we saw in Chapter 8 the service and retail economies frequently demand a great deal from employees and their bodies through the concept of emotional labor (Hochschild, 1983). Especially in the customer service arena, the interactions between employees and customers are often carefully managed in order to maximize profits. Companies attempt to harness and control employee expression of emotions (an intimate aspect of one's identity) in order to enhance customers' experiences and thus maintain their loyalty. While Hochschild's original study focused on flight attendants, the principles of control over emotions, the body, and sexuality are not that different from Loe's experience at Bazooms. And I suspect that anyone reading this book who has worked in a customer service position of any kind will recognize managerial efforts to control and shape emotional expression and performance of body and sexuality.

Sociologist Millian Kang (2010) provides an extremely interesting ethnographic study of the instrumental use of female employees' bodies in nail salons. Kang extends Hochschild's notion of emotional labor by examining the forms of "body labor" in which the mostly Asian (Korean and Vietnamese) nail salon workers must engage in their work. For me, this study is interesting and compelling because it is written from the perspective of the nail salon workers and provides insight into how their bodies are placed on the line every day to provide a cosmetic service for the (mostly female) clientele. When we discussed this book in one of my classes, many of the female students indicated that it profoundly changed their perception of workers in nail salons and made them think twice about using this service industry. Getting one's nails "done" is a good example of a "technology of the body," discussed in Critical Technologies 10.1.

Finally, and in a somewhat different organizational context, Peter Fleming's (2007) qualitative study of a call center shows how the organization deliberately engineers a "culture of fun" in which flirting, dating, and wearing hip and sexy outfits are encouraged among the mostly 20-something employees. Here, there is an effort to link the sexuality of employees (including creating an organizational culture that is gay friendly) directly to the profitability of the company. Interestingly, some of the employees found this "fun" work environment oppressive because of the perceived sleaziness of the flirting culture and the constant pressure to dress in a hip manner in order to be considered among the "cool kids" in the workplace.

Critical Technologies 10.1
Technologies of the Body

In an organizational communication textbook, the term *technology* usually denotes some form of electronic or computer-mediated communication. But it doesn't have to. In Chapter 1 we adopted a broad conception of communication technology as "anything that mediates and alters the user's relationship to the world" and extends our sense of identity into the world. Certainly, electronic communication technologies are the most obvious and visible example of how we do this, especially through the widespread use of social media, as well as the creation of virtual, online identities that enable us to take on characteristics we cannot embody in everyday, nonmediated life.

However, we can also think of the body itself as a site of technology. "Technologies of the body" involve ways we can construct and perform a particular conception of self in everyday life through augmentations of our bodies. These can include everything from makeup and clothing to tattooing, cosmetic surgery, and body piercings. If, as we have discussed in this chapter and in Chapter 9, gender and difference are both socially constructed and performed, then many different identities can be created through use of various body technologies. And body technologies can both affirm and reproduce mainstream gendered and raced identities, or they can resist and subvert them.

For example, the male business suit is a classic affirmation and reproduction of masculine hegemony in the workplace; however, as workplaces are becoming less bureaucratic and hierarchical, the business suit is increasingly being replaced by "business casual" and even "no-collar" work attire—a shift that perhaps reflects a change in the gendered performance of identity.

One interesting development in body technologies in the past 20 years is in tattooing and piercing (Atkinson, 2004;

Modesti, 2008). It used to be that only sailors, criminals, and bikers got tattoos. Now it's estimated that almost 50% of adults between age 21 and 32 have at least one tattoo or piercing beyond the standard ear piercing (Selvin, 2007). Tattooing and piercing, then, are no longer signs of cultural deviance. They are expressions of individual identity, while at the same time being a part of the growing "body industry"—a multibillion-dollar business that increasingly commodifies the human form through various modifications and an appeal to an (mostly unattainable) ideal (Atkinson, 2004). As one of Martin Atkinson's respondents stated in his study of people who get tattoos, "There's something about a tattoo that screams individuality. . . . It says, 'I want you to watch me'" (p. 135).

However, there's a great deal of variance regarding workplace attitudes toward tattooing and piercing. Some companies such as grocery chain Whole Foods have a fairly liberal policy on tattoos—although, interestingly, the chain's policies vary by geographic region, reflecting the greater conservatism of some areas. At my local Whole Foods, it almost seems that visible tattoos are a requirement to get hired! Not surprisingly, the Disney Corporation has a very strict and conservative appearance code, not only forbidding visible tattoos or piercings beyond standard ear piercings but also adopting strict requirements for hair and sideburn length and style. Jennifer Wesely's (2003) comment that "pressure to technologize the body in service to the ideal is reinforced" (p. 649) could easily be applied to Disney's regulation of the body, even though she makes it in the context of a study of exotic dancers!

Do you have tattoos or piercings? Why did you get them? Do you have any concerns about their effect on your ability to get employment?

From an instrumental perspective, then, we can see that the body and sexuality are used by organizations as a resource that can be rationalized and submitted to various forms of control. Sexuality and the body are viewed positively and productively as long as their expression is consistent with the goals of the organization. In this context, they are carefully monitored and controlled, even to the extent of dictating what employees wear, how they comport themselves, even how they use facial expressions. See Critical Case Study 10.2 for an example of how one particular corporation—Abercrombie & Fitch—uses employee bodies and sexuality in instrumental ways.

Critical Case Study 10.2
Sexing up the Corporate Experience

Employee sexuality is increasingly becoming an explicit, actively encouraged aspect of organizational life. One of the clearest examples of this is the clothing chain Abercrombie & Fitch's (A&F) use of its employees' sexuality and bodies to sell its line of clothes. A few years back, A&F gave itself a "brand makeover" and went from an outdoors-oriented store (think Eddie Bauer) to one that appeals strongly to a younger demographic. One of its most distinctive rebranding features is its focus on the male body and male sexuality, including the use of a shirtless male "greeter" in each A&F store (a little different from the average Wal-Mart greeter!). Needless to say, you must have a particular body type to land this job. In addition, if you go to the A&F website you will see a section called "A&F Casting: Do You Have What it Takes?" As far as I can tell, "having what it takes" means being beautiful and having a toned body; it has little, if anything, to do with actual job skills. Potential employees are asked to upload pictures of themselves, and the website is full of photos of "ordinary people" in sexy, often shirtless poses. Moreover, the A&F website makes an explicit connection between "working in a store and modeling," indicating that being a store employee is a stepping stone to modeling for A&F marketing campaigns.

In October 2007 the comedy group Improv Everywhere engaged in a performance at A&F. Improv Everywhere has become famous for its carefully choreographed performances that disrupt the routine flow of everyday life (the group's motto is "We Cause Scenes"). For example, in one "scene" a group of men rode the New York City subway during the morning commute dressed normally except for an absence of pants; in another, a bunch of people invaded a Best Buy store dressed in khakis and blue shirts and answered customer questions (though not claiming to be Best Buy employees). At the A&F flagship store in New York City, 111 men entered the store at random times and spread throughout the four floors; at exactly 4:37 p.m. they all took off their T-shirts and continued to shop normally (in other words, dressed just like the greeter at the store entrance). The organizer describes what happened next:

> After about 15 minutes, the Abercrombie management decided it was time to kick us out. Security employees started approaching all of our men and

asking them to either put a shirt on or leave. They informed us that the model was a paid employee and his state of undress didn't justify ours. So despite the fact that the store constantly bombards you with the image of the shirtless male, Abercrombie still maintains a "No Shirts; No Service" policy. Some agents protested that they were trying to *buy* a shirt, but the staff countered with the not-so-logical, "If you put on a shirt then you can buy a shirt." Many agents just politely agreed to leave and then walked to another floor to shop some more, getting asked to leave several times before finally heading out.

Some performers were even stopped and asked to leave while in the act of making a purchase at the checkout counter! You can see photos and video of the event, along with a full account, at http://improveverywhere.com/2007/10/17/no-shirts/.

A&F's response to Improv Everywhere's stunt seems to support the contention of some organizational communication researchers that the incorporation of sexuality and the body into organizational life can occur only in specific, corporately prescribed ways. A&F sexualizes its employees and uses the body and sexuality to sell merchandise, but the exhibiting of an unregulated body at the point of consumption is seen as a threat to A&F's business (the male greeter's response to the bare-chested customers is worth reading at the link above).

One further story makes the point about carefully prescribed sexuality. In 2009 A&F was accused of "hiding" a sales assistant in a stockroom at its flagship London outlet because her prosthetic arm did not fit with its "look policy." The employee sued for disability discrimination and was awarded $12,000 by an industrial tribunal.

Discussion Questions

1. How do you feel about A&F's use of sexuality and the body in selling clothes?

2. Do you ever shop at A&F? What's your experience as a customer in the store?

3. In general, have you had any work experiences in which there was an effort by the organization to

incorporate sexuality and the body into the work process? These might be retail or service positions but can be other kinds of work, too.

4. Engage in a broad discussion of the increasing ways that the body, sexuality, and organizations intersect. What are some of the positive and negative consequences of this development?

5. Are there positive, non-exploitive ways in which the body and sexuality can be part of everyday organizational life? What might this look like?

Such instrumental uses of sexuality and the body at work certainly appear to be on the rise, especially as organizations increasingly attempt to break down the barriers between employees' work and private lives and tie their identities more closely to the organization (we will discuss the relationship between personal identity and work in more detail in Chapter 14). In this sense, employees' bodies and sexuality are seen as untapped resources of energy that employers can access to create organizational "brand value."

Sexual Harassment in the Workplace

In the second perspective, sexuality and power are closely connected in the study of **sexual harassment**. Indeed, one could argue that sexual harassment is not really about sexuality at all but more about the ways gender and power come together in organizations to create forms of inequality and exploitation. According to the U.S. Equal Employment Opportunity Commission (2002),

> Unwelcome sexual advances, requests for sexual favors, and other verbal or physical conduct of a sexual nature constitutes sexual harassment when submission to or rejection of this conduct explicitly or implicitly affects an individual's employment, unreasonably interferes with an individual's work performance or creates an intimidating, hostile or offensive work environment.

While women are more likely to experience sexual harassment in the workplace than are men, it is also not unusual for men to be harassed or for same-sex harassment to occur. In addition, sexual harassment is typically exercised by people in power over those who are relatively powerless, although harassment can also occur among colleagues at the same rank in an organization.

Sexual harassment is typically viewed as taking two different forms: (1) **hostile environment** and (2) **quid pro quo**. In the hostile environment form, sexual harassment involves contexts where conduct directed at a person because of her or his sex or sexuality unreasonably interferes with the person's ability to perform her or his job. The quid pro quo (literally, "something for something") form involves situations in which a harasser demands sexual favors with the promise of preferred treatment regarding employment or evaluation.

Almost everyone would agree that sexual harassment is unacceptable and a significant problem in the workplace; however, it is surprisingly difficult for people to agree on when sexual harassment has occurred. Even organization members who have experienced sexual harassment are not always comfortable naming their experience as harassment. Furthermore, one person's perception of behavior as friendly banter can sometimes be framed by another as threatening and intimidating behavior. This is especially true when there is a power differential between the parties involved. There is a much greater chance that a person in a subordinate position will view a particular behavior as harassing than that a person in a more powerful position will. I am sure many of you—particularly the women in the class—have felt uneasy about behavior exhibited toward you by a superior or someone in authority, and I suspect that if you were to confront that person about his or her behavior he or she would be shocked at your interpretation of the actions in question. Of course, such a response does not mean that person's behavior is not harassment (regardless of the intent) or that you are wrong to feel uncomfortable.

There is, thus, a strong interpretive, communicative element to sexual harassment; in other words, what counts as harassing behavior is often open to interpretation and depends on the discursive resources people bring to bear on the issue. For example, if an organizational culture as a whole tolerates and even encourages sexual banter and flirting (as in Fleming's study discussed above), then there is a good chance that someone who feels harassed is more likely to have his or her concerns dismissed. Again, this is not to say that such concerns are not legitimate; rather, it is to suggest that, given the complexities of communication processes, the meanings attached to particular behaviors depend on how they are framed in different social contexts.

Along these lines, Robin Clair has studied how the sexual harassment experiences of organization members are often "sequestered" (i.e., hidden from public view and discussion) by the ways both the people who experience harassment and the institutions that create policies discursively frame (i.e., give meaning to) such behaviors (Clair, 1993a, 1993b). Clair reports that in her interviews with women who had experienced workplace harassment, the women used some common discursive frames to make sense out of their experiences. These frames include, for example, "simple misunderstanding," in which women who experience harassment frame it as an interpretive error on their part (thus shifting blame away from the harassers and to themselves), and "reification," in which sexual harassment is accepted as part of the culture of the organization, as "the way it is."

One might assume that, 20 years after Clair's research, it has become easier for women to identify and confront forms of organizational discrimination, including sexual harassment—especially as women gain a stronger foothold amongst the managerial élite. However, recent research by psychologist Britney Brinkman and her colleagues suggests that this is not the case; women continue to struggle to confront instances in which they experience various forms of gender prejudice (Brinkman, Garcia, & Rickard, 2011; Brinkman & Rickard, 2009). Analyzing daily online diaries kept by 81 college-age women, Brinkman found discrepancies between what the women said they would do and what they actually do in dealing with gender prejudice. Thus, women seem readily able to identify gender prejudice (unlike some of Clair's respondents) but are often loath to confront it directly, expressing concerns about possibly escalating the situation or breaking social norms. This evidence suggests, then, that women still struggle with how to deal with prejudice and harassment, fearing backlash from supervisors and peers.

Resistant/Emancipatory Forms of Sexuality

In the third view of sexuality and organizations, sexuality is seen as having a resistant, perhaps emancipatory function. From a broad social context, the sexual revolution of the 1960s was also very much a political revolution, as many groups in society rejected efforts to impose narrow views of sexuality and sexual behavior. The U.S. Food and Drug Administration's approval in 1960 of the birth control pill allowed women to have much greater control over their own bodies and their identities as sexual beings. The Stonewall bar uprising in Greenwich Village, New York, in 1969—where gay men resisted constant harassment by police—signaled the beginning of the modern gay rights movement. While it is a very complex issue, the ability of people to have sovereignty over their own sexuality and bodies is often tied up with issues of political freedom.

For example, in his novel *1984,* George Orwell creates a dystopian society in which the ruling party of Oceania tries to control every aspect of people's lives, including forbidding sexual relationships, not only because they involve behavior outside party control but also because sexual deprivation creates hysteria that can be used to generate war fever and leader worship. As one of the main characters, Julia, states:

> When you make love you're using up energy; and afterwards you feel happy and don't give a damn for anything. They [the Party] can't bear you to feel like that. They want you to be bursting with energy all the time. All this marching up and down and cheering and waving flags is simply sex gone sour. (quoted in Burrell, 1992, p. 70)

Obviously, it's hard to compare the authoritarian regime depicted in *1984* with the modern organization, but we can still think about sexuality as being a potential point of resistance in contemporary organizational efforts to shape human identity. While this perspective seems to contradict our earlier discussion of the ways organizations utilize pleasure and sexuality for instrumental purposes, we can argue that sexuality enters the organizing process formally only when it can be carefully controlled and linked to productivity. In the context of workplace resistance, sexuality is an "undecidable," unpredictable element of organizational life that can disrupt managerial efforts to shape workplace behavior and sense-making processes. Thus, Gibson Burrell's (1984) claim that "sexual relations at work may be expressive of a demand not to be controlled" can be thought of in this context (p. 192).

© iStockphoto.com/laflor and © iStockphoto.com/squaredpixels

As organizations are becoming less bureaucratic and hierarchical, the business suit is giving way to "business casual" and "no-collar" attire.

© iStockphoto.com/SimmiSimons

Body technologies are a mode of self-presentation through augmentation of our bodies. Tattoos have become a common sight in the workplace.

Gay Workers and "Heteronormativity"

One way to frame resistant and/or emancipatory forms of sexuality is to think about the changing nature of organizational life for gay employees. In many respects, the increasing numbers of openly gay workers resist what can be called **heteronormativity** in organizations—that is, the use of norms of heterosexuality to evaluate and make sense of the world and people around us. Such norms position heterosexuality as the implicit ideal against which other forms of sexuality are measured. And it is still, in many respects, one of the defining features of organizational life.

For example, a couple of years ago, I met with a student who was visiting campus in anticipation of joining our graduate program. She mentioned that she had made the trip with her partner, who was checking out the job possibilities in the area. "What kind of work does he do?" I asked. "*She's* in retail," was her response. It wasn't an egregious error on my part, but I still felt bad that I had simply assumed that the student was heterosexual.

Of course, one of the other lessons from my little story is that the student felt quite comfortable correcting my erroneous assumption about her sexuality. This suggests two things: (1) She was confident enough about her sexuality to reveal it to someone in a position of authority (her potential department chair), and (2) she was confident that she was joining a "gay-friendly" institution. Such organizations "do not merely tolerate lesbian, gay, and bisexual workers, but accept and welcome them in the workplace" (Giuffre, Dellinger, & Williams, 2008, p. 255).

There is certainly little doubt that, by and large, organizations and workplaces have become more gay friendly in the course of the past 20 years. For example, more than 500 companies, including IBM, Disney, Fox Broadcasting, Xerox, and Ben and Jerry's, have extended full benefits to partners of gay employees (Allen, 2003, p. 130). However, the United States lags behind other nations in enacting laws banning employment decisions based on sexual orientation. While 21 states have enacted such laws (Wisconsin was the first to do so in 1982), there is no federally mandated policy. At the federal level, September 20, 2011, saw the repeal of the Armed Forces "Don't Ask Don't Tell" policy, enabling homosexual and lesbian military personnel to be open about their sexuality while serving their country. Again, the United States has lagged behind other nations in this regard, with more than 20 countries permitting openly gay men and women to serve in the military. Extensive research on the issue in both the United States and other countries has provided no empirical evidence that gay men and women serving openly impairs military readiness (Frank, 2010).

Of course, this progress in gay rights in the workplace and in the broader society comes in the wake of more than 40 years of struggle on the part of the gay rights movement, initiated by the Stonewall uprising in 1969, mentioned above. For much of its history, the modern corporation has operated according to the principle of "compulsory heterosexuality" (Rich, 1980). Stuart Seidman (2002) argues that the period 1950 to 1980 was the

© Mikkel Bækhøj Christensen/De/Demotix/Corbis

The success of the gay rights movement has helped create organizational climates that are more open to gay and lesbian workers.

"heyday" of the closet in the United States—a period that corresponds closely to the dominance of the formal, bureaucratic organizational form. During this period workplaces not only operated on heteronormative principles but were often actively homophobic in ways that demonized and stereotyped gay and lesbian workers.

The success of the gay rights movement, then, has certainly helped create organization and corporate climates that are more open to gay and lesbian workers. From a critical organizational *communication* perspective, however, what is most interesting about the presence of gay men and women in organizations is how that presence is communicatively constructed and negotiated. In other words, how, through communication processes, do gay men and women manage their workplace identities, and, in turn, how do heterosexual workers make sense of and give meaning to those identities?

One of the earliest articles in organizational communication to address this issue directly is Anna Spradlin's (1998) essay "The Price of 'Passing.'" As the term **passing** suggests, Spradlin discusses the various communication strategies she used as a way to be identified by others as a straight woman at work and hence remain in the "corporate closet" (Woods, 1993). Spradlin identifies six strategies she used when interacting with her colleagues at work:

- *Distancing*: Removing oneself from informal conversational situations where personal information might arise, including not attending department social events.
- *Dissociating*: Avoiding any interaction or association with other homosexual workers.
- *Dodging*: Using conversational topic shifts to steer discussions away from disclosure of personal information.
- *Distracting*: Employing "identity messages" that bolster one's image as heterosexual. For example, Spradlin would reference the fact that she was once married or that she came from a conservative, religious background.
- *Denial*: Withholding information about one's gay identity. For example, Spradlin listed her parents as her emergency contacts on employment forms rather than her partner and did not have photos of her partner in her office.
- *Deceiving*: Constructing deliberately misleading messages regarding one's sexual identity—for example, referring to one's partner as "he" rather than "she" or inviting a male friend posing as a boyfriend to a social event (what today is referred to colloquially as a "beard") to bolster one's heterosexual credentials.

I have two reactions to Spradlin's essay. First, I'm amazed by the amount of emotional and psychological effort required to engage in this kind of passing behavior. For example, Spradlin describes herself as learning to be a "hyper-attentive listener" so she can be constantly attuned to the need to redirect conversations away from "dangerous" topic areas. Such hyper-attentiveness can be extremely exhausting when practiced 24/7. Second, Spradlin's essay is a great example of how identity is communicatively constructed. Her passing strategies rely on her colleagues' ability to make sense of her through the various verbal and nonverbal communication cues she exhibits. In this sense, Spradlin communicatively performs heterosexuality, but it works only because of the heteronormative frame within which people make sense of her behavior.

More recent research reflects the changing character of organizational life by focusing not as much on "passing" behavior but, rather, on the ways gay and lesbian workers manage their identities in workplaces that are recognized as gay friendly (Giuffre et al., 2008, p. 263; Rumens, 2008, 2010; Rumens & Kerfoot, 2009). Again, this research is interesting because of its focus on how both homosexuality and heterosexuality are communicatively constructed through the everyday interactions of gay and straight organization members.

Management scholar Nick Rumens (2009), for example, focuses his research on how gay men have moved beyond both the closet and being "token" novelties in the workplace. He argues that the new, open workplace culture has provided gay men with the opportunity to "invent themselves afresh" as "respected and openly gay professionals" (p. 775). Rumens's work focuses on the ways gay workers negotiate what it means to be professional; that is, how do they enact a professional identity that incorporates their sexuality and is still recognized by colleagues as "professional"? This negotiation process is quite complex because, in many respects, the still-dominant conception of professionalism is based on a rational male figure who restrains his emotions and keeps private issues out of the office.

Rumens suggests that gay men are very conscious of the need to project a professional image while being open about their sexuality. For example, in his study several gay men indicated that they perceived being too "camp" in the workplace as unprofessional behavior. Moreover, they often viewed the body as a site where professionalism could be enacted. As Rumens (2009) states, "Because the gay male body, rather like the female body, can be at risk of being interpreted as a site of sexual excess, fashioning the body to appear professional is critical" (p. 780). Thus, many gay men choose to project a professional image through the use of expensive, well-made clothes, as well as working out regularly to present a fit body to colleagues. Both of these strategies are used to project an image of workplace competence.

Finally, some researchers have pointed out that, while workplaces have generally become more gay friendly, even those organizations identified as such can engage in forms of discrimination, albeit in ways more subtle than outright homophobia (Giuffre et al., 2008; Ward & Winstanley, 2003). For example, some heterosexual workers feel comfortable asking gay colleagues about aspects of their private lives—including their sex lives—that they would never ask straight coworkers. Sometimes this occurs because openly gay workers are treated as "tokens" and "exotic" creatures in the workplace and, thus, as figures of curiosity. And James Ward and Diana Winstanley (2003) have reported that gay and lesbian workers sometimes experience a workplace silence. That is, while heterosexual colleagues will happily talk about their home lives and weekend activities, they demonstrate little interest in hearing about the equivalent lives of their gay coworkers, in part because they define the latter largely through their sexuality and are afraid of getting details that may make them uncomfortable (even though, as several gay workers indicate, their home lives are every bit as boring and routine as those of their heterosexual colleagues).

❖ CONCLUSION

In this chapter I have tried to suggest to you the complexities of the relationships between difference and organizational communication. I have attempted to show that difference is communicatively constructed; this occurs through the development of discourses that shape the values and meanings that define particular forms of difference. From a communication perspective our interest lies not in the differences per se but, rather, in the ways "the differences that make a difference" become taken for granted and institutionalized in everyday organizational life. It is only by exploring how certain differences become seen as "natural" that we can understand the processes through which they are communicatively constructed.

In this chapter we looked at two forms of difference—race and sexuality. We might have looked at a number of others, including class, age, and able-bodiedness. Indeed, one of the dangers of focusing on race and sexuality is that we forget their connections to other forms of difference. For example, it is hard to talk about race without addressing issues of class as well; being a middle-class, professional black man is quite different from being a working-class or unemployed black man in terms of the dynamics of inclusion and exclusion.

In many ways, writing this chapter was quite difficult. I have found that students are often quite comfortable talking about gender (the topic of Chapter 9) and sexuality but get very uncomfortable when asked to discuss race. This in itself suggests how far we have yet to go in addressing issues of race in a forthright and constructive way. For me, the challenge was to write an engaging chapter that raised important issues but didn't alienate the white students among you, or seem hopelessly naïve to students of color. I knew, for example, that I was taking a risk in discussing whiteness, because that meant we could no longer claim that race is an issue only for minorities. It also meant that white students could no longer simply take a "color-blind" perspective ("I don't notice race; I just treat everyone the same")—often the most comfortable position to adopt when addressing race (at least from a white perspective).

Perhaps the most important issue to take from this chapter is that even though we commonly think of difference as individual (U.S. society does heavily emphasize individuality, after all), such individuality can be understood only in the context of the larger organizational and societal forces that shape us. Difference is socially constructed and also shaped by power. The goal, then, as organizational communication scholar Jennifer Mease (2011) has suggested, is to take difference personally *and* think about it institutionally. That is, we need to "develop a critically engaged consciousness that allows [us] to analyze and respond to social constructions of difference and associated power dynamics as personally relevant" (p. 153). This means thinking less about inequality as a function of prejudiced or unmotivated individuals and more about how we, as individuals, personally participate in maintaining, ignoring, or short-circuiting institutional inequalities in our everyday lives.

CRITICAL APPLICATIONS

1. Reflect on your own racial and/or ethnic background. How important has this been in shaping your sense of who you are as a person? See if you can write up an "interrogation" of your own family background along the lines of my own in Critical Case Study 10.1.

2. Share your "interrogation" with someone else in class. What are the points of commonality and difference in your respective racial/ethnic personal narratives? Can you come to any conclusions about the ways race is socially constructed?

KEY TERMS

difference   230

heteronormativity   249

hostile environment   245

invisible knapsack   239

managing diversity   233

outsider within   235

passing   251

quid pro quo   245

sexual harassment   243

whiteness   237

STUDENT STUDY SITE

Visit the student study site at **www.sagepub.com/mumbyorg** for these additional learning tools:

- Web quizzes
- eFlashcards
- SAGE journal articles
- Video resources
- Web resources

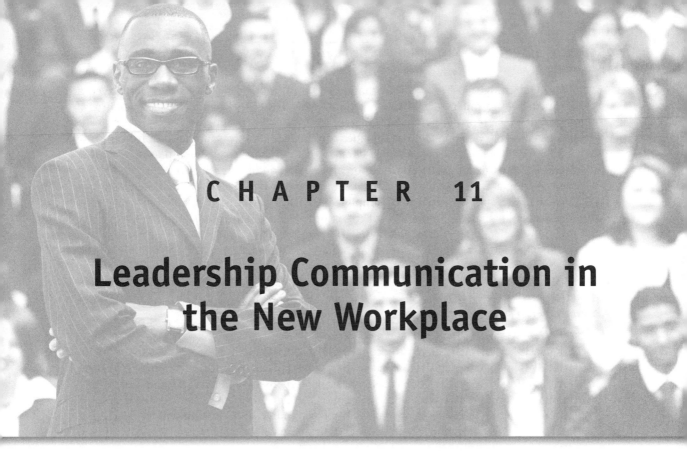

What makes a good leader? It's more complex than you might think.

CHAPTER 11

Leadership Communication in the New Workplace

The death of charismatic and iconoclastic Apple CEO Steve Jobs brought into sharp focus the issue of organizational leadership. The media endowed Jobs with almost mystical powers in his ability to produce the latest iconic technology that would profoundly change the communication and cultural landscape—the Mac, the iPod, the iPhone, the iPad. Will Tim Cook, his successor as CEO, be able to continue the kind of unprecedented success that Apple has had in the past 15 years?

The media stories around Jobs's death represent common-sense understandings of what it means to be a leader and what strong leadership entails. Typically, we think of leadership as a trait of a special individual who, through the sheer force of his (and we usually think of strong leaders as male) personality and charisma, is able to shape people and circumstances to his vision of the world. We often link the success of organizations to specific individuals—hence, the stories about Jobs and similar stories about other "larger-than-life" leaders, such as Jack Welch at General Electric, Lee Iacocca at Chrysler, and Herb Kelleher at Southwest Airlines (can you think of any "larger-than-life" female CEOs?). If you've watched the comedy show *30 Rock*, you know that the Alec Baldwin character, Jack Donneghy, typifies this kind of leader—alpha male, highly driven, Machiavellian, and believing strongly in his ability to shape the world in his image (Alec Baldwin played a character with similar traits in a more dramatic role in the 1992 movie *Glengarry Glenross*).

While these representations of leadership are appealing in their ability to present leaders as colorful characters whose qualities can be distilled into some kind of formula (for sale at your nearest Barnes & Noble bookstore), the reality of leadership as an everyday feature of organizational communication processes is quite different. So in this chapter we will develop a more complex (and, I hope, more reality-based) conception of leadership—one that presents leadership not simply as a trait of gifted individuals but, rather, as a phenomenon that captures many of the issues we have addressed in earlier chapters—meaning, power, and communication.

First, let's look at some of the research that has emerged in leadership studies over the past several decades.

❖ TRADITIONAL PERSPECTIVES ON LEADERSHIP

I suspect that for many of you the concept of "leadership" plays quite a prominent role in your lives as college students. As you develop your credentials for the anticipated transition into a professional career, you probably hear regularly that you need to develop "leadership experience" and "leadership skills." No doubt you have thought about how your résumé can be developed to reflect your leadership background, and I'm sure you will hope that any letters of recommendation from your instructors will talk about how you have shown strong leadership initiative in your time in school.

What does it mean, however, to possess leadership skills or to be a good leader? Surprisingly, there is little consensus about the concept of leadership or the criteria for good leadership; indeed, there are almost as many definitions of leadership as there are scholars doing leadership research. Management scholar Annie Pye (2005, p. 32) cites Dubrin's (2000) claim that there are 35,000 definitions of leadership in the academic literature.

So how do we approach a phenomenon that is apparently so messy and ambiguous? From a critical communication perspective we must recognize that leadership is not simply an objective phenomenon, the facts of which need to be established so we know definitively how to be a good leader. Rather, we need to think of leadership as a socially constructed phenomenon, the study of which has its roots in particular social, political, and economic conditions. In this sense, "leadership" is a discourse that has been created by researchers, popular culture, the media, and industry, and that functions to "frame" the world for us in particular ways. Management scholar Simon Western (2008) claims that "leadership is a growth industry and remains a 'sexy concept' and a buzz word in Business Schools, organizations, and social/political arenas. However, much of the mainstream literature is adapted and recycled theory; old news under a new headline" (p. 25). He argues that leadership ideas packaged into simple solutions are easier to sell in the "leadership industry."

From this critical perspective, leadership research is less about establishing a body of scientific evidence and more about perpetuating an industry that thrives on creating a culture where everyone is convinced that strong leadership skills are the answer to a lot of problems. Management scholar Keith Grint (2010, p. 1) gives an indication of the success of this industry when he points out that an October 2003 search for books on leadership on Amazon.com yielded 14,139 results; just over 6 years later, that number had risen to 53,121. When I did my own search in August 2011 the figure was 68,736. Clearly, then, there is a sense that a lot of people have a vested interest in making sure that "leadership" is kept in the public eye!

One of the goals of this chapter, then, is to problematize the very idea of leadership as a coherent, clearly identifiable phenomenon (with essential features), and to explore it as complex, ambiguous, and uncertain (Alvesson & Spicer, 2011; Western, 2008). In this section, then, we will examine several different perspectives on leadership, looking at the historical context out of which these perspectives emerged. What does each of these perspectives tell us about the place of leadership in organization and society? In the following section we will examine leadership as a communication phenomenon and aim to provide some useful guidelines about how you should approach questions of leadership in your own life.

First, let's provide a fairly generic, baseline definition of **leadership**. More than 60 years ago, Stodgill (1950) defined leadership as "the process of influencing the activities of an organized group in its efforts toward goal setting and goal achievement" (p. 3). This definition contains three elements—influence, group, and goal—that are generally considered central to leadership. But this definition also raises the question of exactly *how* such influence occurs, why someone is considered influential, and if, indeed, there is any measurable, causal connection between a leader and the behavior of followers (and, as we will see later, the very idea of separating "leaders" and "followers" is problematic).

Below, we will examine three broad leadership perspectives that have developed over the past 100 years or so, each of which attempts to isolate the factors that explain leadership as a phenomenon. These three approaches are (1) the trait approach, (2) the style approach, and (3) the situational approach.

The Trait Approach

Leadership scholar Keith Grint (2010) argues that the modern study of leadership can be traced to Scottish philosopher and essayist Thomas Carlyle's (1841/2001) work *On Heroes, Hero Worship and the Heroic in History*, which promoted the idea of the leader as a heroic figure who embodied the virtues of a society and stood head and shoulders above mere mortals. This was the "great man" approach to leadership. Although Carlyle was writing about historical figures, his work resonated with the emerging industrial society and its need for strong and "larger-than-life" leaders who embodied the values of entrepreneurial capitalism.

In its early decades, then, leadership research was dominated by an effort to establish the personal qualities, or traits, of these successful "captains of industry" (a term coined by Carlyle)—people such as J. P. Morgan, Andrew Carnegie, and John D. Rockefeller. From the perspective of the **trait approach**, leaders are born rather than made. Generally speaking, research focused on three main categories of personal characteristics: physical appearance, abilities (intelligence and fluency of speech), and personality (Bryman, 1996). For example, Grint (2010) uses the acronym THWαMP (tall, handsome, white alpha-males of privilege)

Edward N. Jackson, *Popular Science Monthly* Volume 58, and William Ten Eyck Hardenbrook

19th century "captains of industry" were the rock stars of their day—crowd surfing optional.

to describe the archetypal leader in Western society. Certainly, there are exceptions to this rule, but the THWαMP is still very much a dominant figure in leadership roles. Grint (2010, p. 69) even cites research that correlates every extra inch of height with a 1% increase in income (a finding that makes me happy, given that I'm 6 feet 5 inches tall!).

Other traits that research identified as important for successful leaders include intelligence (but there must not be too much of a gap between leaders and followers, otherwise the latter will feel inadequate and alienated from the leader), talkativeness (the "gift of the gab" is a skill many successful leaders possess), self-confidence, a willingness to take the initiative, and sociability/extroversion (not too many successful leaders are shy and retiring types). I suspect that most of us would recognize these traits as generally desirable and indicative of someone we might identify as a leader. And although paying attention to physical characteristics seems superficial, one has only to look at a list of CEOs of large corporations or heads of state to see that the nonwhite and/or female leader is still very much in the minority.

Trait research, however, proved to have too many limitations to provide an adequate explanation of successful leadership. Although it remained heavily influential until the early 1940s, Stodgill's (1948) review of that body of research and his outlining of its shortcomings largely signaled an end to programmatic research in that area. So what were its problems?

First, there was a huge amount of inconsistent and contradictory findings in trait studies; no consensus could be arrived at regarding the key traits of a successful leader. Second, the trait approach attempted to establish a universal set of leadership characteristics that were relevant regardless of the context in which they were applied. As we will see below, many researchers viewed the social and organizational context as a key issue in determining effective leadership. Third, trait research completely ignored the role of "followers"; in other words, leaders are only leaders when they have followers, and so understanding what works as effective leadership depends in good part on explaining the role of followers in the leadership process. Finally, from an ethical perspective, there's something rather unsavory about the idea that leaders are born rather than made. Such a perspective condemns people to the vagaries of their genes. Moreover, the fact that THW αMPs are identified as archetypal leaders is self-serving in its maintenance and reproduction of a system that privileges a white-male view of the world.

Finally, it's worth noting that our old friend Frederick Taylor put something of a monkey wrench in the "great man" theory of leadership with his declaration that successful organizations were not dependent on heroic captains of industry but on decidedly unheroic managers trained to apply scientific principles to the work process. As we will see, as the idea of the rational, bureaucratic organization became the dominant institution in society, the careful, rational analysis of leadership as an acquired skill and set of behaviors took center stage.

The Style Approach

The **style approach** to leadership was the dominant mode of research from the late 1940s through the 1960s (Bryman, 1996). In this perspective, specific leadership behaviors became the focus of study, and emphasis shifted from selecting leaders who had "the right stuff" to training people in skills associated with good leadership. A number of theories emerged out of this approach, but I will mention three very briefly.

First, in research at the University of Michigan, Kurt Lewin distinguished among three different styles of leadership—autocratic, laissez-faire, and democratic (Grint, 2010; Lewin

& Lippett, 1938; Western, 2008). In a series of experiments with Boys' Clubs, Lewin discovered that laissez-faire ("hands-off") leadership was ineffective, whether the leader was present in the task situation or not. On the other hand, with an autocratic (highly controlling) leadership style, followers would focus on tasks when the leader was present but slack off when he or she was not. Finally, Lewin argued that the democratic style was the most effective, as it promoted active involvement and group decision making and encouraged participation in tasks whether the leader was present or absent. However, while the democratic style promoted the most satisfaction, the autocratic style was most effective in terms of productivity.

This tension between satisfaction and productivity (a focus of research since the Hawthorne studies) was taken up in a couple of other style-based approaches. First, researchers at Ohio State University established two main components of leadership behavior: *consideration*, in which leaders demonstrate a concern for subordinates as people and are responsive to their needs, and *initiating structure*, in which leaders focus closely on the task, defining precisely what subordinates are required to do. Perhaps not surprisingly, research showed that leaders who emphasized consideration had subordinates with higher morale, while leaders who emphasized initiating structure had more productive subordinates. Further research came to the conclusion that leaders who demonstrated *both* kinds of leadership style tended to be the most effective.

This finding is elaborated in more detail by psychologists Robert Blake and Janet Mouton's (1964) well-known managerial grid. Blake and Mouton use the two dimensions of "concern for people" and "concern for production" (basically the same as the "consideration" and "initiating structure" styles) to create a grid that identifies five different leadership styles (see Figure 11.1). The five styles are (1) impoverished (low concern for both production and people), (2) country club (high concern for people, low concern for production), (3) authority compliance management—sometimes called "produce or perish" (low concern for people, high concern for production), (4) team leader (high concern for both production and people), and (5) middle-of-the-road (a compromise position that maintains the status quo by focusing on production without overlooking team morale). As Grint (2010) indicates, despite the lack of empirical evidence to support Blake and Mouton's model, their grid has enjoyed continued popularity, popping up in management and organizational communication textbooks (including this one!) to the present day.

Although the style approach to leadership is considered an advance on the trait approach, it still has important limitations. First, the emphasis is still very much on designated and formal leaders—a focus that ignores the fact that much organizational leadership occurs in an informal manner among employees who are not considered leaders in the formal sense. Second, once again the results of style research tended to be inconsistent. As with trait research, it proved incredibly difficult to demonstrate a consistent causal connection between specific leadership styles and increased performance by subordinates (Bryman, 1996). Finally, and perhaps most significant for leadership research, critics argued that it was difficult to establish universal leadership styles, because this ignored the fact that effective leadership was often influenced by situational factors. These critiques led, in the 1970s, to the emergence of the situational approach to leadership.

Figure 11.1   Blake and Mouton's Managerial Grid

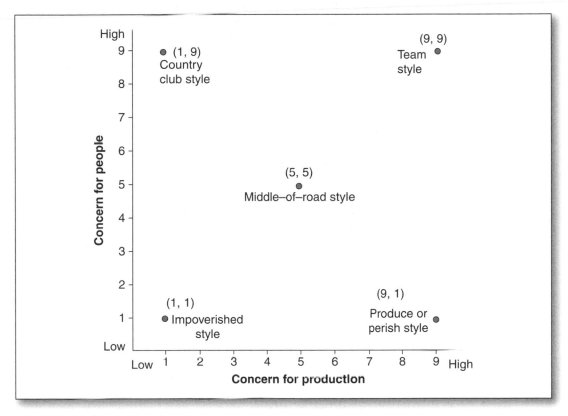

SOURCE: Blake and Mouton (1964).

The Situational Approach

The **situational approach**, or contingency approach, to leadership is an effort to move beyond a universal, "one-size-fits-all" perspective, answering the question, "What makes a good leader?" with, "It depends." In brief, the situational approach argues that contextual factors such as the structure of the task at hand, the power of the leader, and the size of the work group have a mediating effect on the leadership approach that different leaders adopt. Thus, no single leadership style or trait will be effective across different situations.

The most famous situational perspective is psychologist Fred Ficdler's (1967, 1997) contingency model of leadership. For Fiedler, the effectiveness of an organization depends on two interacting factors: (1) the personality of the leader and (2) the extent to which the leadership situation provides the leader with influence and lack of uncertainty. Fiedler measures the personality of leaders along two dimensions: (1) leaders who are relationship oriented and strive to accomplish tasks through maintaining good relations with group members, and (2) leaders who are task oriented and prefer tangible evidence of their competence (i.e., completion of tasks). The organizational situation is measured along three dimensions: (1) leader–member relations (the degree to which the leader feels supported by group members), (2) the structure of the task (how clear-cut or ambiguous it is), and (3) position power (the ability of the leader to reward or punish group members).

Fiedler determines leader personality through an instrument called least-preferred coworker (LPC), in which leaders are asked to think of the person they have been able to work with least well and to rate that person on numerous 8-point scales, such as "friendly–unfriendly" and "cooperative–uncooperative." Leaders with high LPC scores have a strong relational orientation, while leaders with low LPC scores have a strong task orientation. Thus, the effectiveness of these two leader personality types depends on how favorable the situation is to them. Fiedler argues that in uncertain situations, relationship-oriented (high-LPC) leaders will first seek support from group members and then focus on the task once support is ensured. On the other hand, task-oriented (low-LPC) leaders will deal with situational uncertainty by focusing primarily on the task and, once task accomplishment is ensured, will then focus on relational management with subordinates. Fiedler's research led him to conclude that task-oriented leaders are most effective in high-control and low-control situations, and that relationship-oriented leaders do best in moderate-control situations.

Fiedler's model portrays leadership as a psychological process rather than a social process, with his focus on leader personality types. Indeed, it served as the catalyst for a surge in psychological models of effective leadership. There are numerous critiques of Fiedler's perspective (leading to its waning influence in the early 1980s), but three are worth mentioning briefly. First, his focus is exclusively on formal, designated leaders, so there is virtually no attention to informal, emergent leadership processes. Second, because his model focuses on leadership personality, and since personality is notoriously hard to change, he appears to be suggesting that it is necessary to fit work situations to leaders rather than developing leaders who can adapt to various work situations. Third, there have been numerous critiques of the validity of contingency research due to inconsistent findings, including questions about the reliability of his LPC measure.

Summary

This concludes the discussion of what, to be honest, I consider to be some of the more boring, tedious approaches to leadership—social scientific research that, despite decades of trying, has largely failed to demonstrate direct connections between specific kinds of leader behavior and employee performance (Perrow, 1986). By and large, this research operates with rather conservative notions about leaders, followers, and how communication operates. Leaders tend to be viewed as formally designated individuals who act in some official organizational capacity to influence subordinates in particular ways. For the most part, followers are missing from the analysis of leadership processes; while often surveyed regarding their preferred leader behaviors, they are generally not adequately accounted for in the leadership process itself. Moreover, when communication is examined, the model adopted is rudimentary, with communication conceived as the transmission of information between leaders and subordinates.

Finally, this research uncritically accepts the ideas of leader and leadership as given features of organizational life that need to be empirically measured and explained (i.e., subject to prediction and control). As we will see in the rest of this chapter, these very ideas have been increasingly questioned as organizations have evolved from the hierarchical, bureaucratic forms of the mid-20th century.

Let's now turn to more recent leadership perspectives that reflect these changes.

❖ NEW APPROACHES TO LEADERSHIP

Beginning in the early 1980s, **new leadership** (Bryman, 1996; Parry & Bryman, 2006) has been used as an umbrella term referring to a host of different orientations to leadership that emerged around some broad themes. These themes include the following:

- A view of leadership as symbolic action. The leader is conceived as a manager of meaning.
- The emergence of "transformational leadership" and a "neo-charismatic" approach. This signals the return of the heroic "great man," but in a different organizational context.
- A greater focus on "followership," where the role of the follower in leadership processes is more thoroughly examined.
- A shift away from the formal aspects of leadership to a study of leadership as an everyday, informal process.
- A view of leadership as a socially constructed phenomenon rather than an objectively existing set of behaviors.
- The questioning of the very idea of leadership as commonly understood.

Let's examine some of these issues in more detail.

Leadership as Symbolic Action

The concept of the leader as engaged in **symbolic action** emerged largely at the same time as the corporate culture perspective we discussed in Chapter 6. This makes sense if you think about it, as the corporate culture approach—exemplified by Peters and Waterman's (1982) *In Search of Excellence*—stressed the importance of strong, visionary leaders in implementing and maintaining the organization's strong culture and system of values. Historically speaking, this new approach to leadership emerged precisely when globalization was becoming an issue, and the rise of Japan as an economic power was shaking U.S. companies out of their complacency regarding their preeminence in the global marketplace.

Given this context, many leadership researchers shifted from a narrow focus on controlled laboratory experiments and survey questionnaires that tried to establish key leadership behaviors, and turned instead to developing a grander vision of leadership that portrayed leaders as shapers of symbolic realities. In some respects, we see a return of the heroic, visionary leader of the late 19th and early 20th centuries, but remodeled for a late-20th century economic and social reality.

Adopting this perspective, management scholars Linda Smircich and Gareth Morgan (1982) argue that

> leadership is realized in the process whereby one or more individuals succeed in attempting to frame and define the reality of others. . . . Leadership depends on the existence of individuals willing . . . to surrender, at least in part, the powers to shape and define their own reality. (p. 258)

It is thus the role of leaders to engage in sense making for others and to help develop a consensus among organization members around the resulting meanings (Pfeffer, 1981a; Pondy, 1978; Smircich & Morgan, 1982).

In this conception, leadership is socially constructed through interaction and emerges as a result of the sense making and actions of both the leaders and the led. A key feature of this approach, then, is that leadership is not a thing but, rather, a *process* that emerges and is reproduced in an ongoing manner through the daily sense-making activities of organization members.

For example, the IBM story we discussed in Chapter 7 involving a confrontation between Lucille Burger, a security guard, and CEO Tom Watson Jr. illustrates how leadership as the management of meaning can operate. The telling of this story to organization members does not command them to act in a particular way but, instead, operates as a sense-making device, constructing organizational reality around the issue of following rules at IBM. In this sense, the story can be used to serve a leadership function by shaping organizational reality and thus shaping the actions of organization members.

The conception of leadership as symbolic action thus fits well with the cultural, interpretive approach to the study of organizations; leaders engage in sense making on behalf of others and help shape their organizational reality. From this perspective, "the key challenge for a leader is to manage meaning in such a way that individuals orient themselves to the achievement of desirable ends" (Smircich & Morgan, 1982, p. 262). Thus, managers and leaders not only play a central role in shaping the sense-making process but also in making sure the organizational reality constructed serves the goals of the organization. Management scholar Edgar Schein (1992) puts this idea more bluntly when he claims that "the unique and essential function of leadership is the manipulation of culture" (p. 317).

For example, in Chapter 6 we saw how managers at Disneyland got into trouble because they lost control over the sense-making process of organization members and, hence, their ability to shape the culture. While the official organizational reality utilized the drama metaphor, with its emphasis on show business and Disney as a profit-making company, the employees made sense of Disneyland through the alternative metaphor of family, which conflicted with the business approach. Thus, from a leadership as symbolic action perspective, managers at Disneyland failed in their efforts to define organizational reality for employees, with conflict and industrial action being the result of their failure.

Transformational Leadership

Transformational leadership emerged in the 1980s partly as a response to the perceived need for visionary leaders in U.S. industry (Bass, 1985, 1990; Bass & Riggio, 2006; Burns, 1978; Burns & Avolio, 2004). As such, a number of scholars distinguished between a manager and a leader. According to Bryman (1996), the difference lies in the orientation of each to change. True leadership involves an "active promotion of values which provide shared meanings about the nature of the organization" (p. 277). Management, on the other hand, concerns itself primarily with the here and now and is not concerned with broader issues of organizational purpose and identity, as leaders are. Gary Yukl (1989, p. 253) states this in a slightly different way, arguing that leaders influence and promote commitment, while managers simply carry out position responsibilities and exercise authority.

James MacGregor Burns (1978), the originator of transformational leadership, distinguishes between two leadership approaches that reflect this distinction. First, transactional leadership involves exchanges between leaders and organization members in which the former sets goals and expectations and provides the latter with rewards (pay, recognition, etc.) when these goals are met—a model of leadership that reflects a "managerial" worldview. In the transactional model, "transactions [are] typically based on satisfying both the leader's self-interest and the self-interest of his or her followers" (Burns & Avolio, 2004). Transactional leadership thus entails a "quid pro quo" relationship between leader and follower; a psychological exchange occurs in that the leader clarifies the expectations and the follower delivers, receiving the appropriate reward.

On the other hand, transformational leadership involves binding the leader and members together in a higher moral purpose. The leader raises the aspirations of followers such that they think and act beyond their own self-interests. Followers are elevated from their everyday selves to their "better selves" (Yukl, 1989, p. 271). Transformational leaders are more concerned with the collective interests of the organization (or even society) rather than their own self-interests.

In refining Burns's model of transformational leadership, industrial psychologist Bernard Bass (1985, 1990) argued that this leadership style involves (1) charisma/inspiration, (2) individualized consideration, and (3) intellectual stimulation. First, a transformational leader is charismatic, commanding the attention of followers and inspiring them to carry out the vision of the leader. Second, the transformational leader must, through individualized consideration, get to know followers' needs, aspirations, abilities, and so forth so they can be challenged to exceed themselves and take on leadership roles in their own right. Finally, a transformational leader must intellectually stimulate followers by challenging their basic assumptions and values; in this way, followers can be stimulated to think about work in novel ways. Bass thus views transformational leaders in terms of their effects on followers; the latter become more aware of the importance of organizational goals, and they become more self-actualizing.

The transformational approach to leadership became dominant beginning in the mid-1980s and is still very influential today. Again, Peters and Waterman's (1982) study helped propel its popularity, as the excellent companies they profiled (Apple, Disney, IBM, etc.) generally had a transformational, visionary leader at their helms. Indeed, transformational leadership signals something of a return to the "leader-as-hero" approach, leading some researchers to label this perspective the "neo-charismatic" approach, given its focus on the larger-than-life leaders of corporations who inspire their followers to great deeds by articulating a higher moral purpose (e.g., Fairhurst, 2007). As such, it's worth noting that transformational leadership became popular during a time of crisis for U.S. corporations—consistent with Weber's (1978) view of charismatic authority as coming to the fore during crises in societies (see Chapter 3).

However, it should be noted that the charismatic leader and the transformational leader are not the same. Charisma is a necessary but not sufficient condition for transformational leadership to occur. While the charismatic leader can sometimes produce dependence among followers, the goal of transformational leadership is to give followers the skills to engage in their own forms of critical thinking and empowered behavior. Moreover, with charismatic leadership the focus is on the individual leader as opposed to the leadership process itself; in transformational leadership the idea is to share leadership among multiple leaders rather than keeping the spotlight on a single leader.

Followership

Finally, under the broad umbrella of "new leadership" studies, there has been a significant and growing amount of research on what is called **followership** (Baker, 2007; Chaleff, 1995; Howell & Shamir, 2005; Kelley & Bacon, 2004; Manz & Sims, 2000; Meindl, 1995; Shamir, Pillai, Bligh, & Uhl-Bien, 2007). This research takes seriously the idea that leaders do not exist without followers and that a *dialectical* relationship exists between the two; that is, leaders and followers are mutually defining and constructing.

This interest in followership arose in part because of the changed circumstances of U.S. businesses. In the posts–World War II economic boom of the 1950s and 1960s and the global preeminence of U.S. businesses, the social contract prevailed and corporations promised employees lifelong employment in return for loyalty, obedience, and hard work. The stability of the economy left little need to empower workers by reframing the leader–follower relationship (Baker, 2007). However, the more unstable nature of the world economy over the past 30 years has generated an interest in exploring alternative leadership models.

In some ways, followership research is an effort to undermine the continued dominance of "the leader" both as a focus of leadership research and as a dominant construct in the media and popular culture. As we have already discussed, there is a common, widely accepted notion that organizations succeed or fail on the basis of high-profile leaders who impose their will and personality on the organization. For example, Jack Welch, former CEO of General Electric, typifies this kind of leader, and there is a veritable publishing industry devoted to packaging his leadership philosophy. A quick search turns up the following titles: *Jacked Up: The Inside Story of How Jack Welch Talked GE Into Becoming the World's Greatest Company* (Lane, 2008); *Jack Welch Speaks* (Welch, 2008); *Jack Welch and the 4Es of Leadership* (Krames, 2005); *29 Leadership Secrets from Jack Welch* (Slater, 2003); and *The Jack Welch Lexicon of Leadership* (Krames, 2002). The goal here is less to disseminate successful leadership skills to a broader public and more to create the image of Jack Welch as a corporate rock star whose very name on the cover of a book will guarantee sales. The image created in all this popular discourse is that Welch achieved his goals single-handedly and without the collaboration of thousands of employees!

Followership studies, on the other hand, take seriously the idea that "most of us are more often followers than leaders" (Kelley, 1988, p. 143). Management scholar Dennis Tourish and his colleagues have even suggested that business schools should stop marketing themselves as producers of "transformational" corporate leaders and focus instead on training "enlightened followers" who have a more critical orientation to business and leadership practices (Tourish, Russell, & Armenic, 2010). Such an approach would arguably provide better, more pragmatic, and more realistic training for students bound for the work world.

Of course, the problem with the idea of followership (at least in the individualistically oriented culture dominant in the United States) is that the term has quite negative connotations. For the most part, no one wants to be known as a follower, the implication being that one is a passive "yes person" who needs to be told what to do and never has an original or creative thought. Indeed, when was the last time you saw "strong followership skills" listed on someone's résumé?

What, then, are some of the elements of a followership approach? The initial stimulus for this perspective came from Robert Kelley's (1988) essay "In Praise of Followers" in the *Harvard Business Review*. Kelley developed a two-dimensional model that mapped out five different kinds of followership roles. The two dimensions are (1) independent critical thinking vs. dependent, uncritical thinking, and (2) positive energy and active engagement vs. negative energy and passive engagement.

Kelley maps out five followership roles using these two dimensions (see Figure 11.2). First, "sheep" are both passive and uncritical, need to be told what to do, and avoid responsibility. Second, "yes people" or "conformists" are active and full of energy but are uncritical and need to be told what to do. Such people, Kelley argues, can be very deferential or even servile. Third, "alienated followers" have critical thinking skills but tend to be passive and have to be told what to do; they are often cynical and disgruntled and exhibit negative energy. Fourth, "pragmatic followers" or "survivors" cluster around the intersection of the two dimensions and adapt themselves to the prevailing conditions of the organization. They avoid taking strong positions and are constantly monitoring which way the wind is blowing in the organization. Kelley argues that they are the ultimate survivors, regardless of the level of organizational change. Fifth, and finally, "star" or "exemplary" followers are the ideal followers. These employees are highly committed to the organization, self-managing, willing to provide honest, independent, and constructive critique to leaders, and hold themselves to higher performance standards than others do, constantly working to upgrade their skills. Exemplary followers will also work proactively, looking to identify overlooked problems.

It's important to keep in mind that these five categories indicate followership roles and not personality types; thus, it is quite possible for the same person to exhibit different roles in different organizational contexts. An employee who takes on a star follower role in one context, for example, might become an alienated follower in another context if her boss or the tasks she performs do not make full use of her talents. Critical Case Study 11.1 provides a cute and funny example of how "leadership" is a social construction heavily shaped by other people's willingness to be followers.

Figure 11.2   Kelley's Model of Followership Roles

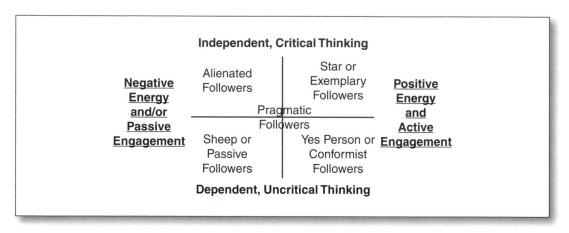

SOURCE: Kelley (1988).

Another interesting take on the concept of followership is provided by management researcher James Meindl and his colleagues in their development of a **romance leadership** perspective (Meindl, 1995; Meindl, Ehrlich, & Dukerich, 1985). In this approach, attention is placed squarely on followers, and in some ways the actual activities of leaders are a secondary factor. Meindl is concerned primarily with how followers construct leaders, arguing that leaders are romanticized such that followers exaggerate their importance and influence. In this sense, Meindl focuses on the idea of leadership as a construct that helps organization members make sense of and comprehend the complexities of organizational life.

In Meindl's romance model, leadership is a product of the ways organization members interact with one another. While most of the leadership perspectives we have discussed attempt to provide empirical evidence for a causal connection between leader behaviors and follower attitudes and performances, Meindl argues that the relationship between leaders and followers is a constructed one; leadership emerges out of a form of "social contagion" in which the reputation of a particular person spreads amongst organization members, rather like an influenza virus. In this sense, the charisma of a leader is not necessarily an objective feature of his or her personality and behavior but, rather, exists in the sense-making processes of followers.

One important implication of Meindl's theory is that the behavior of followers is much less under the control of leaders than other perspectives suggest. Meindl indicates that while the media, business periodicals, and organization members romanticize the role and effectiveness of leaders, such effectiveness exists only as long as the network of relations around the leader constructs them as effective. Once the tide of public opinion turns against a leader, there's not much he or she can do about it.

A followership approach to leadership, then, has a couple of virtues in enabling us to think in different ways about leadership processes in the new workplace. First, as indicated

Critical Case Study 11.1

Leadership Lessons From "Dancing Guy"

One of my favorite YouTube videos is about 2 1/2 minutes long. It doesn't involve cats or babies being cute ("Charlie bit my finger!") but, instead, is a rather shaky video of a guy dancing enthusiastically in a field at a music concert. Dancing on his own. Like a complete dork. The people around him are sitting around, chilled out, listening to the music, and completely ignoring him; they're probably embarrassed for him and his crazy gyrations. Then something weird and truly amazing happens. Suddenly another guy comes running up and starts dancing with him in a similarly dorky manner. Is he being ironic and making fun of him, or is he a fellow dorky dancer? It doesn't really matter. Within a few seconds several more people come rushing up and start dancing with Dancing Guy and his comrade. Now there's momentum. Pretty quickly the people sitting around start to get up and get in on the act. Then, people are literally running over to join in the fun. In no time at all anyone who's not up and dancing looks like a complete killjoy. A movement is born. You can watch the video at the link below. Make sure you have the sound turned up so you can hear the voice-over commentary.

http://www.youtube.com/watch?v=fW8amMCVAJQ

So what happened here? How did Dancing Guy go from an eccentric "lone nut" to the leader of a movement in a few seconds? The video commentary talks about the importance of the "first follower." That is, the first guy who comes and joins Dancing Guy creates the leadership context and, hence, the possibility for followers. In this sense, the video is a great example of the social construction of leadership in microcosm. There's no formal, designated leader and no followers—just a bunch of people sitting around with one eccentric guy following the beat of his own internal drummer. There's not even a connection between "leader" and "followers," except the shared context of a music venue.

In essence, this event is about the management of meaning and a changing of the interpretive frame in operation. Once the "first follower" comes forward, then the frame is changed, and it's okay for others to become associated with Dancing Guy. As the video commentary suggests, it takes courage to associate yourself with the "lone nut," but once that occurs, momentum develops and "lone nut" becomes "cool Dancing Guy"—not because of anything *he* did but because of the shift in interpretive frame for the people around him. In this instance, leadership is indeed in the eye of the beholder. Dancing Guy doesn't attract followers by leading; he acts in a particular way and at a certain point gets defined as a leader engaged in behavior worth following. The rest is history.

Discussion Questions

1. Watch "Leadership Lessons From Dancing Guy" on YouTube. What's your reaction to what happens?

2. Think about your own ideas about leadership. Where do these ideas come from? What do you expect from a leader? Describe your experiences with both good and bad leaders. What differentiates them?

3. Think about your experiences as a "follower." How would you categorize yourself in terms of Kelley's follower roles? What factors influenced your role behavior?

4. In groups, discuss two of the leadership perspectives addressed in this chapter. How might they influence the way you interact with people in organizational settings?

earlier, it "decenters" the idea of the great, heroic leader and instead looks at leaders and leadership as a socially constructed process in which leaders and followers mutually constitute each other. As Brad Jackson and Ken Parry (2011) pithily state it, "Leaders keep on winning largely because their followers perceive them to be winners" (p. 52). Leaders can be effective only if followers construct them as such. Second, followership research decenters leadership in another way. If leaders are no longer positioned as the paragons of brilliance and "derring-do" (Google it!), then followers come to play a crucial role in organizational decision making. If followers played a role of "constructive dissent rather than destructive consent" (p. 65), then perhaps many of the corporate scandals that occurred over the past few years (Enron, Worldcom, the bank mortgage crisis, the Wall Street bailout, and so forth ad nauseam) would have been less likely to occur.

Gary Gemmill and Judith Oakley (1992) have gone so far as to argue that "the concepts of 'leader' and 'leadership' have become psychic prisons" (p. 114) and that much writing on leadership arises from a "deepening sense of social despair and massive learned helplessness" (p. 115). The return of neo-charisma and trait theories in transformational leadership has created the illusion that leaders are in control of events and allows followers to escape responsibility for their own actions. This acceptance of the "leader myth" and the resulting lack of responsibility "promotes alienation, deskilling, reification of organizational forms, and dysfunctional organizational structures" (p. 124). Gemmill and Oakley argue that rather than providing empirical support for the value of leadership, leadership research mainly offers ideological support for the existing social order. The followership perspective allows us to escape at least some of these problems by "reskilling" followers and reframing what leadership is. Let's address further this increasing skepticism about current leadership research by developing a critical communication perspective on leadership.

❖ A CRITICAL COMMUNICATION PERSPECTIVE ON LEADERSHIP

Most of the research we have discussed so far fits fairly comfortably into a "managerial" perspective on leadership. In other words, regardless of the theoretical approach—trait, style, contingency, "new" leadership, and so on—each perspective is interested in studying leadership as a phenomenon that can create more effective and efficient organizations and hence improve the organizational bottom line. But rather than ask the question, "What is leadership and how can we improve its outcomes?" what if we asked a different question? Following Alvesson and Deetz's (2000) critical approach, we will address the question, "What can we see, think, or talk about if we examine leadership from a communication perspective?" In other words, what if we abandoned the idea of leadership as a thing possessed by certain people and instead explored it as a dynamic communication process?

Let's briefly indicate the implications of this **critical communication perspective** and then explore them in more detail:

- A communication approach rejects the traditional separation of leader and follower (Collinson, 2005). Both "leader-centric" and "follower-centric" approaches are rejected in favor of a view of leadership as coproduced among organization members.
- From a communication perspective there is no "essence" of leadership to discover (as in traditional approaches); rather, leadership is examined as a socially constructed process in which social actors interdependently create what leadership means in specific organizational contexts (Fairhurst, 2007; Fairhurst & Grant, 2010).

Critical Technologies 11.1
E-Leadership

Communication technologies (CTs) present particular challenges and possibilities for organizational leadership. On the one hand, CTs provide leaders with many more opportunities and media to communicate with organization members—e-mail, various social media, teleconferencing, and so forth. Moreover, today's organization leaders have greater access to real-time information, and there are many more opportunities to build more-individualized relationships with both customers and employees in far-flung locations.

On the other hand, such a communication-rich environment creates challenges for leaders, including greater pressure to be responsive to various stakeholders, including employees and customers; rapidly changing customer demands, leading to more work being done in temporary work teams that often lack cohesiveness; virtual work teams with individuals working at a distance from one another, with similar cohesiveness issues; and decisions regarding appropriate use of the various communication media.

Management researchers Robert Lengel and Richard Daft (1988) describe selection of appropriate media to communicate with employees as an important leadership skill. Through a theory of "media richness," they argue that communication media vary in their capacity to convey information. The "richness" of a particular CT is measured by its ability (1) to handle multiple information cues simultaneously (verbal, nonverbal, etc.), (2) to facilitate rapid feedback, and (3) to establish a personal focus. Thus, there is a hierarchy of media richness, with face-to-face communication with actual physical presence as the most

media rich, followed by interactive media such as Skype, FaceTime, and so forth, then the telephone, followed by text messaging, e-mail, and then more "lean" CTs such as various social media, electronic bulletin boards (craigslist, etc.), and physical bulletin boards.

Lengel and Daft argue that the skilled "E-leader" is not the one who spends a lot of time in face-to-face conversations but, rather, the one who can best match the communication medium with routineness (or lack thereof) of the message. Consideration must be given to the fit between social context, the communication medium, and the issue at hand. For example, firing someone by posting a message on his or her Facebook wall shows poor judgment (duh!). Similarly, announcing a routine meeting by visiting every person's desk personally is a poor use of a manager's time. The point is that various CTs are not simply neutral channels for conveying information but contain an interpretive element; people make sense of communication processes by paying attention not only to the message but also to its medium.

Consistent with the "leader as manager of meaning" perspective discussed in this chapter, Lengel and Daft also suggest that leaders should use rich media to develop and extend their "social presence"; that is, the degree to which employees interpret their communication efforts as warm, trustworthy, sociable, sensitive, and so forth. Thus, if an executive rarely engages in face-to-face conversations and hides behind e-mails and memos, then he or she is likely to have low social presence and create much psychological distance between him or herself and employees.

- Communication is central to the ways leadership is socially constructed; examination of various communication processes (talk, texts, stories, metaphors, etc.) enables us to see this construction process "at work."
- A communication perspective is a "post-heroic" view of leadership that "decenters" the dominant and romanticized model of the "great man" as leader; instead, leadership is seen as distributed throughout the organization.
- A *critical* communication perspective on leadership both challenges traditional research and focuses on issues of power and control, including possibilities for leadership as a form of resistance (Collinson, 2011; Zoller & Fairhurst, 2007).

Given traditional research and popular conceptions of leadership, it's hard to give up (and hard not to write about!) the idea of leadership as a thing and leaders as specific people who exercise authority over others. However, we will discuss leadership not as something that is inevitable but, rather, as an ongoing process communicatively constructed by organization members (Fairhurst, 2007; Fairhurst & Grant, 2010). In this sense, we will adopt what management scholars Mats Alvesson and André Spicer (2011) refer to as an "ambiguity-centered" approach to leadership—one that focuses on leadership as a complex process that can be used in different ways by different people. In this way, we will challenge the idea that conventional ideas of leadership are inherently good and necessary for all organizations.

We will investigate four different areas within a critical communication approach to leadership: (1) leadership and disciplinary power, (2) resistance leadership, (3) narrative and leadership, and (4) gender and leadership.

Leadership and Disciplinary Power

In this book we've spent a lot of time talking about organizational control processes, and for the most part that has been framed in terms of managers and managerial systems of thought exercising various kinds of control over employees. The reality, however, is that managers and corporate leaders are subject to various forms of control as well. As we saw in Chapter 8, and as we will discuss in more detail in Chapter 14, one of the features of the new, postbureaucratic workplace is that white-collar and "no-collar" workers are increasingly subject to forms of discipline and control that focus on their identities as organization members—for example, the "entrepreneurial self," in which employees see themselves as projects that need to be branded and sold like any other commodity. In a similar way, leaders and corporate executives are subject to forms of disciplinary power in which they are constantly appraised and assessed in terms of their ability to lead employees and produce change. As leadership scholar Gail Fairhurst (2007) points out, in today's corporations, true leaders now have to be "change masters."

When critically examining the relationship between leadership and disciplinary power, then, we need to think about the ways leaders and corporate executives are socially constructed by broader societal discourses. As we have already seen in this chapter, managerial discourse and research on leadership has constructed the leader differently in different historical and economic contexts, responding to the particular needs of organizations. The social construction of leadership has shifted from the "great man" to the rational planner to the symbolic manipulator and so forth. Today, as organizations exist in increasingly turbulent economic environments, executives are constructed as valuable intellectual capital, managing strategic change in the most difficult of circumstances; on the other hand, employees are constructed as expendable through downsizing and cost saving (Fairhurst, 2007).

Because of their value to the company, these executives are subject to constant forms of appraisal and evaluation. In this sense, they are continuous objects of knowledge, through both formal tools for evaluation and their own self-scrutiny. Gail Fairhurst (2007) has shown how three widely used technologies—performance appraisal, 360-degree feedback, and executive coaching—render the manager and executive constantly visible and subject to evaluation, thus inducing a sense of insecurity about their performances.

I can attest to many of these disciplinary practices from my own leadership experience. A couple of years ago I was selected to be a Leadership Fellow at UNC's Institute for the Arts and Humanities. As part of the fellowship I attended a weeklong residential program at the Center for Creative Leadership in Greensboro, North Carolina. In preparation for that experience I had to go through a battery of evaluations, including the FIRO-B, which measures interpersonal style; the MBTI (Meyers-Briggs Type Indicator), which measures personality and decision-making style; and 360-degree feedback, which provides evaluations of leadership effectiveness from subordinates, peers, and supervisors and also includes a self-assessment element. Thus, I got to compare my assessment of myself with others' assessments.

In some ways, the 360-degree feedback evaluation is quite similar to Foucault's notion of the Panopticon. It's a tool that renders you visible to yourself, as seen through other people's eyes. It makes you incredibly self-conscious; you become an object of knowledge, both to yourself and to others. Obviously, such evaluations are not intrinsically bad and, in fact, can be quite useful in identifying issues that one was not aware even existed. However, they are part of an increasing tendency to leave no stone unturned in constructing bodies of knowledge about organizational employees (Holmer Nadesan, 1997). And not coincidentally, a vast and very profitable industry has grown up around such evaluation processes, as companies seek a competitive edge.

If you haven't experienced any of these evaluation tools yet, you are likely to experience them at various points in your professional life. The results of such tests may well lead employers to draw conclusions about whether you have "leadership potential" or not.

Resistance Leadership

There is, however, another way to think about the relationship between leadership and disciplinary power. For the most part, critical scholars have tended to treat leadership as part of the system of domination, due largely to the fact that leadership research comes mostly from a managerial perspective that accepts the existing systems of power and authority in organizations. However, organizational communication scholars Heather Zoller and Gail Fairhurst have challenged this conception and made the case for what they call **resistance leadership** (Fairhurst & Zoller, 2008; Zoller & Fairhurst, 2007). They argue that leadership is not simply about "managing dissent" and getting people to coordinate their behavior; rather, dissent itself can be viewed as a form of organizational leadership.

Zoller and Fairhurst thus disconnect leadership from management and frame the former as a political act that contributes to the well-being of a community. They argue that "leadership is not about the person in charge but about the way one or more actors engages the community and its mores in collective action" (Zoller & Fairhurst, 2008, p. 1339). In this sense, leadership challenges conventional assumptions and the existing power relations. For example, from a traditional managerial perspective, an organizational whistle-blower (someone who, in the public interest, reveals information about organizational misdeeds) is a disloyal employee who needs to be managed and even disciplined or fired (there is a long history of whistle-blowers being treated extremely harshly by organizations, even in cases where they expose practices that hurt the organization as well as members of the public). From a resistance leadership perspective, however, a whistle-blower is someone who challenges existing power relations and engages organization members in thinking about and perhaps changing the way things are done.

For example, in the 1999 movie *The Insider*, Russell Crowe plays Jeffrey Wigand, a vice president for research and development at Brown and Williamson tobacco company who, at great personal risk, reveals documents showing how tobacco companies deliberately manipulate the ingredients in cigarettes to increase the amount of nicotine that smokers receive. In essence, Wigand's testimony revealed that the seven CEOs of "Big Tobacco" had perjured themselves before a congressional hearing in 1994 when each of them stated for the record that nicotine is nonaddictive. Wigand's act of whistle-blowing opened the door for massive lawsuits that resulted in a multibillion-dollar settlement by tobacco companies. Wigand's actions were a form of resistance leadership.

The idea of resistant leadership, then, gets at the way everyday organization members can challenge taken-for-granted realities and, through communication and action, create possibilities for change. Leadership becomes a political act because dissenters engage with other organization members in a dynamic manner and potentially produce a new reality (Kassing, 2011).

Narrative Leadership

Earlier in this chapter we discussed the idea of leaders as managers of meaning, in which much of the "art" of leadership involves the ability to frame reality for organization members. In Chapter 6 we discussed the role of stories in creating organizational culture, and in recent years researchers have discussed how stories can be an important framing mechanism for organizational leaders to use with followers (e.g., Fairhurst & Sarr, 1996). Stories are useful because they make abstract ideas more concrete and can also provide organization members with guiding principles and morals regarding appropriate and inappropriate organizational behavior (e.g., Martin, Feldman, Hatch, & Sitkin, 1983). As we saw in the case study in Chapter 7, the famous IBM story about Lucille Burger, a security guard, confronting CEO Thomas Watson Jr. provides IBM employees with a lesson about the importance of following organizational rules and policies.

From a leadership perspective, the IBM story is a great example of a follower, or "distributed," model of leadership in operation—what might be called **narrative leadership**. That is, although Lucille Burger is a low-level employee, she still demonstrates leadership in working to preserve the integrity of IBM rules about security, regardless of who is trying to circumvent the system. The fact that the story became part of IBM lore attests to its effectiveness in serving as a frame for employee sense making.

Another example of an organizational story that performs a similar framing function comes from FedEx:

The Fedex courier did not intend to go swimming during the work day, especially with the harsh winds and rain covering much of Honolulu, Hawaii. However, when a gust of wind plucked a package from the back of his truck and flung it into the ocean, James did not think twice about diving in. James recovered the package and, soaking wet, delivered it to the customer. (Parry & Hansen, 2007, p. 281)

Again, this story depicts the leadership qualities of a regular employee as he takes ownership of a problem and deals with it himself. Interestingly, when I explored FedEx's website, there was a section about "everyday heroes" that included stories of FedEx employees going "above and beyond the call of duty," not only to serve customers but to contribute to the wider community. At the top of the page was a picture of a FedEx employee pulling a stranded motorist from his flooded vehicle. These kinds of stories serve to frame FedEx not only for employees but also for customers, who are told a story of FedEx as more than just a business but as a corporate citizen that contributes in positive ways to the broader community. Since my exploration of the site, however, the "everyday heroes" campaign seems to have ended—an indication, perhaps, of how companies have to constantly manage the meanings and stories that customers associate with them in order to maintain a dynamic presence in their market.

Management scholars Alan Parry and Hans Hansen (2007) argue that organizational stories are more than simply a tool that leaders can use to frame organizational reality; instead, stories themselves play a leadership role. In this sense, Parry and Hansen provide the ultimate example of a communicative model of leadership, in which leadership is no longer located in people at all but in the communication processes that constitute the organization. Of course, they do not mean that stories literally become leaders but, rather, that stories "exhibit the functions of leadership" (p. 287). Basically, Parry and Hansen argue that organizational stories get told and then are "set free to spread among the organizational community" (p. 292). As such, their position is much like the "social contagion" model of romance leadership discussed previously. If stories are powerful and "charismatic," then they will be told and retold; in other words, they possess "followability." Thus, "leaders may come and go, but an enduring corporate story can last the life of the company, and just as everyone enacts their interpretation of a leader's vision, they enact the vision a story provides" (p. 290).

Consistent with the "ambiguity-centered" conception of leadership discussed earlier, this idea of stories as leaders encapsulates the ways organizational meanings and realities are often "up for grabs." That is, there is never a single interpretation of a story (or indeed any organizational symbol or artifact), and thus the way a story performs a leadership function might vary, depending on how organization members make sense of it. Furthermore, it's quite possible that organization members will create counter-narratives—everyday organizational stories that resist the dominant corporate vision communicatively constructed in the officially sanctioned corporate narrative. For example, in Smith and Eisenberg's (1987) study of an industrial dispute at Disneyland, discussed earlier and in Chapter 6, the employees were able to generate a counter-narrative through the metaphor of family that challenged the official corporate vision of Disney as a business enterprise built on the enactment of a drama. We can therefore say that organization members are "imaginative consumers" of leaders' visions for an organization (Linstead & Grafton-Small, 1992).

Gender and Leadership

The relationship between gender and leadership has been a focus of research for leadership scholars for many decades. Particularly as more women executives started to enter the workforce, researchers began to speculate about whether women leaders brought a different style of communication to organizations (Baxter, 2010; Chin, 2007; Eagly & Johannesen-Schmidt, 2001; Holmes, 2006; Sinclair, 2005). In a now-famous article called "Ways Women Lead," management scholar Judy Rosener (1990) describes an alternative women's leadership style that is different from the "command-and-control," authoritarian style she argued is typical of male executives. Rosener claims that as a result of their socialization, which emphasizes nurturing, support, and cooperation skills, many women executives engage in a leadership style that encourages participation in decision making by subordinates, maintains open lines of communication and shares power, and works to energize subordinates and enhance their self-worth. Rosener calls this style "interactive leadership" because women leaders "actively work to make their interactions with subordinates positive for everyone involved" (p. 120).

While Rosener's perspective is useful for thinking about alternatives to dominant masculine forms of leadership, there are a number of problems with her approach when examined from a critical communication perspective. First, she's guilty of the same errors that have been attributed to other theories regarding leadership style—such style approaches tend to ignore context and don't recognize that different situations, tasks, and employees require different leadership skills. Second, Rosener turns a gender stereotype into a virtue. The idea that because of their upbringing women bring different leadership skills to organizations provides a rather two-dimensional view of gender that ignores the multiple identities both women and men bring to work (as we discussed in Chapter 9). Third, Rosener's view of women leaders ignores organizational power relations; her perspective runs the risk of marginalizing women executives in leadership roles that require nurturing, "touchy-feely" skills, such as human resources and personnel management— roles that often pay less than other executive positions traditionally occupied by men, such as research and development or marketing.

Management scholar Joyce Fletcher (1998, 1999) provides some interesting insights into the idea that women leaders provide an alternative leadership communication style. She argues that although there has been a movement in organizations toward "post-heroic" leadership processes that downplay the manager as hero, when women leaders actually enact this "distributed" process of leadership, they "get disappeared." That is, their contribution to the organization is not recognized or rewarded in the same way as the contribution of executives who adopt "heroic" leadership styles.

Fletcher's study of an engineering firm showed that behaviors such as fostering a strong team environment, allowing others to get credit for work accomplished, and working on weekends to keep a project on schedule were routinely overlooked or dismissed by senior managers, largely because they were not a routine part of the culture and, thus, not perceived as valuable by those in power. In other words, the traditional model of "heroic" leadership was dominant in this organization. Fletcher (2004) refers to this issue as "the paradox of post-heroic leadership," arguing that while organizations may strongly advocate distributed and follower models of leadership, the gendered (i.e., masculine) culture of many organizations means that the kind of "relational practice" connected with the post-heroic leadership philosophy is associated with powerlessness.

To conclude our discussion of gender and leadership, let me briefly introduce a new concept that has recently entered the lexicon of leadership studies—the **glass cliff**. In

Chapter 9 we discussed the widespread phenomenon of the glass ceiling (the invisible barrier that limits women managers' advancement) as well as the glass escalator (the rapid advancement of men in feminized professions such as nursing and teaching). Developed by management scholars Michelle Ryan and Alex Haslam, the glass cliff refers to the precarious position women managers often find themselves in once they have succeeded in "shattering" the glass ceiling (Bruckmüller & Branscombe, 2010; Haslam & Ryan, 2008; Ryan & Haslam, 2007).

Based on their analysis of the appointment and subsequent tenure of numerous women CEOs, Ryan and Haslam argue that companies are more likely to appoint men as CEOs when the company is stable and thriving and more likely to appoint women as CEOs in times of crisis. Ryan and Haslam claim that companies tend to operate with the formula, "Think manager—think male; think crisis—think female" (Ryan & Haslam, 2007). This means that women are often appointed to senior positions associated with a greater risk of failure. Thus, "women were more likely than men to be placed in positions *already associated* with poor company performance" (p. 556).

The glass cliff, then, refers to an *additional* form of discrimination that women may face once they have broken through the glass ceiling—successful women are more frequently placed in precarious positions and, thus, potentially set up for a fall. They tend to be overlooked when safe or "cushy" positions are available. Susanne Bruckmüller and Nyla Bascombe (2011) argue that CEOs such as Carly Fiorina of Hewlett-Packard, Kate Swann of W. H. Smith, and Carol Bartz of Yahoo have all been subject to the glass cliff phenomenon.

Although not referring to a female CEO, the idea of the glass cliff is perfectly summed up in a satirical "news story" with the headline "Black Man Given Nation's Worst Job" (2008), printed in *The Onion*:

> African-American man Barack Obama, 47, was given the least-desirable job in the entire country Tuesday when he was elected president of the United States of America. . . . As part of his duties, the black man will have to spend four to eight years cleaning up the messes other people left behind. The job comes with such intense scrutiny and so certain a guarantee of failure that only one other person even bothered applying for it. Said scholar and activist Mark L. Denton, "It just goes to show you that, in this country, a black man still can't catch a break."

❖ CONCLUSION

In this chapter we have addressed a number of perspectives on leadership, showing how research has evolved over the course of several decades (Table 11.1 provides a handy summary of the various approaches). Leadership research has tended to develop in ways that reflect the changing economic, political, and cultural climate in which organizations and corporations find themselves. In broad terms, theories have evolved from strongly "leader-centric" perspectives, in which the idea of the "heroic leader" is front and center; through "follower-centric" approaches, which recognize that leaders don't exist without followers; and finally to a dynamic, dialectical approach, which focuses

Table 11.1 Comparing Leadership Perspectives

Approach	Trait	Style	Situational	Symbolic Action	Transformational	Followership	Resistance	Narrative
View of leadership	Innate property of "great men"; leader as charismatic	Set of skills that can be learned; focus on formal leaders	Determined by work context, situational factors; psychological model	Ability to frame reality for followers; leader as visionary; leadership as process	Ability to articulate higher moral purpose for followers; return of charisma	"Decenter" leader; leaders socially constructed by followers	Leadership as political act; resistance and dissent as leadership	Contained in the stories that organization members tell; distributed among many employees
View of communication	Means to impart wisdom to followers; use of persuasion through oratory	Provides direction; helps create supportive work context	Shaped by task and leader personality; use to provide direction and support	Process through which meaning and reality are created and framed	Frames reality and creates organizational vision	Process through which followers construct leaders	Use of communication to challenge taken-for-granted organizational realities	Narrates and constructs organizational values and reality
Leader–follower relations	Leader has hero status for followers	Balance concern for followers with productivity	Shaped by nature of task and personality of leader	Co-construct corporate reality, with leader framing employee sense making	Leader empowers followers to be leaders themselves; creates multiple leaders	Followers create leader success; followers play role of "constructive dissent"	Resistance leader engages his/her community in collective action	Leadership not in people but in the stories people tell
View of organization	Product of vision of "great man"	Sites of task accomplishment and work relations	Sites of task accomplishment and work relations	Cultural system of beliefs and values	System of beliefs and values where higher moral purpose is realized	Socially constructed through leader-follower relations	A moral community where freedom must be realized	Organization created and exists in stories members tell

on the social construction of leaders and followers, with the "heroic" leader completely "decentered."

And this is perhaps one of the most important lessons to take away from this chapter: While many leadership approaches attempt to demonstrate a direct, causal relationship between leader behavior and follower attitudes, performance, and commitment, the reality is much more complex and ambiguous. Moreover, one can argue that many of the problems in corporations today can be traced to "alpha-male" leaders who truly believe they can control every aspect of organizational life around them. The kind of leaders depicted in anthropologist Karen Ho's (2009) ethnography of Wall Street are recruited from élite institutions and are told from Day 1 that they are special, the best and the brightest. Such socialization does not make for humility and fosters an absolute belief in one's decision-making ability.

Consistent with the critical communication perspective adopted in this chapter, perhaps the optimal approach to leadership is to recognize that one can manage meaning and empower people to a certain degree but that, ultimately, as meaning-making creatures, humans will always create a version of reality that fits with their own individual and collective experience. Given this situation, let's end the chapter with a critical-communication–oriented definition of leadership (drawing on several leadership scholars) that I hope provides some food for thought:

> Leadership is a coordinated social process through which people communicatively construct and experiment with new possibilities for thought and action. Such possibilities are recognized by the group or organization as moving beyond self-interest and meeting a collective, higher good. Within this communication process, individuals may be constructed as leaders who help guide and facilitate decision-making and action.

The question is, what kind of leader will you be? Do you have what it takes to be not only a good leader (in the broadest, ambiguity-oriented sense) but an "enlightened follower," too? In the course of your professional career you are likely to have several leadership opportunities and be confronted with many difficult decisions and scenarios. Do you have the courage of "Dancing Guy," as well as that of his comrade, the first follower?

CRITICAL APPLICATIONS

1. Interview someone in a position of leadership. Ask that person about his or her "leadership philosophy" and how he or she came to develop this particular perspective. Can you identify this philosophy in any of the leadership theories we have discussed in this chapter?

2. Think about your own experiences in positions of leadership. What are/were the particular challenges you faced? What is/was most rewarding and most frustrating about the experience? In what ways has this chapter helped you put these experiences in context?

KEY TERMS

critical communication
perspective   270

followership   266

glass cliff   276

leadership   257

narrative leadership   274

new leadership   263

resistance
leadership   273

romance leadership   268

situational approach   261

style approach   259

symbolic action   263

trait approach   257

transformational
leadership   265

STUDENT STUDY SITE

Visit the student study site at **www.sagepub.com/mumbyorg** for these additional learning tools:

- Web quizzes
- eFlashcards
- SAGE journal articles

- Video resources
- Web resources

CHAPTER 12

Branding and Consumption

Shopping malls are the "cathedrals of consumption" in the age of branding.

> *A democratic civilization will save itself only if it makes the language of the image into a stimulus for critical reflection—not an invitation for hypnosis.*
>
> —Eco (1979, p. 12)

About a 15-minute drive from where I live in Chapel Hill, North Carolina, there's a place called the Streets at Southpoint. For anybody who likes to shop (and let's face it, who doesn't?) it represents a cornucopia of possibilities for satisfying our consumption cravings. In addition to major department stores such as Nordstrom's and Sears, all the major clothing brands are represented—Gap, Banana Republic, J. Crew, Ann Taylor, Anthropologie, and so on—as well as various "lifestyle" stores such as Bose (high-end audio), Pottery Barn (home furnishings), and Williams-Sonoma (expensive kitchen stuff). There are also lots of chain restaurants, as well as a 12-screen cinema. In short, it's a shopper's dream.

But there's also something a bit odd about Southpoint. You see, Southpoint didn't exist 10 years ago, and there aren't really any streets, as we would understand them in the conventional sense—places where people walk and talk freely in public. "The streets" are actually a real estate developer's ideal of what a downtown area might look like with all the grime and messiness and urban feel taken away. So, in addition to the usual indoor, climate-controlled space we think of when we hear the word *mall*, shoppers can also step outside where the "streets" are lined with stores and restaurants, a fountain, a town square complete with a bandstand. There are even fake, intentionally faded billboard ads for quaint old products painted on the sides of buildings to enhance the urban vibe of the place. There are also kids playing. But wait—those kids are curiously immobile and don't act like kids at all. In fact, the "kids" in question are actually statues frozen in the act of doing what kids do—riding scooters, playing with the pet dog, and just goofing around. I suspect that if real kids tried doing what the statues are doing, they would be immediately removed from the premises by one of the numerous security guards that control the area.

Welcome to the 21st century conception of the marketplace—a place where not only are branded goods on sale but the entire experience of shopping and consumption is branded. Gone are the traditional conceptions of "the streets," where we think of people being "streetwise" or having "street knowledge" or "taking it to the streets" (a phrase associated with rebellion and social transformation as, for example, with the civil rights movement). All these terms and associations make us think of an environment where ideas and opinions freely circulate, where people congregate (perhaps in cafés, perhaps on street corners) to get together with friends, argue about the issues of the day, or protest injustice. Indeed, for hundreds of years "the marketplace" has been a public space where the free exchange of both goods and ideas has occurred (the latter sometimes literally from atop a soapbox!).

In the 21st century the marketplace has been largely privatized and branded to create a reality that is very much a reflection of corporate efforts to control the meanings people associate with their everyday experiences. In this chapter I will make the argument that, while meanings and realities are always mediated in some manner (by friends, family, education, and so forth), today much of what we experience and the realities we inhabit and take for granted are largely the product of corporate branding efforts. Corporations, in this sense, not only shape reality for their employees but also for their customers. Of course, on the face of it this is hardly news—corporations have been attempting to influence the way we think (especially to get us to buy their products) for a long, long time. However, I will argue that the corporate meaning management process has reached a point where it profoundly influences our sense of who we are and the world we inhabit.

In addressing the phenomenon of branding, then, we will discuss it as a primarily communicative process that involves the efforts of corporations to shape human identity and influence the cultural and social landscape in order to sell consumer products. Our lives are saturated with corporate, manufactured meanings that, in many respects, lie largely out of our control. What is interesting about this corporate meaning management process is that companies have very much taken to heart the idea that communication is not about transmitting information from A (company) to B (consumer)—a process characteristic of early advertising and branding—but, rather, is about creating complex systems of meaning that shape social realities and people's identities. Corporations are incredibly sophisticated in their methods of meaning management. As such, it is extremely important that as consumers we are equally sophisticated in our ability to decode and critique the ways such meanings are constructed. In addition, it's important that we appreciate the extent to which we participate in this meaning construction process, and how we engage in a "dialogue" with the brands we purchase (Fiske, 1989).

This chapter, then, will be a communication analysis of the branding and consumption process, examining how corporations construct and manage not only meaning systems but also the very identities of consumers; indeed, the fact that we think of ourselves as "consumers" should give us some insight to the degree to which "consumption" and "identity" are closely tied. First, let's talk about the very idea of branding.

❖ BRANDING

© Bettmann/CORBIS

In the early days of branding, the "housewife" was the target consumer for branded goods, especially household products.

In the second half of the 19th century branding emerged as a revolutionary way for companies to market their products to an increasingly literate working population (Olins, 2000). As capitalism and industrialization expanded and new markets developed, companies competed to secure shares of the newly emerging consumer class. Branding their products was the principal way to develop customer loyalty and increase customer base. Quickly, however, branding became a way not only to create customer loyalty but also to create customer needs. The expansion of capitalism is dependent on the creation of new consumer markets, as old and established markets become saturated and less profitable. Consumers not only need to be continually persuaded to fulfill their needs and desires but also must be continually convinced of new needs and desires they were previously unaware they had!

In the early days of branding, the "housewife" was the primary audience for advertising, given her role in determining household purchases. In fact, according to brand expert Wally Olins (2000), for about the first 100 years of modern advertising the very notion of the brand was intimately connected with perishable household items such as laundry detergent, soap, jam, butter, toothpaste, and so forth—precisely the products that homemakers purchased. Of course, for the most part the various kinds of laundry detergent or toothpaste were virtually indistinguishable from one another, and so the brand—via mass advertising—became the only means that one company's product could be distinguished from another's.

As Olins (2000, 2003) indicates, companies developed a brand formula that highlighted what the advertising industry referred to as the "unique selling proposition" (USP) of a product—a uniqueness often rooted in highly questionable claims. Such USPs, however, were—and still are—an essential part of the effort to establish a distinct brand identity. According to Olins (2003, p. 53), USPs were based on the following formula, aimed at homemakers:

1. This product is better because it contains X (secret, magic, new, miracle) ingredient that will make it work more effectively.

2. If you use it, your home will look more beautiful or your food will taste much better or you will be even more glamorous than ever before.

3. This will leave you more time to remain even more desirable and attractive for your lovely husband and family.

What I find interesting about this 100-year-old formula is that while branding generally has become far more sophisticated, advertising for household products today pretty much sticks to these principles. TV ads for household products are still almost exclusively aimed at women, who are depicted in commercials as completely obsessed with dirt, odors, and food! My current favorite commercial (though probably long off the air by the time you read this) depicts the efforts of a forlorn, lovesick floor mop that has been cast aside by a homemaker in favor of a more modern floor-cleaning implement. The mop keeps trying to win back the affections of the homemaker who has discarded "him." But, of course, she rebuffs his wooing efforts—how could she possibly subject her family to an inferior cleaning tool? There's so much wrong (not to say plain weird) about depicting a mop as a woman's former love interest that I won't even begin to analyze it (you might have fun doing this yourself). Suffice it to say that the branding of household products attempts to engage (even exploit) women's emotions in very particular ways (later we will discuss the idea of "emotional branding"). But in essence, and consistent with the USP described above, all such branding efforts attempt to position women as better, smarter, more caring people by virtue of their purchase of a certain branded product.

One further example of how the USP and the process of need creation were brought together in the early 20th century involves the mouthwash Listerine. Listerine had actually been around for several decades as an ordinary household disinfectant before someone at the company had the bright idea of marketing it as a mouthwash. So, in the 1920s, the company began an aggressive marketing campaign to convince people that halitosis was a serious social problem—a "problem" that, prior to the marketing campaign, was not publically recognized as requiring attention. Similarly, deodorants were first aggressively marketed in the 1920s through an effort to make natural human body odor a problem to be addressed.

Given these examples, then, how might we define a **brand**? A brand is "the total constellation of meanings, feelings, perceptions, beliefs and goodwill attributed to any market offering displaying a particular sign" (Muniz, 2007). In this sense, a brand can be distinguished from a product. While the latter refers to an item that provides a function or a service for people (cars to be driven, clothes to wear, food to eat, etc.), the former refers to the particular relationships and meanings that a company attempts to construct around its product. So, a product can also be a brand, but from a corporation's perspective the brand—not the product—is the most important thing. Indeed, Phil Knight—Nike's former CEO—has argued that Nike makes brands and lifestyles, not products. Thus, as sociologist Janette Webb (2006) points out, automobile companies such as Ford and GM long ago abandoned the idea that they simply make cars and trucks. Instead, through marketing, advertising, and branding, they focus on "organizing social dependencies on the ownership of a car, and . . . creating the perception that car ownership symbolises status, independence, mobility and opportunity" (p. 56).

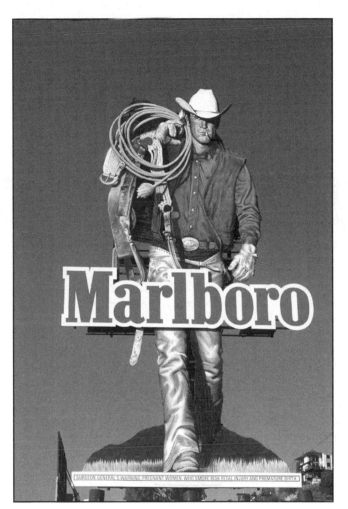

Cigarette brands run the gamut of meanings from ruggedly masculine (Marlboro) to sexy and feminine (Virginia Slims).

© Carl & Ann Purcell/CORBIS

A brand, then, is a constructed set of meanings that a company attaches to a particular product. Such meanings are extremely carefully constructed, and sometimes literally billions of dollars (in the case of the pharmaceutical industry, for example) are spent on the careful development of such meanings. What's interesting about this process, however, is that the meanings associated with products are, by and large, completely arbitrary; that is, there is little or no natural or intrinsic connection between a product and the way it is branded with meanings (recall the discussion of semiotics from Chapter 2).

For example, cigarette brands run the gamut of meanings from rugged and masculine (Marlboro) to patriotic (American Spirit) to sexy and feminine (Virginia Slims); tobacco itself is none of these things in and of itself until millions of dollars are spent on branding it in these ways and creating emotional attachments between the product/brand and the consumer. Hardee's "Thickburgers" are branded as a masculine product that "real men" eat (notice the emphasis on size and weight in Hardee's commercials), even though there's nothing "naturally" masculine about eating ground-up cow between two pieces of bread. As such, brands are created through what is referred to as the **floating signifier effect**. In other words, literally any meaning or quality can be attached to any object or product, including dirt and water (see Critical Case Study 12.1 for an extended example of how the floating signifier effect works).

Critical Case Study 12.1
Diamonds Are Forever?

Perhaps the best and most interesting example I can provide of the floating signifier effect involves the diamond industry and, in particular, the selling of diamond rings (I should warn all the women reading this part of the chapter that there's a good chance they will be very upset with me when I've finished explaining this!). Common sense tells us that diamonds are expensive because they are both inherently valuable and very rare. Surprisingly, this is not the case; diamonds are actually incredibly plentiful and have been since the discovery of extensive diamond fields in Southern Africa beginning in the late 19th century (Epstein, 1981, 1982). Furthermore, as a society we instinctively associate diamonds with romance, love, and marriage; most women would probably say that at some time in their lives they've imagined the moment when a man would get down on bended knee and ask her to marry him, expensive engagement ring in hand.

So, how do these two facts come together—that is, the ready availability of diamonds and their connection to love and romance? First, when diamonds began to be discovered in great quantities the various mining companies quickly realized that if they didn't act fast the price of diamonds would fall precipitously; so, in order to preserve the value of their commodity (and maintain the illusion of scarcity), they created a cartel of companies—called DeBeers—that could control the flow of diamonds onto the market and, thus, their price. With the value and distribution of diamonds secured, DeBeers had to figure out how to sell its (now plentiful) product in a way that would not

reduce its value. Indeed, despite the existence of the cartel, the price of diamonds had fallen steadily in the first part of the 20th century due to economic crises.

In the late 1930s, however, DeBeers hired an advertising firm—N. W. Ayer—to do two things. First, the firm branded diamonds in a way that created a strong tie with love and romance. They did this in part by employing the new medium of film to show movie idols symbolizing their love for "leading ladies" with diamonds. For example, N. W. Ayer wrote a memo to DeBeers suggesting that the cartel contact screenwriters to encourage them to write into movies scenes of men buying engagement rings for their girlfriends. The agency also recommended giving diamonds to public personalities and even to the Queen of Great Britain to cement the public's perception of diamonds as symbols of romance and indestructible love.

Second, it was extremely important for the stability of the diamond market that consumers were convinced diamonds should be kept as family treasures and keepsakes, not resold. An estimated half-billion karats of diamonds are privately owned—about 50 times the yearly output of the diamond industry. Imagine what would happen to the market price of diamonds if this half-billion karats (or even a portion of it) went back on the market? To prevent this, N. W. Ayer initiated a campaign around the phrase, "A diamond is forever." This phrase, created in 1952 by an N. W. Ayer copywriter, is perhaps the most famous phrase in advertising history (even inspiring a James Bond novel and film!) and was incredibly persuasive in creating the image of diamonds not as a valuable commodity to be bought and sold but as a precious item that is eternal and should be kept for generations.

One final example from the diamond industry effectively demonstrates the power of branding to shape social realities. In the mid-1960s the advertising firm J. Walter Thompson began a campaign to sell diamond engagement rings in Japan. The interesting thing about Japan is that for 1,500 years Japanese culture had followed the Shinto tradition of arranged marriage, with no real prenuptial courtship and romance as we would understand it in the West. In fact, in 1967 less than 5% of Japanese women wore engagement rings. So the Thompson agency began a campaign that branded engagement rings as a symbol of Western modernism and a break from traditional Japanese life. Print ads featured men and women dressed in European clothes, often driving European-model cars, and engaged in nontraditional (for Japan) activities such as hiking, camping, and swimming. The message of the ad campaign was clear—wearing diamonds is a symbol of entry into modern life and a break with the traditions of a premodern Japan. By 1972 27% of Japanese women wore engagements rings; in 1978 this figure had risen to 50%, and by 1981 the figure was about 60%. So, in the space of a mere 14 years, the advertising campaign had displaced 1,500 years of cultural tradition.

In summarizing the branding of diamonds, then, I want to reiterate two points about the floating signifier effect. First, the connection between diamonds and love and romance is an arbitrary, socially constructed relationship that is a result of the diamond industry's need to market what had become, by the 1930s, a plentiful commodity. Second, and related, in order to prevent the market price of this plentiful product from falling, diamonds had to be branded as precious heirlooms that

signified eternity—"a diamond is forever." If you watch diamond commercials even today, you will see the same "branding" efforts in operation—diamonds are eternal; if you give a diamond to your loved one, your love will also be eternal. So that common-sense, almost instinctive association that most women make between diamonds and love/romance is a socially constructed association; it is the invention of an industry anxious to preserve the illusion that diamonds are rare and precious and intrinsically valuable.

The branding of diamonds is an extremely successful example of how companies manage meanings for consumers, but the reality is that such corporate meaning management is such a routine feature of our everyday lives that we barely notice it.

Discussion Questions

1. What are the expectations, feelings, and sentiments that you associate with a diamond engagement ring? Where do these come from?

2. How many of you (men and women) have been involved in purchasing a diamond engagement ring? What were you told by friends, family, and diamond sellers about the rules and norms for purchasing diamond rings?

3. Analyze commercials from diamond retailers (Zales, Kay Jewelers). How do they construct love and relationships?

4. In groups, brainstorm other examples of consumer products that have been successful in constructing systems of meanings that have become part of our culture. How do these products use the idea of the floating signifier to create meanings? How have these products shaped our lives?

Just to make things a little more complicated, however, not only products are branded; companies are branded, too. Indeed, companies are increasingly aware that consumers not only purchase particular products/brands but also "buy" the company behind the brand (Christensen, Morsing, & Cheney, 2008, p. 64). Many companies therefore rely on the strength of their corporate brand to engage in **brand extension**; that is, leveraging the meanings and emotions associated with the company to a variety of different products— products that frequently bear little relationship to one another.

For example, the British company Virgin, which began in the 1970s as a record store, has extended its brand to include an airline (Virgin Atlantic), rail services, cell phones, and financial services, among many others. As you can see, there is little direct connection amongst these various products. But in the spirit of the "floating signifier" these products are connected by the Virgin brand that, as Olins (2003) has described it, is "all attitude" (p. 95). Embodied in the maverick personality of its founder and CEO, Sir Richard Branson, Virgin brands itself as the cool, counterculture, upstart, renegade company that defends the little person against the corporate giants (even though Virgin is now a massive corporate empire!). This attitude was illustrated in Virgin Atlantic's rivalry with British Airways (whose image is one of tradition and elitism—its company slogan is "Upgrade to BA"), in which Virgin accused BA of running a "dirty tricks" campaign against Virgin to undermine its success. Virgin even went as far as painting "No Way BA" on the sides of its planes. Virgin won a court libel action against BA, receiving millions in damages and further cementing its image as the scrappy underdog fighting the corporate giants.

Not only things and companies are branded; so are people. Michael Jordan is one of the earliest examples of a single individual becoming a brand that extends across a range of companies (Nike, Gatorade, Wheaties, Hanes, etc.). Tiger Woods is an interesting example of branding, especially in the wake of his 2009 sex scandal. When the news reports about his marital infidelity first broke, one of the first issues discussed was how his behavior would impact his brand image, and a lot of the reporting detailed his various corporate sponsors' reactions to the scandal Buick severed ties with him largely because of its brand focus on family-oriented, more-conservative automobiles and its older consumer base. Finally, Kim Kardashian is an example of a person who is almost all brand and no substance; she exists because of her branding, not because of any talent or skill that was deemed marketable and branded. Indeed, her short-lived marriage to basketball player Kris Humphries (broadcast as a two-part special on E! Entertainment Television) was widely reported to be a publicity stunt aimed at extending the Kardashian brand—an interesting example of how branding and consumption drive even the most personal aspects of people's lives.

Olins (2003) and others have argued that such is the power of branding that the real wealth and capital of a company lie with the brand rather than with the company's actual economic assets. As Olins indicates, this means that "many successful corporations are shifting their ground from making and selling to being—to representing a set of values" (p. 18). A Niketown, for example, is less a retail store that sells sports apparel and more "a three-dimensional expression of Nikeness" (p. 67). Even the name, "Niketown," suggests a place that people inhabit—a space that embodies a certain set of values, beliefs, and meanings. A Niketown store is "Just Do It" brought to life.

The notion that the brand is where the real wealth of a company is located is effectively illustrated by Ford Motor Company's purchase in 1989 of the British car company Jaguar. Ford purchased the company for $2.5 billion, or $13.32 a share—twice the actual market value of Jaguar (Prokesch, 1989). How could such a deal be justified from a business perspective, especially when, at the time it was purchased, Jaguar was barely breaking even and making fewer than 52,000 cars a year? Ford executives made it clear that they were principally interested in the Jaguar brand, which is associated with luxury, elegance, and prestige.

After it purchased Jaguar, Ford radically altered its construction, building the cars with a Ford chassis and many Ford components so a Jaguar was, in many respects, no longer a

Jaguar. But, of course, in a branded world the actual product is much less important than the image and meanings associated with it. Thus, if Ford were able to use its vast resources to construct large volumes of Jaguars, with some models in the price range of the average middle-class consumer, then many more people would be able to connect themselves to a luxury item (despite the decidedly blue-collar reputation of its parent company). In 2008, however, Ford sold Jaguar to Tata, an Indian automobile manufacturer, for $2.3 billion, having spent a further $10 billion trying to revive the Jaguar brand.

A 2008 report in *USA Today* provides a sense of how a company's efforts to extend its brand identity can sometimes result in failure and economic disaster:

> Ford spent a fortune acquiring Jaguar. . . . It paid $2.5 billion for Jaguar in 1990 after a bidding war of sorts with General Motors. Industry experts at the time estimated that was about $1.2 billion more than Jaguar was worth. Ford has since said the deal was worse than that. . . .
>
> Meanwhile, Jaguar's U.S. sales fell from 35,000 to a forecast 17,000 by the end of the year. . . . Despite current sales, Lindland says, both brands have strong images. "It's the brands that make it worth the money. They're iconic brands with really storied histories." Still, she says, "It's a little bit like Wal-Mart buying Prada." (Carty, 2008)

I suspect that for most of us the final sentence of this quotation puts company branding into sharp relief. If we know anything about consumption, we know that Wal-Mart and Prada are at opposite ends of the brand spectrum—the former is the dominant retailer in high-volume, low-cost items, while the latter is a high-end fashion company whose clothes and accessories are status symbols for its consumers. Wal-Mart, by definition, would never stock Prada items, and Prada customers would mutiny if its clothes were sold at Wal-Mart, even if the clothes/bags and their labels (extremely important!) remained the same.

Thus, we can say that some brand associations are good, while others contaminate the brands with meanings that are deadly to the health of both brands. Thus, we can speculate that, amongst other factors, Ford's acquisition of Jaguar failed because it extended Ford's core brand identity too far away from its historical identity as a producer of cheap, reliable vehicles (remember that the "Model T" Ford was the world's first mass-produced car). It's interesting to note that Ford also purchased Volvo in the late 1990s but sold it to a Chinese auto manufacturer in 2010—another sign of its failure to extend brand identity.

A final example illustrates how companies will sometimes purchase other companies not only because of their perceived brand value but also because it allows them to expand into markets far removed from their original reason for being in business. In 1988 Philip Morris tobacco corporation purchased Kraft foods for about 6 times its actual asset value—a decision based purely on the perceived brand strength of Kraft (Klein, 2001). Of course, this takeover also enabled Philip Morris to move into a market—food products—that is far removed from the product with which it is synonymous, especially at a time when tobacco companies were coming under increasing pressure from class-action suits and legislation. I suspect that all of us would have a difficult time buying food and snacks from a tobacco company, but the Kraft brand allows us to do just that and feel okay about it.

It's clear, then, that the branding process is murky and complex—something to be expected given that companies are dealing with the ways meanings and identities are constructed and communicated. Meaning, as we have discussed, is inherently ambiguous, and it is impossible fully to control and determine how customers take up brand meanings. However, what *is* clear is that when consumers purchase a particular brand they are not only purchasing a product to be used for something but also engaging in an act of identity construction. In this sense, in developing brands, companies are very consciously exploiting the human desire for affiliation and identification. In the next section we explore in more detail the complex relationship between branding and human identities.

❖ BRANDING AND IDENTITY

Wally Olins (2003) argues that brand affiliation has in many respects replaced religious belief as a central element of human identity. By extension, the shopping mall is perhaps the cathedral of a (post)modern consumer-oriented economy (Ritzer, 2005, 2007). It is not hard to see why some social commentators might make this argument, given that shopping has become the principal leisure activity of many people; where once shopping was something that had to be done out of necessity, now it is a defining activity in people's sense of self. President George W. Bush even encouraged people to shop as a way to help them overcome the sense of national malaise and personal trauma in the wake of the 9/11 terrorist attacks.

The central role of consumption in creating a sense of self is supported by the work of sociologist Robert Putnam (2000) in his widely read book *Bowling Alone*. Putnam argues that in the past few decades Americans have experienced a decline in "social capital"; that is, the sense of well-being and identity derived from our social networks and involvement in our communities. As our memberships in clubs and societies have declined, so has the amount of time we spend actually interacting with other human beings in social contexts, and so we feel increasingly isolated from one another and disconnected from the communities in which we live. We might argue, then, that consumption has at least partially replaced the role of clubs and societies in our sense of identity and well-being. Consumption provides us with a sense of psychological and emotional security and provides connection—albeit superficial—to the world and other people. Thus, where people once joined bowling clubs, softball leagues, and voluntary associations, today they pay a visit to the postmodern cathedral of consumption—the mall—in order to gain a sense of identity and connectedness.

This may seem like an exaggerated claim about the power of consumption (and, hence, of corporations) in our lives, but it is worth exploring further the ways corporations attempt to create a sense of connection between their brands and the consumers who identify with and purchase them. As Olins (2003) has indicated, branding is an act of seduction, and in order to win a share of the market, companies must win a share of people's minds. This act of seduction is fundamentally a communication process.

As I hope I have made clear, corporations do not want us simply to buy products; they want us to enter into a relationship with a brand that we see as an expression of who we are as people. For example, it says something about our identities that we choose to purchase Ralph Lauren or Tommy Hilfiger clothing rather than Diesel or Sean John or Ted Baker. Brand guru Marc Gobé (2001) probably best captures this relationship with his description of what he calls **emotional branding**:

> Emotional branding provides the means . . . for connecting products to the consumer in an emotionally profound way. It focuses on the most compelling aspect of the human character; the desire to transcend material satisfaction, and experience emotional fulfillment. A brand is uniquely situated to achieve this because it can tap into the aspirational desires which underlie human motivation. (p. xv)

According to Gobé, buying a particular brand can take us beyond mere material satisfaction and move us to a higher plane of existence—one that fulfills us in an emotionally profound way. While perhaps rather fanciful, statements such as Gobé's do provide interesting insights into how brand managers attempt to tap into and influence our sense of who we are. From a communication perspective, it's interesting to explore how brand managers think about the way this process of influence works. Gobé (2001) argues that "emotional branding is a means of creating a personal dialogue with consumers. Consumers today expect their brands to know them—intimately and individually—with a solid understanding of their needs" (p. xxii).

Here we see that branding is not simply a matter of imposing meaning and identity on passive consumers but, rather, involves thinking about the "brand relationship" in active and dynamic terms—the consumer enters into a *dialogue* with the brand. Notice here how both the consumer and the brand are conceived as having agency—the brand is not viewed simply as some*thing* that has meaning to the consumer but, rather, as an active (human?) participant in an ongoing dialogue. Gobé's quote above even implies a high level of intimacy and connection between the brand and the consumer, very like a close friendship or even a romantic relationship.

In developing successful brands, then, companies have taken to heart a very important lesson about how communication works. Back in Chapter 1 we discussed the limitations of a conduit, or transmission, model of communication, arguing instead that communication is a dynamic process of creating complex meanings. Companies understand that simply transmitting the idea behind a brand to consumers is less effective than getting consumers to be active participants in the meaning creation process. In this sense, brands are, to a certain degree, "open texts" that allow for individual interpretations.

A classic example of this kind of brand is Hello Kitty. Since 1974, when this image was created, it has helped turn the Japanese Sanrio company into a billion-dollar corporation. About 10,000 Hello Kitty items are available in North America, all emblazoned with the simple drawing of the mouthless, blank-faced cat with the red bow in her hair. Why is this image so wildly popular, adored by children and adults alike? As journalist Rob Walker (2008) points out, Hello Kitty doesn't have a strong personality we can identify with, such as that of Mickey Mouse or Snoopy; in fact, she has no definable character at all. In short, as Walker states, "Hello Kitty stands for nothing. Or perhaps for anything" (p. 17). Hello Kitty is, in this sense, an open text, "waiting to be interpreted." Her very simplicity allows consumers to project whatever thoughts, feelings, or emotions they wish onto Hello Kitty—she can be seen as cute, welcoming, solemn, cool, camp, and so on. As such, Hello Kitty is a great example of a brand that exploits humans' desire to construct a world that is meaningful to them; it taps into consumers' ability to engage *actively* in sense-making practices that are consistent with their own sense of identity. See Critical Case Study 12.2 for an example of how the "open text" nature of branding can sometimes have negative consequences for those brands.

 Critical Case Study 12.2
When Brands Run Amok

As we've discussed in this chapter, a company's brand is considered a crucial part of its wealth. Some commentators estimate that up to 75% of a company's wealth is tied up in its brand, and any company will go to great lengths to protect that brand. Companies thus spend millions of dollars in their efforts to cultivate and nurture the meanings attached to their brands. However, one thing I hope you have learned about communication and meaning is that it is completely impossible to corral and control the ways meanings work. The meanings of brands (or anything else) are inherently ambiguous and are thus always open to reinterpretation and change.

Sometimes companies deliberately manage shifts in meaning of their brands in order to appeal to a different demographic. In recent years, for example, Nike and Adidas have strategically shifted from a purely sports brand toward a fashion brand associated with "streetwear" and "urbanwear." These companies and others have carefully cultivated what some have called "gangster chic" (Neate, Wood, & Hinkley, 2011) that appeals to a more youthful—primarily male—demographic.

However, the risks entailed by such shifts in meaning are reflected in what happened during the riots in several cities in the United Kingdom during August 2011. Many of the rioters and looters appeared in the streets in such "urbanwear" and even specifically targeted for looting stores that carried the labels associated with this clothing. A massive public relations disaster occurred for Adidas when a photograph of a rioter dressed entirely in Adidas clothing (and standing in front of a burning car) appeared on the front page of several national newspapers. Adidas was forced to issue a statement saying, "Adidas condemns any antisocial or illegal activity. Our brand has a proud sporting heritage and such behavior goes against

everything we stand for" (quoted in Neate et al., 2011, p. 11). Of course, the fact that Adidas has for many years cultivated an image that has little to do with "sporting tradition" highlights how "meaning management" is a precarious process that can seriously backfire. Adidas and other companies have been eager to exploit an image that draws, in many respects, on a culture that has been associated with disenfranchised and marginalized (poor and minority) populations, and then they are shocked when their strategy comes back to bite them in the butt.

On a much more frivolous (but related) note, Abercrombie & Fitch recently offered to pay "The Situation" (of *Jersey Shore* fame) to stop wearing its clothing, arguing that he was harming the company's brand. In this case, I suspect that Abercrombie & Fitch was engaged in a creative public relations stunt as a way to draw attention to its brand. However, it is another indication of the degree to which companies are sensitive to any negative meanings and interpretations that may get attached to their brands.

Discussion Questions

1. Reflect on your own consumption habits. Are there particular brands that you buy consistently? Why?

2. What meanings are, for you, associated with the brands you purchase? How did these associations arise?

3. Are there brands you would not purchase? Why?

4. Reflect in general on your consumption habits and the ways the brands you use make you feel. What does this tell you about your identity as a consumer in the broader society? How is your life shaped by your consumption practices?

❖ MARKETING, "MURKETING," AND CORPORATE COLONIZATION

One of the biggest changes that have occurred in the past decade or so in the process of branding and consumption is the way companies market their products to consumers. Relatively speaking, achieving brand visibility used to be a fairly straightforward process; companies thought in terms of mass audiences who were watching TV, listening to the radio, or reading newspapers and magazines. The trick was to market brands in a way that had a wide appeal and developed a large, loyal group of consumers. In this context, the consumers themselves were viewed as fairly passive recipients of marketing messages (think of the stereotypical Homer Simpson-like "couch potato" who's glued to the TV and is a brand manager's dream in terms of susceptibility to advertising).

Then, along came what Walker (2008) calls the "click" phenomenon. With the emergence of new communication technologies (the Internet, digital video recorders, smartphones, etc.) audiences are no longer "captive" in the way they once were—entertainment and media choices are almost unlimited, and audiences are one "click" away from choosing a new form of distraction. In such a media/marketing environment, traditional branding methods are ineffective. Why spend millions of dollars on TV commercials if viewers simply digitally record their favorite shows and fast-forward right through them? So marketers had to get creative, inventing what Rob Walker describes as **murketing**.

Whereas in traditional marketing strategies a fairly clear distinction exists between the programming of a particular medium and advertising (we know when we're watching a "commercial break" and when we're watching an actual program), with murketing the distinction is basically erased. At one level, murketing has been around for a long time; companies have used "product placement" in TV shows and movies to increase "brand awareness" (next time you go to a movie see how many examples of product placement you can identify). In the past few years, however, the extent to which branding and everyday life have merged together has exploded. From a corporate perspective, the point is that if, indeed, consumers can exercise much greater freedom in choosing brands and integrating them into their "lifestyles," then developing brand loyalty requires a much more sophisticated set of marketing strategies.

With murketing the trick is to blend a brand seamlessly into everyday life and popular culture—to be successful, a brand must become an integral part of the way people express their identities. Again, we are back to the idea that consumers do not buy products but, rather, extensions of their own sense of self and relationship to the world and others. In murketing, then, the relationship between cultural expression and commercial expression is blurred.

In addition, murketing relies on a much more dynamic relationship between brand and consumer. While corporations have long relied on consumer feedback and brand research strategies such as focus groups to hone their brand image, now consumers play an active role in promoting and branding products. For example, companies will frequently recruit unpaid volunteers to engage shoppers in casual conversations about particular products. Indeed, it's quite possible that you've had such conversations in stores yourselves, unaware that the person to whom you were speaking had a vested interest in promoting a particular product.

Axe men's deodorant (owned by the British conglomerate Unilever) has developed a phenomenally successful campaign that heavily depends on blurring the relationship between everyday culture and branding. For example, it has made fake documentaries about skateboarders (complete with moves that incorporate and are named after Axe products), has created its own "girl band" complete with MTV-style videos (the Bom Chicka Wah Wah Girls), and has its own YouTube channel, currently featuring an Axe graphic novel called *Axe Anarchy* (check it out at http://www.youtube.com/user/axe?blend = 3&ob = 4). Recently, Axe has promoted a campus-focused "Axe Undie Run Challenge," described on Axe's Facebook page as "the world's sexiest charity event." On this same Facebook page, you could pay a visit to the Women's Attention Deficit Disorder Research and Prevention Center.

What's fascinating about this entire branding campaign is that it says little or nothing about Axe's quality as a product ("It keeps you dry"; "It smells good") but, rather, constructs a set of meanings to which the product itself is secondary. In fact, Axe's branding strategy was deliberately aimed not to compete against other deodorants on the market. As one of its brand managers stated,

> To be successful as a youth brand is to realize that [deodorant] is not what you're competing against. . . . You're competing against things like movies, television shows, sporting events, other advertisers, the Internet. . . . You have to become part of pop culture. (quoted in Walker, 2008, pp. 132–133)

In other words, Axe is not selling a deodorant but a particular young masculine identity that taps into (and creates) popular culture expressions.

One final way to get a sense of how branding is weaving itself into the very fabric of popular culture and human identity is to explore how corporations engage in brand research. You are probably familiar with (and may even have been involved in) focus-group research. Companies (or at least their brand management consultants) bring together groups of people from the demographic they are targeting and get their opinions on a particular branded product. This could involve anything from taste-testing a new soda to viewing a yet-to-be released Hollywood movie.

These days, however, such tried-and-tested methods have been supplemented by more sophisticated techniques as companies seek to get an edge in ever more competitive and crowded markets. As such, **brand ethnography** has become a commonly used research method for developing branded products. In an earlier chapter we talked about ethnography as a field method used by culture researchers to explore the meanings and identities of members of a given culture. In the context of brand development, ethnography is used to examine how people interact with and use products in their everyday lives.

For example, in her study of children and consumption, Juliet Schor (2004) reports that brand researchers now regularly visit people's homes to study the way products get used once they are purchased. In marketing products to children, researchers spend hours interacting with kids at home, asking questions and observing how they use products ranging from online games to bath soap. In one ethnographic study, Schor reports that brand researchers recommended to a manufacturer of bubble bath that it repackage its product to better take advantage of kids' tendency to turn soap containers into toys—a finding that could not have been made without direct observation and questioning in the home environment.

Ethnography is now also used extensively at the point of purchase in stores. Brand researchers spend many hours observing people as they walk around stores and interact with products. Schor even provides examples of researchers fitting kids with hidden cameras to document their behavior as they walk around stores. The researchers then watch the footage with the kids and ask them questions about why they looked at certain products, what they liked/didn't like, and so forth. Such information provides companies with important information about consumers' relationship with their products. For example, Paco Underhill (1999), one of the pioneers of the ethnographic study of consumer behavior, heads a company that records about 20,000 hours of in-store behavior annually. As a result of this systematic observation, he has developed principles such as "the law of the invariant right turn" (consumers invariably turn right rather than left when they enter a store) and the "decompression zone" (the area where we all pause, right after entering a store, to take stock of the situation and decide what we want to do). While such principles may seem relatively banal, they provide companies with incredibly important information about consumer behavior and how that might affect the placement of particular products and brands in stores.

In this section, then, we have focused on how, as an extension of efforts to link branding and individual identities, companies are increasingly attempting to blur the distinction between branding and everyday life. Indeed, brands no longer try simply to reflect popular culture—they attempt to shape it in their own image. For brands to be truly successful and powerful, they must become part of the ways people/consumers engage in everyday sense making and meaning construction. But like the 2010 Leonardo DiCaprio movie *Inception*, the real trick is to provide people with a sense of agency while at the same time shaping their sense of reality and the choices they make—such is the power of 21st century branding.

❖ ORGANIZATIONS, BRANDING, AND THE ENTREPRENEURIAL SELF

One of the very core ideas at the center of the branding process is the notion of the **sovereign consumer**. Going well beyond the age-old slogan that "the customer is always right," this idea envisions a brand-new (excuse the pun!) relationship between production and consumption in which companies strive to anticipate and adapt to a fast-moving and global consumer market. As we have already seen in this chapter, this new relationship is very much framed in terms of an intimate, almost romantic connection between producer and consumer in which brands meet the most important identity needs and desires of the sovereign consumer. Indeed, books on branding with titles such as *Romancing the Customer: Maximizing Brand Value Through Power Relationship Management* (Temporal & Trott, 2001); *Primal Branding: Create Zealots for Your Company, Your Brand, and Your Future* (Hanlon, 2006); *Passion Brands: Getting to the Heart of Branding* (Edwards & Day, 2005); and *Emotional Branding* (Gobé, 2001) provide much insight into how companies frame the producer–consumer relationship as one that exists at a deep—even primitive—emotional level.

However, the idea of the sovereign consumer has not only altered the producer–consumer relationship but has also fundamentally changed the way organizations operate. As we saw in Chapter 8, the "soulless" bureaucratic form has increasingly given way to the fast-moving, adaptive, decentralized organizational form that is responsive to changing environments and consumer tastes. While unchanging bureaucratic structures could meet the needs of the easily pleased consumers of the Fordist era ("You can have any color car as long as it's black"), the constantly changing needs of the postmodern, post-Fordist consumer require flexible organizations that can shift gears quickly.

One of the consequences of this "cult[ure] of the consumer," as sociologists Paul Du Gay and Graeme Salaman (1992) have described it, is that the very idea of branding and the sovereign consumer is increasingly applied to organization members themselves. While in Fordist organizations employee success was predicated on loyalty, technical skill, and seniority (as well as blending in to the prevailing corporate culture), in the post-Fordist company success is heavily dependent on employees taking an entrepreneurial approach to their work and identities. In other words, employees are increasingly required to brand themselves as a way to become distinct and provide "value-added" performance for the company. In the (post)modern corporation, everyone must adopt and cultivate an **entrepreneurial self**. Du Gay argues that this shift has involved imposing a model of customer–producer relations on internal organization processes, hence blurring the spheres of production and consumption.

When employees are asked to brand themselves, then their work and nonwork selves become increasingly interrelated, with work becoming a constant performance of a carefully nurtured professional identity that visibly contributes to the company's bottom line. In this context, the employee's body can be a key element in such branding, as the employee strives to present a particular corporate image through dress and bodily comportment.

A number of commentators have pointed out that this new discourse of enterprise and self-branding has a distinct moral tone to it, such that "becoming a better worker is represented as the same thing as becoming a more virtuous person, a better self" (Du Gay & Salaman, 1992, p. 626). Thus, as well as the "sovereign customer" there is also the "sovereign worker" who is responsible for making him or herself into "a more virtuous and empowered human being" (p. 627) through efforts to add value to the company he or she works for. In this scenario, workers are responsible for their successes and failures, for their own careers; they are framed as self-actualizing individual agents who engage in personal acts of choice, much like the sovereign customers whom they serve (including their fellow coworkers).

I suspect that many of you reading this chapter have been asked on more than one occasion to think about ways you can "brand" yourselves in a way that's different from other college graduates in a competitive job market. Of course, there is nothing wrong with developing a distinct set of abilities that make you stand out from the crowd, but oftentimes such "branding" is less about particular skills and more about the packaging—just like consumer products, students are increasingly being asked to focus on image rather than substance as a way to "market" themselves. In other words, they are being asked to engage in a "discourse of enterprise" where the focus is marketing and branding rather than engaging in an educational process. Our discussion in Chapter 1 of David Brooks's (2001) essay "The Organization Kid" is an example of how pervasive this discourse of enterprise has become among college students.

For example, I suspect that most of you reading this have, at one time or another, complained about a final grade you received in a class. If you are honest with yourselves, you might admit that sometimes your complaint was based less on the feeling that the quality of your work deserved a better grade and more on your concern about how a "C" on your transcript would affect your personal brand—your image and meaning in the eyes of a potential employer. When a discourse of enterprise pervades even an educational environment, then one of the consequences is that education becomes less about developing critical thinking skills and more about producing employees/consumers who can perform to meet the needs of a constantly shifting image and symbolic environment.

In the final section of this chapter we will discuss the relationship between branding and organizational ethics.

Critical Technologies 12.1
Do You Have Klout?

I'm writing this on Cyber Monday—the "officially" designated day after Black Friday when everyone is supposed to shop online and receive huge savings on purchases. I guess shopping online is safer than actually going to the stores, especially given the violent incidents that are now a routine part of the media reporting on Black Friday—this year a woman at a Wal-Mart in Los Angeles used pepper spray on fellow customers to clear her way to the Xbox console she craved.

Of course, the Internet and social media have had a massive impact on branding and marketing. As we discussed in this chapter, "the click factor" (Walker, 2008) completely changed the ways brands needed to market themselves, requiring a much greater level of interactivity between customer and brand. It's estimated that as of 2011, 80% of companies engage in some form of social media marketing, such as Twitter and Facebook campaigns (Manjoo, 2011).

One of the newest developments in the world of marketing and social media is the Klout score. Developed by the online company it's named for, your Klout score is a measure between 1 and 100 that indicates your personal influence online. According to Klout, your score consists of three elements: (1) *true reach*, or the number of people you influence; (2) *amplification*, or how *much* you influence people (how many people spread your messages further); and (3) *network*, or the influence of the people in your "true reach" (klout.com/corp/kscore). For example, Justin Bieber's Klout score is a perfect 100; President Obama's is 87 (Manjoo, 2011). No irony there, then. Apparently, some people are putting their Klout scores on

their résumés—another bizarre example of how personal branding and the entrepreneurial self are seen as increasingly important. Do you know what your Klout score is? Without checking, I'm pretty certain mine is 1.

But how does a Klout score help companies sell stuff? Klout ("Measuring influence since 2008") works on the principle that "our friendships and professional connections have moved online, making influence measurable for the first time in history. When you recommend, share, and create content you impact others" (http://klout.com/corp/about). Klout has collected data on the influence of more than 100 million people online. Companies come to Klout so they can target messages to potential customers who they know have a high degree of social media impact. For example, Klout can identify for Nike the most influential people in Los Angeles who talk about athletic shoes; Nike can then direct marketing messages to these people, and Klout can track how, via the "klout" of these influential people, the marketing messages spread across the social media landscape. Company marketing of brands is thus mediated through professional and personal relationships. Again, according to Klout, 90% of customers trust peer recommendations, while only 33% trust ads.

From a company's perspective, there's no way of measuring precisely how such use of social media impacts sales—unlike with more conventional advertising, where data can show the return of every dollar spent on advertising. However, this does not seem to bother companies—it is estimated that money spent on social media advertising will increase from $2.1 billion in 2010 to $8 billion in 2014.

❖ THE ETHICS OF BRANDING

This chapter has provided a critical examination of corporate branding. However, is it fair to say that all branding is problematic or even unethical? Branding has been with us for 150 years, and there is little doubt that it will continue to define our relationship to organizations and corporations. One might argue that branding in and of itself is not unethical; rather, certain branding practices are. The reality is that in contemporary organizational life branding is an intrinsic element of what all organizations do on a routine basis. Any organization that needs to maintain a relationship with various stakeholder groups (customers, employees, shareholders, community members, etc.) has to articulate a set of meanings to those groups that enables them to identify with the organization in a particular way. Indeed, most corporations and their employees would probably argue that they believe strongly in the values embodied in their brand.

And, of course, branding is by no means limited to for-profit organizations. Nonprofit, volunteer, charitable, even government and public institutions engage in branding in an effort to cultivate stakeholder relationships. As a department chair at a public university I am constantly aware of the need to raise funds to support my department's teaching and research missions. And, as my development officer frequently tells me, such fundraising is most successful when the department has a strong "brand" that it can pitch to potential donors. As students at colleges and universities, you are probably aware of branding efforts at your own institution that attempt to pitch it to consumers (i.e., you!) in a certain way. For example, your college or university might develop a brand that highlights its friendly, "family" atmosphere (easier to do when there are 3,000 students on campus rather than 60,000!) or its tradition of a strong liberal arts education or its belief in putting students' needs first. Or it might have an unofficial brand as a "party" school!

None of these branding efforts are intrinsically unethical; this occurs only when there is a contradiction between an organization's branding efforts and its everyday organizational practices. For example, if a university brands itself as student oriented, with frequent contact between faculty and students, and then new students discover that teaching is neglected in favor of faculty research, one might argue that such a university behaves unethically in trying to part students from their hard-earned tuition dollars. Or if a company brands itself as environmentally responsible as a way to increase its profits but then exploits nonrenewable resources (a practice described as "greenwashing"), one might legitimately accuse that company of unethical behavior.

However, not all ethical questions are quite so straightforward in the world of branding. At the beginning of this chapter I provided a description of the consumer experience provided by the "Disneyesque" environment of the Streets at Southpoint. Are the developers of this shopping destination unethical? Not in any straightforward sense, and the consumers would probably describe an enjoyable retail/leisure experience. As a critical theorist, though, I am concerned with a broader set of ethical issues regarding the relationship between branding and the role of the modern corporation in everyday life, or with what we identified in an earlier chapter as the process of "corporate colonization" (Deetz, 1992a). That is, to what extent should corporations play a role in defining who we are and how we see ourselves as connected human beings who are members of broader communities? Who gets to decide what is important and what is not in our lives?

My sense is that the ultimate goal of corporate branding efforts is to mediate as many aspects of human experience and identity construction as possible. Certainly, the development of murketing suggests that the days of a relatively clear separation of corporate advertising and everyday life are long gone. We live in an environment that is completely saturated with mediated, branded meanings. It's almost as though nothing is meaningful until it is framed for us by a corporate sponsor. As such, corporations and the meaning systems they create play a disproportionately large role in defining who we are as people.

Some brand theorists have argued that branding and democracy are tied together in a positive manner (Gobé, 2002). Marc Gobé (2007), for example, argues that

> [branding] is not about money: branding is about life, it is about respect, it is about success, it is about love, freedom, and hope. It is about building bonds everyone can trust. . . . There is an economic and psychological divide that exists between societies. If brands are the great equalizer, shouldn't they then inspire, motivate, problem solve? Shouldn't brands be part of the solution, not the problem? Shouldn't brands continue to foster freedom of choice? (pp. 65, 66)

Obviously, such a perspective makes a close connection between consumption and democracy. But do we really want to live in a society where freedom is defined in terms of the ability to purchase consumer goods that help us feel good about ourselves? Is having the choice between hundreds of different brands of soft drinks (a significant factor in obesity rates) or being able to choose how you want your burger prepared an appropriate litmus test for freedom and democracy? If, as Gobé suggests, Coca-Cola via its branding provides a message of optimism and freedom, and if Nike is a symbol of infinite possibilities (Just Do It!), then what does that say about the nature of democracy in the 21st century?

One of the issues that brand theorists such as Gobé consistently ignore is that, ultimately, branding is about making profits for corporations and their shareholders. While it is possible to argue that brands embody principles of freedom and democracy, such a perspective adopts a very superficial view of democracy, overlooking at least two issues. First, because of the floating signifier effect, any meaning attached to a brand is purely arbitrary and, thus, the product of careful marketing—a brand signifies freedom only to the extent that its corporate parent wants it to! Second, in genuine democracies, ordinary people have a strong voice in the ways their political and civil interests are represented. As such, consumption is a form of pseudo-democracy that provides the illusion of participation and empowerment but is carefully mediated and managed by corporate interests.

Benjamin Barber (2007) has argued that "consumer empowerment" (a favorite phrase among brand managers) basically involves choice without consequences. We can feel empowered by our choice of a particular clothing brand, or in voting for our favorite *American Idol* contestant (more people vote for that show's contestants than for presidential candidates), but it's an activity that ultimately is intensely private and isolated. Genuine democracy involves engaged, informed citizens participating with one another in the public sphere and vigorously debating the issues of the day. As we argued earlier, the goal of branding is to get us to respond in emotional rather than rational ways to products. Indeed, the phenomenon of "buyer remorse," which we've all experienced, is a great illustration of how our rational faculties kick in once it's too late!

In many ways, such brand relationships stand in opposition to strong democracy, which requires careful and thoughtful examination of issues and active engagement with other members of our communities. As Barber (2007) argues, however, "shopping seems to have become a more persuasive marker of freedom than voting . . . and what we do alone in the mall counts more importantly in shaping our destiny than what we do together in the public square" (p. 37).

Perhaps the most important test of ethical or unethical behavior involves how companies treat the most vulnerable members of society—children. There is strong evidence suggesting that corporations are increasingly targeting children and teenagers directly and attempting to by-pass the influence of parents. In her book *Born to Buy*, sociologist Juliet Schor (2004) argues that "kids and teens are now the epicenter of consumer culture" (p. 9) and U.S. children are "bonded to brands." Research shows that the average 10-year-old knows 300 to 400 brands and that in 2004 $15 billion in brand marketing was directed at children.

Corporations are fully aware of the revenue opportunities that children represent, and, indeed, the purchasing power of kids has risen considerably in the past two decades or so. Schor (2004) reports that

> children aged four to twelve made $6.1 billion in purchases in 1989, $23.4 billion in 1997, and $30 billion in 2002. . . . Older kids, aged twelve to nineteen, spend even more: they accounted for $170 billion of personal spending in 2002, or a weekly average of $101 per person. (p. 23)

In order to gain their share of this revenue, corporations have become increasingly sophisticated in their branding efforts. Schor (2004) reports on a fascinating interview she conducted with Nancy Shalek, president of the Shalek Agency—a brand management firm. In speaking about advertising brands to children, Shalek stated the following:

> Advertising at its best is making people feel that without their product, you're a loser. Kids are very sensitive to that. If you tell them to buy something, they are resistant. But if you tell them that they'll be a dork if they don't, you've got their attention. You open up emotional vulnerabilities and it's very easy to do with kids because they're the most emotionally vulnerable. (p. 65)

It's interesting to compare this quote with Gobé's earlier comments about emotional branding and the need to provide consumers with "emotional fulfillment." The problem with adopting the same approach with children, however, is that their identities are very much in flux and unformed, and they have no clear sense of what emotional fulfillment means, except when they are provided with adult guidance and strong, nurturing role models. Advertisers and brand managers understand this and frequently attempt to circumvent the parental gatekeeper role in appealing to children.

For example, brand industry analysts understand the importance of the **nag factor** in purchases; that is, the power children possess in pestering their parents to buy certain products. According to the original "nag factor" study conducted in 1998, 70% of parents are susceptible to kids' pestering for purchases. Indeed, marketers advise their clients that many products will not sell unless kids request them. And this does not apply just to products aimed at kids. Even expensive consumer items such as cars are marketed to children because advertisers understand the powerful role children play in purchase decisions. Thus, one of the reasons you see so many kids in car commercials is not so that parents will identify with the carmaker; rather, it increases the possibility that kids will identify with the brand of automobile and influence their parents' choice! Some brand analysts would even maintain that no food product has been truly successful unless it has been marketed to kids rather than mothers, even though parents make the food purchases for the household. Such is the "nagging" power of children.

One might argue, then, that branding is unethical when it develops strategies that attempt to exploit the psychological and emotional insecurities of children. Kids need a sense of security and the knowledge that they're loved in order to develop into stable adults. When advertisers deliberately exploit these insecurities in the name of kid "empowerment," when they market products in ways that tell kids they are uncool if they don't own them, I would argue they are acting unethically. Similarly, pitching brands to children in an effort to circumvent parental authority and deliberately exploit the "nag factor" is also unethical.

In sum, I would suggest that branding is not, by definition, unethical; all organizations have both the right and the responsibility to construct meaningful relationships with their various stakeholders, and branding is one part of that process. Branding does become ethically suspect, however, when organizations adopt communication and meaning construction strategies that (a) contradict their actual business practices; (b) deliberately exploit the vulnerabilities of less powerful members of society; or (c) present consumption as an empowering, defining feature of who we are as people. Consumption is a *dis*empowering act to the extent that it undermines our sense of ourselves as engaged citizens and makes a fetish out of our relationships to objects (the Miller Lite commercial featuring the guy who can't tell his girlfriend he loves her but has no problem expressing his love for his Miller Lite, while funny, exemplifies this fetishism). Consumption makes us all a little more private, a little more isolated, and a little more disengaged from the world and the people around us.

❖ CONCLUSION

One of the ironies of this chapter is that by the time you read it many of the examples I have used to illustrate branding are likely to be outdated. Brands, by definition, have to stay current in order to maintain their market share. More important, brands constantly have to create new "needs" that consumers take up as part of their identities. Thus, for example, where once everyone drank water from the faucet, now we drink branded water from bottles, even though the water purchased in bottles is often inferior in quality to water from the faucet (it's amazing to me that the bottle of water one carries around can be a status symbol!). The latest development is "smart water" (notice again how brands are given human qualities to make them appealing). Water, by its very nature, is a blank canvas on which all kinds of meanings (floating signifiers) and identity associations can be constructed.

If, in a postmodern, consumption-oriented society, brands and identities are tied closely together, then the constantly shifting nature of the branding process leads to a constant sense of slippage and insecurity regarding our sense of who we are in the world. While brand managers can speak of "empowering" consumers through their brands, the reality is that it is a fleeting and superficial sense of empowerment that offers little in the way of a genuine connection to self, others, and the communities we inhabit. The branded identity that gave us a sense of security last year doesn't provide that same sense of security this year. As Rob Walker (2008) points out, such a relationship between branding and identity leads to "terminal materialism" as we engage in a constant, fruitless, and ultimately unsatisfying search for the next consumption high. Tying our identities to consumption practices pretty much guarantees we will be in constant search of an always elusive sense of security about who we are.

The same sense of insecurity around identity issues occurs in the workplace. In a postmodern, post-Fordist organizational environment, the branding process goes beyond consumer products to include employees as well, who must constantly brand and rebrand themselves in a constantly changing, turbulent organizational environment. This notion of an "entrepreneurial self" (Holmer Nadesan & Trethewey, 2000) means that employees must constantly strive to be better, always have an edge over other employees, always be selling themselves. As a *Fortune* magazine article states, "Forget old notions of advancement and loyalty. In a more flexible, more chaotic world of work you're responsible for your career" (quoted in Holmer Nadesan & Trethewey, 2000, p. 228). Of course, such a sense of self is frequently unsustainable, leading to increased stress, a lack of work–life balance, and overall poorer life quality (perhaps in spite of more disposable income).

Branding, then, is a fundamentally communicative process that plays a pivotal role in how we view ourselves and the world around us. For some, branding is precisely what gives the world meaning and significance. But this meaning and significance is superficial. Because branding is such a pervasive and all-encompassing element of our world, it is important that we understand the fundamentally communicative processes through which branding works.

Of course, as educated people we would probably claim to be largely immune to the siren call of advertising messages, but the reality is that we are all susceptible to branding in some way. We are all loyal to some degree to particular brands or get excited by the release of a new branded item. Indeed, while I was writing this chapter, thousands of people were spending hours in line outside Apple stores to purchase the new iPad. As *New York Times* reporter Brad Stone stated after talking to people standing in line to purchase the iPad, "No one can really say what they're going to do with the iPad, but they're getting one anyway" (Gallagher, 2010).

The important thing about branding, I think, is that we are aware of the extent to which it shapes our lives and are thus able to be more reflective about our relationship to a world of images, symbols, and meanings mediated by corporate interests. As Rob Walker (2008) states, "Considering yourself immune to advertising and branding is not a solution, it's part of the problem."

CRITICAL APPLICATIONS

1. Choose a brand with which you are familiar and perform an analysis of the brand identity it cultivates. Who does the brand appeal to? What meanings do you associate with the brand? Why? What are the various communicative elements that make up the branding process? How does the brand appeal to elements of popular culture?

2. Take a trip to the mall. Reflect on your experience as you walk around the stores. How do you feel? If you choose to purchase something, reflect on the experience; what were your feelings before, during, and after the purchase? Can you identify various ways you are encouraged to make purchases?

KEY TERMS

brand   285

brand ethnography   294

brand extension   287

emotional branding   291

entrepreneurial self   296

floating signifier effect   286

murketing   293

nag factor   300

sovereign consumer   295

STUDENT STUDY SITE

Visit the student study site at **www.sagepub.com/mumbyorg** for these additional learning tools:

- Web quizzes
- eFlashcards
- SAGE journal articles

- Video resources
- Web resources

CHAPTER 13

Organizational Communication, Globalization, and Democracy

Globalization has transformed the relationships among people, organizations, and communication processes.

Part-time barista wanted. Must speak Danish.

—Sign on the door of a café in Copenhagen, Denmark, 2011

There's an old saying, attributed to the Irish playwright George Bernard Shaw, that Britain and America are "two countries separated by a common language." When I first arrived in the United States from the United Kingdom in the early 1980s to go to graduate school, I was constantly reminded of this phrase. In some ways it was easier for me to make myself understood in Paris, France, than in Carbondale, Illinois, and my French isn't that great! Of course, part of this "separation" was due to differences in U.K. and U.S. vernacular for everyday objects: car bonnet, not car hood; chips, not french fries; potato crisps, not potato chips; a jumper is a sweater, not a dress; pants are underwear, not outerwear; and so on. My most embarrassing (and funny) moment came when, in my first semester of teaching,

I told students to bring to the midterm exam a pencil and a rubber (Britspeak for eraser). I think they wondered what kind of exam it would be!

But what most made me feel like a fish out of water was a profound feeling of isolation from my native culture: TV was quite different (More than four channels? How do I navigate all this? And what's with the commercials every 5 minutes?); the supermarkets made no sense (Why do I need 50 different breakfast cereals to choose from? And why is milk in those massive 1-gallon containers?); and I had no way of keeping up with news back home, other than the 2-week-old British newspapers at the library and the weekly letters (yes, letters) from my mom (international calls cost about $1 per minute in the early 1980s, and I was living on a meager grad-student stipend).

The picture I've painted of my early experiences in the United States now seems rather quaint; in the past 30 years globalization processes have profoundly transformed our relationship to the world and one another. Indeed, my own experience of the U.S.–U.K. relationship is very much one of cultural convergence, in which the two societies have grown increasingly similar in lots of ways, both profound and superficial. An American visiting the United Kingdom today would see many familiar consumer-culture landmarks: McDonald's, Pizza Hut, Domino's, The Disney Store, Gap, Abercrombie & Fitch, Starbucks, and so on. Similarly, British culture has migrated across the Atlantic in a big way; the "British Invasion" that started with The Beatles has become a veritable flood. It's hard to turn TV on these days without seeing a British personality (Simon Cowell, John Oliver on *The Daily Show*, Craig Ferguson on *The Late Show*, and so on), and there's even a TV channel called BBC America. And most important, at least to me, Fox Soccer Channel and ESPN broadcast live English Premier League football ("soccer") games, so I can watch my beloved Liverpool play.

So things have changed a lot over the past 30 years, and sometimes at a speed that's hard to comprehend. For much of my adult life the Internet and World Wide Web did not exist; many of you reading this book have known nothing else. It still boggles my mind that I can sit in a café in Copenhagen, Denmark, and access research databases via the UNC library website.

In this chapter we will address through the lens of globalization many of the transformations that have occurred in the world around us. More specifically, we will examine the relationship between organizational communication and globalization. Indeed, one might argue that it is the organizational—mainly corporate—form along with revolutions in communication processes that have driven the processes of globalization. Some commentators even argue that the corporation has eclipsed the nation-state as the most significant institution in the world today, precisely as a result of globalization processes. Given this, an additional issue will concern us in this chapter; that is, what is the relationship between organizations and democracy in the context of a globalizing world?

First, however, we will examine the idea of globalization, exploring definitional issues as well as some of the debates that have emerged out of the effects of globalization on our understanding of the world.

❖ DEFINING GLOBALIZATION

The world is in a rush, and is getting close to its end.

—Archbishop Wulfstan, 1014 (quoted in Giddens, 2001, p. 1)

Trying to define **globalization** is like trying to pick up mercury with chopsticks—it's a slippery and complex concept that doesn't lend itself to easy categorization. It's also a highly charged term that evokes a wide range of opinions and emotions—some people see globalization as a democratizing force that is making the world smaller and more interconnected, while others view it as a new form of cultural imperialism and economic colonization of indigenous cultures by Western corporations.

As you might guess, the picture is more complex than either of these positions suggests. So, in this section we will try to get a handle on some of the issues that are addressed by scholars across a number of different fields—communication, sociology, economics, geography, and political science, to name a few—as they grapple with globalization. Thus, because scholars from numerous disciplines have attempted to explain globalization, we will necessarily take an interdisciplinary approach in order to get a more complete picture of globalization.

First, it's important to recognize that globalization in not a *thing*; that is, it is not a structure or a condition with a stable set of characteristics that can be enumerated one by one. It is much too fluid and dynamic a process to be characterized in this way. Rather, following geographer David Harvey (1995), we can think of globalization as a *process*. In this way, we shift the focus from addressing the question, "What is globalization?" and instead ask, "How is globalization occurring?"

A useful definition comes from sociologist Roland Robertson, who argues that "globalization as a concept refers both to the compression of the world and the intensification of consciousness of the world as a whole . . . both concrete global interdependence and consciousness of the global whole" (quoted in Waters, 2001, p. 4).

This definition focuses not on specific features of globalization but, rather, on the overall transformation of space and time on the one hand and changes in human consciousness of the world on the other hand. Globalization has compressed the world through communication technologies and speed of travel, and, as a result, our consciousness of other places and our place in the world as a whole is intensified.

Robertson expands this definition by focusing on how globalization generates two competing but related forces: "What is involved in globalization is a complex process involving the interpenetration of sameness and difference—or, in somewhat different terms, the interpenetration of universalism and particularism" (Robertson & Khondker, 1998, p. 28).

This conception captures many of the arguments that circulate around the globalization process. On the one hand, advocates of globalization argue that the creation of an increasingly universal and homogeneous world with shared economic interests and values leads to a more stable and cosmopolitan global society (e.g., Friedman, 2005; Giddens, 2001). On the other hand, critics of globalization argue that it is an all-consuming force that destroys unique, indigenous cultures and erases difference, while also increasing the gulf between the haves and the have-nots (e.g., Klein, 2001, 2007). Organizational communication scholar Cynthia Stohl (2001) frames this central issue in a slightly different way when she states that in globalization, "the environmental and technical pressures on contemporary organizations to become more and more similar clash with the proprietary pull of cultural identifications, traditional values, and conventional practices of social life" (p. 326).

This idea of competing forces is taken up by other scholars. Sociologist Anthony Giddens (2001) argues that "the battleground of the 21st century will pit fundamentalism against cosmopolitan tolerance" (p. 4). Giddens claims that fundamentalism—which he defines as "beleaguered tradition" (p. 49)—is actually a *product* of globalization and did not exist prior to it. In other words, fundamentalism has emerged as a response to the changes that modernity and globalization have wrought in the world. In this sense, fundamentalism (which, for Giddens, is not the same as religion but can be any unquestioned system of values) has emerged as an effort to defend tradition by asserting ritual "truths" in the face of a globalized, modern world that "asks for reasons" (p. 49). Giddens thus sees fundamentalism as the enemy of cosmopolitan values and tendencies toward increasing democratization.

Benjamin Barber (1995) makes a similar case in arguing that globalization is characterized by two competing worldviews: "Jihad" and "McWorld." However, his position is much more pessimistic than Giddens's regarding the relationship between globalization and democracy. Barber argues that McWorld is a global process that is increasingly dominant everywhere and that constructs the individual as a consumer. McWorld is an economic and cultural form that focuses on lifestyle, knowledge, and services rather than material goods, and, hence, the object of McWorld is human identity—a position consistent with our discussion of branding in the previous chapter. McWorld has helped create an MTV culture in which patience, careful analysis, and argument have given way to simplified debate and the dominance of visual imagery. Jihad, Barber argues, is the child of McWorld and represents a turn toward communalism, tribalism, and tradition (Giddens's notion of fundamentalism). Barber sees Jihad as a response to the consumerist, homogeneous, and shallow culture of McWorld.

A further complication in discussing and defining globalization, however, is that its processes are occurring in multiple interrelated realms of human activity. Understanding globalization requires that we explore each of these spheres more closely. In the next section, then, we will examine globalization processes in the spheres of (1) economics, (2) politics, (3) culture, and (4) gender.

❖ SPHERES OF GLOBALIZATION

Globalization and Economics

The ideas of globalization and capitalism as an economic system have historically gone hand in hand. In the 19th century Marx showed how, in order to increase profitability and surplus value, capitalism, by its very nature, needed to expand its markets constantly, finding new domains to colonize. Indeed, much of the imperialist expansions of countries such as Britain, Spain, Portugal, and France in the 1600s, 1700s, and 1800s were not only about cultural imperialism and the spread of certain values but also about economic imperialism and the capture of working populations and raw materials.

Over the past 40 years the emergence of globalization has been associated with an economic philosophy called **neoliberalism**. This philosophy grew out of the writings of economist Milton Friedman and other members of the Chicago School of economics with which he was associated (Friedman, 1970, 1982; Klein, 2007). Since the early 1970s, the ideas of neoliberalism have been increasingly influential on many Western governments as they have begun to reject the principles of the previously dominant economic philosophy of **Keynesianism**, named after the British economist John Maynard Keynes.

Keynesianism became accepted economic policy in most Western nations after World War II. In brief, it was an effort to limit the "boom-and-bust" cycles of free market capitalism that had led to great economic hardship for many and resulted, amongst other things, in the Great Depression of the 1930s. Keynesianism advocated a "mixed economy," in which state intervention created a welfare system (unemployment benefits, pensions, health care, etc.) and a mixture of publicly (state) and privately owned companies, the former typically being services such as railways, gas, water, and electricity companies. Moreover, labor contracts were put in place that ensured long-term job stability and cooperation between workers and capitalists. Such an economic system is more collectivist in the sense that the freedom of the individual capitalist to engage in the free market is limited by government policies that protect the broader society.

Neoliberalism rejects this economic philosophy and argues for the sovereignty of the free market. In a famous essay in *New York Times Magazine*, Friedman (1970) argued that

> there is one and only one social responsibility of business—to use its resources and engage in activities designed to increase its profits so long as it stays within the rules of the game, which is to say, engages in open and free competition without deception or fraud.

From a neoliberal perspective, such a responsibility could be carried out only if the market were allowed to regulate itself, free from any kind of government intervention and restrictions on trade. Any kind of collectivism that required corporations to be socially responsible is, according to Friedman, "fundamentally subversive" in a free society. In this sense, and as indicated by the title of his famous book *Capitalism and Freedom*, Friedman (1982) argued for an essential link between unrestricted capitalism and the ability of individuals to exercise free choice, unfettered by any restraints of the collective.

The tenets of neoliberalism have been widely practiced over the past three decades. Led by the United States and the United Kingdom (under the leadership of Ronald Reagan and Margaret Thatcher, respectively) many Western countries introduced neoliberal economic policies that included selling off publicly held companies to private corporations, implementing tax cuts, cutting support for welfare systems, reducing the power of trade unions, and reducing restrictions on global trade. As British Prime Minister Margaret Thatcher famously said in a 1987 radio interview, "There is no such thing as society"—a statement that succinctly embodies the principles of neoliberal economics, where the individual is sovereign.

The result of neoliberal economics, many commentators have argued, has been the transformation of how business gets conducted both globally and nationally, with a massive increase in global trade, the "offshoring" of production to countries where labor is cheaper, huge movements of migrants seeking work, and trillions of dollars in investments being traded around the world every day. It is estimated that transnational corporations (TNCs) account for 70% of trade globally and that 51 of the 100 largest economies in the world are corporations (El-Ojeili & Hayden, 2006. p. 65).

There is considerable debate about the benefits of neoliberalism. Commentator Thomas Friedman (2005)—no relation to Milton—argues that the combination of neoliberal economic policy and new communication technologies has created a "flat world" in which previously "backward" nations such as India have now become global players. Moreover, the opening up of more and more countries to capitalism and free trade (e.g., countries of the former Soviet Union) has, it is argued, created more democratic political structures. The opening of a McDonald's in the early 1990s in Red Square in Moscow is often taken as an iconic example of the connections among capitalism, globalization, and democracy.

On the other hand, critics of neoliberalism have pointed to how it has increased inequality—both between nations and within nations—as the gap between rich and poor has become wider and wider (see Figure 13.1). As we have seen in earlier chapters, in addition to increasing income disparities, globalization has created a U.S. workforce that is more subject to job insecurity through downsizing, outsourcing of jobs, reduction of benefits, and so forth, as companies move their business interests offshore.

Figure 13.1   Change in Average Incomes of Top 1% Versus Average Overall Wages, 1979–2009

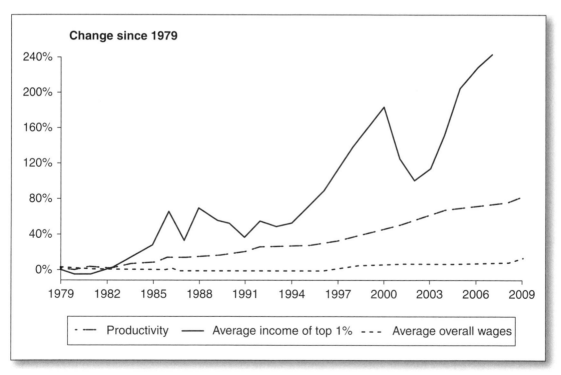

© Mother Jones

Productivity has surged, but income and wages have stagnated for most Americans. If the median household income had kept pace with the economy since 1970, it would now be nearly $92,000, not $50,000.

At a global level, critics point to greater disparities between nations. Journalist Naomi Klein (2007), for example, provides a devastating critique of what she calls "disaster capitalism" as she explores the ways neoliberal economic policies, employed by the International Monetary Fund (IMF), have actually created greater poverty in many nations because of high-interest loans and the restrictions the IMF imposes on countries as a condition for receiving loans.

Critics of neoliberalism have also pointed to a number of other factors. George Soros (2002), for example, argues that with fewer government restrictions economic markets tend to spiral out of control because they are based largely on speculation rather than knowledge—something we saw with the subprime mortgage crisis in 2008. In this sense, under neoliberalism, market speculation tends to function like the kind of deviation-amplifying system we discussed in Chapter 5—a type of system that always ends up crashing at some point. Moreover, Scholte (2000) claims that only about 5% of foreign exchange dealings involve transactions in real goods, with about 95% of all dealings being speculative in nature—greatly increasing the possibility of such crashes and bringing little or no economic benefit to anyone other than the market traders and stock owners.

Critics also point out that neoliberal policies create great human hardship for billions of people as the global flow of wealth creates mass migrations of people looking for work (something we discuss next). In addition, production gets relocated to "Free Trade Zones" in developing countries where wages are low, work and environmental regulations are minimal, and conditions for workers are frequently terrible. For example, as recently as 10 years ago Apple made its computers in the United States, but then the company outsourced this process to Southern China, to companies such as Foxconn, renowned for its repressive labor conditions. In the first 6 months of 2010, 11 Foxconn workers committed suicide and 1 died after working a 34-hour shift (Daisey, 2011; Fleming, 2010). Indeed, criticism of Apple's relationship with Foxconn has been so widespread that Apple CEO Tim Cook personally visited one of its factories in March 2012, perhaps more as a way of reassuring consumers than actually to examine its labor practices.

Finally, in case you think a discussion of economics is a long way from communication issues, it is worth noting that, in many respects, the social world we inhabit is largely written in economic and market language; we are now all framed as consumers first and citizens second. Indeed, in a real sense, economic consumption and democracy are equated. As we saw in Chapter 12, brand guru Marc Gobé (2002) even argues that brands themselves are citizens that can contribute to a "consumer democracy." There is perhaps no clearer indication of how much economic discourse shapes us.

Globalization and Politics

The politics of globalization has also been a significant point of debate among commentators (Beck, 2000; Giddens, 2001; Robertson, 1990; Waters, 2001). Much of this debate has revolved around the relationship between globalization processes and the nation-state. Put simply, a nation-state "possesses external, fixed, known, demarcated borders, and possesses an internal uniformity of rule" (Cochrane & Pain, 2007, p. 6). The nation-state has been a defining feature of modernity, providing stable political institutions and systems of government around the world, as well as functioning as a mediating mechanism between the individual and capitalist organizations. For example, it is at the level of the nation-state that, particularly in the first half of the 20th century, restrictions were placed on the more exploitive aspects of capitalism (e.g., by passing labor laws), worker unions were legalized, and a welfare system was put in place.

However, as sociologist Ulrich Beck (2000) and others have pointed out, the nation-state is a geographic, territorial state, while globalization is a **deterritorializing** process that transcends national borders. Thus, according to some, globalization undermines the importance of the nation-state because it is based on a multiplicity of communication networks, lifestyles, and financial systems, none of which are tied to a particular place. Given this, it is argued that TNCs have become more powerful global actors than nation-states. As Beck (2000) states, the globalization process has political implications because it "permits employers and their associations to disentangle and recapture their power to act that was restrained by the political and welfare institutions of democratically organized capitalism" (p. 2).

Beck, then, sees dangers to democracy in the power that TNCs gain through globalization. Indeed, he goes even further, claiming that as the role of the nation-state declines and as corporations abdicate their role as citizens and "national champions" (El-Ojeili & Hayden, 2006, p. 64) for their home countries, they become "virtual taxpayers," paying a lower and lower percentage of the tax burden while simultaneously laying off more workers ("reengineering") and demanding more and more perks from the countries in which they are located. Beck (2000) thus describes globalization as "capitalism without work plus capitalism without taxes" (p. 5). Certainly, Figure 13.2 below supports his position, showing the steadily declining share of U.S. federal tax revenue paid by corporations.

Figure 13.2 Corporate Share of Federal Tax Revenue, 1950–2010

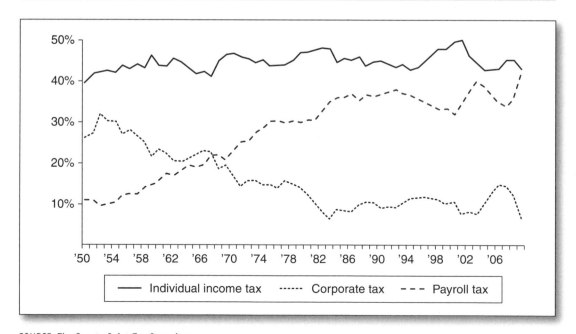

SOURCE: The Senate Joint Tax Committee.

Anthony Giddens (2001) takes a somewhat different position from that of Beck, arguing that nation-states and the institutions that make them up "have become inadequate to the tasks they are called upon to perform" (p. 19). In this sense, they are "shell institutions" (p. 19). For Giddens, globalization provides opportunities for increasing levels of democracy around the world, fueled by developments in communication that compress the world and make it increasingly difficult for authoritarian governments to hide information from their citizens. Moreover, as the power of the nation-state weakens in the face of globalization, the demand for rights and autonomy of local cultures increases. Thus, Giddens argues that although globalization may threaten local cultures, this very threat "is the reason for the revival of local cultural identities in different parts of the world" (p. 13).

One of the outcomes of this revival of local cultural identities is the emergence of various kinds of political resistance to globalization. Below we look at a couple of examples of the forms resistance to globalization has taken.

Globalization and Resistance

Researchers who study resistance to globalization examine collective responses to some of the effects of globalization around the world. Organizational communication scholars Shiv Ganesh, Heather Zoller, and George Cheney (2005) argue that it is critical to examine resistance "from the point of view of movements that work to resist and transform ideologies, practices, and institutions that support and constitute neo-liberalism" (p. 170).

As Ganesh et al. (2005) indicate, this resistance is sometimes referred to as **globalization from below** (Appadurai, 2000). In other words, where globalization is often framed as various forms of imperialism "from above" in which TNCs are turning the world into one global marketplace, the "globalization from below" movement is conceived as a grassroots effort to resist these imperialist tendencies and provide possibilities for more democratic forms of life. In particular, globalization from below argues that the power of TNCs is undemocratic because it is not subject to the governance of nation-states nor to popular will. In this sense, social movements against globalization are just as much opposed to the neoliberal economic policies we talked about earlier as they are to specific corporations (although corporations, as the beneficiaries and practitioners of neoliberalism, are frequently the target of antiglobalization protesters).

Ganesh et al. (2005) thus argue that "globalization from below" involves "collective resistance efforts that aim for the transformation of power relations in the global economy" (p. 172). Here, transformation refers to the ability to "effect large-scale, collective changes in the domains of state policy, corporate practice, social structure, cultural norms, and daily lived experience" (p. 172).

There are numerous examples of "globalization from below" in which can be seen collective efforts to resist the process of globalization. The most recent and visible example is the Occupy movement, which began as an occupation of Wall Street to protest the unregulated excesses of capitalism that led to the 2008 financial meltdown and has become a global movement. As of January 2012, 2,773 Occupy sites existed worldwide (http://en.wikipedia.org/wiki/Occupy_movement). The movement's protests focus on how, over the past 30 years, the richest 1% of the population has increased its wealth by around 240% while the income of the remaining 99% has stagnated (see Figure 13.1). The Occupy movement sees the lack of regulation of global capitalism as the origin of this problem.

© saccophotography/Demotix/Demotix/Demotix/Corbis

The Occupy movement is a recent example of "globalization from below."

While it's hard to identify concrete changes in economic policy that the Occupy move-ment has inspired, its slogan of "We are the 99%" has had a significant effect on the political landscape, with politicians and political commentators now openly discussing inequities in the distribution of wealth. I even saw a program on CNN the other day called "Is Capitalism Broken?" And presidential candidate Mitt Romney suffered attacks from his Republican primary challengers for the "corporate raider" tactics he used as CEO of Bain Capital—exactly the kind of critiques of capitalism that the Occupy movement has been making. An interesting (and inspiring) video on the Occupy movement can be seen at http://www.youtube.com/watch?v = n2-T6ox_tgM.

A very different kind of resistance to globalization—one rooted in consumption prac-tices—is the phenomenon known as **culture jamming** (Klein, 2001, 2005). Associated with the Canadian group Adbusters (who initiated the Occupy movement), culture jamming is an effort to use the advertisements and billboards of corporations against the corporations themselves by reworking their meaning. On its website Adbusters describes itself as "a global network of culture jammers and creatives working to change the way information flows, the way corporations wield power, and the way meaning is produced in our society" (http://www.adbusters.org/abtv/occupy-wall-st-vs-fox-news.html).

Journalist Naomi Klein (2005) reiterates this sentiment, stating that "culture jamming baldly rejects the idea that marketing—because it buys its way into public spaces—must be passively accepted as a one-way information flow" (p. 438). Thus, the idea behind cul-ture jamming is to seize back public space that has been colonized by advertising. Indeed, culture jammers describe what they do as a kind of semiotic jujitsu. Jujitsu is a Japanese martial art that uses the opponent's momentum to defeat him or her. Similarly, culture jammers use the power of corporate advertising against the corporations, creating new meanings that subvert the intended meanings. It's in this sense that they reverse the one-way flow of information from corporation to consumer, creating ads that enable consumers to critique corporations.

Numerous examples of culture jamming can be viewed at www.adbusters.org, but some of the more interesting ones include ads that parody the "Joe Camel" ads, showing "Joe Chemo" in various settings, including in a hospital bed, hooked up to an IV machine, and so forth; a Marlboro billboard ad featuring two cowboys, with one saying to the other, "I miss my lung, Bob"; and hundreds of New York City taxicab rooftop ads selling "Virginia *Slime*" cigarettes. As Klein (2005) indicates, these ads don't just parody the real ones; rather, they are "interceptions—counter-messages that hack into a corporation's own method of communication to send a message starkly at odds with the one that was intended" (p. 438). Critical Case Study 13.1 provides an extended example of one person's culture-jamming effort against Nike.

Globalization and Culture

From a communication perspective, perhaps the most interesting element of globalization is its effect on cultural processes and practices. Like political systems, particular cultures have traditionally been tied to specific geographic territories. However, culture and geography have lost some of their intrinsic connections as globalization processes diffuse and integrate geographically dispersed cultures.

From a critical perspective, globalization is often associated with cultural imperialism (El-Ojeili & Hayden, 2006). That is, because the process of globalization is dominated by Western countries, especially the United States, there tends to be a predominantly one-way flow of cultural products from the West to other nations, resulting in the steady eradication of local cultures and the creation of a single world "monoculture." Terms such as *Disneyfication*, *Coca-colonization*, and *McDonaldization* are all intended to capture the ways the dominant culture industries of the Western nations are colonizing indigenous cultures.

Moreover, this critical perspective emphasizes the degree to which the globalization process is rooted in promoting an identity of consumption, where social actors' identities are framed not in terms of work and family but in terms of a consumption lifestyle. Cultural imperialism, in this sense, promotes the idea that societies are not democratized and liberated until their members can drink Starbucks coffee, watch *American Idol* (available in more than 40 countries), and buy clothes at Gap and Banana Republic.

However, the concept of cultural imperialism is challenged by a number of scholars who argue that this apparent convergence of cultures into a single monoculture is highly exaggerated. First, there is plenty of evidence to suggest that in the process of globalization, cultural flows are not just one way. Most Western nations, for example, have many immigrant populations that have introduced their native cultures to their new homelands. For

Critical Case Study 13.1
Culture Jamming Nike

Perhaps the most interesting example of a culture jam that addresses concerns about globalization is the one attempted by Jonah Peretti, who used the fact that Nike enables people to personalize their Nike sneakers when they order them. Jonah asked for the word *sweatshop* to be stitched under the "swoosh" on his new sneakers. He received the following e-mail in response to his online order:

Your NIKE iD order was cancelled for one or more of the following reasons.

1) *Your Personal iD contains another party's trademark or other intellectual property.*

2) *Your Personal iD contains the name of an athlete or team we do not have the legal right to use.*

3) *Your Personal iD was left blank. Did you not want any personalization?*

4) *Your Personal iD contains profanity or inappropriate slang, and besides, your mother would slap us.*

If you wish to reorder your NIKE iD product with a new personalization please visit us again at www.nike.com
Thank you, NIKE iD

Jonah responded in the following manner:

Greetings,

My order was canceled but my personal NIKE iD does not violate any of the criteria outlined in your message. The Personal iD on my custom ZOOM XC USA running shoes was the word "sweatshop."
Sweatshop is not:

1) *anothers party's trademark,*

2) *the name of an athlete,*

3) *blank, or*

4) *profanity.*

I choose the iD because I wanted to remember the toil and labor of the children that made my shoes. Could you please ship them to me immediately.
Thanks and Happy New Year, Jonah Peretti

Nike responded:
Dear NIKE iD Customer,
Your NIKE iD order was cancelled because the iD you have chosen contains, as stated in the previous e-mail correspondence, "inappropriate slang".
If you wish to reorder your NIKE iD product with a new personalization please visit us again at www.nike.com
Thank you, NIKE iD
Jonah's response was:
Dear NIKE iD,
Thank you for your quick response to my inquiry about my custom ZOOM XC USA running shoes. Although I commend you for your prompt customer service, I disagree with the claim that my personal iD was inappropriate slang. After consulting Webster's Dictionary, I discovered that "sweatshop" is in fact part of standard English, and not slang. The word means: "a shop or factory in which workers are employed for long hours at low wages and under unhealthy conditions" and its origin dates from 1892. So my personal iD does meet the criteria detailed in your first email.
Your web site advertises that the NIKE iD program is "about freedom to choose and freedom to express who you are." I share Nike's love of freedom and personal expression. The site also says that "If you want it done right ... build it yourself." I was thrilled to be able to build my own shoes, and my personal iD was offered as a small token of appreciation for the sweatshop workers poised to help me realize my vision. I hope that you will value my freedom of expression and reconsider your decision to reject my order.
Thank you, Jonah Peretti
(http://www.cleanclothes.org/news/4-compa nies/979-nikes-love-of-freedom-and-personal-expression)
And so it continues, until Nike simply states that Jonah's order contains material "that we simply do not want to place on our products." Of course, the irony of Nike's refusal to honor Jonah's order is that the e-mail thread it produced has probably been circulated to far more people than would ever have seen Jonah's sneakers! The other irony is that Nike's stated commitment to freedom of expression, captured by their "just do it" slogan, clearly does not extend to efforts to draw attention to their labor practices. When it became clear that Nike would not

honor Jonah's order, he sent a final e-mail stating, "I have decided to order the shoes with a different iD, but I would like to make one small request. Could you please send me a color snapshot of the ten-year-old Vietnamese girl who makes my shoes?"

Discussion Questions

1. In groups, discuss your various reactions to Jonah's culture jam. To what extent do you think it was effective? What might he have done differently?

2. Think about the culture-jamming phenomenon in terms of broader issues of globalization. How might it relate to some of the issue discussed in the chapter, including globalization and politics; globalization and culture; and gender, work, and globalization?

3. Go online and examine some of the Adbuster culture-jamming ads. What is your response to them? Do they affect the way you think about certain products?

example, in a speech celebrating "Britishness," former British Foreign Secretary Robin Cook (2001) declared that

> Chicken Tikka Massala is now a true British national dish, not only because it is the most popular, but because it is a perfect illustration of the way Britain absorbs and adapts external influences. Chicken Tikka is an Indian dish. The Massala sauce was added to satisfy the desire of British people to have their meat served in gravy.

This is a perfect example of what globalization scholars refer to as **cultural hybridity**, or hybridization (Appadurai, 2000; Bhabha, 1994). Hybridity is a process in which two or more cultures intersect, producing cultural artifacts that did not previously exist in either culture. Thus, Chicken Tikka Massala, which has been identified as the most popular dish in the United Kingdom, is an example of cultural hybridity—it is an Indian dish, adapted to British tastes, that does not exist in India.

The idea of cultural hybridity thus suggests that, rather than increased cultural uniformity, there is actually more heterogeneity, or variety, amongst cultures. Indeed, critics of the cultural imperialism viewpoint argue that it ignores the degree to which social actors who consume artifacts actively interpret and reinterpret them. In other words, the mere act of consumption does not necessarily mean that members of a culture are mindless consumers, uncritically buying the ideology of "Disneyfication" or "McDonaldization."

Finally, the cultural imperialism thesis has been critiqued because it ignores the fact that no culture is ever pure and pristine, and is inevitably a hybrid mixture of various cultures, subcultures, and traditions. In this sense, the question of precisely what culture is adulterated by the process of globalization is often hard to answer. Indeed, if Giddens is correct that tradition is a modernist creation, then the assumptions of the cultural imperialism perspective become even more suspect.

Perhaps the best approach to the relationship between globalization and culture is to recognize that neither a cultural imperialist perspective nor a celebration of local cultures' ability to resist globalization and consumer culture quite captures the dynamics of the globalization process. What is needed, then, is an approach that moves beyond the binary logic of homogeneity versus heterogeneity, convergence versus divergence. Let's examine one such approach—sociologist George Ritzer's work on the "globalization of nothing."

The Globalization of Nothing

Ritzer (2004) provides an extension of his work on "McDonaldization" (see Chapter 3) with an analysis of how this process has been globalized. His discussion can be viewed as a way to think in a more global context about the issues around branding and consumption that we addressed in the previous chapter.

In describing the process of globalization, he argues that it is the result of two intersecting and interrelated processes: (1) *glo*calization and (2) *gro*balization. **Glocalization** refers to the intersection of local cultures and globalization processes, with a hybrid culture being produced that is reducible neither to the indigenous culture nor the global culture. The concept of glocalization recognizes globalization as a reality but attributes active roles to the members of indigenous cultures, suggesting that they are not simply passive recipients of an all-powerful globalization process. Instead, they appropriate the products of globalization for their own use, creating new cultural artifacts, as we saw above with the hybrid dish of Chicken Tikka Masala.

The idea of **grobalization**, on the other hand, refers to "the imperialistic ambitions of nations, corporations, organizations, and the like and their desire, indeed need, to impose themselves on various geographic areas" (Ritzer, 2004, p. 15). *Grobalization* is a term that addresses processes of cultural *convergence*, whereby there is an increasing homogeneity across cultures as a result of globalization processes. Ritzer argues that grobalization itself involves three interrelated processes: (1) capitalism, (2) McDonaldization, and (3) Americanization. As we have already discussed, in a capitalist economic system companies must grow (*gro*balization) or die, hence the ongoing search for new markets. Second, McDonaldization as a set of principles (efficiency, predictability, calculability, control through technology) has been applied globally to a wide range of industries, from fast food to hotel services to university education. Third, Americanization refers to the predominance of American ideas, customs, industry, and politics around the world. For example, the dominance of Hollywood movies worldwide would be an example of Americanization, as too would efforts to sell the National Basketball Association and National Football League worldwide.

For Ritzer, then, the process of globalization involves the ongoing tensions and conflicts between grobalization and glocalization processes, as depicted in the diagram below:

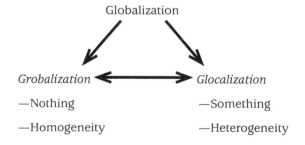

Ritzer (2004) argues that, in terms of the construction of cultural forms, grobalization is associated with "nothing," which he defines as "a social form that is generally centrally conceived, controlled, and comparatively devoid of distinctive, substantive content" (p. 36).

On the other hand, glocalization produces "something"—that is, "a social form that is generally indigenously conceived, controlled, and comparatively rich in distinctive substantive content" (p. 38). Grobalization, then, is about the worldwide diffusion of mass-produced and homogeneous artifacts, services, brands, lifestyles, and so forth. Glocalization, on the other hand, entails the creation of distinctive products and services that are unique to a particular context.

For example, a Big Mac is an example of the grobalization of nothing—a generic, mass-produced burger that is the same regardless of location. On the other hand, down the road from me in Raleigh, North Carolina, is a company called Raleigh Denim that uses local products and artisanal methods to make jeans, all of which are designed, cut, and sewn under one roof. The company makes only small runs of jeans, and each pair is individually numbered and signed like a work of art. In Ritzer's sense, Raleigh Denim produces "something."

Ritzer argues that the something–nothing relationship is a continuum that can be measured along several dimensions: complexity (something is unique; nothing is generic), spatiality (something has local geographic ties; nothing has a lack of local ties), temporality (something is specific to the times; nothing is time free), humanity (something is humanized; nothing is dehumanized), and magic (something is enchanted; nothing is disenchanted). For example, Raleigh Denim products are complex, requiring careful artisanship; have local ties, using local workers and materials; are time specific, made by certain humans in particular relationships; are humanized, in that the company is owned by a couple who are interested in contributing to the local community; and are enchanted, in that the products are tied to old traditions of denim making (e.g., the machines and the workforce that make the denim jeans are right in the store; when you buy a pair, you're told not to wash them for 2 months to get them properly worn in!). It's hard to associate any of these qualities with a pair of mass-produced jeans from Old Navy or Gap.

Ritzer argues that it is precisely the branding of products that attempts to deal with the problem of "nothingness" in the global process of consumption. In other words, and as we saw in the previous chapter, branding is an effort to instill meaning in a product or service that is otherwise generic and largely devoid of any unique identity.

The globalization of nothing, then, reflects the ways, at a worldwide level, struggles over meanings and identities occur. Particularly at the level of culture and meaning, the grobalization process involves attempts to imbue generic products and services with branded meanings that transcend national and cultural boundaries. At the same time, the glocalization process creates distinctive cultural meanings that resist the homogeneity of grobalization, often interacting to create new, hybrid cultural forms.

Gender, Work, and Globalization

What is interesting about the relationship among gender, work, and globalization is that it runs counter to the dominant narrative and media reports of globalization, which focus mainly on the "upper circuits of global capital" (Sassen, 2003, p. 254)—that is, the "hypermobile" capital, people, and investments in the fast-paced world of global finance. In contrast to this, the alternative narrative of gender and work in a global context tells the tale of southern, "Third World" women—a "lower circuit" of global capital and work—who provide the labor that enables that "upper circuit" to be maintained. Thus, although accounts of globalization tend to present it as gender neutral (Acker, 2004), the reality is that the globalization process has had a profound effect on the gender dynamics of work (Ehrenreich & Hochschild, 2003).

As Barbara Ehrenreich and Arlie Hochschild (2003) state, as a result of globalization, "women are on the move as never before in history" (p. 2). But this movement is not the kind of upward mobility that has seen the movement of many women into managerial positions in the past 30 years. Indeed, as Ehrenreich and Hochschild point out, while an élite group of successful "First World" women enjoy the benefits of a high-consumption, "jet-set" lifestyle, a much larger flow of migrant women are taking on the roles of nannies, maids, and even sex workers. This "female underside of globalization" (p. 3) involves a form of migration that sees women from poor southern countries taking on the child-rearing and home-maintenance tasks that many women from northern nations no longer perform. This is due in part to the fact that as household incomes in the United States have declined steadily in real terms since the 1970s, women have increasingly moved into the workforce to make up the income shortfall.

Ehrenreich and Hochschild argue, however, that this "feminization of migration" is largely invisible because unlike factory workers or taxi drivers, female migrant workers are often hidden away in private homes, working as maids and nannies to the children that professional dual-career couples don't have the time to look after. Moreover, the dominance of the ideology of individualism in U.S. society means that professional women are frequently loath to advertise their use of maids and nannies, instead perpetuating the myth of the "superwoman" and the idea of the "CEO Mom" who can have it all.

In examining the relationship of gender, work, and globalization, then, we get a close-up view of the ways the economics and politics of the globalization process come together in the everyday lives of real people—in this case, mostly women who are providing (often invisible) support services that maintain the machinery of global capitalism.

Sociologist Saskia Sassen has written a great deal about the dynamics of gender, work, and globalization, focusing in particular on what she calls **global cities** (Sassen, 1998, 2000, 2003, 2005). Sassen argues that while much of globalization theory focuses on the compression of time and space and the "virtual" nature of global processes, little attention has been paid to the fact that a whole infrastructure of activities and services has to be in place in order for the global economy to function. She advocates a focus on what she calls "counter-geographies of globalization" that shift the globalization lens to include not only the mobile professionals and knowledge workers but also the low-wage support workers who labor alongside them (Sassen, 2005).

Sassen (2005) argues that the global city reflects the fact that "the globalization of economic activity entails a new kind of organizational structure" (p. 28). Rather than nation-states functioning as the principal players in the global economy, global cities have become the primary "production sites for the leading information industries of our time" (Sassen, 2006, p. 109). Global cities such as New York, London, Paris, Tokyo, Amsterdam, Hong Kong, Zurich, and Sao Paulo are the new dominant financial centers that coordinate the flow of money and knowledge. This is where the highly paid knowledge professionals work and communicate with one another across borders of time and space.

Sassen argues, however, that such time–space flexibility would be impossible without the reproductive work necessary to maintain this system. Thus, working right alongside the highly paid knowledge workers are the nannies, domestics, custodial staff, restaurant workers, and so forth who engage in the labor that constitutes the service infrastructure of the global cities. In this sense, the global city draws attention to issues of power and inequality, as the rich and the poor live side by side.

In examining the situation of women who migrate to the north from the south, Sassen (2003) argues that there are two sets of dynamics at work.

First, in relation to the global city, globalization has created a demand for low-wage workers to take jobs that offer few opportunities for advancement—positions that native workers will typically not take. Given the increasing demand for high-level professional jobs in global cities, more and more women have entered the professions. In addition, high-income, dual-career couples often prefer urban living for family life, leading to an expansion of high-income residential areas in global cities. One of the consequences of this is the "professional household without a wife" (Sassen, 2003, p. 259) and, hence, the return of servant classes to global cities, working as nannies, maids, domestics, and restaurant workers to serve the consumption practices of high-income professionals (eating out regularly, weekends away, regular trips abroad, etc.).

Much of this labor is part of a large informal economy where many of the workers are illegal immigrants. As such, they have little recourse when it comes to poor treatment by employers, and, in addition, much of the work tends to be temporary and unpredictable. Susan Cheever (2003), for example, provides a poignant depiction of the life of a nanny in New York City. "Dominique" emigrated from the Caribbean and was lucky enough to get a green card through one of the first families she worked for. However, she still has had eight jobs in 8 years and must commute from her apartment in Brooklyn to Manhattan, where her various employers live. Cheever also describes nannies facing the "attachment factor," in which both nannies and children become strongly attached to each other. However, nannies are often let go when children begin school, and both children and nannies can be devastated by the separation. As Nikki Townsley (2003) points out, the "commodification of love" is a basic feature of the global child-care industry, where children are portrayed as gaining experience of another culture and nannies are portrayed as exotic and maternal.

But as Sassen's description of the second dynamic indicates, this picture is not as rosy as suggested. Sassen argues that in conjunction with the global city, there is what she calls the dynamic of the "survival circuit." In this feature of globalization there has been a "feminization of survival" in which households, communities, and even nations are increasingly dependent on women's migration and subsequent income for survival. Given the stagnation and shrinking of many southern economies, alternate ways of making a living and generating revenue become essential for the countries from which these women migrate. Frequently, the migration system is organized by third parties, including government and illegal traffickers (the latter specializing in trafficking women and girls for the global sex tourism industry). Governments frequently develop programs to encourage women to migrate to more affluent countries, reasoning that women are more likely than men to return their earnings to their home countries. Ehrenreich and Hochschild (2003) report on a Sri Lankan government program that even commissioned a song to encourage migration, the first two and the last lines of which are, "After much hardship, such difficult times / How lucky am I to work in a foreign land. . . . I promise to return home with treasures for everyone" (p. 7).

Currently, about half of the estimated 191 million legal and illegal migrants are women and girls, and women migrants outnumber men in developed countries. According to the United Nations, the most recent (2005) estimate of money sent home by migrants to developing countries is $167 billion, although given the "multiplier effect" of this money on local economies, the total money sent home by migrants is equivalent to about $500 billion.

It is important to note that many of these women are not simply looking for adventure and an exciting life in a foreign land. Rather, they are typically forced to migrate because of conditions in their home countries. Sometimes this is because of war, but many times it is because of difficult economic situations often caused by debt-reduction programs put in place by the IMF. As Sassen (2003) indicates, often the first things to be cut in such austerity measures are education and health care programs, which heavily affect women and children. Women, then, frequently migrate to find work so they can provide for their families.

In the next section we will examine some of the research on organizational communication and democracy. In some ways, the process of globalization makes such an examination even more imperative, given the preeminence of the corporation in a globalizing world. If commentators such as Anthony Giddens and Ulrich Beck are correct in arguing that the nation-state is playing a decreasing role in people's lives, then it seems especially important to explore how organizations and corporations can potentially function as sites of democracy and participation in decision making. Indeed, scholars and practitioners have argued that if they are to survive in a more volatile and unstable global climate, organizations need to move beyond the old, bureaucratic hierarchy and develop structures and processes that are flexible, decentralized, and adaptive (Stohl & Cheney, 2001).

Critical Technologies 13.1
Work, Technology, and Globalization in the Call Center

In some ways the call center is the quintessential global worksite—it is the place where communication technology, organization, and globalization processes converge. There was even a short-lived situation comedy based in a call center. Called *Outsourced*, the "comedy" focused on the trials and tribulations of a U.S. manager in an India-based call center and his efforts to navigate the intercultural pitfalls of life in a foreign country. While the call center was the primary location for the comedy, not much time was spent on the work itself, except when comic mileage could be extracted from conversations between operators and customers.

The reality of work in the global call center is, of course, quite different. Call centers "are emblematic of the uncertainties created by globalization" (Batt, Holman, & Holtgrewe, 2010, p. 454). They are located in remote parts of the world, offer services via a combination of phone and computer technology, and have heavily displaced face-to-face service in local communities. Moreover, call centers require relatively little capital investment, other than a rented building and computer/phone equipment, so they can be relocated fairly easily in response to shifts in the global economy. Finally, call centers embody the post-Fordist shift to a service economy with a heavy use of emotional labor; while call centers do not involve face-to-face service, they depend on the ability of workers to provide customer satisfaction while handling a high volume of calls. In the United States alone, more than 4 million people (3% of the workforce) work in call centers. It's no wonder, then, that a number of organization and management researchers have focused on call center work (Brophy, 2011; Fleming, 2007; Taylor & Bain, 1999, 2003).

Call centers are an example of what some Marxist thinkers have called "cognitive capitalism" (Brophy, 2011), in which language is "put to work" and labor involves the production of knowledge and communication. In this sense, call centers are a classic example of "the production of communication by means of communication" (Virno, 2001, quoted in Brophy, 2011, p. 412). Brody argues that call centers are an essential communication apparatus for managing the relationship between the corporations of cognitive capitalism and its consumers. Call centers act as the tools for selling various products, manage concerns and complaints about those products, and then act as long-distance digital debt collectors when consumers fail to maintain payments for those products.

But while call center work is often classified as "knowledge work," it is also largely deskilled labor exemplifying the "Taylorization" of white-collar work. Workers are constantly monitored, have to follow scripts carefully in interacting with customers, and are under constant pressure to meet quotas and move on to the next customer in the "queue" on their computer screens. Indeed, Phil Taylor and Peter Bain (1999) have described call center work as "an assembly line in the head" (p. 109)—a phrase that fits nicely with the idea of cognitive capitalism and also captures how white-collar work can be every bit as soul destroying as factory work. Indeed, the image of the call

center operator desperately trying to catch up with the callers stacked up in her or his queue is eerily reminiscent of the early scene in Charlie Chaplin's film *Modern Times*, where the "little tramp" flips out trying to keep up with the machine parts passing in front of him (later parodied in an episode of *I Love Lucy* set in a chocolate factory).

Taylor and Bain (1999) provide a compelling and poignant description of the typical call center employee:

> The typical call centre operator is young, female and works in a large, open plan office or fabricated building. . . . Although probably full-time, she is increasingly likely to be a part-time permanent employee, working complex shift patterns which correspond to the peaks of customer demand. . . . In all probability, work consists of an uninterrupted and endless sequence of similar conversations with customers she never meets. She has to concentrate hard on what is being said, jump from page to page on a screen, making sure that the details entered are accurate and that she has said the right things in a pleasant manner. The conversation ends and as she tidies up the loose ends there is another voice in her headset. The pressure is intense because she knows her work is being measured, her speech monitored, and it often leaves her mentally, physically, and emotionally exhausted. (p. 115)

You might want to think about this description the next time you need to talk to someone in a call center.

❖ COMMUNICATION AND ORGANIZATIONAL DEMOCRACY

Addressing questions of organizational democracy and participation takes us back to the central theme of this book regarding the relationships among communication, organization, and control. In essence, this section addresses the question, "What would organizations look like if they focused less on processes of control and practiced participatory democracy?"

As we saw earlier in this chapter, the problems and possibilities surrounding globalization raise important issues regarding the nature of democracy in the 21st century. Anthony Giddens (2001), for example, argues that "globalisation lies behind the expansion of democracy" (p. 5). He reasons that in a world based on active communication processes, where people have access to huge amounts of information, "hard power" (i.e., coercive, repressive forms of power) loses its edge. Certainly, as we have seen recently in the case of the so-called "Arab Spring," the hard power of the regimes in Egypt, Tunisia, and Libya was ultimately no match for the ability of ordinary people to organize collectively for greater democracy and freedom, with communication in the form of various social media playing a central role in this democratizing effort.

However, Giddens also claims that a paradox exists at the center of this global tendency toward democratic reform and revolution. That is, while democracy is an increasingly global phenomenon, there is greater disillusionment among citizens in the older democracies in North America and Europe regarding democratic processes. Certainly, the recent emergence of various movements in the United States and Europe, such as the Tea Party, Occupy Wall Street, and UK Uncut (http://www.ukuncut.org.uk/), suggest that people are looking for alternatives to the traditional forms of representative democracy that have been in place in the older nation-states for 150 years or more.

So how can we think about organizations and organizational communication processes in the context of this apparent shift in how we think about democracy? What role might organizations play in this movement? In reviewing various approaches to organizational communication, from scientific management through human relations and human resource management to the postmodern/post-Fordist organization, we have seen how management theories have tried various methods to get workers to participate in the work process. However, most of these efforts were less about increasing worker participation and more about developing increasingly sophisticated forms of workplace control. What, then, would genuine organizational participation and democracy look like? Scholars in a number of different fields, including organizational communication, have recently begun to examine this question (Ashcraft, 2001; Cheney, 1995, 1999; Deetz, 1995; Mason, 1982; Rothschild-Whitt, 1976, 1979; Stohl & Cheney, 2001).

In the rest of this section we will examine three approaches to organizational democracy: (1) Mason's theory of workplace participatory democracy, (2) Stohl and Cheney's conception of the paradoxes of workplace participation, and (3) Deetz's stakeholder model of organizational democracy.

Mason's Theory of Workplace Participatory Democracy

A good starting point is **Mason's theory of workplace participatory democracy**. Political scientist Ron Mason (1982) argues that

> what distinguishes a system as democratic is the way in which decisions are reached. . . . Democracy is a type of community rule in which the process of decision making generally entails widespread and effective participation of community members. (p. 153)

Mason argues that *community* refers to "a group of people bound into self-conscious units by common interests, concerns and problems" (p. 153). A community, then, is not limited to formal organizations such as workplaces, government agencies, and so forth but can include families, neighborhoods, voluntary groups, and social movements, for example. Indeed, a community can even be geographically dispersed, given the availability of modern forms of communication technology; the social movement UK Uncut is undoubtedly a community but organizes almost exclusively via social media.

According to Mason (1982, pp. 154–156), the degree of participation in a community (and, for our purposes, an organization) can be assessed along five dimensions:

1. *Extensity* is the proportion as well as the absolute number of members who participate in decision making in their community or workplace. The greater the percentage or number of members participating in decision making, the more democratic a community is. If a few élite members of an organization make all the important decisions, then democracy is not an integral part of that organization's philosophy.

2. *Scope* is the number and type of issues available for the members of the workplace community to determine. If most organization members' participation in decision making is limited to issues such as the color of the cafeteria walls or where the annual holiday party will be held, the level of participation and scope of decision making are low. If, however, organization members participate broadly in issues that are central to the organization's function, such as developing organizational philosophy and mission, setting production targets, deciding on systems of remuneration, and so forth, then the level of participation is high.

3. *Mode* is the form that participation assumes. If members are limited to placing ideas in a suggestion box that is opened once a month (or never!), then the mode of participation is not very democratic. On the other hand, if all major decisions are made on the basis of face-to-face discussion with all members present and a complete consensus required for decisions to be implemented, then levels of democratic participation are very high (this form of decision making is adopted by The Religious Society of Friends, or Quakers). Of course, once a community gets larger than around 15 members, such a high degree of participation is difficult, but it is still possible to develop structures that maximize participation, including decentralized decision making, flatter hierarchies, and so forth.

4. *Intensity* refers to the degree of psychological involvement of individuals in the act of participation. Mason argues that as the mode of participation becomes more direct, the level of intensity increases. Thus, members of organizations that make decisions based on consensus developed in face-to-face meetings are likely to have a strong psychological involvement in these decisions. On the other hand, organizations that make decisions with little member input are likely to discover that their members have little psychological investment in those decisions or, indeed, in the organization itself.

5. *Quality* involves the extent to which participation actually has an impact on decisions made in the workplace. Organizations that solicit members' input on decisions and then fail to take such input into consideration are engaged in "pseudo-participation," according to Mason. On the other hand, if members are able to witness ways in which their participation changes how the organization operates, then the quality of participation is high.

As a political scientist, however, Mason does not directly address the role of communication in creating organizational participation and democracy. Given this omission, let's examine two approaches to participation that not only address communication but see it as an essential feature of what it means to develop democratic and participatory organizational forms.

Stohl and Cheney's Paradoxes of Participation

Organizational communication scholars Cynthia Stohl and George Cheney (2001) provide an interesting, communication-centered perspective on organizational participation and democracy. Their approach is useful and insightful because they explore the inherent complexities and, indeed, paradoxes involved in efforts to develop participatory organizational forms. Stohl and Cheney argue that a communication perspective sees participation as "constituted by the discretionary interactions of individuals or groups resulting in cooperative linkages that permeate traditional worker/manager boundaries" (p. 356). Participation, then, ideally transcends normal worker–manager distinctions and goes beyond typical workplace interaction tied to formal job descriptions and work activities.

Given this conception, Stohl and Cheney (2001) define worker participation as comprising "organizational structures and processes designed to empower and enable employees to identify with organizational goals and to collaborate as control agents in activities that exceed minimum coordination efforts normally expected at work" (p. 357). As "control agents," then, workers do not simply occupy roles in an organizational hierarchy but participate actively in creating an empowering organizational environment. Moreover, Stohl and Cheney argue that "participation is a special case of organizational communication," in that it is more than simply an attitude toward work or a particular organizational structure that facilitates workplace involvement. Rather, participation is communicative because it involves a set of interactions that go well beyond what is typically expected of workers in the routine performance of their jobs.

However, Stohl and Cheney (2001) recognize that while the implementation of a participatory model of organizational decision making leads to greater worker commitment to decisions and a higher-quality work experience, it also leads to a more complex communication environment—as they put it, "more people talking to more people about more things more of the time" (p. 358). As such, participation as enacted through communication processes tends to involve many complexities and paradoxes that shape how the dynamics of workplace participation unfold. Stohl and Cheney discuss numerous **paradoxes of participation** but argue that they fall into four main categories: (1) paradoxes of structure, (2) paradoxes of agency, (3) paradoxes of identity, and (4) paradoxes of power. Let's briefly examine each of these.

A paradox is a situation in which two apparently conflicting views have to be reconciled. For example, if someone states, "I always lie," we are faced with a paradox; is the statement itself a lie, therefore negating itself? Or do we believe the statement at its face value, thus negating the speaker's self-declared status as a serial liar? The paradox is irreconcilable. In discussing various paradoxes Stohl and Cheney focus on what are called "pragmatic paradoxes"—that is, paradoxes that are the product of human relationships and interactions. For example, in ordering someone to "be spontaneous!" the command function of the message negates the possibility of actually being spontaneous and produces a paradoxical social context. Organizationally speaking, an example of a pragmatic paradox would be the implementation of a new communication technology designed to increase work efficiency that ends up consuming lots of work time.

Paradoxes of Structure

Stohl and Cheney characterize structure as the "architecture" of organizational participation—that is, the rules, procedures, and guidelines for the participative process. Stohl and Cheney argue that sometimes the attempt to put in place organizational structures that encourage worker participation actually ends up defeating its purpose. For example, the paradox of design involves situations in which upper-level management design a participatory organizational structure but do not seek input from the very people who will be asked to implement and participate in this structure. When they do not have a say, workers often do not feel part of the system and, indeed, simply view it as a manipulative effort on the part of management to get them to work harder.

For example, David Collinson's (1988) study of a group of truck factory workers showed how the new U.S. owners' efforts to implement a more friendly and participative work culture by personalizing worker–manager relations was met with suspicion and hostility by the shop-floor workers. The workers saw such an effort as an attempt to co-opt them, calling it a "let's be pals act" (p. 187). Thus, an effort to loosen the traditional organizational hierarchy had the paradoxical effect of increasing worker–manager tensions and intensifying the hierarchical difference between workers and management.

Paradoxes of Agency

Paradoxes of agency refer to the tension between individuals and groups in participative contexts. As Stohl and Cheney indicate, many participatory workplaces are rooted in group or team structures (Barker, 1999; Sinclair, 1992), which complicate the role of the individual worker in the organization. For example, in the sociality paradox members who are highly committed to the participatory process often find themselves so involved in various activities and projects that they get burned out and are unable to perform their work to the best of their ability. The paradox of agency suggests that when workers are empowered and control their own work lives, other aspects of their lives (e.g., family and social life) frequently suffer.

On the other hand, the paradox of agency also points to the way that, particularly in an individualistic culture such as that of the United States, workers often have a hard time dealing with the fact that group or team, rather than individual, performance is often the focus of the reward system in a participatory structure. Some of you may have experienced this in the context of class group projects. While you may feel that your performance in the group had the biggest impact on the final evaluation, you receive the same grade as another group member who was simply along for the ride. Thus, in a paradox of agency, workers are required to give up a certain degree of autonomy, or agency, in order to serve the broader goals of the team and organization.

Paradoxes of Identity

Paradoxes of identity concern "the fundamental challenges of establishing selfhood and individuality while being part of groups" (Stohl & Cheney, 2001, p. 379). For example, the paradox of commitment details organizational contexts in which participatory values require full commitment and conformity such that voices of dissent are minimized or eliminated. This is paradoxical given that one of the purposes of participatory organizations is to encourage forms of communication in which diverse opinions and perspectives are expressed, maximizing the full range of member skills and resources. Under such circumstances, as Stohl and Cheney indicate, participatory work teams can simply become rubber stamps for management policy.

Another paradox of identity, the representation paradox, pays lip service to the idea of participation in that employees are often given trendy names such as "associate" or "self-manager" while being given little actual access to organizational decision making. On the other hand, paradoxes of representation can also develop in contexts where employees participate with managers in making important decisions. However, such employees often stop identifying themselves as workers and fail to represent their fellow employees' voices adequately, thus undermining the reason for establishing the participatory structure.

Paradoxes of Power

Paradoxes of power address questions of access to organizational resources, opportunities for voices to be heard, and shaping of employee attitudes and behaviors. For example, the control paradox illustrates situations in which the very system of participation and decentralized decision making ends up exercising more control over workers than traditional hierarchical forms. As we saw in Chapter 8 in our discussion of Jim Barker's work on concertive control, the implementation of autonomous work teams created a system of control that was more oppressive than in the old supervisory system.

In a similar analysis that Cynthia Stohl and I conducted, we found that workers in teams in a New Zealand tire company were far more demanding of one another in conforming to rules (e.g., regarding absenteeism) than were supervisors under the traditional organizational hierarchy (Mumby & Stohl, 1992). Of course, from a managerial perspective employee internalization of such control mechanisms is largely seen as unproblematic. However, such control hardly reflects the spirit of genuine participation. Moreover, the fact that concertive control often proves to be more constraining than bureaucratic forms does little to take advantage of the employee creativity and knowledge that participatory models are meant to explore.

Stohl and Cheney, then, enable us to reflect on the complexities of participatory models of organization. The strength of their analysis lies in its exploration of participation as a communicative process that frequently produces paradoxical outcomes. But, as they indicate, paradox is not necessarily a bad thing; indeed, it can actually function as a generative mechanism to get us to think creatively and innovatively about organizing processes.

Deetz's Stakeholder Model of Organizational Democracy

A final model we will address is **Deetz's stakeholder model of organizational democracy** (Deetz, 1995; Deetz & Brown, 2004). Deetz's model is important because it frames the issue of organizational democracy in a broader context, making it about more than simply democracy *in* organizations. Instead, organizations are seen as the site of competing stakeholder interests from the wider society that must be coordinated. As such, Deetz's model takes an explicitly political turn, recognizing that the framing of organizational and corporate life in largely economic terms severely limits our understanding of the ways corporations affect people's lives at an everyday level.

As we saw in discussing Deetz's work in an earlier chapter, he views the modern corporation as eclipsing the government, family, and community in terms of its effects in shaping human identities, decision making, and meaning formation. As such, everyday life suffers from a process of "corporate colonization" (Deetz, 1992a). One of the products of this process of colonization is that the corporate model of instrumental rationality and economic logic comes to pervade society as a whole. As such, people view themselves less as citizens in a nation-state and more as consumers in a market system, families become extensions of corporations or are run like corporations, and education is viewed as an instrumental means to an end in which the "student as consumer" and research dollars are the primary products (McMillan & Cheney, 1996).

Deetz's stakeholder model is thus an effort to rethink the role of the modern corporation in society. He expands the definition of the corporation to include a wider array of stakeholders with wider outcome interests. Rather than viewing the corporation through a purely market, economic lens, Deetz (1992a) positions it as a political actor that shapes perceptions and interests through the "money code"—that is, as constructing all stakeholders in terms of how they affect the bottom line. As he states, "The politics of representation is fully hidden in economic representation" (p. 45). In other words, corporations disguise their political role by framing every stakeholder group—employees, community, shareholders, and so on—economically. On the other hand, "If modern corporations are political bodies that make significant decisions for the public, we must consider how they relate to the various groups that they affect and how, if at all, these groups are represented in decision making" (p. 43). Such a perspective is directly opposed to Milton Friedman's position, discussed earlier, that a corporation's only role is to make a profit for its shareholders.

Deetz (1995) argues that if we reframe the role of corporations in society they can be seen as "positive social institutions providing a forum for the articulation and resolution of important social conflicts regarding the use of natural resources, the production of meaningful goods and services, and the development of individuals" (p. 36). Through this frame, the various stakeholder groups (listed below) are seen as internal (rather than external) to the corporate system; stakeholder interests are not seen as limits to the corporation but as part of its goals. However, stakeholders don't have fixed goals to be won but are rather part of a deliberative process in which corporate goals are codetermined. In this context, the development of a strong stakeholder model positions managers as coordinators of conflicting stakeholder interests rather than controllers of organizational goals that stakeholders must adapt to or oppose. Thus, each stakeholder makes an important claim on the organization, in that each invests in and is affected by corporate decisions.

As you can see from Deetz's stakeholder model, depicted in Figure 13.3, the corporation is reconceived as a set of stakeholder groups whose conflicting interests are coordinated by a managing process, thus producing a set of potential outcomes that are much broader than the usual goods, services, and profits. According to Deetz, these various outcomes can serve as an expanded measure of corporate success. In terms of the various stakeholders,

- *consumers* have an interest in companies producing needed quality goods and services at a fair price, as well as an expectation that these goods and services are produced using ethical, non-exploitive practices;

- *workers* desire a fair wage and safe working conditions, work that is meaningful, the chance to participate in organizational decision making, and a balance between work and private life;
- *investors* have a stake in a reasonable return on their investment and an expectation that corporations are ethically stewarding their investments;
- *suppliers* have an interest in a stable demand for their resource at a reasonable price;
- *host communities* have a stake in a strong quality of life, including fair taxation, creation of jobs, responsible integration of the company into the life of the community rather than destruction of public resources, and so forth;
- the *general society* has a vested interest in equitable treatment of its citizens, economic stability, the development of civility among its citizens, maintaining high-quality life, and so on; and
- the *world ecological community* has a stake in the extent to which corporate decision making has a global impact, particularly with regard to its effect on environments, global climate, and vulnerable communities.

For example, under this stakeholder model corporations would not exclusively determine income distribution. Rather, they would be determined through a process of deliberation

Figure 13.3 Deetz's Stakeholder Model of the Corporation in Society

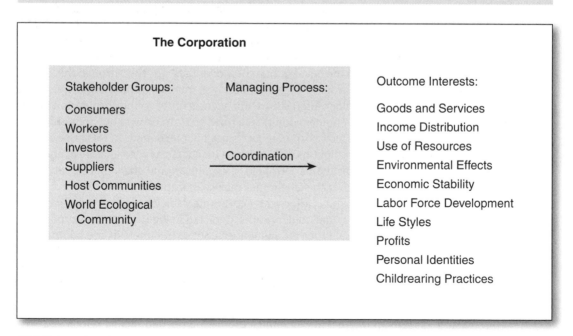

SOURCE: Deetz (1995).

and codetermination among various stakeholders. Given that CEOs of large corporations currently earn around 300 times what the average worker earns and that many executives receive multimillion-dollar bonus packages even when their companies underperform or even fail, it is clear that the current unilateral decision-making model of managerial control is ineffective and counter-productive.

Indeed, we could argue that the current Occupy movement is in part a recognition that corporations, narrowly conceived, can no longer be permitted to frame unilaterally economic issues and how they have an impact on other stakeholders. Executives sometimes make decisions to downsize their companies, for example, not because they are unprofitable or poorly run but because they know that downsizing invariably strengthens company stock and pleases stockholders. Employees are thrown out of work not because they perform poorly but because they are victims of the pressure to produce a healthy quarterly report. Income distribution, then, is an outcome in which numerous stakeholders have a legitimate investment.

Deetz's model is clearly the most ambitious and utopian, asking us as it does to rethink completely the role of the corporation in contemporary society. But, then, many ideas once considered utopian have come to pass, including democracy itself. If nothing else, it does get us to think in other ways about how we have multiple stakes in the way corporations function—not just as employees and consumers.

❖ CONCLUSION

In this chapter we have discussed the phenomenon of globalization, examining its relationships with the economic, political, and cultural spheres. We also looked at some of the ways the globalization process has created gendered effects on work. Finally, we examined some of the research on organizational democracy, exploring some alternative ways to think about our relationship to the process of organizing.

So how do we connect globalization and organizational democracy? If it is indeed true that neoliberal economic policies and processes of globalization have created more powerful corporations while at the same time weakening the role of national governments in people's lives, then it is important that we can understand, evaluate, and critique this expanding role of the corporation.

Anthony Giddens (2001) has argued that democracy is like a three-legged stool, with the government, corporations, and civil society (family, education, the media, public debate, etc.) each representing a leg. If one of those legs is broken, the stool isn't functional. In some ways we live in a period when the corporation wields more power than any institution ever has. It has colonized every aspect of our lives in ways that are detrimental to who we are as people, citizens, family members, and so forth. Perhaps it is time for us to make efforts—large and small—to regain our sense of self from the ever-expanding influence of the corporation.

Speaking of selves, in the final chapter we will address how work and organizations have a profound impact—both positive and negative—on our sense of identity. We will address the question, "How do we find meaning in the context of work and organizational life?"

CRITICAL APPLICATIONS

1. Visit the Slavery Footprint website at http://slaveryfootprint.org/. Take the survey on your "slavery footprint" and have a discussion about the ways we are connected in invisible ways to abusive labor practices around the world.

2. Read the story on bottled water at the following link: www.guardian.co.uk/society/2011/jul/22/had-our-fill-of-water. How does it influence your view of bottled water consumption? What does this say about the relationship between the "upper" and "lower" circuits of capital that Saskia Sassen talks about?

KEY TERMS

cultural hybridity   317

culture jamming   314

Deetz's stakeholder model of organizational democracy   328

deterritorializing   312

global cities   320

globalization   307

globalization from below   313

glocalization   318

grobalization   318

Keynesianism   309

Mason's theory of workplace participatory democracy   309

neoliberalism   308

paradoxes of participation   326

STUDENT STUDY SITE

Visit the student study site at **www.sagepub.com/mumbyorg** for these additional learning tools:

- Web quizzes
- eFlashcards
- SAGE journal articles
- Video resources
- Web resources

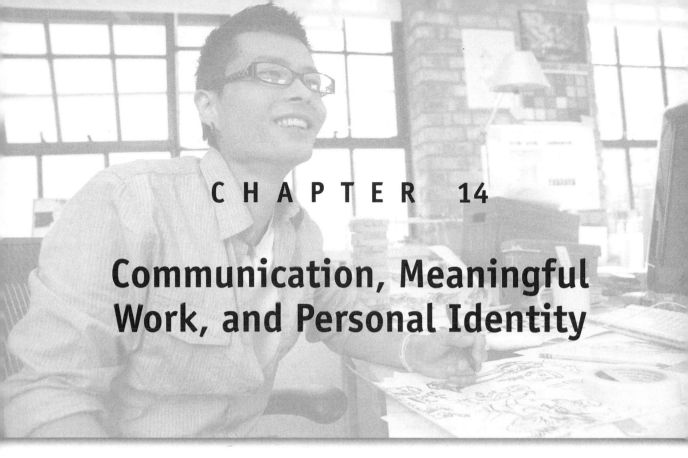

CHAPTER 14

Communication, Meaningful Work, and Personal Identity

Our relationship to work shapes our identities as well as
our sense of how meaningful our lives are.

*All societies have had work at their centre; ours is the first to suggest that it could
be something much more than a punishment or a penance.*

—Alain De Botton (2009, p. 106)

I suspect that everyone reading this book has had the experience of being asked the question, "What do you do?" Of course, we all understand that the appropriate answer to this question is never, "I read novels, hang out in coffee shops, and go running every day." Instead, we know that the person asking the question wants to know how we are employed; in other words, what do we do to earn a living? That this question generally comes pretty early in the conversation on first meeting someone provides a strong indication of the degree to which our identities—our sense of who we are as valued people—are closely tied to how we earn a living. It's also interesting that we all feel compelled to ask this question of people we meet; it's almost as though we are unable to categorize appropriately and make sense of someone unless we know how he or she is employed. As sociologists Ashforth and Kreiner (1999) state, "Job titles serve as prominent identity badges" (p. 417).

From a 21st century perspective it's hard for us to comprehend that work—or at least the kind of employment most of us experience—was not always closely tied to our sense of identity and the leading of a meaningful life. Indeed, one might argue that it was only with the emergence of the industrial age that such connections were made. Max Weber, in his famous book *The Protestant Ethic and the Spirit of Capitalism*, argued that the capitalist economic system was undergirded by religious principles that made the pursuit of profit a calling that defined people's relationship to God. As Joanne Ciulla (2000) argues:

> The Protestants endowed work with the quest for meaning, identity, and signs of salvation. The notion of work as something beyond mere labor . . . indeed as a calling, highlighted its personal and existential qualities. Work became a kind of prayer. More than a means of living, it became a purpose for living. (pp. 52–53)

For the most part, this is the conception of work that remains with us. What we do for a living heavily shapes our sense of self, and, thus, we want to do something that is fulfilling and feeds our perception of self-worth. Because from a young age we've been asked, "What do you want to be when you grow up?" (the right answer is never, "I want to be a good person"), it is an article of faith for us that we need to be engaged in meaningful work, however that might be defined. And there is plenty of evidence to suggest that work is an ever-increasing presence in how we define our lives and our sense of selves.

❖ MEANINGFUL WORK

How, then, might we define meaningful work? One answer might be that such a thing is in the eye of the beholder—if work is meaningful to the person who is doing it, then, by definition, it is meaningful. However, it is perhaps possible to identify some general principles that apply broadly to work. After all, while meaningful work may not necessarily have any objective features, there are nevertheless social norms that define different kinds of work in different ways. Such norms are communicatively constructed; in other words, we can think of meaningful work as symbolically created by individuals and groups as well as by larger societal discourses that circulate through society in various media (Cheney, Zorn, Planalp, & Lair, 2008).

What, then, are some of the features of meaningful work that we can identify? Cheney et al. (2008) suggest the following criteria that, while by no means exhaustive, provide a starting point for our discussion.

A Sense of Agency

People experience work as meaningful to the extent that they have control over the way their work is conducted. Using this criterion, working on a production line would be less meaningful than, for example, working as a doctor. On a production line, machines dictate the tasks performed and the worker simply functions as an appendage to the machines.

Like Charlie Chaplin's character in *Modern Times*, such work can lead to alienation because, as we saw in Chapter 3, the mind is disengaged from both the work itself and the worker's own body; the two function largely independently. On the other hand, when someone experiences a high degree of agency in their work, their sense of self is confirmed and they feel directly connected to the work being performed; mind and body tend to work as one.

However, we should be careful not to equate professional, white-collar work with agency and blue-collar, manual labor with lacking such agency. Much white-collar work can be profoundly alienating and lacking in agency, while blue-collar work can provide significant experience of control and integration of mind and body. For example, the classic "pencil pusher" who spends all day completing forms and the data processor who mindlessly inputs numbers into a computer would probably not consider themselves as having much agency, while a skilled craftsperson who produces his or her own work would no doubt describe him or herself as having considerable agency.

Indeed, in the past few years there has been a renewed interest in the kind of work traditionally regarded as "blue collar," especially that in which skilled workers grapple with difficult and complex problems. Writer Matthew Crawford notes current media fascination with shows such as *The Deadliest Catch*, *Ice Road Truckers*, *Dirty Jobs*, and so on, all of which depict dangerous and grueling blue-collar work. He argues that such fascination stems in part from the fact that most of us occupy boring white-collar jobs in which we rarely see any tangible product of our labors and that, by comparison, the work on these shows seems downright exotic (Crawford, 2009a, 2009b). In referring to work that most Americans do, Crawford (2009b) asks the rhetorical question, "What exactly have you accomplished at the end of any given day?" (p. 1). He suggests that shows such as *The Office* and movies such as *Office Space* ("We need to talk about your TPS reports") "attest to the dark absurdism with which many Americans have come to view their white-collar jobs" (p. 1).

Crawford argues that "the useful arts" (car mechanic, plumber, electrician, etc.) have been wrongly stigmatized as a career path and that most 18-year-olds are scared (by parents, counselors, friends) into believing that a prestigious college is the only path to career success. Trades suffer from low prestige, he says, because "dirty jobs" have been equated with stupidity and lack of education. However, speaking as the owner of a motorcycle repair shop, he makes a case for "working with your hands," engaging directly with a material world problem that can be solved only by utilizing hands and brain together. Moreover, he argues that there is economic security in such jobs because they can't be outsourced, unlike many white-collar jobs (car repair can't be done over the Internet or by phone via a call center located in India).

Philosopher of work Alain de Botton (2009) nicely captures what it means to exercise this kind of agency over one's work:

> How different everything is for the craftsman who transforms a part of the world with his own hands, who can see his work as emanating from his being and can step back at the end of a day or lifetime and point to an object . . . and see it as a stable repository of his skills and an accurate record of his years, and hence feel collected together in one place, rather than strung out across projects which long ago evaporated into nothing one could hold or see. (p. 182)

Furthermore, a sense of agency in one's work is tied to the distinction between "clock time" and "task time" that we discussed in Chapter 3. The more one's work is dictated by clock time, the less sense of agency one experiences. Indeed, the extent to which one is considered to be a professional (along with the autonomy that comes with that status) is determined in part by adherence to a task rather than to the clock. Thus, a surgeon would not quit an operation in the middle because her shift was over. As Ciulla (2000) states, "The defining moral aspect of what it means to be a professional is dedication to the task, not the clock" (p. 181).

Enhances Belonging or Relationships

Another characteristic of meaningful work is that it enhances our sense of connection to others. For the most part, work is not simply about the execution of tasks but also about developing relationships with other people in the process of accomplishing those tasks. In this sense, work is very much a communal affair where we gain a sense of identity and connection from our relationships with others. Of course, work varies considerably in this regard. For example, while working on a production line might allow little connection with others during work itself, a sense of connection can be created during breaks, on the company softball team, after work, and so forth. On the other hand, working in a cubicle along with dozens of other fellow employees in a so-called "knowledge-intensive" work environment can be a soul-destroying experience rather than a way to enhance connections with others.

However, it is also clear that for many people the relationships they develop at work are an important part of their lives. Many companies have recognized this and encourage the development of personal relationships in the workplace. This is a far cry from the old model of the formal, bureaucratic organization where personal connection was frowned on as a distraction from task accomplishment. Thus, even in contexts where the work itself is not intrinsically meaningful, companies spend a great deal of time and money attempting to make workers feel connected to one another and, more important, to the company (Fleming, 2007). In this sense (and as we will discuss in more detail), meaningful work is at least in part connected to a sense of identification with what we do or the company for which we work.

Finally, Melissa Gregg's (2011) recent study of the meaning of work perhaps indicates the future of work relationships and personal connection for many people. She suggests that, for many workers (especially those who change jobs frequently) the main source of connection to others "at work" is via the Internet. With increasing amounts of work being conducted virtually and from home, the only stable work community that many people experience is that which exists online via social media. For workers who are "free agents," their online communities move with them from job to job, providing a feeling of professional stability and some ontological security. Critical Technologies 14.1 addresses further how communication technologies affect our experience of work.

Creates Opportunities for Influence

Work is also meaningful if we are awarded opportunities to affect the organization for which we work. To the degree we are simply subject to influence and unable to exercise influence over others, chances are we will not find the work we do particularly meaningful

Critical Technologies 14.1
How Does Communication Technology Affect Our Experience of Work?

There's a lot of debate about the effect of communication technology (CT) on how we experience work, as well as on the relationship between work and home life. As is the case for a lot of phenomena that haven't been around that long, the evidence is mixed (Coget, 2011). Some suggest that CT, and particularly mobile technologies, are increasing the amount of stress on employees and further blurring the relationship between work and home, with the ubiquitous "Crackberry" user serving as the poster child for what's wrong with the CT–work relationship (Tarafdar, Tu, Ragu-Nathan, & Ragu-Nathan, 2011). In contrast, some have suggested that CT has *improved* workers' abilities to negotiate the work–home relationship (Wajcman & Rose, 2011; Wajcman, Rose, Brown, & Bittman, 2010).

On the negative side, we even have a term for what workers experience—*technostress*. According to Monideepa Tarafdar and his colleagues (2011), CTs can make employees "feel *compulsive* about being connected, *forced* to respond to work-related information in real time, trapped in almost habitual *multitasking* and left with *little time* to spend on sustained thinking and creative analysis" (p. 114). The conditions that create technostress include

- techno-overload (information overload, work interruptions, multitasking),
- techno-invasion (being accessible anywhere and having a need for constant connection, including at home and during family vacations),
- techno-complexity (time spent learning new applications and the terminology that goes with them),
- techno-insecurity (a fear of losing one's job to others who seem more tech-savvy with new CT), and
- techno-uncertainty (constant changes and upgrades of information systems limit employee ability to develop a base of experience; knowledge becomes rapidly obsolete) (pp. 116–117).

According to Tarafdar and his colleagues (2011), technostress is linked to reduced job satisfaction and productivity, decreased innovation, and reduced commitment to organizational values.

On the other hand, Judy Wajcman and Emily Rose argue that workers are not just passive victims of CT (as the technostress study suggests). Instead, they "interpret employees' relationship with communication technologies as one of extensive control over a complex communication ecology" (p. 950). Studying the daily work activities of knowledge workers in a high-tech company, they show how employees' workdays are largely defined by interruptions and changes in work activity (on average about 86 times a day), with only 3% of work episodes lasting 30 minutes or more. Moreover, more than 50% of work consists of activities that take 10 minutes or less, with 5 minutes being the average length of a work episode. Interestingly, out of the 86 average work interruptions, only 9 are from communication media such as e-mails or text messages.

However, knowledge workers do not experience work as fragmented. Indeed, Wajcman and her colleagues report that workers view "interruptions" and multitasking as an integral part of the workday. As two different knowledge workers in the study state, "It's the interruptions which form the genesis of the work," and "I view that as actually workflow; it's work coming to me." Thus, rather than CTs dictating work, this study suggests that knowledge workers adapt and integrate them into a work environment that is already complex.

Finally, Wajcman and her colleagues (2010) suggest in another study that rather than creating more stress in the work–home relationship, CTs help employees better manage that relationship. Counter-intuitively, the study found that the more a worker uses CT at home for work purposes, the lower the worker's sense that work negatively impacts home life. This is because workers in the study viewed the ability to work from home as a way to connect better with family.

I suspect both positions contain elements of truth. Either way, there's little doubt that we will continue to have to negotiate the relations among work, CTs, and our private lives.

or rewarding. If we toil away in jobs we know make little difference to the company or the lives of others, then we are unlikely to feel that our work is meaningful. For example, Conrad (1985) describes the case of an employee who worked on an automobile production line and whose job was to monitor engine piston cases and discard those that weren't up to specifications. She was soon admonished for rejecting too many and told that she should not exceed a rejection rate of 1 %. So, even though she knew that many more did not meet specs, she simply rejected every hundredth piston case that passed in front of her on the conveyor belt and used the extra time to compose songs in her head. In other words, she recognized that the act of actually doing her job to the best of her ability had zero influence on the organization; indeed, she actually inconvenienced it by working diligently. It's hard to imagine anyone feeling that their work is meaningful under such circumstances.

In general, opportunities for influence increase with one's rise up the corporate hierarchy. At one extreme, one could make the case that Steve Jobs engaged in incredibly meaningful work because he not only deeply influenced the direction Apple has taken as a company but also profoundly shaped the wider culture and society in which we all live with the production of the iconic Apple devices. However, most of us settle for a much more mundane and smaller sphere of influence in our work. For example, as a department chair, I have been able to have a stronger influence on the department and university in which I work than I had as a regular faculty member. Thus, one of the rewarding things about my job is the ability to use the resources (economic and political) that my position gives me to improve my colleagues' quality of life. Of course, such influence also has a downside, because you cannot always meet the expectations of those you want to help.

Permits Use and Development of Talents

We all want to be in jobs and careers where our talents are put to good use and allowed to flourish. We quickly tire of jobs that are easy to perform and don't really stretch and test us. Of course, the nature of the post-Fordist economy we all inhabit means that frequent changing of jobs has become a normal part of the career cycle. Richard Sennett (1998, p. 22) claims that the average worker with 2 years of education after high school will change jobs about 11 times during the course of his or her working life. Such an uncertain work environment does not necessarily lend itself to the kind of progressive skill development that is more typical when the employment landscape is more stable and long-term. Indeed, under such precarious employment conditions, movement from job to job can be lateral or even downward rather than consistently upward.

On the other hand, sociologist Richard Florida (2003) has argued that it is precisely this kind of "horizontal hypermobility" (a fancy way of referring to frequent, lateral changing of jobs) that characterizes the "creative class" of workers (currently around 30% of the population), who are much more interested in "quality of place" (What's there? Who's there? What's going on?) than in specific jobs. As such, identification and long-term employment with a specific organization are much less important than the quality of experiences provided by a particular geographical location.

Offers a Sense of Contribution to a Greater Good

We would all like to think that the work we do contributes to making the world a better place, even if only in a small way. De Botton (2009) puts this issue succinctly when he states, "When does a job feel meaningful? Whenever it allows us to generate delight or reduce suffering in others" (p. 78). Interestingly, this comment is made in a chapter devoted to the manufacture of cookies!

Clearly, contributing to the greater good is easier in some professions than in others. Doctors, teachers, nurses, and people in similar professions have a relatively easy time thinking of their work as meaningful in terms of the contributions they make to society. On the other hand (and going to the other extreme), someone who works as an account executive for a tobacco company and whose job is to market cigarettes might have a much harder time making such a case. Such a person may well meet the other criteria we have talked about, but how might he or she claim to be making a contribution to the greater good?

De Botton (2009) gives us some insight into how people in such professions might make sense of the work they do. His interview with the creator and account executive for cookies called "Moments" reveals the ways he sees himself contributing to a better life for people:

> Laurence had formulated his biscuit [cookie] by gathering some interviewees in a hotel . . . and, over a week, questioning them about their lives, in an attempt to tease out of them certain emotional longings that could subsequently be elaborated into the organising principles behind a new product. . . . [A] number of low-income mothers had spoken of their yearning for sympathy, affection and what Laurence termed simply, with aphoristic brevity, "me-time." The Moment set out to suggest itself as the plausible solution to their predicament.
>
> While the idea of answering psychological yearnings with dough might seem daunting, Laurence explained that in the hands of an experienced branding expert, decisions about width, shape, coating, packaging and name can furnish a biscuit with a personality as subtly and appropriately nuanced as that of a protagonist in a great novel. (pp. 72–73)

Of course, having read the chapter on branding and consumption, you should not be surprised at the ways something as mundane as a chocolate-covered cookie is invested with strong meanings (and backed by a $5-million development program). Nevertheless, De Botton's description shows us how sense making and meaning construction processes can frame work as contributing to a better world (in this case, providing stressed, low-income moms with "me-time"), at least by the people who occupy such jobs.

Provides Income Adequate for a Decent Living

This is clearly the most basic criterion for making work meaningful; doing volunteer work feels good, but it doesn't put bread on the table. Of course, what counts as a "decent living" is very much in the eye of the beholder. The U.S. Census Bureau indicates that in 2008 the median household income in the United States was $52,029. On the other hand, in 2010 the U.S. Department of Health and Human Services placed the poverty threshold in the United States at $10,830 for one person, $14,570 for two people, and $22,050 for a family of four. Do you think you would be able to live on these figures?

Interestingly, this criterion for making work meaningful is often the most difficult to talk about. When I ask my students what is important to them in a career, very few are willing to talk openly about "earning lots of money" as important, although a number will say that they want to earn enough not to have to worry about money. As we saw in the chapter on branding and consumption, however, we live in a society where the power to consume is viewed as a necessary prerequisite for a happy and meaningful life, and, as a consequence, a large percentage of the population lives in perpetual debt with little or no savings. Thus, people are prepared to live well beyond their means in order to pursue what they define as a meaningful life.

All the criteria discussed above assume that in order for us to be happy, work must be a meaningful part of our lives. For most people this is probably the case, but for a significant proportion of the population work is simply a means to an end; that is, it is the thing they must do in order to earn the money that allows them to do other things in their lives. For such people, the idea of a "career" is not a defining feature of their lives. For example, my older brother Ken has had numerous jobs in his working life, including working in a steel foundry, serving as a police officer, driving a delivery truck, being a nontraditional student, being a postal worker, and working with special needs children. Looked at in total, it's hard to frame these jobs as a "career." However, for Ken, they allow him to pursue the things in life that are really important to him: supporting his family, spending time with his grand-daughter, traveling, and so forth. In many respects one might argue that my brother has a much healthier relationship to work than those of us who have devoted a lifetime to building a successful career.

So, the issue we need to address more closely is the relation between work and meaning in people's lives. Or, as Ciulla (2000) puts it, "What is the relationship between meaningful work, a meaningful life, and happiness" (p. 208)? This means that rather than thinking about the meaning of work as an individual and often idiosyncratic issue, we need to think about the larger social forces that shape not only the meaning of work itself but also other spheres of our lives. In addition, we need to examine more closely the relationship between work and human identity; that is, how do we make sense of work as an integral part of who we are as human beings? How do we communicatively construct ourselves and others in relation to our work and professional lives? And how does work construct us?

❖ MANAGING WORK IDENTITY: SOME HISTORICAL CONTEXT

The rather neat criteria for "meaningful work" that we laid out above get a lot more complex when placed in historical context. While it is fairly easy to think about the meaning of work in the context of stable, long-term employment and a relatively unchanging economic and political system, such a coherent picture becomes much more elusive in an environment where organizations are less stable, workers change jobs more regularly than they change their cars, and the relationship between work and other dimensions of our lives seems to get ever more complex and fuzzy.

A number of social commentators and theorists have argued that the changes in work and society over the past 50 years have led to a condition in which our sense of self, or identity, is much less stable, such that we are in a constant process of searching for a coherent and grounded sense of who we are (Bauman, 2000; Beck, 1992; Giddens, 1991; Kuhn,

2006; Sennett, 1998). Many of these commentators have used the term **reflexive modernization** to describe this condition, in which traditional stability-maintaining structures of class, family, and industrial forms of production have waned, placing greater pressure on people to create their own sense of stability. The sociologist Anthony Giddens (1991) refers to this as a search for "ontological security"; people look for an experience of life that emphasizes order, continuity, and relative stability across time.

However, the current state of the global political and economic environment means that such stability and continuity are increasingly hard to achieve. Indeed, as sociologist Richard Sennett (1998) points out, while uncertainty in people's lives used to be mostly the product of some kind of human or natural disaster (war, famine, destructive weather conditions, etc.), today it is woven into the everyday practices of "vigorous capitalism." This is in part because the dictates of the market mean that long-term thinking is virtually impossible, and success is gauged in increasingly short time frames. Thus, organizations need to assess themselves constantly and make changes (e.g., in corporate structure, target consumers, branding, etc.) whenever deemed necessary.

The result is that long-term planning has been replaced by short-term thinking, frequently dictated by the quarterly report. Where the success of a company was usually connected to the quality of its products and services, these days it is more likely to be dictated by shareholder return on investment—returns that are measured on a quarterly basis. Indeed, CEOs will often attempt to influence quarterly reports by engaging in practices such as layoffs, "reengineering," "right-sizing," and so forth—activities that please shareholders but for which employees typically bear the brunt.

The sociologist Zygmunt Bauman (2000) uses the term **liquid or light modernity** to describe the social, political, and economic conditions that characterize life today and that shape how we relate to ourselves, one another, work, and consumption. He contrasts this condition with what he calls **solid or heavy modernity**, characteristic of the Fordist period. As he states:

> Fordism was the self-consciousness of modern society in its "heavy", "bulky", or immobile and "rooted", "solid" phase. At that stage in their joint history, capital, management, and labour were all, for better or worse, doomed to stay in one another's company for a long time to come, perhaps forever—tied down by the combination of huge factory buildings, heavy machinery, and massive labour forces. . . . Heavy capitalism was obsessed with bulk and size, and, for that reason, also with boundaries, with making them tight and impenetrable. (pp. 57–58)

Such "heavy capitalism" tied workers spatially and temporally to one place and time, and to a career with a single organization (in Henry Ford's case, the introduction of the $5/day wage was the chain that helped secure workers to the labor process). On the other hand, "liquid modernity" is the era of disengagement and elusiveness; it is "those free to move without notice, who rule" (Bauman, 2000, p. 120). In contrast, "it is the people who cannot move quickly, and more conspicuously yet the category of people who cannot at will leave their place at all, who are ruled" (p. 120).

Because the disembodied labor of liquid modernity no longer ties capital to a specific location, it allows it to be free from spatial restraints; it can move anywhere, and very quickly: "Capitalism can travel fast and travel light and its lightness and motility have turned into the paramount source of uncertainty for all the rest. This has become the present-day basis of domination and the principal factor of social divisions" (Bauman, 2000, p. 121).

From an employee perspective this means that the ontological security once provided by the social contract between workers and employers and its accompanying lifetime employment has largely disappeared, replaced by rules of the game that are constantly shifting. Career events such as promotions and dismissals are no longer grounded in clear and stable hierarchies and corporate rules but can occur in seemingly random and whimsical ways as the latest economic and/or cultural shift changes the way organizations do business.

In this context, more and more responsibility is placed on employees to be flexible and adapt to these changing conditions, or be considered dinosaurs and thus expendable. The problem is that there is frequently no way to know or understand what the "next big thing" will be, and so employees remain in a constant state of disequilibrium as they attempt to be "good employees" without necessarily knowing the criteria by which they are being judged. Such insecurity is intensified by a business climate in which the life cycle of management fads has, in the past 30 years, shrunk from 10 years to 1 year (Micklethwait & Wooldridge, as reported in Ross, 2003, p. 96).

It is easy to see how such cycles of continuous change can have a corroding effect on any employee's sense of professional self and identity, particularly when such change cycles frequently contradict one another. Business rhetoric might stress the need for constant reinvention and reengineering, but the human consequences of such a philosophy can be far-reaching, with mass layoffs and the destabilization of families and even whole communities. A discourse of constant change that constructs successful people as always adapting undercuts the ability of employees to feel any real sense of stability and security in their work lives (and, by implication, other realms of their lives).

Richard Sennett (1998) has argued that the kind of short-term thinking and constant change that characterizes modern capitalism results in what he terms the **corrosion of character**. He claims that the strong influence of Wall Street and the stock market on corporate decision making means that companies are continually expanding and contracting to meet the demands of the market, and employees thus become much more expendable. Hence, the traditional corporate values of trust, loyalty, and commitment, shared reciprocally by employees and their organizations, have been discarded, to the detriment of both employees and the firms themselves. On the one hand, organizations lose the institutional knowledge that long-term employees develop; on the other hand, employees themselves are unable to engage in the long-term planning and organization that gives their lives a sense of stability and coherence. In other words, as Sennett states, it becomes difficult for people to develop a stable "life narrative" around which their sense of character is built.

Indeed, one might argue that the stable, bureaucratic organization has been replaced by constantly changing institutional forms that value disloyalty, irresponsibility, and immediate gratification. As Sennett (1998) argues, "Detachment and superficial cooperativeness are better armor for dealing with current realities than behavior based on values of loyalty and service" (p. 25). Short-term capitalism thus threatens to corrode those qualities that bind humans to one another and furnish a stable and sustainable sense of self.

Finally, it is worth noting that, according to Andrew Ross (2008), there appears to be a negative relationship between job security and managerial efforts over the past 50 years to make work more meaningful and rewarding. One of the central, defining aspects of organizational life we have addressed in this book is the phenomenon of control and the ways theories of management have evolved from efforts to discipline and sanction workers directly to more recent attempts to exercise control through providing worker autonomy from rigid rules and bureaucratic structures. As Ross states:

> As the workplace became more inclusive, free or self-actualizing for employees, it became less just and equal in its provision of guarantees. This was as true for production workers, reorganized into teams exercising a degree of decision-making around their modules, as for white-collar employees, encouraged to be self-directing in their work applications. In either case, the managerial program to sell liberation from drudgery was accompanied by the introduction of risk, uncertainty and nonstandard work arrangements. (p. 35)

In the next section we turn to examine more closely the organizational environments in which people work and the ways they manage their organizational and professional identities in the face of this insecurity and instability.

❖ CREATING AND MANAGING WORK IDENTITIES

The "crisis of identity" we have discussed is further intensified because organizations have constructed a close link between employee identity and control (Alvesson & Willmott, 2002; Casey, 1995). As we have discussed throughout this book, corporations have shifted from behavioral forms of control (requiring the worker to act in a specific way) to control processes that focus much more heavily on the "soul" of the individual employee. As Stan Deetz (1995) has indicated, the modern business of management often involves managing "the 'insides'—the hopes, fears and aspirations—of workers, rather than their behaviors directly" (p. 87). At precisely the time that our own sense of identity is "up for grabs," corporations step into the breach to create forms of control that exploit that insecurity.

In this sense, we can think about employees not simply as possessors of skill sets who perform specific tasks for the organization but, equally important, as **identity workers** who are asked to incorporate the latest managerial discourse into their own narratives of self-identity (Alvesson & Willmott, 2002, p. 622). As a simple example, corporate efforts to get workers to think and speak of themselves as "team members," "family members," or "associates," rather than employees, reflects corporate efforts to encourage workers to construct a certain narrative of work identity—a narrative that fits with the goals of the organization.

However, such efforts to shape employee identity are by no means a simple case of employees uncritically accepting management discourses of work identity. As management scholars Mats Alvesson and Hugh Willmott (2002) argue, "The organizational regulation of identity . . . is a precarious and often contested process involving active identity work. . . . Organizational members are not reducible to passive consumers of managerially designed and designated identities" (p. 621).

There is, therefore, a more complex relationship between employee identity and forms of organizational control in the post-Fordist organization than in the traditional Fordist bureaucracy. Part of this complexity is due to the fact that we have shifted from a society in which selves are **ascribed** to one in which selves are **achieved** (Collinson, 2003). In other words, pre-capitalist societies tended to be characterized by institutional forms in which people's roles were fixed and assigned—serf, aristocrat, peasant, slave, and so on—with little or no room for movement to a higher place in the social order. Even well into the 20th century the class structure in many societies left little room for maneuvering in the social and economic hierarchy. While ascribed identities limited social mobility, they neverthe-less provided a sense of ontological security that enabled a more stable sense of self. Furthermore, work relationships between capitalists and labor, while often antagonistic, were long term. Moreover, a strong sense of stability and security was gained through membership in a union and/or association with an occupational group—groups that tradi-tionally have fought to protect the rights of their members.

On the other hand, achieved selves reflect more fluid social structures in which greater onus is placed on the ability of the individual to carve out a relatively stable, coherent iden-tity. Thus, due to the precarious nature of contemporary life, much of our activity involves *identity work*, where we are "continuously engaged in forming, repairing, maintaining, strengthening or revising the constructions that are productive of a precarious sense of coherence and distinctiveness" (Alvesson & Willmott, 2002, p. 626).

However, the very fluidity of social structures means that individuals constantly reflect on and question their identity as the grounds of a coherent identity shift ("Am I successful enough?" "Does my boss like me?" "Should I change jobs?" "Do I have time for a social life?" "Does my butt look big in these jeans?" and so forth). In this sense, societies characterized by achieved selves are a double-edged sword: They provide the possibility of social mobil-ity, but the choice making that this entails produces existential anxiety and the kind of ontological insecurity we discussed above. Under the conditions characteristic of "liquid" modernity and postmodernity, we can say that identity management is about seeking sta-bility within fluid social structures. How do people develop a coherent and stable sense of self under societal conditions that promote insecurity and instability?

Given the focus of this book on the relationship between communication and organiza-tion, we will examine such achieved work and organizational identities as communica-tively constructed. In other words, identities will be examined not as some internal "essence" of each individual, or even as a cognitive (i.e., mental) phenomenon; instead, we will think about identity as meaning-centered and rooted in social practices. That is, how do people reflect on and make sense of who they are, and how does this sense making get enacted through their communicative practices? In this sense, identity is personal ("Who am I?"), social ("How am I the same as or different from other people, and in what impor-tant or trivial ways?"), and societal ("What larger societal discourses and meanings make possible or limit the kind of person I experience myself as?").

Identity, Identification, and Disidentification

Organization members, then, spend a lot of time engaged in "identity work." However, as we indicated above, such work is a dynamic process that involves active negotiation and sense making on the part of employees. Workers are therefore not the passive recipients of the identities organizations present to them. What, then, are the elements of identity work?

1. *Identity is thoroughly social.* That is, we always develop identities and do ongoing identity work in relation to other people. We have no sense of self except as shaped by significant others around us. Identity is not a self-contained "essence" exclusive to us.

2. *Identity is always contingent and ongoing.* It is never fixed and finalized. Our identities change and adapt to the shifting social contexts in which we find ourselves. Indeed, multiple identities can be performed in a single day.

3. *Identity draws on various macro discourses that enable us to develop a self-identity that is meaningful and coherent.* For example, a macro discourse of "enterprise" can be drawn on to provide a sense of professional self that focuses on self-improvement and self-branding.

4. *Identity involves struggle.* That is, both employees and employers compete over the particular conception of workplace identity that will prevail. This struggle is primarily meaning based and involves competing interpretations and sense-making practices. For example, some workers may not buy into the "family" culture of an organization and choose to create a work identity that distances itself from many of the behaviors required of someone who is a "family member." Identity, then, is a primary site of organizational control and resistance.

5. *Identity is a communication phenomenon.* Workers perform identities through daily communication practices, and companies attempt to shape workers' identities by developing strategic communication processes that attempt to provide a coherent work narrative in which workers can invest.

Given these elements of work identity, we can argue that there are three distinct but related processes: (1) managing identity, (2) identification, and (3) disidentification. In other words, in the process of (1) managing and negotiating their identities, workers will (2) develop differing levels of identification with their organization and/or will (3) engage in various forms of disidentification in separating their sense of self from the work identity a company demands of its employees. Because of the complexities of the relationships among work identity, meaning, and organizing, it's quite possible that employees will experience both identification with and disidentification from various aspects of their work lives. For example, employees might identify strongly with a work subculture to which they belong (e.g., software engineers, or even an office bowling team) while disidentifying with the company's effort to engineer the workplace culture to improve commitment and productivity.

For our purposes, the importance of this tension between identification and disidentification is that it provides insight into how identity has become a focal point for both corporate control processes and employee efforts to maintain a sense of agency and autonomy. If, indeed, "the self" is the "last frontier of control" (Ray, 1986), then it is important to understand how, particularly in post-Fordist conditions of relative insecurity, employees attempt to maintain a coherent and stable sense of self in the face of such control efforts. David Collinson (2003) provides one way to think about this process, arguing that there are three principal forms of work identity that people communicatively enact: (1) conformist selves, (2) dramaturgical selves, and (3) resistant selves.

Conformist Selves

Conformist selves involve efforts by organization members to portray themselves as valued objects in the eyes of those in authority. Under conditions of insecurity, one way to gain security is to demonstrate a level of performance that makes one indispensable to the organization. Under such conditions, the goal is very much to subordinate one's sense of identity to the needs and goals of the organization.

Anthropologist Karen Ho's (2009) ethnographic study of Wall Street investment bankers provides a fascinating example of a profession in which the need to perform a "conformist self" is extremely important to success. She shows how, first, Wall Street firms recruit from an extremely narrow demographic group, concentrating mainly on Ivy League schools—Harvard and Princeton in particular. Then, she explores how new recruits are expected to devote their entire lives to their companies, sometimes working 100 hours a week in the quest to close deals and make lots of money for the company. As Ho suggests, what counts as acceptable and appropriate professional identity management is very carefully defined:

> In an investment bank the presentation of self is crucial. Not surprisingly, the range of possibilities for self-representation is extremely narrow . . . the limitation and boundaries on one's image repertoire are more onerous and the consequences of straying over them are much more dire for women and people of color. (p. 120)

What is fascinating, however, is that this remarkable level of commitment to work and careful cultivation of a Wall Street identity is not rewarded with job security. Wall Street investment banks are notorious for adopting short-term strategies (or, as Ho points out, *no* business strategy at all) and hiring or firing people as they see fit and as investment fads come and go (the recent subprime mortgage fiasco is a great example of this). As a result, employees can make extreme levels of commitment to their employer but still find themselves with no job. Indeed, job insecurity is practically built into the culture of Wall Street.

As Ho points out, it is impossible to live a normal and balanced life under such work pressures. Wall Street employees are frequently young, single, and prepared to do anything to get ahead and make their fortunes by the time they are 40. As such, their commitment and development of conformist identities can frequently result in ill health and burnout due to the stress of work and the long hours, as well as an extremely skewed sense of life priorities.

Wall Street investment bankers are perhaps an extreme example of devotion (albeit self-interested) to a profession. However, it is not unusual for people to adopt such an approach to work. As we indicated above, many people are consumed with the idea of "career success," and such an orientation to work often demands that every sphere of life become subordinated to the project of "career." In his study of accountants, for example, management scholar Chris Grey (1994) shows how, as one becomes more successful,

> it becomes necessary to sublimate one's whole life to the development of career. Friends become transformed into "contacts," and social activity becomes

"networking.". . . The transformation of the non-work sphere into a specific aspect of career development is seen as crucial to success. (p. 492)

Note that it is not simply the case that work takes over other realms of life; rather, all other realms get reframed and are *made meaningful* through a lens of career advancement and success. Grey even reports that the (mostly male) accountants he studied talked about their spouses in terms of how much they helped or hindered career progress. In Deetz's (1992) sense, the discourse of career colonizes the life-world of community and friendship, defining it in an instrumental manner.

Conformist selves thus often view their professional identities as ongoing projects that need to be constantly maintained and improved. In this sense, in the language of the post-Fordist organization, they are "entrepreneurial selves" whose focus is not only the work they do but also their own "brand" and professional image. Thus, such workers *are* their own projects (Du Gay & Salaman, 1992; Holmer Nadesan & Trethewey, 2000).

As Joanne Ciulla (2000) points out, however, one of the ironies of the modern organization is that "the less stability and loyalty companies have to offer employees, the more commitment they demand from them" (p. 153). Workers may perform the conformist self as their principal professional identity but, as we saw previously with Ho's Wall Street bankers, such conformism by no means guarantees job stability. The irony of the conformist self, then, is that the commitment and hard work they engage in is not reciprocated by the organization in terms of commitment to the employee.

Dramaturgical Selves

Dramaturgical selves frequently emerge in organizational contexts where employees "feel highly visible, threatened, defensive, subordinated, and/or insecure" (Collinson, 2003, p. 538). When employees employ the dramaturgical self, they engage in communicative performances aimed at enabling them to survive and prosper in the workplace. Frequently, such performances are a response to work environments where surveillance is high and the workers are highly visible—a common condition in the post-Fordist organization.

In Karen Ho's study of Wall Street discussed above, for example, employees not only had to conform to a clearly defined work culture but also had to demonstrate—through their "onstage" performances—that they had fully internalized the work culture. This included fairly mundane activities such as wearing the regulation "power suit" but also involved more subtle elements such as eating lunch and dinner at your desk to demonstrate to others (and your boss) that you were fully immersed in the intense work culture. It also involved the ability to employ the language of Wall Street fluently, thus demonstrating one's competence and immersion in the culture.

Similarly, in Fleming and Spicer's study of a call center, one way the mainly 20-something employees responded to management's introduction of a "culture of fun" was to dress in hip, sexy clothes at work and openly engage in flirting with coworkers (Fleming, 2007; Fleming & Spicer, 2007). In this context, conformity to the workplace culture was very much a matter of consciously and visibly performing a "trendy" self, thus bringing the nonwork self into the work environment.

However, the deployment of a dramaturgical self in the workplace does not necessarily mean that one is attempting to conform to the culture of the organization. It is also possible that dramaturgical selves can be used as a way to resist the dominant organizational culture. For example, in Taylor and Bain's (2003) study of a call center, they show how an openly gay and very camp employee used humor as a way to resist managerial control efforts. He satirized managers, using his campy persona as a way to undermine their authority. He was able to get away with this behavior "because he would exploit both his own popularity and managers' stereotypical expectations of a gay man" (p. 1503). Thus, this employee was able to engage in a very public performance of "satirical gay employee" as a deliberate strategy of resistance.

The dramaturgical self thus places a heavy emphasis on the public performance of particular work identities that can either demonstrate conformity and commitment to company norms or directly resist them. In either case, the dramaturgical self illustrates the extent to which "identity is a matter of claims, not character; persona, not personality; and presentation, not self" (Ybema et al., 2009, p. 306).

Resistant Selves

Finally, **resistant selves** are employed in organizational contexts where employees are attempting to resist managerial control efforts. As we have seen already, in the post-Fordist organization, the employee self and sense of identity are central to corporate efforts to develop commitment to and identification with the organization. Thus, rather than employing explicit and/or collective efforts at resistance (e.g., through strikes or work slowdowns), employees in such organizations respond by engaging with the organizational meaning system that undergirds corporate efforts to control employee identity. In this sense, resistant selves attempt to negotiate or subvert the dominant, or official, meanings that organizations attempt to foster.

Resistant selves use a number of different communicative strategies, including cynicism, humor, and irony—all tactics that operate at the level of meaning—in an effort to exploit the ambiguity that exists in all corporate efforts to shape organizational reality (Collinson, 1988, 1992; Fleming & Spicer, 2003, 2007; Rhodes & Westwood, 2007). Certainly, David Collinson's study of working-class male shop-floor humor discussed in an earlier chapter is a good example of this kind of resistant self; here, workers use humor to construct a meaning system and sense of work identity directly opposed to management efforts to develop a corporate culture that emphasizes cooperation and higher productivity. Similarly, Bell and Forbes's (1994) account of university secretaries' use of "office graffiti" (Xeroxed cartoons) illustrates how they use self-parody ("I have PMS and a handgun—any questions?") to critique and resist the formal organizational bureaucracy in which they work. Interestingly, this study shows how the office workers in the study perform largely conformist selves in terms of their work routines and responsibilities but exhibit resistance in the informal "spaces" of the workplace.

Resistant selves are interesting (especially from a critical perspective) because they demonstrate the extent to which employees engage in efforts to maintain a sense of personhood that is distinct and separate from the corporate self. If the self is the last frontier of corporate control, then it would seem important (if only from the perspective of personal well-being) that corporations not be allowed to colonize completely our sense of who we are. For this reason, employees will often act ("onstage") the part their employer expects them to play while at the same time holding on to feelings of cynicism and resentment and engaging in "backstage" acts of resistance through humor, irony, and so forth.

For example, Gideon Kunda's (1992) famous study of a high-tech engineering firm illustrated how seasoned employees carefully managed "role embracement" (onstage performance that conformed to the corporate culture) and "role distancing" (maintaining a backstage, "authentic" self that was critical of corporate demands on the employee's sense of identity). By knowing when to engage in these different ways of managing identity, employees could maintain a coherent sense of self that was not completely owned by the company.

Resistant selves, then, highlight the degree to which employees are able to "penetrate" corporate efforts at control and self-consciously manage their identities, thus maintaining a degree of autonomy. However, as management scholars Peter Fleming and André Spicer (2003) have pointed out, it's quite possible that efforts at disidentification through communicative practices such as cynicism and irony simply serve to maintain organizational control. In other words, employees who practice cynicism (e.g., pinning up Dilbert cartoons in their cubicles) still engage in the daily activities of the workplace and maybe even perform their work with a high degree of competence. In such cases, cynicism might be not so much a form of workplace resistance as an ideological device that enables employees to feel as though they are "putting one over" on their bosses while unwittingly reaffirming existing hierarchies of power.

There is some evidence for this view of irony and cynicism because, as Fleming and Spicer (2009) point out, "the latest wave of management gurus invites employees to simply be themselves, even if that means being cynically against the values of the firm" (p. 303). In other words, it is precisely the mavericks and cynical, tattooed, counter-culture types that "bleeding edge" companies want to hire! The philosophy here, of course, is that such employees are deemed to add value to the company precisely because they think "outside the box" and bring innovative ideas to the table.

In her research on temporary workers, organizational communication scholar Loril Gossett (2003) provides one final twist in this rather complicated picture. She suggests that with an increasingly unstable work environment, it is actually not in the best interests of organizations to cultivate strong feelings of identification in all their workers. With the temporary workforce growing and companies increasingly relying on agency workers, it makes no sense for companies to encourage these workers to identify with them. Gossett shows how, through certain communication strategies, companies will actually actively work to keep such workers "at arm's length." Strategies include denying temporary workers access to the symbolic artifacts that would identity them as members of the company culture (e.g., not allowing temp employees to have an internal e-mail account even if they work at the company for several months) and denying temporary employees the opportunity to engage in any decision making or provide feedback to the company. Moreover, Gossett shows that temporary workers rarely experienced identification with their employment agency, especially as they had little regular contact either with other temps or with employers at the agency.

Thus, it is worth remembering that while millions of employees must negotiate the intricacies of identity management on a daily basis, there are also millions more for whom identification with their employer is not an option; indeed, many organizations employ a deliberate strategy of limiting employee identification in order to maintain organizational flexibility and simplify the hiring and firing process. Imagine, then, the quality of work life for those temporary employees who must suffer the indignities of being marginalized on a daily basis! No wonder—as Gregg's (2011) study, discussed earlier, suggests—such workers look to their online communities for a sense of identification and ontological security.

It is clear, then, that "managing identities" at work is a complex and sometimes contradictory process—conformist selves can sometimes turn out to resist corporate control processes, and resistant selves can inadvertently maintain the status quo. Much of this complexity arises from the fact that so much of the organizing process is concerned with the communicative construction and management of meaning. Companies are in the business of meaning production, both for consumers through branding of products and for employees through the internal branding of culture and the "ideal employee." Because organization members are rarely simply passive recipients of such branding efforts, employees will work hard to create their own autonomous "space" within the complexities of organizational meaning systems. Managing work identity, then, is a key aspect of the negotiation of organizational meaning.

In the final section of this chapter we'll take a brief look at the relationship between work and other aspects of people's lives.

© iStockphoto.com/RapidEye

U.S. workers work more hours and get less vacation time than workers in almost every other nation on earth.

No Collar, No Life

In her book *The Overworked American*, sociologist Juliet Schor provides some rather sobering statistics regarding Americans' relationship to work. She argues that the average employed person works an additional 163 hours (1 extra month) per year now than in 1969. Furthermore, there is a distinct gender gap in this increase—men work 98 hours more per year, while women work 305 hours more per year (Schor, 1993, p. 29). Moreover, a Families and Work Institute survey showed that the average workweek increased from 43.6 hours in 1977 to 47.1 hours in 1997 (Useem, 2000). While accurately measuring the amount of time people work is notoriously difficult and some authors have challenged the claims of Schor and others (e.g., Robinson & Godbey, 1999), it is clear that many Americans are consumed by work (for a different perspective on a nation's relationship to work, see Critical Case Study 14.1). And, typically, the higher one goes up the socioeconomic ladder, the more consumed one is; thus, upper-middle-class, no-collar workers tend to report having less leisure time than do blue-collar workers (Robinson & Godfrey, 1999).

A number of years ago sociologist Arlie Hochschild's (1997) book *The Time Bind* addressed the question of why Americans seemed to be working more than workers in other industrialized nations, including the workaholic Japanese (on average, Americans work 137 hours more per year than the Japanese and 260 hours—6.5 weeks—more than the British; yes, we're a lazy lot!). Interestingly, she discovered that this had little to do with companies requiring workers to put in lots of overtime; in fact, many companies reported having a hard time getting employees to go home at the end of the day. Rather, Hochschild put forward the counter-intuitive explanation that people often preferred to be at work rather than at home because, in many ways, work provided a sense of identity that home did not. At work, one does not have to worry about dysfunctional relationships and problems with children; rather, one can focus on the job and experience the camaraderie of workmates.

Whether one accepts Hochschild's thesis or not, it is clear that many people experience **time famine** (Robinson & Godbey, 1999). We never appear to have enough time, and our identities are very much tied up with managing time. I'm always amazed when I catch a glimpse of students' daily planners in class and see how they are completely filled with appointments from early morning until late in the evening—recall the students at Princeton in Chapter 1 who made appointments with their friends to hang out! And in the no-collar, creative economy that many of you will join, time management seems to be a particularly pressing issue.

Richard Florida (2003) reports that well-paid blue-collar workers appear to have the most leisure time while no-collar workers have the least. Why? Florida suggests that with the creative economy's focus on "novelty, variety, and customization" (p. 147) change is paramount; thus, there is constant pressure on no-collar workers to be flexible and adaptive and come up with ideas for new products. And here we are not simply talking about information technologies such as smartphones and laptops; even consumer products such as sneakers, cereal, and clothing are constantly being upgraded to ensure that consumers don't get jaded. Such constant innovation makes for long hours and pressurized work environments. Moreover, because no-collar workers generally earn salaries rather than wages, they are paid the same whether they work a 40-hour or a 60-hour week. Thus, companies

Critical Case Study 14.1
A Tale of Two Countries

While I was working on this book, I spent 4 months as a guest professor at Copenhagen Business School (CBS) in Denmark. It was an eye-opening experience in many ways. Denmark regularly appears at or near the top of rankings regarding quality of life and happiness of citizens, and it's easy to see why. It has universal health care (which I had access to while I was there), a fabulous public transportation system, free education through college, and a low crime rate. In Copenhagen, more than 50% of the workforce rides bicycles to work every day (less than 10% of adults in Denmark are obese, compared with 34% in the United States). Of course, Danes pay high taxes for this high quality of life, but for the most part they do it willingly, believing that it benefits everyone to have a system that promotes mental and physical health.

One of the issues I found most interesting during my stay in Denmark was Danish attitudes toward work and, in particular, its relationship to other aspects of people's lives. The first day I showed up at CBS a department manager gave me a sheet of paper with a list of all the dates of public holidays in Denmark; I counted 12 in all. These holidays are in addition to the guaranteed 6 weeks of paid vacation (basically, few people in Denmark work during the month of July). Now, don't get me wrong—Danes work hard; however, they seemed to have a better sense of how work should be balanced with family and leisure activities. For instance, the Danes are "joiners"—92% of them belong to some kind of group or social club; compare that with the declining rate of participation in social groups in the United States (Putnam, 2000). Work, then, is positioned as part of a broader social identity and does not have the kind of all-encompassing, all-consuming quality it has in the United States.

Perhaps most significant, however, are Danish attitudes toward work and careers. In the United States there is a relatively clear hierarchy regarding the prestige of various types of career—everyone, I think, would classify a sanitation worker or garbage collector as lower in prestige

than, say, a physician or lawyer. In Denmark, however, such distinctions are much more blurry, and "low-prestige" jobs are not stigmatized in the way they are in the United States. Being a server in a restaurant, for example, is a well-paid job with full benefits (part of the reason why eating out is expensive in Denmark) and tips are not expected. A garbage collector is not viewed with disdain or as doing "dirty work" but, rather, as an important member of the community in which he or she works.

Is such a view of work and identity sustainable in the United States? It's hard to say. My first-hand observations seem to suggest that, in general, Danes are happier because of their perspective on the work–life relationship. And they even have to deal with crappy, long winters.

Discussion Questions

1. How do you see your college life relating to your future career? How did you choose your major, and how did you explain this choice to your parents, friends, etc.?

2. In group discussion, talk about your daily schedules. How would you describe your relationship between work and leisure? What commonalities and differences exist among group members?

3. What kinds of pressures do you feel in adopting a particular career path? Are there career choices you would like to make but don't feel able to because of peer and family pressure?

4. In general, what's your experience of communication about work and career identity? What are the various sources of your information about "meaningful work?"

5. Google "Denmark" and see what you can find out about the economic, political, and cultural aspects of this country. How does it compare with your experience of your own country?

have little incentive to hire more workers to create shorter workweeks, as the overtime of salaried workers is essentially free to the employer.

There is also an interesting dimension to the ways we socially construct time for ourselves and its relationship to our personal and professional identities. In Chapter 3 we discussed the rise of "industrial consciousness" along with clock time, and in many ways our 21st century experience of time is that it is parsed into ever-smaller increments. We not only plan work but also plan our leisure and time with family and friends. Moreover, the blurring of work–life boundaries means that our relationship with time is more complicated. For example, in her book *Finding Time*, Leslie Perlow (1997) reports the case of a female project leader at an engineering firm who arranged to work from home 1 day a week. Even though the arrangement worked extremely well for both her and the company, she soon found herself moved to a less-prestigious project that required her presence at the office every day, and she was passed over for an expected raise. Perlow explains this by noting that the firm granted time flexibility only in an ad hoc way and that a great deal of importance was placed on presence in the workplace. Hence, workers resorted to tactics such as leaving jackets and bags at their desks to give the appearance of being present.

In a similar case, Erica Kirby and Kathy Krone's (2002) study of a corporate parental leave policy shows how the temporal link between work and personal life is socially constructed by the employees. In this instance, while the company has a generous (for the United States) official parental leave policy, employees of the company make sense of it by indicating that "the policy exists but you can't really use it." The employees' everyday talk about leave policies is framed largely in terms of the added responsibilities coworkers must take on when a colleague is on leave. In other words, such a policy is framed not as workplace benefit that improves quality of life but as a discriminatory practice that increases the "time famine" for workers without child-care responsibilities.

So what does this all mean for your life after college? Let's try to pull things together below.

❖ CONCLUSION

In this chapter we have taken a close look at the relationships among communication, work, and identity. In our 21st century organizational age we are, to a large extent, defined by the work we do. As we have seen, however, the nature of our work identities and their relationship to other spheres of our lives is a complicated one; while work is a significant part of our identities, it can also pose a serious threat to a coherent sense of self by colonizing other aspects of our lives. In addition, the likely continuing instability of the economic environment means that the relationship between work and identity can be highly volatile and lacking in any real sense of security. So as you think about your professional lives beyond college, how can the issues discussed in this chapter help you make sense of the world you can expect to face? Or, as Richard Sennett (1998) puts it, "How can a human being develop a narrative of identity and life history in a society composed of episodes and fragments?" (p. 26).

As you are already aware, your work life will not look like those of your parents or grandparents but will likely consist of "horizontal hypermobility" (Florida, 2003). But does this new, post-Fordist, "postindustrial" environment mean that young people just beginning their careers are inevitably facing a chaotic and insecure work environment? Is the "corrosion of character" that Richard Sennett talks about an inevitable outcome of the passing of the Fordist era?

On the one hand, we will probably never return to a time when a career spent at one or two organizations was the norm—the global economy has changed too much for that to be the case. On the other hand, there are certainly possibilities for a different kind of coherence and stability—one perhaps less dependent on our relationship to particular organizations.

Richard Florida (2003) argues that the age of organization is over and that "place" has become the key organizing factor in shaping people's lives. Based on an extensive study of numerous locations throughout the United States, Florida claims that for a significant minority of the working population (more than 30%), career decisions are influenced not by the quality of particular organizations but by the quality of the geographical location where organizations are based. How does Florida define "quality"? He argues that three criteria, or measures, are highly predictive of a high-quality living and working environment—one that will attract talent and experience sustained economic growth. These criteria are (1) technology, (2) talent, and (3) tolerance. Technology refers to the amount of "high-tech" and innovative industry concentrated in a geographic region (e.g., Silicon Valley, Silicon Alley, Research Triangle), talent refers to the concentration of the creative class in a region, and tolerance refers to the extent to which a region welcomes gays and lesbians.

Florida argues that members of the creative class use these criteria in deciding where to live. With the criterion of tolerance, Florida is not saying that members of the creative class are predominantly gay but, rather, that the presence of a significant gay community in a region is a sign of diversity and a rich and interesting local culture. Interestingly, he has lots of data to back up his claims. Now, what this says to me is that many people are developing lives and establishing a meaningful and coherent identity beyond the workplace, and in ways not characterized by retreat behind the fences of a gated community. Many urban areas are experiencing growth and transformation, and lots of people want to be part of that experience.

A few years ago Arlie Hochschild was quoted in a *Fortune* magazine article expressing her concern about the rise of the corporate campus and workplaces that take care of all our identity needs: "It's basically privatizing the village green . . . and denuding the real community outside the corporate realm" (Useem, 2000). Florida's argument seems to suggest a different—and more hopeful—scenario, in which individual identity is rooted in a more organic sense of community that emerges from diverse groups of people. It would be nice if Florida was right.

CRITICAL APPLICATIONS

1. Given our discussion of the meaning of work in this chapter, reflect on your own career desires and possible trajectory. In what ways did this chapter ring true for you? With what aspects of it do you disagree?

2. What, for you, makes work meaningful? What would you add to the criteria in this chapter?

KEY TERMS

achieved self   344

ascribed self   344

conformist selves   346

corrosion of
character   342

dramaturgical selves   347

identity workers   343

liquid or light
modernity   341

reflexive
modernization   341

resistant selves   348

solid or heavy
modernity   341

time famine   351

STUDENT STUDY SITE

Visit the student study site at **www.sagepub.com/mumbyorg** for these additional learning tools:

- Web quizzes
- eFlashcards
- SAGE journal articles

- Video resources
- Web resources

Glossary

achieved self: Achieved selves reflect more fluid social structures where greater onus is placed on the ability of individuals to create stable, coherent identities. Demands on the self are constantly changing and thus create precarious identities.

ascribed self: Ascribed selves are identities assigned at birth because of social or class position; unchangeable but providing a clear, stable sense of identity.

autopoiesis: The property of all systems, according to Niklas Luhmann, that enables them to engage in self-reproduction through communication processes.

brand: The total constellation of meanings, feelings, perceptions, beliefs, and goodwill attributed to any market offering displaying a particular sign. A brand is a carefully constructed set of meanings that a company attaches to a particular product, including the company itself.

brand ethnography: The use of field research by marketers to investigate how consumers interact with brands in the course of their everyday lives.

brand extension: The process of leveraging the meanings and emotions associated with a particular company to a variety of different products that don't necessarily have any relationship to one another.

capitalism: A mode of production in which owners of capital ("capitalists") purchase labor power from workers at the market rate in order to produce surplus value and hence make profit. In this system, workers are "expropriated"; that is, because they do not own the means of production, they must sell their labor power in order to survive.

charismatic authority: The ability of a particular individual to exercise authority over others by virtue of their special abilities. Charismatic figures often emerge at times of instability and social unrest.

circular response: Mary Parker Follett's radical, dynamic conception of communication that conceives of it as a system of relating. It addresses the idea that when two or more people communicate, the very act of communicating changes everyone involved. An early conception of communication as creating reality.

clock time: A form of time developed through industrialization in which time is no longer passed but spent. Time is a valuable currency that defines the employer–employee relationship and over which struggles occur.

closed systems: A system is open or closed to the degree that it can exchange information and energy with its environment. A closed system cannot adapt to environmental changes and is more likely to move toward entropy.

communication: The dynamic, ongoing process of creating and negotiating meanings through interactional symbolic (verbal and nonverbal) practices, including conversation, metaphors, rituals, stories, dress, and space.

community power debate: Debate in the field of political science about the nature of power that existed in society. The two camps in the debate were the elitists and the pluralists.

concertive control: An employee-generated system of value premises that shapes employee behavior in team situations. Concertive control is generated by the team itself rather than imposed by an outside party.

conformist selves: Efforts by organization members to portray themselves as valued in the eyes of those in authority. Under conditions of insecurity, one way to gain security is to demonstrate a level of performance that makes one indispensable to the organization.

corporate colonization: The spread of corporate ideologies and discourses to every aspect of our lives, including who we are as human beings. Corporate discourses have "colonized" other institutions such as the family and higher education, thus defining other, traditionally noncorporate spheres of our lives.

corrosion of character: The result of the shift to the new form of capitalism, in which loyalty and long-term employment are no longer key to professional success and a strong work identity. It is difficult for people to develop a stable "life narrative" on which to build a sense of character.

crisis of representation: A challenge to the idea that knowledge consists of a body of facts that represent an objectively existing reality, independent from human perception and experience.

critical communication perspective (of leadership): Rejection of leader- or follower-centric view of leadership. Focus on leadership as dynamic communication process involving everyone. Leadership is socially constructed through communication. A "post-heroic" view of leadership, with a focus on power and control and possibilities for leadership as resistance.

critical feminism: A focus on the processes through which organizations and society are gendered. Gender is viewed as socially constructed and performed though power relations. How do both men and women "do gender"?

critical theory: A "discourse of suspicion" that views the world as socially constructed through communication but sees underlying systems of power as shaping how this social construction process occurs.

cultural hybridity: A process in which two or more cultures intersect, producing cultural artifacts that did not previously exist in either culture. Rather than increased cultural uniformity, hybridity points to more heterogeneity, or variety, amongst cultures.

cultural pragmatist: A view of organizational culture as a variable that can be manipulated to impact employee commitment and performance. Culture and organization are seen as separate. A managerial approach to organizational culture.

cultural purist: A root metaphor approach to organizations. Culture is not a thing an organization possesses; rather, an organization *is* a culture. A researcher approach to organizational culture.

cultural studies: The study of everyday popular culture and systems of meaning. How do people construct meaningful lives in the context of systems of power and control?

culture industry: The mass production of popular culture, administered from above, that creates needs in people that they would not otherwise have. The culture industry maintains the status quo and limits people's critical abilities.

culture jamming: Attempts to use the advertisements and billboards of large, multinational corporations against the corporations themselves by reworking their meanings; "semiotic jujitsu."

Deetz's stakeholder model of organizational democracy: A view of democracy that sees organizations as consisting of multiple stakeholders, each of whom has a legitimate stake in organizational decision making. Organizations are seen as central to the larger system of democracy in society.

deterritorializing: The process of globalization in which money, information, and people flow around the world without regard for national boundaries. Globalization is based on virtual communication networks rather than geographic regions.

dialectical theory: An approach developed by the Frankfurt School to explore the complex relations between economics, culture, and politics. There is no one-to-one correspondence between these elements; instead, they interact in complex ways to create social reality.

difference: A social construction used to classify human beings into separate, value-based categories.

disciplinary power: The form of power associated with the postmodern, post-Fordist organization; a "bottom-up" form of power that focuses on employees' own production of a particular sense of self and work identity. Originates with philosopher Michel Foucault.

double-interacts: Weick's notion of the basic unit of organizing (A-B-A) through which organization members reduce information equivocality.

dramaturgical selves: The employment of visible communicative performances aimed at enabling employees to survive and prosper in the workplace. They frequently emerge in organizational contexts where employees feel under constant surveillance, threatened, defensive, subordinated, and/or insecure.

economic determinism: A classic Marxist position that views the culture and ideas of a society as heavily shaped by the economic structure of that society.

elitists: A group of scholars involved in the "community power debate" who claimed that power is concentrated in the hands of a privileged few who controlled political agendas.

emotional branding: A term used by marketers to describe efforts to connect brands to customers in an "emotionally profound way"; a strategy to strengthen the "brand relationship" to customers.

emotional labor: The management of feeling to create a publicly observable facial and bodily display. Emotional labor functions in the service of organizations to increase profitability.

enactment, selection, and retention: Weick's model of the organizing process through which equivocality, or uncertainty, in organization members' information environment is reduced.

entrepreneurial self: The increasing expectation that company employees will brand themselves through constant performance of a carefully nurtured professional identity that visibly contributes to the company's bottom line; involves an increasing blurring of the professional and private self.

entropy: The second law of thermodynamics, whereby over time a system naturally moves toward chaos and disorder, and dissipates. An open system staves off entropy through adaptation to change and is hence *negentropic.*

equifinality: The ability of an open system to reach the same final state from differing initial conditions and by a variety of paths.

equivocality (uncertainty) reduction: The means by which, through the process of enactment, selection, and retention, organization members reduce the information uncertainty in their environments.

ethnography: The study of naturally occurring human behavior through a researcher's immersion into the culture of a group or organization; an exploration of how humans engage in meaning construction through communication processes.

expropriation: The condition of workers under capitalism who do not own their own means of production and have only their labor power to sell.

facts: A body of social knowledge, shared by members, that enables them to navigate the culture on a daily basis.

feminism: A "discourse of empowerment" that sees reality as socially constructed through gender-based communication processes that have mostly excluded women from participation in organizations and institutions; need to empower women in order to escape oppression.

floating signifier effect: The notion that the meaning of any particular brand is arbitrary. Literally any meaning or quality—any "floating signifier"—can be attached to any object, product, company, or person.

followership: A leadership approach in which leaders don't exist without followers; most people are followers most of the time. Exemplary followers are highly committed to the organization, self-managing, and willing to provide honest, independent, and constructive critique to leaders.

Fordism: The dominant mode of production and organization in the 20th century, characterized by a hierarchical, bureaucratic, centralized decision-making system; deskilled labor; large economies of scale; standardization of products; and lifetime employment.

four-systems approach: Rensis Likert's classification of organizations into four systems (exploitative–authoritative, benevolent–authoritative, consultative, participative), with each representing an increasing level of worker participation in decision making.

functionalism: A "discourse of representation" that views the world as existing separately from knowledge claims and human perception; the dominant discourse in the human sciences.

gender accountability: The process through which we are judged and evaluated (i.e., held accountable) on our appropriate performance of gender identities. Such accountability occurs in an everyday, ongoing fashion.

general system theory: Defined by von Bertalanffy as "the general science of wholeness"; the study of living (including social) structures as interdependent, goal-oriented systems that are irreducible to their basic elements.

glass ceiling: An invisible institutional barrier that limits professional women's progress into the upper echelons of an organization.

glass cliff: The precarious position women managers often find themselves in once they have succeeded in "shattering" the glass ceiling. Women are often appointed to senior positions associated with a greater risk of failure and thus are often set up to fail.

glass escalator: The experience of faster upward mobility of men in traditionally female occupations.

global cities: The primary sites where the leading, global information industries are located. Global cities (London, New York, Paris, Tokyo, etc.) have become more powerful than nation-states in shaping global economies.

globalization: A political, economic, and cultural process that involves the intensification of consciousness of the world as a whole and an increased interdependence between nation-states and cultures.

globalization from below: Efforts by grassroots organizations and peoples around the world to resist the economic and cultural imperialism often associated with globalization; focus on transforming power relations and empowering local groups.

glocalization: Ritzer's term to describe the intersection of local cultures and globalization processes, with the result that a hybrid culture is produced that is reducible neither to the indigenous culture nor the global culture; associated with "something".

goal orientations: All systems are goal oriented, and through the process of feedback (both positive and negative), they are able to adjust their activities in order to maintain progression toward their goal.

grobalization: Ritzer's term describing the imperialistic ambitions of nations, corporations, organizations, and their desire to impose themselves on various geographic areas, resulting in greater cultural convergence; associated with "nothing".

Hawthorne effect: The primary finding of the Hawthorne studies, suggesting a causal connection between the psychological state of a worker and his or her productivity ("A happy worker is a productive worker").

Hawthorne studies: A famous series of experiments, conducted from 1924 to 1933 at the Western Electric Hawthorne plant in Cicero, Illinois, that established the importance of social relations in work; inspired decades of group and leadership research.

hegemonic masculinity: The historically dominant, socially constructed form of masculinity—characterized by physical prowess, individuality, aggressive heterosexuality, and independence—against which other forms of masculinity are measured.

hegemony: The struggle over the establishment of certain meanings and ideas in society. A group maintains hegemony when it is able to create a worldview that other people and groups actively support, even though that worldview may not be in their interests. Hegemony operates when the taken-for-granted system of meanings that everyone shares functions in the best interests of the dominant group.

heteronormativity: The use of norms of heterosexuality to evaluate and make sense of the world and people around us. Such norms position heterosexuality as the implicit ideal against which other forms of sexuality are measured.

hidden transcripts: Employee discourse and behavior that occur "offstage" and outside the immediate view of those in power in an organization; a form of employee resistance to managerial control efforts.

hierarchy: Systems are not structured on a single level but, rather, process information and function dynamically across multiple levels. Any system is made up of interrelated and interdependent subsystems and is itself a subsystem within a larger suprasystem.

historical materialism: Marx's analysis of history according to the different "modes of production" used in a society (e.g., slave, feudal, capitalist, etc.).

holism: The systems principle of "nonsummativity"—the whole is different from the sum of its parts. The elements of a system, functioning interdependently, cannot be aggregated; they can be understood only through their dynamic interaction.

homeostasis: The ability of an open system to maintain a steady state by adapting to changes in its environment.

homosocial reproduction: The tendency of the dominant men in organizations to reproduce themselves in their own image through their hiring practices.

hostile environment: A form of sexual harassment where conduct directed at a person because of her or his sex or sexuality unreasonably interferes with the person's ability to perform her or his job.

human relations school: A group of management researchers who focus on the social, interactional dimensions of work rather than its technical dimensions.

identity workers: What most workers are required to become—in addition to performing work tasks—by developing a professional identity that meets the needs and goals of the organization.

ideology: The system of attitudes, beliefs, ideas, perceptions, and values that shape the reality of people in society. Ideology does not simply reflect reality as it exists but shapes reality to favor the interests of the dominant class. Ideology does this by (1) representing particular group interests as universal, (2) obscuring contradictions in society, and (3) naturalizing social relations through the process of reification.

industrial democrats: A group of early 20th century social thinkers who believed that organizations could be a force for positive change if they were made more democratic and empowered ordinary people more.

integration: Follett's conception of conflict resolution that moves beyond domination and compromise to provide a creative "win-win" solution.

interpretivism: A "discourse of understanding" that views the world as socially constructed through communication process. Communication creates reality. Research focus is on the role of communication in human sense-making processes.

invisible knapsack: A set of privileges and practices that white people carry around with them that largely protects them from everyday injustices.

kaizen: A Japanese system of continuous work improvement that focuses on the work process rather than the product (literally, "change for the better").

Keynesianism: An economic philosophy that advocates a "mixed economy," in which government intervention creates a welfare system (unemployment benefits, pensions, health care, etc.) and a mixture of publicly (state) and privately owned companies. Its intent is to limit extreme economic cycles of "boom and bust."

law of the situation: Follett's view of exercising power or giving orders, in which authority arises out of the needs of the situation, not a specific person's power or authority.

leadership: The process of influencing the activities of an organized group in its efforts toward goal setting and goal achievement.

liberal feminism: An approach to gender and power that focuses on creating equal opportunities for women in all spheres of life—work, home, and education.

liquid or light modernity: Bauman's view of the current state of capitalism in which change is constant, the social contract no longer exists between employers and employees, and the powerful are those free from geographical constraints.

managing diversity: A term used to describe efforts to create a workforce that reflects the gender, racial, and ethnic differences in the wider society.

Mason's theory of workplace participatory democracy: A theory of democracy based on the five principles of extensity, scope, mode, intensity, and quality of participation in workplace decision making.

metaphors: The understanding and experiencing of one kind of thing in terms of another. Organizational cultures can be experienced as families, teams, machines, and so forth.

metatheoretical framework: A "theory about theories" that enables us to compare and contrast the different assumptions on which competing theories and perspectives on organizational communication are based.

modernism: Both a historical epoch and a way of thinking in which science, rationality, and progress are the dominant themes. Each individual, through rational thought, can come to understand the world and thus be emancipated from myth and superstition.

multifinality: The ability of a system to reach multiple goals and states from the same initial conditions and inputs.

murketing: A marketing strategy that attempts to integrate brands into the expression of individual identities by blurring the distinction between marketing and everyday life and popular culture.

nag factor: The strategic marketing of products to children to encourage them to "nag" their parents to buy those products.

narrative leadership: A "decentered" model of leadership that sees stories as exhibiting a leadership function and playing a central role in shaping organizational vision.

negative entropy: A state that counters entropy, or disorder. An open system staves off entropy through adaptation to change and is hence *negentropic.*

neoliberalism: An economic philosophy that argues for the sovereignty of the free market without any government intervention. The sole responsibility of a company is to make a profit for its shareholders.

new leadership: A broad term that describes innovations in leadership research, including leadership as symbolic action, followership, transformational leadership, and a view of leadership as socially constructed.

no-collar worker: A "free agent" worker with a nontraditional career path who engages in creative, "knowledge work" and rejects the idea of stable, long-term employment at a single company; creation of ideas ("symbol manipulators"), not things.

normative control: The attempt to elicit and direct the required efforts of members by controlling the underlying experiences, thoughts, and feelings that guide their actions.

one-dimensional view of power: Power is exercised through direct influence of one person or group over another. Overt conflict is necessary for power to be exercised. "A has power over B to the extent that A can get B to do something that B would not otherwise do."

open systems: A system is open or closed to the degree that it can exchange information and energy with its environment. A more open system can adapt to environmental changes.

operative closure: An autopoietic system's exclusive communicative

principles that enable it to maintain its difference from its environment and other systems.

ordinary management: Management by rule of thumb and use of arbitrary principles to regulate the labor process; the system of management Frederick Taylor was attempting to eliminate.

organizational communication: The process of creating and negotiating collective, coordinated systems of meaning through symbolic practices oriented toward the achievement of organizational goals.

organizational control: The dynamic communication process through which different organizational interest groups struggle to maximize their stake in an organization.

organizational ethics: An exploration of how, by virtue of their structure as systems of competing interests and power relations, organizations are continuously in the process of making decisions that affect people's lives in often fundamental ways.

organizational storytelling: A symbolic, narrative representation of an organization's culture that provides members with a moral imperative about appropriate and inappropriate organizational behavior.

outsider within: The experiences and perceptions of a person with minority status from a position within a dominant culture.

paradoxes of participation: Although the implementation of a participatory model of organizational decision making typically leads to greater worker commitment to decisions and a higher-quality work experience, it also leads to a more complex communication environment that can create irreconcilable conflicts for workers.

participant-observation: A form of ethnography in which the researcher studies an organization while participating in its everyday cultural practices.

passing: The various communication strategies adopted by minority group member (e.g., by sexuality, race, or class) in order to gain social acceptance within a majority group.

pluralists: A group of scholars involved in the "community power debate" who argued that power was equitably distributed throughout society and that no particular group had undue influence over decision-making processes.

post-Fordism: The late 20th century successor to Fordism, characterized by flatter structures; decentralized decision-making systems; small economies of scale; "niche" production; increasing commodification of everyday life; more insecure, unstable employment; and a blurring of the distinction between work and life.

postmodernism: A "discourse of vulnerability" that rejects any single overarching social reality. Reality is constructed in multiple ways by multiple, competing voices. Reality is textual: "There is nothing outside of the text."

power: A dynamic process in which relations of interdependence

exist between actors in organizational settings.

practices: The everyday behavior that enables members to accomplish the process of organizing and enacts the organizational culture.

precariat: Workers in all segments of the workforce who are in extremely precarious economic environments and are constantly under threat of losing their jobs.

quid pro quo: A form of sexual harassment in which the harasser demands sexual favors with the promise of preferred treatment regarding employment or evaluation.

radical feminism: A "woman-centered" approach that revalues feminine qualities that have been devalued in patriarchal society; focuses on the creation of alternative, women-centered organizations that attempt to operate independently from patriarchal society.

rationalization: The process by which all aspects of the natural and social world become increasingly subject to planning, calculation, and efficiency. We are all subject to the "iron cage of bureaucracy."

rational–legal authority: Exercise of authority through the impersonal system of rules and responsibilities that come with the holding of a bureaucratic office; "rule of the bureau".

realist democrats: A group of thinkers, opposed to the industrial democrats, who took a more conservative position on organizations and advocated the use of

administrative élites in developing industrial policy and worker–manager relations.

reflexive modernization: A new period of modernity in which the traditional stability-maintaining structures of class, family, and industrial forms of production have waned, placing greater pressure on people to create their own sense of stability and identity.

relevant constructs: Important terms and phrases that help organize the experience of members of a culture; differentiate what is important from what is less important.

resistance leadership: A non-managerial approach to leadership that views acts of resistance as a form of leadership that can contribute to the well-being of a community or organization.

resistant selves: Employed in organizational contexts where employees are attempting to resist managerial control efforts. Resistant selves attempt to negotiate or subvert the dominant, or official, meanings that organizations attempt to foster.

retrospective sense making: Weick's view of how people construct rational accounts of organizational behavior after the fact—"how do I know what I think until I see what I say?"

rites and rituals: Regular, repeated organizational symbolic practices that create order and predictability in organization members' lives and produce a shared reality.

romance leadership: A perspective that focuses on how leaders are socially constructed by followers. Leaders are romanticized such that followers exaggerate their importance and influence.

scientific management: Development of the "one best way" to engage in a work process using the scientific principles established by Frederick Winslow Taylor.

semiology/semiotics: The scientific study of systems of representation and meaning. Meaning is not in the relation between a symbol and what it refers to but in the relationship between symbols. Meaning arises out of difference (e.g., traffic lights).

sexual harassment: Unwelcome sexual advances, requests for sexual favors, and other verbal or physical conduct of a sexual nature constitutes sexual harassment when submission to or rejection of this conduct explicitly or implicitly affects an individual's employment; unreasonably interferes with an individual's work performance; or creates an intimidating, hostile, or offensive work environment.

situational approach: Rejects the idea of a universal leadership style or trait; views contextual factors such as the structure of the task at hand, the power of the leader, and the size of the work group as shaping the leadership approach adopted.

solid or heavy modernity: The old, Fordist style of modernity based in the social contract, where relations between management and employees were clearly defined. Solid modernity

was rooted in bulk and size and mass production of solid goods.

sovereign consumer: The term used to describe the new relationship between brands and consumers in a fast-changing global economic environment; involves efforts to increase the level of intimacy between the brand and the customer.

style approach: A leadership approach that argues there is a specific set of skills managers can learn to become effective leaders.

surplus value: The difference between the value of the labor power as purchased by the capitalist and the actual value produced by the laborer; the source of profit for capitalists.

symbol manipulators: Workers who create ideas and knowledge and find ways to transform them into branded, marketable products.

(leadership as) symbolic action: A conception of leadership that focuses on the ways the leader is able to frame and define reality for others. Leadership is conceived as a process of interaction rather than a thing.

systematic soldiering: The deliberate and coordinated effort of workers to restrict output by limiting the speed at which they perform work. Workers engage in systematic soldiering to prevent piece rates being cut.

task time: An organic sense of time in which work is shaped by the demands of the task to be performed. For example, work in a farming community is shaped by the seasons.

Theory X: McGregor's term for the dominant management philosophy that sees workers as having an inherent dislike of work and needing to be coerced to be productive.

Theory Y: McGregor's own philosophy of management, which treats workers as motivated, creative, engaging in self-direction, and enjoying work as much as play.

Therbligs: The basic units of motion that make up work tasks; created by Frank and Lillian Gilbreth to analyze and redesign work tasks, thereby reducing unnecessary motion and worker fatigue.

thick description: The writing of narrative accounts that provide rich insight into the complex meaning patterns that underlie people's collective behavior; associated with ethnographic research.

three-dimensional view of power: Conflict (either overt or covert) is not a necessary condition for the exercise of power. Power operates at a "deep-structure" level by shaping people's interests, beliefs, and values.

time famine: The increasing sense that time is at a premium, requiring that we constantly engage in managing time. Our identities, including leisure activities, become tied up with effective time management and getting the most out of our time.

tokenism: A condition in which a person is visibly identified as a minority in a dominant culture. These people are identified as representative of their minority groups, and any failure is viewed as a failing of the minority group to which they belong. Tokenism is a creation of the perceptual and communication practices of those who shape the dominant culture of the organization.

traditional authority: The inherited right of individuals to expect loyalty and obedience from others; authority based in custom and tradition.

trait approach: A leadership approach that argues that the qualities of a leader are embodied in his or her innate personal characteristics—physique, intelligence, and personality. Leaders are born, not made.

transformational leadership: The active promotion of values to provide a shared vision of the organization. Leader and members are bound together in a higher moral purpose. The leader raises the aspirations of followers such that they think and act beyond their own self-interests.

two-dimensional view of power: Power is exercised by setting agendas and "mobilizing bias" to support one's position. Covert, but not overt, conflict is necessary for power. "A has power over B when A prevents B from doing something that B would otherwise do."

vocabulary: The use of a specific jargon that is exclusive to members of a culture and functions as a badge of identification, distinguishing members from other cultures.

whiteness: A socially constructed racial category that consists of institutionalized practices and ideas that people participate in consciously and unconsciously. Whiteness is simultaneously taken for granted, largely invisible, and a yardstick for judgment of behavior and ideas.

work teams: A collection of individuals who are interdependent in their tasks, who share responsibility for outcomes, and who see themselves and are seen by others as an intact social entity embedded in one or more large social systems.

References

Acker, J. (1990). Hierarchies, jobs, bodies: A theory of gendered organizations. *Gender and Society, 4,* 139–158.

Acker, J. (2004). Gender, capitalism and globalization. *Critical Sociology, 30,* 17–41.

Acker, J., & Van Houten, D. R. (1974). Differential recruitment and control: The sex structuring of organizations. *Administrative Science Quarterly, 19,* 152–163.

Ackman, D. (2004, June 23). Wal-Mart and sex discrimination by the numbers. *Forbes.* Retrieved from www.forbes.com/2004/06/23/cx_da_0623topnews.html

Adorno, T. (1973). *Negative dialectics* (E. B. Ashton, Trans.). New York: Continuum.

Agger, B. (1991). *A critical theory of public life: Knowledge, discourse and politics in an age of decline.* London: Falmer Press.

Allen, B. J. (1996). Feminist standpoint theory: A black woman's (re)view of organizational socialization. *Communication Studies, 47,* 257–271.

Allen, B. J. (1998). Black womanhood and feminist standpoints. *Management Communication Quarterly, 11,* 575–586.

Allen, B. J. (2000). "Learning the ropes": A black feminist standpoint analysis. In P. M. Buzzanell (Ed.), *Rethinking organizational and managerial communication from feminist perspectives* (pp. 177–208). Thousand Oaks, CA: Sage.

Allen, B. J. (2003). *Difference matters: Communicating social identity in organizations.* Prospects Heights, IL: Waveland.

Allen, B. J. (2007). Theorizing communication and race. *Communication Monographs, 74,* 259–264.

Alvesson, M. (1993). *Cultural perspectives on organizations.* Cambridge, UK: Cambridge University Press.

Alvesson, M., & Deetz, S. (2000). *Doing critical management research.* Thousand Oaks, CA: Sage.

Alvesson, M., & Spicer, A. (2011). Theories of leadership. In M. Alvesson & A. Spicer (Eds.), *Metaphors we lead by: Understanding leadership in the real world* (pp. 8–30). London: Routledge.

Alvesson, M., & Willmott, H. (2002). Identity regulation as organizational control: Producing the appropriate individual. *Journal of Management Studies, 39,* 619–644.

Anderson, E. (2009). *Inclusive masculinity: The changing nature of masculinities.* New York: Routledge.

Appadurai, A. (2000). Grassroots globalization and the research imagination. *Public Culture, 12,* 1–19.

Argyle, M. (1953). The Relay Assembly Test Room in retrospect. *Occupational Psychology, 27,* 98–103.

Ashcraft, K. L. (1998). "I wouldn't say I'm a feminist, but . . .": Organizational micropractice and gender identity. *Management Communication Quarterly, 11,* 587–597.

Ashcraft, K. L. (2000). Empowering "professional" relationships: Organizational communication meets feminist practice. *Management Communication Quarterly, 13,* 347–392.

Ashcraft, K. L. (2001). Organized dissonance: Feminist bureaucracy as hybrid form. *Academy of Management Journal, 44,* 1301–1322.

Ashcraft, K. L. (2005). Resistance through consent?: Occupational identity, organizational form, and the maintenance of masculinity among commercial airline pilots. *Management Communication Quarterly, 19,* 67–90.

Ashcraft, K. L. (2007). Appreciating the "work" of discourse: Occupational identity and difference as organizing mechanisms in the case of commercial airline pilots. *Discourse & Communication, 1,* 9–36.

Ashcraft, K. L. (2011). Knowing work through the communication of difference: A revised agenda for difference studies. In D. K. Mumby (Ed.), *Reframing difference in organizational communication studies: Research, pedagogy, practice* (pp. 3–30). Thousand Oaks, CA: Sage.

Ashcraft, K. L., & Allen, B. J. (2003). The racial foundation of organizational communication. *Communication Theory, 13*, 5–38.

Ashcraft, K. L., Kuhn, T., & Cooren, F. (2009). Constitutional amendments: "Materializing" organizational communication. *Academy of Management Annals, 3*, 1–64.

Ashcraft, K. L., & Mumby, D. K. (2004). Organizing a critical communicology of gender and work. *International Journal of the Sociology of Language, 166*, 19–43.

Ashforth, B., & Kreiner, G. (1999). "How can you do it?": Dirty work and the challenge of constructing a positive identity. *Academy of Management Review, 24*, 413–434.

Ashforth, B., Kreiner, G., Clark, M., & Fugate, M. (2007). Normalizing dirty work: Managerial tactics for countering occupational taint. *Academy of Management Review, 50*, 149–174.

Atkinson, M. (2004). Tattooing and civilizing processes: Body modification as self-control. *Canadian Review of Sociology and Anthropology, 41*, 125–146.

Axley, S. (1984). Managerial and organizational communication in terms of the conduit metaphor. *Academy of Management Review, 9*, 428–437.

Bachrach, P., & Baratz, M. (1962). Two faces of power. *American Political Science Review, 56*, 947–952.

Bachrach, P., & Baratz, M. (1963). Decisions and nondecisions: An analytical framework. *American Political Science Review, 57*, 641–651.

Baker, S. D. (2007). Followership: The theoretical foundation of a contemporary construct. *Journal of Leadership and Organizational Studies, 14*, 50–60.

Ball, K. (2005). Organization, surveillance and the body: Towards a politics of resistance. *Organization, 12*, 89–108.

Banta, M. (1993). *Taylored lives: Narrative production in the age of Taylor, Veblen, and Ford*. Chicago: University of Chicago Press.

Bantz, C. R. (1993). *Understanding organizations: Interpreting organizational communication cultures*. Columbia: University of South Carolina Press.

Barber, B. R. (1995). *Jihad vs. McWorld*. New York: Ballantine.

Barber, B. R. (2007). *Con$umed: How markets corrupt children, infantilize adults, and swallow citizens whole*. New York: W. W. Norton.

Barker, J. R. (1993). Tightening the iron cage: Concertive control in self-managing teams. *Administrative Science Quarterly, 38*, 408–437.

Barker, J. R. (1999). *The discipline of teamwork: Participation and concertive control*. Thousand Oaks, CA: Sage.

Barnard, C. (1938). *The functions of the executive*. Cambridge, MA: Harvard University Press.

Barrett, D. (2011). *Leadership communication*. New York: McGraw-Hill Irwin.

Barthes, R. (1972). *Mythologies*. London: Cape.

Bass, B. M. (1985). *Leadership and performance beyond expectations*. New York: Free Press.

Bass, B. M. (1990). *Bass and Stogdill's handbook of leadership: Theory, research, and managerial applications* (3rd ed.). New York: Free Press.

Bass, B. M., & Riggio, R. E. (2006). *Transformational leadership*. Mahwah, NJ: Lawrence Erlbaum.

Bateson, G. (1972). *Steps to an ecology of mind*. New York: Ballantine.

Batt, R., Holman, D., & Holtgrewe, U. (2010). The globalization of service work: Comparative institutional perspectives on call centers. *Industrial and Labor Relations Review, 62*, 453–488.

Bauman, Z. (2000). *Liquid modernity*. Cambridge, UK: Polity Press.

Baxter, J. (2010). *The language of female leadership*. London: Palgrave Macmillan.

Beck, U. (1992). *Risk society: Towards a new modernity*. London: Sage.

Beck, U. (2000). *What is globalization?* (P. Camiller, Trans.). Cambridge, UK: Polity Press.

Bederman, G. (1995). *Manliness and civilization: A cultural history of gender and race in the United States, 1880–1917*. Chicago: University of Chicago Press.

Beede, D., Julian, T., Langdon, D., McKittrick, G., Kahn, B., & Doms, M. (2011, August). *Women in STEM: A gender gap to innovation* (ESA Issue Brief #04-11). Washington, DC: U.S. Department of Commerce.

Bell, E. L., & Forbes, L. C. (1994). Office folklore in the academic paperwork empire: The interstitial space of gendered (con)texts. *Text and Performance Quarterly, 14,* 181–196.

Bennis, W. (1995). Thoughts on "The essentials of leadership." In P. Graham (Ed.), *Mary Parker Follett—prophet of management: A celebration of writings from the 1920s* (pp. 177–181). Boston: Harvard Business School Press.

Bergquist, W. (1992). *The postmodern organization: Mastering the art of irreversible change.* San Francisco: Jossey-Bass.

Bhabha, H. (1994). *The location of culture.* London: Routledge.

Bird, S. R. (1996). Welcome to the men's club: Homosociality and the maintenance of hegemonic masculinity. *Gender & Society, 10,* 120–132.

Black man given nation's worst job. (2008, November 5). *The Onion.* Retrieved from http://www.theonion.com/articles/black-man-given-nations-worst-job,6439/

Blake, R. R., & Mouton, J. S. (1964). *The managerial grid: Key orientations for achieving production through people.* Houston, TX: Gulf.

Boden, D. (1994). *The business of talk.* Cambridge, UK: Polity Press.

Bogle, K. A. (2008). *Hooking up: Sex, dating, and relationships on campus.* New York: New York University Press.

Boje, D. (1991). The storytelling organization: A study of story performance in an office-supply firm. *Administrative Science Quarterly, 36,* 106–126.

Boje, D. (1995). Stories of the storytelling organization: A postmodern analysis of Disney as "Tamara-Land." *Academy of Management Journal, 38,* 997–1035.

Boje, D., & Rosile, G. A. (1994). Diversities, differences, and authors' voices. *Journal of Organizational Change Management, 7*(6), 8–17.

Boltanski, L., & Chiapello, E. (2005). *The new spirit of capitalism* (G. Elliott, Trans.). London: Verso.

Bolton, S. C. (2005). *Emotion management in the workplace.* Houndmills, Basingstoke: Palgrave Macmillan.

Borch, C. (2011). *Niklas Luhmann.* New York: Routledge.

Bormann, E. G. (1983). Symbolic convergence: Organizational communication and culture. In L. L. Putnam & M. Pacanowsky (Eds.), *Communication and organizations: An interpretive approach* (pp. 100–115). Beverly Hills, CA: Sage.

Boudens, C. (2005). The story of work: A narrative analysis of workplace emotion. *Organization Studies, 26,* 1285–1306.

Boulding, K. (1985). *The world as a total system.* London: Sage.

Bourdieu, P. (1977). *Outline of a theory of practice* (R. Nice, Trans.). Cambridge, UK: Cambridge University Press.

Bramel, D., & Friend, R. (1981). Hawthorne, the myth of the docile worker, and class bias in psychology. *American Psychologist, 36,* 867–878.

Braverman, H. (1974). *Labor and monopoly capital: The degradation of work in the twentieth century.* New York: Monthly Review Press.

Brewis, J., & Linstead, S. (2000). *Sex, work and sex at work: Eroticizing the organization.* London: Routledge.

Brinkman, B., Garcia, K., & Rickard, K. (2011). "What I wanted to do was . . ." Discrepancies between college women's desired and reported responses to gender prejudice. *Sex Roles, 65,* 344–355.

Brinkman, B., & Rickard, K. (2009). College students' descriptions of everyday gender prejudice. *Sex Roles, 61,* 461–475.

Brooks, D. (2001, April). The organization kid. *Atlantic Monthly,* 40–54.

Brophy, E. (2011). Language put to work: Cognitive capitalism, call center labor, and worker inquiry. *Journal of Communication Inquiry, 35,* 410–416.

Brown, A. (1998). Narrative, politics and legitimacy in an IT implementation. *Journal of Management Studies, 35,* 35–58.

Brown, A. (2006). A narrative approach to collective identities. *Journal of Management Studies, 43,* 731–753.

Brown, M. H. (1990). Defining stories in organizations: Characteristics and functions. In J. A. Anderson (Ed.), *Communication yearbook* (Vol. 13, pp. 162–190). Newbury Park, CA: Sage.

Browning, L. D. (1992). Lists and stories as organizational communication. *Communication Theory, 2,* 281–302.

Bruckmüller, S., & Branscombe, N. R. (2010). The glass cliff: When and why women are selected as leaders in crisis contexts. *British Journal of Social Psychology, 49,* 433–451.

Bruckmüller, S., & Branscombe, N. R. (2011). How women end up on the "glass cliff." *Harvard Business Review, 89*(1/2), 26.

Brummans, B. (2007). Death by document: Tracing the agency of a text. *Qualitative Inquiry, 17*, 711–727.

Bruner, J. (1991). The narrative construction of reality. *Critical Inquiry, 18*, 1–21.

Bryman, A. (1996). Leadership in organizations. In S. Clegg, C. Hardy, & W. R. Nord (Eds.), *Handbook of organization studies* (pp. 276–292). London: Sage.

Burawoy, M. (1979). *Manufacturing consent: Changes in the labor process under monopoly capitalism.* Chicago: University of Chicago Press.

Burns, J. M. (1978). *Leadership.* New York: Harper & Row.

Burns, J. M., & Avolio, B. J. (2004). Transformational and transactional leadership. In G. R. Goethals, G. J. Sorenson, & J. M. Burns (Eds.), *Encyclopedia of leadership* (pp. 1558–1566). Thousand Oaks, CA: Sage.

Burrell, G. (1984). Sex and organizational analysis. *Organization Studies, 5*, 97–118.

Burrell, G. (1988). Modernism, postmodernism and organizational analysis 2: The contribution of Michel Foucault. *Organization Studies, 9*, 221–235.

Burrell, G. (1992). The organization of pleasure. In M. Alvesson & H. Willmott (Eds.), *Critical management studies* (pp. 66–89). Newbury Park, CA: Sage.

Burrell, G., & Morgan, G. (1979). *Sociological paradigms and organisational analysis.* London: Heinemann.

Buzzanell, P. M. (1994). Gaining a voice: Feminist organizational communication theorizing. *Management Communication Quarterly, 7*, 339–383.

Calás, M. B., & Smircich, L. (1991). Voicing seduction to silence leadership. *Organization Studies, 12*, 567–602.

Calás, M. B., & Smircich, L. (1996). From "the woman's point of view": Feminist approches to organization studies. In S. R. Clegg, C. Hardy, & W. R. Nord (Eds.), *Handbook of organization studies* (pp. 218–257). Thousand Oaks, CA: Sage.

Carey, A. (1967). The Hawthorne studies: A radical criticism. *American Sociological Review, 32*, 403–416.

Carlone, D. (2006). The ambiguous nature of a management guru lecture: Providing answers while deepening uncertainty. *Journal of Business Communication, 43*, 89–112.

Carlone, D., & Larson, G. (2006). Locating possibilities for control and resistance in a self-help program. *Western Journal of Communication, 70*, 270–291.

Carlone, D., & Taylor, B. (1998). Organizational communication and cultural studies. *Communication Theory, 8*, 337–367.

Carlyle, T. (2001). *On heroes, hero worship and the heroic in history.* London: Electric Books. (Original work published 1841)

Carter, B. K. (1992). Mary Parker Follett and the self-defining community. *Women and Politics, 12*(2), 59–89.

Carty, S. S. (2008, March 26). Tata motors to buy Jaguar, Land Rover, for $2.3B. *USA Today.* Retrieved from http://www.usatoday.com/money/autos/2008-03-25-ford-sells-jaguar-land-rover-tata_N.htm

Casey, C. (1995). *Work, self and society: After industrialism.* London: Sage.

Chafkin, M. (2009, May 1). The Zappos way of managing. *Inc.* Retrieved from http://www.inc.com/magazine/20090501/the-zappos-way-of-managing.html

Chaleff, I. (1995). *The courageous follower: Standing up to and for our leaders.* San Francisco: Berrett-Koehler.

Chaudhuri, S. (2008a, November 6). Most influential women in web 2.0. *Fast Company.* Retrieved from http://www.fastcompany.com/articles/2008/11/influential-women-web.html

Chaudhuri, S. (2008b, November 11). Sexist, sexist and more sexist: Digg responds to Fast Company's Women in Web 2.0. *Fast Company.* Retrieved from http://www.fastcompany.com/blog/saabira-chaudhuri/itinerant-mind/sexist-stupid-and-downright-offensive-digg-community-responds-

Cheever, S. (2003). The nanny dilemma. In B. Ehrenreich & A. Hochschild (Eds.), *Global woman* (pp. 31–38). New York: Metropolitan Books.

Cheney, G. (1991). *Rhetoric in an organizational society: Managing multiple identities.* Columbia: University of South Carolina Press.

Cheney, G. (1995). Democracy in the workplace: Theory and practice from the perspective of communication. *Journal of Applied Communication Research, 23*, 167–200.

Cheney, G. (1999). *Values at work: Employee participation meets market pressure at Mondragon.* Ithaca, NY: Cornell University Press.

Cheney, G., & Tompkins, P. K. (1987). Coming to terms with organizational identification and commitment. *Central States Speech Journal, 38,* 1–15.

Cheney, G., Zorn, T., Planalp, S., & Lair, D. (2008). Meaningful work and personal/social well-being: Organizational communication engages the meanings of work. In C. Beck (Ed.), *Communication yearbook 32* (pp. 137–185). Thousand Oaks, CA: Sage.

Chin, J. L. (Ed.). (2007). *Women and leadership: Transforming visions and diverse voices.* Malden, MA: Blackwell.

Christensen, L., Morsing, M., & Cheney, G. (2008). *Corporate communication: Convention, complexity, critique.* London: Sage.

Ciulla, J. B. (2000). *The working life: The promise and betrayal of modern work.* New York: Times Books.

Clair, R. P. (1993a). The bureaucratization, commodification, and privatization of sexual harassment through institutional discourse. *Management Communication Quarterly, 7,* 123–157.

Clair, R. P. (1993b). The use of framing devices to sequester organizational narratives: Hegemony and harassment. *Communication Monographs, 60,* 113–136.

Clegg, S. (1989). Radical revisions: Power, discipline and organizations. *Organization Studies, 10,* 97–115.

Clegg, S. (1990). *Modern organizations: Organizations in a postmodern world.* Newbury Park, CA: Sage.

Clegg, S. (1994). Weber and Foucault: Social theory for the study of organizations. *Organization, 1,* 149–178.

Clegg, S., Courpasson, D., & Phillips, N. (2006). *Power and organizations.* Thousand Oaks, CA: Sage.

Cochrane, A., & Pain, K. (2007). A globalizing society. In D. Held (Ed.), *A globalizing world? Culture, economics, politics* (2nd ed., pp. 5–46). London: Routledge/Open University.

Cockburn, C. (1984). *Brothers.* London: Verso.

Coget, J.-F. (2011). Techno-phobe vs. techno-enthusiast: Does the internet help or hinder the balance between work and home life? *Academy of Management Perspectives, 25*(1), 95–96.

Cohen, S. G., & Bailey, D. E. (1997). What makes teams work: Group effectiveness research from the shopfloor to the executive suite. *Journal of Management, 23,* 239–290.

Collinson, D. (1988). "Engineering humor": Masculinity, joking and conflict in shop-floor relations. *Organization Studies, 9,* 181–199.

Collinson, D. (1992). *Managing the shop floor: Subjectivity, masculinity, and workplace culture.* New York: De Gruyter.

Collinson, D. (2003). Identities and insecurities: Selves at work. *Organization, 10,* 527–547.

Collinson, D. (2005). Dialectics of leadership. *Human Relations, 58,* 1419–1442.

Collinson, D. (2011). Critical leadership studies. In A. Bryman, K. Grint, D. Collinson, B. Jackson, & M. Uhl-Bien (Eds.), *The SAGE handbook of leadership* (pp. 181–194). Los Angeles: Sage.

Connell, R. W. (1993). The big picture: Masculinities in recent world history. *Theory and Society, 22,* 597–623.

Connell, R. W. (1995). *Masculinities.* Berkeley: University of California Press.

Conrad, C. (1985). *Strategic organizational communication: Cultures, situations, and adaptation.* New York: Holt, Rinehart, & Winston.

Cook, R. (2001, April 19). Robin Cook's chicken tikka masala speech. *The Guardian.* Retrieved from http://www.guardian.co.uk/world/2001/apr/19/race.britishidentity

Cooren, F. (2000). *The organizing property of communication.* Amsterdam, Netherlands: John Benjamins.

Covey, S. R. (1989). *The seven habits of highly effective people: Restoring the character ethic.* New York: Simon & Schuster.

Crawford, M. B. (2009a, May 21). The case for working with your hands. *New York Times.* Retrieved from http://www.nytimes.com/2009/05/24/magazine/24labor-t.html

Crawford, M. B. (2009b). *Shop class as soulcraft: An inquiry into the value of work.* New York: Penguin Press.

Crenshaw, C. (1997). Resisting whiteness' rhetorical silence. *Western Journal of Communication, 61,* 253–278.

Crozier, M. (1964). *The bureaucratic phenomenon.* London: Tavistock.

Culler, J. (1976). *Ferdinand de Saussure.* London: Fontana.

Czarniawska, B. (1997). *Narrating the organization.* Chicago, IL: University of Chicago Press.

Dahl, R. (1957). The concept of power. *Behavioral Science, 2,* 201–215.

Dahl, R. (1958). A critique of the ruling elite model. *American Political Science Review, 52,* 463–469.

Dahl, R. (1961). *Who governs? Democracy and power in an American city.* New Haven, CT: Yale University Press.

Daisey, M. (2011, October 6). Against nostalgia. *New York Times.* Retrieved from http://www.nytimes.com/2011/10/06/opinion/jobs-looked-to-the-future.html?emc = eta1

De Botton, A. (2009). *The pleasures and sorrows of work.* New York: Vintage Books.

Deal, T. E., & Kennedy, A. A. (1982). *Corporate cultures: The rites and rituals of corporate life.* Reading, MA: Addison-Wesley.

Deetz, S. (1973a). An understanding of science and a hermeneutic science of understanding. *Journal of Communication, 23,* 139–159.

Deetz, S. (1973b). Words without things: Toward a social phenomenology of language. *The Quarterly Journal of Speech, 59,* 40–51.

Deetz, S. (1992a). *Democracy in an age of corporate colonization: Developments in communication and the politics of everyday life.* Albany: State University of New York Press.

Deetz, S. (1992b). Disciplinary power in the modern corporation. In M. Alvesson & H. Willmott (Eds.), *Critical management studies* (pp. 21–45). Newbury Park, CA: Sage.

Deetz, S. (1994a). The micropolitics of identity formation in the workplace: The case of a knowledge intensive firm. *Human Studies, 17,* 23–44.

Deetz, S. (1994b). The new politics of the workplace: Ideology and other unobtrusive controls. In H. W. Simons & M. Billig (Eds.), *After postmodernism: Reconstructing ideology critique* (pp. 172–199). Thousand Oaks, CA: Sage.

Deetz, S. (1994c). Representational practices and the political analysis of corporations: Building a communication perspective in organizational studies. In B. Kovacic (Ed.), *New approaches to organizational communication* (pp. 211–244). Albany: State University of New York Press.

Deetz, S. (1995). *Transforming communication, transforming business: Building responsive and responsible workplaces.* Cresskill, NJ: Hampton Press.

Deetz, S. (2001). Conceptual foundations. In F. M. Jablin & L. L. Putnam (Eds.), *The new handbook of organizational communication: Advances in theory, research, and methods* (pp. 3–46). Thousand Oaks, CA: Sage.

Deetz, S., & Brown, D. (2004). Conceptualising involvement, participation and workplace decision processes: A communication theory perspective. In D. Tourish & O. Hargie (Eds.), *Key issues in organizational communication* (pp. 172–187). London: Routledge.

Deetz, S., & Mumby, D. K. (1985). Metaphors, information, and power. In B. Ruben (Ed.), *Information and behavior* (Vol. 1, pp. 369–386). New Brunswick, NJ: Transaction.

Deetz, S., & Mumby, D. K. (1990). Power, discourse, and the workplace: Reclaiming the critical tradition. In J. Anderson (Ed.), *Communication yearbook* (Vol. 13, pp. 18–47). Newbury Park, CA: Sage.

Dempsey, S. E. (2009). NGOs, communicative labor, and the work of grassroots representation. *Communication and Critical/Cultural Studies, 6,* 328–345.

Derrida, J. (1976). *Of grammatology* (G. Spivak, Trans.). Baltimore, MD: Johns Hopkins University Press.

DeSantis, A. D. (2003). A couple of white guys sitting around talking: The collective rationalization of cigar smokers. *Journal of Contemporary Ethnography, 32,* 432–466.

DeSantis, A. D. (2007). *Inside Greek U.: Fraternities, sororities, and the pursuit of pleasure, power, and prestige.* Lexington: University Press of Kentucky.

Dixon, T. (1996). Mary Parker Follett and community. *Australian Journal of Communication, 23*(3), 68–83.

Doorewaard, H., & Brouns, B. (2003). Hegemonic power processes in team-based work. *Applied Psychology: An International Review, 52,* 106–119.

Drucker, P. F. (1995). Mary Parker Follett: Prophet of management. In P. Graham (Ed.), *Mary Parker Follett—prophet of management: A celebration of writings from the 1920s* (pp. 1–10). Boston: Harvard Business School Press.

Du Gay, P. (2000). *In praise of bureaucracy: Weber, organization, ethics.* Thousand Oaks, CA: Sage.

Du Gay, P., & Salaman, G. (1992). The cult[ure] of the consumer. *Journal of Management Studies, 29,* 615–633.

Dubrin, J. (2000). *Leadership.* London: Houghton Mifflin.

Duneier, M. (1999). *Sidewalk*. New York: Farrar, Straus & Giroux.

Eagly, A. H., & Johannesen-Schmidt, M. C. (2001). The leadership styles of women and men. *Journal of Social Issues, 57*, 781–797.

Eco, U. (1979). Can television teach? *Screen Education, 31*, 1–20.

Edwards, H., & Day, D. (2005). *Creating passion brands: Getting to the heart of branding*. London: Kogan Page.

Edwards, R. (1979). *Contested terrain: The transformation of the workplace in the twentieth century*. New York: Basic Books.

Ehrenreich, B., & Hochschild, A. (2003). *Global woman: Nannies, maids, and sex workers in the new economy*. New York: Metropolitan Books.

Eisenberg, E. (1984). Ambiguity as strategy in organizational communication. *Communication Monographs, 51*, 227–242.

El-Ojeili, C., & Hayden, P. (2006). *Critical theories of globalization*. Basingstoke, UK: Palgrave Macmillan.

Epstein, E. J. (1981). The marketing of diamonds: How a successful cartel turned a worthless rock into a priceless gem. *Harper's*. Retrieved from http://www.stayfreemagazine.org/ml/readings/diamonds.pdf

Epstein, E. J. (1982). *The rise and fall of diamonds: The shattering of a brilliant illusion*. New York: Simon & Schuster.

Eugenides, J. (2002). *Middlesex*. New York: Farrar, Straus & Giroux.

Ezzamel, M., & Willmott, H. (1998). Accounting for teamwork: A critical study of group-based systems of organizational control. *Administrative Science Quarterly, 43*, 358–396.

Ezzamel, M., Willmott, H., & Worthington, F. (2001). Power, control and resistance in "the factory that time forgot." *Journal of Management Studies, 38*, 1053–1078.

Fairhurst, G. (2007). *Discursive leadership: In conversation with leadership psychology*. San Francisco: Jossey-Bass.

Fairhurst, G., & Grant, D. (2010). The social construction of leadership: A sailing guide. *Management Communication Quarterly, 24*, 171–210.

Fairhurst, G., & Sarr, R. A. (1996). *The art of framing: Managing the language of leadership*. San Francisco: Jossey-Bass.

Fairhurst, G., & Zoller, H. M. (2008). Resistance, dissent and leadership in practice. In S. P. Banks (Ed.), *Dissent and the failure of leadership* (pp. 135–148). Cheltenham, UK: Edward Elgar.

Faludi, S. (1991). *Backlash*. New York: Anchor Books.

Ferguson, K. (1984). *The feminist case against bureaucracy*. Philadelphia: Temple University Press.

Fiedler, F. E. (1967). *A theory of leadership effectiveness*. New York: McGraw-Hill.

Fiedler, F. E. (1997). Situational control and a dynamic theory of leadership. In K. Grint (Ed.), *Leadership: Classical, contemporary, and critical approaches* (pp. 126–154). Oxford, UK: Oxford University Press.

Finder, J. (1987, February 22). A male secretary. *New York Times Magazine*, 68.

Fineman, S. (2000). *Emotion in organizations* (2nd ed.). London: Sage.

Fisher, W. R. (1985). The narrative paradigm: An elaboration. *Communication Monographs, 52*, 347–367.

Fiske, J. (1989). Shopping for pleasure: Malls, power, and resistance. In J. Schor & D. B. Holt (Eds.), *The consumer society reader*. New York: New Press.

Flax, J. (1990). *Thinking fragments: Psychoanalysis, feminism, and postmodernism in the contemporary west*. Berkeley: University of California Press.

Fleming, P. (2007). Sexuality, power and resistance in the workplace. *Organization Studies, 28*, 239–256.

Fleming, P. (2009). *Authenticity and the cultural politics of work: New forms of informal control*. New York: Oxford University Press.

Fleming, P., & Spicer, A. (2003). Working at a cynical distance: Implications for power, subjectivity, and resistance. *Organization, 10*, 157–179.

Fleming, P., & Spicer, A. (2007). *Contesting the corporation*. Cambridge, UK: Cambridge University Press.

Fleming, P., & Spicer, A. (2009). Beyond power and resistance: New approaches to organizational politics. *Management Communication Quarterly, 21*, 301–309.

Fleming, R. (2010). Another Foxconn employee dies after 34 hour shift. *Digital Trends*. Retrieved from http://www.digitaltrends.com/international/another-foxconn-employee-dies-after-34-hour-shift/

Fletcher, J. K. (1998). Relational practice: A feminist reconstruction of work. *Journal of Management Inquiry, 7*, 163–186.

Fletcher, J. K. (1999). *Disappearing acts: Gender, power, and relational practice at work*. Cambridge: MIT Press.

Fletcher, J. K. (2004). The paradox of postheroic leadership: An essay on gender, power, and transformational change. *Leadership Quarterly, 15,* 647–661.

Florida, R. (2003). *The rise of the creative class: And how it's transforming work, leisure, community, and everyday life.* New York: Basic Books.

Follett, M. P. (1924). *Creative experience.* New York: Longmans, Green.

Follett, M. P. (1995a). Constructive conflict. In P. Graham (Ed.), *Mary Parker Follett—prophet of management: A celebration from the 1920s* (pp. 67–95). Boston: Harvard Business School Press.

Follett, M. P. (1995b). Power. In P. Graham (Ed.), *Mary Parker Follett—prophet of management: A celebration of writings from the 1920s* (pp. 97–119). Boston: Harvard Business School Press.

Follett, M. P. (1995c). Relating: The circular response. In P. Graham (Ed.), *Mary Parker Follett—prophet of management: A celebration of writings from the 1920s* (pp. 35–65). Boston: Harvard Business School Press.

Follett, M. P. (1998). *The new state.* University Park: Pennsylvania State University Press. (Original work published 1918)

Foucault, M. (1972). *The archaeology of knowledge and the discourse on language* (A. M. S. Smith, Trans.). New York: Pantheon.

Foucault, M. (1973). *The order of things: An archaeology of the human sciences.* New York: Vintage.

Foucault, M. (1979). *Discipline and punish: The birth of the prison* (A. Sheridan, Trans.). New York: Vintage.

Foucault, M. (1980a). *The history of sexuality: An introduction* (R. Hurley, Trans., Vol. 1). New York: Vintage.

Foucault, M. (1980b). *Power/knowledge: Selected interviews and other writings 1972–1977* (C. Gordon, L. Marshall, J. Mepham, & K. Soper, Trans.). New York: Pantheon.

Foucault, M. (1988). *Madness and civilization: A history of insanity in the age of reason* (R. Howard, Trans.). New York: Vintage.

Francke, R. H., & Kaul, J. D. (1978). The Hawthorne experiments: First statistical interpretation. *American Sociological Review, 43,* 623–643.

Frank, N. (2010). What does the empirical research say about the impact of openly gay service on the military? A research memo. Santa Barbara, CA: Palm Center.

Frankenberg, R. (1993). *White women, race matters: The social construction of whiteness.* Minneapolis: University of Minnesota Press.

Freiberg, K., & Freiberg, J. (1996). *Nuts! Southwest Airlines' crazy recipe for business and personal success.* New York: Broadway Books.

French, J. R. P., & Raven, B. (1959). The bases of social power. In D. Cartwright (Ed.), *Studies in social power* (pp. 150–167). Oxford, UK: University of Michigan Press.

Friedan, B. (1963). *The feminine mystique.* New York: Dell.

Friedman, M. (1970, February). The social responsibility of business is to increase its profits. *New York Times Magazine.*

Friedman, M. (1982). *Capitalism and freedom.* Chicago: University of Chicago Press.

Friedman, T. (2005, April 3). It's a flat world, after all. *New York Times.* Retrieved from http://www. nytimes. com/2005/04/03/magazine/ 03DOMINANCE. html?pagewanted = 1%27s a flat world aftre all &sq = It&st = cse&scp = 1&adxnnlx = 1317903 299-jlh/RxVLC6VhgT uRxvuw

Frost, P. J., Moore, L. F., Louis, M. R., Lundberg, C. C., & Martin, J. (Eds.). (1985). *Organizational culture.* Beverly Hills, CA: Sage.

Fry, L. W. (1976). The maligned F. W. Taylor: A reply to his many critics. *Academy of Management Review, 1*(3), 124–129.

Gadamer, H.-G. (1989). *Truth and method* (J. W. D. G. Marshall, Trans. 2nd ed.). New York: Continuum.

Gallagher, D. (2010, April 3). Live blogging the iPad's big day. http://bits.blogs.nytimes. com/2010/04/03/live-blogging-the-ipads-big-day/?scp = 1&sq = apple ipad release&st = cse

Ganesh, S., Zoller, H. M., & Cheney, G. (2005). Transforming resistance, broadening our boundaries: Critical organizational communication meets globalization from below. *Communication Monographs, 72,* 169–191.

Geertz, C. (1973). *The interpretation of cultures.* New York: Basic Books.

Geertz, C. (1983). *Local knowledge: Further essays in interpretive anthropology.* New York: Basic Books.

Gemmill, G., & Oakley, J. (1992). Leadership: An alienating social myth? *Human Relations, 45,* 113–129.

Giddens, A. (1979). *Central problems in social theory: Action, structure and contradiction in social analysis*. Berkeley: University of California Press.

Giddens, A. (1991). *Modernity and self-identity: Self and society in the late modern age*. Stanford, CA: Stanford University Press.

Giddens, A. (2001). *Runaway world: How globalisation is reshaping our lives* (2nd ed.). London: Profile Books.

Gilbreth, F. B. J., & Carey, E. G. (1948). *Cheaper by the dozen*. New York: Thomas Y. Crowell.

Gilbreth, L. M. (1927). *The home-maker and her job*. New York: D. Appleton.

Gill, R., & Pratt, A. (2008). In the social factory? Immaterial labour, precariousness and cultural work. *Theory, Culture & Society, 25*(7–8), 1–30.

Giuffre, P., Dellinger, K., & Williams, C. L. (2008). "No retribution for being gay?" Inequality in gay-friendly workplaces. *Sociological Spectrum, 28*, 254–277.

Gledhill, C. (1997). Genre and gender: The case of soap opera. In S. Hall (Ed.), *Representation: Cultural representations and signifying practices* (pp. 337–384). London: Sage/Open University Press.

Gobé, M. (2001). *Emotional branding: The new paradigm for connecting brands to people*. New York: Allworth Press.

Gobé, M. (2002). *Citizen brand: 10 commandments for transforming brands in a consumer democracy*. New York: Allworth Press.

Gobé, M. (2007). *Brandjam: Humanizing brands through emotional design*. New York: Allworth Press.

Golden, D. (2006). *The price of admission: How America's ruling class buys its way into élite colleges—and who gets left outside the gates*. New York: Crown.

Golden, T. D., & Fromen, A. (2011). Does it matter where your manager works? Comparing managerial work mode (traditional, telework, virtual) across subordinate work experiences and outcomes. *Human Relations, 64*, 1451–1475.

Gossett, L. (2003). Kept at arm's length: Questioning the organizational desirability of member identification. *Communication Monographs, 69*, 385–404.

Gossett, L., & Kilker, J. (2006). My job sucks: Examining counterinstitutional web sites as locations for organizational member voice, dissent, and resistance. *Management Communication Quarterly, 20*, 63–90.

Graham, L. (1993). Inside a Japanese transplant: A critical perspective. *Work and Occupations, 20*, 147–173.

Graham, L. D. (1997). Beyond manipulation: Lillian Gilbreth's industrial psychology and the governmentality of women consumers. *Sociological Quarterly, 38*, 539–565.

Graham, L. D. (1999). Domesticating efficiency: Lillian Gilbreth's scientific management of homemakers, 1924–1930. *Signs: Journal of Women in Culture and Society, 24*, 633–675.

Graham, P. (Ed.). (1995). *Mary Parker Follett—prophet of management: A celebration of writings from the 1920s*. Boston: Harvard Business School Press.

Gramsci, A. (1971). *Selections from the prison notebooks* (Q. Hoare & G. N. Smith, Trans.). New York: International.

Grant, D., & Oswick, C. (Eds.). (1996). *Metaphor and organizations*. London: Sage.

Gregg, M. (2011). *Work's intimacy*. Cambridge, UK: Polity Press.

Grey, C. (1994). Career as a project of the self and labour process discipline. *Sociology, 28*, 479–497.

Grimes, D. S. (2001). Putting our own house in order: Whiteness, change and organization studies. *Journal of Organizational Change Management, 14*, 132–149.

Grimes, D. S. (2002). Challenging the status quo? Whiteness in the diversity management literature. *Management Communication Quarterly, 15*, 381–409.

Grint, K. (2010). *Leadership: A very short introduction*. Oxford, UK: Oxford University Press.

Hall, S. (1985). Signification, representation, ideology: Althusser and the poststructuralist debates. *Critical Studies in Mass Communication, 2*, 91–114.

Hall, S. (1991). Brave new world. *Socialist Review, 21*(1), 57–64.

Hall, S. (Ed.). (1997a). *Representation: Cultural representations and signifying practices*. London: Sage/Open University Press.

Hall, S. (1997b). The work of representation. In S. Hall (Ed.), *Representation: Cultural representations and signifying practices* (pp. 13–64). London: Sage/Open University Press.

Hamilton, J., Baker, S., & Vlasic, B. (1996, April 29). The new workplace. *Businessweek*, 109–117.

Hanlon, P. (2006). *Primal branding: Create zealots for your brand, your company, and your future*. New York: Free Press.

Harrison, T. (1994). Communication and interdependence in democratic organizations. In S. Deetz (Ed.), *Communication yearbook* (pp. 247–274). Newbury Park, CA: Sage.

Harvey, D. (1989). *The condition of postmodernity: An enquiry into the origins of cultural change.* Oxford, UK: Basil Blackwell.

Harvey, D. (1991). Flexibility: Threat or opportunity. *Socialist Review, 21*(1), 65–77.

Harvey, D. (1995). Globalization in question. *Rethinking Marxism, 8*(4), 1–17.

Haslam, S. A., & Ryan, M. K. (2008). The road to the glass cliff: Differences in the perceived suitability of men and women for leadership positions in succeeding and failing organizations. *Leadership Quarterly, 19*, 530–546.

Hawes, L. (1977). Toward a hermeneutic phenomenology of communication. *Communication Quarterly, 25*(3), 30–41.

Hearn, J. (1996). Deconstructing the dominant: Making the one(s) the other(s). *Organization, 3*, 611–626.

Hearn, J., Sheppard, D., Tancred-Sheriff, P., & Burrell, G. (Eds.). (1989). *The sexuality of organization.* London: Sage.

Helmer, J. (1993). Storytelling in the creation and maintenance of organizational tension and stratification. *Southern Communication Journal, 59*, 34–44.

Hill Collins, P. (1991). *Black feminist thought: Knowledge, consciousness and the politics of empowerment.* New York: Routledge.

Ho, K. (2009). *Liquidated: An ethnography of Wall Street.* Durham, NC: Duke University Press.

Hochschild, A. (1983). *The managed heart: The commercialization of human feeling.* Berkeley: University of California Press.

Hochschild, A. (1997). *The time bind: When work becomes home and home becomes work.* New York: Metropolitan Books.

Holmer Nadesan, M. (1997). Constructing paper dolls: The discourse of personality testing in organizational practice. *Communication Theory, 7*, 189–218.

Holmer Nadesan, M., & Trethewey, A. (2000). Performing the enterprising subject: Gendered strategies for success (?). *Text and Peformance Quarterly, 20*, 223–250.

Holmes, J. (2006). *Gendered talk at work : Constructing gender identity through workplace discourse.* Malden, MA: Blackwell.

hooks, b. (1981). *Ain't I a woman: Black women and feminism.* Boston: South End Press.

hooks, b. (2000). *Feminism is for everybody: Passionate politics.* Boston: South End Press.

Horkheimer, M., & Adorno, T. (1988). *Dialectic of enlightenment* (J. Cumming, Trans.). New York: Continuum.

Howell, J. M., & Shamir, B. (2005). The role of followers in the charismatic leadership process: Relationships and their consequences. *Academy of Management Review, 30*, 96–112.

Humphreys, M., & Brown, A. D. (2002). Narratives of organizational identity and identification: A case study of hegemony and resistance. *Organization Studies, 23*, 421–447.

Hunter, F. (1953). *Community power structure.* Chapel Hill: University of North Carolina Press.

Jablin, F. (2001). Organizational entry, assimilation, and exit. In F. Jablin & L. L. Putnam (Eds.), *The new handbook of organizational communication: Advances in theory, research, and methods* (pp. 732–818). Thousand Oaks, CA: Sage.

Jackson, B., & Parry, K. W. (2011). *A very short, fairly interesting and reasonably cheap book about studying leadership.* London: Sage.

Jacques, R. (1996). *Manufacturing the employee: Management knowledge from the 19th to 21st centuries.* London: Sage.

Jameson, F. (1984). Foreword. In J.-F. Lyotard, *The postmodern condition* (pp. vii–xi). Minneapolis: University of Minnesota Press.

Janis, I. L. (1983). *Groupthink: Psychological studies of policy decisions and fiascoes.* Boston: Houghton Mifflin.

Jay, M. (1973). *The dialectical imagination.* Boston: Little, Brown.

Jensen, J. V. (1996). Ethical tension points in whistleblowing. In J. A. Jaksa & M. S. Pritchard (Eds.), *Responsible communication: Ethical issues in business, industry, and the professions* (pp. 41–51). Cresskill, NJ: Hampton Press.

Jermier, J. M., Knights, D., & Nord, W. R. (Eds.). (1994). *Resistance and power in organizations.* London: Routledge.

Kalberg, S. (1980). Max Weber's types of rationality: Cornerstones for the analysis of rationalization processes in history. *American Journal of Sociology, 85*, 1145–1179.

Kalleberg, A. L. (2009). Precarious work, insecure workers: Employment relations in transition. *American Sociological Review, 74*, 1–22.

Kang, M. (2010). *The managed hand: Race, gender and the body in beauty service work*. Berkeley: University of California Press.

Kanter, R. M. (1977). *Men and women of the corporation*. New York: Basic Books.

Kanter, R. M. (1995). Preface. In P. Graham (Ed.), *Mary Parker Follett—prophet of management: A celebration of writings from the 1920s* (pp. xiii–xix). Boston: Harvard Business School Press.

Kassing, J. W. (2011). *Dissent in organizations*. Cambridge, UK: Polity Press.

Katz, D., & Kahn, R. L. (1966). *The social psychology of organizations*. New York: Wiley.

Kelley, R. E. (1988). In praise of followers. *Harvard Business Review, 66*(6), 142–148.

Kelley, R. E., & Bacon, F. (2004). Followership. In G. R. Goethals, G. J. Sorenson, & J. M. Burns (Eds.), *Encyclopedia of leadership* (pp. 504–513). Thousand Oaks, CA: Sage.

Kellner, D. (1989). *Critical theory, Marxism, and modernity*. Baltimore, MD: Johns Hopkins University Press.

Kersten, A. (1991). *Ethics and values in the organization of the future: A critical perspective*. Paper presented at the annual meeting of the International Communication Association, Chicago, IL.

Keyton, J. (2011). *Communication and organizational culture: A key to understanding work experiences* (2nd ed.). Thousand Oaks, CA: Sage.

King, R. T., Jr. (1998, May 20). Jeans therapy: Levi's factory workers are assigned to teams, and morale takes a hit. *Wall Street Journal*, pp. A1, A6.

Kirby, E., & Harter, L. (2002). Speaking the language of the bottom-line: The metaphor of "Managing Diversity." *Journal of Business Communication, 40*(1), 28–49.

Kirby, E., & Krone, K. (2002). "The policy exists but you can't really use it": Communication and the structuration of work–family policies. *Journal of Applied Communication Research, 30*, 50–77.

Klein, N. (2001). *No logo*. London: Flamingo Press.

Klein, N. (2005). Culture jamming. In L. Amoore (Ed.), *The global resistance reader* (pp. 437–444). London: Routledge.

Klein, N. (2007). *The shock doctrine: The rise of disaster capitalism*. New York: Metropolitan Books/ Henry Holt.

Knights, D. (1990). Subjectivity, power and the labor process. In D. Knights & H. Willmott (Eds.), *Labour process theory* (pp. 297–335). London: MacMillan.

Knights, D., & McCabe, D. (2000a). 'Ain't misbehavin'? Opportunities for resistance under new forms of "quality" management. *Sociology, 34*, 412–436.

Knights, D., & McCabe, D. (2000b). Bewitched, bothered and bewildered: The meaning and experience of teamworking for employees in an automobile company. *Human Relations, 53*, 1481–1517.

Knights, D., & Willmott, H. (Eds.). (1999). *Management lives: Power and identity in work organizations*. London: Sage.

Koch, S., & Deetz, S. (1981). Metaphor analysis of social reality in organizations. *Journal of Applied Communication Research, 9*(1), 1–15.

Kolb, D. M., Jensen, L., & Shannon, V. L. (1996). She said it all before, or what did we miss about Ms. Follett in the library. *Organization, 3*, 153–160.

Kondo, D. K. (1990). *Crafting selves: Power, gender, and discourses of identity in a Japanese workplace*. Chicago: University of Chicago Press.

Krames, J. A. (2002). *The Jack Welch lexicon of leadership*. New York: McGraw-Hill.

Krames, J. A. (2005). *Jack Welch and the 4Es of leadership: How to put GE's leadership formula to work in your organization*. New York: McGraw-Hill.

Krizek, R. L. (1992). Goodbye old friend: A son's farewell to Comiskey Park. *Omega, 25*(2), 87–93.

Krone, K. (2005). Trends in organizational communication research: Sustaining the discipline, sustaining ourselves. *Communication Studies, 56*, 95–105.

Kuhn, T. (1970). *The structure of scientific revolutions* (2nd ed.). Chicago: University of Chicago Press.

Kuhn, T. (2006). A "demented work ethic" and a "lifestyle firm": Discourse, identity, and workplace time commitments. *Organization Studies, 27*, 1339–1358.

Kuhn, T., Golden, A., Jorgenson, J., Buzzanell, P., Berkalaar, B., Kisselburgh, L., et al. (2008). Cultural discourses and discursive resources for meaning/ ful work: Constructing and disrupting identities in contemporary capitalism. *Management Communication Quarterly, 22*, 162–171.

Kunda, G. (1992). *Engineering culture: Control and commitment in a high-tech corporation*. Philadelphia: Temple University Press.

Lakoff, G., & Johnson, M. (1980). *Metaphors we live by*. Chicago: University of Chicago Press.

Lamphere, L. (1985). Bringing the family to work: Women's culture on the shop floor. *Feminist Studies, 11*, 519–540.

Lane, B. (2008). *Jacked up: The inside story of how Jack Welch talked GE into becoming the world's greatest company*. New York: McGraw-Hill.

Langellier, K., & Peterson, E. (2006). "Somebody's got to pick eggs": Family storytelling about work. *Text and Performance Quarterly, 73*, 468–473.

Leidner, R. (1993). *Fast food, fast talk: Service work and the routinization of everyday life*. Berkeley: University of California Press.

Leith, S. (2011, August 15). The plot thickens. *The Guardian,* pp. 17–19.

Lengel, R., & Daft, R. (1988). The selection of communication media as an executive skill. *Academy of Management Executive, 11*, 225–232.

Lewin, K., & Lippett, R. (1938). An experimental approach to the study of autocracy and democratic leadership. *Sociometry, 1*, 292–300.

The liberated, exploited, pampered, frazzled, uneasy new American worker [Special issue]. (2000, March 6). *New York Times Magazine*.

Liebow, E. (1967). *Tally's corner: A study of Negro streetcorner men*. Boston: Little, Brown.

Likert, R. (1961). *New patterns of management*. New York: McGraw-Hill.

Linder, M., & Nygaard, I. (1998). *Void where prohibited: Rest breaks and the right to urinate on company time*. Ithaca, NY: ILR Press.

Linstead, S., & Grafton-Small, R. (1992). On reading organizational culture. *Organization Studies, 13*, 311–355.

Loe, M. (1996). Working for men—at the intersection of power, gender, and sexuality. *Sociological Inquiry, 66*, 399–421.

Lorde, A. (1984). *Sister outsider*. Trumansburg, NY: Crossing Press.

Lucas, K. (2011). The working class promise: A communicative account of mobility-based ambivalences. *Communication Monographs, 78*, 347–369.

Luhmann, N. (1995). *Social systems* (J. John Bednarz, Trans.). Stanford, CA: Stanford University Press.

Luhmann, N. (2005). The concept of autopoiesis. In D. Seidl & K. H. Becker (Eds.), *Niklas Luhmann and organization studies* (pp. 54–63). Copenhagen: Copenhagen Business School Press.

Lukács, G. (1971). *History and class consciousness: Studies in Marxist dialectics* (R. Livingstone, Trans.). Cambridge: MIT Press.

Lukes, S. (1974). *Power: A radical view*. London: MacMillan.

Lutgen-Sandvik, P. (2003). The communicative cycle of employee emotional abuse: Generation and regeneration of workplace mistreatment. *Management Communication Quarterly, 16*, 471–501.

Lynch, O. H. (2002). Humorous communication: Finding a place for humor in communication research. *Communication Theory, 12*, 423–445.

Lyon, A. (2011). Reconstructing Merck's practical theory of communication: The ethics of pharmaceutical sales representative–physician encounters. *Communication Monographs, 78*, 53–72.

Lyon, A., & Mirivel, J. C. (2010). The imperative of ethical communication standards in an era of commercialized medicine. *Management Communication Quarterly, 24*, 474–481.

Lyotard, J.-F. (1984). *The postmodern condition: A report on knowledge* (G. Bennington & B. Massumi, Trans.). Minneapolis: University of Minnesota Press.

MacKinnon, C. A. (1979). *Sexual harassment of working women: A case of sex discrimination*. New Haven, CT: Yale University Press.

Maguire, M., & Mohtar, L. F. (1994). Performance and the celebration of a subaltern counterpublic. *Text and Performance Quarterly, 14*, 238–252.

Mandela, N. (1995). *Long walk to freedom: The autobiography of Nelson Mandela*. Boston: Back Bay Books, Little, Brown.

Manjoo, F. (2011, July–August). (Like) + (Retweet) = $$$? *Fast Company,* 86–117.

Mansnerus, L. (1999, November 21). It takes a village to make an office. Ask Mother Merck. *New York Times,* pp. 1, 8.

Manz, C. C., & Sims, H. P. (2000). *The new superleadership: Leading others to lead themselves*. San Francisco: Berrett-Koehler.

Marks, S. R. (1999). The gendered contexts of inclusive intimacy: The Hawthorne women at work and home. In R. G. Adams (Ed.), *Placing friendship in context* (pp. 43–70). Cambridge, UK: Cambridge University Press.

Martens, W. (2006). The distinctions within organizations: Luhmann from a cultural perspective. *Organization, 13*, 83–108.

Martin, J. (1985). Can organizational culture be managed? In P. Frost, M. Louis, J. Martin, &

C. Lundberg (Eds.), *Organizational culture* (pp. 95–98). Beverly Hills, CA: Sage.

Martin, J. (1990). Deconstructing organizational taboos: The suppression of gender conflict in organizations. *Organization Science, 1*, 339–359.

Martin, J. (1992). *Culture in organizations: Three perspectives*. New York: Oxford University Press.

Martin, J., Feldman, M., Hatch, M. J., & Sitkin, S. J. (1983). The uniqueness paradox in organizational stories. *Administrative Science Quarterly, 28*, 438–453.

Martin, J., Knopoff, K., & Beckman, C. (1998). An alternative to bureaucratic impersonality and emotional labor: Bounded emotionality at The Body Shop. *Administrative Science Quarterly, 43*, 429–469.

Martin, J. N., & Nakayama, T. K. (Eds.). (1999). *Whiteness: The communication of social identity*. Thousand Oaks: Sage.

Martino, J.-M. (1999). *Diversity: An imperative for business success*. New York: Conference Board.

Marx, K. (1967). *Capital* (S. Moore & E. Aveling, Trans.). New York: International Publishers.

Marx, K., & Engels, F. (1947). *The German ideology*. New York: International.

Marx, K., & Engels, F. (2008). *The communist manifesto*. London: Pluto Press.

Maslow, A. H. (1987). *Motivation and personality*. New York: Addison-Wesley Longman.

Mason, R. (1982). *Participatory and workplace democracy: A theoretical development in critique of liberalism*. Carbondale, IL: Southern Illinois University Press.

May, S. K., Cooren, F., & Munshi, D. (Eds.). (2009). *The handbook of communication and ethics*. New York: Routledge.

McGregor, D. (1960). *The human side of enterprise*. New York: McGraw-Hill.

McIntosh, P. (1990). White privilege: Unpacking the invisible knapsack. *Independent School, 49*(2), 31.

McMillan, J., & Cheney, G. (1996). The student as consumer: The implications and limitations of a metaphor. *Communication Education, 45*, 1–15.

McMillan, J., & Northorn, N. A. (1995). Organizational codependency: The creation and maintenance of closed systems. *Management Communication Quarterly, 9*, 6–45.

McRobbie, A. (2000). *Feminism and youth culture*. New York: Routledge.

Mease, J. (2011). Teaching difference as institutional and making it personal: Moving among personal, interpersonal, and institutional construction of difference. In D. K. Mumby (Ed.), *Reframing difference in organizational communication studies: Research, pedagogy, practice* (pp. 151–171). Thousand Oaks, CA: Sage.

Meindl, J. R. (1995). The romance of leadership as a follower-centric theory: A social constructionist approach. *Leadership Quarterly, 6*(3), 329–341.

Meindl, J. R., Ehrlich, S. B., & Dukerich, J. M. (1985). The romance of leadership. *Administrative Science Quarterly, 30*, 78–102.

Mill, J. S. (1970). The subjection of women. In A. S. Rossi (Ed.), *Essays on sex equality* (pp. 123–142). Chicago: University of Chicago Press. (Original work published 1869)

Miller, A. (1949). *Death of a salesman: Certain private conversations in two acts and a requiem*. New York: Viking Press, 1968.

Mills, A. J., & Chiaramonte, P. (1991). Organization as gendered communication act. *Canadian Journal of Communication, 16*, 381–398.

Mills, C. W. (1951). *White collar: The American middle classes*. New York: Oxford University Press.

Mills, C. W. (1956). *The power elite*. New York: Oxford University Press.

Modesti, S. (2008). Home sweet home: Tattoo parlors as postmodern spaces of agency. *Western Journal of Communication, 72*, 197–212.

Mohrman, S. A., Cohen, S. G., & Mohrman, A. M. (1995). *Designing team-based organizations: New forces for knowledge work*. San Francisco: Jossey-Bass.

Monge, P. R. (1982). Systems theory and research in the study of organizational communication: The correspondence problem. *Human Communication Research, 8*, 245–261.

Morgan, G. (2006). *Images of organization*. Thousand Oaks, CA: Sage.

Morris, M. (1998). *Too soon too late: History in popular culture*. Bloomington: Indiana University Press.

Morrison, K. (1995). *Marx, Durkheim, Weber: Formations of modern social thought*. London: Sage.

Moss, G. (Ed.). (2010). *Profiting from diversity: The business advantages and the obstacles to achieving diversity*. Basingstoke, UK: Palgrave Macmillan.

Mumby, D. K. (1987). The political function of narrative in organizations. *Communication Monographs, 54*, 113–127.

Mumby, D. K. (1988). *Communication and power in organizations: Discourse, ideology, and domination*. Norwood, NJ: Ablex.

Mumby, D. K. (Ed.). (1993). *Narrative and social control: Critical perspectives*. Newbury Park, CA: Sage.

Mumby, D. K. (1998). Organizing men: Power, discourse, and the social construction of masculinity(s) in the workplace. *Communication Theory, 8*, 164–183.

Mumby, D. K. (2005). Theorizing resistance in organization studies: A dialectical approach. *Management Communication Quarterly, 19*, 1–26.

Mumby, D. K. (2007). Organizational communication. In G. Ritzer (Ed.), *The encyclopedia of sociology* (pp. 3290–3299). London: Blackwell.

Mumby, D. K. (2011a). Ethics and power. In G. Cheney, S. May, & D. Munshi (Eds.), *The handbook of communication ethics* (pp. 84–98). New York: Routledge.

Mumby, D. K. (Ed.). (2011b). *Reframing difference in organizational communication studies: Research, pedagogy, practice*. Thousand Oaks, CA: Sage.

Mumby, D. K., & Stohl, C. (1992). Power and discourse in organization studies: Absence and the dialectic of control. *Discourse & Society, 2*, 313–332.

Muniz, A. (2007). Brands and branding. In G. Ritzer (Ed.), *The Blackwell encyclopedia of sociology*. Oxford: Blackwell.

Murphy, A. G. (1998). Hidden transcripts of flight attendant resistance. *Management Communication Quarterly, 11*, 499–535.

Murphy, A. G. (2003). The dialectical gaze: Exploring the subject–object tension in the performances of women who strip. *Journal of Contemporary Ethnography, 32*, 305–335.

Nakayama, T., & Krizek, R. (1995). Whiteness: A strategic rhetoric. *Quarterly Journal of Speech, 81*, 291–309.

Neate, R., Wood, Z., & Hinkley, S. (2011, August 13). Love affair with gangster-chic turns sour for top fashion brands. *The Guardian*, p. 11.

Norton, M. I., & Ariely, D. (2011). Building a better America—one wealth quintile at a time. *Perspectives on Psychological Science, 6*(1), 9–12.

O'Connell, V. (2008). Stores count seconds to trim labor costs. *Wall Street Journal*. Retrieved from http://online.wsj.com/article/SB122651745876821483.html

O'Connor, E. (1999a). Minding the workers: The meaning of "human" and "human relations" in Elton Mayo. *Organization, 6*, 223–246.

O'Connor, E. (1999b). The politics of management thought: A case study of the Harvard Business School and the human relations school. *Academy of Management Review, 24*, 117–131.

Olins, W. (2000). How brands are taking over the corporation. In M. Schlutz, M. J. Hatch, & H. L. Mogens (Eds.), *The expressive organization: Linking identity, reputation, and the corporate brand* (pp. 51–65). Oxford, UK: Oxford University Press.

Olins, W. (2003). *Wally Olins on brand*. London: Thames & Hudson.

Orbe, M., & Harris, T. M. (2001). *Interracial communication: Theory into practice*. Belmont, CA: Wadsworth.

Pacanowsky, M. (1988). Communication in the empowering organization. In J. Anderson (Ed.), *Communication yearbook* (Vol. 11, pp. 356–379). Thousand Oaks, CA: Sage.

Pacanowsky, M., & O'Donnell-Trujillo, N. (1982). Communication and organizational cultures. *Western Journal of Speech Communication, 46*, 115–130.

Parker, L. D. (1984). Control in organizational life: The contribution of Mary Parker Follett. *Academy of Management Review, 9*, 736–745.

Parker, M., & Slaughter, J. (1988). *Choosing sides: Unions and the team concept*. Boston: South End Press.

Parker, P. S., & Mease, J. (2009). Beyond the knapsack: Disrupting the production of white racial privilege in organizational practices. In L. Samovar, R. Porter, & E. McDaniel (Eds.), *Intercultural communication: A reader* (12th ed., pp. 313–324). New York: Wadsworth.

Parry, K. W., & Bryman, A. (2006). Leadership in organizations. In S. Clegg, C. Hardy, T. B. Lawrence, & W. R. Nord (Eds.), *The SAGE handbook of organization studies* (2nd ed., pp. 447–468). London: Sage.

Parry, K. W., & Hansen, H. (2007). The organizational story as leadership. *Leadership, 3*, 281–300.

Perlow, L. A. (1997). *Finding time: How corporations, individuals, and families can benefit from new work practices*. Ithaca, NY: ILR Press.

Perrow, C. (1986). *Complex organizations* (3rd ed.). New York: Random House.

Peters, T. (1988). *Thriving on chaos: Handbook for a management revolution*. New York: Harper & Row.

Peters, T., & Waterman, R. M. (1982). *In search of excellence*. New York: Harper & Row.

Pfeffer, J. (1981a). Management as symbolic action: The creation and maintenance of organizational paradigms. *Research in Organizational Behavior, 3,* 1–52.

Pfeffer, J. (1981b). *Power in organizations*. Cambridge, MA: Ballinger.

Phillips, N. (1995). Telling organizational tales: On the role of narrative fiction in the study of organizations. *Organization Studies, 16,* 625–649.

Pierce, J. L. (1995). *Gender trials: Emotional lives in contemporary law firms*. Berkeley, CA: University of California Press.

Pondy, L. (1978). Leadership is a language game. In M. W. McCall & M. M. Lombardo (Eds.), *Leadership: Where else can we go?* Durham, NC: Duke University Press.

Prasad, P., & Prasad, A. (2000). Stretching the iron cage: The constitution and implications of routine workplace resistance. *Organization Science, 11,* 387–403.

Pringle, R. (1989). *Secretaries talk: Sexuality, power and work*. London: Verso.

Prokesch, S. (1989). Ford to buy Jaguar for $2.38 billion. *New York Times*. Retrieved from http://www.nytimes.com/1989/11/03/business/ford-to-buy-jaguar-for-2.38-billion.html?pagewanted = all&src = pm

Putnam, L. L. (1983). The interpretive perspective: An alternative to functionalism. In L. L. Putnam & M. Pacanowsky (Eds.), *Communication and organizations: An interpretive approach* (pp. 31–54). Beverly Hills, CA: Sage.

Putnam, L. L., & Nicotera, A. M. (Eds.). (2008). *Building theories of organization: The constitutive role of communication*. Oxford, UK: Routledge.

Putnam, L. L., & Pacanowsky, M. (Eds.). (1983). *Communication and organizations: An interpretive approach*. Beverly Hills, CA: Sage.

Putnam, R. (2000). *Bowling alone: America's declining social capital*. New York: Simon & Schuster.

Pye, A. (2005). Leadership and organizing: Sensemaking in action. *Leadership, 1,* 31–50.

Quindlen, A. (2003, October). Still needing the F word. *Newsweek,* 74.

Ray, C. A. (1986). Corporate culture: The last frontier of control? *Journal of Management Studies, 23,* 287–297.

Ray, R., Gornick, J., & Schmitt, J. (2008). *Parental leave policies in 21 countries: Assessing generosity and gender equality*. Washington, DC: Center for Economic and Policy Research.

Raz, A. E. (2002). *Emotions at work: Normative control, organizations, and culture in Japan and America*. Cambridge, MA: Harvard University Asia Center and Harvard University Press.

Redding, W. C. (1988). Organizational communication. In E. Barnouw (Ed.), *International encyclopedia of communications* (Vol. 3, pp. 236–239). New York: Oxford University Press.

Reich, R. (1991). *The work of nations*. New York: Vintage Books.

Rhodes, C., & Westwood, R. (Eds.). (2007). *Humor, organization, and work*. London: Routledge.

Rich, A. (1980). Compulsory heterosexuality and lesbian existence. *Signs, 5,* 631–660.

Ritzer, G. (2000). *The McDonaldization of society*. Thousand Oaks, CA: Pine Forge Press.

Ritzer, G. (2004). *The globalization of nothing*. Thousand Oaks, CA: Sage.

Ritzer, G. (2005). *Enchanting a disenchanted world: Revolutionizing the means of consumption* (2nd ed.). Thousand Oaks, CA: Pine Forge Press.

Ritzer, G. (2007). *The globalization of nothing 2*. Thousand Oaks, CA: Pine Forge Press.

Robertson, R. (1990). *Globalization*. London: Sage.

Robertson, R., & Khondker, H. H. (1998). Discourses of globalization: Preliminary considerations. *International Sociology, 13,* 25–40.

Robinson, J. P., & Godbey, G. (1999). *Time for life: The surprising ways Americans use their time*. University Park: Pennsylvania State University Press.

Rockmann, K., & Pratt, M. G. (2011). *Rethinking telecommuting and the distributed work organization*. Paper presented at the Academy of Management, San Antonio, TX.

Roediger, D. R. (2005). *Working toward whiteness: How America's immigrants became white*. New York: Basic Books.

Roethlisberger, F. J., & Dickson, W. J. (1939). *Management and the worker*. New York: Wiley.

Rosen, M. (1985). "Breakfast at Spiro's": Dramaturgy and dominance. *Journal of Management, 11*(2), 31–48.

Rosen, M. (1988). You asked for it: Christmas at the bosses' expense. *Journal of Management Studies, 25*, 463–480.

Rosener, J. B. (1990). Ways women lead. *Harvard Business Review, 68*, 119–125.

Ross, A. (2003). *No-collar: The humane workplace and its hidden costs.* New York: Basic Books.

Ross, A. (2008). The new geography of work: Power to the precarious? *Theory, Culture & Society, 25*(7–8), 31–49.

Ross, R. (1992). *From equality to diversity: A business case for equal opportunities.* London: Pitman.

Roth, D. (2000, January 10). My job at The Container Store. *Fortune,* 74–78.

Rothschild-Whitt, J. (1976). Conditions for facilitating participatory-democratic organizations. *Sociological Inquiry, 46*, 75–86.

Rothschild-Whitt, J. (1979). The collectivist organization: An alternative to rational bureaucratic models. *American Sociological Review, 44*, 509–527.

Roy, D. (1959). "Banana time": Job satisfaction and informal interaction. *Human Organization, 18*, 158–168.

Rumens, N. (2008). Working at intimacy: Gay men's workplace friendships. *Gender, Work and Organization, 15*, 9–30.

Rumens, N. (2010). Workplace friendships between men: Gay men's perspectives and experiences. *Human Relations, 63*, 1541–1562.

Rumens, N., & Kerfoot, D. (2009). Gay men at work: (Re)constructing the self as professional. *Human Relations, 62*, 763–786.

Rushe, D. (2007, September 16). Forget work, just have some fun: Office jollity is replacing drudgery for today's office staff. *Sunday Times.*

Ryan, M. K., & Haslam, S. A. (2007). The glass cliff: Exploring the dynamics surrounding the appointment of women to precarious leadership positions. *Academy of Management Review, 32*, 549–572.

Sassen, S. (1998). *Globalization and its discontents: Essays on the new mobility of people and money.* New York: New Press.

Sassen, S. (2000). Women's burden: Counter-geographies of globalization and the feminization of survival. *Journal of International Affairs, 53*, 503–524.

Sassen, S. (2003). Global cities and survival circuits. In B. Ehrenreich & A. Hochschild (Eds.), *Global woman* (pp. 254–274). New York: Metropolitan Books.

Sassen, S. (2005). The global city: Introducing a concept. *Brown Journal of World Affairs, 11*(2), 27–44.

Sassen, S. (2006). *A sociology of globalization.* New York: W. W. Norton.

Sathe, V. (1983). Implications of corporate culture: A manager's guide to action. *Organizational Dynamics, 12*(3), 5–23.

Sathe, V. (1985). *Culture and related corporate realities: Text, cases, and readings on organizational entry, establishment, and change.* Homewood, IL: R. D. Irwin.

Scheibel, D. (1992). Faking identity in clubland: The communicative performance of "fake ID." *Text and Performance Quarterly, 12*, 160–175.

Scheibel, D. (1996). Appropriating bodies: Organ(izing) ideology and cultural practice in medical school. *Journal of Applied Communication Research, 24*, 310–331.

Scheibel, D. (1999). "If your roommate dies, you get a 4.0": Reclaiming rumor with Burke and organizational culture. *Western Journal of Communication, 63*, 168–192.

Schein, E. H. (1992). *Organizational culture and leadership* (2nd ed.). San Francisco: Jossey-Bass.

Schivelbusch, W. (1986). *The railway journey: The industrialization of time and space in the 19th century.* Leamington Spa, UK: Berg.

Schlosser, E. (2002). *Fast food nation: The dark side of the all-American meal.* New York: Perennial.

Scholte, J. A. (2000). *Globalization: A critical introduction.* Basingstoke, UK: Palgrave MacMillan.

Schor, J. (1993). *The overworked American: The unexpected decline of leisure.* New York: Basic Books.

Schor, J. (2004). *Born to buy: The commercialized child and the new consumer culture.* New York: Scribner.

Scott, J. C. (1990). *Domination and the arts of resistance: Hidden transcripts.* New Haven, CT: Yale University Press.

Seidl, D. (2005). The basic concepts of Luhmann's theory of social systems. In D. Seidl & K. H. Becker (Eds.), *Niklas Luhmann and organization studies* (pp. 21–53). Copenhagen: Copenhagen Business School Press.

Seidl, D., & Becker, K. H. (Eds.). (2005). *Niklas Luhmann and organization studies*. Copenhagen: Copenhagen Business School Press.

Seidl, D., & Becker, K. H. (2006). Organizations as distinction generating and processing systems: Niklas Luhmann's contribution to organization studies. *Organization, 13*, 9–35.

Seidman, S. (2002). *Beyond the closet: The transformation of gay and lesbian life*. New York: Routledge.

Selber, K., & Austin, D. M. (1997). Mary Parker Follett: Epilogue to or return of a social work management pioneer? *Administration in Social Work, 21*(1), 1–15.

Selvin, M. (2007, August 10). Setting degrees of tattoo taboos is no easy task. *Los Angeles Times*. Retrieved from http://blog.nwjobs.com/career-center/setting_degrees_of_tattoo_taboos_is_no_easy_task.html

Sennett, R. (1998). *The corrosion of character: The personal consequences of work in the new capitalism*. New York: W. W. Norton.

Sewell, G. (1998). The discipline of teams: The control of team-based industrial work through electronic and peer surveillance. *Administrative Science Quarterly, 43*, 397–428.

Shamir, B., Pillai, R., Bligh, M. C., & Uhl-Bien, M. (Eds.). (2007). *Follower-centered perspectives on leadership: A tribute to the memory of James R. Meindl*. Greenwich, CT: IAP.

Shannon, C. E., & Weaver, W. (1949). *The mathematical theory of communication*. Urbana: University of Illinois Press.

Sinclair, A. (1992). The tyranny of a team ideology. *Organization Studies, 13*, 611–626.

Sinclair, A. (2005). *Doing leadership differently: Gender, power and sexuality in a changing business culture* (2nd ed.). Melbourne, Australia: Melbourne University Press.

Skyttner, L. (2005). *General systems theory: Problems, perspectives, practice* (2nd ed.). Singapore: World Scientific Press.

Slater, R. (2003). *29 leadership secrets from Jack Welch*. New York: McGraw-Hill.

Smircich, L., & Morgan, G. (1982). Leadership: The management of meaning. *Journal of Applied Behavioral Science, 18*, 257–273.

Smith, A. (1937). *An inquiry into the nature and causes of the wealth of nations*. New York: Random House. (Original work published 1776)

Smith, D. (1970). The fallacy of the "communication breakdown." *Quarterly Journal of Speech, 56*, 343–346.

Smith, F. L., & Keyton, J. (2001). Organizational storytelling: Metaphors for relational power and identity struggles. *Management Communication Quarterly, 15*, 149–182.

Smith, J. H. (1998). The enduring legacy of Elton Mayo. *Human Relations, 51*, 221–249.

Smith, R., & Eisenberg, E. (1987). Conflict at Disneyland: A root metaphor analysis. *Communication Monographs, 54*, 367–380.

Soares, R., Regis, A., & Shur, Y. (2010). 2010 Catalyst census: Fortune 500 women executive officers and top earners. Retrieved March 27, 2012, from http://www.catalyst.org/publication/459/2010-catalyst-census-fortune-500-women-executive-officers-and-top-earners

Soros, G. (2002). *On globalization*. New York: Public Affairs.

Spradlin, A. (1998). The price of "passing": A lesbian perspective on authenticity in organizations. *Management Communication Quarterly, 11*, 598–605.

Stark, D. (2009). *The sense of dissonance: Accounts of worth in economic life*. Princeton, NJ: Princeton University Press.

Stevens, A., & Lavin, D. (2007). Stealing time: The temporal regulation of labor in neoliberal and post-Fordist work regime. *Democratic Communiqué, 21*(2), 40–61.

Stewart, R. (1996). Why the neglect? *Organization, 3*, 175–179.

Stivers, C. (1996). Mary Parker Follett and the question of gender. *Organization, 3*, 161–166.

Stivers, C. (2006). Integrating Mary Parker Follett and public administration. *Public Administration Review, 66*, 473–476.

Stodgill, R. M. (1948). Personal factors associated with leadership: A survey of the literature. *Journal of Psychology, 25*, 35–71.

Stodgill, R. M. (1950). Leadership, membership and organization. *Psychological Bulletin, 47*, 1–14.

Stohl, C. (2001). Globalizing organizational communication. In F. Jablin & L. L. Putnam (Eds.), *The new handbook of organizational communication: Advances in theory, research, and methods (pp. 323–375). Thousand Oaks, CA: Sage.

Stohl, C., & Cheney, G. (2001). Participatory processes/paradoxical practices: Communication and the dilemmas of organizational democracy. *Management Communication Quarterly, 14,* 349–407.

Tannenbaum, A. S. (1968). *Control in organizations.* New York: McGraw-Hill.

Tarafdar, M., Tu, Q., Ragu-Nathan, T. S., & Ragu-Nathan, B. S. (2011). Crossing to the dark side: Examining creators, outcomes, and inhibitors of technostress. *Communications of the ACM, 54*(9), 113–120.

Taylor, B. C., & Trujillo, N. (2001). Qualitative research methods. In L. L. Putnam & M. Pacanowsky (Eds.), *The new handbook of organizational communication: Advances in theory, research, and methods* (pp. 161–196). Thousand Oaks, CA: Sage.

Taylor, F. W. (1934). *The principles of scientific management.* New York: Harper. (Original work published 1911)

Taylor, P., & Bain, P. (1999). "An assembly line in the head": Work and employee relations in the call centre. *Industrial Relations Journal, 30,* 101–117.

Taylor, P., & Bain, P. (2003). "Subterranean worksick blues": Humour as subversion in two call centres. *Organization Studies, 24,* 1487–1509.

Temporal, P., & Trott, M. (2001). *Romancing the customer: Maximizing brand value through powerful relationship management.* New York: Wiley.

Therborn, G. (1980). *The ideology of power and the power of ideology.* London: Verso.

Thompson, E. P. (1967). Time, work-discipline, and industrial capitalism. *Past and Present, 38,* 56–97.

Thrift, N. J. (2005). *Knowing capitalism.* London: Sage.

Tompkins, P. K., & Cheney, G. (1985). Communication and unobtrusive control in contemporary organizations. In R. D. McPhee & P. K. Tompkins (Eds.), *Organizational communication: Traditional themes and new directions* (pp. 179–210). Beverly Hills, CA: Sage.

Tong, R. (1989). *Feminist thought: A comprehensive introduction.* Boulder, CO: Westview Press.

Tourish, D., Russell, C., & Armenic, J. (2010). Transformational leadership education and agency perspectives in business school pedagogy: A marriage of inconvenience? *British Journal of Management, 21,* S40–S59.

Townley, B. (1993a). Foucault, power/knowledge, and its relevance for human resource management. *Academy of Management Review, 18,* 518–545.

Townley, B. (1993b). Performance appraisal and the emergence of management. *Journal of Management Studies, 30,* 221–238.

Townley, B. (1994). *Reframing human resource management: Power, ethics and the subject at work.* London: Sage.

Townsley, N. C. (2003). Love, sex, and tech in the global workplace. In B. J. Dow & J. T. Wood (Eds.), *The SAGE handbook of gender and communication* (pp. 143–160). Thousand Oaks, CA: Sage.

Tracy, S. (2000). Becoming a character for commerce: Emotion labor, self-subordination, and discursive construction of identity in a total institution. *Management Communication Quarterly, 14,* 90–128.

Tracy, S. (2005). Locking up emotion: Moving beyond dissonance for understanding emotion labor discomfort. *Communication Monographs, 72,* 261–283.

Tracy, S., Lutgen-Sandvik, P., & Alberts, J. (2006). Nightmares, demons, and slaves: Exploring the painful metaphors of workplace bullying. *Management Communication Quarterly, 20,* 148–185.

Tracy, S., & Scott, C. (2006). Sexuality, masculinity, and taint management among firefighters and correctional officers: Getting down and dirty with "America's heroes" and the "scum of law enforcement." *Management Communication Quarterly, 20,* 6–38.

Trethewey, A. (1997). Resistance, identity, and empowerment: A postmodern feminist analysis of clients in a human service organization. *Communication Monographs, 64,* 281–301.

Trethewey, A. (2001). Reproducing and resisting the master narrative of decline: Midlife professional women's experiences of aging. *Management Communication Quarterly, 15,* 183–226.

Trice, H. M., & Beyer, J. M. (1984). Studying organizational culture through rites and ceremonials. *Academy of Management Review, 9,* 653–669.

Trist, E. L., & Bamforth, K. W. (1951). Some social and psychological consequences of the long-wall method of coal-getting: An examination of the psychological situation and defences of a work group in relation to the social structure and technological content of the work system. *Human Relations, 4*(1), 3–38.

Trist, E. L., Higgin, G. W., Murray, H., & Pollock, A. B. (1963). *Organizational choice: Capabilities of groups at the coalface under changing technologies.* London: Tavistock.

Trujillo, N. (1992). Interpreting (the work and talk of) baseball: Perspectives on ballpark culture. *Western Journal of Communication, 56,* 350–371.

Trujillo, N., & Dionisopoulos, G. (1987). Cop talk, police stories, and the social construction of organizational drama. *Central States Speech Journal, 38,* 196–209.

Underhill, P. (1999). *Why we buy: The science of shopping.* New York: Simon & Schuster.

U.S. Department of Health and Human Services. (2010, August). *The HHS poverty guidelines for the remainder of 2010.* Washington, DC: Author. Retrieved from http://aspe.hhs.gov/poverty/10poverty.shtml

U.S. Equal Employment Opportunity Commission. (2002). Facts about sexual harassment. Retrieved March 28, 2012, from http://www.eeoc.gov/facts/fs-sex.html

Useem, J. (2000, January 10). Welcome to the new company town. *Fortune,* 62–70.

Van Maanen, J. (1991). The smile factory: Work at Disneyland. In P. J. Frost, L. F. Moore, M. R. Louis, C. C. Lundberg, & J. Martin (Eds.), *Reframing organizational culture* (pp. 58–76). Newbury Park, CA: Sage.

Van Maanen, J. (1995). Style as theory. *Organization Science, 6,* 133–143.

Viskovatoff, A. (1999). Foundations of Niklas Luhmann's theory of social systems. *Philosophy of the Social Sciences, 29,* 481–516.

von Bertalanffy, L. (1968). *General system theory.* New York: George Braziller.

Waggoner, C. E. (1997). The emancipatory potential of feminine masquerade in Mary Kay Cosmetics. *Text and Performance Quarterly, 17,* 256–272.

Wajcman, J. (2010). Feminist theories of technology. *Cambridge Journal of Economics, 34,* 143–152.

Wajcman, J., & Rose, E. (2011). Constant connectivity: Rethinking interruptions at work. *Organization Studies, 32,* 941–961.

Wajcman, J., Rose, E., Brown, J. E., & Bittman, M. (2010). Enacting virtual connections between work and home. *Journal of Sociology, 46,* 257–275.

Walker, R. (2008). *Buying in: The secret dialogue between what we buy and who we are.* New York: Random House.

Walsh, M. W. (2000). Where G.E. falls short: Diversity at the top. *New York Times,* pp. 1, 13.

Walther, J. B., & Bunz, U. (2005). The rules of virtual groups: Trust, liking and performance in computer-mediated communication. *Journal of Communication, 55,* 828–846.

Ward, J., & Winstanley, D. (2003). The absent presence: Negative space within discourse and the construction of minority sexual identity in the workplace. *Human Relations, 56,* 1255–1280.

Waters, M. (2001). *Globalization* (2nd ed.). London: Routledge.

Watzlawick, P., Beavin, J., & Jackson, D. D. (1967). *Pragmatics of human communication: A study of interactional patterns, pathologies, and paradoxes.* New York: W. W. Norton.

Webb, J. (2006). *Organisations, identities and the self.* Houndmills, Basingstoke, Hampshire: Palgrave Macmillan.

Weber, M. (1958). *The Protestant Ethic and the spirit of capitalism.* New York: Scribner's.

Weber, M. (1978). *Economy and society: An outline of interpretive sociology* (G. W. Roth & C. Wittich, Trans.). Berkeley: University of California Press.

Weick, K. E. (1979). *The social psychology of organizing* (2nd ed.). Reading, MA: Addison-Wesley.

Weick, K. E. (1988). Enacted sensemaking in crisis situations. *Journal of Management Studies, 25,* 305–317.

Weick, K. E. (1989). Organized improvization: 20 years of organizing. *Communication Studies, 40,* 241–248.

Weick, K. E. (1990). The vulnerable system: An analysis of the Tenerife air disaster. *Journal of Management Studies, 16,* 971–993.

Weick, K. E. (1993). The collapse of sense-making in organizations: The Mann Gulch disaster. *Administrative Science Quarterly, 38,* 629–652.

Weick, K. E. (1995). *Sense-making in organizations.* Thousand Oaks, CA: Sage.

Weick, K. E. (2001). *Making sense of the organization.* Oxford, UK: Blackwell.

Welch, J. (2008). *Jack Welch speaks: Wisdom from the world's greatest business leader.* Hoboken, NJ: Wiley.

Wesely, J. K. (2003). Exotic dancing and the negotiation of identity: The multiple uses of body technologies. *Journal of Contemporary Ethnography, 32,* 643–669.

West, C., & Zimmerman, D. (1987). Doing gender. *Gender and Society, 1,* 125–151.

Western, S. (2008). *Leadership: A critical text.* Los Angeles: Sage.

Whyte, W. F. (1981). *Street corner society: The social structure of an Italian slum.* Chicago: University of Chicago Press.

Whyte, W. H. (1956). *The organization man.* New York: Simon & Schuster.

Wiener, N. (1948). *Cybernetics or control and communication in the animal and the machine.* New York: John Wiley.

Williams, C. L. (1992). The glass escalator: Hidden advantages for men in the "female" professions. *Social Problems, 39,* 253–267.

Wilson, F. (1996). Organizational theory: Blind and deaf to gender? *Organization Studies, 17,* 825–842.

Witten, M. (1993). Narrative and the culture of obedience at the workplace. In D. K. Mumby (Ed.), *Narrative and social control: Critical perspectives* (pp. 97–118). Newbury Park, CA: Sage.

Wolfe, T. (1976, August 23). The "me" decade and the third great awakening. *New York.*

Wolfinger, R. E. (1971). Nondecisions and the study of local politics. *American Political Science Review, 65,* 1063–1080.

Wollstonecraft, M. (1975). *A vindication of the rights of woman.* New York: W. W. Norton. (Original work published 1792)

Woods, J. D. (1993). *The corporate closet: The professional lives of gay men in America.* New York: Free Press.

Ybema, Y., Keenoy, T., Oswick, C., Beverungen, A., Ellis, N., & Sabelis, I. (2009). Articulating identities. *Human Relations, 62,* 299–322.

Young, E. (1989). On the naming of the rose: Interests and multiple meanings as elements of organizational culture. *Organization Studies, 10,* 187–206.

Yukl, G. (1989). Managerial leadership: A review of theory and research. *Journal of Management Studies, 15,* 251–289.

Yukl, G. (2006). *Leadership in organizations.* Upper Saddle River, NJ: Pearson/Prentice Hall.

Zavella, P. (1985). "Abnormal intimacy": The varying networks of Chicana cannery workers. *Feminist Studies, 11,* 541–564.

Zoller, H. M. (2003). Working out: Managerialism in workplace health promotion. *Management Communication Quarterly, 17,* 171–205.

Zoller, H. M., & Fairhurst, G. (2007). Resistance leadership: The overlooked potential in critical organization and leadership studies. *Human Relations, 60,* 1331–1360.

Index

Note: In page references, p indicates photos, f indicates figures, and t indicates tables.

About the Author

Dennis K. Mumby is Professor and Chair of Communication Studies at the University of North Carolina at Chapel Hill, and a Fellow of UNC's Institute for the Arts and Humanities. His research focuses on the relationships among discourse, power, gender, and organization. He has published five books and over 50 articles in the area of critical organization studies in journals such as *Academy of Management Review, Management Communication Quarterly, Communication Monographs,* and *Human Relations.* He is a past chair of the Organizational Communication Division of the National Communication Association and a six-time winner of the division's annual research award. Most recently, he served as Chair of the Organizational Communication Division of the International Communication Association. His most recent book is titled *Reframing Difference in Organizational Communication Studies: Research, Pedagogy, Practice.* Mumby is a National Communication Association Distinguished Scholar and a Fellow of the International Communication Association.

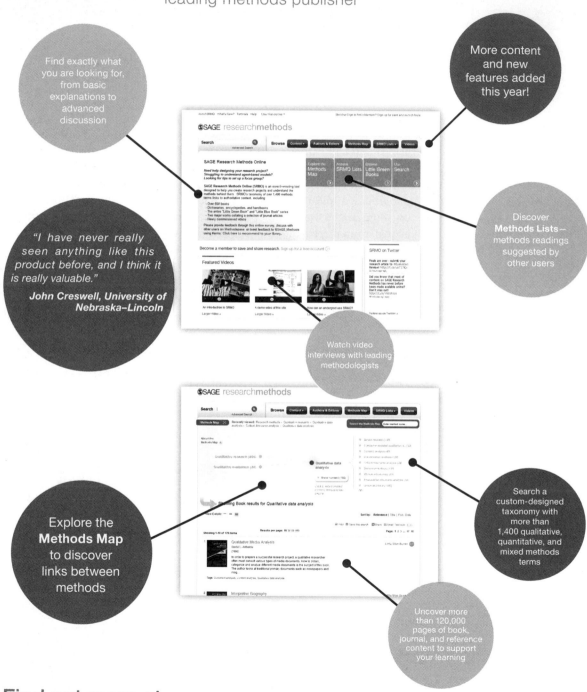